Skeptical Linguistic Essays

Skeptical Linguistic Essays

Paul M. Postal

OXFORD
UNIVERSITY PRESS

2004

OXFORD
UNIVERSITY PRESS

Oxford   New York
Auckland   Bangkok   Buenos Aires   Cape Town   Chennai
Dar es Salaam   Delhi   Hong Kong   Istanbul   Karachi   Kolkata
Kuala Lumpur   Madrid   Melbourne   Mexico City   Mumbai   Nairobi
São Paulo   Shanghai   Taipei   Tokyo   Toronto

Published by Oxford University Press, Inc.,
198 Madison Avenue, New York, New York 10016

www.oup.com

Oxford is a registered trademark of Oxford University Press

Library of Congress Cataloging-in-Publication Data
Postal, Paul Martin, 1936–
Skeptical linguistic essays / Paul M. Postal.
p. cm.
Includes bibliographical references and index.
ISBN 0-19-516672-8; ISBN 0-19-516671-X (pbk.)
1. Grammar, Comparative and general.   2. English language—Syntax.   3. Chomsky,
Noam.   4. Linguistic analysis (Linguistics)   I. Title.
P151.P655 2003
415—dc21   2003040455

2 4 6 8 9 7 5 3 1

Printed in the United States of America
on acid-free paper

CONTENTS

Skeptical Linguistic Essays

INTRODUCTION

$\mathbf{T}$his collection of essays is concerned with syntactic questions, with certain general features of grammatical theory related to syntax, here and there with semantic issues, and quite a bit with questions of appropriate standards in pursuing research in the previously mentioned domains. It has almost nothing to say about phonology. The immediately following remarks are to be interpreted against the background of this restricted understanding of what 'linguistic' is here intended to denote.

A prospective reader might ask "what is a *skeptical* linguistic essay?" I would answer that it is one based on a deep and long-standing view that much nonetheless prestigious current linguistics has in fact made very restricted descriptive and explanatory progress and, in some areas where great things have been claimed, no real substantive progress at all. This lack of true progress holds, I maintain, despite the fact that the literature of modern linguistics and its ancestors is replete with boasts of at least grand-sounding accomplishments; see in particular the discussion of (2) of chapter 8.

Consider (1) for example:

(1) Epstein and Hornstein (1999: xi)
     "GB's very success, however, dramatically alters the methodological landscape. It has
     spawned a consensus that principles-and-parameters accounts may well answer Plato's
     problem in the domain of language. This general and surely tentative consensus allows
     the other sorts of measures of success to guide minimalist theory construction and (self-)-
     evaluation. In effect, given a principles-and-parameters setting, simplicity, elegance,
     parsimony, and naturalness move from background to foreground concerns in the con-

3

struction and evaluation of analyses. To put matters more tendentiously than is warranted: given that principles-and-parameters models 'solve' Plato's problem, the paramount research issue becomes which of the conceivable principles-and-parameters models is best, and this issue is (in part) addressed using conventional (not uniquely linguistic) criteria of theory evaluation."

Various hedges notwithstanding, the authors of this passage clearly communicate the view that the government binding (GB) framework has been a deep success and has even in some sense solved the problem of natural language (hereafter: NL) acquisition ('Plato's problem'). This is in my view so far from reality as to be little more than a dream.[1] The claim that GB has been a success is not backed up, and I claim could not be, by any citation of substantive factual results for the grammar of English, for example.[2] Chapters 2, 3, 5, 7, and 8 consider in fact cases where some factual success in these terms seems to have been proclaimed and I suggest that they show that the claims are groundless. Note that passages like (1) make no attempt to consider criticisms of the favored view nor do they deal with arguments, many of considerable detail and depth, that other, competing views of NL syntax are far superior to the GB view. Work in lexical functional grammar (LFG) and head-driven phrase structure (HPSG), categorial grammar, and so on, is unmentioned. In short, such passages partake more strongly of the character of factually empty propaganda than of serious scholarship.

Beyond any substantive questions, many of the essays that follow thus express even more serious skepticism about the standards that seem to govern the way much linguistic research is evaluated, justified, and promoted. Lack of actual progress is unfortunate but at least remediable. But inadequate standards can undermine the entire enterprise of linguistic inquiry by even eating away at a clear conception of what an actual result might be. One non-negligible aspect of this damaging development is seen in remarks like (2):

(2)   Chomsky and Lasnik (1995: 28)
      "The shifts in focus over the years alter the task of inquiry considerably and yield different conceptions of what constitutes a 'real result' in the study of language. Suppose we have some collection of phenomena in a particular language. In the early stages of generative grammar, the task was to find a rule system of the permitted form from which these phenomena (and infinitely many others) could be derived. That is a harder task than the ones posed in pregenerative grammar, but not an impossible one: there are many potential rule systems, and it is often possible to devise one that will more or less work—though the problem of explanatory adequacy at once arises, as noted.

      "But this achievement, however difficult, does not count as a real result if we adopt the P&P approach as a goal. Rather, it merely sets the problem. The task is now to show how the phenomena derived by the rule system can be deduced from the invariant principles of UG with parameters set in one of the permissible ways. This is a far harder and more challenging task. It is an important fact that the problem can now be posed realistically, and solved in interesting ways in some range of cases, with failures that are also interesting insofar as they point the way to better solutions. The departure from the long and rich tradition of linguistic inquiry is much sharper and more radical than in early generative grammar, with problems that are quite new and prospects that appear promising."

The notion to be critically commented on here is that in the linguistics advocated by the authors, constructing a grammar of a NL that gets the facts right putatively "does not count as a real result." Rather, supposedly, a genuine result is only achieved when a successful rule system is deducible from universal grammar. While such remarks sound impressively deep, their implications *at this stage* threaten an elimination of the constraints on linguistic theorizing by precluding a serious factual basis for it. How much can anyone be expected to labor to actually try to account for the facts of actual NLs, internal to a point of view that proclaims at the start that success in such an endeavor is not even a result? But, as stressed long ago (Chomsky, 1957: 11), proper understanding of NL universals depends on *successful* descriptions: "More generally, linguists have been concerned with the problem of determining the fudamental underlying properties of successful grammars."

The thinly disguised contempt for getting the facts right manifest in a passage like (2) emerges particularly clearly when one is told that "failures are also interesting" and "point the way to better solutions."[3] Such claims can only be seen as self-serving defensive attempts to make descriptive failure seem acceptable. *Some* failures (of some kind) *might* be interesting in some way, 'interesting' being monumentally subjective, and *some* might point the way to a better solution. Others might just be hopelessly wrong, misguided, contradictory, ludicrous, and hence incapable of pointing to anything positive whatever. But since supposedly even descriptive failures are valuable, then, assuming descriptive successes are of at least *some* value, too, passage (2) would appear to embody the overall idea that *anything* done in this framework is progress. While this view would be marvelously convenient for its supporters, it is evidently illusory!

Implicit in (2) is the fantastic and unsupported notion that descriptive success is not really that hard and so not of much importance. Were such a claim true, it would be straightforward to show that it is. The authors would merely need to document the existing proper descriptions (since supposedly "it is often possible to devise one that will more or less work"). For of course they could not know that proper descriptions are easily obtained unless they had such available. Given the now *very* long period of work in the advocated terms, successful descriptions should be abundant. Since their current position is explicitly a development of decades of effort by hundreds of people, with English the favored domain of study, correctness of their point of view would, one would think, almost *inevitably* have yielded some (many?) concrete descriptive results, at least for English.

But they offer nothing of the sort and it is not that common to see such things even attempted in recent years. One is a very long way indeed from concern with realizing the earlier goal (Chomsky, 1957: 13) of a grammar that would describe all the well-formed sequences and none of the ill-formed ones. Moreover, one need only look at various syntactic areas where the authors themselves have worked, passives, expletives, *wh* constructions, object raising constructions, parasitic gaps, control phenomena, crossover phenomena, ellipsis, negation, and so on to see that there is no subdomain, even in English, where a genuinely successful description can be said to have been achieved. This is argued in considerable detail for crossover phenomena and passives in chapters 7 and 8. In such a context, talk about 'real results' that go *beyond* successful grammars is largely make-believe.

Challenged here, though, is not the idea that there are higher level results to be sought that would involve a reduction of aspects of successful descriptions to universal principles. Rather, at issue is the merit of skepticism about the ill-supported assumption that successful grammatical descriptions are relatively straightforwardly come by, thereby rendering notions of deducing such descriptions from universal principles currently meaningful. Perhaps the most negative aspect of claims that descriptive success is not a real result and that it is appropriate at this stage of linguistics to concentrate on higher order explanatory goals is that it undermines understanding of (i) the need for truly intensive factual study and (ii) the lack so far even in well-studied NLs like English of serious descriptive understanding. If one had achieved an adequate description of English passive phenomena, for example, in the almost half a century of work in the terms the authors favor, it would make sense to inquire into the general principles from which such a description followed. But as touched on in chapter 8, the actual descriptions offered in these frameworks so far are not only not successful but also so bad as to hardly merit being taken seriously. Just so with issues of the strong crossover phenomenon, as treated in chapter 7. Many claims of virtues for such descriptions are achieved only via a disregard for serious standards. But if there are no actual defensible descriptions, talk of deducing such from universal grammar or the like is evidently more like make-believe than serious inquiry.

A last point: Dismissiveness with respect to the difficulty and importance of reaching adequate descriptions can only undermine the proper valuation of real work that actually advances descriptive adequacy. I am thinking here, for example, specifically of work on negative polarity, which I have tried to educate myself about over the last half-dozen years or so. Here it is uncontrovertible that really serious insights have been gained, specifically in the rich descriptive and theoretical studies partially and inadequately referenced by Atlas (1996, 1997, 2000), Beghelli (1994), Fauconnier (1975a, 1975b, 1976, 1979), Giannakidou (1998, 1999, 2001), Heim (1984), Hoeksema (1983, 1986, 1996, 2000), Horn (1995, 1996a, 1996b, 2001), Horn and Kato (2000), Horn and Lee (1995), Israel (1996, 1998), Kempson (1985), Krifka (1990, 1994, 1995), Ladusaw (1980, 1996a, 1996b), Linebarger (1981, 1987, 1991), van der Wouden (1994, 1997), and Zwarts (1995, 1996, 1999). But enormous problems remain and no one who even samples the literature on this topic can, I believe, be long deluded into shallow assumptions about the *ease* of finding viable descriptions. Anyone who dares to speak in such terms should, I suggest, be faced with the simple requirement of presenting a characterization of the distribution of, for example, English negative polarity <u>any</u> that, as in (2), "will more or less work."

The fourteen essays found here, only one of which was previously published, fall into two categories. Part I contains six chapters that purport to be positive contributions to the study of English syntax, with implications for general syntactic theory. While the point is not made explicitly in any of them, I do not think it possible to reflect on their content without seeing how far one remains in the year 2003 from serious understanding of English grammar.

Chapter 1 deals with the vexed question of English so-called *locative inversion* structures like (3):

(3)   a. Under the rock was lying a large snake.
      b. In the sphere could be seen several space aliens.
      c. At that time were invented new forms of defensive rhetoric.

This chapter, mostly written in 1994–1996, arose as a response to Bresnan (1994), which argued that the initial PPs in (3a, b) are subjects. Chapter 1 develops a range of evidence that they are not and that such clauses have invisible expletive subjects. An interesting consequence of these conclusions, if true, is that the evidence that Bresnan (1994) took to show the subjecthood of the relevant PPs actually argues that these phrases fall under the category of *noncanonical* DP behavior, known principally in the case of 'unexpected' or 'quirky' case marking, for example, dative for subjects. The discussion reveals that it is all too easy to draw an erroneous conclusion on the basis of a few (real) arguments that favors a position one finds pleasing because that pleasing character may deter one from seeking evidence against that position. In effect, one is always balancing the pros and cons of various proposals and one must beware of prematurely concluding P on the basis of evidence for it if one has not systematically considered the question of available evidence against it.

Chapter 2 addresses a notable convergence of views among the GB, LFG, and HPSG frameworks. For quite distinct theoretical reasons, all three of these positions developed during the 1980s came to embody the claim that there can be no phenomenon in NL syntax that could be informally characterized as "raising to complement/object of P." This *might*, for instance, be the proper analysis of cases like (4), as in fact suggested in Postal (1974: 363, note 7):

(4)   Dora was depending on James to bring the wine.

It is argued, morever, that despite the theoretical convergence cited that would preclude any raising treatment for (4), that is actually the correct analysis. If so, the theoretically 'forbidden' phenomenon exists in English. While many might be disturbed by controversy and lack of agreement in syntax, this essay could be taken to justify a certain skepticism about theoretical *concord*.

Chapter 3, which originated as a lecture given at the University of Maryland in May 2000, deals with a curious set of restrictions initially visible in certain interactions with Complex DP Shift and Right Node Raising constructions and illustrated by contrasts like (5) and (6):

(5)   a. I believe [the woman who is favored to win]$_1$ to have screamed.
      b. I believe [the woman who is favored to win]$_1$ to be a doctor.
      c. I believe [the woman who is favored to win]$_1$ to be you.

(6)   a. I believe t$_1$ to have screamed [the woman who is favored to win]$_1$.
      b. I believe t$_1$ to be a doctor [the woman who is favored to win]$_1$.
      c. *I believe t$_1$ to be you [the woman who is favored to win]$_1$.

Here while in general the arguably raised (to object) subject of an infinitival complement with a main verb like <u>believe</u> can be the target DP of the Complex DP Shift
phenomenon, not so in cases like (5c). This chapter explores the reasons for this
apparent anomaly and its connections to a number of other peculiar restrictions. There
emerge grounds for skepticism both about views that see Complex DP Shift and Right
Node Raising as fundamentally distinct from left extractions and about those that
reject the notion of invisible resumptive pronouns, and there also emerges a straightforward argument for a 'nonderivational' property of these constructions.

Chapter 4 argues for the existence of a grammatical category distinction in English DPs that both traditional grammar and more modern research seem mostly not
to have recognized. This distinction is taken to underlie such a priori puzzling contrasts as (7):

(7)   a. Tanya attended (in the matriculation sense) some school/*something/it.
      b. Tanya discussed some school/something/it.
      c. Tanya discussed some school$_1$/*something$_1$ after attending (in the matriculation
         sense) it$_1$.

This chapter could be said to be skeptical of the possibility of an adequate account of
English syntax that does not appeal to the posited category distinction.

Chapter 5 grew out of research begun jointly with Haj Ross and took more form
as a talk "On the Grammar of <u>Squat</u>" given at the Yale University Department of
Linguistics Reunion on November 10, 2000. The skeptical morals here are severalfold.
There is the general implication that much less is understood about the grammar of
even well-studied NLs than is often implied. In this case, now quite current slang
forms are shown to have hitherto largely unstudied and surprising properties relevant
not only to their own analysis but also to that of central standard forms. Further,
evidence emerges that even systematic morphological relations characteristic of a
class of forms can be quite deceptive as to their implications for the grammatical
analysis of those forms.

The reader will notice that inter alia the topics of chapters 1–5, if developed as
promised, will flesh out and support the claims at the beginning of this introduction that it is not serious to imagine that linguists are today in possession of, or
even close to, adequate descriptive accounts of syntax, even for a heavily studied
NL like English.

Chapter 6, while raising serious issues of linguistic theory, is also in a sense tran-
sitional to the concerns of part II, as it uncovers an unpleasant feature of much common linguistic theorizing, namely, deep question begging. It is argued that a critical
claim about the role of the lexicon that underlies the assumption that NLs could have
generative grammars in the technical sense is supported in a literature that dates to
the mid-1950s only by begged questions. This situation is not what one would expect to find in real linguistics but is entirely expected internal to the topic of part II,
which is something specious that masquerades as linguistics. This chapter presents
arguments based on a variety of phenomena that NLs have a property called *openness*, which precludes the possibility of their having proof-theoretic/generative grammars. The phenomena at issue include direct discourse.

Part II contains eight essays, seven of which purport to uncover something that I claim is justifiably called *junk linguistics*. The latter is defined not by the substantive matters it touches on but by the standards, more accurately lack of same, that govern what to a significant extent only purports to be linguistic inquiry. It is one thing to lack insight, to propose defective principles, to suggest generalizations that do not stand up. All this is a regrettable but nearly inevitable part of normal inquiry. It is a quite different thing to flout minimal standards of scholarly procedure; to ignore the literature; to claim such and such generalization holds when one knows or should know it does not; to generalize to grand claims from a few selected cases; to develop techniques, rhetorical and otherwise, for avoiding falsification; to deliberately cite certain facts that support one's proposals while deliberately not citing those that do not; to fail to respond to criticisms and to restate criticized positions as if no critique existed not because the challenges do not merit a response but because one lacks a viable response; to utilize other people's ideas without credit; to claim that someone whose work one is criticizing has said such and such when there is no basis for such a claim[4]; and so on. Combinations of various of these and other unacceptable procedures inevitably yield something that, while purporting to be linguistics, is actually junk linguistics.[5] The latter claims to advance the understanding of NL, but it is a pretense and fundamentally a deception.[6]

That junk linguistics should not exist is uncontroversial, and it would be soothing and thereby quite tempting to think that it does not. Moreover, the contemporary culture of linguists is, I believe, unwisely unreceptive to any claims that it does. Especially, this culture is certainly extremely defensive about questioning the standards of the influential and powerful.

But facts about linguistics aside, this would be a puzzling state of affairs. For scientific fraud and fakery in general is hardly rare and whole works are devoted to its dissection; see for instance the excellent volume by Broad and Wade (1982).[7] After all, the term *junk science* on which *junk linguistics* is calqued has a well-known non-null extension. By what miracle could one expect that the field of linguistics would be free of such things? To give one concrete example, Postal and Pullum (1997) document a clear case where a major linguistic figure distorted to a biographer (the latter a person in general untutored in linguistics and its history) the history of that figure's own department, a history in which I was marginally personally involved. The distortion, not surprisingly, made the figure appear far more positively with respect to the (remarkably marginal and minor) issues at stake than reality indicates. The validity of the historical claims in Postal and Pullum (1997) has never been challenged. But after it appeared, I received a note from the chairman of a major Department of Linguistics in the United States. Therein the chairman expressed distaste and fatigue with the sort of quarrelsome content of our article and expressed worries about its negative effect on students. No negative feeling was directed toward the dishonesty we had documented. That is, the chairman's critical attitude challenged exclusively the revelation and correction of falsehood, not the falsehood itself, although nothing that addressed the conclusion of falsehood was presented. In my experience, this attitude, which sees *exposure* of misbehavior (at least that by a favored few) as in bad taste while ignoring or finding some strained justifcation for the behavior itself is not isolated. But a field that allows the pseudovalue of consensus that includes at least a dictated silence about misdeeds primacy over the truth, some of which may be displeasing, is all too likely to obtain a lot more consensus than truth.

Junk linguistics of course attempts to impersonate real linguistics as junk science in general attempts to impersonate real science. My view is that the best defense against junk linguistics is precisely the skeptical attitude referenced in the title of this work. Here there are several aspects. First, one must of course intellectually challenge, at least to oneself, claims that such and such generalization or princple holds either for a particular NL or, more grandly, for all. One wants to know where this has been shown, what data sets support it, what data sets if any attack it, and so on. When one is told that so and so has shown such and such, one needs to demand references, specifically page references.[8] Second, one must try to analyze as clearly as possible the logic of the purported support for various proposals. However, certain aspects of junk linguistics are more insidious than simply inadequately supported or false claims. A recurring feature is utilization of a pretentious terminology to make grandiose-*sounding* claims that, on analysis, turn out to involve no factual propositions about the subject matter at all. Good examples of this with respect to the study of passivization are found in chapter 8. One different example should suffice for illustration here.

Smith (1999: 1) begins his investigation of the linguistic contributions of a leading contemporary figure by stating flatly that "he has shown that there is really only one human language." This claim is then repeated (1999: 214) at the end of Smith's laudatory volume, indicating that it is meant to represent an important accomplishment. Notable is that nowhere is there any citation of a work or even part of a work where a demonstration of this seemingly remarkable property could be found. Nor is there any even attempted analysis of what the claim of 'only one language' could mean. Evidently, it is not intended to signify that we all speak Mohawk.[9] What could show that it is false and that there are, say, two, nine, or sixteen hundred languages? Given the undeniably vast diversity among the totality of attested NLs, such a claim can only mean that there are certain similarities among them. The situation is entirely analogous to that for the totality of known human beings, which reveals a vast diversity and yet an enormous core of common features (hence, e.g., the possibility of medical science). But is any biologist going to claim thereby that there is only one human being?

Evidently then, the relevant claim is empty, mere use of an unanalyzed terminology ('one language') with presumed deep and important connotations to cover a claim no less devoid of content than would be a 'one human being' claim. Such empty puffery is typical of junk linguistics. Especially disturbing is that such vacuous 'accomplishments' can be claimed, discussed, published, reviewed, and so forth, all without any outcry, as if the difference between such pretense and real inquiry was not noticed.[10] This should be a warning that the rot of junk linguistics is widespread and little recognized. But another aspect of the invocation of contentless accomplishments like the 'one language' claim deserve stress. Research that has *real* scientific accomplishments has no need to cite such empty pseudoresults. Their invocation should be regarded, first, as an attempt to fill the gap left by the lack of actual results and, second, consequently, in effect as an unintended admission of the lack of same. Remarkable then is the apparently widespread inability to hear the admission.[11]

Relevant to an understanding of this situation, no doubt, are the mind-clouding effects of (i) the repetition of claims, (ii) the association of claims with prestigeful figures, and (iii) the creation by the process of education of interest groups whose career success depends as much or more on the conformity of expressed views with certain doctrines as on their validty and scientific grounding. Here one should, for instance, look most carefully at the recent discussion of the introduction and wide-spread acceptance of the so-called minimalist program, arguably successfully intro-duced with no groundings in descriptive success whatever.[12] The fact that one finds a claim repeated in ten, twenty, or one hundred works cannot, no one doubts, in itself legitimize the claim. But there is nonetheless a tendency to attribute serious-ness to widely cited claims. My experience suggests, though, that wide affirma-tion of a claim is in current linguistics not even ground for confidence that it is serious, still less that it is well supported or true. As already indicated, chapter 2, though not concerned with junk linguistics, documents a case of broad cross-framework agreement that a certain syntactic phenomenon, arguably found in English, is universally impossible.

Chapter 7 examines a popular and widely cited purported explanation of the strong crossover effect, a phenomenon apparently first made explicit in Postal (1971). The junk linguistic character of this proposal is revealed sharply inter alia by the fact that the so-called explanatory account can be shown to fail not on the basis of data from some exotic NL but merely because of English data, already published (in Postal, 1971) a decade *before* the essential junk claim appeared. Ominously, this state of affairs in no way interfered with a long and happy acceptance of the junk claim. That is, for a junk linguistic proposal, having been, in effect, already shown to be false before it was even formulated appears to be no current barrier to success.

Chapter 8 considers a range of transformational grammar views about English passives. It is argued that they manifest a characteristic combination of junk features that includes seemingly strong claims actually rendered empty by rhetorical dodges, grotesque factual incompatibility of claims if interpreted in a way with factual con-tent, and an overall deep contempt for the facts, standards of argument, the litera-ture, and readers. It is shown, for instance, that some strong (if interpreted factually) transformational claims about passives of the 1970s were not only already known in the 1950s to be false but also known to be such by the author of the later claims.

Chapter 9, previously published in 1988, takes the form of a series of parodies of junk linguistic claims, although the term 'junk linguistics' was not used. But the parody form should not obscure the serious intent. Herein is cited inter alia what is, one hopes, the only case in the history of inquiry where an author states that a propo-sition A *is a theorem of* certain assumptions B, then states that he has no proof of A from B, and then adds that it is unlikely any proof can be constructed. A twenty-first-century reader might imagine that such incoherence could, at worst, only have appeared outside of a parody in some marginal outlet, a very bad beginning student paper, a set of parochial working papers, or a missupervised thesis in, maybe, a de-prived or isolated third world university, and so on. Not at all; it was published in what many might consider the then (and now) most prestigious current journal of theoretical linguistics. Moreover, despite the absurdity, in the intervening twenty-four years, neither the author nor the editor who approved its publication have, to my knowledge, in any way recognized the junk linguistic character of the passage, which thus remains unrepaired.[13] Except for its place in my parody and a citation in Postal (1982), I do not know that it is ever mentioned. The implication is, evidently, that even the most obvious junk linguistic failure, one trivially discernible independent of facts and entirely on internal grounds, is cost-free for its perpetrator. Anyone who doubts that junk linguistics is a real and longstanding phenomenon should try to find an alternative account for all of (i) the production and writing of the set of claims just cited, (ii) their unimpeded passage before the eyes of several readers for this prestigious journal, (iii) their satisfaction of the editor's standards for publication, and (iv) their survival over decades without correction. A key conclusion is that, unlike the parallel situation with junk work in many other fields, junk linguistics seems to incur no sanctions.

Chapter 10 argues for the intrusion of junk linguistics into the refereeing process for the National Science Foundation. A specific referee report is analyzed in detail and argued to be a nearly perfect model of junk linguistic thinking disguised as refereeing.

Chapter 11 focuses on issues of ethics and honesty in a passage putatively concerned with the foundations of linguistics. Here is junk linguistics arguably at its absolute worst with an author contradicting himself internal to the passage, contradicting other nearly contemporary work of his own, contradicting his own accurate remarks of decades earlier, scorning fundamental and universally acclaimed results of modern logic, and ignoring criticisms of his position he evidently cannot answer, all in aid of a foundational position that is straightforwardly incoherent. The reader who for whatever reasons a priori doubts the existence of junk linguistics might well be advised to begin here.

Chapter 12 undertakes a bit of lexicographic analysis of arguably curious and obscure usages of linguists themselves, ones like "X follows automatically from Y," "X virtually holds," and "X is natural." It is suggested that these usages in themselves reveal a strong underlying current of junk linguistic thinking.

Chapter 13, the final substantive essay of part II, investigates recent claims that such and such supposed feature of NL is (*virtually*) *conceptually necessary*. It is suggested that such jargon is a substantively empty means, hence one to be expected in junk linguistics, of promulgating claims in the absence of any serious argument or evidence for them. It is argued in detail that certain claims of this type are not only unsupported but also unsupportable, since they are false. A key issue involved is what amounts to rhetorical facilitation of serious and very longstanding question begging about the nature of NL grammars.

Chapter 14 provides a brief set of schematic personal suggestions of how one should in principle deal with junk linguistics. As signaled in this book's title, a key component should be a thoroughgoing skepticism, one that begins with one's own views. Those who have different ideas about how to react to junk linguistics should be urged to make them public.

STUDIES IN LINGUISTICS

A Paradox in English Syntax

1. Introduction

1.1. Paradoxes

The notion of 'paradox' relevant to this essay is nicely defined in (1):

(1) Sainsbury (1988: 1)
     "This is what I understand by a paradox: an apparently unacceptable conclusion derived
     by apparently acceptable reasoning from apparently acceptable premises. Appearances
     have to deceive, since the acceptable cannot lead by acceptable steps to the unaccept-
     able. So, generally, we have a choice: Either the conclusion is not really unacceptable,
     or else the starting point, or the reasoning, has some nonobvious flaw."

Early sections of this study argue that common, perhaps even standard assumptions about English grammar yield a paradox in this sense when combined with certain observations about a puzzling class of sentences. It is ultimately claimed that
one can resolve the paradox by adopting a particular set of grammatical assumptions;
a partial development of these makes up section 9.

1.2. Factual background

A characteristic feature of one rather formal style of English is the existence of structures I refer to with considerable theoretical prejudice as *null expletive subject* (NEX)
clauses. They are illustrated by the sentences in (2):

(2) a. Under the table was lying an elderly crocodile.
     b. Toward the island advanced the huge enemy armada.
     c. Aissen and Hankamer (1972: 502)
        Under this verb is embedded the S containing the cyclic subject.
     d. Aissen and Hankamer (1972: 502)
        To these causes are attributed most of the financial catastrophes of the decade.
     e. Aissen and Hankamer (1972: 502)
        To the social director fell the task of finding accommodations for all the visiting icthyologists.
     f. Green (1985: 117)
        To every VP rule with certain properties corresponds an S rule with related properties.

A rough atheoretical characterization of NEX clauses is as follows: They consist of a preverbal PP, henceforth the *X-PP*, a verbal expression, possibly other elements, and a postverbal DP expression that determines the finite verb agreement. Hereafter, I refer to this DP as the *P(otential)-subject*, since, in general, each NEX clause corresponds to a non-NEX clause where the P-subject is in standard subject position (and the X-PP possibly postverbal). NEX clauses were probably first analyzed in modern terms in Emonds (1970, 1976).

NEX clauses have rather curious properties linked to the notion subject just mentioned as follows. Most English (finite) clauses have an unambiguously identifiable element one can refer to as a *standard superficial subject* (hereafter S3). The S3, typically a DP,[1] precedes the finite verb in nonsubject/auxiliary inversion clauses, determines verb agreement, concords with a tag if one is present, corresponds to the raised element in a raising construction with verbs like <u>seem</u>, occurs postposed to the first auxiliary in subject/auxiliary inversion clauses, and so on. It is plausible to suggest, at least for English, that principle (3) holds:

(3) Every finite clause has one and only one S3.[2]

NEX main clauses challenge (3) in that there is no clear candidate for S3 status. To this challenge there are in effect several logical responses and various proposals actually found in the literature. One response would simply reject (3) and take NEXs to have no S3s. If though (3) is maintained there are at least three subpositions with respect to NEXs, represented in (4):

(4) a. The S3 is an invisible expletive; see Coopmans (1989), Lawler (1977), and Postal (1977).
     b. The S3 is the postverbal DP that detemines verb agreement, that is, the P-subject (e.g., <u>the huge enemy armada</u> in (2); see Bresnan (1976, 1977), Kathol and Levine (1993), and Levine (1989)).
     c. The S3 is the X-PP.

Although (4c) might, given widely accepted assumptions about the nature of S3s, a priori seem far-fetched, such a position was proposed in Stowell (1981: 269–276) and accepted in Pesetsky (1981/1982: 330). Moreover, in a number of works, Bresnan

(1989, 1991, 1994, 1995) and Bresnan and Kanerva (1989, 1992) consider all of (4), present arguments against (4a), and conclude that (4c) is the correct analysis of NEX clauses. More precisely, this is concluded about the restricted subclass of NEX clauses dealt with, those where the fronted phrase is a locative or directional PP, which Bresnan references under the rubric *locative inversion*. As mentioned later, this terminology is hardly ideal, as there is a wide range of otherwise structurally similar NEX clauses whose elements are not subsumed by even the broadest interpretation of 'locative'. Bresnan's conclusions were based inter alia on two important observations she has made about the interactions of NEXs with extraction constraints. These appear to show that the X-PPs in NEXs obey constraints on extracted subjects, that is, on extracted S3s. This evidence is strengthened later.

But the burden of this essay is to argue that rather than justifying conclusion (4c), Bresnan's work in effect reveals a paradox in English syntax. This arises when one considers (i) certain common assumptions about English grammar, (ii) the strengthened evidence from extraction facts that seemingly indicate that the X-PPs in NEX clauses are subjects, and (iii) a variety of evidence, which Bresnan did *not* consider, that X-PPs are *not* subjects. As with other intellectual paradoxes, the recognition of this one is ultimately not a negative result but rather a genuine opportunity to understand something deeper about the subject matter. For if, as it turns out, given a background set of assumptions A, different factual assumptions suggest both that certain phrases in certain sentences have and do not have certain properties P (here, those defining subjecthood in a specific sense), at least one of A must be false. So I agree with Bresnan (1994) that NEX clauses tell us something important about the 'architecture of universal grammar', as well as about English grammar in particular, but for very different reasons. There is little overlap between the conclusions I draw and those induced in Bresnan's recent work. Where the latter concludes that NEX cases support the version of the Lexical Functional Grammar (LFG) framework she advocates, I will appeal to a quite different set of assumptions.

As already mentioned, the class of NEX clauses on which Bresnan focuses are those commonly and not unnaturally called locative inversion cases. 'Locative' in this sense is characterized by Bresnan (1994: 75) as subsuming "a broad range of spatial locations, paths, or directions, and their extensions to some temporal and abstract locative domains." This seems to me an inadequate and rather arbitrary way to slice up the class of NEX clauses. Even taking into account the vague and unclarified 'extensions' and 'abstract' locative domains, this kind of description does not give a real sense of the richness of the class of PPs that define NEX structures.[3] That characterization seems, for instance, to have no obvious application to many relatively banal NEX examples:

(5)   a. Lawler (1977: 502)
           To the states is entrusted the power to regulate education (by the Constitution).
      b. For that perverted cause were slaughtered thousands of innocents.
      c. From condition (i) can be deduced the fact that every verb contains two vowels.
      d. During the reign of Queen Lulu II were built many fabulous monuments.
      e. With this pen seems to have been written the first verse of that famous sonnet.
      f. Against that proposal can be objected the fact that no one is entirely logical.

g. Throughout that period were undertaken some impressive feats of irrigation.
h. To those questions correspond the following answers.
i. On this election may well depend the future of our entire planet.

Here, at least examples (5a, b, c, e, f, and h) do not seem to be subsumed by Bresnan's characterization. Nonetheless, the basic properties that define what appears to me to just be the locative inversion subpart of the NEX construction are equally found in structures that do not involve locatives, like those of (5); these properties include, as will be shown, the extraction facts that loom so large in Bresnan's conclusion that the X-PPs of NEX clauses are (functional) subjects. It is not clear that there is any English-internal justification for picking out locative inversion cases as a separate construction; in any event, I do not do so here.

2. Subject properties of X-PPs

2.1. Remarks

Although Bresnan (1976, 1977) assumed (4b),[4] her recent works adopt assumption (4c), as specifically interpreted internal to the LFG framework. Under this interpretation, the X-PPs in NEX clauses are subjects at the (grammatical) function level (functional structure) but not phrase structure subjects at the surface level, since in effect they have been extracted. I certainly agree with Bresnan as well as other work that the X-PPs are extracted. In cases like (2), the extraction can presumably be identified with PP topicalization. But although the bulk of work on NEX clauses seems limited to PP topicalization cases, otherwise parallel clauses manifest other types of extraction, highlighted in (6):[5]

(6)   a. Aissen and Hankamer (1972: 502)
          They are planning to destroy the old church, *under which* are buried six martyrs.
       b. Aissen and Hankamer (1972: 503)
          These are the causes *to which* are attributed most of the financial catastrophes of the decade.
       c. *On what wall* should be hung the portrait of Generalissimo Francisco Franco?
       d. *During what period* were first developed effective pork-preservation methods?
       e. It was *there* that were first developed effective pork-preservation methods.
       f. *No matter where* he thinks were first developed pork-preservation methods, . . .

That X-PPs are extracted, a point on which Bresnan and I are in total agreement, thoroughly undermines any argument for the subjecthood of X-PPs based on subject raising, that is, based on facts like (7):

(7)   a. On the wall were standing two large blackbirds.
       b. On the wall seemed to be standing two large blackbirds.
       c. On the wall I believe to have been standing two large blackbirds.
       d. On the wall are believed to have been standing two large blackbirds.
       e. *I believed on the wall to have been standing two large blackbirds.
       f. *It is impossible for on the wall to have been standing two large blackbirds.

For, as partially noted in Lawler (1977: 234–235), this array of facts is what would be expected under view (4); in particular, in each grammatical case, the X-PP can be analyzed as being in an ordinary extraction position. Notably, (6e and f), where this is not the case, are ungrammatical, which can be attributed to the well-known incompatibility of infinitival clauses with domain internal extraction. Given these long-known facts, the claim of Bresnan (1994: 96) that "inverted locative phrases undergo subject raising (Postal 1977)" is unfounded, since such an assertion cannot be supported merely on the basis of data like that in (6) and Bresnan provides no other grounds. While the facts in (6) are *consistent* with the view that their X-PPs are subjects, they are no less consistent with the view that an invisible expletive is the raised subject. Hence such facts play no known role in differentiating the viability of views (4a) and (4c). Arguments like that of Pesetsky (1981/1982: 330) simply do not go through: "As Joan Bresnan and Donca Steriade have pointed out to me, the idea that these PPs and adverbials move to subject position is supported by the fact, noted by Postal (1977) that these elements can undergo Subject-to-Subject raising."[6]

If, however, raising facts like (6) contributes nothing to arguing for the subjecthood of X-PPs in NEX cases, Bresnan has developed two rather striking and unexpected types of argument that seemingly do.

2.2. The Anticomplementizer Constraint argument

One goes back to the observation in Bresnan (1977: 186) that, as Bresnan (1994: 97) states it: "[T]he preposed locatives in locative inversions show the constraints on subject extraction adjacent to complementizers":

(8) a. It is in these villages that we all believe __ can be found the best examples of this cuisine.
     b. *It is in these villages that we all believe that __ can be found the best examples of this cuisine.

Thus the X-PPs in NEX structures seem to manifest the so-called that-trace effect, otherwise linked only to subject extraction. So *(8b) behaves like the regular subject extraction case *(9a) and not like the regular adjunct extraction case (9b):

(9) a. *It is these villages that we all believe that __ contain the best examples of this cuisine.
     b. It is in these villages that we all believe (that) the best examples of this cuisine can be found.

I refer to facts like those in (9a) as the *Anticomplementizer Constraint*. Bresnan's widely neglected discovery that the X-PPs in locative inversion NEX clauses manifest the Anticomplementizer Constraint is a striking argument for the subjecthood of those PPs, given the not heretofore seriously challenged (but see later text) assumption that in all other English cases the extracted elements that manifest the Anticomplementizer Constraint are S3s.

Before continuing, it is worth observing that the Anticomplementizer Constraint holds as well for NEX clauses that do not fall under the locative inversion rubric:

(10)   a. To these causes I believe (*that) are attributed most of the financial catastrophes of the decade.
        b. To the social director I believe (*that) fell the task of finding accommodations for all the visiting icthyologists.
        c. During the reign of Queen Lulu II I believe (*that) were built many fabulous monuments.
        d. On this election I believe (*that) may well depend the future of our entire planet.

2.3. The Parallelism Constraint argument

The Anticomplementizer Constraint argument alone is a serious basis for Bresnan's adoption of conclusion (4c). And it takes on greater force in combination with another rather parallel argument she has developed. This involves what she calls the *Parallelism Constraint* on across-the-board extraction from coordinate constituents. This constraint (see Falk, 1983; Gazdar, 1981; and Woolford, 1987) is illustrated by Bresnan (1994: 98) with data like (11):

(11)   a. She's someone that __loves cooking and __ hates jogging.
        b. She's someone that cooking amuses __ and jogging bores __.
        c. *She's someone that cooking amuses __ and __ hates jogging.
        d. She's someone that cooking amuses __ and I expect __ will hate jogging.

According to Bresnan, the generalization is that "subject gaps at the top level of one coördinate constituent cannot occur with any other kind of gap in the other coördinate constituent." This generalization distinguishes (11a), in which both the gaps correspond to subjects, and (11b), in which they both correspond to objects, from the bad (11c), in which a subject gap is mixed with a nonsubject gap. (11d) is then nonetheless well formed, because the subject gap is not at the highest level of the conjunct that contains it.[7]

Bresnan then goes on to note insightfully that the X-PPs in locative inversion cases obey the Parallelism Constraint, citing such data as (12):

(12)   Bresnan (1994: 100)
        a. That's the old graveyard, in which __ is buried a pirate and __ is likely to be buried a treasure.
        b. That's the old graveyard in which workers are digging __ and a treasure is likely to be buried __.
        c. *That's the old graveyard, in which workers are digging __ and __ is likely to be buried a treasure.
        d. That's the old graveyard, in which workers are digging __ and they say __ is buried a treasure.

As Bresnan observes, the pattern in (12) matches that in (10), which would follow from the Parallelism Constraint if the X-PPs are subjects, as (4c) claims.[8]

As with the Anticomplementizer Constraint argument, the properties Bresnan has documented are not limited to the locative inversion subset of NEX clauses:

(13)   a. That is the period during which were built many large monuments __ and were
          proved to have been fought several fierce battles.
       b. That is the period during which many large monuments were built and several fierce
          battles were proved to have been fought.
       c. *That is the period during which many large monuments were built and were proved
          to have been fought several fierce battles.
       d. That is the period during which many large monuments were built and they say
          were proved to have been fought several fierce battles.

One might accept, though with great reluctance, that either the Anticomplementizer Constraint argument facts or the Parallelism Constraint facts for NEX cases
are some kind of fortuitous accident. But that both constraints hold for NEX cases as
well as standard subject cases renders recourse to such a position at the least highly
implausible.

2.4. The Complementizer Effect argument

Moreover, there is in effect a third argument from extraction facts parallel to Bresnan's
that also seems to support the claim that X-PPs are subjects. This is based on
complementizer facts found inter alia in relative clauses, including those occurring
in cleft structures. The generalization is that when a subject is extracted *in the absence of a relative pronoun*, the complementizer that is obligatory, but not so when
nonsubjects are extracted. Since this is something of the opposite of the situation
described by the Anticomplementizer Constraint, call it the *Complementizer Effect*:

(14)   a. They were discussing the spaceship that/Ø the scientists built.
       b. They were discussing the spaceship that/*Ø attacked the town.

Clefts are then crucial because they permit the extraction of PPs. Notably then, the
Complementizer Effect is found when the a clefted constituent is the X-PP of a NEX
structure, although not when it is an arbitrary PP:

(15)   a. It was those towns that/Ø he studied.
       b. It was those towns that/*Ø were studied.
       c. It was those towns that/Ø she talked about.
       d. It was in those towns that/Ø she learned the best techniques for drying fruit.
       e. It was in those towns that/*Ø were learned the best techniques for drying fruit.

2.5. The Adverb Effect

The correctness of Bresnan's insight that the extracted PPs of NEX clauses obey the
Anticomplementizer Constraint is corroborated by what work of Culicover (1991,
1993a, 1993b) refers to as the *Adverb Effect*. Roughly, Culicover notes that in the presence of certain fronted adverbials the Anticomplementizer Constraint is not found. Significantly for our purposes here, Culicover (1993a: 104) notes that the same nullification
of the Anticomplementizer Constraint by a fronted adverbial occurs in NEX cases:[9]

(16)   a. Standard Anticomplementizer Constraint

*Robin met the man who$_1$ Leslie said that t$_1$ was the mayor of the city.

   b. Adverb Effect (Culicover, 1993a: 98)

Robin met the man who$_1$ Leslie said that for all intents and purposes t$_1$ was the mayor of the city.

   c. Standard Anticomplementizer Constraint in NEX Case (Culicover, 1993a: 104)

*[On which table]$_1$ were you wondering whether t$_1$ had been put the books that you had bought

   d. Adverb Effect in NEX Case (Culicover, 1993a: 104)

[On which table]$_1$ were you wondering whether under certain circumstances t$_1$ might have been put the books that you had bought

These parallelisms further strengthen Bresnan's original observation and indicate beyond much doubt that X-PP extraction in NEX cases is governed by the Anticomplementizer Constraint.

2.6. Summary

It appears then that the X-PPs of NEX clauses obey the three extraction constraints, the Anticomplementizer Constraint, the Parallelism Constraint, and the Complementizer Effect. This is a substantial basis for concluding that (4c) is correct and provides serious motivation for Bresnan's recent adoption of that position.

3. Nonsubject properties of X-PPs

3.1. Remarks

However, while a body of real evidence that argues for the subject status of the X-PPs of NEX clauses has been assembled, this is by no means the end of the matter. For except for consideration of the presence of a P and the failure to determine finite verb agreement, two very *nonsubjectlike* properties of these putative PP subjects, Bresnan's work that attempts to justify (4c) has been largely inattentive to a number of other discernible ways in which the putative PP subjects *fail* to behave like subjects (S3s). This is true, I believe, despite her remark (1994: 97, note 36) that indicates the change of position represented by Bresnan (1994): "Since inverted locatives show the same effect as subjects, but differ in some other respects from subjects, Bresnan 1977 concludes that the extraction constraint cannot reflect syntactic subject status." When, however, a collection of such properties is attested, it becomes apparent that an immediate conclusion from the materials of section 2 that X-PPs are subjects in the same sense as standard S3s is premature at best. Let us then consider nonsubject features of the putative subjects.

3.2. Failure to determine finite verb agreement

Failure to determine finite verb agreement renders the forms anomalous under a subject analysis, since there seem to be no other attested S3s with this property.

3.3. PP subjects

The presence of a P or, equivalently, the fact that the putative subjects are PPs is also an anomaly, since again no other attested S3s seem to have this property, either. I agree with Bresnan (1994: 110–111) that examples like (17) that involve initial PPs and predicate nominals are consistent with this claim:

(17)   a. Under the table is a good place to put the box.
      b. Under the table seems to be a good place to put the box.
      c. He believes under the table to be a good place to put the box.
      d. Is under the table a good place to put the box?

For, as (17d) shows, these apparent PP subjects, unlike the X-PPs of NEX cases, can appear in postauxiliary position and also in clear nonextracted positions like that of (17c). I agree with Bresnan's suggestion that cases like (17) most likely involve some form of invisible DP head and noun, so that (17a) would have a subject DP of schematically the form [a place under the table].[10]

Beyond the support for this view given in Bresnan (1994: 110–111), consider:

(18)   a. [Under the table]$_1$ looks/seems like it$_1$ is a good place to put the box.
      b. *[Under the table]$_1$ looks/seems like it$_1$/there$_1$/Ø$_1$ was placed the missing box.

That is, the phrase in the construction of (17) can, like an uncontroversial S3, antecede a resumptive pronoun in the look/seem + like construction, returned to briefly in chapter 3, but the X-PP of a NEX case cannot.

3.4. Standard floating quantifiers

The proper type of S3 can, of course, link to standard floating quantifiers (SFQs), all, both, and each, found in VP-internal positions, an ability that is unaffected when the subject is extracted. But X-PPs can never link to SFQs:[11]

(19)   a. Those women have all/both/each filed a complaint.
      b. Those women, I am sure __ have all/both/each filed a complaint.
      c. To those women were (*all/*both/*each) proposed a distinct alternative.
      d. Under those chairs I believe have (*both) been found that kind of dust.
      e. During their reigns were (*each) annexed a wealth-producing adjacent territory.

In further support of the contrast between X-PPs and PP subjects like those in (17), the latter can link to SFQs:

(20)   a. Under the table and under the bed would both be good places to store our ski equipment.
      b. Under the table and under the bed was/were (*both) stored our ski equipment.

This further attacks the subjecthood of X-PPs.

3.5. Nonstandard floating quantifiers

By nonstandard floating quantifiers (NFQs) I refer to those instances of <u>each</u> that are semantically linked to one NP but occur postposed (possibly cliticized) to another, as in (21):

(21)   He sent those girls three photos each.

NFQs can, of course, link to S3s, even when these are extracted:

(22)   a. Those girls, I am sure __ sent him three photos each.
　　　 b. It was those girls who I am sure __ sent him three photos each.
　　　 c. It was those girls who I am sure __ were sent three photos each.

As (22c) indicates, S3s that would be regarded as 'derived' in transformational terms can also link to NFQs.
　　Notably, though, NFQs never link to X-PPs:[12]

(23)   a. Under those tables were sitting two frogs (*each).
　　　 b. To the two officers fell three complicated tasks (*each).
　　　 c. At those tanks were fired three rockets (*each).

Compare the following contrast between an uncontroversial S3 and an X-PP based on lexically and semantically identical DPs with the same verb:

(24)   a. Those candidates (he learned) had been sent three questionnaires (each).
　　　 b. To those candidates (he learned) had been sent three questionnaires (*each).

3.6. Floating emphatic reflexives

Standard S3s can link to floating emphatic reflexives (FERs), a possibility that is also unaffected when the subject is extracted:

(25)   a. Those women have themselves filed complaints.
　　　 b. Those women, he believes __ will soon themselves file complaints.

But X-PPs never link to FERs, contrasting again with the cases of (17):

(26)   a. To those women were (*themselves) given the opportunity to resign.
　　　 b. Under that sofa may (*itself) have been lying two snakes.
　　　 c. Under the table may (itself) have been a good place to hide a snake.

3.7. Controllers

S3s can, of course, function as the antecedents for control, that is, can be par excellence controllers for subjects of nonfinite adjuncts, for example:

(27) a. [Those women]$_1$ were given the opportunity to file complaints without $\emptyset_1$ having to reveal their identities.

   b. [The two men]$_1$ stood near Jane and Clarissa after $\emptyset_1$ entering the room.

But this is in general not possible for X-PPs:

(28) a. *To [those women]$_1$ was given the opportunity to file complaints without $\emptyset_1$ having to reveal their identities.

   b. *Near [Jane and Clarissa]$_1$ stood the two men after $\emptyset_1$ entering the room.

   c. *At the fortress$_1$ were fired seven rockets while $\emptyset_1$ being attacked by tanks.

   d. [The chimp]$_1$ was handed a banana without $\emptyset_1$ being handed a peach.

   e. *[To the chimp]$_1$ was handed a banana without $\emptyset_1$ being handed a peach.

In this respect, X-PPs again contrast with the sort of true PP S3s of cases like (17), since, as noted in Hornstein (2001: 78), the latter can be controllers:

(29) [In the bathroom]$_1$ is a great place to hide without $\emptyset_1$ really being a good place to live.

3.8. Reflexive/Reciprocal X-PPs

English S3s cannot be reflexives or reciprocals bound by other elements of their clause. Most theories of reflexives are designed to yield this as a consequence; see, for example, Chomsky (1981) and Pollard and Sag (1992, 1994). Call this the Reflexive/Reciprocal S3 Constraint. This constraint is unaffected by extraction of the offending form:[13]

(30) a. *Himself$_1$ discussed Mike$_1$ with the other students.

   b. *It was himself$_1$ that __ discussed Mike$_1$ with the other students.

   c. *Himself$_1$, they said __ discussed Mike$_1$ with the other students.

   Consider then:

(31) a. *To Mike$_1$, himself$_1$ should never be described.

   b. ?To himself$_1$, Mike$_1$ should never be described.

   c. ??To himself$_1$ is said to have been unexpectedly described the only guy$_1$ who thought he was handsome.

The point here is no doubt subtle. While (31c) is hardly acceptable, its quality seems much closer to the less than perfect non-S3 case (31b) than to the totally impossible Reflexive/Reciprocal S3 Constraint violation (31a).

   A less fuzzy paradigm is seen in (32):

(32) a. Those tapes seem to have been bought by Ed$_1$ for himself$_1$.

   b. ?For himself$_1$ three of the tapes in question seem to have been bought by Ed$_1$.

   c. For himself$_1$ seem to have been bought by Ed$_1$ three of the tapes in question.

For me, notably, (32c), which would be a Reflexive/Reciprocal S3 Constraint violation under the proposal that X-PPs are subjects, is, if anything, *better* than (32b).

The reciprocal facts are also relatively clear:

(33)   a. Those guys$_1$ bought such things for each other$_1$.
      b. For each other$_1$ those guys$_1$ would never buy such things.
      c. ?For each other$_1$ such things would never be bought by those guys$_1$.
      d. ?For each other$_1$ would never have been bought by those guys$_1$ the things in question.
      e. *Each other$_1$ would never buy such things for those guys$_1$.

Here (33d) does not seem appreciably worse than (33c) and so it lacks the utter impossibility of a Reflexive/Reciprocal S3 Constraint violation such as *(30a) or *(31a) or *(33e). See also:

(34)   a. Those girls$_1$ would never show such things to each other$_1$.
      b. *Each other$_1$ would never show such things to those girls$_1$.
      c. *Each other$_1$ would never be shown such things by those girls$_1$.
      d. ?Those girls$_1$ would never be shown such things by each other$_1$.
      e. ?To each other$_1$ such things would never be shown by those girls$_1$.
      f. ?To each other$_1$ would never be shown by those girls$_1$ the sort of things in question.

The bottom line is that none of (31c), (33c), (33d), or (34f) is anything like as bad as a standard Reflexive/Reciprocal S3 Constraint violation.

3.9. Reflexives/Reciprocals anteceded by X-PPs

Consider now something of the reverse of the situation in section 3.8, namely, where reflexives or reciprocals are anteceded by X-PPs of NEX clauses. Since hypothesis (4c) claims X-PPs are S3s and S3s are the best possible reflexive or reciprocal antecedents, at first glance the ungrammaticalities in (35) seem to count against the position:

(35)   a. Sally and Louise were described to themselves/each other.
      b. To Sally and Louise were described the two doctors/*themselves/*each other.

However, this is not obvious since a defender of (4c) might attribute these to the independent fact that P-subjects in NEX clauses cannot be definite pronouns. So the bad cases of (35b) would be so for the same reasons, for example, as (36):

(36)   *To Sally and Louise were described you/them/us.

But even if this move successfully defends (4c) against cases like (35b), it does not work in general. For parallel reflexive/reciprocal facts involve conjoined DPs and there exists no ban on a P-subject as a conjoined DP one of whose conjuncts is a pronoun; see Iwakura (1978: 329). Thus facts like (37) really do argue against the S3-hood of X-PPs:

(37)   a. Sally and Louise were described to Mike and themselves/each other.
       b. Sally and Louise were described to themselves/each other and Mike.
       c. To Sally and Louise were described Mike and us/you/them.
       d. *To Sally and Louise were described Mike and themselves/each other.
       e. *To Sally and Louise were described themselves/each other and Mike.

Observe that the ill-formed (37e) is parallel to (38c):

(38)   a. Mary talked about Sally/*himself to Fred.
       b. *Mary talked about Sally and himself to Fred.
       c. *To Fred, Mary talked about (Sally and) himself.

3.10. Unembedded subject topicalization

Under position (4c) advocated in Bresnan (1994), an example like (39) involves a topicalized PP subject:

(39)   Above the ranch was hovering a standard type of flying saucer.

However, while standard S3s are capable of topicalization, as in (40b), there is no reason to believe that in (40a) the first NP can, still less must, be analyzed as topicalized:

(40)   a. A standard type of flying saucer was hovering above the ranch.
       b. That type of flying saucer, they never learned was hovering above the ranch.

That is, there seems to be a gap in topicalization paradigms that corresponds to an S3 of a main clause.

Moreover, the intuitive view that cases like (40a) do not involve any kind of extraction is supported by a telling argument developed in Lasnik and Saito (1992: 110–111) on the basis of certain reflexivization facts. These authors argue specifically that while 'long' topicalization of a subject is possible, as in, for example, (40b), 'short' topicalization of a subject is impossible. Their strongest argument for this conclusion depends on paradigms like (41):

(41)   a. *John$_1$ thinks that Mary likes himself$_1$.
       b. John$_1$ thinks that himself$_1$, Mary likes.
       c. *John$_1$ thinks that himself$_1$ likes Mary.
       d. *John$_1$ thinks that himself$_1$, likes Mary.

The argument runs as follows: Topicalization 'rescues' certain otherwise impossible reflexives, as in (41b). But such examples involve *object* topicalization. The parallel subject cases are illustrated by (41c and d).

As Lasnik and Saito observe, if 'short' topicalization of subjects were possible (necessary), then the principles that allow (41b) should also allow (41d). Since the latter are barred, the hypothesis that 'short' subject topicalization exists should be rejected. Given that, the fact that (4c) requires obligatory topicalization of its putative subject PPs shows that in still another respect the putative subjects of that analysis are anomalous.

3.11. 'Extraposed' phrases

3.11.1. 'Extraposed' relative clauses

A property of uncontroversial English S3s is that they permit 'extraposition' of relative clauses, however one analyzes that theoretically. This phenomenon is entirely compatible with extraction of the relevant S3. But the X-PPs of NEX clauses, putative S3s under hypothesis (4c), never permit this:

(42) a. [What woman]$_1$ did they claim was t$_1$ served beer (who$_1$ had ordered wine)?
      b. [To what woman]$_1$ did they think t$_1$ was served beer (*who$_1$ had ordered wine)?
      c. [What bridge]$_1$ t$_1$ collapsed (that had cost over a billion dollars to build)?
      d. [Under what bridge]$_1$ did they think t$_1$ lived a troll (quite happily) (*which had cost over a billion dollars to build)?

This also counts against the view that X-PPs are subjects in the sense of S3s.

3.11.2. 'Extraposed' exceptive phrases

Parallel to relative clause 'extraposition', uncontroversial English S3s permit 'extraposition' of 'exceptive' phrases, regardless of whether the S3 is extracted. But again, this is impossible with the X-PPs of NEX clauses:

(43) a. [Who else except me]$_1$ are you sure t$_1$ was sent candy?
      b. [Who else]$_1$ are you sure t$_1$ was sent candy (except me)?
      c. [To who(m) else]$_1$ are you sure t$_1$ was sent candy (*except me)?

3.11.3. Summary

I hope to have shown then that there is a range of evidence that clearly counts against the view that X-PPs are S3s.

4. The paradox: X-PPs as both subjects and nonsubjects

Within the perspective developed by Bresnan (1989, 1991, 1994, 1995), the extraction arguments of section 2 show that the X-PPs of NEX cases are subjects. The limited nonsubject behavior of X-PPs that she deals with can then be treated as minor or peripheral features to be explained in various ways. Thus Bresnan (1994: 117–118) attributes the failure of X-PPs to manifest the normal S3 determination of finite verbal agreement to the absence of certain syntactic features on PPs.

Whatever plausibility that general strategy had given the limited range of nonsubject properties of X-PPs mentioned by Bresnan, it has essentially none given the systematic failure of X-PPs to manifest the numerous subject (S3) properties cataloged in the previous section. It is not just a question of finding some alternative accounts for the lack of these S3 properties. Even (highly implausible) success in that venture would not obscure the fact that the supposed X-PP subjects of analysis (4c) simply do not behave like uncontroversial S3s in many clear ways. This collection of facts forms a paradox when combined with the extraction evidence assembled by Bresnan and strengthened in the previous section to the effect that X-PPs are subjects.

Reversing Bresnan's logic also leads to paradox. For assuming that the evidence of section 3 indicates that X-PPs are not subjects clashes with the extraction evidence, which then seemingly becomes a web of unexplained anomalous correlations.

The paradox then is that there appears to be no acceptable conclusion as to the subject status of the X-PPs of NEX clauses. Since, as indicated in (1), this is a theoretically intolerable situation, it must be due not merely to the sort of factual observations that underlie sections 2 and 3 but also to some false assumption(s) that have colored their interpretation. It must be assumed that if one can find and reject these incorrect premises, a consistent treatment of all the facts will emerge. Before focusing directly on that step, I consider further data that greatly strengthens the view that X-PPs are *not* S3s and thus suggests that the proper area to search for the false and paradox-inducing assumptions lies in the previously assumed interpretation of the extraction patterns of section 2.

5. Null expletive analyses of NEX clauses

5.1. Criticisms of null expletive analyses

Postal (1977) proposed that the S3 of NEX clauses was an invisible expletive NP, specifically an invisible variant of presentational there; that is, a version of (4a) was advocated. Although Bresnan herself notes (1994: 99) that an expletive subject analysis explains various facts that are problematic for her own X-PP as subject treatment, facts that include agreement determination, she (1994: 98–103) criticizes expletive analyses and ultimately concludes that they are inferior to her alternative. One can divide her criticisms into two categories. The first simply stresses that (previous) expletive subject analyses offer no basis for the facts of section 2, that is, in general, for the fact that extracted X-PPs obey extraction constraints otherwise apparently exclusively linked to subjects. This category of criticism is surely sound as far as it goes; no extant *expletive* analysis has offered any basis for the fact that X-PPs obey the extraction constraints otherwise linked to subject extraction.

The second category consists of all Bresnan's other criticisms, and these are, I will argue, largely without force. Consideration of them ultimately strengthens the case made in section 3 that X-PPs ae not subjects.

5.2. Lack of expletive 'sources'

Bresnan (1994: 99) claims that an obvious problem for the expletive subject view is that certain types of locative inversion NEX cases, particularly those that involve directionals, cannot occur with overt expletive subjects. At issue are contrasts like the following:

(44)   Bresnan (1994: 99 [76])
    a. Into the room (*there) ran Mother.
    b. Out of it (*there) steps Archie Campbell.
    c. About a half an hour later in (*there) walk these two guys.
    d. Home (*there) came John.

Similar data were noted earlier by Green (1985: 125-126).[14]

Bresnan (1994: 100) concludes from these data that many NEX clauses "lack a plausible source." However, the term 'source' here is neither defined nor explicated. This term has (or had) a standard usage in transformational work. But Bresnan herself has long since abandoned such frameworks. Moreover, even internal to those ideas, at least as widely interpreted, contrasts like those in (44) would hardly impose the view that the shorter versions could not be related to structures that contain invisible variants of the parenthesized elements. For instance, while it may be false that (45a) has a 'source' in which the fronted phrase is in postverbal position, surely (45b) does not suffice to show that:

(45)   a. No matter what Ed does turns out badly.
    b. *Ed does < (no matter) what > turns out badly.

In short, Bresnan has failed to spell out the logic of the supposed criticism of the expletive analysis from facts like (44) and her appeal to a vague term like 'source' makes it seem like there is some straightforward basis for the conclusion when there is not.

An advocate of the expletive analysis is free to say about (44) that nothing more is at issue than the conditions under which the expletive must (as opposed to can) be invisible. Bresnan herself (1994: 99) notes that many locative inversion cases have alternates that contain a visible <u>there</u>. An even stronger connection was noted much earlier:

(46)   Green (1985: 121–122)
    "For the most part, V-inversions correspond to <u>there</u>-constructions, with or without an initial non-subject phrase. That is, for almost every inversion sentence of the form of (16a), there is a <u>there</u>-sentence of the form (16b) or (16c), or both, where C is in (A, P, V):
    16a. CP ... V NP W
    16b. CP there ... V NP W
    16c. There ... V NP CP W"

I return to such correlations later. Thus an overall grammar of English must specify the conditions of alternation in some way. Unless Bresnan can argue that the expletive hypothesis about NEX clauses complicates this task or renders it impossible, which she has not attempted, the conclusion that (44) infirms a null expletive analysis borders on the non sequitur.

A similar remark holds for the point that Bresnan recalls from Aissen (1975) to the effect that the definiteness constraint on the P-subject that occurs with expletive there is not really found in NEX cases:

(47) a. *In the closet there still sat Fido.
      b. In the closet still sat Fido.
      c. *Suddenly there ran out of the woods Bob and Louise.
      d. Out of the woods suddenly ran Bob and Louise.

But again there is no argument for the conclusion that contrasts like (47) are problematic for the null expletive view of NEX clauses ("show that [47b and d] lack sources" in Bresnan's terms).

For the advocate of such an analysis can say that the definiteness constraint, highly mysterious and poorly understood despite a great deal of work (see, e.g., Reuland and ter Meulen, 1987; and Safir, 1985), is stated in such a way as to be sensitive in part to the difference between visible and invisible expletives, more plausibly, perhaps, to other structural factors that determine that. Note, too, that the sensitivity is partial, in that there are many fine there cases with definite DPs; see, for example, Rando and Napoli (1978) and examples like (48):

(48) a. Into that cave (there) just crawled the largest snake I have ever seen.
      b. At that time (there) was said to have been rounded up the entire membership of the Communist Party.
      c. Under those conditions (there) will certainly still remain the problem of repatriating the refugees.

5.3. Typological implausibility

5.3.1. The logic of the case

Another in principle very weak sort of objection to the null expletive hypothesis that Bresnan makes is that such an analysis is *typologically implausible*. This is based on facts about other languages that allow null subjects in a range of positions where English does not. The point involves the claim that "[n]o other properties of English point to the presence of such null 'pro' subjects" (1994: 102). Even if this assertion were true, the argument against a null expletive analysis would be weak. An advocate of such could simply claim that not enough is known about NL grammar to ground any principle that would exclude an NL with the following two properties: (i) it has no finite clauses with null subjects that are not parallel to NEX clauses and (ii) it has clauses parallel to NEX clauses that have null expletive subjects. In the absence of such principles, Bresnan's rejection of the null expletive analysis on typological grounds has little weight.

5.3.2. The facts of the case

Moreover, a much stronger defense against the typological criticism is available, since the assumption that English has no null subject finite clauses outside the realm of NEX clauses, though no doubt accepted by others beside Bresnan, is arguably false.

I suggest that there are several types of such clauses and, ironically, Bresnan's thesis (1972: 136) already has discussed one of them.

Let us examine first what are called _as-Parentheticals_ (A-Parentheticals) in Postal (1994b). These are illustrated in (49):

(49)   a. Lasers can, as he has long felt, cut through stone walls.
      b. Lasers can, as he feared, cut through animate tissue.
      c. Lasers cannot, as it first appeared, cut through stone walls.

The instances of _as_ in these forms roughly correspond to the _that_ clauses of indepen-dent clauses. Note, for instance, that as in (49c), A-Parentheticals are formed from expressions that occur essentially only with _that_ clauses:

(50)   a. It appeared that lasers could cut through that wall.
      b. *It appeared a vision/something/many colors/those possibilities.

Consider then cases like (51):

(51)   a. Lasers can, as is obvious, cut through stone walls.
      b. Lasers can, as was proved by Mike, cut through stone walls.

With adjectival and passive predicates, A-Parentheticals occur without an obvious candidate for S3 status. Let us for convenience refer to these cases as _M(ysterious)-A-Parentheticals_. There are at least three reasonably straightforward proposals about their structures:

(52)   a. The _as_ in M-A-Parentheticals is an extracted S3.
      b. The _as_ in M-A-Parentheticals is an extracted non-S3 and there is a null (exple-tive) S3.
      c. The _as_ in M-A-Parentheticals is indifferently an extracted S3 or non-S3.

Incidentally, nothing relevant here is changed if (as in Potts, 2002), instead of re-garding _as_ as an extractee, it is taken to be some grammatical element, for example, a P, that is cooccuring with an invisible extracted phrase. I suspect that the common view would be (52a); see Kayne (1984: 67) and Tellier (1988: 134–135). This is pretty much the obligatory choice for anyone who adopts Bresnan's (1994) position, since either (52b or c) recognizes that English has at least some null subject finite clauses.

But there is evidence that (52b) is correct and that cases like (51a and b) involve _invisible extraposition expletives_ of the type that otherwise show up as _it_, as in (49c) and (53b):

(53)   a. It seemed to everyone that lasers could cut through stone walls.
      b. Lasers cannot, as it had previously seemed to everyone, cut through stone walls.

In (53b), the _as_ clearly corresponds to a nonsubject, given that the _that_ clause comple-ment of a verb like _seem_ can never appear as its subject:

(54)   *That lasers can cut through stone walls had seemed to everyone.

Thus a manifest property of English syntax is:

(55)   A-Parentheticals *can* be formed from nonsubjects.

Important evidence that bears on the status of (55) derives from a class of complement-taking verbs discussed in Chomsky (1981: 122), Marantz (1984: 133), Postal (1986a: 96–99; 1998: chapter 4, note 12); Williams (1981); and see chapter 8, section 8. These verbs do not permit their complements to appear as their subjects (in passives). Members of this class include <u>feel</u>, <u>hold</u>, <u>say</u>, <u>suppose</u>, and <u>think</u>:

(56)   a. Everyone intelligent feels/holds/says/supposes/thinks that gold is rare.
       b. *That gold is rare is felt/held/said/supposed/thought by everyone intelligent.
       c. It is felt/held/said/supposed/thought by everyone intelligent that gold is rare.

Nonetheless, these verbs permit passive M-A-Parentheticals just like complement-taking verbs such as <u>believe</u>, which are not subject to the constraint blocking (56b):

(57)   Gold is not, as is deeply felt/widely held/sometimes said/usually supposed/generally thought, extremely rare.

The existence of M-A-Parentheticals like (57) combines with the facts in (56) to support much more than (55). Such cases argue that the <u>as</u> in passive M-A-Parentheticals does *not* correspond to structures like (56b), that is, those with passive <u>that</u> clause subjects, but rather to those like (56c), that is, those with (extraposition) expletive subjects (S3s). If so, (52a) is wrong and (52b) arguably the correct position.

The point is strengthened because the verbs in (56) also do not permit object-raising versions of transitive clauses with complement objects. Nonetheless, M-A-Parentheticals that correspond to those are possible:

(58)   a. That Herb is a complete hypocrite is easy to believe/*feel/*hold/*say/*suppose/*think.
       b. Herb was not, as was (nonetheless) easy to believe/?feel/hold/say/suppose/think, a complete hypocrite.
       c. It is easy to believe/feel/hold/say/suppose/think that Herb is a complete hypocrite.

These data also argue that gaps in M-A-Parentheticals like those of (58b) correspond to nonsubjects, here to structures like those of (58c).

Further support for this view emerges as follows. The facts of (56)–(58) are consistent with a much stronger position than (55), namely:

(59)   A-Parentheticals can *only* be formed from nonsubjects.

I suggest that (59) is true, which excludes analysis (52a) independently of facts like (56)–(58). One sort of evidence for (59) could take the form of complement-taking verbs that do not, in simple clauses, permit their complements to be nonsubjects but do permit them as subjects. According to (59), such verbs could not permit (any) A-Parentheticals—in particular, no passive M-A-Parentheticals. As observed in Grimshaw (1982) and discussed in Dowty and Jacobson (1988: 103), Hukari and Levine (1991: 116–117), Jacobson (1992b), and Postal (1998: 108–114), such a class of verbs (see chapter 8, section 8) is represented by capture, express, and reflect:

(60) a. *This theory captures/expresses/reflects that languages have verbs.
      b. *It is captured/expressed/reflected by this theory that languages have verbs.
      c. That languages have verbs is captured/expressed/reflected by this theory.

Given these facts, (59) predicts, correctly, that these verbs preclude A-Parentheticals:[15]

(61) a. *Languages do (not) have, as this theory captures/expresses/reflects, the sort of verb in question.
      b. *Languages do (not) have, as is captured/expressed/reflected by this theory, the sort of verb in question.[16]

Further evidence with the same essential logic derives from data like (62):

(62) a. That she is greedy strikes me as the problem.
      b. *It strikes me as the problem that she is greedy.
      c. *She is greedy, as strikes me as the problem.

That is, (62a) indicates that a subject that clause is possible, while (62b) shows that extraposition of the subject is not. Hence the complement can only appear as subject. And (62c) documents that a corresponding M-A-Parenthetical is impossible, as (59) determines.

Principle (59) receives independent support from the fact that it can be taken as a special case of a more general principle that covers not only A-Parentheticals but also those called N(ull)-Parentheticals in Postal (1994b). These are illustrated in (63):

(63) a. Jerome is, I believe, quite intelligent.
      b. Jerome is, it is believed, quite intelligent.
      c. Jerome is, it is obvious, quite intelligent.

The relevant point is that the gap in an N-Parenthetical can never correspond to a subject:

(64) a. *Jerome is, is believed, quite intelligent.
      b. *Jerome is, is obvious, quite intelligent.
      c. *Jerome is, appears to me, quite intelligent.

Some principle must thus guarantee this characteristic, and a priori (65a) is preferable to the less general (65b):

(65)   a. English parentheticals can only be formed from nonsubjects.
       b. English N-Parentheticals can only be formed from nonsubjects.

But (65a) trivially entails (59), which is then arguably just a special case of a broad generalization about English parenthetical formation.

So far then, triple evidence has been amassed for the view that passive M-A-Parentheticals involve an invisible subject that corresponds to the extraposition expletive and not to the that clause or as—in other words, that in these cases as does not represent an extracted subject. First, in (57) and (58) M-A-Parentheticals are good, although the verbs in question bar subject that clauses, while allowing extraposed ones. Second, in (61) and (62) M-A-Parentheticals are bad, although the verbs in question allow subject that clauses, while banning nonsubject ones, including extraposed ones. Thus the formation of A-Parentheticals patterns with extraposed that clauses, not with subject that clauses. Third, it is independently supported by the facts of N-Parentheticals that English parentheticals cannot involve subject extraction. The view consistent with this evidence is (52b), while (52a) is inconsistent with it.

Despite the evidence just referred to, a defender of Bresnan's position that there are no null (expletive) subject clauses in English might still try to maintain (52a) in some way. However, beyond what has been argued so far, this is in effect *impossible* internal to Bresnan's overall set of assumptions about NEX clauses, given the facts illustrated in (66):

(66)   a. Such pistols are, as was obvious and Frank just demonstrated, quite deadly.
       b. Such pistols are, as Frank just demonstrated and was obvious anyway, quite deadly
       c. Such pistols are, as has long been suspected and Frank just demonstrated, quite
          deadly.

I find all of these perfect. But, according to (52a), the first conjuncts of (66a and c) each involve an extracted subject, while the second involves an extracted nonsubject, both at the highest level of coordination. That analysis *violates* the Parallelism Constraint, one of Bresnan's basic arguments for the X-PP as subject view of NEX structures, discussed in section 2.3. Example (66c) shows that the order of conjuncts is irrelevant. On the contrary, under the null (extraposition) expletive analysis of (66) advocated here, consistency with the Parallelism Constraint is *maintained*, as extraction from both conjuncts involves nonsubjects in all cases.

The evidence in (66) is strengthened by a contrast between these as facts and partly parallel facts that involve sentential which, often contrasted with as in other ways; see Postal (1994b), Potts (2002), Rizzi (1990: 15), and Ross (1984):

(67)   a. *He said cyanide pistols are quite deadly, which is obvious and I have always believed.
       b. *He said cyanide pistols are quite deadly, which I have always believed and is obvious.
       c. *He said cyanide pistols are quite deadly, which was long suspected and Frank just
          proved.
       d. *He said cyanide pistols are quite deadly, which Frank just proved and was long
          suspected.

The (66)/*(67) contrast will follow from the assumption that the former correspond to constituents extracted from extraposed positions, while the latter require extraction from standard DP positions. It is easily seen that, independently, sentential which cannot be formed from an extraposed position:

(68) a. *That he was sick seemed to everyone.
      b. It seemed to everyone that he was sick.
      c. *He was sick, which it had seemed to everyone.

Overall then, an additional argument for (52b) and against (52a), hence against the claim that English does not allow null expletive clauses, is that such a view is incompatible with the Parallelism Constraint.

The status of a view of M-A-Parentheticals that involve (52a) and is consistent with Bresnan's overall assumptions about English clause structure in general and NEX cases in particular is even worse than so far indicated, as shown by (69):

(69) a. Ted was cheated, as I assumed (*that) was obvious.
      b. Ted was cheated, as I thought (*that) had been proved by Michelle.

Examples (69a and b) show that the very M-A-Parentheticals that the distributional evidence from verb/that clause restrictions shows involve constituents extracted from extraposed positions, not from subject positions, and would violate the Parallelism Constraint if they did involve extracted subjects *nonetheless obey the Anticomplementizer Constraint*. Although not directly about NEX cases, this fact is, I take it, ultimately devastating for Bresnan's approach to NEX cases. For it indicates that a primary assumption that underlies her conclusion that X-PPs are subjects, the view that both the Anticomplementizer Constraint and the Parallelism Constraint are defined on subjects (S3s), is just false. The interaction between A-Parentheticals and these constraints combined with the multiple grounds for denying that M-A-Parentheticals involve subject extraction shows this cannot be the case.

5.3.3. Comparative cases

The evidence cited so far in section 5 that involves A-Parentheticals can essentially be duplicated with comparative structures. Key data is already found in Bresnan (1972: 136), which supplied the following paradigms, crediting in part William Leben:

(70) a. More is known than it seems.
      b. *More is known than __ seems.
      c. *More is known than it is necessary.
      d. More is known than __ is necessary.
      e. More is known than __ seems to be necessary.

A key point for our purposes here is that these patterns match significantly those of A-Parentheticals:

(71) a. He knew that, as it seemed.
      b. *He knew that, as seemed.
      c. *He did that, as it was necessary.
      d. He did that, as was necessary.
      e. He did that, as seemed to be necessary.

Examples like (71a) show that with comparatives English grammar permits the non-appearance of any remnant of a _that_ clause complement. As with A-Parentheticals, the question then arises whether this phenomenon of complement vanishing is possible corresponding to subject complements.

Evidence to the negative is that A-Parenthetical/comparative parallels extend to the unique classes of verbs that support the claims that A-Parentheticals preclude subject extraction, that is, that support the claim that M-A-Parentheticals involve null expletive subjects:

(72) a. More is known than (*it) is generally felt/held/said/supposed/thought.
      b. More is known than is explained/*captured/*expressed/*reflected by this theory.

All these facts support the view that like both types of parentheticals, vanished complement comparatives cannot correspond to subject complements. In short, there is every reason to think that comparative examples like (71d), which parallel M-A-Paentheticals, do not involve subject extraction but rather null expletive subjects. And like A-Parentheticals, these cases then show that the Anticomplementizer Constraint is not uniquely linked to subject extraction, since such effects manifest in comparative cases of this kind:

(73) a. More is known than he believes (*that) is necessary.
      b. More is known than he said (*that) had been reported.

5.4. Further evidence for a null expletive analysis of M-A-Parentheticals

5.4.1. Remarks

Beyond the arguments in section 5.3, a number of other rather clear grounds clash with the view that M-A-Parentheticals involve extracted S3s. These also show, rather, that the _as_ in such cases corresponds to an extraposed clause and that the S3 is an invisible extraposition expletive.

5.4.2. Number agreement

Conjoined subject _that_ clauses can determine _plural_ verb agreement, which is impossible with the extraposition expletive:

(74) a. That the company is bankrupt and that he is responsible are/is obvious.
      b. It is/*are obvious that the company is bankrupt and that he is responsible.

The M-A-Parenthetical facts parallel the extraposition cases and contrast with the subject ones:

(75)   The company is bankrupt and he is responsible, as is/*are (both) obvious.

5.4.3. Standard floating quantifiers

Conjoined subject that clauses can link to SFQs; extraposed clauses cannot:

(76)   a. That the company is bankrupt and that he is responsible are both obvious.
        b. *It is/are both obvious that the company is bankrupt and that he is responsible.

Again, the facts for M-A-Parentheticals match those of the extraposed cases:

(77)   *The company is bankrupt and he is responsible, as is/are both obvious.

5.4.4. Floating emphatic reflexives

Subject that clauses can link to FERs; extraposed clauses cannot:

(78)   a. That the company is bankrupt and that he is responsible are themselves obvious.
        b. *It is/are itself/themselves obvious that the company is bankrupt and that he is responsible.

Once more, M-A-Parentheticals match extraposed structures:

(79)   *The company is bankrupt and he is responsible, as is/are itself/themselves obvious.

5.4.5. Summary

The facts of plual agreement, SFQs, and FERs further confirm the conclusion that M-A-Parentheticals do not involve extracted S3s but rather represent instances of an extracted constituent that corresponds to an extraposed clause, with a null extraposition expletive functioning as S3.[17]

5.5. Results

The implications of this brief look at A-Parentheticals and subjectless comparatives appear to be very strong. First, English arguably has null expletive clauses independently of the analysis of NEX structures. So any attempt to exclude a null expletive analysis on grounds of plausibility, 'typological' or otherwise, collapses. More strongly still, the assumption that the Anticomplementizer Constraint and the Parallelism Constraint are both defined on subjects (S3s), which is absolutely central to Bresnan's conclusion that the X-PPs of NEX structures are subjects, is independently untenable for English and thus cannot be appealed to in the analysis of NEX cases.

6. The NEX clause paradox partially resolved

The conclusions of section 5 suggest, I believe, a resolution of the paradox that involves the subject status of X-PPs in NEX clauses. One term of the paradox arose principally from Bresnan's striking apparent demonstration that extracted X-PPs apparently alone among extracted elements that are not *obviously* subjects behave like extracted subjects. This led Bresnan to the conclusion that X-PPs are subjects. The other term arises from the fact, argued in section 3, that in a wide variety of other ways X-PPs behave like nonsubjects.

A solution has become visible based on the conclusion that the extraction evidence does not show that X-PPs are subjects because it is not true that the Anticomplementizer Constraint and the Parallelism Constraint are both defined on subjects (S3s). Rather, the A-Parenthetical facts show clearly that the former is *not* defined (exclusively) over S3 extraction. This evidence leaves how the latter is defined open. But overall, the new situation now makes it reasonable to see the problem in terms entirely different from Bresnan's. The question is not whether X-PPs are subjects; they clearly are not. The question is how the extraction constraints are to be stated in such a way that subjects and X-PPs but not other arbitrary constituents are subject to them. This formulation is not even quite correct. As section 5 indicated, it is also necessary to subsume nonsubject extraction of certain <u>as</u> and comparative cases under the Anticomplementizer Effect. I return to the formulation of the extraction constraints in section 9. First, I consider additional facts about NEX cases that both contribute further to undermining Bresnan's assumptions and further support the view that these involve null expletive subjects.

7. Further evidence for invisible expletives in NEX clauses

7.1. Remarks

Further grounds for analyzing NEX clauses as having null expletive subjects can take the form of direct evidence for the presence of invisible expletives. This will involve chiefly respects in which NEX clauses share properties with clauses that contain *visible* expletive <u>there</u>. A good way to begin is by consideration of some further arguments of Bresnan (1994) *against* the presence of null expletives, which I will argue do not show anything of relevance.

7.2. Two arguments from Hoekstra and Mulder

Section 5 already considered Bresnan's definiteness and 'typological plausibility' arguments. Bresnan (1994: 102) considers two further arguments against null expletives, due in effect to Hoekstra and Mulder (1990). The first is based on examples like (80):

(80)   a. We all witnessed how down the hill came rolling a huge baby carriage.

        b. We suddenly saw how into the pond jumped thousands of frogs.

These are supposed to show that it is not possible to capture the fact that NEX clauses manifest the Anticomplementizer Constraint by claiming that the null expletive subject is "licensed only by a locative PP in the same position as WH-extracted phrases." I do not really follow how this argument yields an objection to null expletives; it is supposed to depend on the idea that cases like (80) show that the position of extracted WH-phrases (SPEC, CP) is already filled, by the how.

But I believe examples like (80) are irrelevant, since the best analysis of this type of how is probably that it is a restricted complementizer, thus parallel to that and not to a WH-phrase. It is surely not a question form of a manner adverbial. Observe such contrasts as the following:

(81)   a. They may wonder how else we could proceed.
       b. Did they witness how (*else) down the hill came rolling a baby carriage?

(82)   a. They may ask how on earth a bright light could have shone into the room.
       b. They did not testify how (*on earth) into the room suddenly shone a bright light.

In any event, I see no clear way in which these facts bear on the posit of a null expletive in NEX clauses.

The second argument is more straightforward:

(83)   Bresnan (1994: 102)
       "questioning the inverted locative fails to trigger auxiliary inversion (I-to-C movement), which is obligatory where there is a subject and impossible where the subject itself has been extracted."

That is, a paradigm like (84) parallels a standard subject one like (85), where both contain unstressed auxiliaries:

(84)   a. On which wall hung a portrait of the artist?
       b. *On which wall did hang a portrait of the artist?

(85)   a. Which wall contained a portrait of the artist?
       b. *Which wall did contain a portrait of the artist?

That the locative behaves likes an extracted S3 argues that it is such, incompatible with the view that there is a null expletive subject.

While this argument from unstressed auxiliaries is sound as far as it goes, it doesn't go far enough. For consider question S3 extraction when the auxiliary do is stressed:

(86)   Which wall (must we conclude) DID contain a portrait of the artist?

In this case, a (stressed) auxiliary is possible in the presence of an extracted subject. If then the X-PP of a NEX clause were an S3, one would expect it to be compatible in the question case with a stressed auxiliary do. But this is impossible:

(87)   a. On which wall HUNG a portrait of the artist?
       b. *On which wall (must we conclude) DID hang a portrait of the artist?

In short, the two auxiliary arguments seem to cancel each other out. While the X-PP resembles an S3 in weak auxiliary behavior, its strong auxiliary behavior resembles that of a non-S3. No conclusion about the subject status of X-PPs can thus so far be drawn from auxiliary presence or absence data.

7.3. Presentational there properties reflected in NEX clauses

7.3.1. Setting

My position is that NEX clauses are a variety of presentational there structure in which, for reasons returned to in section 9, the expletive is invisible. Evidence for this view involves properties that NEX clauses share with presentational there structures. The recognition of such sharing is hardly new; recall Green (1985). And Coopmans (1989: 743) asserts: "Many of the restrictions on stylistic inversion in the context of preposed adverbial PPs also hold for the inversion in the presentational there construction . . ."

7.3.2. P-subject properties

As Bresnan (1994: 99, 107) herself notes, the postverbal NPs of presentational there clauses determine verb agreement, so a null expletive account of NEX clauses reduces the agreement properties of these, really anomalous under Bresnan's account, to the independently needed principles operative in presentational-there structures:

(88)   On the rock (there) *was/were sitting two giant frogs.

Second, the postverbal NPs of presentational there clauses cannot be definite anaphoric pronouns (see Bresnan, 1994: 86 for recognition of the restriction in NEX cases), isolated indefinite pronouns like someone, or single-word wh pronouns.[18] NEX structures share all these features:

(89)   a. *On the rock (there) was sitting him/someone.
       b. *Who said that on the rock (there) was sitting who?

Third, consider tags in yes/no questions. As Bresnan (1991) observes, in tag questions a declarativelike clause is followed by a tag that consists of an auxiliary verb and a pronoun that agrees with the S3 of the declarative constituent:

(90)   a. Guns are dangerous, aren't they/*it/*you?
       b. Selma will cry, won't she/*they/*us?

Bresnan then cites an observation from Bowers (1976: 237) that the latter took to argue against the S3 status of the P-subject of NEX clauses. This is the grammaticality of tag question variants of NEX cases like (91), in which the tag pronoun is there:

(91)   a. In the garden is a beautiful statue, isn't there?
      b. In the garden stood/lay a beautiful statue, didn't there?

Bresnan (1991) asserts that "the hypothesis that the inverted locative is the topicalized subject would explain this situation." She is thus claiming that the choice of the tag pronoun there supports hypothesis (4c).

But these facts of course fail to support (4c) over the view that NEX clauses involve an invisible expletive otherwise identical to there. Moreover, when one considers *nonlocative* NEX cases, Bresnan's claim breaks down in that there are topicalized phrases in such cases that would not determine there in anaphoric contexts and yet whose best tag must contain there:

(92)   a. That task fell to Gloria$_1$ but it shouldn't have fallen to her$_1$/*there$_1$.
      b. To Gloria will fall a number of unpleasant tasks, won't *her/?there?
      c. They built a number of warships [at that time]$_1$, but they didn't deploy them then$_1$/*there$_1$.
      d. At that time were built a number of warships, weren't *then/there?
      e. The following answer corresponds to [that question]$_1$, but he didn't ask it$_1$/*there$_1$.
      f. To that question might correspond an interesting answer, mightn't *it/?there?

Facts like those in (92) argue that the matching between the tag pronoun and the NEX clause involves an expletive there and not the topicalized PP. If so, the tag facts do not, contrary to Bresnan's claim, support position (4c) but actually contribute to undermining it.[19]

7.3.3. Context parallels

7.3.3.1. PREDICATE NOMINALS   Presentational there clauses and NEX clauses are subject to much the same sort of overall global constraints on the predicate classes that permit them. First, neither type of structure can be formed with intransitive predicates that take *predicate nominals*:[20]

(93)   a. Many women are lawyers in New Zealand.
      b. *In New Zealand (there) are lawyers many women.

(94)   a. Certain unfortunate individuals turn into werewolves after sundown.
      b. *After sundown (there) turn into werewolves certain unfortunate individuals.

7.3.3.2. ADJECTIVAL PREDICATES   Second, neither presentational there clauses nor NEX clauses can be based on adjectival predicates:[21]

(95)   a. That sort of heroin addict is prone to accidents on the highways.
      b. *On the highways (there) is prone to accidents that sort of heroin addict.

(96)   a. The majority of young people are hesitant about that in Mexico.
      b. *In Mexico (there) are hesitant about that the majority of young people.

A corollary of the ban on adjectival NEX clauses is that there are no NEX versions of adjectival passives, a type of structure discussed in, for example, Bresnan (1982c), Dryer (1985), Levin and Rappaport (1986), Siegel (1973), Wasow (1977), and Williams (1981):[22]

(97)   a. Regular Passive: Several boxes were loaded with cookies.
       b. Adjectival Passive: Several boxes remained loaded with cookies.
       c. In that room (there) were loaded with cookies several large, square metal boxes.
       d. *In that room (there) remained loaded with cookies several large, square metal boxes.

(98)   a. Regular Passive: Several bottles of wine were being tasted in that kitchen.
       b. Adjectival Passive: In that kitchen several bottles of wine went untasted.
       c. In that kitchen (there) were being tasted several bottles of rare wine.
       d. *In that kitchen (there) went untasted several bottles of rare wine.

7.3.3.3. COMPLEMENT CONTEXTS   A significant fact about NEX structures noted in Bresnan (1995) is that in no case can the P-subject be a complement clause, that is, a non-WH infinitive or that clause:[23]

(99)   Bresnan (1995)
       a. (The warning) that enemies were coming was written on the roof.
       b. On the roof was written the warning that enemies were coming.
       c. *On the roof was written that enemies were coming.

(100) a. The task of calling Sam fell to Mary.
       b. It fell to Mary to call Sam.
       c. To Mary fell the task of calling Sam.
       d. *To Mary fell to call Sam.

(101) a. From that testimony can be deduced the fact that he is a thief.
       b. *From that testimony can be deduced that he is a thief.

(102) a. At that conference was suggested a new line of research.
       b. *At that conference was suggested that we abandon the project.

Notably, though, identical restrictions hold for clauses with explicit presentational there:

(103) a. On the roof there was written the warning that enemies were coming.
       b. *On the roof there was written that enemies were coming.

(104) a. To Mary there fell the task of calling Sam.
       b. *To Mary there fell to call Sam.

(105) a. From that testimony there can be deduced the fact that he is a thief.
       b. *From that testimony there can be deduced that he is a thief.

(106)   a. Only at that conference was there suggested a new line of research.

b. *Only at that conference was there suggested that we abandon the project.

One might state these facts as simply indicating uniformly that the extraposition expletive is <u>it</u>, not <u>there</u>.

7.3.3.4. PREVENT CONTEXTS   Third, despite earlier examples like (7c), in which NEX structures can be formed on raising to object structures, there are various partly parallel environments where both <u>there</u> and NEX clauses are impossible:

(107)   a. Ellen prevented there from being a riot.

b. *There was prevented from being a riot.

The generalization of relevance about this environment is that expletive <u>there</u> is unpassivizable in it. Most other NPs, even expletive ones, are not:[24]

(108)   a. Students were prevented from rioting.

b. It was prevented from raining (by Zeus).

c. It must be prevented from becoming obvious that we are spies.

Notably then, presentational <u>there</u> and NEX clauses both seem to share this constraint:

(109)   a. *Ellen prevented there from dashing into the meeting three angry students.

b. *Into the meeting (*there) were prevented from dashing three angry students.

Of course, the generalization specified does not account for *(109a); there may be a more general constraint that bans even unpassivized expletive <u>there</u> of the presentational type. If so, NEX clauses share this constraint as well, as (110) indicates:

(110)   *Into the room he prevented from dashing three angry students.

Compare:

(111)   a. Into the meeting she believed (there) to have dashed three angry students.

b. Into the meeting (there) were believed to have dashed three angry students.

7.3.3.5. COUNT/DEPEND/RELY ON CONTEXTS   Next consider the environment in (112):

(112)   a. You can count/depend/rely on her to tell the truth.

b. You can count/depend/rely on it to rain during the picnic.

c. You can count/depend/rely on it to be unclear whether he is guilty.

d. *You can count/depend/rely on there to be a riot.

e. *You can count/depend/rely on there to have arrived some penguins by that time.

The generalization appears to be that, with these verbs, the object of <u>on</u> with a following infinitive cannot, for the most part, be expletive <u>there</u>, although other expletives are permitted. Limitations on this constraint are discussed in chapter 2. The relevant constraint extends to pseudopassives of such cases:

(113) a. It can be counted/depended/relied on to rain/to be obvious that he is guilty.
       b. *There can be counted/depended/relied on to be a riot/to have arrived some penguins by that time.

Strikingly, both active and passive versions of NEX structures obey the constraint as well:

(114) a. *On the bench you can count/depend/rely on to be sitting two penguins.
       b. *By that time can be counted/depended/relied on to have arrived some penguins.

7.3.3.6. PERCEPTION VERB CONTEXTS   Next, consider perception verb contexts like the following:

(115) a. I sometimes heard/saw/watched her being hassled in Jane's class.
       b. In Jane's class, I sometimes heard/saw/watched her being hassled.

Notably, it is not possible to form NEX structures on this model:

(116) *In Jane's class, I sometimes heard/saw/watched being hassled the kid you are talking about.

This parallels (117):

(117) *In Jane's class, I sometimes heard/saw/watched there being hassled the kid you are talking about.

Actually, the claim about NEX structures and perception verbs is too general. There are cases where the two can combine. But, notably, in those cases, the variant with <u>there</u> is also found:

(118) a. In Portugal, I saw a new religion arise.
       b. In Portugal, I saw (there) arise a new religion.
       c. In Portugal, I saw (there) develop a great revulsion toward foreigners.

So again the distribution of NEX clauses closely matches that of <u>there</u> structures.

7.3.3.7. A RESUMPTIVE PRONOUN ENVIRONMENT   Another environment that links NEX clauses to presentational <u>there</u> ones was touched on in section 3; see (18):

(119)   a. It looks/sounds like it is impossible to do that.
        b. It looks/sounds like it will rain.
        c. There looks/sounds like there is going to be a riot.
        d. There looked/sounded like there were two cats fighting in the yard.
        e. *There looks like there fell to Ruth the task of cleaning the pots.
        f. *There sounds like there were fighting two wild boars.

Here the constraint appears to bar the expletive there of (only) presentational there structures, including that of P-there structures. But NEX forms are also barred:

(120)   a. *To Ruth looks/sounds like (there) fell the task of cleaning the pots.
        b. *In the woods sounds like (there) are fighting two wild boars.

7.3.3.8. MIDDLES   Another link between NEX clauses and there structures is that both are incompatible with middle formation, which contrasts in this respect with participial passives:[25]

(121)   a. In this institution, inmates bore easily.
        b. *In this institution (there) bore easily many inmates.

(122)   a. At home, many such new products prepare quite rapidly.
        b. At home, many such new products can be prepared quite rapidly.
        c. *At home, (there) prepare quite rapidly many such new products.
        d. At home, (there) can now be prepared rapidly many such new products.

(123)   a. In that state, all multiple murderers used to hang.
        b. In that state, all multiple murderers used to be hung.
        c. *In that state, (there) used to hang all multiple murderers.
        d. In that state, (there) used to be hung many multiple murderers each year.

7.3.3.9. GET PASSIVES   English participial passives appear in at least two forms, with main verb be or get:

(124)   a. In that field dozens of partisans were/got executed.
        b. In that way several new recruits were/got trained.

But neither presentational there nor NEX structures are possible with the get varieties:

(125)   a. In that field (there) were/*got executed dozens of partisans.
        b. In that way (there) were/*got quickly trained a number of new recruits.

7.3.3.10. OTHER PASSIVES INCOMPATIBLE WITH NEX STRUCTURES   Bresnan (1994: 79–80) observes insightfully that although passives are a very productive source of well-formed NEX cases, not all passives permit NEX variants. In particular, she claims that pseudopassives (prepositional passives) never allow this:

(126)   Bresnan (1994: 79)
    a. We fought for these rights in these very halls.
    b. These rights were fought for in these very halls.
    c. *In these halls were fought for these rights.
    d. In these halls were fought tremendous battles for equal rights.

While I am not entirely sure that Bresnan's claim holds for the full class of NEX passives, I believe that whenever a NEX variant of a pseudopassive is barred, a parallel constraint holds when an explicit there is present:

(127)   a. In the hall, some touchy issues about women's rights were being considered/discussed/debated/argued about/talked about/fought about (by the delegates).
    b. In the hall, (there) were being considered/discussed/debated/*argued about/*talked about/*fought about in a raucous way some touchy issues about women's rights.

See also:

(128)   a. In that hospital, many victims of the explosion are being treated/taken care of/worked on/looked after by only three doctors.
    b. In that hospital, (there) are being treated/*taken care of/*worked on/*looked after many of the victims of the explosion.

Next, consider passives based on double object verb constructions. Postal (1986a) characterized the three types of passive possible with certain double object verbs as in (129):

(129)   a. Marsha gave Louise the books.
    b. Marsha gave the books to Louise.
    c. *Primary Passive* The books were given to Louise.
    d. *Secondary Passive* Louise was given the books.
    e. *Tertiary Passive* The books were given her/Louise.

While many current speakers do not accept any tertiary passives, many, including the present writer, do; see chapter 8. Bresnan (1994: 79, note 9) observes in effect that NEX structures cannot be formed on secondary passives, which she ultimately attributes to a putative basic constraint on NEX structures that the 'shifted' element (my P-subject) must be a *thematic* direct object:[26]

(130)   a. In that hall were given to Louise insightful books on wart prevention.
    b. *In that hall were given them yesterday several recent graduates.

Bresnan did not observe though that even for speakers who *accept* tertiary passives, there are no NEX variants of the latter, even though these would meet all of the conditions on the formation of such she adduces. Notably then, parallel constraints hold for presentational there structures:

(131) a. In that hall (there) were given to Louise insightful books on wart prevention.
       b. *In that hall (there) were given Louise/her insightful books on wart prevention.

Some might argue that cases like (131b) violate the constraint that NEX structures are not possible in the presence of a direct object. However, it can be argued, I believe, that, for example, <u>Louise</u> in (131b) is an indirect object, not a direct object, so that no violation of a direct object constraint could exist.

There are other cases, typically nonagentive, where passives do not permit NEX variants, for currently obscure reasons. These also seem to systematically preclude variants with explicit <u>there</u>. Compare:

(132) a. At that time (there) were reached/*hated certain conclusions.
       b. During the period in question (there) were discovered/*forgotten several important theorems.

7.3.3.11. MULTIPLE RAISING   It has been known since Cantrall (1969: 124) (see Aoun, 1985: 81–83; Dresher and Hornstein, 1979; Postal, 1974: 198–204) that there are constraints on multiple raisings of certain types of DPs, including expletive <u>there</u>. Compare:

(133) a. Jerome continues to seem to support the director.
       b. It continues to seem to be impossible to find her.
       c. *There continue to seem to be riots in Bananastan.

(134) a. The captain appeared to start to be interested in Greta.
       b. It appeared to start to be possible to treat that disease.
       c. *There appeared to start to be riots in Bananastan.

(135) a. Clara is believed to continue to undergo therapy.
       b. It is believed to continue to be impossible to square a circle.
       c. *There are believed to continue to be riots in Bananastan.

Where earlier evidence seems to have always involved existential <u>there</u>, such constraints also hold for presentational <u>there</u>:

(136) a. Into that cave there crawled strange-looking frogs.
       b. Into that cave there continue to crawl strange-looking frogs.
       c. *Into that cave there continue to seem to crawl strange-looking frogs.
       d. *Into that cave there are believed to continue to crawl strange-looking frogs.

Once again, the constraint on presentational <u>there</u> is mirrored in constraints on NEX structures, which also resist multiple raising:

(137) a. Into that cave crawled strange-looking frogs.
       b. Into that cave continue to crawl strange-looking frogs.

    c. *Into that cave continue to seem to crawl strange-looking frogs.

    d. *Into that cave are believed to continue to crawl strange-looking frogs.

       7.3.3.12. PARTICLE ORDER   In transitive structures, a typical particle can appear either before or after a direct object:

(138) a. Henry figured out the answer.
       b. Henry figured the answer out.
       c. Henry finished off the vodka.
       d. Henry finished the vodka off.

However, in presentational there structures the P-subject must always follow a particle. Consider first intransitive cases:

(139) a. In the Senate, there will come about a reasonable compromise.
       b. *In the Senate, there will come a reasonable compromise about.
       c. In that house, there grew up a future president.
       d. *In that house, there grew a future president up.

Note that the violations here cannot be attributed to some heaviness constraint, as objects identical to those in (139) can precede particles in direct object structures:

(140) Henry picked a future president up (at his house).

      Even more strikingly, P-subject particle order is impossible in passives, even when that order is fine in the corresponding actives with the same lexical/semantic items:

(141) a. To Henry they handed over the key documents.
       b. To Henry they handed the key documents over.
       c. To Henry there were just handed over the key documents.
       d. *To Henry there were just handed the key documents over.

(142) a. She cut out several figures from that picture.
       b. She cut several figures out from that picture.
       c. From that picture there had been cut out several figures.
       d. *From that picture there had been cut several figures out.

The generalization that bars P-subject + particle order holds as well for NEX clauses. That is, the patterns of well-formedness/ill-formedness in (139)–(142) are preserved when the expletive there is suppressed from each example that contains it.

      7.3.3.13. ENVIRONMENTS FROM LEVIN (1993)   In her exceptionally extensive study of English verb classes, Levin (1993) provides significant information about verb classes that occur with what she calls 'There Insertion' and what she calls 'Locative Inversion'. As far as I can determine, every class Levin lists that permits one of these permits the other and every class she lists that precludes one precludes the other. These are:

(143) a. Page 237 verbs of substance emission (e.g., <u>drip</u>) allow both.
 b. Pages 245–246 other alternating verbs of change of state (e.g., <u>defrost</u>) preclude both. /
 c. Pages 247–248 verbs of calibratable changes of state (e.g., <u>fluctuate</u>) preclude both.
 d. Page 248 lodge verbs (e.g., <u>dwell</u>) preclude both.
 e. Pages 249–250 verbs of existence (e.g., <u>remain</u>) allow both.
 f. Pages 250–251 verbs of entity-specific modes of being (e.g., <u>froth</u>) allow both.
 g. Pages 251–252 verbs of being that involve motion (e.g., <u>vibrate</u>) allow both.
 h. Page 252 verbs of sound existence (e.g., <u>resonate</u>) allow both.
 i. Pages 253–254 swarm verbs (e.g., <u>swarm</u>) allow both.
 j. Pages 255–256 verbs of spatial configuration (e.g., <u>perch</u>) allow both.
 k. Page 256 meander verbs (e.g., <u>stretch</u>) allow both.
 l. Page 258 appear verbs (e.g., <u>materialize</u>) allow both.
 m. Page 259 reflexive verbs of appearance (e.g., <u>present</u> [<u>itself</u>]) preclude both.
 n. Page 260 verbs of disappearance (e.g., <u>vanish</u>) (according to Levin) only weakly allow both.
 o. Pages 260–261 verbs of occurrence (e.g., <u>happen</u>) allow both.
 p. Page 262 verbs of assuming a position (e.g., <u>crouch</u>) preclude both.
 q. Pages 265–266 run verbs (e.g., <u>jog</u>) allow both.

I do not wish to give the impression that Levin's data reveals a *perfect* correlation between verbs that permit a <u>there</u> construction and those that permit a corresponding NEX structure. The correlations cited in (143) do not support such a strong conclusion because they are stated in terms of verb <u>classes</u> and her account does not indicate whether both are possible or impossible for each verb of the various classes. In certain cases, she specifically indicates that constructions are possible only for some members of a class. Nonetheless, the data in (143) is still quite strong support for a systematic connection between <u>there</u> and NEX structures of the sort that only (4a) among the analyses here at issue recognizes.

This point is supported further by the fact that in certain cases I disagree with Levin's categorizations. For instance, on page 246 she claims that the change of state verb <u>dry</u> is not possible in either <u>there</u> or NEX forms. I disagree, but the key point is that I find both types possible:

(144) On the line (there) were drying some of the most beautiful shirts I ever saw.

Overall then, I believe Levin's data provides excellent support for the claim that NEX clauses are a variant of <u>there</u> structures.

7.3.3.14. SOME RANDOMLY CHOSEN ENVIRONMENTS   Various other difficult to classify environments also reveal, I believe, a fundamental connection between NEX structures and P-<u>there</u> ones. So, for example, contrast the two verbs <u>fall</u> and <u>occur</u>, both of which take human <u>to</u> phrases. The former permits a presentational <u>there</u> structure and, correspondingly, a NEX clause. The latter permits neither:

(145) a. To Jenny (there) fell the task of contacting the parents.
        b. *To Jenny (there) occurred the idea of contacting the parents.

A similar set of correlated contrasts exists for <u>go</u> versus <u>appeal</u>:

(146) a. To Jenny (there) will go the poetry prize.
        b. *To Jenny (there) will appeal the handsome waiter.

See also <u>happen</u> and <u>matter</u>, which preclude both presentational <u>there</u> and NEX structures, and <u>flow</u>, which allows both:

(147) a. *To Jenny (there) happened all sorts of terrible things.
        b.*To Jenny (there) matter many things that seem unimportant.
        c. To Jenny (there) flowed all of the profits from that venture.

Further, Napoli (1993: 75) gives the following presentational <u>there</u> data that involves intransitive verbs:

(148) a. There strode into town the ugliest gunslinger alive.
        b. There went up a cry of protest.
        c. There appeared a man in the doorway.
        d. There lived a king in days gone by that I must tell you about.
        e. There stood a little boy in the corner.
        f. There suddenly burst in five policemen.
        g. *There telephoned a hysterical victim.
        h. *There spoke an imposing woman in favor of ozone.
        i. *There painted a woman on the bridge over the Seine.

This distribution of grammatical and ungrammatical structures is exactly matched by corresponding NEX cases (I ignore Napoli's "??" vs. "*" markings in (149), which do not correspond to anything in my judgments):

(149) a. Into town strode the ugliest gunslinger alive.
        b. In the hall went up a cry of protest.
        c. In the doorway appeared a man.
        d. In days gone by lived a king that I must tell you about.
        e. In the corner stood a little boy.
        f. At that point suddenly burst in five policemen.
        g. *In the corner cried a little boy.
        h. *From the scene telephoned a hysterical victim.
        i. *At the meeting spoke an imposing woman in favor of ozone.
        j. *Throughout the storm painted a woman on the bridge over the Seine.

7.3.3.15. IDIOMATIC OBJECTS   A notable characteristic of both NEX and presentational there clauses is that they are incompatible with at least a wide range of idiomatic objects, even those that are passivizable:

(150)   a. At that reunion a great deal of money/attention was paid to the new director.
         b. At that reunion (there) was paid to the new director a great deal of money/*attention.
(151)   a. During that week (some) strong beverages were kept near the children.
         b. During that week (there) were kept near the children (some) strong beverages.
         c. During that week very close tabs were kept on the children.
         d. *During that week (there) were kept on the children very close tabs.

(152)   a. During that exhibition a very strong impression was made on the paper/the audience.
         b. During that exhibition (there) was made on the paper/*the audience a very strong impression.

7.3.3.16. METAPHORICAL INTERPRETATIONS   A striking and as far as I know never previously observed fact about both presentational there and NEX structures is that they seem broadly incompatible with at least many metaphorical interpretations of verbs. Thus for a verb that has both literal and metaphorical interpretations and permits passives of both, the corresponding presentational there and NEX structures nonetheless may well permit exclusively the literal readings:

(153)   a. At that orgy many innocent tourists were killed.
         b. At that orgy a lot of time was killed in arguments.
         c. At that meeting a lot of fine proposals were killed.
         d. At that orgy (there) were killed many innocent tourists.
         e. *At that orgy (there) was killed a lot of time (in arguments).
         f. *At that meeting (there) were killed a lot of fine proposals.

(154)   a. At that meeting several women were screwed by licensed physicians.
             (i) The physicians had sex with the women.
             (ii) The physicians did something rotten to the women.
         b. At that meeting (there) were screwed a large number of women.
             (i) Unspecified people had sex with the women.
             (ii) *Unspecified people did something rotten to the women.

(155)   a. On Friday the Yankees were massacred by the Red Sox.
             (i) The Red Sox murdered the Yankees in a violent way.
             (ii) The Red Sox beat the Yankees by a wide margin in a game.
         b. On Friday (there) were really massacred several minor-league teams.
             (i) Unspecified murdered the members of several minor-league teams.
             (ii) *Unspecified beat several minor-league teams by wide margins in games.

(156)   a. At that meeting several officials will apparently be roasted.
             (i) The officials will be cooked.
             (ii) The officials will be strongly criticized.

    b. At that meeting (there) will apparently be roasted several notorious officials.
       (i) The officials will be cooked.
       (ii) *The officials will be strongly criticized.

(157) a. During that barbecue an enormous number of beers/crazed ideas were swallowed.
       b. During that barbecue (there) were swallowed an enormous number of beers/*crazed ideas.

It is bizarre that such constraints should have to be stated once in a grammar. But a view that fails to link NEX clauses to presentational <u>there</u> ones would seem committed to stating them twice.[27]

       7.3.3.17. SUMMARY   Bresnan (1994: 103) claimed:

(158) "In summary, we have seen that many locative inversions in English lack a plausible expletive source, that a null subject leads to loss of generalizations over subject extractions, that English lacks other characteristics of null-subject languages, and that a null expletive cannot in any event explain the contrasts between English and Chichewa. For these reasons, I reject the expletive subject hypothesis for English locative inversions."

But it has been shown here that talk of 'sources' is irrelevant, that the subject extraction generalizations cannot be stated over S3s, that the claimed lack of null expletive subject characteristics is only partially true, and that the evidence that links NEX clauses to presentational <u>there</u> clauses is broad, diverse, and sufficiently thoroughgoing as to undermine any account that fails to systematically relate these two types of structures. But that is exactly what an analysis like (4c) does. Only a null expletive treatment of NEX clauses seems to have a chance of capturing their similarities with presentational <u>there</u> structures.[28] One is left then with the issues of the relation between English NEX clauses and structures in other NLs and the unresolved issue of the proper way to state the extraction constraints that led Bresnan to the view that X-PPs were subjects (S3s). Before dealing with the latter obviously crucial issue, I turn to the foreign NL question and argue that, with respect to the choice between (4a, b, and c), it cannot cut the way Bresnan has claimed.

8. Foreign tongues

One of Bresnan's (1994) arguments for a subject analysis of X-PPs depends on cross-linguistic considerations—in particular, similarities between English NEX cases, more precisely the locative inversion subpart of this construction, and certain structures from the Bantu language Chichewa, which Bresnan takes to instantiate the same universal locative inversion pattern. Apparently, Chichewa locative inversion structures parallel NEX cases in a number of specific properties and yet it is, according to Bresnan, clear that the corresponding locative forms are subjects. Hence the argument is that only the subject analysis of the X-PPs of English NEX cases captures the generalizations that cover both English and Chichewa.

If one accepts the premises about Chichewa locative inversion cases and parallelisms with English NEX cases, this argument might seem to have a good deal of force. Its logic is roughly this. There are two parallel constructions, English NEX cases and Chichewa locative inversion cases in which locative constituents behave in special ways. In English, the status of these constituents, that is, X-PPs, is unclear and controversial, as we have seen. But in Chichewa, their subject status can be taken as established. This supports the subject status of X-PPs, since it permits stating the generalizations about the specific properties as properties of locative inversion subjects.

But the ability of this line of argument to show something about English is dependent on many other factors. An objector could well claim that the parallelisms between English NEX clauses and Chichewa locative inversion clauses are at least partially fortuitious or due to factors that can be captured without taking English X-PPs to be subjects. This sort of objection could be justified if one could find other NLs that have constructions that also share properties with English NEX clauses but where it is clear that their analogs of X-PPs are *not* subjects.

I claim that French is such a language, as illustrated initially in (159):

(159)   Examples essentially from Gross (1975: 93–94)
      a. Un certain nombre d'ennuis résulteront de ta décision.
         "A certain number of problems will result from your decision"
      b. De ta décision résulteront un cetain nombre d'ennuis.
         "From your decision will result a certain number of problems"
      c. Cette question correspond à cette réponse.
         "This question corresponds to this response"
      d. A cette question correspond cette réponse.
         "To this question corresponds this response"
      e. Des primes s'ajouteront à ce salaire.
         "Bonuses will be aded to that salary"
      f. A ce salaire s'ajouteront des primes.
         "To that salary will be added bonuses"
      g. Une chemise à fleurs sort de son pantalon.
         "A flowered shirt is sticking out of his pants"
      h. De son pantalon sort une chemise à fleurs.
         "From his pants is sticking out a flowered shirt"
      i. Des dossiers sont disposés sur la table.
         "Files are placed on the table"
      j. Sur la table sont disposés des dossiers.
         "On the table are placed files"
      k. Des personnes bien disposées interviendront à ce moment-là.
         "Well-intentioned people will intervene at that moment"
      l. A ce moment là interviendront des personnes bien disposées.
         "At that moment will intervene well-intentioned people"

This construction is also found with passives and interacts with raising in the same way as NEX cases:

(160) a. Des fleurs ont été mises sur la table.
          "Flowers have been placed on the table"
       b. Sur la table ont été mises des fleurs.
          "On the table have been placed flowers"
       c. Sur la table semble avoir été mises des fleurs.
          "On the table seem to have been placed flowers"

Surely, in examining cases like these, it is hard to imagine that this French construction is not *at least* as close to English NEX structures as Chichewa locative inversion cases are. If so, then valid cross-linguistic generalizations should treat French and English structures in parallel ways.

But it seems impossible to analyze French cases like (159) and (160) in a fashion parallel to the way *Bresnan* analyses NEX structures, that is, with the preverbal PP treated as a subject (S3). For French also has an analog of the English Anticomplementizer Constraint; as a body of work makes clear, this is represented by the so-called que/qui alternation; see, for example, Kayne (1976; 1984: 69–71; 94–98); Moreau (1971); and Pesetsky (1981/1982). That is, where the standard French equivalent of the English finite complementizer that is que, the complementizer qui is required in cases of straightforward *subject* extraction:

(161) a. l'homme que je crois que/*qui Marie déteste
          "the man that I believe that Marie detests"
       b. l'homme que je crois *que/qui déteste Marie[29]
          "the man that I believe detests Marie"

If then it were appropriate to analyze the French analog of NEX structures as involving PP subjects, one would expect that these cases would, like their English analogs, determine the Anticomplementizer Constraint, that is, behave like subject extractions. *But they do not*:

(162) a. la table sur laquelle je crois qu'/*qui ont été mises des fleurs
          "the table on which I believe have been placed flowers"
       b. A quelle question croit-il que/*qui correspond cette réponse?
          "To what question does he think corresponds that answer"

Thus if one adopts the very logic Bresnan appeals to and insists that English must be analyzed parallel to the straightforward analysis of an NL that contains a construction that parallels NEX structures, one is led to reject Bresnan's subject analysis of X-PPs in favor of an analysis that is also applicable to French. This is an analysis that treats the French cases as involving null expletives and hence only *nonsubject* extraction in examples like (162). Since it is surely no less obvious that the French/English parallels are genuine than that the Chichewa/English ones are, at best the French facts undermine any argument for the analysis of NEX clauses based on Chichewa. If, as I believe, it makes much *more* sense to treat the French and English constructions the same than it does the Chichewa and English ones, the French facts provide a positive argument against Bresnan's analysis of NEX clauses.

And the French situation suggests in another way that a key problem in the treatment of NEX cases is the proper formulation of the English Anticomplementizer Constraint. One now sees that this is not completely parallel to the French Anticomplementizer Constraint in that in English, but not in French, the relevant effects are found in structures like NEX clauses. One key question that needs to be addressed then is what factor differentiates English NEX clauses from their French parallels in such a way that the former yields the Anticomplementizer Constraint, but the latter does not. Nothing in Bresnan's proposal addresses this issue, which is treated at the end of the following section.

9. A novel account of NEX structures

9.1. Capturing the similarities

Previous sections have, I believe, shown that the X-PPs of NEX structures are not S3s and that such clauses have invisible expletive S3s of the there type. In these terms, the failure of X-PPs to manifest *most* subject properties and the broad sharing of properties between NEX clauses and presentational there clauses that has been supported are entirely expected. *Not* expected is that NEX clauses obey the three extraction constraints of section 2. It has already been argued that the apparently conflicting implications of the cooccurrence of these two sets of facts are not paradoxical, inter alia because, as independently supported by the A-Parenthetical data, the extraction constraints cannot be uniquely defined over S3 extraction. But that has left open just how they can be defined in such a way as to capture the English-internal generalizations. And the previous section has revealed that it is in addition reasonably requisite that the proper solution for that also provide a means of specifying that the French analog of NEX clauses does *not* yield in particular (the analog of) the Anticomplementizer Constraint.

My suggested solution to these problems, in effect an answer to Bresnan's (1994) claim that an expletive S3 analysis of NEX clauses fails to account for the extraction data, appeals to the following logic: The (extracted) X-PPs of NEX clauses, unlike all other extracted PPs, are treated by the three extraction constraints of section 2 like extracted S3s despite not being extracted S3s, because X-PPs *share certain abstract grammatical properties with S3s*, properties that are not shared with other constituents like direct objects and arbitrary other PPs. These properties can, I suggest, be characterized within an appropriate theoretical framework in terms of a view of the abstract syntactic structure that underlies case.

It seems fair to say about both traditional notions of case marking and modern applications and extensions of them that at least two different levels of ideas are involved. First, there is a syntactic aspect. At this level, one can for example recognize that there is some close relation between subject and nominative case, between direct object and accusative case, and so forth. On a different level, there is the question of the morphological nature of case marking, whether it is even morphologically present and, if so, where, whether it involves prepositions, postpositions, infixes, inflections, and so on. It should not be terribly controversial to hold that these two aspects are in principle independent. I have nothing to say about the morphological aspect here. My concern is exclusively with the syntactic aspect. Since my notions about this are quite nonstandard, I take the never-pleasing step of denoting the relevant concepts by a novel term, *Quace*. It will ultimately be claimed that each of a range of core grammatical relations, subject, direct object, indirect object, and such, defines a syntactic object called a Quace and, moreover, that these objects can be associated with certain other constituents (e.g., complementizers) via a type of agreement. The idea will be that, for example, final subjects determine for themselves a default type of Quace, call it subject-Quace (hereafter1-Quace and, in general, Quace types will be defined by the R-signs of [168] later), but that final subjects can also have a partially distinct Quace, and that elements that are not final subjects can have a type of 1-Quace as well.

With respect to NEX structures, application of the ideas just invoked can be introduced highly informally as follows: Viewed from the vantage point of other phrases, both X-PPs and the invisible expletives of NEX clauses I have argued for are unusual. The former are unusual in two respects: They are obligatorily extracted and, although non-S3s, are subject to the three constraints otherwise largely but not completely characteristic of extracted S3s. The latter are unusual in that they are obligatorily invisible, whereas, of course, other instances of expletive <u>there</u> not only need not be but also cannot be:

(163)   a. There suddenly broke out violent disagreements.
        b. *Suddenly broke out violent disagreements.
        c. Harriet prevented there from being an argument.
        d. *Harriet prevented from being an argument.

Now, it is known that there is a domain of unusual or special behavior for nominal expressions instantiated in particular under notions of *noncanonical* case marking; see Aikhenvald, Dixon, and Onishi (2001) for a recent survey of this domain. Normally, talk of noncanonical behavior is invoked in cases where a nominal expression has an unexpected or *quirky* case, for example, when a subject is dative or an object is nominative. But if one hypothesizes that there is a specific type of syntactic structure that underlies the relevant sort of case marking as well as more expected kinds (call the latter *straight* cases), one can appeal to a more general notion of quirky behavior even in contexts where no *morphological* case marking is present. This is the idea that underlies my proposal about English NEX constructions. Specifically, if the syntactic structure that underlies case marking is characterized in terms of the notion Quace, to be elaborated, then the idea is that there is, more fundamentally, straight and quirky Quace. The assumption then is that while the expletives I have argued are S3s of these constructions are subjects, they are quirky Quace subjects, that is, subjects with a Quace distinct from 1-Quace, the quirkiness being what underlies their nonstandard property of invisibility. In an NL with case marking, one would in such terms expect that the analogs would have some quirky case, that is, a non-nominative one.

Just so, while the X-PPs of NEX constructions are not S3s and thus would not in standard terms have the structure that determines nominative marking, I assume that they, too, have quirky Quace, in particular, quirky 1-Quace. This will mean that they exceptionally possess in part the sort of overlain syntactic structure that determines nominative case on S3s regularly. In these terms, NEX clauses represent two types of jointly cooccurring quirky nominal structures; in addition, it must be assumed that by and large *each of them is only possible in the presence of the other*. The solution of the paradox developed earlier, with X-PPs sharing some (the extraction) properties with S3s but contrasting with true S3s in a host of other features, then takes the following form. The extraction constraints of relevance, which treat X-PPs and subjects (S3s) alike, will be claimed to be defined not directly over (final) subjects (S3s) but over a slightly larger domain, namely, that of phrases with a restricted type of 1-Quace. It can then be claimed that the elements of A-Parentheticals and comparatives, which were shown to also obey some of the extraction constraints that X-PPs and S3s do, also have 1-Quace. More precisely though still obviously totally informally, in English all and only S3s, X-PPs, A-Parenthetical <u>as</u> forms, extracted comparative elements, and fronted adjectival and participial phrases, which also induce the Anticomplementizer Constraint (see [179] later), will have 1-Quace.

9.2. A few generalities about the Metagraph framework

To develop the ideas alluded to so far in a more precise (but still highly sketchy and incomplete) way, I will appeal to a development of an *arc-based* conception of syntactic structure like that of Johnson and Postal (1980) and Postal (1986a, 1990a, 1992, 1996), which, following Postal (1992), I refer to as *Metagraph Grammar*. The basic Metagraph idea about syntactic structure is that sentences are built of objects called *arcs*, *nodes*, and two primitive grammatical relations between arcs called *Sponsor* and *Erase*. Each arc represents the existence of a grammatical relation that holds between the object that is the head of the arc and the object that is the tail of the arc. Which relation an arc represents is indicated by its label, called a *R(elational)-sign*. That is, an arc is a pair that consists of a primitive *edge* plus an R-sign. Each edge is paired with two *nodes*, one a *head* node, one a *tail* node.[30]

The following remarks hold for the two primitive relations between arcs. They are each binary and irreflexive. Moreover, some arcs are sponsored (stand as second arguments of the Sponsor relation), while others are not; the latter are called *initial* arcs. Sponsored arcs have exactly one sponsor. If arc A sponsors arc B and they have the same head node, then B is a *successor* of A (reciprocally, A a *predecessor* of B). Any relation between arcs A and B is *local* if and only if A and B have the same tail node, meaning their head nodes are sisters; such arcs are called *neighbors*. Otherwise a relation between arcs is *foreign*. For any relation R between arcs, the logical *ancestral* (a reflexive relation) of R is denoted by *Remote-R*. So, for instance, if D is a successor of C, C a successor of B, and B a successor of A, then each of A, B, C, and D is a remote successor of itself, D is in addition a remote successor of A, B, and C, C is in addition a remote successor of A and B, and B is in addition a remote successor of A.

Some arcs have erasers (that is, stand as the second arguments of the Erase relation); others do not. No arc has more than one eraser. The Erase relation plays a key role in picking out from the total set of arcs in a sentence V a subset that represents the superficial structure of V. A necessary condition for membership in this subset of arcs is that an arc *not* be erased.

To illustrate a bit, assume that a clause like (164) involves an unaccusative verb, which in Metagraph terms means one whose only initial argument, here realized as <u>Dragons</u>, heads an (initial) 2-arc:

(164)   Dragons die.

Since that phrase is a superficial subject, the overall structure of the clause would include at least the elements of (165, fig. 1.1):

(165)

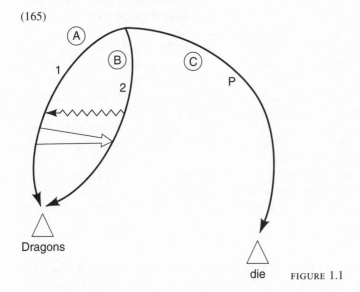

die   FIGURE 1.1

In (165) and later, the Sponsor relation is graphically represented by a wiggly arrow with the sponsored arc at its point, the Erase relation by a double arrow with the erased arc at its point. Here arcs B and C have no sponsors, while B sponsors A. By the definition, the 1-arc A here is a local successor of the initial 2-arc B, also a remote (local) successor of it. In this simplified representation, A and C would qualify as superficial arcs, since both lack erasers, but B would not, as it does have one, namely, A.

In (165), A, the successor of B, erases its predecessor. From a purely logical viewpoint, nothing precludes the inverse situation, erasure of a successor by its predecessor. While this pattern was claimed to be impossible in Johnson and Postal (1980), subsequent work, which included Postal (1992, 1996), has assumed that such relations are possible. And that assumption is crucial for specification of the notion of Quace presented here. I thus distinguish at least two subtypes of successor relations:

(166)   Definition
   a. A is a *type I successor* of B (reciprocally, B a *type I predecessor* of A) if and only if A is a successor of B and A erases B.
   b. A is a *type II successor* of B (reciprocally, B a *type II predecessor* of A) if and only if A is a successor of B and B erases A.

Given what was said about the relation between the Erase relation and superficial structure, it can be seen that type I predecessors, like B in (165), are *never* candidates for inclusion in superficial structure. Therefore, type I successor/predecessor pairs can represent inter alia different types of 'changes of status'; one instance is that of a phrase that, like <u>Dragons</u> in (165), is an object at one level of a fixed constituent but a subject at another 'later' one, with only the 'later' status having the possibility of determining a superficial status. Another is that where a phrase that is an initial and final subject of one clause 'raises' into a higher one, which, in Metagraph terms, indicates that that constituent will head an arc that is a type I foreign successor of the final 1-arc it heads. This means then that the constituent *can* be a *superficial* constituent of the higher clause but not of the lower one, although it is a constituent of both.

However, for type II predecessors, no such remarks hold. For an arc A to have a type II successor has no direct implication at all for the potential superficial status of A. One might say then, entirely informally, that type II successor structures provide a sort of 'covert' status for a phrase, one that not only is not but also cannot be directly represented in its surface status. So, heading a type I successor arc whose R-sign is Q gives a phrase the possibility of being a surface Q. But heading a type II successor arc whose R-sign is Q does not; it merely offers the possibility of sharing some properties with surface Qs.

A crucial notion for this discussion is that of *final arc*. I will, generalizing a bit the statement in Postal (1992), take a final arc to be one that has no eraser arc internal to the constituent defined by its tail node, but see later comments and also note 35. More precisely:

(167)   Definition
        An arc A is *final* if and only if no Remote Branch of any neighbor of A erases A.

Since A is a *branch* of B if and only if A's tail node is identical to B's head node, a final arc is defined as one that is either not erased at all or erased by some arc that cannot be reached from A by 'traveling' down branches that start at A or any neighbor of A.

I assume further that there is a class of *Nominal-arcs*, defined by their R-signs, which includes at least those of (168). Hereafter, arcs that represent the relevant relations are named by their R-signs; so arcs that represent the subject relation are 1-arcs, and so on:

(168)   Nominal-arc R-signs and the Relations They Characterize
        1   subject
        2   direct object
        3   indirect object
        4   subobject (see Postal, 1990a)
        5   semiobject (see Postal, 1990a)
        6   quasiobject (see Postal, 1990a)
        8   chomeur
        9   extraposed clause
        Oblique$_1$
        Oblique$_2$
        . . .
        Oblique$_n$

My assumption is that it is (only) (possibly a subset of) Nominal-arcs that define the domain of 'primitive' Quace determination. Other types of arcs will, as touched on presently, receive Quace, but only via what I take to be agreement phenomena.

9.3. The notion of Quace

My assumption is that each final Nominal-arc determines a default Quace structure. Specifically, a final 2 should determine default 2-Quace, a final 3 default 3-Quace, and so on. To define such a default structure, I see at least two possibilities. Under one, call it *Proposal A*, the default Quace of a final R-arc A could simply be taken to be some *equivalent* type II local successor of A, where two arcs are equivalent if and only if they have the same R-signs. Under another, *Proposal B*, the default Quace of a final R-arc A could be induced from A itself. That is, one could introduce a definition in which a final R-arc has by definition R-Quace, with no need to postulate an equivalent type II local successor for A, as in Proposal A. Proposal A might seem clumsy and "redundant," as it requires every final Nominal-arc to have an equivalent type II local successor. Moreover, it requires a condition like (169):

(169)   Condition 1. Equivalent Quace
        If A is a final Nominal-arc, then there is a B that is an equivalent *type II* local successor of A.

Proposal B would not require (169). These formal factors indicate that it is worthwhile trying to develop an account of Quace in terms of Proposal B. But attempts along that line have not been very successful and thus here I adopt Proposal A. To understand the issue, it is necessary to recognize that ultimately it seems correct to take the Quace structure of a final arc A to consist of a sequence of arcs, certainly including some type II local successors. This fact makes Proposal A seem more motivated than it would simply in isolation because, in contrast to Proposal B, it permits the sequence of arcs to consist of nothing but type II local successors, the simplest situation.

One can take advantage of the ancestrals of basic relations such as Remote-Successor, to define Quace structure as follows internal to Proposal A:

(170)   Definition: Quace Marker
        A sequence of arcs $\{Q_1 \ldots Q_n\}$ *is the Quace Marker of an arc A* if and only if
        a. A is not a type II local successor, and
        b. A is a type II local predecessor of Q_1, and
        c. Q_n is *not* a type II local predecessor, and
        d. for all i, $1 \leq i \leq n$, Q_{i+1} is a Nominal-arc type II remote local successor of Q_i.

The key points about a definition like (170) are, first, that it does not determine that an arbitrary arc has a Quace Marker. However, second, combined with Condition 1, it does determine that every final Nominal-arc has one. In such cases, the Quace Marker of a final arc A consists of the *maximal* sequence of Nominal-arc type II remote local successors of A. In no case can a Quace Marker be null. Third, while Definition (170) determines that the Quace Marker of a final Nominal-arc A could consist exclusively of B, the single equivalent type II local successor of A whose existence Condition 1 guarantees, it also allows for richer possibilities in which B itself has a type II local successor.

The former situation in which there is a Quace Marker with one member will be taken to define what was called the default situation, that is, *straight* Quace. The latter possibility can be taken to define the notion *quirky* Quace. Put differently, one can specify that a particular type of final constituent in a particular context has quirky Quace by specifying that the final arc A that defines such a final constituent has not only the equivalent type II local successor determined by Condition 1 but also at least one nonequivalent type II remote local successor whose R-sign is distinct from A's. Under the assumption that the notions relevant to Quace are limited to the domain of nominals, (170) limits all members of Quace Markers to Nominal-arcs. The exclusion of A itself from this specification is needed, as will be seen, to allow, for example, the arcs headed by complementizers, which are not Nominal-arcs, to have Quace Markers, a possibility instantiated, I suggest, only through *agreement* in Quace. Possibly, more generally, Quace Markers for non-Nominal-arcs of any type arise only through Quace agreement.

Many questions evidently arise about Quace Markers, but the search for their answers is in general beyond the scope of these remarks. Certain of these questions concern more generally type II local successors. One is whether a single arc can have more than one. I suggest not, a state of affairs imposed by Condition 2.

(171)   Condition 2. Type II Local Successor Uniqueness
         If A and B are type II local successors of C, then A = B.

No analog of Condition 2 is necessary to exclude the case where one arc has two *type I* local successors, excluded by the uniqueness of the Erase relation. That is, an arc that has two type I successors, local or not, violates the Unique Eraser Law of Johnson and Postal (1980), which limits each arc to a maximum of one eraser.

While Condition 1 specifies that each final Nominal-arc has a relationally equivalent type II local successor, it does not itself specify that no final Nominal-arc has any relationally nonequivalent type II local successor. That is, it requires situation (172a, fig. 1.2a) but would alone be satisfied by (172b, fig. 1.2b):

(172)   a.

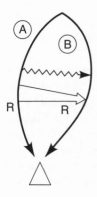

A is a final Nominal-arc

FIGURE 1.2a

b.

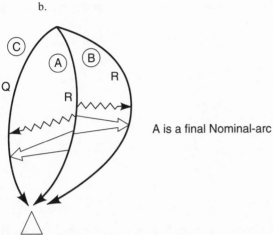

A is a final Nominal-arc

FIGURE 1.2b

But (172b) could exist only if a type II predecessor could have distinct type II local successors, which, so far purely on grounds of conceptual neatness and lack of known instantiations, is barred by Condition 2.

Another question is whether type II local successors can themselves have type II local successors. The development here ends up requiring this. But I propose minimal limitations on this situation, in particular, eliminating the case where a type II local successor has an *equivalent* type II local successor. This can be done more generally by requiring cases where a local successor and its predecessor have the same R-sign to be such that the predecessor is not a type II local successor and its successor is.

(173)   Condition 3. Local Successor Equivalence
         If A is an equivalent local successor of B, then A is a type II local successor and B
         is not.

This excludes such situations as (174a, b, figs. 1.3a, b):

(174)   a. An equivalent type I local predecessor/successor pair:

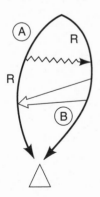

FIGURE 1.3a

b. An equivalent type II local predecessor/successor pair where the predecessor is also a type II local successor.

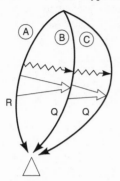

FIGURE 1.3b

Condition 3 not only bars a type II local successor from having an equivalent type II local successor; it also bars the apparently never motivated and redundant situation, which unhappily did not follow from anything independent in the system of Johnson and Postal (1980), where an arc has an equivalent type I local successor. This state of affairs would be consistent with arbitarily long sequences of useless local successors like B in (174a), none of which can influence the surface status of a constituent.

Other questions that arise from the notion defined in (170) are specific to Quace Markers. For instance, one wants to know about bounds on their size, on the possibility of the same R-sign being repeated in the sequences (though given Condition 3, necessarily at best only in nonadjacent Quace Marker positions), and so on.

Returning to descriptive issues, the intention is that in these terms, a quirky case, say dative, final subject would instantiate substructure (175, fig. 1.4), under the plausible view that dative case is determined by 3-arc Quace:

(175)

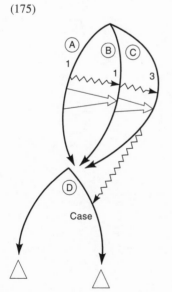

FIGURE 1.4.

In a structure like (175), A's Quace Marker = [B, C] contains two distinct arcs. Let us say in such circumstances to simplify discussion that for a final arc A whose Quace Marker contains arcs B, C, and so on, that B and C are *Quaces of A* and also that if B is an R-arc, that *A has R-Quace*. In a multiple arc Quace Marker, the different arcs do not have symmetrical status and it is important to distinguish them, which one can do terminologically as follows:

(176)   Definition
        A member, A, of a Quace Marker M is *finished* if and only if A has no (type II) local successor (that is, is the final arc of M).

So in (175) C is finished, but B is not.

Structure (175) sketches a possible view of the relation between case and Quace. Although an investigation of the morphological structure of case is (far) beyond this discussion, the analysis in (175) has case represented in part by an arc (here D) with R-sign Case, where D is sponsored by an arc of which it is a branch. Moreover, the sponsor is a Quace-arc and, further, a finished Quace-arc. One can speculate that these conditions are lawful. It would, I think, be bizarre in a structure otherwise like (175) to have D sponsored by, for example, B. For that would mean that the case is unrelated directly to the quirky Quace-arc. Under the narrower view, it might then be possible to simply define the core cases, at least nominative, accusative, and dative, as those sponsored by finished Quace-arcs with, respectively, the R-signs 1, 2, and 3.

With the apparatus just (very partially) specified in hand, one can approach the descriptive conclusions about NEX clauses argued for in earlier sections. What I want to say is that English allows a variety of final Nominal-arcs, which include 5-arcs, 6-arcs, 8-arcs, Oblique$_1$arcs, . . . Oblique$_n$-arcs, to have quirky 1-Quace, that is, to have Quace Markers with a finished Quace 1-arc. But this is subject to several conditions. The first, is that the relevant phrases are ultimately *extracted*, which, in this framework, means those final arcs are remote foreign predecessors of certain arcs (called *Overlay-arcs* in Johnson and Postal [1980]), which include Wh Q-arcs, Wh-Rel-arcs, Topic-arcs, and such. The second is that the final Nominal-arc with quirky 1-Quace is a neighbor of a final 1-arc that itself has some kind of quirky Quace. I will specify *with some arbitrariness* that this is 4-Quace.[31] Third, it is assumed that a final 1-arc with 4-Quace is only possible in this construction if it is a neighbor of a final Nominal-arc with quirky 1-Quace. Fourth, I assume that the final 1-arc with 4-Quace, which must be a sister of the arc with quirky 1-Quace, is headed by an *expletive* and, moreover, exceptionally requires its head node to have a null phonological realization.[32] This is still not sufficient to characterize the NEX construction. It must, in addition, be specified that the relevant expletive is there and not one of the expletive it found in English. A full specification of the latter condition would require a full understanding of the difference between expletive there and the various expletive it. I do not possess such. However, it may be possible to specify that a there type expletive arc is one that is a remote successor of a 2-arc sponsored by a neighboring 2-arc whose head represents a DP that is not a complement clause.

Therefore, the NEX clause defining structure will include *at least* the elements of (177) fig. 1.5:

(177)

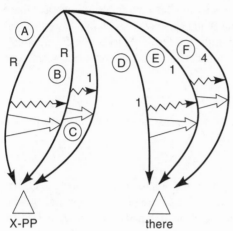

X-PP   there

A is a final Nominal-arc   FIGURE 1.5.

In this structure, I artificially ignore, as I will in what follows, the fact that X-PPs are PPs. This matter raises a variety of issues about the description of PPs that, though important and relevant, are not central to this discussion, so I will not seek to deal with them here. In (177), arc A is the final R-arc, which determines that X-PPs are not S3s. B is the type II local successor required by Condition 1, which represents default Quace, and C is the finished Quace-arc that specifies that A has quirky 1-Quace. E is the default Quace-arc required by Condition 1, while F is the arc that represents that D has finished quirky 4-Quace.

I will assume that the conditions just discussed on NEX clauses are a consequence of several distinct principles of English grammar. First, there is a specifically NEX clause characterizing condition that I take to specify three necessary conditions for a final Nominal-arc, like A in (177), which is *not* a 1-arc, to have finished 1-Quace:

(178)   Condition 4. NEX Clause Constraints
        If A is a final Nominal-arc but non-1-arc, then A's Quace Marker's final element is a (finished) 1-Quace arc only if
        (i) there is a distinct neighboring final *expletive* 1-arc, B with finished 4-Quace; and
        (ii) A's R-sign is a member of $\{5, 6, 8, \text{Oblique}_1, \ldots \text{Oblique}_n\}$; and
        (iii) A is a type I remote foreign predecessor of an Overlay-arc.

Notable about (178) is that it does not restrict the existence of final expletive 1-arcs with finished 4-Quace to NEX clauses and is consistent with their occurring in any sort of clause whatever. This is obviously inadequate, since I assume that it is precisely finished 4-Quace on a 1-arc that leads to an expletive subject not being pronounced. I will propose, however, that the conditions needed here are relevant more generally than to NEX clauses and are needed at least for those as clauses and comparative clauses shown in section 5 to also involve null expletives.

Moreover, I assume that the same conditions hold for fronted participial constructions like (179), which induce the Anticomplementizer Constraint just as NEX clauses and the others do but which space precludes discussing in detail:[33]

(179)   Lying on the table (he is sure) (*that) were two sick gerbils.

I take this to mean that the participial constituent heads a final P-arc, which has quirky 1-Quace. I thus propose:

(180)   Condition 5. Quirky Expletive Subject Constraints
        If A is final expletive 1-arc, then A has finished 4-Quace only if there is a neighboring final arc with finished quirky 1-Quace.

This constraint simply requires that finished 4-quace on an expletive arc only occur in a clause that contains some final arc with quirky 1-Quace. However, (180) fails to embody the informal assumption that all those expletives that head final 1-arcs with quirky 4-quace are not pronounced. So in particular Condition (180) does not specify that the expletive in NEX clauses is null. Typically, in the Metagraph framework, a null realization of some constituent K is represented by the erasure of (all) the arcs headed by K. That view always raises the question of the identity of the relevant erasers, which, in this case, is not obvious.

Certain conclusions are possible, though. Since internal to present assumptions, the quirky 4-Quace constituent, that is, the invisible expletive, needs to be associated with a final arc, the relevant eraser of at least one of the arcs headed by the expletive would not necessarily be internal to the minimal clause that contains that expletive. For given the definition of 'final arc' in (167), such erasure would mean that the arc was not final. That conclusion is, moreover, seemingly strengthened since, as seen earlier, the expletive in question can arguably raise, meaning that the 1-arc it heads can have a type I foreign successor. This needs to be assumed for raising cases like (181), argued in section 1 *not* to show that the X-PPs were subjects:

(181)   a. To Jerome seem/*seems to have been sent several threats.
        b. To Jerome *seem/seems to have been sent a threat.

Moreover, the expletives posited for as cases, comparative cases, and predicate ones like (179) arguably also can raise:

(182)   a. Jerome is mad, as appears to have been obvious to everyone.
        b. Jerome was angrier than appears to be consistent with his mental health.
        c. Lying on the table seem/*seems to have been two sick gerbils.
        d. Lying on the table *seem/seems to have been a sick gerbil.

Since X-PPs have been shown not to be subjects, to embed cases like (181) and (182) in the general raising pattern, which involves the raising of final complement subjects, one must assume the invisible expletive has raised. By taking there type expletives to agree in number with the DPs they share a relation with, cases like (182c and d) are regular under an analysis that posits raising of the expletive. That would mean then that the final 1-arc headed by the expletives in the (have) (been) sent clause of (181) has no eraser in that clause. Rather, it would seem that the ultimate expletive arc that is erased would have to be at least as high as the seem/seems clause. The only thing in that clause that is really particular to the NEX clause structure is the X-PP that has extracted through the seem clause to its ultimate overlay position. This might suggest that the eraser of the relevant expletive 1-arc is one of the 30-arcs.

But I reject that idea. My assumption is that the invisibility of the there in NEX clauses as well as other English cases of null expletive subjects is, rather, to be assimilated to the *general* invisibility of final 1 expletives in NLs like Italian and Spanish, which in general occur with nothing like an X-PP. Arguably then, the eraser for all such expletive arcs has to be the P-arc of the highest clause in which they occur. If so, then it is on various grounds necessary to revise the definition of 'final arc' so that the sort of erasure just posited does not preclude an arc being final. One way to do this would be to add a specification that the 'Remote Branch' referenced in (167) is a Nominal-arc. At any rate, the idea is then:

(183)   Condition 6. Invisibility of Expletives That Head Quirky-Quace Marked Final 1-arcs
        If A is a final expletive 1-arc with finished 4-Quace whose neighboring P-arc is B, then if A is not erased by an arc distinct from B, A is erased by B.[34]

The motivation for the second 'if' clause is precisely the raising instances discussed earlier where final expletive 1-arcs of the sort at issue have type I foreign successors when they are in the infinitival complements of seem clauses.

9.4. Stating the extraction constraints

9.4.1. Remark

The claim of this section is that the three extraction constraints of section 2 treat the X-PPs of NEX clauses in the same way that they treat S3s because of the fact that the former, exceptionally, have quirky 1-Quace, while S3s, which represent the heads of final 1-arcs, regularly have (straight) 1-Quace. Logic then requires that the three constraints each be stated in a way that takes advantage of *the sharing of 1-Quace*, which means that none of the three constraints can be properly stated via exclusive reference to *final* 1-arcs. The following three subsections sketch analyses of the three constraints in Quace terms.

9.4.2. The Anticomplementizer Constraint

The Anticomplementizer Constraint in its English variant says in effect that the complementizer of a *nonrelative* type finite clause must be null under a specific condition Q. The constraint will then have two sorts of effects, given a background claim that of the various English finite complementizers only that has a null variant. The others, as if/how/if/like/when/whether, do not permit this. Therefore, in any overall context where condition Q holds, the Anticomplementizer Constraint will force the null variant of the <u>that</u> complementizer and will render ungrammatical a clause with one of the other finite complementizers. The pattern will be like that of (184a–f):

(184) a. No gorilla did he believe *that/Ø would solve the problem.
       b. No gorilla did it look *as if/*Ø would solve the problem.
       c. No gorilla did he see *how/*Ø solved the problem.
       d. No gorilla did he like it *if/*Ø solved the problem.
       e. No gorilla did he like it *when/*Ø solved the problem.
       f. No gorilla did he know *whether/*Ø had solved the problem.
       g. Culicover, (1993a: 104)
          [On which table]$_1$ were you wondering whether under certain circumstances t$_1$ might have been put the books that you had bought
       h. That is the tiger which$_1$ they saw how at a key moment t$_1$ had helped his trainer.

However, when, as in the Adverb Effect environment illustrated in Culicover's (1993a) example (16d) repeated as (184g), or in (184h), subject extraction does not require a null complementizer, compatibility with a complementizer other than <u>that</u> is possible.

Leaving aside how the issue of null realization for different complementizers is to be described, the core of the formulation of the Anticomplementizer Constraint then reduces to specification of condition Q. My suggestion is that the basic constraint is that a complementizer, C_n, is in the relevant environment Q if and only if there is some final Nominal-arc A of the highest clause of which C_n is the complementizer, which has two properties: (i) A has finished 1-Quace and (ii) the head constituent represented by A is extracted past C_n.

Moreover, I will take the latter to mean that A is the foreign predecessor of a specific type of arc that defines extractions; assume these to be defined, as in Postal (2001a), by the R-sign 30. The idea then is roughly that any *ordinary* (see the discussion of 40-arcs later for a bit of explication of this hedge) extraction involves a minimum of three types of arcs. First, there is an arc that is *not* a 30-arc and has a 30-arc type I foreign successor. Call this a *Start* arc. In cases of nominal extraction, the Start arc will typically be a final Nominal-arc.[35] Second, there is a (non-null, possibly unitary) sequence of 30-arcs, the first a type I foreign successor of the Start arc and each subsequent one, if any, a type I foreign successor of the previous 30-arc. Assume that any type I foreign successor of a 30-arc is itself a 30-arc; call this the *Uniformity Condition*. Finally, there is some arc, a member of the class called *Overlay-arcs* in Johnson and Postal (1980), that is a type I local successor of the last 30-arc foreign successor.

I will also assume, quite crucially, that extraction always involves successive immediate constituencies; more precisely, an extracted element must be a constituent of every constituent between its original and final positions. So:

(185) Condition 7. Extraction Limitation
       If B is a foreign successor of A, then there exists an arc C such that B is a neighbor of C and A is a branch of C.

That is, extractions must be like (186a, fig. 1.6a) and never like (186b, fig. 1.6b):

(186)   a. Licit Extraction

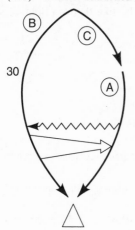

FIGURE 1.6a

b. Illicit Extraction

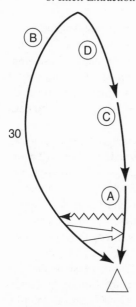

FIGURE 1.6b

In (186b) the type I foreign successor of A, B, defining the extraction is not, as required, a neighbor of an arc A is a branch of, since A is a branch of C but only a remote branch of D.

The conditions that determine the Anticomplementizer Constraint could be made more compact and cross-linguistically expected if it were possible to state a (hopefully universal) condition that links a complementizer to extractions from the clause it marks. This would be possible if there is in effect a kind of *agreement* between complementizers and (certain) phrases extracted from their clauses. Such a general agreement pairing has been previously recognized in, for example, Irish and Chamorro; see Chung (1998) and Chung and McCloskey (1987). Moreover, it is also known that there is agreement between complementizers and elements of the clause they mark (e.g., subjects) independently of extraction; see Watanabe (2000) for examples, discussion, and references. The possibility for complementizers to agree thus seems clear.

I assume here, moreover, that English complementizers manifest at least agreement *in Quace* and, further, that this agreement is mediated through the following (hypothesized) informally specified state of affairs:

(187)   30-arcs *agree in Quace* with their predecessors (perhaps better and more generally:
If A is a remote successor of a 30-arc and A is a successor of B, A *agrees in Quace* with B).

The generalization in parenthesis here extends the claim of Quace agreement to successors of A, like, for example, A_6 in (191b). Thus the more general version says that a 30-arc agrees in Quace with its Start-arc predecessor, that every remote successor of that 30-arc agrees with its predecessor, and that the ultimate local successor of the last 30-arc in the sequence agrees with the latter in Quace. Thus Quace would be in effect passed up from the Start arc to each intervening 30-arc and finally to the ultimate remote successor of the Start arc, an Overlay-arc.

To make sense of claim (187), though, it is requisite to give a precise interpretation of the highlighted word sequence. To do this, one can first define an auxiliary notion for a fixed Quace Marker, as in (188):

(188)   Definition
If $M = \{Q_1, \ldots, Q_n\}$ is a Quace Marker, then a sequence of R-signs $\{R_1, \ldots, R_n\}$ is *the Relational Marker of M* if and only if for all i, $1 \leq i \leq n$ Q_i is an R_i-arc.

That is, a Relational Marker of a fixed Quace Marker QM is simply the total R-sign sequence defined by the successive R-signs of the successive members of QM.

Assuming the notion Relational Marker, one can take a specification of the form (189a) to mean (189b):

(189)   a. Arc A agrees in Quace with arc B.
b. If B's Quace Marker = $\{Q_1, \ldots Q_n\}$, then the Relational Marker of A's Quace Marker = $\{R_1, \ldots R_n, \ldots\}$.

That is, agreement in Quace between two arcs means that the agreeing arc must have a Quace Marker whose *initial sequence* of arcs matches in R-sign the *full* set of arcs of the Quace Marker of the determining arc.

At this point then, (187) requires that a 30-arc foreign successor, A, of a Start 1-arc with only straight Quace itself have a type II 1-arc local successor and if A has a (type I foreign) successor, that 30-arc also will have to have a type II 1-arc local successor, and so on. That is, in effect, the Relational Marker of a Nominal-arc Start arc is passed on to each member of any sequence of its 30-arc successors. Then, assuming that complementizers head arcs with the R-sign CT, it is possible to say something like (190):

(190)   Condition 8. Complementizer Agreement in Quace
A CT-arc A agrees in Quace with an arc B if and only if B is a 30-arc neighbor of A.

Given (190), a simple subject extraction case of the sort relevant to the Anticomplementizer Constraint like (191a) will involve a structure that includes a subpart like
(191b, fig. 1.7). To simplify diagrams for comprehensibility, however, here and later
*I suppress drawing separate type II local successor arcs for 30-arcs and sometimes
for CT-arcs as well.* Instead, I draw such arcs with complex R-sign combinations of
the form 30/1/. . . , CT/1/2, and so on. This should be taken to mean that the first arc
has a type II 1-arc local successor and if there is a third symbol, say 2, that 1-arc has
a type II 2-arc local successor, and so forth:

(191)   a. I know who they claimed (*that) supports Saddam.
         b.

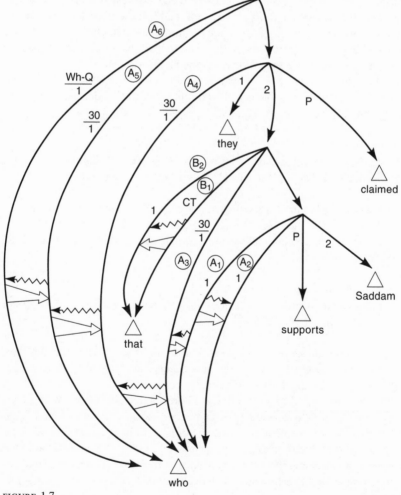

FIGURE 1.7

A nonsubject extraction, say one like (192a), whose Start is a 2-arc, would be a model of (192b, fig. 1.8):

(192)   a. I know who they claimed (that) Saddam supports.
         b.

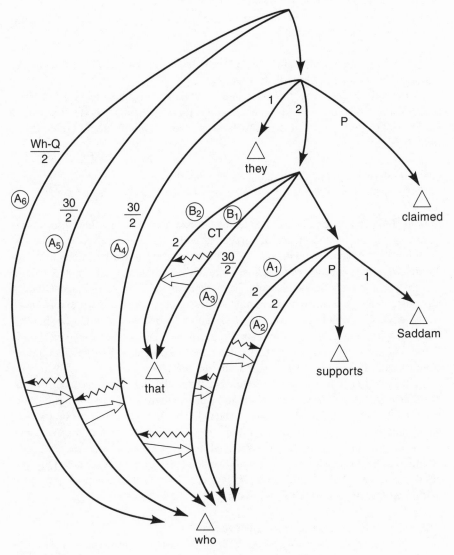

FIGURE 1.8

Notably, in (192) the CT-arc ends up via Quace Agreement with finished 2-Quace, not finished 1-Quace, as in (191).

At this point, the tools are largely available to indicate initially that both subject and X-PP extraction out of a complement clause must, ignoring the Adverb Effect and another restriction discussed later, yield a null complementizer. For at this point the relevant CT-arcs whose heads must be unpronounced have Quace Markers with finished 1-Quace.[36] The descriptive task can then be accomplished apparently by having the relevant 1-Quace arc erase the CT-arc.

(193)   Condition 9 Nonrelative Clause CT-arc Erasure
         A CT-arc of a *nonrelative clause* with finished 1-Quace is erased by the arc it agrees with in Quace.[37]

Given (193), the head of CT-arc B_1 in (191b) will have to be erased by the 30-arc A_3, although this erasure is not indicated there.

However, despite what has been said, in at least two subcontexts the description constructed so far fails to work correctly. First, for subjects extracted from a clause deeper than that the CT-arc is directly associated with, there are contrasts like (194a, b):

(194)   a. the terrorist who I believe (*that$_1$) threatened Ernie
         b. the terrorist who I believe (that$_2$) Ernie claimed (*that$_1$) threatened you.

In both (194a and b) the CT-arcs headed by complementizer that$_1$ should seemingly have 1-Quace as a consequence of agreement with the 30-arc, call it A, headed by the relative pronoun who, with that 1-Quace being determined by the fact that the 30-arc is a remote successor of the final 1-arc of the complement of claimed. But the CT-arc whose head corresponds to that$_2$ apparently must not have 1-Quace, although it is a neighbor of a 30-arc that is a remote successor of A and thus, by previous specifications, that is, principles (187) and (190), should agree with it in Quace. In other terms, despite the fact that subject extraction is present, the complementizer that$_2$ in (194b) does not manifest the Anticomplementizer Constraint, and this fact and its contrast with the case for that$_1$ is so far unaccounted for.

I suggest one can handle this contrast without altering anything said so far by positing an additional principle of restricted Quace determination by main predicates from whose complements things are extracted. This takes account of the fact that under previous assumptions the 30-arc that is a neighbor of the CT-arc, A, associated with that$_2$, unlike that CT-arc associated with that$_1$, is a (remote) successor of a 30-arc, B, which is a neighbor of a P-arc (one that corresponds to the verb claimed in (194b). I suggest then that the 30-arc B is forced by a further principle *to have an additional Quace-arc*, which I will hypothesize is a 2-Quace:

(195)   Extraction Quace Assignment (first version)
         If A is a 30-arc whose Start is a final arc with finished 1-Quace and A is a neighbor of a P-arc, then A has finished 2-Quace.

This principle can in general be satisfied by a 30-arc only if the latter's Quace Marker consists of the sequence {. . . , A, B}, where A is a type II 1-arc local successor and B is a type II 2-arc local successor of A. This is a reason why, as noted earlier, one must allow some type II local successors to themselves have type II local successors.

Given this new principle, the 30-arc remote successor of the 1-arc that might have been expected to determine (via the agreement specified in [190]) 1-Quace on the highest CT-arc in (194b) actually determines finished 2-Quace on that arc. Such a CT-arc is then properly *not* required by (193) to be erased.

That is, the relevant parts of (194b) would include the elements of (196, fig. 1.9):

(196)

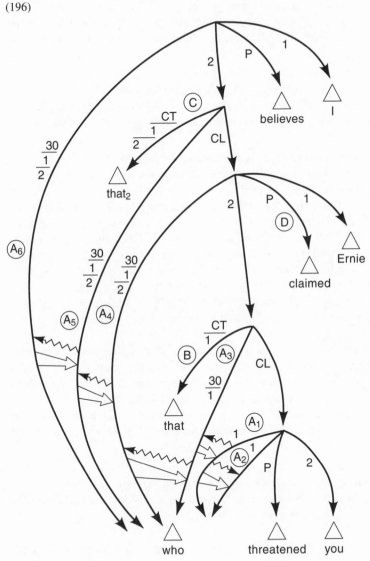

FIGURE 1.9.

Here the CT-arc B must have finished 1-Quace, via agreement with its neighboring 30-arc, A_3, which is not a neighbor of any P-arc and thus has no source of 2-Quace. But the 30-arc A_4 is a neighbor of the P-arc D and thus must have finished 2-Quace.

Hence, by further agreement, A_5 has finished 2-Quace, and thus the CT-arc C has it by agreement with A_5. In these terms, it is not an accident that the higher instances of that do not yield the Anticomplementizer Constraint, for their CT-arcs are neighbors of 30-arcs that are remote successors of a 30-arc that is a neighbor of some P-arc, which requires finished 2-Quace via principle (195).

A virtue of the approach to the (194a, b) contrast just sketched is that it likely can be extended to the second so far untreated issue, which is the Adverb Effect. Recall that in the presence of many fronted adverbs, as first noted by Bresnan and stressed in later work by Culicover, the Anticomplementizer Constraint is not found:

(197)   a. the nurse who he believes (*that) would watch her father
        b. the nurse who he believes that under those conditions would watch her father
        c. *the nurse who he believes Ø under those conditions would watch her father.

Here, though, there are actually two phenomena. First, unlike the ordinary subject case of (197a), the that of the grammatical (197b) is not *required* to be null. Second, unlike other (e.g., object extraction) cases, the that is not *permitted* to be null, so that (197c) is ill formed. Why should these properties hold? A partial answer, I believe, lies in the following circumstance, which is partially parallel to that which holds in cases like 194b). In the latter, as represented in (196), the complementizer that fails to behave as if it had finished 1-Quace, that is, $that_2$, heads CT-arc B. As already discussed, the head of B is separated from the position of the head of the Start arc of the 30-arc with which B agrees in Quace by an intermediate verb, which heads some P-arc, there D. I have claimed that that P-arc determines that a neighboring 30-arc with 1-Quace has finished 2-Quace; so A_4 is required to have finished 2-Quace.

Notably then, in (197b, c) the fronted adverb that nullifies the Anticomplementizer Constraint is intermediate in position between the position of the head of the Start 1-arc and that of the complementizer, which fails to be null. This means that under past assumptions some 30-arc that accounts for the extraction of the 1 will be a neighbor of the arc headed by the adverb. Assuming that the R-sign of this adverbial arc is of a systematically specifiable type, say Z, then one can simply extend (195) to say:

(198)   Condition 10 Extraction Quace Assignment (Final Version)
        If A is a 30-arc whose Start is a final arc with finished 1-Quace and A is a neighbor of a P-arc or a Z-arc, then A has finished 2-Quace.

Given (198), it is now predicted that (197b) is possible, since the complementizer heads a CT-arc whose finished Quace will be 2-Quace, which does not invoke principle (193). The proposal is thus that the fronted adverbs that nullify the Anticomplementizer Constraint also determine non-1-Quace as the finished Quace on a CT-arc just as higher predicates do. The relevant structure of (197b) would be (199, fig. 1.10):

(199)

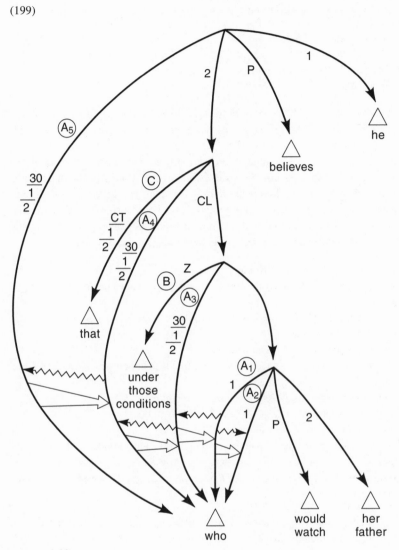

FIGURE 1.10.

In (199), the key arc is A_3, which, as a neighbor of the Z-arc B, is forced by (198) to have an extended Quace Marker with finished 2-Quace. That means that A_4, the successor of A_3, is forced to have finished 2-Quace, which determines that the CT-arc C has it, guaranteeing that it need not be null.

Further support for the view embodied in (198) arises when attention is turned to the Parallelism Constraint and the Complementizer Effect.[38] Before turning to the other constraints that extracted X-PPs share with extracted S3s, one should briefly note parallelisms between this description of the Anticomplementizer Constraint and Kayne's (1984: 6–7) account of what I claim is a related phenomenon. Kayne dealt with the marginal and perhaps largely archaic option of marking a subject interrogative or relative pronoun as <u>whom</u>, noting cases like (200a):

(200) a. the man who(m) I believe has left
       b. the man who(*m) left
       c. Who(m) do you believe left first?
       d. Who(*m) left first?

A key fact is that (200a and b) clearly contrast, as do (200c and d). In Kayne's transformational terms, cases like (200a and c) were the result of a second cyclic case assignment into Comp.

   In this framework, the extra objective case marking is arguably possible in just the context seen earlier to determine finished 2-Quace on a 30-arc, that is, in a context where a WH form achieves its final position only by raising past the locus of a predicate (here, <u>believe</u>).[39] If the parallelism is genuine, one would also expect that the contexts of the Adverb Effect, unified with the higher predicate context in (198), would permit the case marking seen in (200a, c). I believe this is at least weakly the case:

(201) a. a woman who(*m) might be hired
       b. a woman who(??)m under the sort of conditions you have just referred to might
           be hired
       c. a woman who(??m) at the time the police believe the crime was committed was
           thought to be in Istanbul
       d. I don't know who(*m) might be hired.
       e. I don't know who(??m) under the sort of difficult conditions you have just referred
           to might manage to get hired.
       f. a politician who(*m) looks ill whenever I see him
       g. a politician who(?m) whenever I see him looks ill.
       h. someone who(*m) is now the ruler of the country
       i. someone who(??m) for all intents and purposes is now the ruler of the country
       j. someone who(*m) has supported terrorism for years
       k. someone who(??m), as the *National Review* has recently documented, has supported
           terrorism for years

While (201b, c, e, g, i, and k) are hardly lovely, there is, I find, a sharp contrast with the hopeless long versions of (201a, d, f, h, and j).

   Arguably then, the special objective case marking of an extracted S3 found in (200a) should be limited to the head of an Overlay-arc, which, while a remote successor of a Start arc with finished 1-Quace, is also a remote successor of an intermediate 30-arc, which, via principle (198), has finished 2-Quace. Properly then, this possibility cannot be available for the Overlay-arc headed by <u>whom</u> in (200b), which has no way of receiving finished 1-Quace via principle (198).

9.4.3. The Parallelism Constraint

Turn then to the Parallelism Constraint. In its primitive form this prevents a main clause final subject from being combined under coordination with a main clause nonsubject, yielding, for example:

(202)   a. *a woman who sang well and Greg praised
        b. *a woman who Greg praised and sang well

However, the constraint does not bar such combinations if the final subject at issue is an embedded one:

(203)   a. a woman who Greg proved could sing well and Tony wanted to meet
        b. a woman who Tony wanted to meet and Greg proved could sing well

    Bresnan's key observation then was that X-PPs behave in the same way, which she took to support the claim that they are subjects (S3s in our terms here).

(204)   a. *In that cage was lying a gorilla and they then placed a monkey.
        b. In that cage they believed was lying a gorilla and they then placed a monkey.

It has been seen that Bresnan's conclusion is not viable. Moreover, given the Quace assignment principles of this section, no assumption that X-PPs are final 1s is motivated by facts like (204b). All that is required, arguably, to determine that they behave like 1s under the constraint is that the latter be stated in terms of *finished 1-Quace*. While the facts of coordination are too complex to permit here a serious account of the Parallelism Constraint, it seems that the following informal statement is defensible:

(205)   Coordinate combinations of the sort that underlie Bresnan's Parallelism Constraint preclude combinations of two constituents, one of which heads an Overlay-arc with finished 1-Quace and the other of which does not.[40]

    Moreover, formulation (205) explains the difference in (204). That is, in (204a) the underlying PP in the first conjunct, which is a NEX clause, will have finished 1-Quace while that in the second conjunct will not. Combination is thus banned. But in (204b) the PP in the first conjunct has no source of finished 1-Quace and neither does that in the second; violation of (205) is not possible.
    If that is the proper view, then given constraint (198), one would expect that, like the Anticomplementizer Constraint, the Parallelism Constraint should also be *nullified* in environments where the Adverb Effect holds. This seems correct:

(206)   a. *He believes that in that cage they kept a monkey and had already been placed a gorilla.
        b. ?He believes that in that cage they kept a monkey and at some earlier point in time had already been placed a gorilla.

While (206b) is not lovely, it shows considerable improvement over (206a), which would lack any Z-arc to assign finished 2-Quace to the X-PP that is combined with an ordinary PP from the first complement conjunct. See also the parallel:

(207)   a. *Stella claimed that during that era the Arabs had formulated many axioms and had been proved many theorems..

b. ?Stella claimed that during that era the Arabs had formulated many axioms and despite considerable controversy had been proved many theorems.

If something like (205) is correct, it predicts facts like (208) under my assumption, necessary given the inducement of the Anticomplementizer Constraint in cases like (179), that fronted participial phrases in inversion cases represent arcs with finished 1-Quace:

(208) a. Arrested by the police may have been Mickey Cardozo.
       b. Arrested by the police Sally Reynolds is said to have been.
       c. Arrested by the police is said to have been Sally Reynolds.
       d. Arrested by the police Mickey Cardozo may have been and Sally Reynolds is said to have been.
       e. Arrested by the police may have been Mickey Cardozo and is said to have been Sally Reynolds.
       f. *Arrested by the police may have been Mickey Cardozo and Sally Reynolds is said to have been.
       g. *Arrested by the police Sally Reynolds is said to have been and may have been Mickey Cardozo.

In (208d), the participial phrase does not correspond to the predicate of an inversion clause and thus would not head an arc with 1-Quace. In (208e), the participial phrase corresponds to the predicate of inversion clauses in both conjuncts; thus a 1-Quace phrase would be combined with a 1-Quace phrase. But in the ungrammatical case, (208f) the predicate of the first clause would have 1-Quace while that of the second would not, and in the ungrammatical (208g) the predicate of the first clause would not have 1-Quace while that of the second would. Note that in these terms, principle (195) would be irrelevant, since it only determines assignment of 2-Quace to arcs that have 1-Quace, which, given condition (180), is just not the case for the participial phrase arc of the second conjunct of (208f) or the first conjunct of (208g).

9.4.4. The Complementizer Effect

Finally, I turn to the Complementizer Effect, which holds only of relative type clauses and which is something of the opposite of the Anticomplementizer Constraint; that is, it requires that a complementizer be non-null:

(209)   the vampire that/*Ø attacked Tony

It was observed in section 1 that this also holds for X-PPs:

(210)   It was to Larry that/*Ø were sent threatening postcards.

Serious discussion of relative clauses being impossible here, suffice it to say that the fact that this constraint holds for both S3 and X-PP extractions can also be captured by stating the constraint in terms of 1-Quace. Assuming that the relative clause initial that of cases like (210) is a complementizer, agreement principle (190) already determines that CT-arcs like that headed by that in (210) have finished 1-Quace. So an informal version of the constraint needed for relative clauses might say:

(211)   If A is a *relative clause initial* CT-arc and has finished 1-Quace, A is not erased.

If current assumptions are roughly correct, the embedded environments and the Adverb Effect, which both lead to assignment of finished 2-Quace (via condition [198]), should nullify the consequences of (211). This is correct (for the higher complementizer) in the case of the embedded environment (see [212]), but sharply incorrect in the Adverb Effect environment (see [213]):

(212)   a. the vampire (that$_2$) they said (*that$_1$) attacked Tony
         b. a vampire that/*Ø under the right sort of conditions would certainly attack Tony

(213)   a. It was to Larry (that$_2$) they said (*that$_1$) were sent threatening postcards.
         b. It was to Larry that/*Ø at that time were sent threatening postcards.

Although in our terms here, the CT-arcs in both (212b) and (213b) should have finished 2-Quace and so not fall under (211), the Adverb Effect environment has no improving effect in cases like (212b) or (213b). I do not have an account of this fact. The only bright feature of the situation is that X-PP extraction and S3 extraction in the relevant contexts behave the same. To handle this in our terms here, it seems like it would be necessary to modify the Z-arc part of (198) so that it is only satisfied in a *nonrelative* clause. This ad hoc limitation on only part of a condition is evidently ugly and suspicious, but I have nothing better to offer at this point.

9.5. French

Recall that section 8 showed that in French the analog of NEX clauses interacts with the French variant of the Anticomplementizer Constraint, that is, the obligatory mapping of complementizer que to qui in the case of S3 extractions, in such a way that, in contrast to English, the Anticomplementizer Constraint is *not* found in French NEX clauses. Combined with other factors, there is then no evidence that French analogs of X-PPs have any commonalities with French S3s at all. One approach to the facts would then just deny that there is quirky 1-Quace marking of French X-PPs. Another, which would keep the French construction abstractly more similar to the English one, would posit the same 1-Quace marking on X-PPs as has been posited for English but state CT-arc agreement in French, that is, the analog of (190), in a more restricted way, such that perhaps Quace agreement is only defined for non-Quirky 1-Quace, that is, for single-arc Quace Markers. I will not attempt to choose between such approaches here. It suffices that there is no particular mystery apparent in the French facts and no particular problem is raised for our approach to the English NEX clause phenomenon here.

There is one further fact of relevance, though. This is represented by the English/French parallelism in (214):

(214)   a. the dragon (that) I believe (*that) was found
       b. le dragon que/*qui je crois *que/qui a été trouvé

Evidently, just as the English Anticomplementizer Constraint only holds for the mini-mal clause, the one that in this account contains the Start arc for the extraction, just so the French analog only holds there. This would indicate that parallel conditions are at work. In our terms here, it means that 1-Quace assignment to CT-arcs and additional assignment of 2-Quace to certain 30-arcs in contexts of 'deep' extraction are also found in French.

9.6. Final comment

The key evidence that seemingly favors position (4c) is that X-PPs obey the various extraction constraints, the Anticomplementizer Constraint, the Parallelism Constraint, and the Complementizer Effect. I have tried to sketch, though, a method based on the notion of Quace that permits capturing the extension of these constraints, mostly relevant to S3 extraction, to X-PPs without the really radical and ultimately unten-able idea that X-PPs are S3s. Rather, it can be stated that all these constraints pick out the relevant class of forms via specification of the notion of finished 1-Quace. And I further sketched how a parallel treatment was possible for the French analog of the Anticomplementizer Constraint.

To conclude, one really terminological remark might be appropriate. The reader will have noted that in the development here, although it is denied that X-PPs are S3s, each X-PP does correspond to the head of a 1-arc—namely, the 1-arc type II local successor that provides its finished 1-Quace. Despite this, I think it is correct to avoid, as I have throughout, calling such phrases 'subjects'. It is easy to give a gen-eral principle that underlies the choice of terminology (or nonterminology). Namely, a phrase has been called a 'subject' only if it heads a 1-arc of the sort that could be a superficial arc, that is, one that is not necessarily erased. Since every type II local successor is (by definition) erased, the inference is that merely heading a type II local successor R-arc is not grounds for being called an R. Adopted systematically then, this approach to terminology would not call a nominative object, one likely heading a final 2-arc with quirky 1-Quace, a subject and would avoid calling a dative subject, one, say, heading a final 1-arc with quirky 3-Quace, an indirect object. These termi-nological choices are formally clear, given the precise notion of type II local succes-sor, and seem in accord with tradition as far as comparisons are possible. The only caution necessary then is that in an enriched arc framework that recognizes Quace-arcs, it is simply not the case that, for example, merely being the head of an arbitrary 1-arc determines that a constituent is a subject, and so on.

A Putatively Banned Type of Raising

1. Background

Syntacticians are a notoriously argumentative lot given to (sometimes) acrimonious disputes, and few, if any, syntactic conclusions have achieved uniform endorsement. One might therefore assume that a point on that a broad consensus of syntactic opinion *has* been reached is one that can be accorded some confidence. Notable then is that during the 1980s and 1990s proponents of the three most widely appealed to contemporary views of NL syntax, that is, the government binding (GB), lexical-functional grammar (LFG), and head-driven phrase structure grammar (HPSG) frameworks, all came to a common conclusion. Namely, although as a consequence of very different principles internal to each of these views, a certain type of syntactic *raising* was taken to be impossible. One might be tempted then to infer that this conclusion is now a well-established fact of NL syntax. In the framework of skeptical essays, however, caution is evidently in order.

Postal (1974: 363, note 7) mentioned a class of English complement cases of the type shown in (1):

(1)   You can depend on *him* to do something decent,

noting that they were likely part of a larger paradigm that also involves the verbs <u>bet (on)</u>, <u>bank (on)</u>, <u>count (on)</u>, and <u>rely (on)</u>. It was claimed that the highlighted DP in (1) was a superficial main clause subconstituent but an underlying complement subject, hence one raised into the main clause. A similar view was stated in Emonds

(1976: 77). Assuming that <u>on + him</u> in (1) forms a PP, a point to which I return, the suggested analysis would then instantiate what might be called *raising to complement of P* (RCP). Now precisely what the three views mentioned at the outset are agreed on is:

(2)   RCP does not exist in NL.

If so, then the analysis of (1) must involve some distinct type of constructional features. However, the burden of this chapter is that RCP, rightly understood, is the factually supported analysis of a number of English cases like (1) and others as well. If so, it is necessary to gaze at no NL more exotic than English to determine that the agreed upon theoretical conclusion is *wrong*.

The background of the question at issue in this chapter was nicely described in the following:

(3)   McCloskey (1984: 441)
      "The relationship—syntactic and/or semantic—that holds between the matrix subject position and the null position marked by _ in an English example like (1) has been the source of much productive theorizing in the tradition of generative grammar:
      (1)   Pascal appears _ to be playing well tonight
      It was in an attempt to elucidate the central properties of this relationship that the transformation of Subject (to Subject) Raising was first proposed (Rosenbaum 1967, Kiparsky & Kiparsky 1971, Postal 1974). It is with this 'Raising relationship' that I will be concerned in this paper, though in a different language—Modern Irish."

McCloskey then focused the issue more sharply:

(4)   McCloskey (1984: 441–442)
      "The dispute I will be concerned with is that concerning the range of positions to which a complement subject may legally be Raised. What is the range of possible target-positions or host-positions for Raising? It seems to be uncontroversial that NP's may be Raised to subject position. Raising to Object is widely believed to figure in the analysis of English examples such as those in (2):
      (2)   a. The Press believes Mrs. Thatcher to be on the point of calling an election.
            b. I consider Spassky to have been the greatest player of his era.
          What I want to argue here is that the range of permissible options is in fact broader than this summary would suggest, that Raising to (a certain restricted subset of) prepositional object positions also exists. I will argue that the standard criteria for identifying Raising constructions suggest that there is a fairly large group of predicates in Irish that govern Raising, and that the Raised NP appears in a prepositional object position in the matrix clause."

McCloskey had thus raised the issue of the viability of a ban on RCP almost twenty years ago but had done so on the basis of data external to English. In fact, as reiterated in Joseph (1990: 262), Joseph (1979) had still earlier attested an apparent case of RCP in Greek. Joseph (1990) argues in detail for the correctness of such an interpretation.

2. The LFG claim about RCP

The earliest statement I am aware of that explicitly *rejects* the existence of RCP on theoretical grounds is part of the overall LFG view of Bresnan (1982b); see in particular the following (figure numbers have been changed to correspond to placement in this chapter):

(5)   Bresnan (1982a: 348)
      "A further generalization of control follows from this theory. Recall that in lexically induced functional control relations, OBL_θ cannot be a controller. Since the oblique functions are marked by prepositions in English (Bresnan 1979), it follows that prepositional objects cannot be lexically induced functional controllers in English. The following examples were previously given to illustrate this point.
      (69)   a. I presented it to John *dead*.
               b. *1 presented John with it *dead*.
      There are apparent counterexamples to this generalization, such as (70a,b):
      (70)   a. Louise signaled to Ted to follow her.
               b. Mary relies on John to dress himself.

      "However, these are either cases of anaphoric control or cases of Verb-Preposition Incorporation (V-P Incorporation; see chapter 1). For example, the fact that we find *Louise signaled* to *Ted for him to follow her*, in which the subject is a lexically expressed NP, indicates that the complement of *signal* must be anaphorically, not functionally, controlled in (70a). As for *rely on*, it is subject to the rule of V-P Incorporation, which produces the two lexical forms shown in (71 [fig. 2.1]).

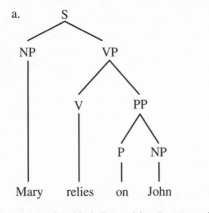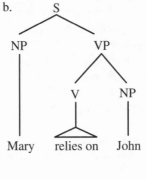

FIGURE 2.1 Verb-Preposition Incorporation

(71)
a. [rely]$_V$,   ($\uparrow$PRED) = 'RELY-ON<(SUBJ)(OBL$_{ON}$)>'
b. [rely on]$_V$,   ($\uparrow$PRED) = 'RELY-ON<(SUBJ)(OBJ)>'
      "The verb with lexical form (71a) is inserted into the structure shown in figure 2.1a; the verb with lexical form (71b) is inserted into the structure 2.1b.
      "In the structure shown in figure 2.1a, *on John* is a constituent, while in the structure shown in figure 2.1b, it is not. Moreover, *John* is an OBL in figure 2.1a, but an

OBJ in figure 2.1b. The former structure accounts for the impossibility of *It is on John that Mary relies*, in which the constituent *on John* is clefted; the latter structure accounts for *John is relied on by Mary*, in which *John* as an OBJ has passivized (chapter 1). The theory of control adopted here predicts that functional control of a complement to *rely on* should be possible only when the preposition is incorporated in the verb as in figure 2.1b. Hence, if the functionally controlled complement is present, *on John* must fail to form a constituent. This explains the contrast between (72a) and (72b) and the possibility of (72c).

(72)   a. *It is on John that Mary relies to dress himself.
       b. It is John that Mary relies on to dress himself.
       c. John is relied on by Mary to dress himself."

In Bresnan's LFG terms, 'functional control' is extensionally equivalent to the union of raising and control structures in most other syntactic approaches. The difference between raising and control is claimed to reduce to different functional identifications. So (Kaplan and Bresnan, 1982: 229): "The wider class of raising verbs differs from equi verbs in just this respect. Thus, the lexical entry for PERSUADE maps the *baby* f-structure in (108) into argument positions of both PERSUADE and GO. The OBJ of the raising verb *expected*, however, is an argument only of the complement's predicate, as stipulated in the lexical entry (112)."

The relevant claim of Bresnan's (5) is then that the position of functional controller, that is, the position ordinarily taken to be the target of raising, cannot bear an Oblique relation. And since in English it is claimed that all DPs that are complements of PPs bear Oblique relations, the result that RCP cannot exist in English is predicted.

With respect to a case like her (70b), Bresnan assumed that while it was a case of functional control of the nonraising type, this would not violate the stated constraints on the latter because such cases were claimed, on one analysis, to involve so-called V-P Incorporation, roughly, what is called reanalysis in other frameworks. According to this view, Bresnan's (70b) would involve a reanalyzed structure in which there is no PP but rather a direct object. That is, in more standard terminology, Bresnan (1982a) was claiming that cases like her (70b) did involve raising of the complement subject into the main clause, as in the raising analysis of Postal (1974) for cases like (6):

(6)   a. Arabella believed six to be a larger number than eight.
      b. Arabella proved six to be a larger number than eight.

The difference between Bresnan's (70b) and (6) was, essentially, only that the former involved a verb that manifested V-P Incorporation. But in both types of case the raised phrase (functional controller) is a main clause object and not at any level of analysis internal to a PP.

Moreover, Bresnan gave one argument for her V-P Incorporation view, namely, that it explained the badness of her (72a), since on the V-P Incorporation structure on + DP would not be a constituent and thus expectably not capable of being the focus of a cleft construction.

However, this argument is undermined by a number of facts, which include several parallel to some invoked in Baltin and Postal (1996) as part of a general critique of reanalysis. In particular, while Bresnan claimed that if the functionally controlled complement (the infinitive) was present, on + DP fail to form a constituent, one finds a range of examples like (7), which are inexplicable under that view:

(7)   a. They were relying, it now appears/without any good reason/despite doubts, on the fifth division to cover their retreat.
      b. They were relying foolishly or at least naively on the fifth division to cover their retreat.
      c. They were relying on one division to cover their left flank and *on* another division to cover their right flank.
      d. They were relying not on the fifth division (to cover their retreat) but *on* the sixth division to cover their advance.
      e. One unit relied on the fifth division to cover the advance, the other *on* the sixth division to cover the retreat.
      f. They were relying on the fifth division or *on* the sixth division to come to their aid.
      g. Although they didn't rely on the fifth division to cover their flank, they did *on* the sixth division.
      h. Napoli (1993: 363)
         On whom did you depend to make the arrangements?

It would clearly not be serious to regard the unique P on in (7a, b) as having incorporated into the verb and even less feasible to regard the (highlighted) second instances of P on in (7c, d, e, f, g) as having done so. Moreover, example (7h) indicates that for some speakers even the sort of extraction restrictions represented by Bresnan's (72a), which she took to argue for a type of reanalysis, are not found (for at least some extractions).

Moreover, observe the contrast in (8):

(8)   a. Ernestine had chastised Lewis during the meeting.
      b. Ernestine had chastised during the meeting—the guy who was opposed to her position.
      c. Ernestine had proved that guy to be an impostor.
      d. Ernestine had proved to be an impostor—the guy who was opposed to her position.
      e. Ernestine had counted/depended/relied on that guy to support you.
      f. *Ernestine had counted/depended/relied on to support you—the guy who was opposed to her position.

That is, the pivot in the clearer raising to object case (8c) can feed the Complex DP Shift phenomenon, like the uncontroversial object in (8a). But the pivot in (8e) cannot. If the pivot, for example, that guy in (8e), is inside a PP, the ill-formedness of (8f) follows from the independently motivated principle, known since Ross (1967/ 1986), that the Complex NP Shift phenomenon cannot strand prepositions. But if (8e) had a non-PP analysis of the sort entailed by Bresnan's reanalysis/P-incorporation view and was really parallel to (8c), the ill-formedness of (8f) would remain unexplained.

The facts gone over then mean that the grounds for the ill-formedness of Bresnan's (72a) must be sought elsewhere.[1] Overall then, Bresnan's proposed universal constraint on functional control combines with her assumption that the cases in her (70b)/(72) involve functional control to just give the wrong answer for English, which provides no viable analysis for paradigms like her (70b)/(72), which include cases like (7) and (8e and f).[2]

3. The HPSG claim about RCP

Both major statements of the HPSG framework so far, Pollard and Sag (1987, 1994), explicitly reject the existence of RCP:

(9)   a. Pollard and Sag (1987: 20)
         "The existence of a syntactic dependency associated with raising explains the other-
         wise mysterious fact that there are no raising verbs with PP controllers analogous to
         PP-controlled equi verbs like *appeal*, for no PP can unify with the NP subject SUBCAT
         element of the verbal complement:
         (27)   Kim appealed to Sandy *to be optimistic*. (*PP* object control)"
      b. Pollard and Sag (1994: 139)
         "In English, there is somewhat sparser evidence for the sharing of syntactic informa-
         tion in raising constructions. One suggestive piece of evidence, however, is the well-
         known fact that in English PP objects may be equi controllers, but not raising controllers.
         That is, there are object equi verbs like *appeal*, whose infinitive complement's subject
         is interpreted on the basis of the object of the prepositional phrase, as in (115):
         (115)   Kim appealed to Sandy to cooperate.
         "But there are no analogous object raising verbs, that is, no verbs whose PP complement
         is not assigned a semantic role. We find no verbs otherwise like the raising verb *be-
         lieve* that take PP complements whose prepositional object is a raising controller. Thus
         there are no verbs in English like the hypothetical *kekieve* in the following examples:
         (116)   a. Kim kekieved to there to be some misunderstanding about these issues.
                 b. Lee kekieved from it to bother Kim that they resigned."

Where Bresnan's LFG claim that barred RCP involved a constraint on so-called functional controllers, Pollard and Sag's also purely theory-based rejection depends on the HPSG framework property that unification is not possible for a PP and the NP/DP subject SUBCAT element of verbal complements. This framework-internal theoretical difference aside, Pollard and Sag's remarks add nothing to the *evidence* for the position that assumes the nonexistence of RCP attempted by Bresnan since they merely assert that the relevant cases do not exist. They made no attempt to analyze, for example, the potential counterexamples suggested in Postal (1974: 363, note 7), one of which was taken up by Bresnan. The lack of factual support offered is not obscured by their discourse, which refers to the putative nonexistence of RCP as a "mysterious fact," a "well-known fact," and even a piece of evidence for a theoretical conclusion. Since, unlike Bresnan (1982a), Pollard and Sag seem to grant that the raised phrases are parts of PPs and since they preclude an RCP analysis, their HPSG analysis would have to take the rely on and similar cases as instances of *control* in the ordinary sense. I will return to the factual viability of such a view.[3]

4. The GB claim about RCP

McCloskey (1984) specifically proposed to argue for the existence of RCP in Irish, against the background of the fact that this was clearly barred by GB framework assumptions, for reasons spelled out in detail as follows:

(10)   a. McCloskey (1984: 444–445)

       "Chomsky (1981) argues for a certain view of the interaction between the notions of subcategorization, of thematic role assignment (θ-role assignment) and the Projection Principle, which has the effect of radically restricting the range of variation in Raising constructions which the theory leads us to expect. One part of the theory of θ-role assignment (the θ-criterion) requires that no expression bear more than one θ-role. Movement from one position which is assigned a θ-role to another such position would result in the moved category being assigned two θ-roles—one from its original position, and one from the position to which it is moved. Therefore movement from a θ-position (a position assigned a θ-role) is possible only if the target of the movement is not a θ-position. It is assumed moreover, within the GB framework, that subcategorization implies θ-marking—that is, that a verb assigns a θ-role to each position in VP for which it is subcategorized. It follows, of course, that movement to a subcategorized position will always give rise to a violation of the θ-criterion and is thus illegitimate. More generally, there can be no movement to any position within VP (Chomsky 1981, p. 46), since other assumptions within the framework in question imply that movement to non-subcategorized positions within VP would also give rise to violations of the θ-criterion."

      b. McCloskey (1984: 445)

       "This combination of assumptions is linked to a much more general principle—the Projection Principle—with broader consequences. The Projection Principle holds that all levels of 'syntactic' representation (D-structure, S-structure and LF) are isomorphic and reflect directly the thematic and subcategorizational properties of lexical items. Raising to a position within VP, would violate this principle, because Raising verbs take only clausal complements at LF as a lexical property, but analyses which include Raising to a position within VP need to provide these verbs with an extra complement NP at D-structure (where it would be empty) and at S-structure (where it would be filled by the Raised NP). Such analyses then imply a mismatch within VP between the properties of this group of verbs at LF on the one hand, and at D- and S-structure on the other."

Having stated clearly how and why the GB system precluded inter alia RCP, McCloskey went on to argue that Irish in fact allowed RCP in certain cases, a claim challenged in Stowell (1989). I will not be concerned with this Irish-internal issue here (see Postal, 1986b). The argument here is that any collection of principles that bar RCP can be shown to be incorrect merely on the basis of English facts, more-over, facts that are rather different in form from those McCloskey and Stowell treated.[4]

5. The English class: <u>bank</u>/<u>bet</u>/<u>count</u>/<u>depend</u>/<u>rely</u> + <u>on</u> + infinitive

5.1. Remarks

My goal is thus to argue that RCP is instantiated in English. As in Postal (1974), I refer to the DP whose status is at stake in the issue of whether a particular case in-volves raising or control (or something distinct) as the *pivot* DP. In the cases here, the pivot is then a PP object.

The clearest evidence of English RCP involves the verbs listed in the heading of this section, hereafter the <u>on</u> verbs.[5] The reasons are as follows. First, as already touched on in section 2, the relevant class of infinitival structures actually involves PPs. These are fairly evidently main clause constituents. So consider:

(11) a. One can count on the ex-president *with a high degree of confidence* to lie on most public occasions.
      b. They were depending on the monster, *apparently*, to rush back into the cave.
      c. Most staff members were relying on the director *in a touchingly naive way* to do the right thing.

In each case, the highlighted modifier is (can be) understood to modify the predicate of the main clause. This makes it implausible in the extreme to regard, for example, <u>on the director in a touchingly naive way to do the right thing</u> to be a complement clause or even a constituent. This conclusion is supported by the fact that such se-quences cannot be the foci of pseudocleft or Right Node Raising constructions:

(12) a. *What most staff members were counting was on the director (in a touchingly naive way) to do the right thing.
      b. *Many managers may have been relying and some workers were certainly relying—on the director (in a touchingly naive way) to do the right thing.

Second, the PP complement in <u>on</u> verb cases like (11) is evidently understood as the subject of the infinitival constituent. There are then two standard conceptuali-zations of such facts. One can either invoke some kind of raising or posit a control relation between an unraised main clause (PP) object constituent and the comple-ment subject, taken, for example, to be some sort of invisible element. In effect, under the raising view, the putatively raised phrase is a syntactic but not a semantic con-stituent of the main clause, while under the control from main clause object view it is both. Acceptance of the raising view in the <u>on</u> verb case of course grants the claim of this investigation. Therefore, it seems that to reject that, one must adopt a control view of cases like (11), as implied in the Pollard and Sag (1987, 1994) materials quoted earlier. To justify this position, it then largely suffices to show that a control analysis of <u>on</u> verb structures is not viable.

5.2. Traditional raising/control differentia

There are of course a number of *traditional* criteria that argue that a pivot is *not* a controller and thus, if one accepts that the only alternative is a raising analysis, that it is a raisee. These criteria hold of the least controversial instances of raising, those where the pivot ends up as the subject of a nonpassive, as with verbs like <u>appear/seem/turn out</u> or adjectives like <u>bound/certain/likely</u>, and so on. The first relevant property is that a controller is normally involved with selections in the main clause, as well as in the complement. Lack of any selectional restrictions with respect to the main clause is then an argument against controller status. Notably then, the PP objects of <u>on</u> verbs at issue do not seem to be selected in the main clause and are extremely free. They can be animate or inanimate, human or nonhuman, count or mass, abstract or concrete:

(13)   a. One can't depend on that gorilla to behave himself.
       b. I depended on my car to start in the winter.
       c. I depended on the nurse to watch over my uncle.
       d. I depended on the alarm to go off at the right time.
       e. I depended on the carrots to peel rapidly.
       f. I depended on the soup to cook properly.
       g. I depended on her understanding to be sufficiently sharp for the job.
       h. Michael relied on that algorithm to properly sort people into friends and enemies.

This situation contrasts with that of an uncontroversial object control type pivot such as the object of, for example, <u>convince</u>, which must, modulo personification, of course be animate:

(14)   a. One can't convince that gorilla to behave himself.
       b. *I convinced my car to start in the winter.
       c. I convinced the nurse to watch over my uncle.
       d. *I convinced the alarm to go off at the right time.
       e. *I convinced the carrots to peel rapidly.
       f. *I convinced the soup to cook properly.
       g. *I convinced her understanding to be sufficiently sharp for the job.
       h. *Michael convinced that algorithm to properly sort people into friends and enemies.

The contrasts between (13) and (14) roughly parallel those between the uncontroversial raising structures with <u>seem/likely</u> and the uncontroversial control structures with <u>want/hope</u>, and so on.

A second criterion, related to the selectional facts just cited, is that control structures are in general incompatible with the possibility of a pivot being an *expletive*. In uncontroversial raising and control cases, this yields well-known contrasts like the following:

(15)   a. There are likely to be spies in the class.
       b. *There want to be spies in the class.

(16)   a. It is likely to be evident that the bomb will not be found.
      b. *It wants to be evident that the bomb will not be found.

(17)   a. It is likely to sleet.
      b. *It wants to sleet.

(18)   a. It is likely to be astounding, the number of people who choose to eat snails.
      b. *It wants to be astounding, the number of people who choose to eat snails.

Significantly then, many, though not all, expletives are possible as the PP objects with on verbs, but none are possible with, for example, convince:

(19)   a. *Amanda counted/depended/relied on there to be spies in the class.
      b. Amanda relied on it to be evident that the bomb would not be found.
      c. Amanda depended/relied on it not to sleet.
      d. Amanda banked on it to be astounding, the number of people who chose to eat snails.

(20)   a. *Amanda convinced there to be spies in the class.
      b. *Amanda convinced it to be evident that bomb would not be found.
      c. *Amanda convinced it not to sleet.
      d. *Amanda convinced it to be astounding, the number of people who chose to eat snails.

This evidence, too, supports the noncontroller status of the PP objects; the fact that expletive there is not always possible where 'expected' does not really undermine this conclusion, since it is easily seen that there are a host of special constraints on there even in clear noncontrol and probable raising cases, such as (21–23):

(21)   a. Herbert made it rain/be possible to travel to other galaxies.
      b. *Herbert made there be a riot.

(22)   a. Herbert watched it rain/get dark/become impossible to get a drink after 11 P.M.
      b. *Herbert watched there be an investigation of his father.

(23)   a. Herbert considered it likely to be impossible to square that circle.
      b. *Herbert considered there likely to be a runoff election.

Moreover, even the more restricted expletive there is sometimes possible in on verb infinitives:

(24)   a. Don't count on there to be that many supporters in the organization.
      b. She should not have depended on there to be as much resistance as she hoped.
      c. It is never a good idea to rely on there to be more favorable opinions than unfavorable ones.
      d. We can't depend on *there* to be enough beer to keep all the students happy.

I am not sure about what picks out that subclass of <u>on</u> verb environments that *allow* expletive <u>there</u>, but it seems to have something to do with the complement that represents a specification of *quantity*.

A third traditionally cited argument against the controller status of a pivot position (and hence in favor of its raisee status) is that raising structures fairly freely allow restricted DPs, for example, idiom chunks, whereas the control cases mostly do not.[6] So there are well-known idiom chunk contrasts like the following:

(25) a. Close tabs were kept/*placed/*maintained on her movements.
      b. They believe close tabs to have been kept/*placed/*maintained on her movements.
      c. *They convinced close tabs to be kept/placed/maintained on her movements.
      d. ?They were counting/depending/relying on close tabs to be kept/*placed/maintained on her movements.
      e. ?Close tabs were being counted/depended/relied on to be kept/*placed/*maintained on her movements.

(26) a. The shit hit/*struck/*collided with the fan. (The * notation here indicates lack of idiomatic meaning = 'something bad happen'.)
      b. They believe the shit to have hit the fan yesterday.
      c. *They convinced the shit to hit the fan yesterday.
      d. They were counting/depending/relying on the shit to hit the fan when the new director arrived.
      e. The shit can be counted/depended/relied on to hit the fan at that time.

(27) a. That finally broke/*crushed/*smashed the ice at the meeting (* = lack of idiomatic meaning = "initial interpersonal tensions were dissolved").
      b. The ice was finally broken/*crushed/*smashed.
      c. *They convinced the ice to finally be broken.
      d. They were counting/depending/relying on the ice to finally be broken.
      e. ?The ice can't be counted/depended/relied on to finally be broken.

(28) a. Her ship/*boat finally came/*floated in (= "she received the life-improving lucky break").
      b. Her ship is likely to come/*float in.
      c. They believed her ship to have finally come/*floated in.
      d. You can't count/depend/rely on your ship to come/*float in just when you want it to.

(29) a. The lovebug bit/*clawed/*grabbed Marsha (= "Marsha fell in love").
      b. The lovebug seems to have bitten/*clawed/*grabbed Marsha.
      c. It is a mistake to believe the lovebug to have bitten/*clawed/*grabbed Marsha.
      d. It is a mistake to count/depend/rely on the lovebug to bite/*claw/*grab Marsha in time.

(30) a. *Her ship wants to come/float in.
      b. *They convinced her ship to come in.

(31) a. *The lovebug wants to bite Marsha.
      b. *They convinced the lovebug to bite Marsha.

(32) a. All hell broke loose/*broke up/*broke down.
      b. All hell seems to have broken loose/*up/*down.
      c. It is a mistake to believe all hell to have broken loose/*up/*down.
      d. You can count/depend/rely on all hell to break loose/*up/*down at that time.

That is, the on verb + PP object + infinitive cases behave like the uncontroversial raising cases with seem/likely/believe, not like uncontroversial control cases.

5.3. Nontraditional raising/control differentia

I believe several infinitival characteristics *not* standardly cited, systematically differentiate raising and control structures. One involves the property originally taken in Postal (1970) to be characteristic of control structures, namely, that the controlled complement has an invisible (weak definite) *pronominal* subject.[7] This then theoretically differentiates such complements from those of raising structures in which, in the general case, the complement subject simply is the main clause pivot DP, which, of course, need not be a pronoun.[8] Therefore, this theoretical difference would in principle permit factual differentiation of the two structures in specific cases if one could find independent grammatical features that reveal the presence or absence of (invisible) weak definite pronouns.

A feature of this type that I have made much of in other contexts involves what I have called *antipronominal contexts*, those that reject the presence of weak definite pronouns.[9] If one finds a context, in this case, in particular, an antipronominal subject context, then the theoretical distinction between raising and control complements in the terms of Postal (1970) would lead one to expect (33):

(33) Whereas, modulo note 7, a raising complement should be indifferent to whether its
      subject position is antipronominal, a control structure should be ungrammatical when
      the complement subject position is antipronominal.

Unfortunately, I have not found many subject positions that are antipronominal, which renders the task of testing (33) rather difficult. Still there are some. Two include the subject positions of be the matter/wrong with:

(34) a. Something/That/Lots of things are the matter with my transmission.
      b. Something$_1$ is the matter with my transmission, but that sort of thing/*it$_1$ is not the
         matter with his.
      c. That kind of thing/Nothing is wrong with her values.
      d. *He said something$_1$ was wrong with her values and it$_1$ is wrong with them.

Given that the subject positions of be the matter with and be wrong with appear to be antipronominal, one can test (33) with uncontroversial raising and control cases.

Significantly then, one observes first that such contexts do not combine with clear control structures:

(35) a. (Its) Being common doesn't mean that that problem/something/anything is serious.
      b. *(Its) Being the matter with my transmission doesn't mean that something/anything is serious.
      c. *Something/Lots of things can be the matter with your transmission without being the matter with mine.

(36) a. (Its) Being harmful may indicate that something is detectable.
      b. *(Its) Being wrong with your liver may not mean something is detectable.
      c. *That can be detectable without being wrong with your liver.

And equally clearly, they do combine with a variety of clear raising structures:

(37) a. Something/Lots of things/Nothing seem(s) to be the matter with your transmission.
      b. Many things are likely to be the matter with your transmission.
      c. What they proved to be the matter with your transmission is not serious.

(38) a. Did that appear to be wrong with Mike's liver?
      b. Such a thing is bound to be wrong with someone's liver.
      c. They didn't believe anything to be the matter with her liver.

Against this background, it is thus possible to test whether the behavior of the on verb structures resembles those of clear control cases or those of clear raising cases:

(39) a. You can count on that not to be the matter with your transmission.
      b. He wasn't depending on anything of the sort to be the matter with the enemy's missile defense system.
      c. We can't rely on that many things/all those things to be wrong with their intelligence network.

The evidence then shows that the infinitival complements of on verb structures behave like the uncontroversial raising cases and contrast with the uncontroversial control forms.

A second nontraditional way of testing the difference between raising and control cases relates to the possibility of the complement representing a *middle* structure, which, I suggest, is subject to condition (40):

(40) A control complement cannot be a middle clause.

It is apparent that this divides up uncontroversial cases properly:

(41) a. Harry bribed Uruguayan police.
      b. Uruguayan police bribe cheaply/easily.

    c. Uruguayan police seem/are likely to bribe cheaply/easily.
    d. *Uruguayan police hope/try/want to bribe cheaply/easily.
    e. *Bribing cheaply/easily pleases Uruguayan police.
    f. Hugh proved Uruguayan police to bribe easily/cheaply.
    g. *Hugh persuaded Uruguayan police to bribe easily/cheaply.
    h. *Some policemen can be poor without bribing easily.
    i. *Uruguayan policemen often apologize to foreigners for not bribing cheaply.

(42)   a. They frightened the wimp.
    b. Certain wimps frighten easily.
    c. Certain wimps seem/are likely to frighten easily.
    d. *Certain wimps don't try/want to frighten easily.
    e. *Frightening easily worries certain wimps.
    f. They proved certain wimps to frighten easily.
    g. *They persuaded certain wimps to frighten easily.
    h. *Good soldiers can be inexperienced without frightening easily.

(43)   a. They sold the beer easily.
    b. Such beer sells easily.
    c. *Selling easily made that sort of beer expensive.
    d. *That kind of beer can be cheap without selling easily.

Note, too, clear correlations like (44):

(44)   a. They prevented there from being a riot.
    b. They prevented Uruguayan police from bribing cheaply.
    c. *They discouraged there from being a riot.
    d. *They discouraged Uruguayan police from bribing cheaply.

That is, traditionally prevent is analyzed as inducing raising (to object) (see Postal, 1974: 154–163; and Postal and Pullum, 1988: 655–657), supported by the expletive object of (44a), which analysis is then consistent with (40) given the grammatical middle complement of (44b). On the contrary, discourage, which as (44c) illustrates, precludes expletive objects, and is traditionally taken to induce control, allows no middle complement, as (44d) indicates.

    Significantly then, the infinitival complements of on verbs can be middles:

(45)   a. Hugh was counting/depending/relying on Uruguayan police to bribe easily/cheaply.
    b. They counted on/depended on/relied on certain wimps to frighten easily.
    c. She was counting on that sort of beer to sell easily.

These data thus also support the view that on verb structures are of the raising, not the control, type.

    The argument from middle distribution in favor of a raising analysis of on verb infinitival structures can be a bit strengthened as follows. The facts with the on verb instances of middle infinitives with pivot DPs inside PPs contrast with other pivot instances inside PPs, that is, with real control cases, which are ungrammatical, as (40) specifies:

(46) a. *The president appealed to/proposed to/suggested to Uruguayan police to bribe cheaply.
     b. *The president pleaded with Uruguayan police to bribe cheaply.

One potential problem with the argument for a raising analysis of <u>on</u> verb cases based on principle (40) has been pointed out to me by Idan Landau (personal communication of July 16, 2000). He observed that the infinitive in the case of the infinitival complements of the main verbs <u>claim</u> and <u>pretend</u> *can* be a middle, providing examples (47a and b), to which I add others:

(47) a. Linguists usually claim to discourage easily.
     b. Many linguists pretend to discourage easily.
     c. Uruguayan police claim not to bribe cheaply.
     d. Uruguayan police pretend to bribe cheaply.

I agree that these are fine. If, as usually assumed, these are control cases, they obviously falsify (40), raising then the issue of why the other control cases are bad. Idan Landau offered the suggestion that the right generalization takes account of the fact that (47a and b), unlike typical control cases, involve complements that *represent propositions*.

One must then consider an alternative to hypothesis (40) of the following form:

(48) An infinitival or gerundive complement that is nonpropositional cannot be a middle.

Differentiating the factual viability of this generalization, which would not help differentiate raising and control structures, from that in (40) is not so easy because most infinitives are nonpropositional. Still there are a few pretty clearly propositional ones:

(49) a. Sheldon demonstrated/proved to us to know Spanish (= that he knew Spanish).
     b. Gwen swore to us to be a government agent (= that she was a government agent).

These structures are not predicted by (48) to *bar* middles, any more than (47a and b) do, while (40) claims that middles should be impossible. The latter is correct:

(50) a. *Corrupt police try to demonstrate to their clients to bribe cheaply.
     b. *Even cowards may swear to TV reporters not to frighten easily.

Further, when one looks at gerundive clauses that represent propositions, middles are also impossible as (40) specifies, while (48) would allow them to be good:

(51) a. Being a vampire (= 'that she is a vampire' = 'that it is true that she is a vampire') proves Jane not to be a vegetarian.
     b. *Bribing cheaply proves Uruguayan police to be desperate.

    c. *Frightening easily makes wimps unreliable.

    d. *Rattling so easily makes a TV announcer appear foolish.

Moreover, observe that middles are impossible in clearly proposition-denoting controlled adjuncts:

(52) a. Uruguayan police can be corrupt (without looking guilty/*without bribing easily).

     b. Uruguayan police were criticized for being dishonest/*bribing too cheaply.

My suggestion is thus that one should accept the incompatibility of middles and control structures and therefore take the grammaticality of (47) to falsify *not* (*33*) but rather the traditional view that such cases are control structures. I propose instead that they are raising structures associated with the additional feature (quite exceptional in English) that the raised form, understood as bound by the main clause subject, is invisible.[10] It is not irrelevant, I think, that these verbs do take infinitival complements transparently not interpretable as control cases but easily seen as raising ones, less marginally so in the case of claim:

(53) a. *She claimed that to be the case.

     b. *They claimed biological weapons to be too terrible to use.

     c. *Irving pretended something to be bothering him.

     d. That, he claimed to be the case.

     e. Biological weapons, they claimed to be too terrible to use.

     f. What did they claim to be too terrible to use?

     g. What Irving pretended to be bothering him was his neighbor's drum playing.

     h. No matter what they pretend to be impossible, don't believe them.

     i. That, he may have only pretended to be the case.

While straightforward cases like (53a, b, and c) are obviously ungrammatical, they arguably manifest what was called in Postal (1974: 305) the *Derived Object Constraint* (DOC). This bars certain raised objects from remaining in the standard main clause postverbal object position. But cases like (53d, e, f, g, h, and i), which satisfy DOC, seem fine. Thus a consistent analysis can claim that these two verbs, not mentioned in Postal (1974), are also subject to DOC.

    Consider then:

(54) a. *Marilyn claimed herself to be intuitive.

     b. *Marilyn pretended herself to be intuitive.

These would surely be regularly ruled out by any formulation of DOC capable of blocking (53a, b, c). Suppose, though, continuing to assume these are raising cases, that these two verbs allow, and arguably in fact require, raised *reflexive* objects bound by their main clause subjects to be invisible.[11] This would properly differentiate the following:

(55) a. *Herself$_1$, Marilyn$_1$ claimed to be intuitive.

     b. Herself$_2$, Marilyn$_1$ claimed to have talked to Jane$_2$ about.

   c. *Herself$_1$, Marilyn$_1$ pretended to be intuitive.

   d. Herself$_2$, Marilyn$_1$ pretended to have talked to Jane$_2$ about.

A further bit of evidence that the infinitival complements of the verb <u>claim</u> are raising, not control, structures is that they permit the same type of passives as less controversial raising inducers such as <u>believe</u> and <u>prove</u>:

(56) a. The gorilla was claimed/believed by Austin to be telepathic.

     b. Such things are often claimed/proved by scientists to be dangerous.

     c. That program was claimed to have been written in Cobol.

     d. It was claimed to have been hidden from the people that he was a werewolf.

     e. *It was pretended to be the case.

     f. *That was pretended to be impossible.

There is clearly no way to regard such <u>claim</u> cases, which, it should be observed, satisfy DOC, as control structures, since uncontroversial instances of the latter cannot correspond to such passives:

(57) a. Herb hopes/longs/tries to be brave/help the handicapped.

     b. *Those people are hoped/longed/tried by Karen to be brave

Left open of course is why the putative raising complement of <u>pretend</u> does not permit passivization, a question not directly relevant to our concerns here.

A virtue of an obligatory *reflexive* deletion view of what I am arguing are raising cases like (53d, e, f, g, and h) is that it is consistent with the fact that such cases are *understood de se*, a systematic feature of true control structures.[12] This might seem to argue against a raising analysis but does not if the latter is limited, as here suggested for these cases, to reflexive structures, which also are well known to have the *de se* requirement; see Higginbotham (1992: 87). That is, with respect to *that* feature, the following pairs do not differ:

(58) a. Glen expects himself to win the first match.

     b. Glen expects to win the first match.[13]

     c. Glenda wants herself to develop better muscle tone.

     d. Glenda wants to develop better muscle tone.

A third poorly known property that distinguishes control from raising cases involves certain metonymous stock (price) structures:

(59) Microsoft went up.

In this case, a company name DP appears as a subject with certain predicates but is understood to refer to the stock of that company, in turn to the price of the stock of that company. So (59) is equivalent to (60a), in turn equivalent to (60b):

(60) a. Microsoft stock went up/down/dropped/rose (in price).

     b. The price of Microsoft stock went up/down/dropped/rose.

Now, relevantly, the usage in (59) does *not* interact freely with complement types and for uncontroversial cases, a generalization *initially* statable as (61) holds:

(61)   The 'stock' usage of company name DPs like that in (59) is not possible in control structures.

This generalization is supported by data like (62):

(62)   a. Microsoft seems/is likely to have gone up.
        b. They proved Microsoft to have gone up.
        c. *Microsoft hopes/plans/tried/wants to go up.
        d. *Going up pleased Microsoft.
        e. *They persuaded Microsoft to go up.
        f. Microsoft hired Michael Downs without knowing that/*going up.
        g. Microsoft hired Michael Downs to impress the government/*go up.
        h. *Microsoft fired its chairman after going down.
        i. *Microsoft denied the story without shooting up/rising much.

And here also the usage in question is perfectly possible in the infinitival complements of <u>on</u> verbs:

(63)   a. The labor union was counting on Microsoft to go up toward the end of the year.
        b. No one should depend on Enron to go down/drop any further.
        c. I can't rely on Enron to rise this year.

So constraint (61) also argues for the raising and against a control analysis of the infinitives with <u>on</u> verbs.

It is important to dispel a possible objection to (61). Despite ill-formedness like that in (62c–i), control cases like (64) are perfectly grammatical:

(64)   a. Microsoft went up today after going down yesterday.
        b. Going up yesterday did not cause Microsoft to go down today.

This shows that the initial extremely informal formulation in (61) is inadequate. However, I do not think such cases cast doubt on the reality of a control restriction on the relevant stock usage. For it is easy to see that cases like (64) differ in a specific way from the ungrammatical control structures taken to support (61). Namely, in the latter the controller company name DP as it were stands alone in a position where in general a DP that denotes stock or its price would be ungrammatical. That is, it appears in a position that selects mind-possessor denoting DPs, with companies being taken to be of that category. In (64), however, the controller is a company name DP that is itself understood to denote the stock or stock price of the relevant company.

My partially speculative suggestion is that one can give a superior replacement of (61) that allows (64a, b) as follows. Assume that the stock (price) interpretation of a company name DP simply involves a specific type of *possessor ascension* so that there is a structure for cases like (64), in which the DP <u>Microsoft</u> is the possessor of a larger DP headed by a noun that means "stock" and that that larger DP is in turn the possessor of one whose head noun means "price." Schematically then, (65a) would have a representation like (65b):

(65)   a. Microsoft went up.
       b. Microsoft's$_1$ stock's$_2$ price$_3$ went up.

Now, under this three DP analysis, grammatical cases like (64a and b) are represented as (66a and b), respectively, while an ungrammatical one like (62c) is represented as (66c):

(66)   a. Microsoft's$_1$ stock's$_2$ price$_3$ went up today after [it]$_3$ going down yesterday.
       b. [It's]$_3$ Going up yesterday did not cause Microsoft's$_1$ stock's$_2$ price$_3$ to go down today.
       c. *Microsoft$_1$ wants its$_1$ stock's$_2$ price$_3$ to go up.

The key point then is that under this speculative analysis, in the ungrammatical (62c) = (66c), the controller is a company denoting DP, while in the grammatical (64a, b) = (66a, b) the controller is not a company denoting DP but one that denotes price. This suggests that the right elaboration of (61) would be something like (67):

(67)   A proper noun-headed company-denoting DP cannot be the antecedent (controller or not) of a pronoun that is a (possessor ascended) company denoting DP.

I have generalized (67) beyond controllers to cover as well facts like (68):

(68)   a. *Microsoft$_1$ hired Bevins because it$_1$ had gone down recently.
       b. *Microsoft$_1$ claimed that it$_1$ would go up.
       c. *He wants to work for Microsoft$_1$ because it$_1$ will soon go up.

Compare:

(69)   Microsoft went down recently because it had gone up so much before.

As with the control cases (64a and b), (69) is good because the antecedent of the pronoun can be taken to be a larger DP that contains the company name phrase, one that denotes stock price. Inter alia, (67) accounts for the lack of ambiguity of the long form of (70), whereas the short form is ambiguous:

(70)   Jerome bought Microsoft$_1$ (because it$_1$ went down).

That is, the short version has readings where what is bought is the company or the stock of the company, but the long version has only the stock reading.

Another virtue of the formulation in (67) that covers pronouns and reflexives is that it can account for the fact that the stock usage in question does not seem acceptable with the verbs claim and pretend, argued earlier to involve raising not control:

(71)   a. *Microsoft claims to have gone up.
        b. *Microsoft pretended to drop.

Given the earlier proposal that claim/pretend infinitival structures involve invisible raised *reflexives* bound by the subject, what is wrong with (71a and b) is that they violate the same constraint seen in (72):

(72)   a. *Microsoft$_1$ claimed that that was the case after it$_1$ went up.
        b. *Harry wants to work for Microsoft$_1$ because it$_1$ is going to go way up.
        c. *Microsoft believes itself to have gone up.

That is, very roughly, it does not seem possible for a pronominal form, reflexive or not, that designates the stock or price of the stock of a company to be anteceded by a DP that designates that company. That is, given the formulation in (67), cases like (72) are blocked under either a control or a raising analysis.

Just as was remarked apropos of constraint (40), support for (67) is also increased when it is observed that clear instances of control that involve pivots internal to PPs contrast with on verb cases like (63):

(73)   a. *The president appealed to/proposed to/suggested to Microsoft to go up.
        b. *The president pleaded with Microsoft to go up.

It must be stressed that the English grammatical constraint here reconstructed as (67) can *not* be understood in general semantic terms. What I mean can be indicated with respect to (74):

(74)   *Microsoft intends to go up.

It might occur to some to suggest that what is wrong with such a case is that there is a semantic clash between the controller, a DP that denotes a company, and the controlee, which designates a stock or its price. But it can be shown beyond serious doubt that this is not the relevant factor. This is possible because a variety of other metonymy cases with the same semantic clash property characteristic of the stock cases *are grammatical*. Here are two:

(75)   a. I am parked on Twenty-sixth Street (= "my car is parked on Twenty-sixth Street").
        b. I didn't want/intend to be parked on Twenty-sixth Street.

(76)   a. That pitcher is hard to hit (= "That baseball pitcher's pitches are hard to hit").
        b. That pitcher wants/intends to be hard to hit.

In (75b) the controller denotes a person, but the controlled form denotes a vehicle; in (76b) the controller also denotes a person, but the controlled form denotes (baseball) pitches. Hence it is clear that there is no general principle that requires some sort of semantic matching that could fail in the stock case. Consequently, one must appeal to a construction-specific constraint for the latter such as (67).

A fourth property that distinguishes uncontroversial control and raising structures from each other but is not part of the traditional battery of tests for the distinction is called *partial control* in Landau (2000, 2002). This is the phenomenon seen in cases like the following:

(77) a. *The director met at noon.
      b. The director wants to meet at noon.

(78) a. *I got together yesterday.
      b. I wanted to get together yesterday.

That is, with intransitive verbs that normally require a plural or conjoined subject, like meet, get together, join together, divorce, and so on, it is possible to find cases where they occur as the heads of infinitival complements of what are universally analyzed as control structures *where the controller is a singular*. Taking these complements to have invisible subjects, the interpretation then is that the denotation of the controller is understood to be (only) one element of the set denoted by the invisible subject, the others being unspecified.

The relevance of this phenomenon, treated in detail in Landau (2000), is that, as he states clearly, *it is impossible in uncontroversial raising cases*:

(79) a. *Myron$_1$ seems [ ]$_{1,\ldots n}$ to have met at noon.
      b. *Myron$_1$ is likely [ ]$_{1\ldots n}$ to get together tomorrow.
      c. *I believe Myron$_1$ [ ]$_{1,\ldots n}$ to have met at noon.
      d. *They proved Myron$_1$ [ ]$_{1,\ldots n}$ to have gotten together at that time.
      e. *They prevented Myron$_1$ from [ ]$_{1,\ldots n}$ getting together at that time.

Testing then how the PP structures that occur with on verb infinitivals behave with respect to partial control, one finds that they fall together with the uncontroversial raising cases and contrast with control cases:

(80) a. *I can't count on Myron$_1$ [ ]$_{1,\ldots n}$ to get together when we want to.
      b. Myron$_1$ refused [ ]$_{1,\ldots n}$ to get together when I wanted to.

(81) a. *One shouldn't depend on Myron$_1$ [ ]$_{1,\ldots n}$ to meet at all.
      b. Myron$_1$ hoped [ ]$_{1,\ldots n}$ to meet before the demonstration.

(82) a. *They were relying on Myron$_1$ [ ]$_{1,\ldots n}$ to get together after the party.
      b. Myron$_1$ worried about [ ]$_{1,\ldots n}$ getting together without her.

Here also then the evidence supports the raising character of on verb infinitival structures, not a control analysis.[14]

As with the earlier arguments, this support for a raising analysis of on verb infinitives can be broadened by again noting the contrast with clear control cases that have pivots internal to PPs. So compare (80)–(82) with (83):

(83) a. Carla appealed to/proposed to/suggested to Larry$_1$ [ ]$_{1,\ldots n}$ (not) to meet without her.
      b. Carla pleaded with Larry$_1$ [ ]$_{1,\ldots n}$ not to meet without her.

An evident implication of the combination of the view that partial control is impossible in raising structures with my claims that the verbs <u>claim</u> and <u>pretend</u> that occur with infinitival complements represent raising, not control, structures is that partial control should be *impossible* in forms like, for example, (84):

(84) a. *The department chairman$_1$ claims [ ]$_{1,\ldots n}$ to have gotten together/met yesterday.
      b. *The department chairman$_1$ pretended [ ]$_{1,\ldots n}$ to meet yesterday.

I find these to indeed be ungrammatical. However, Landau (2002) cites the following as grammatical:

(85) The chair$_1$ claimed [ ]$_{1,\ldots n}$ to be gathering once a week.

But I find (85), if anything, even worse than (84a).

One way, perhaps, to sharpen the issue is to note that the control view, which would take (85) to be good, predicts a clear *difference* in such sets as (86):

(86) a. *The department chairman$_1$ claimed [ ]$_{1,\ldots n}$ to have gotten together last week.
      b. *The department chairman$_1$ was claimed [ ]$_{1,\ldots n}$ to have gotten together last week.
      c. *The department chairman$_1$, they claimed [ ]$_{1,\ldots n}$ to have gotten together last week.

Since it is clear that the latter two examples cannot involve control but must be raising structures, for me all three should be undifferentiated, which is how I judge them.

5.4. A problematic type of restriction

While the evidence cited so far seems to fairly relentlessly support the raising nature of <u>on</u> verb infinitival complements and disconfirm any view that they involve control structures, one set of facts might seem to raise difficulties. It was suggested in Rosenbaum (1967) that an effective test for the raising/control distinction is the way the two types of cases interact semantically with passivization. When all relevant DPs are definite referential expressions, active and passive are semantically (truth functionally) equivalent:

(87) a. Glen tickled Betty.
      b. Betty was tickled by Glen.

That is, one of these can represent a true assertion if and only if the other does. When such passives interact with clear raising/control structures, though, equivalence is found only in the former:

(88) a. Glen seems to have defended Betty =
      b. Betty seems to have been defended by Glen =
      c. It seems that Glen defended Betty.

      d. Glen wants to defend Betty ≠
      e. Betty wants to be defended by Glen.

The same story holds for the object cases like (89):

(89)   a. Stan expects Glen to defend Betty =
       b. Stan expects Betty to be defended by Glen.
       c. Stan persuaded Glen to defend Betty ≠
       d. Stan persuaded Betty to be defended by Glen.

The equivalence between (88a and b) would follow from the simple passive equivalence if the meaning of the (88a) case were that of the full that clause case, that is, if the pivot NP in the (88a) case with seem played no semantic role. By parity of reasoning then, the structure of the (88d) case should be different and in particular should be such that the pivot NP *does* play a semantic role in the main clause. For then the nonequivalent passives will involve two different NPs in the main clause, and that is how they differ semantically. That is, in (88c) the sentence is about a want of Glen's but in (88d) about a want of Betty's.

    According to this reasoning then, equivalence under passivization is a test for raising structures. Attempting to apply this idea to on verb cases, one finds, however:

(90)   a. Stan was counting/depending/relying on Glen to defend Betty.
       b. ?*Stan was counting/depending/relying on Betty to be defended by Glen.

The first point is that whereas (90a) are normal sentences, the sentences in (90b) seem unacceptable. Second, cutting through the obscurity determined by its ungrammatical status, (90b) does not seem equivalent to the corresponding case of (90a). Roughly, the latter seems to indicate that the focus of the 'reliance' is on the entity denoted by the raised DP Betty, while the former indicates that the focus is on the entity denoted by the raised DP Glen. This state of affairs is not consistent with what Rosenbaum dealt with.

    Now, encounters with instances of this problem are of long date:

(91)   Postal (1974: 363–364)
       "An interesting set of cases relevant to assumption linkage involves a set of verbal elements with the form Verb + *on*, including *bet on, depend on, bank on, count on, rely on.* Consider *depend on*. This occurs with both gerundive and infinitival complements:
       (i) a. You can depend on him to do something decent.
           b. You can depend on him doing something decent.
                          his
       "I should like to argue that sentences like (i)a are, in fact, derived by Raising. However, examples like (i)a and (i)b are not strict paraphrases. Compare the following:
       (ii) a. ?You can depend on that corpse to remain here for another hour.
           b. You can depend on that corpse's remaining here for another hour.
       "It seems clear again that the putative Raising examples entail the analogous unraised examples, but not conversely. That is, there seems to be an assumption linked with

Raising application for *depend on*. Roughly this is that the dependable state of affairs is so because of the will(s) of the entities designated by the raised NPs. Hence (ii)a is anomalous because corpses have no wills, etc. Since it is easy to show that the post-*on* NP with infinitival complements in such cases is a main clause constituent, the alternative to a Raising analysis would involve distinct underlying structure types for the *a* and *b* examples in such pairs, a highly unsatisfactory account. I think that these verbal examples with *on* should thus provide a fruitful domain for studying the interaction between Raising application and particular linked semantic assumptions."

These remarks were made internal to a section that discussed a number of cases that putatively involved raising being associated with particular semantic assumptions. I cannot claim to understand much more about these matters than when I wrote the preceding. However, if it is accepted that such linkages of raising with implicatures are a real phenomenon, then the facts in (90) would not really bear on the fundamental issue of these remarks, which is the existence of RCP and its support from on verb structures.

Significantly then, I argued a bit in the section cited here that even uncontroversial raising structures can reveal the kind of linked semantic assumption seemingly found with on verbs that take infinitives. So compare the following:

(92)　a. Joseph Stalin seemed to me to be an evil monster.
　　　b. It seemed to me that Joseph Stalin was an evil monster.

For someone like me, who had the good fortune to never encounter Mr. Stalin, use of an example like (92a) is strange. The reason, I think, is that raising with this experiential verb is associated with the implicature that the entity denoted by the verb's logical subject (here me) has had some direct experience of the entity (if any) denoted by the raised DP. On the contrary, (92b), which involves no raising and hence no implicature, is neutral and usable by anyone, regardless of his or her experience with Mr. Stalin. Since cases with seem are, though, the archetype of generally accepted raising structures, it would follow that the implicature linkage is not an indication of the nonexistence of raising, hence not an argument for a control analysis, for example.

Taking that as the case, there is no reason to think that facts like (90) attack the view here that the on verb structures are instances of raising, not of control. Still, there is a mystery in (90b) beyond the mere facts of implicature linkage, namely, why the anomaly. This contrasts, for example, with seem structures:

(93)　a. Stan seemed to Glenda to have defended Betty
　　　b. Betty seemed to Glenda to have been defended by Glen.

Here the b. example in no way seems anomalous. Not really understanding the nature of the implicatures linked to the raising cases, I can do no better than speculate that the difference lies in the nature of the linked assumptions. In the on verb cases, I suspect, as already speculated almost thirty years ago, that the assumptions involve reference to the will of the entity denoted by the raised DP, while this is not the case in the seem assumption. If so, then possibly what is wrong with (90b) is that the state of affairs denoted by a passive is normally not attributable to the will of the entity denoted by the subject of the passive, even if there is such an entity and it has a will.

In any case, I suggest that while the <u>on</u> verb cases do not provide a perfect model of the situation, Rosenbaum (1967) took to be a diagnostic for raising, neither do other cases of the sort that are almost uniformly taken to be raising cases. Hence I do not believe the implicature facts bear negatively on the conclusions of this chapter.

6. The structure of RCP cases

The mere recognition of the existence of a raising analysis for cases like (94) leaves many questions about the relevant structures open:

(94)   Winston counted/depended/relied on Isabelle to do the taxes.

In particular, despite what has been argued here, there is in the proper terms no reason to think that the raising involved in RCP actually involves anything that is accurately described as raising to the object position of a P.

Although the claim just made might seem paradoxical, in relational terms, as already discussed in Postal (1986b) and Joseph (1990), it is not. In relational terms, raising itself means (i) that a constituent that heads an arc, say A, in a subordinate constituent (here, an infinitival clause) also heads at least one arc, say B, in the main clause, and that (ii) in a specifiable sense, arc B's status depends on A. In the framework of Johnson and Postal (1980) and Postal (1990a, 1992, 1996), briefly sketched in chapter 1, section 9, which recognizes the primitive relations between arcs called Sponsor and Erase, these conditions can be taken to mean that A sponsors arc B, which erases arc A; technically then, B is a type I *foreign successor* of A.

In such terms then, the reason that the raised DP ends up internal to a PP has to do with the relation that the raisee ends up bearing in the main clause. Simply put, that relation, call it R^{10}, can be taken to be one that in English, unlike, for example, the core relations 1 (subject), 2 (direct object), and 3 (indirect object), requires the PP structure. There are then two possibilities. The more attractive, I believe, is to say that the raising with <u>on</u> verbs is simply raising to the same status as with more standard raising to object verbs like <u>believe</u>, that is, to direct object, 2. This means, in terms of the sketch of the previous paragraph, that B is a type I 2-arc foreign successor of A. One can then posit that <u>on</u> verbs obligatory require (at least certain) 2-arcs to have R^{10}-arc type I local successors. It is possible and maximizes generality to assume that nonraising cases with the same verbs, like (95), then also involve R^{10}-arc type I local successors of 2-arcs:

(95)   Jenny counted/depended/relied on Lucy.

This means that one can take these verbs to occur with initial 2-arcs subject to the same requirement of demotion to R^{10} as holds for the raising cases. The difference is then that in (95) it is initial 2s that demote to R^{10}, while in the cases discussed throughout this chapter it is 2s that result from raising (to object).

Viewed from this perspective, one can easily see that any analog of principles that ban RCP, principles argued here to be untenable just because of English cases like, for example, (94), would be quite strange. Such principles would merely stipulate that, for example, 2-arc foreign successors cannot have local successors with any R-sign that defines a relation that must determine a PP structure. Such a principle would be strange inter alia because the notion of 'relation that must determine a PP structure' does not pick out a universally specifiable set of relations. A particular relation may define a PP structure in one NL but not in another. The point then is that internal to the sort of arc-based ideas relevant to this section there is no independent motivation for any principle that accomplishes the work claimed to be done in LFG, HPSG, and GB frameworks by the various framework-specific assumptions that putatively block RCP. But without the needed stipulations, arc-based ideas, unlike these three views, arguably will not block the sort of raising that results in RCP. This is an obvious virtue if, as argued in earlier sections, RCP is instantiated in English.

While the view that cases like (94) involve raising to 2 with subsequent demotion to R^{10} is attractive, it is not required. A distinct arc-based description would simply say that with on verbs raising is to R^{10}; that is, infinitival complement 1-arcs have type I R^{10}-arc foreign successors, which then determine the PP structure. Again, if this is not possible, in such terms it is only because of apparently fairly stipulative axioms that limit the class of foreign successors of, in particular, 1-arcs, axioms that might exclude R^{10}-arc foreign successors. If such axioms could be justified, then the alternative just mentioned would be excluded and something like the raising to 2 with subsequent demotion to R^{10} might be imposed as the only available raising analysis.

7. Conclusion

While the three most widely invoked syntactic frameworks have, as shown in earlier sections, all claimed as a consequence of fairly deeply rooted principles of those frameworks that RCP cannot be a feature of an NL, it has been argued in this chapter that such a view is falsified merely by an examination of certain facts of English. Such a conclusion then serves as a solid pillar for the fundamental claim of this work that enormous skepticism is justified with respect to current syntactic claims and conclusions.

A New Raising Mystery

1. Background

Some quarter of a century ago a debate took place about the proper analyses to be assigned to various English clauses with *non*finite complements, including those like (1):

(1) a. The doctor considered *the condition* to be untreatable.
      b. Most observers perceived *them* to be nervous.
      c. Isabelle proved *Jerome* to have vampirelike properties.
      d. Lydia wants *Ken* to succeed.
      e. The general wishes *you* to stand at attention.

At issue inter alia was the superficial clausal status of the highlighted DPs, hereafter the *pivot* DPs. Principal works involved include Bach (1977), Bresnan (1976), Chomsky (1973, 1981), Lightfoot (1976), and Postal (1974, 1977). Under the view defended in Postal (1974, 1977) and a bit in Postal and Pullum (1988), the pivot DPs were in one aspect of the structure of such sentences *subjects* of the complement clauses but in another aspect of that structure *objects* of the main clause. Under the view advocated in Chomsky (1973), the pivot DPs were *exclusively* subjects of the complement in every relevant structural aspect. Other positions are logically possible; for example, Pollard and Sag (1994: chapter 3) claim that the pivot DPs in (1) are exclusively main clause objects.

    It is unclear where these matters stand today. With the passage of time, the grammatical assumptions and theoretical commitments that underlay the debate of the

1970s have evolved; no one involved in those discussions holds today a theoretical position entirely like, perhaps even much like, that they held then. Moreover, new facts have of course come to light. It would thus be appropriate to reconsider the whole web of issues that surrounds cases like (1).[1] But that task greatly exceeds the scope of this chapter. Rather, I focus here on a specific range of data that played no role in the earlier discussions but I believe bear significantly on the proper analysis of these constructions.

Before getting to that, though, let me sketch informally my own current position on these matters. This is not so easy for the major reason that I think about such issues in terms of a relational or *arc*-based view of syntactic structure that is not widely known. Anyone interested should consult works like Johnson and Postal (1980), Postal (1990a, 1992, 1996), and chapter 1, section 9. It is not possible to discuss this conception in detail here. That is a major reason that what I will say will be quite informal.

The original controversy took place internal to a certain number of assumptions that defined what was then called *transformational grammar*. Not accidentally, the subtitle of Postal (1974) included the phrase "One Rule of English Grammar," a reference to a particular transformational operation whose existence was argued for. I have, however, long since rejected the idea that transformational rules, whether schematized as in Chomsky's *Move α* formulations of recent decades or not, play any role in NL. More generally, I claim that there is no motivation for any *generative* apparatus at all. An NL grammar should, I believe, be regarded as an *axiom system* whose elements are statements to which truth values can be assigned, not as a sentence formation machine implementable as a computer program. I cannot defend this view here, but I hope to have at least made it clear that among the ideas I reject are those that both the opposing position and mine *shared* in the 1970s debate. See chapters 6 and 13 for further discussion of the issue of generative versus nongenerative grammars.

Despite these differences from my 1974 framework, much of the substance of the earlier raising view of the relevant English clauses can be extracted from a transformational position and formulated in terms of a nongenerative conception of grammars and an arc-based conception of sentential structure. And if this is done, I believe the essence of the 1974 claims to be correct, even though some of the arguments for them were unsuccessful. The preservable substantive view is informally that stated at the beginning. The pivot DPs in cases like (1) are in one aspect of sentence structure subjects, in fact, typically what relational frameworks call *final subjects*, of the complement clauses, but also *noninitial* objects of some kind of the main clause. In arc terms, the pivot DPs head 1-arcs in the complement and *noninitial* 2-arcs in the main clause.

Incidentally, one simple argument for a raising analysis that was *not* unsuccessful is that based on the *particle-positioning* facts in (2):

(2) a. Helen *made* there out to be seven gorillas in the clearing.
  b. Helen *made* it out to be seven miles to the next gas station.
  c. Helen *figured* it out to be impossible to square most circles.

The point was that the highlighted main verbs and particle <u>out</u> are lexically linked even though the latter follows the pivot DP. Under the position taken by Chomsky (1973, 1981) then, an element lexically linked to the main verb would have to be taken to appear inside the complement clause, while under a raising analysis it can be taken to be a normally positioned main clause particle. Remarkably, no defense of Chomsky's position has, as far as I am aware, ever addressed this argument.

By including cases like (1d and e) under the raising to object umbrella, I enter into especially controversial territory, for a number of writers, most notably Bach (1977) and Lightfoot (1976) in their reviews of Postal (1974), claimed that whatever the status of the raising claim for cases like (1a–c), which involve what I called *B-verbs*, that for cases like (1d and e), which involve what I called *W-verbs*, is much worse. Both invoked an earlier analysis from Bresnan (1972), which appealed to distinctions in complementizer status for the two cases. This line of thinking receives a modern interpretation in Lasnik and Saito's (1991) work, which recognizes some kind of raising for the B-verb case while still denying it for the W-verb structures. The view that the pivot DP is a main clause constituent in both B-verb and W-verb cases, contra the view of Chomsky (1973), is supportable, though, by the grammaticality of cases like (3):

(3)   a. Herbert proved Henry *without any difficulty* to be a spy.
       b. Herbert desires/wants/wishes Henrietta *with all his heart* to recover.

Under any straightforward implementation of Chomsky's view, the highlighted main clause modifying adverbials are inside a subordinate clause, an IP in some instantiations, which is of course otherwise unknown.

As a last background remark, I should state that my current view actually recognizes a scope for the raising of subjects into nonsubject status in English even *broader* than was central to the earlier discussion. For, as discussed in detail in chapter 2, I take all of the *prepositional phrase* cases in (4) to instantiate such raising:

(4)   a. We can't count on *there* to be enough beer to keep all the students happy.
       b. One cannot depend on *the lovebug* to bite him just when it would be convenient for us.
       c. You can rely on *all hell* to break loose when the regional director shows up.
       d. Stan arranged for *there*, despite my misgivings, to be a meeting with the students.

Such cases were barely touched on in the 70s. But as was discussed in chapter 2, not only Chomsky's GB framework but also the HPSG framework of Pollard and Sag and Bresnan's LFG framework have all been explicitly constructed so as to *bar* a raising analysis of cases like (4); apparently the former two frameworks would impose instead a *control* analysis, while the latter appeals to a variant of 'reanalysis' that is not viable. The expletive pivot DPs in (4a and d) and the idiom chunk pivot DPs in (4b and c) already cast considerable doubt on a control analysis, and as shown in chapter 2, there is much other evidence as well against a control view of such cases.

2. Some puzzling facts

The central topic of this chapter is introduced by data like (5):

(5)   a. (I am sure that) The woman who is favored to win screamed.
       b. (I am sure that) The woman who is favored to win is a doctor.
       c. (I am sure that) The woman who is favored to win is you.

English clauses like (5a–c) seem initially parallel; each apparently involves a different type of predicate phrase that occurs with an instance of the same subject. But these apparently identical subjects fail to behave identically in a variety of constructions, as shown in (6)–(10); here and throughout, indexed subscripted letters t, pg are used to indicate extraction gaps/parasitic gaps, with *no* theoretical implications about the existence of traces, and so on.

(A) *Topicalization*

(6)   a. [The woman who is favored to win]$_1$ I am sure t_1 screamed.
        b. [The woman who is favored to win]$_1$ I am sure t_1 is a doctor.
        c. *[The woman who is favored to win]$_1$ I am sure t_1 is you.

(B) *Clefting*

(7)   a. It is the woman who is favored to win who$_1$ I am sure t_1 screamed.
        b. It is the woman who is favored to win who$_1$ I am sure t_1 is a doctor.
        c. *It is the woman who is favored to win who$_1$ I am sure t_1 is you.

(C) *Object Raising*

(8)   a. [The woman who is favored to win]$_1$ is hard to believe t_1 to have screamed.
        b. [The woman who is favored to win]$_1$ is hard to believe t_1 to be a doctor.
        c. *[The woman who is favored to win]$_1$ is hard to believe t_1 to be you.

(D) *Object Deletion*

(9)   a. [The woman who is favored to win]$_1$ is too old for us to believe t_1 to have screamed.
        b. [The woman who is favored to win]$_1$ is too old for us to believe t_1 to be a doctor.
        c. *[The woman who is favored to win]$_1$ is too old for us to believe t_1 to be you.

(E) *Parasitic Gaps*

(10)   a. the guy who$_1$ they will arrest t_1 after proving pg_1 to have screamed
         b. the guy who$_1$ they will arrest t_1 after proving pg_1 to be a doctor
         c. *the guy who$_1$ they will arrest t_1 after proving pg_1 to be you

While initially anomalous-seeming, the differences in (6)–(10) can apparently be reduced to regularities under well-motivated assumptions, given the facts in (11), which show up when one replaces the subjects of the relevant clauses in (5) with *weak definite pronouns*:

(11)   a. (He noticed [the woman who is favored to win]$_1$ because) she$_1$ screamed.
         b. (He noticed [the woman who is favored to win]$_1$ because) she$_1$ is a doctor.
         c. *(He noticed [the woman who is favored to win]$_1$ because) she$_1$ is you.

These data show that the subject position in (5c) but not those in (5a and b) is an *antipronominal context* in the terminology of Postal (1993a, 1993b, 1994a, 1994b,

1998, 2001a, 2001b), a position from which *weak* definite pronouns are, for whatever reason, barred. This can explain the contrasts in (6) and (7) under the assumption argued in Postal (1994a, 1998) that both DP topicalization and DP clefting in
English are what were called *B-extractions*. These *obligatorily* link to invisible
resumptive pronouns in their extraction sites. For if, as also argued in some of those
publications, resumptive pronouns are weak definite pronouns, it follows that
B-extraction sites and antipronominal contexts should in general fail to intersect. The
works just cited argue that this is the case, but see Levine (2001) for a skeptical rejection of these ideas. I believe that what follows not only appeals to the notion of
B-extractions but also in fact supports their recognition.

Six examples that involve antipronominal contexts distinct from that in (5c) are
given in (12)–(17):

(12) a. Herman was speaking French/it.
      b. Herman was speaking in French/*it.
      c. [Which language]$_1$ was Herman speaking (in) t$_1$?
      d. French$_1$, Herman was definitely speaking t$_1$.
      e. *French$_1$, Herman was definitely speaking in t$_1$.

(13) a. Ethel was inside of the sphere/it.
      b. Ethel was inside the sphere/*it.
      c. [Which sphere]$_1$ was Ethel inside (of) t$_1$?
      d. [That sphere]$_1$, Ethel was inside *(of) t$_1$.

(14) a. Marjorie quit that police unit/*it/*them.
      b. [Which police unit]$_1$ did Marjorie quit t$_1$?
      c. *[That police unit]$_1$, Marjorie quit t$_1$ last week.

(15) a. She gave those walls a coat of paint because he would not give them a coat of
         paint/*it.
      b. [Which coat of paint]$_1$ did she give those walls t$_1$? (answer: the second).
      c. *[That coat of paint]$_1$, I gave those walls t$_1$.

(16) a. There were particles of plutonium/*them in the pudding.
      b. [Which kinds of particles]$_1$ were there t$_1$ in the pudding?
      c. *[That kind of particles]$_1$, there were t$_1$ in the pudding.

(17) a. She was unable to tell (= 'determine') the distance to the sound/*it.
      b. [Which distance]$_1$ was she unable to tell t$_1$?
      c. *[The distance to the sound]$_1$, she was unable to tell t$_1$.

The contrasts in (12)–(17) receive a parallel explanation from the same underlying
pronoun contrasts on the assumption that DP topicalization is a B-extraction.

Moreover, if it is accepted, as claimed in, for example, Cinque (1990) and Postal
(1994a, 1994b, 1998, 2001a, 2001b), that the gaps in the *object raising*, *object deletion*, and *parasitic gap* constructions also are invisible weak definite pronouns, the

contrasts in (18)–(23) fall out, as these constructions, too, cannot have as their gaps the antipronominal contexts in (12)–(17):

(18)   a. [That language]$_1$ is difficult to speak (*in) t$_1$.
        b. *[That language]$_1$ is too complex for me to speak (*in) t$_1$.
        c. [Which language]$_1$ did he criticize t$_1$ while speaking (*in) pg$_1$?

(19)   a. [That sphere]$_1$ is impossible to get inside *(of) t$_1$.
        b. [That sphere]$_1$ is too small to get inside *(of) t$_1$.
        c. [Which sphere]$_1$ did Melissa criticize t$_1$ after finding herself inside *(of) pg$_1$?

(20)   a. *[That police unit]$_1$ was difficult for Marjorie to quit t$_1$.
        b. *[That police unit]$_1$ is too well paid for Marjorie to quit t$_1$.
        c. *[Which police unit]$_1$ did Helga join t$_1$ immediately after Marjorie quit pg$_1$?

(21)   a. *[The second coat of paint]$_1$ was difficult for her to give the walls t$_1$.
        b. *[The second coat of paint]$_1$ will be too thick for a child to give those walls t$_1$.
        c. *[Which coat of paint]$_1$ did Marsha criticize t$_1$ after Sally gave those walls pg$_1$?

(22)   a. *[Those particles]$_1$ were impossible for there to be t$_1$ in the pudding.
        b. *[Those particles]$_1$ are too rare for there to be t$_1$ in the pudding.
        c. *[Which (type of) particles]$_1$ did there being pg$_1$ in the pudding lead the FDA to ban t$_1$?

(23)   a. *The distance to the sound was impossible for her tell.
        b. *The distance to the sound was too far for her to be able to tell.
        c. *[What distance]$_1$ did her being unable to tell pg$_1$ lead Jim to try to estimate t$_1$?

The background facts so far might not in themselves merit much further discussion. What does, though, is data not, I believe, previously noticed that relates to previous claims in Postal (1994b) formulable informally as in (24) and (25):

(24)   Right Node Raising DP gaps, in contrast to those that involve, for example, topicalization or clefting DP gaps, are *not* sensitive to antipronominal contexts.

(25) Complex DP Shift gaps are *not* sensitive to antipronominal contexts.

These claims, linked to the view that, unlike, for example, topicalization, neither Right Node Raising nor Complex DP Shift requires resumptive pronouns, indicate that nothing should preclude intersection of the classes of Right Node Raising and Complex DP Shift gaps with antipronominal contexts. Claim (24) can be supported by data like (26), which involves antipronominal contexts already mentioned:

(26)   a. Ted may have spoken (in) t$_1$ and Sandra certainly did speak (in) t$_1$ [that very obscure Oriental language]$_1$.
        b. Ted may have gotten inside (of) t$_1$ and Sandra certainly did get inside (of) t$_1$ [that very peculiar-looking sphere]$_1$.

c. Marjorie certainly quit t_1 last week and Jane will probably quit t_1 this week [that very prestigious police unit]$_1$.

d. Lester may have given those walls t_1 and he certainly gave these walls t_1 [a second coat of paint]$_1$.

e. There may be t_1 in the first sample and there certainly are t_1 in the second sample [the sort of particles at issue]$_1$.

f. Ted may have been unwilling to say she was unable to tell t_1, but she was unable to tell [the distance to the overheard sound]$_1$.

Claim (25) cannot be supported from all of the same antipronominal contexts given the fact first noted in Ross (1967/1986) that Complex DP Shift gaps cannot be complement DPs of prepositional phrases. But (25) is still easily supportable, as in (27):

(27)   a. Ted dyed his eyebrows green/that color/*it yesterday.

b. Ted dyed his eyebrows t_1 yesterday [an awful shade of bright yellow]$_1$.

c. Ted gave that idea a lot of consideration/*it yesterday.

d. Ted gave that idea t_1 yesterday [more consideration than it deserved]$_1$.

e. Marjorie quit t_1 last week [that very prestigious police unit]$_1$.

f. Molly will give that wall t_1 tomorrow [the second coat of paint it needs]$_1$.

g. There were t_1 in the pudding [exactly the sort of particles we had feared]$_1$.

h. Ted was unable to tell t_1 with any exactitude [how far the alien planet was from our solar system]$_1$.

Given this background, the contrasts in (28) and (29) are initially rather bewildering:

(28)   a. Ted may believe t_1 to have screamed and Archie does believe t_1 to have screamed [the woman who is favored to win]$_1$.

b. Ted may believe t_1 to be a doctor and Archie certainly does believe t_1 to be a doctor [the woman who is favored to win]$_1$.

c. *Ted may believe t_1 to be you and Archie certainly does believe t_1 to be you [the woman who is favored to win]$_1$.

(29)   a. I believe t_1 to have screamed [the woman who is favored to win]$_1$.

b. I believe t_1 to be a doctor [the woman who is favored to win]$_1$.

c. *I believe t_1 to be you [the woman who is favored to win]$_1$.

For the good and bad cases of this Right Node Raising and Complex DP Shift data match exactly the pattern of ordinary and antipronominal contexts in (5). That is, the ungrammatical cases of (28) and (29) would apparently be what one would expect if Right Node Raising and Complex DP Shift *were* somehow sensitive to antipronominal contexts. But this is just what (24) and (25) deny, and, as I have illustrated, with real factual motivation. This seemingly points to the ugly conclusion that (28c) and (29c) are bad for (unknown) reasons that have nothing to do with (5) and hence nothing to do with the parallel instances of ill-formedness in the topicalization, clefting, object

116   STUDIES IN LINGUISTICS

raising, object deletion, and parasitic gap paradigms. Such an 'accidental similarity' conclusion is obviously thoroughly implausible, even for a single antipronominal context case like that in (5c).

And the dubious status of an 'accidental similarity' view worsens when it is observed that the same state of affairs exists for other subject antipronominal context cases, like those in (30):

(30)   a. Something is the matter with his fuel pump (*but it is not the matter with mine).
       b. Lots of things are wrong with my liver (*but fortunately they are not wrong with your liver).

As expected, these antipronominal sites are incompatible with topicalization, object raising, and so forth; see (31):

(31)   a. *[Something really terrible]$_1$ they claimed t$_1$ was the matter with the fuel pump.
       b. *[Something like that]$_1$ was impossible to believe t$_1$ to be the matter with the fuel pump.
       c. *It was that which$_1$ they claimed t$_1$ was wrong with her liver.
       d. *That$_1$ is too rare to believe t$_1$ to be wrong with her liver.

And just like the antipronominal context in (5c), those in (30) also correlate with bad Right Node Raising and Complex DP Shift gaps in cases parallel to (28) and (29), that is, in putative raising to object structures like those of (32):

(32)   a. *Ted may have claimed t$_1$ to be the matter with the fuel pump and Joe did claim t$_1$ to be the matter with the fuel pump [something really terrible]$_1$.
       b. *Ted claimed t$_1$ to be the matter with the fuel pump [something probably irreparable]$_1$.
       c. *The doctor may have believed t$_1$ to be wrong with her liver and the nurse did believe t$_1$ to be wrong with her liver [something that required immediate surgery]$_1$.
       d. *The doctor believed t$_1$ to be wrong with her liver [something really terrible]$_1$.

One can summarize the discussion so far as follows. Where it was previously claimed that neither Right Node Raising nor Complex DP Shift gaps are incompatible with antipronominal contexts, conclusions supported consistently by data like (26) and (27), at least one class of subject antipronominal contexts *does* seem to induce Right Node Raising and Complex DP Shift violations under specific conditions, namely, where these define instances of the raising to object construction. So (33) seems to be the case:

(33)   If α is a subject antipronominal context and X is a putative raising to object structure whose complement subject occurs in α, then the derived object position in X is *not* compatible with Right Node Raising and Complex DP Shift gaps.

Assuming that (33) is essentially true, a conclusion for which further evidence will be provided, it can hardly be an accident. The incompatibility of certain raised subjects with Right Node Raising and Complex DP Shift in these particular circumstances must relate to the existence of the relevant subject antipronominal contexts This creates an apparent *paradox*, given (24) and (25), which state that Right Node Raising and Complex DP Shift in general are indifferent to antipronominal contexts and which are supported by considerable data independent of the raising to object constructions at issue.

3. An initial approach to the paradox

One would like to maintain (24) and (25) without any ad hoc exceptions for the raising to object construction or any other and yet still reduce generalization (33) to the fact that the raised phrases are subjects that occur in antipronminal contexts. Securing this result involves initially *four descriptive elements*, informally describable as follows: *Element one* is to continue to assume, as in previous work of mine, that topicalization is, but Right Node Raising and Complex DP Shift are *not*, in general sensitive to antipronominal contexts because the former must, but the latter need not, link to (evidently invisible) resumptive pronouns in their extraction sites. This means that topicalization is a B-extraction but that Right Node Raising and Complex DP Shift contrast in not determining resumptive pronouns.

Element two is to assume that the constructions at issue do involve raising to object. Focus for concreteness on, for example, (34d):

(34)   a. Ted claimed it to be imminent.
      b. Ted claimed t_1 to be imminent [something probably irreparable]$_1$.
      c. Ted claimed something probably irreparable to be the matter with the fuel pump.
      d. *Ted claimed t_1 to be the matter with the fuel pump [something probably irreparable]$_1$.

Given element two, both (34b and d) will involve raising of the lower subject out of the lower clause and into the main clause.

Element three consists of informal assumption (35):

(35)   In the cases where Right Node Raising and Complex DP Shift are bad, the instance of raising to object *involves its own proper (invisible) resumptive pronoun.*

Claim (35) means that in (34d) the raising of <u>something probably irreparable</u> out of the complement requires the presence of a resumptive pronoun as subsequent complement subject, although this is *not* the case in (34b), where the raising is from a context that is *not* antipronominal. So, under current assumptions, the pronouns that end up *violating* the antipronominal context condition on the subject of, for example, <u>be the matter with</u> are resumptive pronouns linked to raising to object, *not* resumptive pronouns linked to Right Node Raising or Complex DP Shift. This means inter alia that in a fuller schematic structure of (34d) there is a resumptive pronoun in the complement but none in the main clause:

(36)   *Ted claimed t_1 <RP$_1$ to be the matter with the fuel pump> – [something probably irreparable]$_1$.

The fact that the resumptive pronoun is an element of the infinitival complement is what guarantees consistency with principle (25). For the Complex DP Shift gap is in the main clause, while the antipronominal context is in the complement.

Significantly, claim (35) cannot be interpreted to mean that the presence of raising-linked invisible resumptive pronouns is *uniformly* associated with raising to object, even for the very main verbs like <u>believe</u> at issue and even for the very antipronominal subject complement types under consideration. The impossibility of such a general conclusion is shown as follows: A variety of raising to object structures whose defining elements raise out of subject antipronominal contexts are perfectly grammatical when the raised form is *not* extracted under Right Node Raising or Complex DP Shift. The latter condition is met if the raised phrase is either left extracted or not extracted at all. So all of (37) are fine, although the lower subject is, as already seen, in each case an antipronominal context:

(37) a. Ernestine believes the person favored to win to be you.
      b. Ernestine believes something grave to be the matter with the fuel pump.
      c. Ernestine believes something probably fatal to be wrong with her liver.
      d. Who$_1$ did Ernestine believe t$_1$ to be you?
      e. [Nothing of the sort]$_1$ did Ernestine believe t$_1$ to be the matter with the fuel pump.
      f. [No matter what]$_1$ Ernestine believed t$_1$ to be wrong with her liver, . . .
      g. Something grave was believed to be the matter with the fuel pump.

To maintain consistency with this antipronominal character, cases such as (37), like (34b) and significantly unlike (34d), must *not* involve complement subject resumptive pronouns. Therefore, a required *element four* is as in (38):

(38) Although (a) raising to object can *in general* link to a complement subject resumptive pronoun or not, (b) a linked subject resumptive pronoun in the complement is *obligatory* if the object formed by raising serves as the extractee for Right Node Raising or Complex DP Shift.

That is, an absolutely essential feature of this four-element proposal about the raising to object cases is that association of a resumptive pronoun with an instance of English raising to object is *conditional* on whether or not the raisee is an extractee in the higher constituent and, moreover, an extractee of the Right Node Raising or Complex DP Shift types. While there are syntactic views that could not incorporate such a 'nonderivational', 'noncyclic' condition, happily a relational framework of the sort described in Johnson and Postal (1980), Postal (1990a, 1992, 1996), and chapter 1, section 9, faces no problems with such an account, which would be quite straightforward.[2] I will argue, though, that what is involved is more general and is not limited to raising to object cases or to those that involve Complex DP Shift or Right Node Raising.

4. Expanding the database

The factual grounding of conclusion (38) is stronger than indicated so far. Further support will derive from any other more or less lexical type of subject antipronominal context. For (38) predicts that any such subject that enters into the raising to object construction will *fail* to permit Right Node Raising or Complex DP Shift of the raised subject. Christopher Potts has pointed out to me several further cases that include, first, the expression in (39a):

(39) a. Nothing/Very little/Little of value/*It came of that proposal.
      b. He believes little of value to have come of that proposal.
      c. *He believes t₁ to have come of that proposal [little of value]₁.
      d. *Frank may believe t₁ to have come of that proposal and Gloria does believe t₁ to have come of that proposal [little of value]₁.

Just as principle (38) predicts, both types of right extraction structures are ill formed. Second, Potts observes the expression in (40a):

(40) (Scientist notices his lab rat has gained incredible strength after its injection):
      a. What! Something strange is going on here! But that/*it was not going on before the injections.
      b. *Dr. Frankenstein believes t₁ to be going on in his lab [something quite strange]₁.
      c. *Dr Frankenstein may believe t₁ to be going on in his lab and he certainly believes t₁ to be going on in your lab [something quite strange]₁.

Again the otherwise anomalous gaps in Right Node Raising and Complex DP Shift paradigms are as predicted by (38).

Third, Potts notes that the sense of the verb <u>eat</u> roughly equivalent to that of <u>bother</u> found in (41a) also has an antipronominal context subject, as supported by the data in (41b):

(41) a. What's eating/bothering Gilbert Grape?
      b. Something is eating/bothering you, Gilbert; I can tell. (But whatever it is, it is not *eating/bothering your sister.)
      c. Donna believes t₁ to be *eating/bothering Gilbert [something incomprehensible to her]₁.
      d. Donna may believe t₁ to be *eating/bothering Gilbert and she certainly believes t₁ to be *eating/bothering Neil [something incomprehensible]₁.

And once more the Right Node Raising and Complex DP Shift paradigm holes predicted by (38) are found.

5. Links to raising to subject structures

So far I have supported descriptive principle (35) with six instances of antipronominal subject contexts. These data, which involve what I consider raising to *object* structures, reveal certain striking parallels to relatively uncontroversial raising to *subject* structures, for example, with the adjectival raising to subject trigger <u>likely</u>. Consider, for example, (5') parallel to (5) and (28') parallel to (28) and (29):

(5')   a. The woman favored to win is likely to scream.
     b. The woman favored to win is likely to be a doctor.
     c. The woman favored to win is likely to be you.

(28')   a. How likely to scream is the woman favored to win?
     b. How likely to be a doctor is the woman favored to win?
     c. *How likely to be you is the woman favored to win?

The antipronominal context, which in (28) and (29) precludes the raised subject in a raising to *object* structure from being an extractee for Right Node Raising or Complex DP Shift, in these raising to *subject* cases is incompatible with the fronting of the adjectival phrase that includes the raising trigger. To see that this parallelism is nonfortuitous, observe that a parallel holds for other antipronominal contexts cited for the object case, as shown in (32'), (39'), (40'), and (41'):

(32')   a. Something serious was likely to be the matter with the fuel pump.
     b. *How likely t_1 to be the matter with the fuel pump was [something serious]$_1$?
     c. *Likely to be the mattter with the fuel pump though [something serious]$_1$ was, . . .
     d. [Something really grave] is likely t_1 to be wrong with her liver.
     e. *How likely t_1 to be wrong with her liver is [something really grave]$_1$?
     f. *Likely to be wrong with her liver though [something really grave]$_1$ was, . . .

(39')   a. Nothing (much)/Very little/Little of value is likely to come of that proposal.
     b. They claimed little of value was likely to come of that proposal (*and likely t_1 to come of that proposal [little of value was]$_1$.
     c. *Likely t_1 to come of that proposal though [little of value]$_1$ was, . . .

(40')   a. Something unexpected is likely to be going on in that lab.
     b. *How likely t_1 to be going on in that lab is [something unexpected]$_1$?

(41')   a. Something seemingly trivial is likely to be eating/bothering Gilbert.
     b. How likely t_1 to be *eating/bothering Gilbert is [something seemingly trivial]$_1$?
     c. Likely t_1 to be *eating/bothering Gilbert though [something seemingly trivial]$_1$ was, . . .

The good variants of (41'b and c) already show that there is no *general* ban on combining the sort of frontings at issue with raising to subject structures. This is evidenced further in (42) and (43):

(42)   a. How likely t_1 to show up late are [some of your students]$_1$?
     b. How likely t_1 to puzzle a child is [something that strange]$_1$?
     c. How likely t_1 to raise eyebrows is [something so risque]$_1$?
     d. Likely t_1 to show up late though [some of your students]$_1$ are, . . .
     e. Likely t_1 to puzzle that child though [something that strange]$_1$ is, . . .

(43)   a. They said that something serious usually tends to be the matter with the carburetor/ to happen at the wrong time.

b. *and tend t_1 to be the matter with the carburetor, [something serious]$_1$ usually does.

c. and tend t_1 to happen at the wrong time [something serious]$_1$ usually does.

d. Something like that is likely to be wrong with her liver/harmful to her liver.

e. How likely t_1 to be harmful to her liver is [something like that]$_1$?

f. *How likely t_1 to be wrong with her liver is [something like that]$_1$?

The raising to subject data apparently ground a descriptive generalization like (44):

(44) If a is a subject antipronominal context and X is a putative raising to subject structure whose complement subject occurs in a, then the adjectival/verbal phrase that contains the raising trigger cannot be left extracted.

6. Generalizing over raising to object and raising to subject structures

Given that it has been found that constraints similar to those for raising to object cases hold for raising to subject ones, questions like those in (45) arise:

(45) a. Why should the subject antipronominal contexts that were looked at in connection with putative raisings to *object* apparently interact with the adjectival and verbal phrase frontings to seemingly block certain raising to *subject* cases?

b. What structural property is shared by (i) Right Node Raising and Complex DP Shift interactions with raising to object and (ii) Adjectival Phrase fronting/raising to subject interactions such that both (38) and (44) hold?

Under the assumption that the sets of structures I have looked at, those with putative raising to object main verbs and those with raising to subject triggers like likely, *both* involve raisings, the following emerges: When a raised subject in the former case is the extractee for Complex DP Shift or Right Node Raising, the raised DP then *linearly follows* its own extraction site, although it does arguably c-command it just as in a non-Complex DP Shift or Right Node Raising case. Moreover, when the whole adjectival phrase that contains a raising to subject trigger is left extracted under questioning, though extraction, and so forth, the raised DP both follows its own extraction site and fails to c-command it. I conclude that at least one of these two partially correlated properties is crucial in predicting the bad results.

But there is a deeper issue. Namely, since the linear precedence facts are common to *all* the cases and yet so far ungrammaticality has only been attested in those where the raising source positions are antipronominal contexts, a key puzzle is the linkage between antipronominal contexts and the constructions that influence word order. The crucial issue, I believe, is to understand how and why antipronominal contexts induce ungrammaticality in just a proper subset of the variety of cases I have documented.

I would like to propose that the linkage is essentially due to a generalization of the point inherent in the four-element proposal made earlier about just the raising to object case. Namely, the structural conditions at issue, which involve Right Node Raising and Complex DP Shift in the raising to object case and left extractions of adjectival/verbal phrases in the raising to subject case, interact with antipronominal contexts because under the very structural conditions at issue it is required that *either type of raising* leave a resumptive pronoun in the complement subject position. These are just the positions where antipronominal contexts have been shown to be associated with ungrammaticality. In short, just as I claimed earlier that, for example, structures like (46a and b) have partially different complement structures in which (46a) need not but (46b) *must* involve a resumptive pronoun, just so one can make a parallel claim for (47):

(46) a. They found something quite trivial to be bothering/eating Gilbert.
     b. They found t_1 <RP_1 to be bothering/*eating Gilbert> [something quite trivial]$_1$.

(47) a. Something quite trivial is likely to be bothering/eating Gilbert.
     b. How likely <RP_1 to be bothering/*eating Gilbert> is [something quite trivial]$_1$.

The posited resumptive pronouns provide the link between the reorderings and the restriction of ungrammaticality to *just those cases where the raising source position is antipronominal.*[3]

To develop the resumptive pronoun claim, it is of course necessary to give an account of the conditions under which raisings *must* link to resumptive pronouns. Since for reasons touched on at the beginning I am not proposing a precise framework for this description, I cannot approach this issue in a truly serious way. Still I suggest something like (48) is probably at work:

(48) The Raising Resumptive Pronoun Linkage Condition
      a. Let the notion *raising* be restricted for this discussion to the case where some DP_x constituent of a complement clause C_1 also appears as a *noninitial* subject, object, or oblique constituent of a constituent K that contains C_1. Then:
      b. If DP_x raises out of C_1 into K from position P, a resumptive pronoun *must* appear in P *unless all of (i)–(iv) hold*:
         (i) DP_x is the last nonresumptive *subject* of C_1.
         (ii) C_1 is *non*finite.
         (iii) If C_1 is a constituent of a clause C_2, distinct from K, K is a constituent of C_2 (that is, C_1 is the *highest* clausal constituent of K).
         (iv) The surface realization of DP_x both c-commands and linearly precedes a surface realization of the (raising) remnant of C_1.

I must leave it open here whether (48) should be interpreted as a universal or merely a principle of English.[4] But the idea is that in ordinary raising to subject cases like that with English <u>likely</u>, all of (48bi–iv) will hold but that a legitimate NL raising construction can fail to satisfy any or all of them provided that a resumptive pronoun, *visible or not*, appears in the raising origin site. Put differently, I am suggesting that (48bi, ii, iii, and iv) are the conditions required for raising that does *not* involve a resumptive pronoun.

To briefly go over the intended claims, (i) essentially picks out the case where the raisee is a subject; (ii) is self-explanatory, while (iii) specifies that the *highest* clause from which raising occurs is is an immediate constituent of the clause of which the raised element is a noninitial constituent. Condition (iv) is the one crucial for this discussion. It requires that any raisee that does *not* link to a resumptive pronoun bear two fixed structural relations to the remnant clause out of which it raises and, moreover, requires these relations to hold at the surface level. Although (48biv) mentions c-command, there is in fact nothing in the English data gone over that really motivates that. For in every bad case of relevance that has been cited, the raisee ends up linearly following the raising remnant. Moreover, arguably, in the case of, for example, raising to object where the raisee is the target of Complex DP Shift or Right Node Raising, the raisee continues to c-command the site of origin for raising. My guess, though, is that for (48biv) to have any cross-linguistic plausibility, something *non*linear would be required.

What (51biv) says is that any grammatical phenomenon that brings about a raising remnant clause not being both c-commanded and linearly preceded by the raisee requires that the instance of raising involve a resumptive pronoun. This will inter alia generate ungrammaticalities in cases where the raising site is an antipronominal context.

There are relevant phenomena of a sort rather different from those so far illustrated that have effects like those referenced by (48biv), for example, the clausal and verbal phrase ellipsis phenomena in (49):

(49) They said Carol was sick, a. as she is/b. which she is/c. and so she is/d. and that she is/
      e. and she is.

If (48) is on the right track, all of these should yield ungrammaticalities when combined with raisings. That is, one should for instance find contrasts in cases like (50):

(50) They said something was bothering/eating Gilbert, as something was/b. which something was/c. and so something was/d. and that something was/e. and something was.

And cases like (51) should just be outrightly bad:

(51) They said something of the sort was wrong with the transmission
      a. as something of the sort was.
      b. which something of the sort was.
      c. and so something of the sort was.
      d. and that something of the sort was.
      e. and something of the sort was.

These are quite subtle data, though, and I leave it to readers to make their own judgments.

While a condition like (48) is motivated by data of the sort I have gone over that involve raising to subject and raising to object in infinitival cases, it has a much broader scope. Limiting attention only to English, it first of all naturally allows a raising analysis of the construction in (52):

(52)   Mike looks/seems/sounds like/as if *he* is a werewolf.

Since the highest clause out of which raising would occur in (52) is finite, (48) forces a resumptive pronoun, arguably represented by the highlighted form. A raising analysis of this construction is moreover supportable via traditional expletive and idiom chunk arguments, as first noted in Rogers (1973) and illustrated in (53) and (54):

(53)   a. There look/*looks like/as if there/*it/*them/*her are/*is going to be problems with the dean.
        b. There *look/looks like/as if there *are/is going to be a problem with the dean.

(54)   a. The chickens look like they have finally come home to roost.
        b. Martha's ship looks like it has come in.
        c. The wolf looks like it is at the door.
        d. The lovebug sounds like it has bitten Mary again.
        e. The shit seems like it is about to hit the fan.
        f. The ball sounds like it is in your court.
        g. Fortune seems like it has finally smiled on Myriam.

I would take the *complement* occurrences of there in (53) to be resumptive pronouns, the rule being evidently that raised there determines a resumptive of the same shape and that a resumptive pronoun agrees with the element it 'resumes' in person, number, and gender. Perhaps the same shape condition can be subsumed under the rule operative for tags like that of (55):

(55)   a. There are gorillas in the field, aren't there/*it/*they?
        b. Into the bar there strode a mean-looking dude, didn't there/*it/*they?

It is rather remarkable that one has seen decades of theorizing about limitations on raising with postulation of principles that would *not* allow a raising analysis of this construction, despite the fact that it has been known for years.[5] Moreover, views that would not allow a raising analysis seem to have offered no alternative.

Further, condition (48) is consistent with the fact that this construction seemingly has instances in which *nonsubjects* raise, although these are restricted, in ways I do not understand; see (56):

(56)   a. Melissa sounds like Bob has been hassling her again.
        b. Melissa's arm looks like the dog has been biting it again.
        c. Melissa looks like Bob has been kicking her in the arm again.
        d. ?Melissa sounds like people want to force her to resign.
        e. Melissa sounds like Bob believes her to have a chance of winning.
        f. *There sounds like Bob believes there to be no chance of her winning.
        g. *The wolf sounds like Bob believes it to be at the door.

Principle (48) can also be taken as a key component in an understanding of the object-raising construction, represented by the once famous sentence in (57):

(57)   John is easy to please.

If, as in early transformational accounts, this is analyzed in terms of raising, since the raisees are in general *non*subjects, (48) forces a resumptive pronoun. This predicts, correctly I believe, that the gaps for this construction are incompatible with antipronominal contexts, already partly supported earlier. One thing that has been claimed to argue *against* a raising analysis of this construction is that it does not allow the raisee to be an idiom chunk, in comparison, for example, to raising with <u>seem</u>; see (58):

(58)   a. Chomsky (1981: 309)
            "We therefore expect it to be resistant to idiom chunks and other non-arguments . . ."
        b. Chomsky (1981: 309)
            *Good care is hard to take of the orphans.
        c. Chomsky (1981: 309)
            *Too much is hard to make of that suggestion.

But while true that such raising is far more restricted, that (58b and c) are bad, and that the construction absolutely bars raising of expletives, as Chomsky noted, there are nonetheless numerous *acceptable* instances of idiom chunk object raising, as illustrated in (59):

(59)   a. The baby is easy to throw out with the bathwater.
        b. The ice is difficult to break at faculty parties.
        c. The cat will be easy to prove to be out of the bag.
        d. The jury is easy to show to still be out on that proposal.
        e. The bottom is now easy to imagine falling out of the cocoa market.
        f. Thatcher's shoes are impossible to imagine anyone like you filling.
        g. ?Stan's ass is not hard to anticipate being in a sling again.
        h. The rug is impossible for me to imagine being pulled out from under a guy like that.
        i. Jacobson (1992b: 271) Careful attention was very hard to pay to that boring lecture.
        j. Jacobson (1992b: 271) ?The cat would be quite easy to let out of the bag.
        k. McCawley (1998: 115) *The cat was easy to let out of the bag.
        l. McCawley (1998: 107) John's leg is easy to pull.
        m. Nunberg, Sag, and Wasow (1994: 517) The law can be hard to lay down.

Two further notes about object raising: While in American English it is, I believe, impossible to object raise a *subject* that has not independently raised to object, this is, I have learned, arguably *not* entirely so in British English. I heard an example essentially like (60) in a televised documentary with a British narrator:

(60)   That attitude made [such a tragedy]₁ all too easy t₁ to happen.

I have checked this with two British speakers, both of whom seem to accept it, whereas for me, and I suspect most Americans, it is entirely impossible. One notes of course that the subject in question is *unaccusative*, and brief investigation suggests that this is required. Even those who accept (63) seem to firmly bar (61):

(61)   *That attitude made [such a tragedy]$_1$ all too easy t$_1$ to devastate Rodney.

I conclude then that both the finite construction of (55) and the object-raising construction are bona fide raising cases required by (48) to involve resumptive pronouns. Of course, even if true, this still leaves open key issues. An obvious one is the visibility of the resumptives in the former and their absence in all the other cases I have dealt with. This suggests that at least English has a principle like (62), where the notation refers back to (48):

(62)   Raising-Linked Resumptive Pronoun Visibility
        A raising-linked resumptive pronoun is visible if and only if C$_1$ is finite.

Note that quite properly, principle (62) requires an *invisible* resumptive pronoun in cases where object raising raises a phrase from a finite clause that is itself embedded in a nonfinite one, as in (63) for that subset of speakers, like me, who accept such:

(63)   Michelle$_1$ will not be that easy [$_{C1}$ to inform them [$_{C2}$ that you plan to dismiss (ok RP$_1$ = Ø/*RP$_1$ = her)]].

7. Earlier data

There are two further issues I want to raise, one that involves a proposal by Lasnik and Saito and another that involves related but more general issues that concern idiomatic DPs. First, Lasnik and Saito (1992: 140–142) cite observations attributed to my colleague Mark Baltin that (64a) and (65a) are bad despite (64b) and (65b). Both contrast with (66a).

(64)   a. *How likely t$_1$ to be a riot is there$_1$?
        b. There is likely to be a riot.

(65)   a. *How likely t$_1$ to be taken of John is [advantage]$_1$?
        b. Advantage is likely to be taken of John.

(66)   a. How likely t$_1$ to win is [John]$_1$.
        b. John is likely to win.

Lasnik and Saito proposed to account for (64a), (65a) and related data via a principle to the effect that a trace must be bound (hence c-commanded) by its antecedent, at every level; see (67):

(67)   Lasnik and Saito (1992: 90) *The Generalized Proper Binding Condition*
        Traces must be bound throughout a derivation.

At first glance, there is a remarkable partial parallelism between the cases in (64) and (65) and the raising to subject cases I cited earlier, for example, (32'c), (39'b, c), (40'b) and (41'b). All involve ungrammaticality *only* when a raising to subject remnant is itself left extracted. The earlier cases involved raising of ordinary DPs from antipronominal contexts. The ones Lasnik and Saito deal with involve expletive and idiomatic DPs. One cannot help but inquire into whether the phenomena dealt with here and those for which Lasnik and Saito invoke (67) are the same. I find that there are solid grounds for thinking they are the same but also problematic issues that I do not currently know how to resolve and that could undermine this conclusion. I will briefly consider both the positive and negative aspects.

Consider first the expletive cases revealed by the <u>there</u> data Baltin noted. Here arguably <u>there</u> does *not* occur in antipronominal contexts. Rather there is reason to consider <u>there</u> itself a weak definite pronoun, as argued by (53a, b) earlier. This might make it appear that there is no way to directly reduce the facts to principle (48). But this is not necessarily so. It is evident that, as required by principle (62), in all the infinitival cases when (48) requires a resumptive pronoun the latter must be invisible. Suppose as I have speculated elsewhere (see Postal, 1993a: 752–753; 1994b: 93–96; 2001a: 237–238) about other types of invisible resumptives, this is due to a type of *control* phenomenon. And suppose principle (68a) holds for everyone while some people have the still stronger (68b):

(68)   a. The expletive <u>there</u> DP cannot control a *resumptive* pronoun.
       b. The expletive <u>there</u> DP cannot control *any* pronoun.

Principle (68b) is motivated by facts in standard adjunct control environments like those of (69):

(69)   a. * (There) being a gorilla in a living room proves there to be a gorilla in the bedroom.
       b. */okThere can be war in the north without (there) being war in the south.

Everyone seems to reject control in (69a). But some speakers, including *me*, accept control in (69b), arguing that (68b) is too general. But even the weaker (68a) would combine with (48) to predict the badness of Baltin's <u>there</u> patttern. For in the environments where (48) forces raising of <u>there</u> to leave a lower resumptive pronoun, (62) in effect requires that pronoun to be controlled, while (68a) in effect forbids that, since the required controller cannot then serve as such. While this account is entirely informal, it seems basically coherent.

Turn next to idiom chunks and proverbial expressions. A variety of these seem to provide a great deal of support for a principle like (48), for a very large number of them involve DPs that occur in antipronominal contexts. Some of these take inherent subjects and some have nonsubject antipronominal contexts that are passivizable and then form subject antipronominal contexts And remarkably, such expressions reveal all the types of restrictions on raising to object and raising to subject I have documented for nonidiomatic antipronominal contexts. A typical example is seen in (70):

(70) a. (She said) [birds of a feather]₁ flock together (*and they₁ do flock together).
      b. She believes birds of a feather to flock together.
      c. *She believes t₁ to flock together [birds of a feather]₁.
      d. *Sally may believe t₁ to flock together and Sonia certainly believes t₁ to flock to-
          gether [birds of a feather]₁.
      e. Birds of a feather are likely to flock together.
      f. *How likely t₁ to flock together are [birds of a feather]₁?
      g. *Likely t₁ to flock together though [birds of a feather]₁ are, . . .

There is a problem relevant to testing, for example, principle (35) against such idiomatic data, which is common though not severe in (70). This involves the fact that most often the relevant idiomatic nominal that appears in an antipronominal context is not particularly 'heavy' in the sense in which this might be a requirement for Complex DP Shift and certainly a preference for Right Node Raising. But in all cases, one can see that the effect in analogs of (70c and d) cannot be reduced to violation of any 'heaviness' requirement.

Consider for instance (71):

(71) a. The cat is out of the bag.
      b. Sonia believes the cat to be out of the bag.
      c. They said the cat was out of the bag and it is out of the bag. (ok literal/*idiomatic)

Both (71a and b) are ambiguous, having either a literal reading about a feline or one that involves a secret. But not so in (72):

(72) a. *Sonia believes t₁ to be out of the bag [the cat]₁.
      b. ?Sonia may believe t₁ to be out of the bag and Harriet certainly does believe t₁ to be
          out of the bag [the cat]₁.

Here there may be violations of heaviness constraints on the pivot nominals for Complex DP Shift and Right Node Raising, although I believe that heavy stress on the pivot renders it acceptable. But independently of that, it is palpable that only the feline reading is possible, which cannot have anything to do with heaviness, since the pivot is equally heavy under either reading. Consequently, some principle must block the idiomatic reading but not the literal one, and a principle that forces a resumptive pronoun combines with the antipronominal character of the subject position of the idiom to play this role.

One can cite a great deal more evidence that supports (48) based on subject antipronominal contexts linked to idiomatic or proverbial nominals. I have given a range of such data in the most restricted form possible. In all cases, strictures about the irrelevance of heaviness factors already touched on should be borne in mind. Moreover, all stars represent only idiomatic or proverbial readings. The data is ordered essentially randomly in (73)–(78):

(73) a. [A great deal of attention]₁ was claimed to have been paid to that (*but it₁ wasn't
          paid to that).

b. *Ernest believes t_1 to have been paid to that [a great deal of attention]$_1$.

c. *How likely t_1 to have been paid to that was [a great deal of attention]$_1$?

(74) a. Sabine said [the chickens]$_1$ had come home to roost (*but they$_1$ hadn't come home to roost).

b. *Sabine may have found t_1 to have come home to roost and Emily certainly found t_1 to have come home to roost [the chickens]$_1$.

c. *Likely t_1 to have come home to roost though [the chickens]$_1$ were, . . .

(75) a. Gwen claims [Tony's heart]$_1$ is in the right place (*and it$_1$ is in the right place).

b. *Gwen may have believed t_1 be in the right place and Nora certainly did believe t_1 to be in the right place [Tony's heart]$_1$.

c. *How likely t_1 to be in the right place was [Tony's heart]$_1$?

(76) a. [Cold water]$_1$ was thrown on your idea (*but it$_1$ wasn't thrown on my idea).

b. *Dana may believe t_1 to have been thrown on your idea and she certainly believes t_1 to have been thrown on my idea [cold water]$_1$.

c. *Likely t_1 to have been thrown on his idea though [cold water]$_1$ was, . . .

(77) a. Myra believes [the early bird]$_1$ gets the worm (*but it$_1$ doesn't get the worm).

b. *Myra believes t_1 to get the worm [the early bird]$_1$.

c. *How likely t_1 to get the worm is [the early bird]$_1$?

(78) a. [The rug]$_1$ was pulled out from under him (*but it$_1$ wasn't pulled out from under me).

b. *Andrea believes t_1 to have been pulled out from under him [the rug]$_1$.

c. *Likely t_1 to have been pulled out from under him though [the rug]$_1$ is, . . .

I must leave it to the reader to determine that entirely parallel data can be found for such further expressions as those in (79):

(79) a. The ball is in your court.

b. A stitch in time saves nine.

c. All hell broke loose.

d. A good time was had by all.

e. The fat is in the fire.

f. The cat has his tongue.

g. The lovebug bit Tony.

h. The shoe is on the other foot.

i. Fortune smiled on Gwendolyn.

j. The bottom fell out of the cocoa market.

k. The buck stops here.

l. The jury is still out on that proposal.

m. The shit hit the fan.

n. The jig is up.

o. The party is over.

p. The good times are about to roll.

q. The worm is going to turn.

r. The tide is turning.

s. All the ducks are in line.

t. The truth will out. Murder will out.

u. The wind has gone out of his sails.

v. The fox is in the chicken coop.

w. The wolf is at the door.

x. The ice was broken at the party.

y. The devil alone knows who did this.

z. His number is up.

z1. Miriam's ship came in.

z2. A pall fell over the gathering.

z3. The baby was thrown out with the bathwater.

z4. Close tabs were kept on her movements.

z5. Unfair advantage was taken of his good nature.

z6. Stan's goose is cooked.

z7. Churchill's shoes will be difficult to fill.

z8. Strings were pulled.

z9. That filthy habit was finally kicked.

z10. Simone's hair stood on end.

z11. The shoe is on the other foot.

z12. The ceiling caved in on Mike.

z13. A damper was put on the evening by Tony's announcement.

So far then, the idiomatic and proverbial expression data just seem to instantiate multiple further instances of antipronominal contexts, all of which bar raising to object and raising to subject under the same conditions already uncovered for other types of antipronominal context. All these data thus initially appear only to strengthen the support for a principle like (48) forcing resumptive pronouns in certain, but only certain, instances of raising.

However, a range of partially different data that involve the same idiomatic and proverbial expressions may call this conclusion into question. It can be illustrated by the facts in (80):

(80) a. He kept close tabs on her movements.
      b. *He believes t_1 to have been kept on her movements [very close tabs]$_1$.
      c. *Ted may have believed t_1 to have been kept on her movements and Fred does believe t_1 to have been kept on her movements [very close tabs]$_1$.
      d. *He kept t_1 on her movements [very close tabs]$_1$.

Hitherto, the data given relevant to the interaction of idiomatic DPs and Complex DP Shift or Right Node Raising was only of the types in (80b and c), where the phrase extracted to the right is a *raisee*. But (80d) illustrates something that turns out to be equally systematically true, namely (81):

(81) No idiomatic/proverbial DP$_x$ can be the extractee for Complex DP Shift or Right Node Raising even when DP$_x$ is *not* a raisee.

Further supporting evidence for (81) is given in (82):

(82)   a. Helen let the cat out of the bag.
      b. Helen let t_1 out of the bag [the cat]$_1$. (ok literal/*idiomatic)
      c. Helen threw cold water on Ted's face/idea.
      d. Helen threw t_1 on Ted's face/*idea [cold water]$_1$.
      e. Helen pulled the rug out from under Ted.
      f. Helen pulled t_1 out from under Ted [the rug]$_1$. (ok literal/*idiomatic)
      g. No one can fill Ted's shoes in this organization.
      h. *No one can fill t_1 in this organization [Ted's shoes]$_1$.
      i. Helen threw the baby out with the bathwater.
      j. Helen threw out the baby with the bathwater.
      k. *Helen threw t_1 out with the bathwater [the baby]$_1$.

The potential problem that generalization (81) raises is this: If there is no way to reduce it to principle (48), then some *other* principle must block the bad cases of (80) and (82). And this principle could then arguably be invoked also for the idiomatic data that seem to support (48), like (80b and c), undermining *some* of the support for (48).

And so far I see no way to reduce (81) to (48) or any way to guarantee that the bad cases of (82) would contain resumptive pronouns in the slots that are arguably antipronominal. For the key to guaranteeing their presence in earlier cases was to invoke conditions under which raisings are required to link to resumptives, and in (82) there are, arguably, no raisings.

Moreover, there is a second class of data that involves idiomatic expressions illustrated by (83):

(83)   a. They said she threw cold water on his head and she did throw it on his head.
      b. *They said she threw cold water on his idea and she did throw it on his idea.
      c. ?They said cold water was thrown on his head and cold water was.
      d. *They said cold water was thrown on his idea and cold water was.
      e. They said cold water was thrown on his head it was thrown on his head.
      f. *They said cold water was thrown on his idea and it was thrown on his idea.
      g. They said cold water was thrown on his head and it was.
      h. They said cold water was thrown on his idea and it was.

It seems that most idiomatic DPs that can appear as subjects reveal a patttern like that seen in (83f and h). While the subject is antipronominal when another piece of the idiom is present in the surface form, the position allows a weak pronoun when no piece of the idiom appears there. Now one might generalize these observations by suggesting that there is a principle for idioms composed of multiple lexical pieces something along the lines of (84):

(84)   The Multiple Lexical Item Idiom Condition
      If a multiple-membered set of lexical items K forms an idiom and one member of K
      has a visible surface realization, then every other member of K must have a surface
      realization and all these surface realizations form a c-command chain (most accurately,
      one that involves a version of c-command that ignores prepositions, as in Pesetsky
      [1995: 172–3]; see for example, [82i, j]).

Such a principle cannot only block data like (83f and h); it also blocks the bad instances of (82) under the well-established assumption that the DP victim of Complex DP Shift ends up in a structure something like (85):

(85)   [[Verb, X, t_1,Y] + DP_1]

The problem then is that (84) not only covers the cases of idiomatic blockages that (48) might, but it also covers those where (48) is irrelevant. Principle (84) thus seems to undermine any support for the earlier analysis *drawn from the idiomatic domain.* This does not, of course, yield grounds for rejecting the overall analysis but does weaken its factual support somewhat.

Notice that (84) properly is consistent with pieces of idioms being passivized DPs or DPs that raise under the construction in (55)/(58) or under object raising, for in these cases a c-command chain is maintained. Similarly, (84) is also consistent with pre- or postparticle word order for idiomatic DPs, as in (82i, j).

8. An earlier proposal

One should compare this proposal with that of Lasnik and Saito (1992), with which it shares key properties but from which it differs in key ways.

(86)   a. *How likely t_1 to be a riot is there$_1$?
       b. There is likely to be a riot.

(87)   a. *How likely t_1 to be taken of John is [advantage]$_1$?
       b. Advantage is likely to be taken of John.

(88)   a. How likely t_1 to win is [John]$_1$.
       b. John is likely to win.

Recall that these authors proposed to account for (86a), (87a), and related data via principle (67), which requires that a trace be bound (hence c-commanded) by its antecedent, "throughout a derivation." As these authors note, (67) raises a problem for standard *GB* analyses of a case like (66a), repeated as (89):

(89)   How likely t to win is John?

For (67) determines that (66a) cannot actually have structure (89), in which the trace would *not* be c-commanded by <u>John</u> at S-structure.

Lasnik and Saito then propose that traditional raising to subject structures like (66b) have dual analyses along the lines of (90a, b):

(90)   a. John is likely t to win.
       b. John is likely PRO to win.

Example (66a) can then be taken to instantiate (91b), which satisfies principle (67), and not the blocked (91a):

(91) a. How likely t to win is John?
      b. How likely PRO to win is John?

In these terms, Lasnik and Saito (1992) claim that (86a) and (87a) are ill formed because of the known general failure (but see [68b]) of, for example, expletives like there and idiomatic NPs like advantage to function as controllers, that is, immediate antecedents of PRO structures, which give data like (92):

(92) a. *There tried PRO to be a riot.
      b. *Advantage wants PRO to be taken of John.

Similarities with the view I have advocated here are thus clear, in that Lasnik and Saito also invoked a type of control. But unlike my proposal, which involves controlled resumptive pronouns, theirs involves the nonresumptive pronoun PRO, in effect first introduced in Postal (1970) as a pronoun with a Doom feature.

However, explication of the deviance of (86a) and (87a) via principle (67) and the proposal that traditional raising structures actually have dual movement/control analyses were certainly not tenable claims in Lasnik and Saito's terms. Unless buttressed by unknown and unstated additions, the proposals block many perfectly grammatical structures. Most strikingly, Lasnik and Saito's analysis undermines the adequacy of GB and, more generally, transformational movement/trace analyses of passives, which they nonetheless endorsed; see their page 127. For under the standard analysis (93a and b) violate (67) as much as, for example, (89) does:

(93) a. Shocked t_1 by the revelations though (they claim that) [Arthur]$_1$ was, . . .
      b. They said [he]$_1$ would be eaten by the shark and eaten t_1 by the shark (I suspect that) [he]$_1$ was.

To maintain (67), Lasnik and Saito would thus have to provide dual analyses for passives, with the novel analysis not involving an object position trace. In this case, PRO cannot provide the second analysis since, as the authors stress (1992: 130), they maintain the earlier GB idea that PRO cannot be governed. So (94b) is not a possible analysis for (94a):

(94) a. He was eaten by the shark.
      b. He was eaten PRO by the shark.

It remains entirely obscure what, if any, analysis distinct from the standard trace one they actually maintained Lasnik and Saito could give for passives so as to allow cases like (93).

The problem just raised for principle (67) as the basis of the subject raising data I have gone over is, evidently, not inherently linked to passives. Clearly it arises in any case where there is the possibility of the left-extraction of a constituent that contains what in GB terms would have to be a subject trace. If, as has often been proposed, middles, unaccusatives, and such, are of this type, then (95a and b), for example, pose the same difficulty that (94a and b) do:

(95)   a. They said [the convertible]$_1$ handled well and handle t$_1$ well (I am sure that) [it]$_1$ did.
      b. They said that [that]$_1$ would happen and happen t$_1$ (they claim that) [it]$_1$ did.

A distinct problem for Lasnik and Saito's proposal is, of course, that it has no way to account for the antipronominal context data. Recall that the crucial point there was that raisings can either involve resumptive pronouns or not, and violations ensue in antipronominal contexts only under those circumstances where such pronouns are *forced*. Consider (96):

(96)   a. Helen believes something exactly like that/*it to have been the matter with the transmission.
      b. Helen believes something exactly like that/it to have been harmful to the transmission.
      c. *Helen believes t$_1$ to have been the matter with the transmission [something exactly like that]$_1$.
      d. Helen believes t$_1$ to have been harmful to the transmission [something exactly like that]$_1$.

There is nothing in Lasnik and Saito's proposal that accounts for contrasts like (96c and d), nothing to link this contrast to the pronoun contrast between (96a and b). Even if in some unknown way they could force PRO in (96c), that would not suffice to block the example, for unlike the expletive and idiomatic data they dealt with, a DP like the pivot in (96a) is a perfectly happy controller of what they would have to take as PRO, as in (97):

(97)   [Something very grave]$_1$ can go wrong on one day without PRO$_1$ going wrong on another day.

Moreover, they would have no way to account for (98):

(98)   *[Something very grave]$_1$ can be wrong with one car without PRO being wrong with another.

In our terms, (98) is of course bad because control involves pronouns, and the controlled subject of <u>be wrong with</u> (but not that of <u>go wrong</u>) is an antipronominal context.

Return to Lasnik and Saito's claim that raising to subject structures have dual analyses and that, for example, (91a) can have a structure like (91b). This is dubious on the basis of the two novel tests for the control/raising distinction introduced in section 5.3 of chapter 2. Recall that it was argued that control complements cannot be middles and cannot be the sort of stock (price) designating metonymy structures represented by company names. These constraints yield control/raising contrasts like (99):

(99)   a. Control: *Uruguayan police want to bribe cheaply.
      b. Raising: Uruguayan police seem to bribe cheaply.

    c. Control: *Microsoft wanted to go up.

    d. Raising: Microsoft seemed to go up.

These factors independently distinguish what are differentiated as raising (that is, trace in Lasnik and Saito's terms) versus control (PRO) structures in GB terms.

If these usages are good tests for the raising/control distinction, Lasnik and Saito's principle (67) account of (91) would then predict that there can be no left extracted cases parallel to (91) with middles or the 'stock' usage in question, since that for them must instantiate PRO and not trace. But the facts are otherwise, as (100) and (101) show:

(100) a. How likely t_1 to go up is [Microsoft]$_1$?

      b. They said Microsoft was likely to go up and likely t_1 to go up [Microsoft]$_1$ still is.

      c. Likely t_1 to go up though [Microsoft]$_1$ is, . . .

(101) a. How likely t_1 to bribe cheaply are [Uruguayan police]$_1$?

      b. They said Uruguayan police were likely to bribe cheaply and likely t_1 to bribe cheaply [Uruguayan police]$_1$ still are.

      c. Likely t_1 to bribe cheaply though [Uruguayan police]$_1$ are, . . .

9. A speculation

Before concluding this chapter, so far restricted to facts from English, I would like to make one rather speculative suggestion of crosslinguistic relevance. A number of NLs, which include Swedish and the West African languages Vata and Yoruba, manifest an interesting property linked to resumptive pronouns. For the facts in the latter, see Carstens (1985a, 1985b), Koopman (1982, 1984), Koopman and Sportiche (1982/1983, 1986), and Stahlke (1974). I will limit my remarks to Swedish. Engdahl (1985, 1986), Engdahl and Ejerhed (1982), Zaenen and Maling (1982), and others observe that Swedish, in contrast to English and even to other Scandanavian languages, does not permit gap-yielding extraction of the subject of an embedded clause with lexical material preceding the subject. Rather, a visible resumptive pronoun must appear, as in the minimal pair in (102):

(102) Zaenen and Maling's (1982) (5a, b)

      Vem$_1$ undrade alla om *t_1/han$_1$ skulle komma i tid?

      Who$_1$ wondered all if   null$_1$/he$_1$ would come on time

      "Who did everyone wonder if he would come on time"

Let us refer to resumptive pronouns of this sort as β-resumptive pronouns.

The relevant works reveal that β-resumptive pronouns like that in the good version of (102) have a number of characteristic properties; specifically, they cannot alternate with epithets, can participate in across-the-board extractions as if they were gaps, can serve as the licensing gaps for parasitic gaps, and do not suppress weak crossover effects, a property that has been noted to be associated with a range of resumptive pronouns by Cinque (1990), Lasnik and Stowell (1991), May (1985), and Postal (1993b). Moreover, β-resumptive pronouns only appear as subjects. In all these respects, β-resumptive pronouns seem to contrast with other Swedish resumptive pronouns and to behave essentially like ordinary extraction gaps; that is, they behave as if they were not there.

The analysis of the puzzling restrictions on English Complex DP Shift and Right Node Raising in connection with raising of subjects out of antipronominal contexts, namely, one that involves conditional determination of resumptive pronouns by the raising, not the extractions, suggests the possibility of a parallel account of Swedish β-resumptive pronouns. Namely, suppose structures like (102) involve ordinary subject extractions that yield ordinary gaps, while the resumptive pronouns are determined conditionally by some kind of raising associated only with subjects. The rule would then be that the raising in question yields a β-resumptive pronoun if and only if the raisee is extracted.

To make this work, it would be necessary to regard the preverbal subject position as one that involves raising, which is not today all that controversial. However, clauses that contain Swedish β-resumptive pronouns would have to involve two raisings, first of the nonresumptive subject, subsequently extracted, and second raising of the β-resumptive. This issue does not arise in the English cases I have discussed because in these the resumptives are invisible. Working out the needed analysis of Swedish is then not without problems but does not seem beyond feasability.

10. Conclusion

I conclude by briefly making four points. First, I believe I have given a new and solid argument for raising to object analyses based on shared properties of raising to object and uncontroversial raising to subject cases. The argument depends on principle (48), which conditionally determines the presence of resumptive pronouns in raising cases, accounting for gaps in both types of raising paradigms where subject antipronominal contexts are found.

Second, the discussion has strengthened the evidence for the recognition of invisible pronouns in topicalization, cleft, object raising, object deletion, and P-gap structures by showing that this assumption plays a key role in accounting for the special type of constraints that is the topic of this essay.

Third, while there are similarities between what is suggested here and the proposal of Lasnik and Saito (1992), the proposal here has been argued to have several clear advantages.

Fourth, of considerable theoretical significance is the nature of the constraint found to link the requirement of a resumptive pronoun for raisings to phenomena that bring it about that the raisee follows the raising constituent remnant. While such a constraint is easily stated in a framework of nongenerative, statement-based description that appeals to a view of sentences as built of arcs and their relations, as in (i) of note 2, the condition would have what I earlier called a 'nonderivational', 'noncyclic' character if one attempted to express it internal to a proof-theoretic/derivational view of grammars. Put simply, in the latter terms one would have to say that the choice of whether a resumptive pronoun is required in the complement is determined nondetermininistically by whether those grammatical phenomena that determine the form of the main clause yield a word order in which the remnant precedes the raisee or not. This yields a sort of necessary 'look-ahead' feature. If the claim that proof-theoretic operations must apply in a cyclic fashion, often taken to be an important principle, has content, 'look-ahead' requiring derivations should be impossible. Cases like those central to this chapter therefore seem to be clear counterexamples and represent by themselves a sharp challenge to such ideas.[6]

Chromaticity

An Overlooked English Grammatical Category Distinction

1. Basics

This essay argues for the existence of an English grammatical category distinction that, as far as I know, has not been previously recognized. This distinction bifurcates the class of nominals into subtypes I will refer to as *chromatic* and *nonchromatic*. Instances of these are seen in (1) and (2):

(1) Chromatic DPs =
    {some fox, any fox, no fox, what fox, whatever fox, many computers, that hat, much soup, some place, some week, what way, what reason, . . .}

(2) Nonchromatic DPs =
    {something, anything, nothing, what, whatever, squat, stuff, someone, everyone, who, somewhere, where, sometime, when, how, why . . .}

Most DPs belong to the chromatic class, which is open. The nonchromatic class consists, though, of a restricted, if not tiny, group of forms.[1] The choice of the terminology adopted is based on the fact that systematically the nonchromatic forms have extremely general and nonspecific meanings, ones, as it were, that lack 'color'. Kishimoto (2000: 563) approaches the same meaning property by speaking of the nouns that underlie nonchromatic DPs as "semantically light" and claiming they are "devoid of lexical meaning." The latter claim seems too strong. So, while both of the objects in (3) are nonchromatic, certainly they differ in meaning:[2]

(3) a. Rhonda criticized something unusually evil.
     b. Rhonda criticized someone unusually evil.

That is, the DP in (3b) restricts the object referent to humans, which that in (3a) does not. If neither had any lexical meaning, how could they differ?

A proper *subset* of nonchromatic DPs is represented by the elements that Kishimoto (2000) argues involve nominal-internal N-raising into the associated D. This N-raising can be taken to underlie at least two properties of the relevant subset, the characterization of which is briefly touched on in section 5.

(4) a. Unlike chromatic DPs, unrestricted in this regard, elements of the subset are systematically single-word forms.
     b. Those nonchromatic DPs that have property (4a) never permit prenominal simplex adjectives.

Following Kishimoto's logic, which I believe is essentially correct, this would follow from a structure for the forms in question along the lines of (5):[3]

(5) $[_{DP} [_D D_x + N] [_{NP} (Adj) [_{Noun} \varnothing]]]$

That is, since the normal position of simplex adjective phrases is prenominal within NP, if the N ends up outside the NP but inside the D it will precede any simplex adjectives. As Kishimoto (2000) observes then, this yields rightly contrasts like (6):

(6) a. some vicious fox
     b. *some fox vicious
     c. something vicious
     d. *some vicious thing

Actually, (6d) is not, of course, in fact ungrammatical. But I would argue that on its good analysis, it represents a chromatic DP; thus a nominal stem thing is found in both the chromatic and nonchromatic categories (whereas, e.g., the stem fox is found only in the former). This dual view of certain N-stems like thing is also advocated by Kishimoto (2000) and is supported further later.

While it is argued here that the chromatic/nonchromatic distinction is a syntactic one, it seems to correlate with some kind of semantic contrast that underlies the choice of terminology. This involves a lack of whatever semantic substance it is that a typical lexical noun contributes. The property shows up clearly in the case of pseudoclefts, as in (7):

(7) a. What Edgar purchased was some house/boat/manuscript.
     b. *What Edgar purchased was something.
     c. What Edgar purchased was not any house/boat/manuscript.
     d. *What Edgar purchased was not anything.
     e. What Edgar purchased was something interesting.
     f. What Edgar purchased was not anything that I would have wanted.

That is, the predicate in a pseudocleft cannot consist of a simple existential non-chromatic DP. It can, however, consist of that plus a modifier, as in (7e, f). The restriction might seem to be that the predicate DP add some semantic substance. If so, the contrast in (8) reveals something important about the 'semantically light' or 'nonchromatic' aspect of the semantics of nonchromatic nouns. That is, while the clearly syntactically nonchromatic form someone is animate and human like the chromatic a person, the former seemingly lacks a semantic property that the chromatic a person has:

(8)   What Edgar saw was *someone/a person.

Perhaps one can appeal to a difference between presupposed or backgrounded meaning and another kind, the former being all that can be associated with nonchromatic nouns. But this topic is beyond the scope of these remarks.

So far three properties that systematically distinguish (a subset of) nonchromatic DPs from more common chromatic DPs have been noted: (i) single-word status, (ii) nominal-internal position of simplex adjective phrases, and (iii) possibility of occurrence as focus of pseudoclefts. A fourth property involves the possibility of combination with pre-D, prenominal modifiers, in particular, even and only. These are only possible with chromatic DPs (here capitalization indicates strong stress):

(9)   a. Even every MAN agreed with that.
       b. *Even everyone agreed with that.
       c. Even some GORILLA spoke Spanish.
       d. *Even someone spoke Spanish.

(10)   a. Only every NURSE advocated such a policy.
       b. *Only everyone advocated such a policy.
       c. Only some CHIMP spoke Spanish.
       d. *Only someone spoke Spanish.[4]

There is, arguably, also a fifth property sensitive to the chromatic nonchromatic DP distinction. This involves the distribution of the form else:

(11)   a. Herb discussed every/some/no problem/issue (*else).
       b. Herb discussed everything/something/nothing (else).[5]
       c. Herb looked in every/some/no place/bar (*else).
       d. Herb looked everywhere/somewhere/nowhere (else).
       e. Did Ethel check any room (*else)?
       f. Did Ethel check anything (else)?
       g. What (*else) bar (*else) did they burn down?
       h. What (else) did they burn down?
       i. Whatever (*else) principle (*else) we adopt, they will reject it.
       j. Whatever (else) we adopt, they will reject it.
       k. Some (*else) linguist (*else) was rejected.

    l. Someone (else) was rejected.
    m. What (*else) linguist (*else) was rejected?
    n. Who (else) was rejected?

It appears, that is, that <u>else</u> is possible (only) with members of the same subset of nonchromatic DPs that is characterized in (4).[6]

Further, consider the issue of which DPs can occur as preposed genitives:

(12)   a. some/every/no doctor's wife
       b. someone's/everyone's/no one's wife
       c. what/which man's wife
       d. whose/who else's wife

With human DPs, preposed genitives are clearly not restricted as to chromaticity. But with nonhuman DPs, contrasts appear:

(13)   a. some/every/no car's carburetor
       b. *something's/everything's/nothing's carburetor
       c. what/which car's carburetor
       d. *what's/*what else's carburetor

(14)   a. some/every/not a single/any person's blood
       b. someone's/everyone's/not a single one's/anyone's blood
       c. what/which person's blood
       d. whose/who else's blood

(15)   a. some/every/not a single/any car's oil
       b. *something's/*everything's/*not a single thing's/*anything's oil
       c. what/which car's oil
       d. *what's/*what else's/*whose (inanimate) oil

(16)   a. that car's motor
       b. *that's motor

    The initial generalization seems to be that for inanimates, genitives are systematically possible on chromatics but blocked on nonchromatics. There is, though, one problem. While <u>whose</u> cannot of course be used as an inanimate interrogative form, it is a fine inanimate relative pronoun:

(17)   a. an integer whose successor is even
       b. an/some explosion whose cause was unknown
       c. no discovery whose origin is at issue

The generalization proposed would then lead one to expect that nonchromatic heads with such relative pronouns would be impossible. But this does not seem to be in accord with the facts:

(18)   a. something whose analysis is incomplete
        b. everything whose cause is unknown
        c. nothing whose origin is at issue

It is argued in section 3.5 that restrictive relative pronouns agree with their heads in chromaticity. If so, then the instances of <u>whose</u> in (18) would all be nonchromatic and the generalization that inanimate genitive nonchromatics are blocked would be false. I have no better solution at this point than to say that the sixth generalization, that which links nonchromatics and inanimate genitives, simply does not hold for relative pronouns. Since it does hold elsewhere, though, an argument for the relevance of the chromaticity dimension in English syntax still emerges.

A seventh grammatical generalization also supports recognition of the chromaticity dimension. This involves a restriction on topicalization illustrated in (19):

(19)   a. Jerome understands something/everything/someone/everyone/stuff.
        b. Jerome understands some movies/every movie/some singers/every singer/cheap stuff.
        c. *Something/*Everything/*Someone/*Everyone/*Stuff, Jerome understands.
        d. Some movies/Every movie/Some singers/Every singer/Cheap stuff, Jerome understands.

The generalization, in effect partly noted in Postal (1993c), appears to be that 'unmodified' nonchromatic DPs, those that consist at most of a combined D + N, cannot be topics.[7]

2. Selections

So far, seven properties have been cited that support the existence of a chromatic DP/nonchromatic DP distinction. However, the most important features that argue for the existence of the grammatical categories of chromatic and nonchromatic DPs involve selections. While standard contexts that permit DPs make no selectional distinction between chromatic and nonchromatic DPs, as in (20), there is, nonetheless, a range of environments that distinguish chromatic and nonchromatic DPs:

(20)   a. Henrietta cooked some fish/something.
        b. The priests offered nothing/no gifts to the demons.

First, various environments permit DPs of the form <u>some</u>/<u>any</u>/<u>no</u>/<u>the</u>, and so on + lexical noun but bar all of the inanimate indefinite pronouns <u>something</u>, <u>anything</u>, and <u>nothing</u>, their <u>wh</u> variants <u>what</u>, <u>whatever</u>, and so on. Examples are given in (21)–(28):

(21)   a. Joe attended some/no/the Catholic school/*something/*nothing/*stuff/*that thing.
        b. Joe didn't attend any school/*anything/*squat.
        c. *Whatever he attended was in Boston.

(22) a. Sue spoke some/every Slavic language/the language/*the thing/*something/*every-
thing/*stuff.
      b. Sue didn't speak any Slavic language/*anything/*squat.
      c. *What (else) do they speak in Bangladesh?

(23) a. Mike scored some baskets/the basket/*the thing/*something/*stuff.
      b. Mike didn't score any baskets/*anything/*squat.
      c. *Whatever Mike scored was not a three pointer.

(24) a. Mike took some time/the time/*something/*everything/*stuff/*the thing to call his
mother.
      b. Mike didn't take any time/*anything/*squat to call his mother.
      c. What *(amount of time) did Mike take to mark the exams?

(25) a. Vanessa committed perjury/*something/*everything/*nothing.
      b. What crime/*What did Vanessa commit?
      c. No matter what crime/*what Vanessa committed, I still respect her.
      d. Vanessa didn't commit any crime/*anything.

(26) a. Glen swore an oath/*something/*everything/*nothing.
      b. What kind of oath/*What did Glen swear?
      c. Whatever oath/*Whatever Glen swore, he was just kidding.
      d. Glen didn't swear any oath/*anything/*a damn thing.

(27) a. Vanessa carried out a threat/some threat/*something.
      b. What threat/*What (else) did Vanessa carry out?
      c. No matter what threat/*what Vanessa carried out, . . .
      d. Vanessa didn't carry out a single threat/any threat/*anything/*a damn thing.

(28) a. Kim spent some part/*something of her life in Topeka.
      b. Kim didn't spend any part/*anything of her life in Topeka.
      c. What part/*What of her life did Kim spend in Topeka?
      d. Whatever part/*Whatever (else) of her life Kim spent in Topeka, . . .

A further case is pointed out by my colleague Mark Baltin:

(29) a. Arnie dissuaded/deterred Rosalie from some course of action/*something/*every-
thing/*stuff.
      b. Arnie did not dissuade/deter Rosalie from any course of action/*anything/*a damn
thing/*squat.
      c. What course of action/*What did Arnie dissuade/deter Rosalie from?
      d. No matter what course of action/*what Arnie dissuaded/deterred Rosalie from, . . .

One can, in the light of earlier remarks, characterize the contexts in (21)–(29) as ones
that *obligatorily require chromatic DPs* or, equivalently, ones that exclude nonchromatic DPs.

Note that the chromatic/nonchromatic distinction may cleave differently for a *morphological* verb depending on its meanings. That is, one meaning may require a chromatic type of DP in a particular context, another meaning not, as illustrated in (30):

(30)   a. He didn't spend $_{<monetary>}$ any money/anything/squat in Hawaii.
        b. He didn't spend $_{<temporal>}$ any time/*anything/*squat in Hawaii.
        c. He didn't assume $_{<logical>}$ any principle/anything/squat.
        d. He didn't assume $_{<physical>}$ any position/*anything/*squat.
        e. He didn't attend $_{<matriculation>}$ any school/*anything/*squat.
        f. He didn't attend $_{<physical\ presence>}$ any lecture/anything/squat at that conference.

So spend in the monetary sense is indifferent to the chromaticity of its object, but spend in the temporal sense requires a chromatic object. Similarly, assume in the logical sense takes either chromatic or nonchromatic objects but in the physical sense requires a chromatic one. The same pattern is seen with attend, whose physical sense is equally compatible with object chromaticity or its absence but whose matriculation sense requires a chromatic object. Such facts seem quite anomalous at first glance but have at least a simple description if one can appeal to the grammatical category distinction argued for here.

A second category of selectional fact that supports chromaticity as a grammatical category dimension in English is that some DP environments require *nonchromatic* DPs. Two such environments are formed by the subjects of the expressions be the matter with + DP and be wrong with + DP, noted to require antipronominal subjects in chapter 3:

(31)   a. Nothing/Something/Everything/(Terrible) Stuff is the matter/wrong with that car.
        b. *Some problem/*Power loss/*Rust/*Old age/*Overuse is the matter/wrong with that car.
        c. I don't believe anything/squat/a fucking thing to be the matter/wrong with that car.
        d. *I don't believe a flat/rust/an oil leak/electrical problems to be the matter/wrong with that car.

Another nonchromatic environment, whose existence I am indebted to Christopher Potts for pointing out to me, is the subject of the use of eat on which it means something like "bother":

(32)   a. Something/(Bad) Stuff/Nothing/Not a damn thing/That (thing) is eating Gilbert.
        b. What (else) is eating Gilbert?
        c. *Some problem/Hair loss/Boredom/Lack of charisma/Overweight is eating Gilbert.
        d. I don't believe anything/squat/jack-shit to be eating Gilbert.

A further environment that selects nonchromatic DPs is seen in (33):

(33)   a. They named their daughter something/that/the same thing I named mine/*some (stupid) name.

b. They did not name their daughter anything/a damn thing.
c. I need to know who named their daughter what (*name).

And further adverbial instances are found in (34) and (35):

(34) a. Trolls resided *some bridge/*every bridge/somewhere/everywhere.
     b. Trolls resided *no bridge/nowhere.
     c. Trolls didn't reside *any bridge/anywhere.
     d. *What bridge/Where (else) did trolls reside?
     e. No matter *what bridge/where trolls resided, . . .

(35) a. Juanita played golf *some way/*some manner during her vacation.
     b. *What way/*What manner/How (else) did Juanita play golf during her vacation?
     c. No matter *what way/*what manner/how (else) Juanita played golf, . . .

Taking it for granted now that there are selections defined on the chromatic/nonchromatic distinction, the question arises of whether all such facts can be taken to involve purely semantic requirements of the selectors in question. This question is relevant, evidently, to the issue of whether all selection is semantic; see, for example, Grimshaw (1979, 1981) and Pesetsky (1995). Consider first a verb like <u>attend</u> on its matriculation sense, which requires a chromatic object. Could this follow from some purely semantic requirement? It is not easy to see how. The relevant requirement would seem to be (36):

(36) The object of matriculation <u>attend</u> denotes an institution of learning.

The problem then is that there is no reason that such a condition would block, for example, (37a and b), given that, as (37c and d) illustrate, there is no general barrier to nonchromatic forms denoting institutions of learning:

(37) a. *Celia attended _{<matriculation>} something/everything/stuff.
     b. *What Celia attended _{<matriculation>} was the University of Vermont.
     c. Celia was discussing something (namely, her high school) with Billy.
     d. What Celia was referring to was the University of Vermont.

Given data like (37c and d), there is no visible reason that the nonetheless clearly deviant (37a and b) would violate what appears to be the semantic condition on the relevant verb, matriculation <u>attend</u>, that represented as (36).

Turning to the opposite sort of selectors, those like <u>matter with</u>, which require nonchromatic subjects, it is also difficult to envisage a motivated purely semantic condition that would block only the bad cases of (38a), especially given the grammaticality of those like (38b):

(38) a. They didn't prove anything/a damn thing/squat/*leukemia/*bulimia/*whooping cough to be wrong with her.
     b. What they proved to be wrong with her was leukemia/bulimia/whooping cough.

My tentative conclusion then is that the selectional constraints that involve the chromaticity dimension are syntactic, entailing more generally that not all selection is semantic.

To conclude this section, the two types of selectional evidence contribute, strongly, I think, to supporting the syntactic reality of the chromatic/nonchromatic distinction. But the sort of evidence that shows this perhaps most strongly of all involves what will be argued to be a range of *agreement* phenomena.

3. Chromatic agreement

3.1. Remark

I believe that several types of constructions in which constituents of type A are known to manifest agreement with others of type B in properties such as person, gender, and number are such that constituents of type A must agree in chromaticity value with those of type B. This state of affairs is harder to show than for agreement that involves person, gender, or number, because what I suggest is chromaticity value agreement has no direct *morphological* realization. That is, no expression B that can be argued to manifest agreement in, say, positive chromaticity value differs in morphological form from the corresponding element that manifests negative chromaticity value. Nonetheless, there are restrictions that seem best characterized as agreement of chromaticity value.

3.2. Chromatic agreement of ordinary visible definite pronouns

First, I suggest that ordinary definite pronouns like it must *agree with their antecedents* in chromaticity value. So, consider (39):

(39)   a. *Jerome spent $_{<temporal>}$ something (namely, Easter) in Bermuda.
        b. Jerome spent $_{<temporal>}$ some holiday (namely, Easter) in Bermuda.
        c. Jerome discussed something (namely, football/bunions/ice cream).
        d. Marsha discussed *something$_1$/some holiday$_1$ because Jerome spent $_{<temporal>}$ it$_1$ in Bermuda.

The already mentioned fact that the *temporal* spend excludes nonchromatic objects accounts for the badness of (39a). But (39c) shows that discuss, like most verbs, is *not* subject to such a constraint. Nonetheless, the nonchromatic version of (39d) is ill formed. Given that the chromatic version is good, this cannot be due to the mere presence of a pronoun in the bad version.

The facts would, though, follow if something like (40a and b) were both true:

(40)   a. An English definite pronominal DP must agree in chromaticity value with its antecedent.
        b. The temporal verb spend requires *any* object DP it occurs with to be chromatic.

To make sense of (40a), one must assume minimally that the English definite pronominal forms it, its, they, them, their, and so on,[8] are analyzed as both chromatic and nonchromatic. In this respect, they would be like the noun thing touched on earlier, which also needs to be taken to have both chromatic and nonchromatic forms, whereas most nouns are only chromatic. The point would then be that while, for example, it has syntactically distinct chromatic and nonchromatic variants, these do not differ morphologically in the way that, for example, the syntactically distinct singular masculine nominative and singular masculine and feminine forms he and she do. This makes chromaticity value agreement less visible than agreement in gender value but not necessarily thereby less real.

Incidentally, the reason that all of the definite pronouns listed are inanimates has to do with the fact that while there are arguments (from else, etc.) that forms like someone are human nonchromatics, I do not know of any environment that *selects* for human chromatics or nonchromatics. Thus there is no environment currently available to show agreement in chromatic value for human DPs.

Another case of the same sort as (39) is seen in (41):

(41)   a. Mike spoke *something/some language.
       b. Mike studied *something$_1$/some language$_1$ despite not speaking it$_1$.
       c. No matter *what$_1$/what language$_1$ Mike praised despite the fact that he did not speak it$_1$, . . .

Here the facts in (41b) would follow from (40a) together with assumption (42):

(42)   The verb speak requires any object DP it occurs with to be chromatic.

A third case is found in (43):

(43)   a. Abdul composed his poems in some African language/*something/*everything.
       b. Abdul did not compose his poems in any African language/*anything/*a damn thing.
       c. What language/*What (the hell) did Abdul compose his poems in?
       d. Zeke was interested in some language$_1$/*something$_1$ because Abdul composed poems in it$_1$.
       e. Whatever language$_1$/*Whatever$_1$ Zeke is interested in, Abdul composes a poem in it$_1$.

A fourth case is (44):

(44)   a. Sheila attended $_{<matriculation>}$ *something/some school.
       b. Sheila's parents looked into *something$_1$/some school$_1$ because Sheila was thinking of attending $_{<matriculation>}$ it$_1$ in the fall.
       c. No matter what$_1$/what school$_1$ Sheila's parents praised, she refused to attend $_{<matriculation>}$ it$_1$.

And a fifth is:

(45)   a. They diagrammed something (= physical position)/some physical position.
       b. They diagrammed *something$_1$/some physical position$_1$ right after Stan assumed $_{<physical>}$ it$_1$.
       c. What$_1$/*What position$_1$ did they diagram right after Stan assumed $_{<physical>}$ it$_1$?

A sixth case is:

(46) a. Their star scored *something/two goals.
      b. When that team needs *something$_1$/a goal$_1$, their star scores it$_1$.

A seventh case is found in (47):

(47) a. Barry drove $_{<baseball>}$ in *something/some runs.
      b. *What did Barry drive $_{<baseball>}$ in?[9]
      c. Barry didn't drive $_{<baseball>}$ in *anything/*a damn thing/any run.
      d. The manager was hoping for *something$_1$/a run$_1$ just before Barry drove $_{<baseball>}$ it$_1$ in.

The strength of the latter case as support for principle (40a) is increased by the fact that the same verb also takes human objects with, strangely, pretty much the same meaning as the nonhuman objects of (47). But the human object position is *not* restricted with respect to chromaticity value. And, notably, analogs of (47d) are then fine:

(48) a. Barry drove $_{<baseball>}$ in someone/a baserunner.
      b. She was pointing at someone$_1$/a baserunner$_1$ just before Barry drove $_{<baseball>}$ him$_1$ in.

I believe that the (arguably) agreement data just gone over support in a clear way the reality of chromaticity value agreement. And this seems true despite the lack of direct morphological manifestation of such agreement. Evidently, though, the existence of such a phenomenon is only possible on the basis of the underlying existence of the chromatic/nonchromatic category distinction itself.

3.3. Chromatic agreement and subject control

The overall set of facts that relate to chromaticity agreement has nontrivial theoretical implications relevant to much-discussed issues. Consider first cases such as (49):

(49) a. Something$_1$/A specific amount of money$_1$ had to be discussed after Ø$_1$ being spent $_{<monetary>}$ in Spain.
      b. *Something$_1$/A specific week$_1$ had to be discussed after Ø$_1$ being spent $_{<temporal>}$ in Spain.

The obvious factual point is that although in (49) there is no superficially visible pronoun to show agreement, the contrast in (49b) is nonetheless strikingly reminiscent of the chromaticity agreement contrast with temporal verb <u>spend</u> seen in (39), while the lack of contrast in (49a) parallels the lack of a chromaticity agreement contrast with the monetary verb <u>spend</u> seen in (50):

(50) Something$_1$/A specific amount of money$_1$ was set aside/saved so it$_1$ could be spent $_{<monetary>}$ on vacations.

One finds in (49) of course an <u>after</u> adjunct with a *controlled* subject. Now, it has been an issue since at least the account in Postal (1970) whether cases of control involve invisible pronominal elements or not. The work just cited argued for the former view. But many have since denied it; see, for example, Chierchia (1984), Chierchia and Jacobson (1985), Jacobson (1992b), and Dowty (1985). What seems to be a chromaticity agreement fact in (49) then supports the invisible pronominal view. For such cases would force an alternative to the invisible pronominal view to somehow account for the contrast in (49) with some further mechanism M distinct from that in (40), where M would have nothing to do with pronominal agreement.

To drive home the relevance of chromaticity constraints to control, it is important to see that (49) is not an isolated or anomalous instance of subject control. Relevantly then, control into subject complements also reveals parallels to clear pronominal chromaticity value agreement:

(51)   a. *Something /A strange position was assumed $_{<\text{physical}>}$ by the gorilla.
       b. Its$_1$ having been assumed $_{<\text{physical}>}$ by the notorious gorilla made *something$_1$/a strange position$_1$/famous.
       c. Ø$_1$ Having been assumed $_{<\text{physical}>}$ by the notorious gorilla made *something$_1$/a strange position$_1$ famous.

(52)   a. *Something/Some language was spoken by the cloned scientist.
       b. Its$_1$ having been spoken by the cloned scientist wouldn't necessarily make *anything$_1$/any language$_1$ of interest to the CIA.
       c. Ø$_1$ Having been spoken by the cloned scientist wouldn't necessarily make *anything$_1$/any language$_1$ of interest to the CIA.

Chromatic relevance to subject control is also seen in structures with too/enough:

(53)   a. Some school$_1$/*Something$_1$ had to be too expensive/cheap enough for it$_1$ to be attended by Sheila.
       b. Some school$_1$/*Something$_1$ had to be too expensive/cheap enough Ø$_1$ to be attended by Sheila.

The point is also made by the sort of subject control found in conjoined clausal structures with then:

(54)   a. Some language$_1$/*Something$_1$ was chosen and then, Stella claims, it$_1$ was spoken by all of the students.
       b. Some language$_1$/*Something$_1$ was chosen and then, Stella claims, Ø$_1$ was spoken by all of the students.

Overall then, it seems clear that chromaticity facts argue for the role of invisible pronouns in a range of subject control structures.

3.4. Chromatic agreement and nonsubject control

Chromaticity value agreement is arguably also involved in several distinct types of nonsubject control. First, there is the type associated with too/enough (see, e.g., Fiengo and Lasnik, 1974; and Postal, 1994b):

(55) a. Some position$_1$/*Something$_1$ was too difficult for Jerome to assume $_{<physical>}$ it$_1$.
      b. Some position$_1$/*Something$_1$ was too difficult for Jerome to assume $_{<physical>}$ Ø$_1$.

Second, chromaticity is relevant to nonsubject control in those purposives of the sort that permit it (see, e.g., Bach, 1982; and Browning, 1987):

(56) a. He composed poems in some Siberian language/*something.
      b. He chose *something$_1$/some language$_1$ for the purpose of composing poems in it$_1$.
      c. He chose *something$_1$/some language$_1$ to compose poems in Ø$_1$.
      d. He studied Mongolian$_1$/*something exotic$_1$ to speak it$_1$ to his mother-in-law.
      e. He studied Mongolian$_1$/*something exotic$_1$ to speak Ø$_1$ to his mother-in-law.
      f. She set aside a week$_1$/some period of time$_1$/*something$_1$ to spend it$_1$ with her fiancé.
      g. She set aside a week$_1$/some period of time$_1$/*something $_1$to spend Ø$_1$ with her fiancé.

Note that the starred form of (56c) is irrelevantly grammatical on a reading where something denotes a location and not an NL, in which case the controlled position also then denotes a location.

Third, the chromaticity dimension is relevant to the sort of marginal 'instruction set' nonsubject control touched on in Postal (1994b):

(57) a. Choose some comfortable position$_1$/*something$_1$ and assume it$_1$ for a short period.
      b. Choose some comfortable position$_1$/*something$_1$ comfortable and assume Ø$_1$ for a short period.

Fourth, chromaticity status is relevant to the nonsubject control characteristic, according to Postal (1993a, 1994b, 2001a, 2001b), of parasitic gaps (but see Levine, Hukari, and Calcagno, 2001, for a strongly opposing opinion):

(58) a. What language$_1$/*What$_1$ did they discuss/argue about t$_1$ immediately after hearing the spy speak it$_1$?
      b. What language$_1$/*What$_1$ did they discuss/argue about t$_1$ immediately after hearing the spy speak Ø$_1$?

(59) a. That is a holiday$_1$/*something$_1$ that Freddy thought fondly of t$_1$ without ever spending $_{<temporal>}$ it$_1$ in Naples.
      b. That is a holiday$_1$/*something$_1$ that Freddy thought fondly of t$_1$ without ever spending $_{<temporal>}$ Ø$_1$ in Naples.

3.5. Chromatic agreement and restrictive relative clauses

Just as restrictive relative pronouns, visible or not, appear to agree with the heads of the nominals they form in gender and number, as illustrated in (60), they can be argued to show agreement along the chromaticity dimension as well:

(60) a. the woman who praised herself/*himself/*themselves
      b. the man who praised himself/*herself/*themselves
      c. the children who praised themselves/*herself/*himself

First, consider cases where the overall DP formed with a restrictive relative is itself chromatic:

(61) a. Some language/*Something that Teresa spoke Ø was discussed at length.
      b. Some position/*Something that the gorilla assumed _{<physical>} Ø was discussed at length.

Evidently, when the overall DP is chromatic, its contained relative clause can contain a relative extraction gap in a position that is required to be chromatic, but this is impossible if the overall DP is nonchromatic. This would follow if the relative pronoun (visible or not) had to agree with the head DP in chromaticity value.

The parallel point is made when one chooses relative clause gaps in positions that are required to be nonchromatic. This is only possible when the head DP is also nonchromatic:

(62) a. The thing/*problem that Ø is eating Gilbert is unknown.
      b. Something strange/*Some strange problem that Ø used to be the matter with my car is now affecting Ted's car as well.
      c. The thing/*name/that they named her Ø was strange.

All these facts would follow if a principle like (63) held:

(63) A restrictive relative pronoun agrees in chromaticity value with its head DP.

3.6. Chromatic agreement and nonrestrictive relative clauses

It should not be surprising at this point to observe that nonrestrictive relative pronouns also manifest chromaticity agreement:

(64) a. Quentin discussed *something/some period of time, which he spent _{<temporal>} in Bermuda.
      b. Quentin diagrammed *something/some position, which he was unable to assume _{<physical>}·
      c. The manager was counting on *something/a run, which Tim was unable to drive in _{<baseball>}·

These nonrestrictive relative contrasts would follow from the independently existing constraints that define chromatic and nonchromatic positions if the following principle holds:

(65) A nonrestrictive relative pronoun agrees in chromaticity value with its head DP.

3.7. Chromatic agreement: conclusion

I have argued that strong grounds for the reality of the chromaticity dimension in English grammar are presented by what I have suggested are agreement phenomena. These are of two types: first, agreement that involves superficially overt items that include ordinary definite pronouns, restrictive relative pronouns, and nonrestrictive relative pronouns; and second, agreement that involves invisible or covert elements that include controlled pronouns and restrictive relative pronouns. In all cases, modulo the fact that the chromaticity dimension is not morphologically marked, the facts of chromaticity value agreement seem parallel to those for person, gender, and number agreement, which argues that chromaticity is a grammatical dimension in the same sense that these traditional categories are.[10, 11]

4. Ellipsis phenomena

I believe the chromaticity dimension also has implications for the description of ellipsis phenomena like Gapping, Nominal Gapping, Pseudogapping, VP Deletion, and Comparative Deletion. Consider:

(66) Gapping (see, e.g., Jackendoff, 1971; Lobeck, 1995; and Nejit, 1980)
   a. Jerome spoke some African language and Carol some Asian one.
   b. Jerome discussed something African and Carol something Asian.
   c. Jerome spoke some African language and Carol some Eurasian language/*something Eurasian.
   d. Something simple is the matter with my car and something complex with Ted's.
   e. *Something simple is the matter with my car and some very bad problem with Ted's.

(67) Nominal Gapping (see Jackendoff, 1971)
   a. Lucille's spending of a week in Bermuda and Janet's of a month in Spain were unusual.
   b. *Lucille's spending of a week in Bermuda and Janet's of something even more indulgent in Spain were unusual.
   c. Lucille's assumption _{physical>} of a common position and Janet's of a hitherto unknown position were unexpected.
   d. *Lucille's assumption _{physical>} of a common position and Janet's of something hitherto unknown were unexpected.

(68) Pseudogapping (see Baltin, 2003; Lasnik, 1999b; and Levin, 1978, 1986)
   a. Although Jerome did not speak any African language, he did some Asian one.
   b. *Although Jerome did not speak any African language, he did something Asian.
   c. Although nothing is the matter with my car, something serious is with Ted's.
   d. *Although nothing is the matter with my car, some serious problem is with Ted's.

(69) VP Deletion (see, e.g., Fiengo and May, 1994; Johnson, 2001; and Sag, 1976)
   a. Some African language Terry did speak, but some Eurasian language/*something well known in America he didn't.
   b. Although nothing seemed to be the matter with my car, something/*some problem/*a serious problem was.

(70)   Comparative Deletion (see Bresnan, 1973, 1975; and Kennedy, 1997a)
        a. Susan has studied the same language that Ted discussed/speaks.
        b. Susan has studied the same thing that Ted discussed/*speaks.
        c. Susan diagrammed a different position than Ted discussed/assumed $_{<physical>}$.
        d. Susan diagrammed a different thing/something different than Ted discussed/
           *assumed $_{<physical>}$.

These data show that the same selectional restrictions found in clauses with visible selectors like speak, the matter with, spending, assumption, and so forth show up in clauses (and nominals) that manifest ellipsis of various sorts determined by phrases that contain those restricted selectors. This supports a view that this sort of ellipsis actually involves invisible versions of the syntactic entities that determine the selections. It also suggests that the zeroed constituents contain actual DPs of the sort that can manifest the chromatic or nonchromatic categorization.

5. Types of nonchromatic DPs

It was seen in section 1 that one type of nonchromatic DP required a single-word combination of D + noun, as argued by the positioning of simplex adjectives after the nonchromatic noun:

(71)   a. Something terrible took place.
        b. Some terrible event took place.
        c. They did not witness anything terrible.
        d. They did not witness any terrible event.

Now, it was claimed but not explicated that the one-word property, analyzed by Kishimoto (2000) in terms of N-raising, is only characteristic of one subtype of nonchromatic DP. Given what has been established about the existence of certain selectional positions that only allow nonchromatic DPs, one can support the earlier claim by showing that in such positions one finds both one-word and multiword DPs, hence multiword nonchromatic DPs.
        Consider then:

(72)   a. (Only) Something minor was the matter with her liver.
        b. *Some problem/*Some disease/*Some rare condition was the matter with her liver.
        c. A terrible thing was the matter with her liver.
        d. The awful thing that was the matter with her liver caused her to be hospitalized.
        e. The only thing that was the matter with her liver was not serious.
        f. That frightening thing was also the matter with my liver.
        g. Certain frightening things might be the matter with his liver as well.[12]
        h. Herb doesn't believe a damn thing to be the matter with her liver.

Cases like (72b) argue, as already indicated earlier, that the subject of the matter with must be a nonchromatic DP. But then cases like (72c, d, e, f, g, and h) show clearly that some nonchromatic DPs do not manifest the D + N as a single-word feature.

I do not have a good understanding of the DP internal structural factors that distinguish the distinct types of nonchromatic DPs, but roughly it may work as follows: First, the single-word feature is clearly not associated with definite DPs, as in (72e, f). Second, it seems that there is a division among *non*definite DPs that cuts along the lines that separate some from a forms. So, informally:

(73)   The single-word feature (N-raising in Kishimoto [2000]'s terms) is associated only with indefinite DPs of the some type.

An obvious observation is that for (73) to have any chance of being viable, it is necessary to analyze a range of Ds that do not manifest surface instances of the morpheme some as being of the some type. These include most obviously anything, nothing, everything, what, and whatever, as in (74):

(74)   a. She doesn't believe anything serious to be the matter with the liver.
        b. She believes nothing serious to be the matter with the liver.
        c. (Just about) Everything conceivable is the matter with the liver.
        d. What does she believe to be the matter with the liver?
        e. No matter what she believes to be the matter with the liver, . . .
        f. Whatever she believes to be the matter with the liver is likely to be serious.

Less obviously, there is also a range of slang forms that include those of (75) and need to be categorized as indefinite some forms:[13]

(75)   a. Harry proved stuff to be the matter with the liver.
        b. Harry proved zilch/zip/zippo/zero to be the matter with the liver.
        c. Harry did not prove beans/crap/dick/diddley/diddley-squat/fuck-all/jack/jack-shit/
           jack-squat/piss-all/poo/shit/shit-all/squat to be the matter with the liver.

These conclusions seem to me to have no known undesirable consequences.

6. Coordination of chromatic and nonchromatic DPs

When DPs of distinct categories coordinate, the resulting complex DP is assigned to a category as a function of the categories of the conjuncts. This is most visible in agreement phenomena. So, in an NL with both dual and plural number, the conjunctive coordination of two singulars yields a dual and the coordination of a singular and dual or plural yields a plural.[14] In English, with no dual/plural distinction, conjunctive coordination of any DPs yields a plural:

(76)   a. Mike is tall.
        b. Roberta is tall.
        c. Mike and Roberta are tall.
        d. Mike and those two runners are tall.

With respect to person, in English and possibly universally coordination of a first person with any person yields a first person (plural) and coordination of a second person DP with any non–first person DP yields a second person DP:

(77)   a. We are proud of ourselves.
       b. You are proud of yourselves.
       c. You and I are proud of ourselves/*yourselves.
       d. Those guys and I are proud of ourselves/*themselves.
       e. You and those guys are proud of yourselves/*themselves.

Strangely, though, it seems that conjunctive coordination of chromatic and nonchromatic DPs yields a complex DP that cannot be taken to be *either* exclusively chromatic or exclusively nonchromatic. The evidence is that apparently no mixed conjunctive coordination of chromatic and nonchromatic DPs can occur in any context restricted to *either* chromatic or nonchromatic forms. This is true both for pure selectional cases and for those that involve what I have taken to be pronominal agreement:

(78)   Required Chromatic Context
       a. Renee attended _{matriculation} some school/*something expensive.
       b. *Renee attended _{matriculation} at various times some private school and something inexpensive.
       c. *Renee described some private school$_1$ and something cheap$_2$ after attending _{matriculation} them$_{1,2}$.

(79)   Required Nonchromatic Context
       a. Something grave/*Some minor problem was eating Gilbert.
       b. *At different times something grave and some minor problem were eating Gilbert.
       c. *Renee described something grave$_1$ and some minor problem$_2$ after learning they$_{1,2}$ were eating Gilbert.

It is unclear to me how one should react to this data. One possibility would involve a claim that such coordinate phrases must be taken to be *both* chromatic and nonchromatic, which indicates that one cannot analyze these in a way equivalent to taking them to be plus and minus values of a single binary feature. Another possibility would be to claim that such coordinations are assigned to *neither* the chromatic nor nonchromatic categories. Not having studied these facts in any detail, I am not in a position to offer anything that chooses between the alternatives or to offer any distinct solution.

7. A prescriptively disfavored type of agreement

Normally, English morphologically singular DPs determine, not surprisingly, morphologically singular pronominal agreement:

(80) a. The doctor$_1$/That doctor$_1$/Some doctor$_1$/Every doctor$_1$ claimed he$_1$ was ethical.

   b. A professor$_1$/This professor$_1$/A certain professor$_1$/No professor$_1$ was sure she$_1$ was right.

Replacing he/she by they in these cases would preclude the antecedent relation that is marked. However, there are cases where plural pronominal agreement that involves they, them, or their is possible, although prescriptively looked down upon:

(81) a. If everyone$_1$/someone$_1$/no one$_1$ thinks they$_1$ are a genius/their$_1$ child is a genius, . . .

   b. Who$_1$ here thinks they$_1$ are a genius?

   c. No matter who$_1$ thinks demons are after them$_1$, . . .

   d. Whoever$_1$ thinks they$_1$ are/their$_1$ child is a genius is probably a moron.

   e. Anyone who$_1$ thinks they$_1$ are a genius is probably a moron.

While the regular, expected singular agreement is also possible in such cases, apparently only the *human* subclass of the same subset of nonchromatic forms that permit else permits this "fake" plural agreement:

(82) a. *If a philospher$_1$/a certain guy$_1$/a specific fellow$_1$ thinks they$_1$ are a genius/their$_1$ child is a genius,

   b. *What guy$_1$ thinks they$_1$ are a genius?

   c. *No matter what guy$_1$ thinks demons are after them$_1$, . . .

Those are at least my judgments. But the "Oddments and Miscellanea" column of the *Vocabulary Review* 3, no. 7 (whose prescriptive motto is "A society is generally as lax as its language"), of July 2001, states:

> Each month, "Oddments and Miscellanea" will focus on a particular matter of faulty grammar, slipshod syntax, or improper punctuation. This month's admonition: Avoid using the plural pronoun *their*, *them*, or *they* following words like *each* and *one*, *every* and *any*, *everyone* and *everybody*, *anyone* and *anybody*, *someone* and *somebody*, and *no one* and *nobody* when the antecedent is clearly singular.

The prescribers then present the following list of putatively bad examples and their proposed improvements:

(83) a. Each of the women during this eight-week program developed their body as well as their mind and emotions. USE *her; her.*

   b. Everyone has their own story. USE *his or her* or *his* or *her.*

   c. No one wants their name and information given to anyone and we at Elante Luggage hold this to be paramount to good business. USE *his or her* or *his* or *her.*

   d. A quick e-mail to thank somebody for their time goes a long way. USE *his or her* or *his* or *her.*

   e. Every international student when they first came to Toorak College must have felt a bit nervous and homesick. USE *he or she* or *he* or *she.*

   f. If you want to see what someone truly feels they deserve, just take a look at what they have. USE *he deserves* or *she deserves* or *he or she deserves*; *he has* or *she has* or *he or she has*.

g. Every one of the contestants wore a patch on their vests. USE *his vest* or *her vest* or *his or her vest*.

h. How do you tell someone that you love them? USE *him or her* or *him or her*.

i. It's time for anyone who still thinks that singular "their" is so-called bad grammar to get rid of their prejudices and pedantry! USE *his or her* or *his or her*.

As prescriptive grammar goes, this is high-quality. The authors provide a rich list of examples and a clear indication of the construction they think should be avoided. Note, though, that while their preexemplification text cites essentially nonchromatic antecedents, of their nine examples only six involve nonchromatic antecedents. For me, such a heterogeneous collection misses a distinction. That is, I regard (83a, e, and g) as truly ungrammatical, while the other six examples are fine. It is unclear that the *Vocabulary Review*'s prescriptive remarks are incompatible with my claim that plural agreement with singulars is only possible with a (subtype) of nonchromatic DP antecedent. Because, arguably, for its authors, all such agreement is ungrammatical. What is unclear is whether the sentences they believe they are proscribing, including (83a, e, and g), really occur and "need" proscribing or whether they have just been made up randomly to illustrate a point by authors concerned only to devalue all plural agreement with singular antecedents.

The evidence in Pinker (1994: 390–391) is also a bit equivocal. Six of the seven examples of 'fake agreement' that he cites have nonchromatic antecedents. The seventh, said to be a quote from J. D. Salinger's *Catcher in the Rye*, was:

(84) He's one of those guys who's always patting themself on the back.[15]

But I find this ungrammatical, which raises the issue of dialect variation.

In any event, my view that the existence of the plural agreement with singular antecedence phenomenon supports the relevance to English grammar of the chromatic/nonchromatic distinction is supported *if* the following holds. There are some speakers like I claim to be who restrict such antecedence to that subtype of nonchromatic antecedents that determine one-word character and sanction a following else.[16]

8. Limitations of informal statements

It will not have escaped the reader that the discussion of this chapter has been entirely informal. I have not provided a precise account of the internal structure of DPs to support the claim that English DPs divide into the chromatic and nonchromatic. Nor have I spelled out mechanisms that could account for the conclusion, argued in some detail, that chromaticity is a dimension relevant for agreement of various types.

These are serious limitations but, fortunately, not ones directly relevant to the chief point of this essay, which is merely to document the existence of the chromatic/nonchromatic distinction, one that past linguistics seems to have overlooked.

One point, though, that is worth expanding is this: Just as, for example, nouns like man/woman, boy/girl, and such must be the core locus of the distinction of grammatical gender, just so nouns must be the core locus of the distinction between chromatic and nonchromatic. Since, however, the distinction ultimately divides large DP constituents into corresponding types, it is evident that a proper grammatical framework must allow for some kind of 'projection' of the lexical noun distinction to one that distinguishes as well their minimal containing DPs. There are various extant approaches to such questions and I have nothing to add to the understanding of the matter here.

The Structure of One Type of
American English Vulgar Minimizer

1. Background

In the summer of 1995, Haj Ross and I began jointly looking into the grammar of the vulgar American English slang forms in (1):

(1) *SQUAT* = Vulgar Minimizers = {beans, crap, dick, diddley, diddley-poo, diddley-squat, fuck-all, jack, jack-shit, jack-squat, piss-all, poo, shit, shit-all, squat}

Some examples of some uses of these forms, taken to be members of the nonchromatic class in chapter 4, are given in (2):

(2) a. Olmstead didn't say dick about the new dean.
     b. Olmstead knows fuck-all about Botswana.
     c. Olmstead didn't contribute jack to the emergency fund.
     d. Olmstead doesn't understand squat about topology.

In naming these expressions as I have, I intend to bring out what I take to be a genuine connection with other *minimizers*, a standard category of negation studies; see Horn (2001: 452–453). Generally, a minimizer is a type of DP that denotes minimal elements on some scale:

(3) Minimizers that are not *vulgar* minimizers include, for example, a drop/a word/a red cent/a finger, as in (4):

(4)   a. Sally didn't drink a drop. (minimal amount of liquid)
      b. Stan didn't say a word. (minimal amount of linguistic utterance)
      c. Sarah didn't have a red cent. (minimal amount of money)
      d. Steve didn't lift a finger. (minimal amount of effort)

One key difference between vulgar minimizers and others such as those in (4) is
that mostly the former are *not* narrowly restricted to *particular* dimensions but can
express minimality along many dimensions not specifically invoking animate things,
because, like most minimizers, all those of (1) form exclusively inanimate nominals.
A few English minimizers, specifically those highlighted in (5), do not:

(5)   a. Spiro didn't see *a soul* on Sunday. (minimal number of people)
      b. Spiro didn't see *a living soul* on Sunday. (minimal number of people)
      c. The police didn't find *a fucking soul* alive in the crack house. (minimal number of
         people)

In discussing a linguistic subject, one normally references the literature on it,
which is easy in this case, given that, as far as I know, grammatical/semantic works
devoted to or containing detailed analyses of English vulgar minimizers are nearly
nonexistent. See, though, Horn (1996b, 2001) for some discussion and Nexis search
examples.

While (1) lists many forms, no doubt most Americans use or even know only a
proper subset. I assume, though, that most American speakers are familiar with at least
one member of SQUAT and thus have introspective access to the phenomenon.[1] Various vulgar minimizers are mentioned in slang dictionaries. There they appear to uniformly be said to mean "nothing," as are other forms not listed in (1) like those in (6):

(6)   Z-minimizers = {zero, zilch, zip, zippo}

See, for instance, Spears (1996: 374), which mentions squat and diddly-squat and
gives only the meaning "nothing."

However, something key is missed by such dictionaries. As already in effect illustrated in (1), while vulgar minimizers do have uses in which they seem to mean "nothing" and in this respect are like the forms of (6), many of them for many speakers also
have different uses in which they function as *negative polarity items* (NPIs), that is,
items that cannot occur in simple non-negative clauses but do occur with negation. This
polarity property is illustrated for the animate minimizer in (5c) in (7):

(7)   a. Claudia did not see a fucking soul.
      b. *Claudia saw a fucking soul.
      c. Claudia did so see someone.
      d. *Claudia did so see a fucking soul.

Notably, none of the Z-minimizers occurs as an NPI in the NPI licensing environment of (7a), as (8) illustrates:

(8)   ??Claudia did not see zilch/zip/zippo.

If (8) is acceptable at all, it can only be as a non-NPI instance of denial negation, with strong stress on <u>not</u>, representing rejection of a previous claim that Claudia saw zilch. Seemingly, even in an NPI-accepting environment, the Z-minimizers can only have the non-NPI meaning "nothing."

But for vulgar minimizers, the situation is different, as illustrated in (9) and (10):

(9)   a. Claudia saw squat.
      b. Claudia did not see squat.

(10) a. Claudia discovered dick.
      b. Claudia did not discover dick.

While the a. forms are consistent with the behavior of Z-minimizers and with the slang dictionary claim that vulgar minimizers mean "nothing," the b. cases seem to indicate that they can also mean "anything."[2] In fact, although Spears (1996) gives only "nothing" as the meaning of <u>squat</u>, one of his two example sentences is of the type in (9b), where <u>squat</u> would naturally be taken to mean "anything" rather than "nothing."

(11) Spears (1996: 374)
      I worked all day on this, and she didn't pay me squat.

Besides raising a problem for slang dictionary meaning claims, pairs like (9) and (10) are truly extraordinary in one clear respect, for they illustrate forms that occur in a fixed position where the presence versus absence of an *overt negation* seems to make no semantic difference. That is, (9a, b) and (10a, b) are logical (truth functional) equivalents. There are few other such forms.[3] The standard and expected situation where presence of a negative yields distinct meanings is seen in (12):

(12) a. Claudia discovered many treasures. ≠
      b. Claudia did not discover many treasures.
      c. Claudia violated every rule. ≠
      d. Claudia did not violate every rule.

Focus then on a logically equivalent pair like (13a and c):

(13) a. Irma understands dick about clones.   =
      b. Irma understands nothing about clones.
      c. Irma does not understand dick about clones. =
      d. Irma does not understand anything about clones.

Given the apparent perfect equivalences here, it is overwhelmingly tempting to attempt to reduce the patterns in the vulgar minimizer cases to that of the standard cases with <u>anything</u> and <u>nothing</u>. The obvious way to do this would be as follows: First, assume that each of the vulgar minimizer pieces of morphology represents a noun stem. Second, claim that the vulgar minimizers are ambiguously analyzable in exactly the same way as either <u>nothing</u> or <u>anything</u>. Assuming that <u>no</u> forms like <u>nothing</u> involve a negative determiner that consists of a syntactic negative (NEG) + <u>some</u>, this means taking one term of the ambiguity for vulgar minimizers to involve something like (14), the other something like (15):

(14) a. nothing = $[_{DP} [_D \text{NEG} + \text{some}] + [_N \text{thing}]]$
      b. squat/dick/ . . . = $[_{DP} [_D \text{NEG} + \text{some}] + [_N \text{squat/dick/} . . .]]$

(15) a. anything = $[_{DP} [_D \text{any}] + [_N \text{thing}]]^4$
      b. squat/dick/ . . . = $[_{DP} [_D \text{any}] + [_N \text{squat/dick/} . . .]]$

The idea for (14b) and (15b) would then be that the determiners that otherwise manifest as <u>no</u> and <u>any</u> are obligatorily *invisible* when they occur with a vulgar minimizer noun.

Let me distinguish terminologically two forms of vulgar minimizers: those of (9a) and (10a) I will refer to for reasons that will emerge as *type Z*, and those of (9b) and (10b) I will refer to as *type A*, this intended to suggest a link with <u>anything</u>. The central goal of this chapter is to argue for the following (at least to me) quite amazing conclusion: Any equation like that in (14b), that is, any analysis that treats the nonpolarity variant of each member of SQUAT as in effect a negative form like <u>nothing</u>, is *completely wrong*. Z-type vulgar minimizers cannot be analyzed as forms having negative quantifiers for determiners and, even more generally, cannot be correctly analyzed as containing any syntactic negatives at all.

2. What type Z vulgar minimizers are not

2.1. Remarks

Thus the goal of this section is to show that in sentences like (13a) the vulgar minimizer <u>dick</u> does not contain a negative quantifier and, more generally, that such sentences contain no syntactic negation whatever. Admittedly, it is unclear that anyone has publicly claimed that they do contain such. The few remarks in the literature about such forms seem quite equivocal about their analysis:

(16) van der Wouden (1997: 78)
      "For instance, one of the many possibilities to affectively strengthen negation doesn't use negation at all."

The author then cites the type Z vulgar minimizer case (17a) and notes that "[a] variant of this sentence does use negation," citing (17b):

(17) a. He knows shit about GB.
      b. He doesn't know shit about GB.

One might take these remarks to deny that (17a) involves negation, but the conclusion is hardly solid. Similarly:

(18)   Hoeksema, Rullman, Sánchez-Valencia, and van der Wouden (2001: viii–ix)
       "The paper includes a discussion of *squat* and similar expressions of scatological origin, which have recently undergone part of the Jespersen Cycle, rendering them negative in force even in the absence of any overt negation: *They told him squat = They didn't tell him squat.*"

Again it is unclear what inference to draw about the authors' view of the role of syntactic negation in the analysis of the first, type Z, example. Finally:

(19)   Horn (2001: 185)
       "The key fact here, as recognized by the OED, is that *squat* can appear either in the scope of a licensing negation as the equivalent of *anything*, or on its own as the counterpart of *nothing*."

Horn refers to the former usage as *licensed* squat, the latter as *unlicensed*. Once more, though, it is not evident whether the remarks should be read as a claim that the correct synchronic analysis of type Z vulgar minimizers involves negation or not.

But regardless of whether anyone *else* has assumed type Z vulgar minimizers involve a syntactic negative, the position to be criticized here is not a straw man, since I myself adopted it as a working hypothesis for many months, struggling vainly to keep the view consistent with the collection of contrary data that continued to accumulate. I will try to indicate why such consistency is not possible by documenting a variety of ways in which type Z vulgar minimizers behave as if syntactic negation was entirely *absent*. It turns out, I believe, that only two indications even *suggest* that type Z vulgar minimizers involve negation. The first is simply the morphological parallelisms between type Z and type A minimizers; the second is the logical equivalence between pairs like (9a, b) and (10a, b). A logic that leads from these facts to a view that type Z vulgar minimizers do contain negation might go something like this: Relevant pairs like (9a, b) and (10a, b) are clearly related morphologically and yield logical equivalents. Given that the type A variants do involve syntactic negation, which is easily shown, then assuming that the logical equivalent of something negative is (double negations aside) something negative, the conclusion is reached. It should be of some general interest that this pattern of reasoning fails, as I will now argue.

2.2. Double negatives

Despite what one heard in school about the evils of double negatives, even standard American English allows double negative cases like (20a), to be sharply distinguished from exclusively substandard cases like (20b); see Postal (in press).

(20)   a. No professor favors NO proposal/NOTHING. (caps = contrastive stress)
       b. substandard: No professor favored no proposal/nothin'. = 'No professor favored any proposal/anything'

The substandard (20b) involves so-called *negative concord*. But the standard (20a) involves something else and is equivalent to (21):

(21)   Every professor favors SOME proposal.

See also the fine (22a), which contrast with the only substandard (22b):

(22)   a. The professor did not favor NO proposal   = 'favored SOME proposal'.
      b. substandard: The professor did not favor no proposal = 'did not favor any'.

Now, since standard English <u>no</u> forms like <u>nothing</u> permit non-negative concord structures like (20a) and (22a), if Z type vulgar minimizers were disguised <u>no</u> forms, they also would presumably permit that; but they do not, as (23a and b) indicate:

(23)   a. *No professor favored SQUAT.
      b. *The professor did not favor JACK.

I believe such examples are ill formed; but in any event, there is no way they can be interpreted like parallel cases with stressed <u>NOTHING</u>. That is, type Z vulgar minimizers do not show the double negative behavior of standard <u>no</u> forms.

2.3. Positive versus negative interrogative tags

A well-known test for the presence of negation first introduced in Klima (1964: 263–265) involves the possibility of a *positive* (negation-free) interrogative tag. Notably though, in this respect type Z vulgar minimizer structures behave like positive forms and contrast with both <u>no</u> forms and type A vulgar minimizer structures:

(24)   a. Janet read some book, *did/didn't she?
      b. Janet read no book, did/*didn't she?
      c. Janet didn't read squat, did/*didn't she?
      d. Janet read squat *did/didn't she?

2.4. Emphatics: <u>too/so</u> versus <u>(n)either</u>

A second known test for negation also found first in Klima (1964: 261–262) involves the possibility of emphatics of the form <u>(n)either</u>, as opposed to positive emphatics of the form <u>too/so</u>. And with respect to this test, too, type Z vulgar minimizer cases behave like positive forms and not like clear negative forms, which include <u>no</u> forms and type A vulgar minimizer expressions:

(25)   a. Janet read some book and Hilda read some book, too/*either.
      b. Janet read no book and Hilda read no book, *too/either.
      c. Janet didn't read squat and Hilda didn't read squat, *too/either.
      d. Janet read squat and Hilda read squat, too/*either.

e. Janet read some book and so/*neither did Hilda.
f. Janet read no book and *so/neither did Hilda.
g. Janet didn't read squat and *so/neither did Hilda.
h. Janet read squat and so/*neither did Hilda.

2.5. The not even + X strengthener

A third known test for negation also introduced in Klima (1964: 262–263) involves the possibility of the strengthening expression not even + X, which requires inter alia a syntactically negative 'antecedent'. Again type Z vulgar minimizers contrast with type A ones and manifest the behavior of non-negatives:

(26) a. Jane read some book yesterday (*, not even the assigned book).
b. Jane read no book yesterday (, not even the assigned book).
c. Jane didn't read squat yesterday (*, not even the assigned book).[5]
d. Jane read squat yesterday (*, not even the assigned book).

2.6. I don't believe/think parentheticals

A fourth test for negation involves parenthetical clauses with negation, which only can modify negation-containing clauses. And once more, type Z vulgar minimizer structures contrast with those that contain type A vulgar minimizers or uncontroversial negation-containing expressions:

(27) a. Jane read some book yesterday (*, I don't think).
b. Jane read no book yesterday (, I don't think).
c. Jane didn't read squat yesterday (, I don't think).
d. Jane read squat yesterday (*, I don't think).

2.7. 'Expression of agreement' clauses: So versus not

A fifth, perhaps less known test for negation, suggested to me by Haj Ross, involves elided clauses that express agreement with the content of a preceding clause. Such clauses manifest an initial yes + so if the clause 'agreed with' is positive but an initial no and final not if it is negative. Again, type Z vulgar minimizer structures manifest positive behavior:

(28) a. Jane read some book yesterday. Yes, I guess so/*No, I guess not.
b. Jane read no book yesterday. *Yes, I guess so/No, I guess not.
c. Jane didn't read squat yesterday. *Yes, I guess so/No, I guess not.
d. Jane read squat yesterday. Yes, I guess so./*No, I guess not.

2.8. Negative polarity licensing

Finally, as the now common jargon has it, no forms can *license* NPIs, a few of which are highlighted in (29):

(29)   a. Helga gave no magazines to *anyone*.
       b. Helga has said nothing to me *in years*.
       c. Helga learned nothing in any convent *at all*.

If then, Z type vulgar minimizers were <u>no</u> forms, they would be expected to also license NPIs. But the contrast between (29) and (30) shows they do not:[6]

(30)   a. *Helga gave squat to anyone.
       b. *Helga has said squat to me in years.
       c. *Helga learned squat in any convent at all.

2.9. Summary

Overall then, the evidence seems quite consistent and compelling. With respect to a range of fact types that independently differentiate negative from positive clauses, type Z vulgar minimizer forms fail to reveal any syntactic indication of involving negation and their containing clauses behave rigorously like positive clauses. Given their relation to type A minimizer forms, logical equivalences, and such, this might seem to yield a bit of a paradox. But the next section argues that it does not.

3. What type Z vulgar minimizers are

Taking it now as justified that type Z vulgar minimizers are *not* analyzable in the same way as <u>nothing</u> and do not even contain negatives, let us return to logically equivalent pairs like (31):

(31)   a. They don't understand squat.
       b. They understand squat.

While a priori it could have well seemed plausible to make sense of such pairs by taking type Z vulgar minimizers to be like <u>nothing</u> and type A ones to be like <u>anything</u>, it has been shown that the former assumption is untenable. How then one analyze type Z vulgar minimizers? My suggestion, stimulated by an idea in Déprez (1997) about certain French forms, is that they should be analyzed as containing a determiner that is not an invisible negation + <u>some</u> but rather an invisible cardinal numeral <u>zero</u>, as in (32):[7]

(32)   type Z <u>squat</u> = $[_{DP} [_D$ zero$] + [_N$ squat $]]$

This analysis motivates the terminology 'type Z vulgar minimizers' that has been adopted.

Analysis (32) permits capturing two crucial aspects of type Z vulgar minimizers. First, without any grammatically present negation, they end up, as required by the facts, being logically equivalent to <u>nothing</u>, given the independent existence of truth functional equivalences like (33):

THE STRUCTURE OF ONE TYPE OF AMERICAN ENGLISH VULGAR MINIMIZER   167

(33)   a. Joanne read no books   ↔   b. Joanne read zero books.

Second, the <u>zero</u> determiner analysis of type Z vulgar minimizers accounts for the fact that they behave grammatically like they contain no syntactic negatives, since they simply don't. More generally, type Z vulgar minimizer structures are seen to essentially share most of the properties of independently occurring DPs with the <u>zero</u> determiner, as (34) shows:

(34)   a. No woman drank *SQUAT/ZERO martinis.
       b. Penelope drank zero martinis/squat, did/*didn't she?
       c. Penelope drank zero martinis/squat and Francine drank zero martinis/ squat, too/ *neither.
       d. Penelope drank zero martinis/squat and so/*neither did Francine.
       e. *Penelope drank zero martinis/squat yesterday, not even weak martinis/ones.
       f. *Penelope drank zero martinis/squat yesterday, I don't think.
       g. Penelope drank zero martinis/squat yesterday. Yes, I guess so.
       h. *Penelope drank zero martinis/squat yesterday. No, I guess not.

The only real contrasts for my idiolect are that in (34a) and that, while as seen earlier, type Z vulgar minimizers cannot license NPIs, <u>zero</u> DPs can:

(35)   a. *Hector sent squat to any of his ex-wives.
       b. Hector sent zero presents to any of his ex-wives.

But as suggested in note 6, some speakers accept cases like (35a), so this may well be an idiosyncrasy of marginal significance. The difference in (34a) shows that type Z vulgar minimizers are more restricted than explicit <u>zero</u> forms with respect to such contrast structures. Since I do not understand such expressions very well, I will not try to say anything more about them.

4. McCawley's puzzle

4.1. The puzzle

McCawley (1998: 607) presented some observations about the distribution of the word <u>nothing</u> with respect to certain sentence properties often, as in section 2, taken since Klima's (1964) work to provide tests for the presence of negation. Specifically, McCawley discussed the contrast between (<u>n</u>)<u>either</u> and <u>so/too</u>, noting, as I did in section 2, that the former is only possible if the clause that actually contains it is negative in a relevant sense.

McCawley's currently relevant observation is that, unexpectedly, with <u>nothing</u> as an object (see later discussion for clarifications) but *not* with <u>no</u> forms in general, it is possible to have either <u>too</u> or <u>either</u>, apparently without meaning difference:

(36)   McCawley (1998: 607)
       a. John said nothing, and Mary said nothing, too.
       b. John said nothing and Mary said nothing, either.

In general, these forms are, of course, not *both* possible in the same context:

(37)   a. Jane cooked no reptile meat and Sheila cooked no reptile meat, either/*too.
       b. Ferdinand chased neither student and Otto chased neither student, either/*too.

Why (36a and b) are both possible is then quite mysterious and McCawley, noting the problematic character of (36a) for his assumptions, simply said: "I will leave this problem unresolved."

   The distinction in (36) is not isolated but illustrates a systematic possibility for the form <u>nothing</u>. Note initially:

(38)   a. John contributed *no idea/nothing and so did Mary. (See Jackendoff, 1972: 364.)
       b. John contributed no idea/nothing and neither did Mary.

4.2. A novel proposal

The analysis of type Z vulgar minimizers proposed in section 3 offers a new and intriguing way to look at the relevant exceptional alternation. For there is evidently an abstract similarity between the data of section 4.1 and that already encountered. In the case of type Z vulgar minimizers, one finds forms that in some vague sense seem to be negative or equivalent to negatives like <u>nothing</u> but behave according to syntactic tests for negation like non-negatives. Arguably, that is just what is found in (36a) and (38a). I suggest then that the two versions of (36) and (38) differ in that the one that can occur with <u>either</u> contains a negation, specifically an ordinary <u>no</u> form, while the one that can occur with <u>too</u> fails to contain a negation.

   What is it then? The answer that previous sections suggest at this point is that it has the structure of a type Z vulgar minimizer. This means that one could allow for a certain case in which the determiner <u>zero</u> + some vulgar minimizer stem is pronounced <u>nothing</u>, which then might have at least the two distinct analyses in (39):

(39)   a. <u>nothing</u> = $[_{DP} [_D \text{NEG} + \text{some}] + [_N \text{ thing }]]$
       b. <u>nothing</u> = $[_{DP} [_D \text{ zero}] + [_{N, \text{ vulgar minimizer}} \text{thing }]]$

Required then would be that at least one usage of <u>thing</u> be a member of the class of regular noun stems and also a member of the restricted class of vulgar minimizer nouns, one of which only takes the <u>zero</u> determiner.[8]

   A problem with (39b), though, is that it requires taking the vulgar minimizer stem that underlies the positive <u>nothing</u> to be an exception to the general rule that the D associated with a vulgar minimizer is phonologically null. And it requires ad hoc morphology that realizies the determiner <u>zero</u> as <u>no</u>.

   A superior alternative would then be to retain the view that that the null realization rule for Ds with vulgar minimizer nouns is absolute and to analyze the non-negative <u>nothing</u> instead slightly differently as in (40):

(40)   <u>nothing</u> = $[_{DP} [_D \text{ zero}] + [_{N, \text{ vulgar minimizer}} \text{nothing }]]$

Analysis (40) has the advantage over (39b) of not complicating the general rule for D invisibility with vulgar minimizer nouns. And it also requires no special irregular realization of the D as no.

Beyond the fact that the proposal to analyze the positive-behaving nothing as a type of vulgar minimizer DP immediately reduces McCawley's (1998) observation (36a) to regularity, it is strongly supported by a variety of other evidence, all of which shows that on one analysis nothing in positions like that of (36) behaves like a negative form and on another like a positive one.

4.3. Evidence for treating some instances of nothing as type Z vulgar minimizers

First, recall that at least in my idiolect type Z vulgar minimizers cannot license NPIs. If then the nothing that goes with too/so is not negative and has the structure of a type Z vulgar minimizer, while that which goes with (n)either is negative, one would expect that NPI licensing is possible for speakers like me only with the latter, which is correct:

(41) a. Claudia said nothing/*squat at any time and I said nothing at any time, either.
     b. *Claudia said nothing at any time and I said nothing at any time, too.
     c. Claudia said nothing at all and I said nothing at all, either.
     d. *Claudia said nothing at all and I said nothing at all, too.
     e. Claudia said nothing to anyone and *so/neither did I.

Second, while no forms can freely be the targets of so-called *negative fronting*, type Z vulgar minimizers cannot be. Notably, when nothing is a negative fronting target, only behavior consistent with the negative analysis is possible:

(42) Nothing/*Squat did Claudia say to Henry and nothing did Louise say, either/*too.

Third, as seen earlier, type Z vulgar minimizers do not, in contrast to negative forms, permit positive tags in questions but, again in contrast to negative forms, do permit negative tags. Notably, tags don't combine freely with too/either; when either is present, only the tag appropriate for a negative clause is possible:

(43) a. Jerome ate nothing and Stan ate nothing, either, *didn't/did he?
     b. Jerome ate nothing and Stan ate nothing, too, didn't/*did he?

Fourth, no forms but not type Z vulgar minimizers can be strengthened with not even phrases. Strikingly though, in the context here, that is possible only with either, not with too:

(44) The president said nothing and the vice president said nothing, either/*too, not even good-bye.

Fifth, <u>no</u> forms but not type Z vulgar minimizers permit negative parentheticals of the form <u>I don't believe/think</u>. And once more, such are compatible with <u>either</u> but not with <u>too</u>:

(45) a. The president said nothing and the vice president said nothing, either/*too, I don't think.
      b. The president said nothing and the vice president said nothing, either/too, I think.

Sixth, <u>no</u> forms but not type Z vulgar minimizers permit the negative version of the 'agreement' clause structure:

(46) a. Karen sent no gifts to them, did she? *Yes, I guess so/No, I guess not.
      b. Karen sent squat to them didn't she? Yes, I guess so/*No, I guess not.

And once more, in this context, <u>nothing</u> can behave like a type Z vulgar minimizer:

(47) a. Karen sent nothing to them, did she? *Yes, I guess so/No, I guess not.
      b. Karen sent nothing to them, didn't she? Yes, I guess so/*No, I guess not.

A different class of arguments can also support the claim that the positive-behaving instances of <u>nothing</u> should be analyzed in the same way as type Z minimizers. These arguments depend on various distributional restrictions on vulgar minimizers that are independent of negation.

First, such minimizers cannot appear as passive <u>by</u> phrase complements and indeed not in many types of PPs:

(48) a. Jerome was shocked by nothing/*squat.
      b. The riot was caused by nothing/*dick.
      c. That claim is supported by nothing/*jack.

Notably then, when found in these environments, occurrences of <u>nothing</u> show only negative behavior, not the positive behavior associated with type Z vulgar minimizers:

(49) a. Jerome was shocked by nothing, was/*wasn't he?[9]
      b. Jerome was shocked by nothing and Irma *was, too/wasn't, either.
      c. Jerome was shocked by nothing, (I don't think) (not even the deception).
      d. Jerome was shocked by nothing. *Yes, I guess so/No, I guess not.

(50) a. Herb sat on top of nothing/*squat.
      b. Herb leaned against nothing/*jack-shit.

(51) a. Herb sat on top of nothing, did/*didn't he?
      b. Herb sat on top of nothing and Jane *did, too/didn't, either.
      c. Herb sat on top of nothing (I don't think) (not even the table).
      d. Herb sat on top of nothing. *Yes, I guess so/No, I guess not.

Further, vulgar minimizers cannot occur as the *first* object of double object constructions:

(52) a. Cynthia gave nothing/*squat that sort of attention.
      b. Cynthia gave nothing/*jack-shit a glance.

And again, when <u>nothing</u> occurs in this environment, it cannot manifest positive behavior:

(53) a. Cynthia gave nothing that sort of attention, did/*didn't she?
      b. Cynthia gave nothing that sort of attention and Jane *did, too/didn't, either.
      c. Cynthia gave nothing that sort of attention (I don't think) (not even her finances).
      d. Cynthia gave nothing that sort of attention. *Yes, I guess so/No, I guess not.

In addition, vulgar minimizers do not permit modifying adjectives, relative clauses, or PPs:

(54) a. They sent nothing/*squat useful/ that I liked/of interest.
      b. They discussed nothing/*jack-shit important/ that I was concerned with/from your book.

And when <u>nothing</u> appears with modifiers, it cannot show positive behavior:

(55) a. They sent nothing useful/that I liked/of interest, did/*didn't they?
      b. Sally sent nothing useful/that I liked/of interest and Jerome *did, too/didn't, either.
      c. Sally sent nothing useful/that I liked/of interest (I don't think) (not even a book).
      d. Sally sent nothing useful/that I liked/of interest. *Yes, I guess so/No, I guess not.

Next, vulgar minimizers are incompatible with so-called *A-adverbs* like <u>absolutely</u>, <u>almost</u>, <u>nearly</u>, <u>just about</u>, <u>practically</u>, and <u>virtually</u>; see Horn (2000: 161); all of these combine happily with ordinary <u>no</u> forms:

(56) a. Harriet saw (*absolutely/*almost/*vitually) squat.
      b. Stan regrets (*just about/*practically) jack.
      c. Harriet saw (absolutely/almost/vitually) no cormorants.
      d. Stan regrets (just about/practically) no decision.

As expected at this point, when <u>nothing</u> is modified by an A-adverb, it can only show negative behavior:

(57) a. Harriet saw absolutely/almost nothing and Ruth saw absolutely/almost nothing, *too/either.
      b. Harriet saw absolutely/almost nothing, did/*didn't she?
      c. Harriet saw absolutely/almost nothing and *so/neither did Ruth.
      d. Harriet saw absolutely/almost nothing. *Yes, I guess so/No, I guess not.

Other environments for some reason preclude clear vulgar minimizers and when <u>nothing</u> appears in these environments, it must show negative behavior:

(58) a. Ted was near nothing/*squat.
      b. Ted was fond of nothing/*squat.

(59) a. Ted was near nothing, was/*wasn't he?
      b. Ted was near nothing and Irma *was, too/wasn't, either.
      c. Ted was near nothing (I don't think) (not even a water fountain).
      d. Ted was near nothing. *Yes, I guess so/No, I guess not.

(60) a. Ted was fond of nothing, was/*wasn't he?
      b. Ted was fond of nothing and Irma *was, too/wasn't, either.
      c. Ted was fond of nothing (I don't think) (not even poetry).
      d. Ted was fond of nothing. *Yes, I guess so/No, I guess not.

It is also the case that for me, type Z vulgar minimizers cannot appear as predicate nominals. And when <u>nothing</u> does, it must show negative behavior:

(61) a. As for that scratch, it is nothing/*squat
      b. It turned into nothing/*jack-shit.

(62) a. That scratch is nothing, is/*isn't it.
      b. The first scratch was nothing and the second *was, too/wasn't, either
      c. The scratch was nothing (I don't think) (not even an annoyance).
      d. The scratch was nothing. *Yes, I guess so/No, I guess not.

Finally, vulgar minimizers seem to be barred from *subject* positions; and when <u>nothing</u> appears there, it cannot display positive behavior:

(63) a. Nothing/*Squat happened.
      b. For nothing/*squat to go wrong would be surprising.
      c. Nothing happened, did/*didn't it?
      d. Nothing happened yesterday and nothing happened today, *too/either.
      e. Nothing happened yesterday. *Yes, I guess so/No, I guess not.

4.4. Conclusion

I hope to have shown in this section that the curious behavior of the form <u>nothing</u> noted by McCawley receives a rather elegant account if it is recognized that in addition to a standard analysis as a DP with a negative quantifier D, <u>nothing</u> has a distinct analysis under which it is in effect a type Z vulgar minimizer based on a noun stem <u>nothing</u> taking the same <u>zero</u> D as other type Z vulgar minimizers. If this account is viable, it shows that the study of vulgar minimizers not only is of interest in itself but also impacts in a positive way the treatment of more standard English forms.

The Openness of Natural Languages

1. Curious implications

It might seem plausible to the nonspecialist that a given NL, NL_x permits one to report linguistic performances, both performances of NL_x elements and those of NLs distinct from NL_x. By "reporting linguistic performances" I refer to nothing more arcane than forming statements like "Amanda just shouted, "Where's my baby?"" It might also seem to a nonspecialist that NL_x permits one to do descriptive linguistics, not only the descriptive linguistics of NL_x but also that of other distinct NLs. By "doing descriptive linguistics" I mean nothing more exotic than forming sentences like "The German word for 'air force' is 'Luftwaffe.'" But while these nonspecialist assumptions might seem not only plausible but also self-evidently true, modern linguistics in its dominant instantiation, *generative grammar*, in fact denies both these claims. Of course, it does this only implicitly and most advocates of generative grammar may be unaware that its doctrines taken literally preclude what any nonspecialist would assume possible. Readers who do not easily accept this conclusion will find their skepticism addressed in what follows, for a major goal of this study is to justify in detail the claim that generative grammar has the evidently intolerable implications just mentioned.

2. Background

Near the beginning of the *generative grammar* movement in linguistics the following claims were made (all emphases mine: PMP):

(1) a. Chomsky (1959: 137)

"A language is a collection of sentences of *finite length* all constructed from a *finite alphabet* (or, where our concern is limited to syntax, a *finite vocabulary*) of symbols."

b. Chomsky (1959: 137)

"Since any language L in which we are likely to be interested is an infinite set, we can investigate the structure of L only through the study of the finite devices (grammars) *which are capable of generating its sentences.*"

c. Chomsky (1959: 138)

"The weakest condition that can significantly be placed on grammars is that F be included in the class of general, unrestricted Turing machines."

Characterization (1a) clearly was not meant to introduce some arbitrary notion 'language' but rather assumed that NLs fell under the conditions given:

(2) Chomsky (1957: 13)

"I will consider a *language* to be a set (finite or infinite) of sentences, each finite in length and constructed out of a finite set of elements. All natural languages in their spoken or written form are languages in this sense, since each natural language has a finite number of phonemes (or letters in its alphabet) and each sentence is representable as a finite sequence of these phonemes (or letters)."

That is, it was in effect claimed in (1a) inter alia:

(3) a. Every NL sentence is finite in size (therefore, e.g., in length).
     b. Every NL sentence is exclusively formed from a fixed, finite vocabulary of symbols.
     c. Every NL is an infinite collection.
     d. Every NL can be generated (recursively enumerated).

Given (3a, b), it is plausible, although not necessary, that the sentence collections that define NLs form (recursively) enumerable sets,[1] and hence (3d) and (1c) might well be true. But they might also be false and (3a, b), interpreted as factual claims about NLs, might also be false. If so, (3d) would be false and hence (1c) would also be false.

However, as observed in Langendoen and Postal (1984: 15), Chomsky then gave no arguments or evidence for (3a, b, d) in the 1950s. Nor has he since. This meant that in the mid- to late 1950s, claim (1c) was *question begging*. Chomsky's never interrupted and current maintenance of it (see later discussion) is arguably *worse*. For Langendoen and Postal (1984, 1985) rejected all of these claims, focusing in particular on (3a, d), and offered a purported proof (whose conclusion was named *the NL Vastness Theorem*) that any NL with productive coordination, that is, apparently every NL, including English, was not only not an enumerable set but also not a set at all. Rather full collections of NL sentences were concluded to be what logicians call *proper classes*; see, for example, Stoll (1979: 319). And it was argued that this was true because, inter alia, NLs not only have individual sentences that are not finite but also contain, contrary to (3a), infinite-sized sentences of every (nonfinite) cardinality.

Purported proofs can, obviously, contain flaws. But these results were reviewed in major journals and, while they were hardly welcomed, no reviewer claimed to have found any error in the argument.[2] Rather, even the unenthusiastic reviews by and large somewhat grudgingly admitted that the argument seemed sound. Moreover, while eighteen years have passed since the publication of the arguments in question, to my knowledge no one has since even claimed to have shown that they were erroneous. Like any proof, that in Langendoen and Postal (1984, 1985) involved fixed premises and a logic. To reject the conclusion, a rational critic would have to reject at least one of these. But the logic of the proof was almost entirely that of a fundamental result in set theory, *Cantor's Theorem*.[3] It stretches plausibility, to say the least, to imagine that *this* aspect of the argument can be undermined. That leaves a rational critic with only two choices: either accept the conclusion or find grounds for rejecting the premise. No one has done the latter and yet the conclusion seems not to be accepted.

In particular, although the formulation in Langendoen and Postal (1984) was specifically and explicitly aimed at Chomsky's various formulations, he has never, to my knowledge, addressed the result.[4] Instead, despite a history of speaking of his own work as "rational inquiry" and sometimes disparaging other work in linguistics as lacking this virtue,[5] he has throughout the intervening period continued to assume, without justification and without dealing with the counterargument, that nothing precludes taking an NL to involve (in fact, as in [4], to *be*) a computational procedure that recursively enumerates a set of expressions.[6] This view is strongly embedded in his so-called minimalist program, which entirely postdates Langendoen and Postal (1984, 1985). So, for instance:

(4)   Chomsky and Lasnik (1995: 14–15)
       "We may think of the language, then, as a finitely specified generative procedure (function) that enumerates an infinite set of SDs. Each SD, in turn, specifies the full array of phonetic, semantic, and syntactic properties of a particular linguistic expression."

But of course, unless the argument of Langendoen and Postal (1984, 1985) is refuted, claim (4) is just what a rational person *cannot* think, since:

(5)   Langendoen and Postal (1984: 72): The NL Nonconstructivity Theorem
       No NL has any constructive (= proof-theoretic, generative, or Turing machine) grammar.

Conclusion (5) is evidently a trivial consequence of the NL Vastness Theorem.

So it appears that the argument of Langendoen and Postal (1984, 1985) to the effect that NLs are (i) not recursively enumerable sets and (ii) are not sets at all and hence (iii) have no generative/constructive/Turing machine grammars, although both factually and logically unchallenged, was too arcane and too much in conflict with deeply held a priori beliefs to be taken seriously within contemporary linguistic theory. The arcane aspect was localized in two points: First, the argument depends on granting the existence of *nonfinite* sentences,[7] whereas the unargued prejudice that all NL sentences are finite is very strong in linguistics.[8] Second, the argument assumed an axiom about the productivity of coordination, a claim that the class of, for example, declarative sentences is closed under coordination, which was not hitherto recognized. From this *closure axiom*, appealing to Cantor's Theorem, the existence of nonfinite sentences can be proven. Now, given these arcane aspects and given the sociological fact that the substantively unchallenged argument has not been accepted, it would be significant if it could be shown *independently of these seeming truths* that NLs fail to be recursively enumerable sets, hence (must) fail to have constructive grammars, on other, less arcane grounds. I believe this can be done by focusing on claim (3b), largely passed over in Langendoen and Postal (1984). Given that no argument or evidence was presented for this in 1959 or since, it obviously should *also* be a major point of suspicion.

The goal of this chapter is to show that (3b) is false; hence by *asserting* (1a) without argument the author had then begged and has continued simply to beg the question in a way Langendoen and Postal (1984) mostly *ignored* of whether NLs could have generative/constructive grammars. By focusing on (3b) it will be possible to present a different type of argument for the claim that no NL has a generative/constructive/proof-theoretic grammar. The attraction of the newer form of argument is that, unlike that of Langendoen and Postal (1984, 1985), it depends neither on recognizing nonfinite sentences nor on accepting the axiom about coordinate closure appealed to there. Moreover, the new argument also does not inherently stand on the conclusion that each NL includes more than $\aleph_0$ sentences, although it provides independent grounds for the latter conclusion. So the goal of this study is to establish the earlier conclusion on different and possibly less controversial grounds.

3. Fixed, finite lexicons

Focus on claim (3b) built into (1), which requires that the sentences of NL NL_i are formed exclusively from forms listed (hence listable) in a fixed, finite lexicon of NL_i (hereafter: LX_i). This doctrine enunciated by its author more than forty years ago and never abandoned by him is maintained in, for example, (6):[9]

(6)   Chomsky (2000c: 120)
       "The I-language consists of a computational procedure and a lexicon. The lexicon is a
       collection of items, each a complex of properties (called features), such as the property
       bilabial stop or artifact. The computational procedure selects items from the lexicon and
       forms an expression, a more complex array of such features."

The author thus makes it clear that the computational procedure he posits as characterizing an NL (or, in his terms, as being an NL) operates by finding items in a lexicon, that is, in some kind of finite list.

One can state the doctrine a bit more precisely, if still informally, as in (7a) or (7b):

(7)   a. For every NL NL_i, every *minimal form* of every sentence of NL_i either is drawn from
          LX_i, or is computable from grammatical mappings of other forms drawn from LX_i.

b. Let a grammar G be some full computational specification of an NL, NL₁ and let F be any arbitrarily chosen minimal form in an arbitrary well-formed sentence of NL₁. Then G *mentions* F.

By 'minimal form' I mean roughly what are called morphemes. The notion 'mentions' of (7b) can be made quite precise in terms of set membership. For instance, one could identify the G of (7b) with an arbitrary *Turing machine* defined as in (8):

(8) Partee, ter Meulen, and Wall (1993: 508)
"A Turing machine M is a quadruple (K, Σ, s, δ), where K is a finite set of states, Σ is a finite set (the alphabet) containing #, s $\in$ K is the initial state, and δ is a (partial) function from K $\times$ Σ to K $\times$ ($\Sigma \cup \{L, R\}$)."

Then to say that G mentions some minimal form F is to say that F either is a member of K or is one of the symbols in the "situations" defined by the partial functions. More perspicaciously perhaps for linguists, one can take advantage of the equivalence of Turing machines and Type 0 grammars (Partee, ter Meulen, and Wall, 1993: 514) and take "mention" to mean that F is one of the nondesignated (e.g., not the arrow) symbols of one of the rules of a Type 0 grammar (that is, an unrestricted rewriting system).

To illustrate the notions, consider that infinitesimally tiny but infinite subpart of English whose initial members are represented by (9):

(9) a. My father died.
     b. My father's father died.
     c. My father's father's father died.
     d. My father's father's father's father died.
     e. My father's father's father's father's father died.

Evidently, the collection of which (9) specifies an initial sequence consists of all and only those sentences of the form (10), where $(X)^*$ is the so-called *Kleene star notation*, which denotes any finite string composed exclusively of occurrences of the symbol string in parentheses in that order:

(10) My + (father+'s)*+ father + die+ ed

A partial grammar of this collection might be given by a totally ad hoc and unprincipled phrase structure grammar of the form (11):

(11) a. S → DP + Verb
      b. DP → my +GenDP + father
      c. GenDP → GenDP + GenDP
      d. GenDP → DP + 's
      e. DP+s → father + 's
      f. Verb → die + ed

Now, assuming that the sentences in (9) consist of all and only the minimal forms my, father, 's, die, and ed, it is clear that every minimal form in the collection (9) is mentioned in (11), in that my and father are among the symbols of rule (11b), 's is one of the symbols of rule (11d), and die and ed are among the symbols of rule (11f).

Let us say then:

(12)   An NL is *closed* if and only if
       a. there is some finite grammar of $NL = G_{NL}$ such that
       b. every minimal form of every sentence of NL is mentioned in G_{NL}.

A still simpler, essentially equivalent way of saying this would be (13a):

(13)   a. An NL is *closed* if and only if there exists some finite list of all the minimal forms of every sentence of NL
       b. An NL is *open* if and only if it is *not* closed.

Clearly, for any collection of sentences, hence any NL, to be enumerable, minimally it must be closed, for devices that recursively enumerate sets, that is, Turing machines or their equivalents, are self-contained. They can only compute an output member of the set to be enumerated by combining elements from a given fixed list, as in claim (6). For (3d) to be true then, it is necessary that NLs be closed.[10] Evidently, the subpart of English specified in (9) is closed. But this tells us nothing about English as a whole.

The essence of the question begging involved in claim (1a)/(6) necessary to justify (3d) is then that its author has never argued that full NLs are closed; nor has anyone else to my knowledge. In what follows I try to show that this logical gap in any argument for (1c)/(3d) cannot be filled for the simple reason that NLs are open, moreover, richly open, in several distinct ways.

4. Direct speech

In the 1951 science fiction film *The Day the Earth Stood Still*, a recently arrived space alien (played by Michael Rennie) at one point speaks to his giant flying saucer defense robot (named Gort). One could report that linguistic event as in (14):

(14)   The space alien said 'klaatu barrada nikto' to Gort.

Example (14) is one of endlessly many sentences of a perfectly well known variety. These contain a complement of a familiar type called *direct discourse* or *direct speech*. It is a standard and quite traditional notion with a traditional Latin name. So Jespersen (1924: 290) indicates: "When one wishes to report what someone else says or has said (thinks or has thought)—or what one has said or thought oneself on some previous occasion—two ways are open to one. Either one gives, or purports to give, the exact words of the speaker (or writer): *direct speech* (oratio recta)." Trask (1993: 83) defines direct speech as "[t]he reporting of what someone has said by quoting her/his exact words, as in 'What time is it?', she asked . . ." The difference between (14) and Trask's example is that the former purports to report the exact words of an instance of performance in a (presumed for argument) NL distinct from that of the report.

In view of this difference, let us informally distinguish three types of direct speech:

(15) a. *a domestic direct speech segment* (*DDSS*): a piece of reported speech that is purported to be in the same NL as the containing report.
b. *a foreign direct speech segment* (*FDSS*): a piece of reported speech that is purported to be in an NL distinct from the containing report
c. *a nonlinguistic direct speech segment* (*NLDSS*): a piece of reported noise that is not purported to be in any NL.

Category (15c) is intended to allow for reports of, for example, noises by animals, noises of inanimate origin, tornadoes, explosions, trains, squeaking doors, and so forth.

Consider now a purported constructive grammar $G_{English}$ of one of the multitude of NLs referred to as "English," say, my English, in which (14) might be a sentence. Since (14) is by assumption an English sentence, then if (3d) is true, $G_{English}$ generates (14) and every other sentence of English, and if so, as already argued, English would have to be closed.

The problem is that any derivation that involves any computational procedure/ Turing machine, for example, that postulated by Chomsky, will fail to yield (14) unless it is able to find the FDSS klaatu barrada nikto (or all of its components if any; see later discussion) in $LX_{English}$.

Keeping doctrine (3d) consistent with data like (14) will apparently (but see later discussion) then require at a minimum maintaining the disjunction in (16):

(16) Either:
a. (14) is *not* an English sentence, or
b. The FDSS 'klaatu barrada nikto' (or its components [if any]) is listed in/an element of $LX_{English}$, that is, is mentioned by $G_{English}$.

Consider first (16a). This would follow from the more general:

(17) (14) is not an NL sentence.

The problem with any attempt to maintain (16a) is this: Surely if, contrary to (17), (14) *is* an NL sentence, it is an English sentence and not, for example, a Turkish or space alienese one. However, (14) seems quite well formed in my English. There is no intuitive fact to ground any rejection of its grammaticality. One does not teach children or foreigners to avoid such constructions. One does not correct such examples. Even the most extreme purist who bemoans linguistic deterioration would never cite examples like (14) as evidence. Popular grammarians never point to such examples as part of their prescriptive enterprise. And as already seen, traditional grammatical discussion recognizes their existence and assigns them to a type (*oratio recta*). There is then no direct factual basis for denial that (14) and similar examples are part of English. Thus (16a) is groundless.

One can then turn to (16b). If doctrine (3b) has any content, then a straightforward interpretation of (16b) is evidently not tenable. For all of (18a–f) and the endlessly many other cases relevantly like them have exactly the same status as (14):

(18)   a. The space alien said 'slatu niraba miktu' to Gort.
      b. The space alien said 'tlato sniraba fiktu' to Gort.
      c. The space alien said 'drato zimboto shiktu' to Gort.
      d. The space alien said 'snato jikmoti puroboton yablotofoo korodor' to Gort.
      e. The space alien said 'grato shilt buzu ftmakvrss muktmwik rabsidobad vagomasitor' to Gort.
      f. The space alien said 'vngmssptkfookytz' to Gort.

If the notion of fixed, finite lexicon is to have any substance at all, that is, if it is genuinely to be part of a computational procedure, the FDSSs of (14), (18), and so on, clearly could not be elements of an included lexicon. For an interpretation of (3b) under which it is consistent with the inclusion of all of these forms is an interpretation under which the notion 'fixed lexicon' excludes nothing. A 'lexicon' needed to cover (14), (18), and so on, could hardly even meet the minimal condition of being finite, given a lack of length bound on pieces of direct speech; see Langendoen and Postal (1984: chapter 3) for a general discussion of the nonexistence of length bounds of any sort in NLs. So nothing precludes distinct, arbitrarily long FDSSs or NLDSSs, of, for example, the form:

(19)   a. The foreigner screamed 'neeeeeeeeeeeeeeeeeeeeeeeeeeeeeeeee. . . .'
      b. The cow went 'moo'/'mooo'/'moooo'/'mooooo'/'moooooo . . .'

That is, there is no viable reason to believe that while, for example, English permits reporting as in (19a) human expressions or as in (19b) cow noises of various lengths, at some point there is a human or cow noise too long to be reported. What rule of English fixes a maximum length on reportable noises? Since it is impossible to specify an actual bound, the answer must be "none." In short, and for several reasons, it is then impossible for every piece of direct speech, every DDSS, FDSS, and NLDSS, to be mentioned in the grammar of any NL.

The points just made were in essence, as I am grateful to Geoffrey K. Pullum for reminding me, noted by Harris (1979) in remarks that subsequent linguistics seems to have ignored (and so, inter alia, never refuted); note the failure of Chomsky's major linguistic works subsequent to Harris (1979), for example, Chomsky (1981, 1986a, 1986b, 1988, 1995b, 2000c), to even reference it.

(20)   Harris (1979: 10–12)
      "Hence the set of sentences, as sequences of elements in a finite discrete set, is denumerably infinite, even though it will be seen below that the matter is complicated by the fact that the set of sentences is not well-defined and is not even a proper part of the set of word sequences."

Harris inserts here a footnote, his 11:

The latter is due to the fact that there are sentences which contain sound sequences that are not words: Any sound can be the subject of a sentence of the form X *is a sound, X is his name, X_1 and X_2 are different sounds even though we cannot hear the difference* (5.4), etc. The set of objects that occupies the positions of X here, and so the set of sentences of the above forms, is not discretely differentiated (aside front the limits of discrimination of hearing and perception) and not necessarily denumerable.

Harris makes it clear here that (i) direct speech expressions can in principle be parts of grammatical sentences, that is, grammaticality will fail only when the non–direct speech portions are improperly formed; and (ii) that for that reason alone, the collection of sentences is not well defined and does not form a recursively enumerable set. He also raised the possibility that the NLs were thereby not denumerable sets but hedged with "not necessarily." Implicit in Harris's remarks is, of course, the claim that NLs are not closed.

While Harris's insightful claims are certainly correct as far as they go, they are too terse to really do justice to the major implications they have. He did not address various indirect moves to which a defender of the closed status of NLs might attempt to appeal.

For despite what has been implied so far, there might seem to be a way of keeping the grammaticality of even infinitely many pieces of embedded direct speech consistent with a finite lexicon. This might appeal to some idea like the vague, undeveloped, repeated claim by Chomsky that an NL grammar assigns a structure to "every possible relevant physical event":

(21)   a. Chomsky (1986b: 26): "[T]he I-language assigns a status to every relevant physical event, say every sound wave."
        b. Chomsky (2000c: 79): "[I]t could turn out that it assigns a specific interpretation to every possible signal."

The application to the issue I am discussing here would be something like this: While it could be granted that there are infinitely many pieces of direct speech, and that these occur as parts of well-formed NL sentences, it could be claimed that (i) these pieces of direct speech are themselves recursively enumerable because (ii) every piece of direct speech merely involves some finite combination drawn from a *fixed finite phonetic alphabet*. An idea like this has already been proposed in passing by Green (1985: 123–124).[11]

These assumptions would permit taking the direct speech piece in, for example, (14) to consist neither of an arbitrary single unit nor of a sequence of, say, three such units. Rather, every direct speech sequence would consist of a fixed string of phonetic elements and every such string could be generated by a trivial infinite grammar finitely schematizable via the Kleene star notation as in (22): The notion 'schematizable' here can be given a precise interpretation in terms of *metagrammars*, computational devices that generate infinite collections interpreted as grammars. For this conception of finite grammars that generate nonfinite grammars, see Langendoen (1976).

(22)   Direct Speech → (Phonetic Segment)*

This assumes the existence of some grammatical category Direct Speech and a recursively enumerable set of phonetic segments. The latter assumption might be claimed to have a certain plausibility if one limits its application to direct speech that involves purely linguistic performances. However, it is by no means obviously true, even for this class. The limited view itself is challenged in Pullum (1983). If there is such a thing, though, then the claim could be that the computational grammar would specify all and only the positions where the category Direct Speech could appear, for example, after verbs like say, whisper, yell, and so on, and after nouns like sound, utterance, form, expression, and such. It would then be necessary to expand the notion of lexicon to include not only the *listed* minimal forms but the entire computational output of (22) plus the principles that spell out the fixed set of phonetic segments.

This would no doubt induce complications in particular versions of the doctrine under attack here. Viewing, for example, klaatu barrada nikto as made up *syntactically* of each of its phonetic segments seems entirely artificial. Is one, for instance, to maintain claims such as that all branching is binary by asserting that this has a huge number of alternative binary bracketings?[12] Further, how are these putative syntactic constituents to be analyzed so as to be consistent with other putative universal constraints on tree structures, for example, X bar theories? In addition, normal syntactic constituents have meanings, but analyzing direct speech into syntactic constituents the size of phonetic segments precludes any assignment of meanings to these constituents.

Finally, it is arguable that entire direct speech segments have meanings, as discussed in section 9, and if this is so, but their syntactic components do *not*, then claims about compositionality also run afoul of these cases. The obvious argument for the claim that direct speech segments have meanings is that, for example, (23a, b), (23c, d), and even (23e, f) (see [23g]) embody distinct propositions, a key point to which I will return:

(23)   a. Elmer grunted 'you'll never take me alive'.
       b. Elmer grunted 'you'll never make me a hive'.
       c. Ellen snarled 'snedo'.
       d. Ellen snarled 'fneto'.
       e. The cow went 'moooo'.
       f. The cow went 'mooooooooooo'.
       g. Don't be silly! The cow went 'moooo,' not 'mooooooooooo'.

But despite these problems, it might still be concluded that any notion that direct speech clashes fundamentally with the claim that NL grammars can be computational has been successfully gotten around.

But even were this approach capable of rendering direct speech compatible with the idea that NL grammars can be proof-theoretic in the case of DDSSs and FDSSs, it still seems hopeless for NLDSSs, since the view that there is a universal computational alphabet capable of representing every nonlinguistic noise that can be reported with direct speech seems impossible to take seriously. I will not belabor this point here since it is taken up in a more general context in section 6 and, as considered in

the following sections, the idea of a purely computational account of performance
reports faces distinct and, if anything, worse problems.

5. Gestural performance

Even if one ignores the direct speech reporting of nonlinguistic noises and accepts
the possibility of a recursive enumeration of phonetic segments for spoken NLs along
the lines of (22), this would *not* suffice to solve the problem of direct speech for a
view that NLs are closed. The reasons involve first nonspoken NLs, for example, the
multitude of signed NLs of the deaf. Even the author of (1), who in the past had written
as if NLs and phonetically performed NLs were coextensive, as in (21a), has recently
said:

(24)   Chomsky (2000c: 121)
    a. "Though highly specialized, the language faculty is not tied to specific sensory
       modalities."
    b. "Thus the sign language of the deaf is structurally much like spoken language."[13]

Given, though, the fact that some NLs systematically use nonphonetic gestures to
create tokens of their sentences, to maintain a claim that NLs as such are closed
even in the face of direct speech, it cannot suffice for there to be a recursive enumeration of *phonetic* segments relevant only for the subgroup of NLs that are in
standard circumstances performed via sound. Rather, under the assumption that
there are analogs of direct speech constituents in nonspoken NLs,[14] there would
have to be as well a recursive enumeration of a gestural equivalent of discrete
phonetic segments for every physical gesture that could underlie the performance
of any nonspoken NL.

   Far from being plausible, this seems chimerical. That it is might well be implicit
in the claim cited in Perlmutter (1986: 523) that pertains to signing:

(25)   Whitney (1875/1979)
    "Among their manifold capacities, they are able to make *gestures, of infinite variety,*
    all of which are reported by the vibrations of the luminous ether to a certain appre-
    hending organ, the eye, both of the maker and of others." (emphasis mine: PMP)

In any event, anyone who claims that there is a recursive enumeration of the gestures capable of serving as parts of performances of *all* signed NLs bears the heavy
(and to my knowledge never assumed) burden of supporting such an idea.

   Second, it can be argued that the demarcation between phonetically expressed
NLs and others like the gesturally signed NLs of the deaf is incomplete. This means
that the logic that shows how gesturally expressed NLs attack the notion that NLs
are closed can be applied *internal to standard phonetically expressed NLs.* That is, I
claim that even basically phonetically expressed NLs like English allow restricted
gestural and other nonvocal forms of expression, specifically in certain direct speech
and related contexts. So there is every reason to take, for example, (26a and b) to be

schemas for endlessly many *English* sentences whose next to final constituent is gesturally signed:

(26) a. The deaf person went ___ yesterday.
      b. The deaf person made the gesture ___ in the living room.

To perform a relevant instance of (26a) one articulates the first four words and then makes at that point (corresponding to the dashes) a gesture appropriately identical to that which is being reported, then pronounces <u>yesterday</u>. Other examples of the same type that have nothing to do with NLs associated with the deaf include (27b), a truth functional equivalent of (27a):

(27) a. When the cop told her to leave, Sheila gave him the finger (twice).
      b. When the cop told her to leave, Sheila went ___ (speaker makes the appropriate gesture) (twice).

So, barring a factually unmotivated claim that instantiations of schemas (26a, b), (27b), and so on are not NL sentences (e.g., sentences of English in this case), to maintain Chomsky's claim (3b) requires again the posit of a recursive enumeration of gestures.

6. Beyond gestures

I have so far considered the implications for claim (3b) of types of NL sentences that involve direct speech and nonphonetic gestural performance. But the situation for a defender of NL closure is more threatening than that entailed by these phenomena. First, as already touched on, there are NL sentences that bear certain similarities to direct speech structures but involve reference not to linguistic performance, that is, in the standard case, to utterances taken to perform sentences, but to other sorts of noises, either vocally produced or not. For instance, (28a) might be a schema of descriptions of the noise made by a person afflicted with serious snoring, while (28b) might schematize the description of the noise associated with a tornado:

(28) a. He goes ___.
      b. It gives off a roar like ___.

The relevance of such cases is that even though the material schematized by the blanks in (28) involves proper performance via the creation of sound waves, there is, evidently, no reason at all to imagine that the full range of such performances is coded by anything like a universal phonetic alphabet. That is, there is no reason to believe that, for example, the class of examples illustrated in (29) that purport to indicate bump-induced car noises is a priori specifiable in a linguistic way:

(29) Pullum and Scholz (2001: 17)
      My car goes 'ehhrgh' when I go over a bump.

This position is consistent with the observation of Kathol and Levine (1993: 210, note 7): "Thus inarticulate cries, imitations of animal or industrial noises, indeed anything producible by the human vocal tract can appear within the fronted quotation."

The point is strengthened if, as, I would claim, it is correct to see such schemas as (28) and the quoted part of cases like (29) as covering NL sentences where the blanks or quoted material are performed even *without* human vocal apparatus, for example, by clapping, or utilizing an arbitrary mechanical means of producing sounds, orchestras, guitars, machine guns, or whatnot. That is, I suggest that while it is certainly proper to perform (29) by making a vocal noise after the word goes, it is just as proper to perform it by playing a recording of actual car noises in that position and just before one pronounces when I go over a bump. If so, any possibility of reducing such cases to consistency with (3b) via analogs of (22) is out of the question.

Support for the view that NL sentences can involve nonvocal apparatus noise is provided by the remarks in (30) about metalinguistic negation:

(30)   Horn (1985: 136, note 12)
       "As Barbara Abbott has pointed out to me, *u* need not even be a specifically linguistic utterance, as seen by the function of metalinguistic negation in the following musical scenario:
       Piano student plays passage in manner μ.
       Teacher: 'It's not [plays passage in manner μ] __ It's [plays same passage in manner μ'].'"

Here Horn's μ, μ' denote some physical characteristics of piano-playing performances. While Horn does not assert that the teacher has performed NL *sentences*, using only the term scenario, his discussion only makes sense on that assumption.

For he is taking the examples to support his view about the nature of metalinguistic negation. This would be illogical unless the performances in question were instances of performance of NL sentences. If the entities involved were *not* NL sentences, that is, not part of the NL being discussed, how could they positively support a claim about the way metalinguistic negation is to be analyzed in that NL? That is, if no NL sentences are involved in the scenarios, they could no more support a claim about metalinguistic negation than, for example, (31a, b) can support a claim that English has verb final transitive clauses:

(31)   a. *Melissa will her roommate cheat.
       b. *The government should the elderly support.

Second, I see, moreover, nothing in the structure of NL itself that limits cases like (28) to *sounds*. For instance, the written medium can be seen to bring out the fact that, again in a regimented set of contexts, even regularly phonetically signed NLs allow graphic or geometric realizations of certain constituents. Thus I claim that (32a and b) *schematize* endlessly many *English* sentences, where the blank denotes some *shape*; one of these can be represented on paper as in (32c):

(32)   a. The professor drew ___ on the blackboard.
        b. The professor drew a figure of the form ___ on the blackboard.
        c. The professor drew a figure of the form Ⓟ on the blackboard.

Each distinct instance of (32a) can be performed by articulating the first three words, then providing some representation of the geometric form and then pronouncing the final three words. For (32b), one pronounces the first eight words, then somehow instantiates the figure and then pronounces the final three words. Hence one instance of (32a) will be truth functionally equivalent to (33):

(33)   The professor drew a circle with the letter *P* in it on the blackboard.

Actual instances of such sentences are found, even in the linguistic literature. Here is one from a recent monograph:

(34)   Culicover (1999: 28)
        "Conversely, the fact that *hotdog* means

        is not predictable from 'hot', 'dog' or the combination."

I see no reason beyond a priori dogma for denying that Culicover has as much instantiated an English sentence with (34) as he did with his following remark, which incorporated no image.

    To avoid an arbitrary claim that (32a and b) do not represent actual NL sentences and that (32c) and (34) are not written representations of actual sentences, maintenance of (3b) would then require not only a recursive enumeration of gestures but also an enumeration of all the geometric forms that could be covered by (32a and b). Given the uncountable character of even the collection of all planar (two-dimensional) forms, whose number is of the order of the real numbers, this is impossible.[15]

    Moreover, any restriction to just *two* dimensions seems artificial, since (35a) could be a truth functional equivalent of one instance of (35b):

(35)   a. The sculptor carved something of the form of a cube out of sandstone.
        b. The sculptor carved something of the form ___ out of sandstone.
        c. The device produced a three-dimensional image just like ___.

To perform a relevant instance of (35b), one pronounces the first seven words, then displays a cube, then pronounces the last three words. The way to perform an instance of (35c) is to pronounce the first eight words and then to in some way introduce the relevant image, for example, by turning on multiple slide projectors, by displaying a holograph, by holding mirrors in a certain way, and so on. But, since the number of three-dimensional objects is, via the logic of note 15, of the order of real numbers, it follows that the class of constituents schematized in (35b, c) is also of that order.

7. Metalinguistic structures

A type of linguistic information-representing sentence distinct from all the various 'direct speech' varieties is relevant to questions of openness, a type represented by, for example, (36):

(36)   a. The French word for milk is 'lait'.
       b. To express ignorance of some topic, one can say in French 'va savoir'.
       c. German 'Kopf' is equivalent to French 'tête'.

Such examples, like standard direct speech representation cases, contain parts that seem to involve NL elements. The difference is that a direct speech sentence purports to describe a particular *performance*; the direct speech report references an object with space/time coordinates. The foreign parts of examples like (36), however, are not putative descriptions of any performance of the NLs referenced. They purport instead to denote elements of those NLs themselves. Let us refer to the relevant parts of such examples as *metalinguistic constituents*.

Clearly, examples like (36) that contain metalinguistic constituents are common and intuitively entirely grammatical. Any denial of their well-formedness would be an act of desperation. Notably, those whose theoretical position might demand such a rejection utilize metalinguistic examples like (36) en masse, without the slightest indication that they are in any way abnormal. Some examples from Chomsky (1988), which contains by a rough count more than *two hundred and forty* others, are displayed in (37):

(37)   a. "The verb *examinar* requires an object, . . ." (page 95)
       b. "One of the traces must be bound by *nos* and the other by *al que*." (page 96)[16]
       c. "Thus (2) must be understood in the manner of (8a), not (8b) (where *lo* stands for *el hombre*)." (page 98)
       d. "Let us first take the case in which the clitic attaches to *afeitar*, forming *afeitarse*." (page 86)

Denial that (37a–d) are English sentences would have such implications as that touched on in section 1, namely, that it would not be possible to express the linguistics of NL_1 in any NL distinct from NL_1.

Given that metalinguistic expressions occur in grammatical sentences, the question arises of how they can be kept consistent with claim (3b). The same pattern of argument involved in the discussion of direct speech segments becomes relevant. While the infinite number of metalinguistic forms obviously cannot be listed in any LX_i, it might be claimed that metalinguistic forms nonetheless fall within the domain of recursive enumerability via appeal to an analog of (22) something like (38):

(38) Metalinguistic Constituent → (Phonemic Segment)*

The choice of phonemic rather than phonetic segments here seems natural (see [2]) but is not crucial. The same artificiality issues would arise with respect to taking the syntactic structures of metalinguistic stretches to be phoneme-sized. More important, the same issues of gestural forms, geometric forms, and such attack any claim that a universal theory of phonemic segments could cover all meta-linguistic constituents. For instance, this is hardly conceivable for instances of schemas like (39):

(39)   a. In the NL of the deaf of Gwambamamba, the gesture ___ means "why not?"
       b. In America, the gesture ___ means "screw you."

Overall then, metalinguistic sentences just strengthen the arguments against (3b) from direct speech structures, gestural structures, and so forth.

8. The controversial constituents as real constituents

One can suspect that there will exist considerable resistance to accepting as real NL sentences the sort of wholly or partially nonphonetically performed objects I have claimed are NL sentences, which include those schematized in (26), (27b), (28), (29), (30), (32a, b, c), (34), (35b, c), and (39). Part of such resistance might just be the traditional association of sentence with its pronunciation, reinforced by frequent repetition of remarks like those in (40):

(40)   a. Chomsky and Halle (1968: 3)
          "The grammar of the language is the system of rules that specifies this sound-meaning correspondence."
       b. Chomsky (1972c: 11)
          "A person who has learned a language has acquired a system of rules that relate sound and meaning in a certain specific way."

Besides what can now be seen to be an exaggeration of the link between NL sentences and *sound* performance in particular, such statements are misleading in another respect. Actual sound can only be produced by a physical object capable of producing a physical disturbance in a medium like air, in this case the speech apparatus. An NL itself cannot directly link structure and sound, since actual noise can only be produced by performance, by setting some physical objects in motion. What an NL can do, and for the most part does,[17] as made clearer in Chomsky (1975a: 18), is link various abstract structures, which include a superficial one that can be interpreted (according to some sort of conventions) as instructions to a certain physical apparatus. From this point of view, the interpretation conventions that associate particular parts of sentences with physical instantiations of particular kinds might be regarded as external to the NL proper. In any event, the interpretation via articulation, nonvocal gestures, or whatever, is not determined by the abstract structure. Given that, there is no reason to assume an inherent relation between NL sentences and sound in particular.

On the positive side, one reason to view the sort of constituents at issue here as real NL objects is because they seem to have key properties of uncontroversial constituents.[18] For instance, all the examples cited so far had the form of independent (in fact, declarative clauses) or simple embeddings. But this is not at all necessary. Such structures can yield questions, commands, and suggestions, can appear as restrictive relative clauses, as complement clauses, as parts of predicate clauses, and so forth, as illustrated in (41)–(43):

(41)   a. Did the alien shout 'klaatu barrada nikto'?
        b. Don't go around whispering 'klaatu barrada nikto'.
        c. I suggest that you never grunt 'klaatu barrada nikto' at that robot.
        d. Every alien who shouted 'klaatu barrada nikto' was executed.
        e. They reported that the alien shouted 'smato marada snikto'.
        f. The right thing to do was to scream 'klaatu barrada nikto'.

(42)   a. Every deaf person who went ___ was arrested.
        b. When did Marsha make the gesture ___ with her right hand?
        c. The facial expression ___ often indicates anger.
        d. They reported that she made the facial expression ___.

(43)   a. No professor who drew ___ on the blackboard was rehired.
        b. The sculptor who carved something of the form ___ was criticized.
        c. A star shaped like ___ is associated with the Jewish religion.
        d. They denied that she drew ___ on the blackboard.

Moreover, constituents of the relevant kind can be coordinated and negated:

(44)   a. The alien shouted 'klaatu barrada nikto' and not 'slatu niraba miktu'.
        b. What did the alien shout? Not 'slatu niraba miktu'.
        c. Carla went ___ or ___.
        d. The alien shouted neither 'slatu niraba miktu' nor 'smatu birada smakto'.
        e. The ASL/English bilingual went 'please have some pie' or ___ twice.
        f. The sculptor carved things of both the forms ___ and ___.
        g. He drew not the shape ___ but rather the shape ___.
        h. The teacher played not ___ on the piano but ___ on the tuba.

Further, constituents with gestural or other nonsound performances can be antecedents for ellipsis:

(45)   a. The space alien went ___ with his right tentacle, but I didn't ___ with mine.
        b. Male space aliens can go ___ with their tentacles faster than female space aliens can ___ with theirs.

    c. Although Mercedes drew the shape ___, I didn't.

    d. While Noriko can't carve a three-dimensional image of the form ___ on Friday, she can on Saturday.

In such cases, it is clear that the ellipsis-containing constituent involves a claim about the same nonverbally performed constituent as the antecedent.[19]

    And such nonverbally performed constituents can also be the antecedents for non-null anaphoric elements, highlighted in (46):

(46) a. The space alien produced an image just like yours, but I did not produce an image anything like *that*.

      b. The space alien produced an image just like ___, but I did not produce an image anything like *that*.

      c. Sheila gave the cop the finger, *which* is a vulgar gesture.

      d. Sheila went ___, *which* is a vulgar gesture.

      e. Sheila gave the cop the finger but I did not make *that gesture*.

      f. Sheila went ___, but I did not make *that gesture*.

      g. Sheila went both___ and ___, but Glen did not make *the latter gesture*.

      h. *I did not make *that gesture*, but Sheila gave the cop the finger.

      i. *I did not make *that gesture*, but Sheila went ___.

Given that performances of such cases yield no sense of grammaticality, seem to have the standard properties of uncontroversial sentence performances (note the parallel ungrammaticality of [46h, i] for violating a constraint that evidently does not allow the anaphoric device to both be in a coconjunct of the conjunct that contains the antecedent and to precede that coconjunct), and provide no general obstacle to formulating a coherent account (see section 10), it seems that their inclusion in NL is deniable only on purely doctrinal grounds.

9. The irrelevance of the historical dynamics of lexicons

A certain range of well-known and undisputed NL phenomena have *not* been cited here as objections to (3b) and should not be. I refer to the omnipresent existence of *lexical accretion and loss*, which over time add new forms to, and more slowly remove old ones from, the lexicons of NLs continuously. So fifty years ago there was no English form laptop referring to a type of computer, no verb suck meaning "to be of minimal value/quality," and so on. Just so, previous to this work the forms open, openness, and so on were not used in the way they are here. But according to Partridge (1970: 153), before 1915 there was a word chuck-up meaning a military salute, a form I had never heard of and which evidently is not part of current English. When one looks at the full range of such phenomena, it might seem that one is also dealing with facts that render the notion of a fixed lexicon incompatible with linguistic reality.

    However, the dynamic sociohistorical processes that alter historical lexicons in this way have nothing to do with the point being argued for in this study, that is, have nothing to do with the issue of whether NLs are open or closed. The reason is that such historical phenomena can be viewed as mappings from one finitely specifiable lexicon LX_1 to another LX_2 such that if each is combined with the remaining elements of an NL, the result consists of two (relatively trivially) distinct NLs.[20] This is entirely consistent with the view that NL variants that differ in lexical elements, like those in (47), also represent trivially different NLs:

(47)   a. British: The bonnet of the Jaguar was scratched/wants washing.
       b. American: The hood of the Jaguar was scratched/needs washing.

Such variation also is irrelevant to the issue of whether NLs are closed.

But lexical change is in no way parallel to the phenomena illustrated by (14). While the former can be viewed as a historical phenomenon that really amounts to the instantiation of (relatively) trivially distinct NLs, it is absurd to imagine that there is a pre-1950s English that excludes the expression klaatu barrada nikto and a post-1950s one that contains it. The absurdity of the assumption is fully revealed by, for example, the infinite open-endedness of the example collection illustrated in (18). That is, direct speech and the related phenomena discussed previously do not involve historical processes of NL change but rather for every NL at every point the possibility of representing infinitely many unconstrained physical performances. Just so, a "dynamic" approach equally lacks any application to cases like (37), since it makes no sense to imagine that every sentence that involves a descriptive remark about a hitherto unmentioned foreign form in NL_5 represents a historical modification of NL_5.

10. Unregimented constituents and the nature of NL sentences

Standard views of NL sentences, fairly represented, I believe, by (1a) and (6), are arguably correct over a certain range of sentences. But such views fail, as argued in earlier sections, when faced with the variety of NL direct speech sentences, metalinguistic sentences, gesturally represented sentences, sentences that incorporate pictorial, geometrical or multidimensional objects, and so on. The standard view has thereby deeply underestimated the richness and expressive potential of NLs. In this section, I wish to show how this richness of expressive power can be given a coherent interpretation internal to what I believe is independently the only viable ontological view of NL sentences, namely, that they are abstract objects and, more specifically, that each NL sentence is a set.[21] I want to suggest that the line between sentences that can be viewed as based on a fixed, finite lexicon, as in (1a), and those that cannot corresponds to several types of division of constituents. The first distinction is that between constituents of NL_x that are, as (1a) requires, wholly based on forms mentioned in the grammar of NL_x. I will call these *lexically pure constituents*. So, in (48), the subject constituent is lexically pure, but the object constituent, the verbal phrase constituent that contains it, the whole clause, and so forth, are not. Call them *alexical constituents*:

(48)   The newly arrived alien shouted 'vlaatu worrada smeikto' at the mailbox.

A second distinction involves the relation between the abstract objects, in fact, sets, that are constituents and any physical events, objects, and such that serve as genuine tokens of constituents. The basic idea is this: One class of constituents, those *normally* considered in linguistics, contains specific elements, in the standard case a phonetic representation, which can be regarded as a recursively enumerated object capable of being interpreted as instructions to a fixed physical apparatus. I will refer to such constituents as *regimented*. There is little need to say more about them here.

But part of the force of earlier sections can be summed up simply by saying that NLs incorporate certain constituents that are *unregimented*; these include direct speech constituents whose performances seem to include arbitrary noises, image constituents whose performances seem to include arbitrary two-dimensional representations, and so on. And the current task is to see how one can make sense of unregimented constituents, specifically in context with the view that sentences are abstract objects of the type set.

Arguably, of the four types of constituents logically constructable from the two distinctions just made, only three are characteristic of NLs. The normally considered constituents are both lexically pure and regimented. While all of the theoretically unusual constituents that have been considered in earlier sections are alexical, many are naturally taken as regimented. Others though, like those schematized in (32b), (35b), and so forth, are clearly not. What I see no way to instantiate, though, is a constituent that is both lexically pure and unregimented, and I assume that there are no such objects.

I therefore concentrate on the question of how to give a theoretical account of the notion of a constituent that is both alexical and unregimented. It has been claimed that sentences are sets, and it is natural and I think correct to assume that sentences have a complex set-theoretical structure, which involves sets with other sets as members as well as some sets whose members are whatever the appropriate primitives for characterizing lexically pure and regimented constituents turn out to be. The question then is how alexical, unregimented constituents can fit into such a set-theoretical framework. The only answer I see is that an alexical, unregimented constituent C must represent a set whose elements include *the physical tokens that make up individual performances of C*. Let us clarify this through maximally simple examples:

(49)   a. Felicia yelled 'smekto'.
        b. Felicia yelled 'smektof'.

The crucial property such examples have from the point of view of maintenance of the conception of sentences as sets is that distinct elements seem to be defined by distinct performances, more precisely by sets of performances. So (49a and b) represent distinct propositions and hence, if one assumes that meanings are parts of sentences, distinct sentences. This entails that the sets that comprise NL sentences must be able to contain as members or submembers something that can instantiate the endlessly distinct physical properties involved in direct speech. The only way I see that this can be the case is if direct speech segments involve sets that contain the physical properties themselves and not, as in the case of more standard (regimented) linguistic elements, symbols that represent instructions (to a fixed physical apparatus) to produce physical things.

What I am claiming is that the object constituent of the unique English sentence represented by (49a) is a set one of whose subsets contains as elements the actual physical sound waves produced by performances of (49). Note that a priori there is nothing strange in talking about sets, abstract objects, at least some of whose elements are physical objects, that is, nonabstract objects. This is common in introductory discussions of set theory. So Halmos (1960: 1) says: "A pack of wolves, a bunch of grapes, or a flock of pigeons are all examples of sets of things." And Allwood, Andersson, and Dahl (1997: 3) indicate: "We might for instance choose to consider the set which consists of the Premier of Sweden, the smallest moon of Mars and the square root of 7." So if there are three marbles on a table, one can speak of the set that consists of exactly those three marbles, and I can speak of the set of all electrons in the universe and ask questions about it, for example, about its cardinality.[22] The fact that the latter might be currently unspecifiable in no way attacks the existence of the set in question. Just so in the case of the unregimented object constituent in (49a) the fact that there is no way to specify the size of the set of sound waves that make up all its tokens in no way argues against the existence of such a set.[23]

Taking an unregimented constituent to involve a set of its tokens is evidently superior to taking it to involve some single, specific token. The latter is incompatible with the fact that no less than regimented constituents, unregimented ones have unlimitedly many potential tokens. So, for example, (49b) can be said repeatedly and no particular sound wave associated as a token of its object has any primacy with respect to the specification of the nature of the object constituent.

The idea that an unregimented constituent involves a set of its tokens receives some support, I believe, when one considers the semantics of cases such as (49) that involve them. I claimed earlier that direct speech constituents had meanings. It would perhaps be better to say "have denotations." For, under the account of unregimented constituents just sketched, these denotations are, in general, informal terms, not hard to specify. The idea is as follows: An ordinary referential constituent, for example, the one associated with that dog, has a denotation that is independent of any token of that constituent. But not so for unregimented constituents. For these, the denotation is one of the set of associated tokens:

(50)   The denotation of an unregimented constituent X one of whose subsets is a set of physical tokens T is some member of T.[24]

So if one specifies that the object constituent of (49a) is defined by a set of physical tokens T_1, an utterance of (49a) by someone at 10 P.M. on October 31, 2002, amounts to the instantiation of a true proposition only if at some earlier point in time Felicia produced a yell that was a sound sequence S, where S is a member of T_1.

While what I have just sketched seems to me to be correct, it does have, I grant, one aspect that might seem like sleight of hand. It is all very well set-theoretically to speak about unregimented constituents being subsets of physical tokens. But since in general these tokens can be neither listed nor recursively enumerated, how are these sets specified? One way to understand this question is to ask what grounds a claim that, for example, (51a and b) are distinct direct speech sentences, accounting, for example, for the sensible character of (51c):

(51)   a. Helen whimpered 'snedo'.
       b. Helen whimpered 'sneto'.
       c. Helen whimpered 'snedo', not 'sneto'.

It appears inevitable that unregimented constituents must be assumed to involve some kind of *equivalence conditions*, not necessarily (and surely not) the same for different types of unregimented constituents. Hence when one produces a token of an unregimented constituent C, one will specify the set that defines that constituent by virtue of the equivalence condition somehow associated with C. Arguably, these associations are derivable from the linguistic contexts in which unregimented constituents occur.

For example, the fact that a constituent C is the object of the specific verb whimper, as in (51), might determine the relevant equivalence conditions. Since whimper describes a form of verbal performance, it is natural that these conditions would then involve some kind of identity of sound features but exclude as irrelevant such properties of verbal noises as those that define individual voices, which involve loudness and so forth, since these are in general properties irrelevant to claims about whether so and so *whimpered* such and such.

Just so, the fact that an unregimented constituent is object of a verb that involves the creation of two-dimensional figures like that in (52) would naturally impose certain equivalence requirements and exclude others:

(52) The professor drew ———— on the blackboard.

Here the equivalences would exclude sound but include properties of two-dimensional objects, geometric characteristics, color, and such.

So the overall idea is roughly that the set of physical tokens taken here to characterize an unregimented alexical constituent C is specified as follows: Any fixed physical performance P interacts with the equivalence conditions EQ imposed by the context of C to define the token set that characterizes C. The logic is simply that the relevant set is the set of all elements X such that EQ holds between X and P.

I cannot attempt here to say more about the required equivalence conditions. But nothing seems to emerge that interferes with the account suggested, in which an unregimented constituent involves a subset of its tokens, where the membership requirement involves crucially equivalence conditions imposed by the meanings present in linguistic context of the unregimented constituent.

To conclude the discussion of the reality of NL constituents that are alexical and unregimented, it is worth mentioning a proposal of Partee (1973: 416). She suggested very briefly that a possible way of describing direct quotes and sentences that seem to contain gestures would involve recognition of invisible demonstratives plus a claim that the direct quote or gesture was actually not part of the sentence but only part of a larger discourse. The idea would then be that, for example, (53a) would be an elliptical form of (53b):

(53)   a. Morris went ——— (where the blank represents a vocal noise X).
       b. Morris went like this: ——— (where the blank represents a vocal noise X).

The connection between the demonstrative and the putative nonsentence part would then be mediated by some sort of contextual algorithm that picks out certain objects in or properties of the whole context as a referent of the demonstrative. Partee's model for this type of description was, specifically, cases like (53a), in which the quoted material referred to by the demonstrative follows everything else in the sentence. This makes the sentence-external view of such at least conceivable. But of course, that property is not at all general and endlessly many cases are not subject to such a treatment:

(54)   a. Everyone who claimed they went ——— may have really gone ——— or at least
          thought they did.
       b. Since the claim that she went ——— has not been refuted, I can assume that some-
          one who went ——— was seen.

Moreover, on other grounds, Partee's sort of account would have no obvious application to cases of the sort dealt with by Jackendoff (1984), discussed later, where no analog with a demonstrative is grammatical:

(55)   a. The sound ——— is grating.
       b. *The sound that is grating: ———.
       c. He discussed the gesture ——— on Friday.
       d. *He discussed the gesture that on Friday: ———.

11. Conclusions

The principal result of the preceding sections has been an array of arguments that support the untenable character of the claims in (1), repeated here:

(1)   a. Chomsky (1959: 137)
          "A language is a collection of sentences of *finite length* all constructed from a *finite*
          alphabet (or, where our concern is limited to syntax, a *finite vocabulary*) of sym-
          bols."
       b. Chomsky (1959: 137)
          "Since any language L in which we are likely to be interested is an infinite set, we
          can investigate the structure of L only through the study of the finite devices (gram-
          mars) *which are capable of generating its sentences.*"
       c. Chomsky (1959: 138)
          "The weakest condition that can significantly be placed on grammars is that F be
          included in the class of general, unrestricted Turing machines."

The key element of (1a) for our concerns here is the view that each NL sentence is constructed from a finite (hence listable) alphabet of symbols or a finite vocabulary of syntactically minimal forms, a fixed lexicon. Accepting (1a) amounts to accepting that NLs have the property I have called *closed*. It has been argued to the contrary that (1a) must be seen as false and NLs regarded as *open* because of diverse facts that involve direct speech, nonphonetic gestures, nonlinguistic noise, geometrical forms, metalinguistic constituents, and so on. All these phenomena reveal that NLs incorporate certain constituents whose minimal elements are not mentioned in any grammars; these are the alexical constituents of section 10.

Several aspects of doctrine (1a) are worth highlighting. First, the logical conjunction of (1a, b, and c) defines the technical aspect of the *generative grammar* view of NLs. The untenability of (1a) thus undermines that general view. Second, (1a) was introduced in the 1950s with no supporting argument Third, it has been maintained by its originator and a multitude of those he has influenced ever since also with no supporting argument. Works like Chomsky (1995b) that advance the minimalist program of the 1990s and later and incorporate (1a) neglect to argue for it, just as did those of the 1950s.

That the doctrine flourishes in the face of this lack suggests that many may have assumed that (1a) is a sort of self-evident truth. But it has been argued here that not only is (1a) not self-evident, but also unchallenged factual properties of NLs incompatible with it (e.g., the existence of various forms of direct speech, metalinguistic constituents) were known long before (1a) was enunciated. This principle seems in short to be nothing more than a (strangely) popular dogma, which is evidently an extraordinary state of affairs. If one were to have asked a priori whether a doctrine incompatible with well-known and traditionally discussed (e.g., by Jespersen, 1924) features of the domain of study could be introduced in the mid–twentieth century in a growing field and successfully take root and maintain itself over a period now approaching a half-century, one would have tended to answer in the negative. But the facts are otherwise.

No doubt one reason that (1a) was so easily maintained in spite of its grave incompatibility with common fact is that the issue it raises was rarely discussed. A notable exception is provided by Hockett (1966: 182–183). Hockett ended up assuming (1a), specifying (1966: 183) as in (56):

(56)   "Any sentence in the language is a string of characters, each of which is one or another of the characters of the fixed finite alphabet."

However, this claim by Hockett was not question begging, since prior to that he had considered the factual adequacy of the claim, characterized it as open, and only specified (56) as a working assumption.

Hockett's discussion was phrased in terms of a striking and insightful implication of (1a) for the logical connection between NL and *typewriters*. He noted (1966: 182):

(57)   "A point of departure for the formalization of language description is afforded by the fact that one can design a typewriter for any human language. . . . The keyboard and type bars give us a small, clearly defined stock of symbols among which we must make our choice for any key-striking. The carriage motion is such that our choices appear in a linear sequence on the paper. The operator can override these arrangements—I have

seen pictures drawn with a typewriter—but let us set aside such aberrations. If the stock of symbols is the correct one for a given language, then we can write practically anything we wish in that language.

"Any linguist who uses a typewriter has had the experience of lacking some symbol he needs and having to improvise or to arrange for his keyboard to be modified. There are two possible interpretations of this. One is that a typewriter's limitations are only a matter of economics. Symbols but rarely needed can more cheaply be written in by hand as the occasion arises, but in principle there is no reason why we should not incorporate everything we will ever need for a given language on a single keyboard. Of course, not everything we put on paper is language. If the supply of useful type faces is indefinitely large only because of charts, graphs, pictures, and other nonlanguage items, the first interpretation can stand. The second interpretation is that the limitation is not merely practical but essential. No matter how large we were to make the keyboard for a particular language, according to this interpretation, we might still encounter a need for symbols not provided on it.

"It is not at all obvious which of these interpretations is empirically correct. It is clear, however, that for purposes of analysis and description the first interpretation is customarily assumed. If the assumption is in fact true, all is well. . . . Our assumption is, then, that if one has the right keyboard one can type, not just *almost* anything one wishes in a given language, but *any* sentence of that language. The keyboard supplies a finite *alphabet* of *characters*. Any sentence in the language is a string of characters, each of which is one or another of the characters of the fixed finite alphabet. On the other hand, not every string of characters drawn from the alphabet is a sentence of the language. The string of symbols that begins with the last capital letter before this and ends with the next period is a sentence of written English. The string that follows the next colon and runs to the following period is drawn from the proper alphabet, but is not, I believe, a sentence of written English: fkwwy qpat emff agvktom. Every sentence is a string of characters from the appropriate alphabet, but not vice versa."

Hockett thus saw with full clarity that there was a factual claim involved in (1a). And his typewriter account permits one to see in a most graphic way the nature of the issue and why the evidence of earlier sections that involved, for example, arbitrary noises, arbitrary gestures, arbitrary pictures, and so forth, that is, unregimented constituents, shows that (1a) cannot be true.

Moreover, Hockett's description of the regimentation issue in terms of typewriters permits a novel and very vivid alternative way of specifying the nature of openness, as follows:

(58)   a. T is an *abstract typewriter/printer* if and only if T consists of finite set of elements called *keys*, $\{k_1 \ldots k_n\}$, each associated with some single symbol $S(k_i)$.

   b. A word string W is *typeable/printable* (*T*) ('printable by T') if and only if W consists of a finite string of symbols [Z] and every member of [Z] (except perhaps 'space') is a member of $\{S(k_1), \ldots, S(k_n)\}$.

   c. An NL, NL_x, is *closed* if and only if there is some abstract typewriter/printer T such that the word string of every sentence of NL is typeable/printable (T).

   d. An NL that is not closed is *open*.

What Hockett did not see then is that evidence that shows the correctness of his 'second interpretation' of the relation between NLs and abstract typewriters was easily at hand. No abstract typewriter provides the means to type/print every sentence of an NL that allows direct speech, gestural or pictorial constituents, and such. Any such NL will have indefinitely many sentences at least one part of which is unprintable.

Moreover, in effect, a perception of the falsehood of (1a) was also reached by Jackendoff (1984). He was concerned with an English construction that I have not so far mentioned, one that he characterized (1984: 25) as consisting "of a definite article and a noun followed without pause by an expression *E* which can be of quite varied character; I will refer to it as the *the N—E* construction. Here is a range of examples, grouped approximately into semantic categories." Jackendoff's large list of examples included those of (59):

(59)   a. the phrase *the phrase*
        b. the word/verb *run*
        c. the prefix *un*
        d. the construction *N of NP*
        e. the sentence *Will you marry me*
        f. the sequence *up a*
        g. the sound p^h
        h. the syllable *pa*
        i. the letter A
        j. the number 14
        k. the note $E^\flat$
        l. the noise ***** [raspberry, imitation of' a goat, etc.]
        m. the pattern *da-dum da-dum da-dum*
        n. the symbol $

Crucial from my perspective here, of course, are cases like (59i, k, l, m, and n), where in our terms the expression E is alexical and in some cases (clearly, l, and n) unregimented.

About such cases Jackendoff (1984: 26) concluded:

(60)   "On the other hand, there are no inherent *syntactic* constraints on E: it need not be a syntactic constituent—as in (1); nor even an expression of English—as in (3). In fact, if the construction is uttered, E need not be expressible in standard orthography (as I have tried to suggest in [8a]); while if the construction is written, E need not have a pronunciation, as in (9). Hence, like the complements of verbs such as *say* and *go* (in the sense 'make a noise'), E is a constituent whose interior is unconstrained by normal rules of syntax and phonology."

Clearly then, Jackendoff had recognized that the constituents he called 'E' were overall unregimented and alexical and thus implicitly that no NL that contains an E-like constituent could satisfy (1a). He thus had in hand nineteen years ago a tool for showing further the entailed falsity of (1b, c). But, like Hockett eighteen years earlier, Jackendoff did not take this step.

Rather, he concluded for some reason that alexical, unregimented constituents could be subsumed internal to the generative apparatus of the time, arguing further:

(61)   Jackendoff (1984: 26)

"We will assume, therefore, that the phrase structure rule responsible for introducing E violates the normal theory of syntactic categories by permitting a totally free expression."

But assumption (61) is impossible. For there can be no phrase structure rule or indeed any generative rule that permits a "totally free expression." Because "totally free" is incompatible with the fact that E subsumes objects whose minimal elements are drawn from no list. But any generative rule ultimately specifies a class that is closed.

Jackendoff's remark might fairly be construed as a confusion that wrongly attributed to a putative generative rule properties that could only hold of a nongenerative, model-theoretic one (see later discussion). Suppose, for example, one offers (62) as a putative phrase structure rule that reconstructs Jackendoff's idea:

(62)   E → anything at all

The intention would be to have a rule that permits a "totally free expression." But contrary to the intention, the characterization of phrase structure rule would allow only one real interpretation of (62) (ignoring that where each character is a separate symbol). Namely, its right-hand side consists of the morpheme string [anything + at + all]. Far from allowing free expression, the rule allows only a single output. To get what Jackendoff wanted, one needs minimally the equivalent of a logical variable over the class that E represents. But phrase structure rules and generative rules in general do not contain such equivalents.

So, while Jackendoff (1984) insightfully uncovered and discussed a relevant class of evidence that showed that (1a, b, and c) were all untenable, unfortunately he did not then grasp the implications of what he had found.[25]

The relation between the false (1a) and (1b) is logically more complex than might appear. Certainly the falsehood of (1a) shows that (1b) cannot be true. Given that NLs are open and hence not recursively enumerable collections, the idea that one can only study them through finite grammars that generate (recursively enumerate) their member sentences is untenable. It cannot sensibly be required that one adopt descriptive mechanisms that must logically fail. Notably, no argument has ever been given by Chomsky (or anyone else as far as I know) for (1b), either. This is fundamental because in fact, once one goes beyond the uncontroversial issue of grammars being finite, even the *truth* of (1a) would not justify (1b).

The reason is that there is nothing inherent in the linguistic goal of specifying the nature of infinite collections of highly structured objects like the sentences of NLs that imposes the methodology of formulating generative/constructive/proof-theoretic grammars. This is an obviously impossible conclusion given the existence of nonrecursively enumerable infinite collections, for example, the real numbers. Formal fields other than linguistics, mathematics, logic, and such, have thus developed ways to study such collections in various ways via appeal to axiomatic systems, model-theoretic satisfaction, and so forth.

The point with specific reference to linguistics has recently been nicely put by Pullum and Scholz (2001: 1):

(63)   "The second half of the 20th century saw the emergence of two quite different types of frameworks for theorizing about the syntax of natural languages. One sprang from the syntactic side of mathematical logic, the other from the semantic side."

By the "syntactic side of mathematical logic" Pullum and Scholz refer to proof-theoretic ('derivational') approaches whose linguistic instantiations are the various versions of generative grammar. By the "semantic side of mathematical logic" Pullum and Scholz refer to model-theoretic/satisfaction approaches. About this they say (2001: 3):

(64)   "It applies model theory rather than proof theory to natural language syntax."

Given the logical existence of these two very different approaches, even if, counterfactually, (1a) were true and NLs were recursively enumerable collections, to justify generative grammar one would *still* need a never supplied argument that their proper grammars are generative/proof-theoretic systems, rather than nonconstructive, axiomatic/model-theoretic ones. Chomsky's claim (1b) thus further begs the question of the superiority of proof-theoretic over model-theoretic approaches to NL grammars, which would still need to be argued *even if (1a) were true*. Since it is false, the missing argument can never be supplied.

Since (1b) is false because (1a) is and (1b) would not follow even if (1a) were true, (1c) cannot, of course, be a tenable condition to impose on grammars. It simply embodies the question begging about the choice between proof-theoretic and model-theoretic approaches to NL grammars. The weakest condition that can reasonably be placed on NL grammars is not the quite arbitrary (1c) but rather that they be systems capable of characterizing the full collections that form NLs. Given the openness of NLs and the arguments that the class of direct speech, geometric, and so forth, NL sentences are of the order of the real numbers, model-theoretic approaches seem to be the only basis for constructing correct NL grammars.

The just expressed conclusion in effect reiterates one already reached in Langendoen and Postal (1984: 77–78), who said:

(65)   "Since the ideas of generative grammar became dominant in the late 1950s, linguistics has in general assumed that the task of grammatical theory involves answering the question: What is the right form of *generative* grammar for NLs? The many disputes which have divided linguists over the past quarter century are then reducible by and large to disputes over claims about 'right form'. Some linguists have believed that NL grammars contain transformational rules; others have denied this. Some linguists have believed that transformational rules are parochially ordered; others have denied this. Some linguists have believed that there are interpretive semantic rules; others have denied this. And so on. Underlying all such disputes has been the assumption that it is

possible through appeal to some combination of proof-theoretical devices to construct *some* generative grammar for each NL."

Langendoen and Postal (1984) rejected this possibility but only reached the conclusion of the untenability of proof-theoretic grammars on the basis of the proof, mentioned at the outset, that NLs were not sets. Given the radical and controversial nature of that line of argument, this work has sought to construct a path to the same conclusion in a different and I hope less controversial way. This path appeals of course to the conclusion that NLs are not closed. Accepting the latter as a fact means that NLs cannot be regarded as recursively enumerable sets and directly yields the result that NL grammars cannot be generative grammars. The proof-theoretic approach to NL grammars, which generative grammar insists on, is thus seen as irreparably flawed independently of the bases of the argument in Langendoen and Postal (1984, 1985).

The seemingly only available alternative then is to develop model-theoretic approaches, as primitively attempted in Johnson and Postal (1980) and Langendoen and Postal (1984: chapter 5.2). See Pullum and Scholz (2001) for many references to more recent sophisticated and formalized approaches to model-theoretic grammars.

Finally, it is worth indicating exactly why a model-theoretic approach to NL grammars is *not* undermined by NL openness in the way that proof-theoretic approaches are. Consider the direct speech case (66):

(66)   Maureen grunted 'fnstribkl'.

A generative grammar cannot characterize such sentences because it cannot find ('look up') the alexical object constituent or its components in its lexicon. Thus no proof-theoretic grammar can, as required for factual adequacy, yield a proof (derivation) of arbitrary grammatical direct speech sentences simply because the unregimented direct speech constituents are unlistable, hence unlisted.

But model-theoretic approaches, as stressed in Pullum and Scholz (2001), embody necessary (and, I would stress, sufficient) conditions for sentencehood. They state what conditions an object must satisfy to be a sentence of the NL described. Therefore, such a grammar can characterize (66) without having to mention fnstribkl or any other direct speech segment. For this to work, it merely must characterize the realizations of the object of direct speech verbs like grunt in such a way that no conditions are imposed that fnstribkl and so forth will fail to satisfy. A nonconstructive grammar can allow alexical constituents, regimented or not, in various contexts simply by failing to state overly specific constraints. For the object context of (66), it will suffice if the grammar requires only that an acceptable object constituent specify a set of actual noises. Thus a collection of endlessly many direct speech objects like that of (66) is characterized without mentioning any of them, engendering no conflict between a finite grammar and a nonrecursively enumerable set of constituents, that is, a class of constituents that have no gödel numbering; see note 9. Put differently, a model-theoretic approach permits accomplishing what Jackendoff's putative but nonexistent phrase structure rule could not. So, while the openness of NLs is strongly incompatible with proof-theoretic approaches to NL grammars, hence with the defining ideas of generative grammar, it is straightforwardly compatible with model-theoretic approaches.

STUDIES OF JUNK LINGUISTICS

7

Junk Syntax 1

A Supposed Account of Strong Crossover Effects

1. Background

The *strong crossover phenomenon*, apparently first treated in Postal (1971), designates binding failures like those in (1):[1]

(1) a. ⊄Who_1 did Frank convince her_1 that you would hire t_1?
   b. ⊄the $principle_1$ $which_1$ I inferred from it_1 that no other principle entailed t_1
   c. ⊄$What_1$ Jane compared it_1 to a model of t_1 was the Eiffel Tower.
   d. ⊄[Generalissimo $Garcia]_1$, no one could persuade him_1 that you were related to t_1.
   e. ⊄It doesn't matter $[who]_1$ they claim she_1 believes you should invite t_1.

Following Wasow (1972, 1979), I refer to the asymmetric relation between antecedent and pronominal form, reflexive or not, as *anaphoric linkage*. Binding is thus a subtype of this. First noticed in 1968, examples like (1) manifested previously unknown restrictions on anaphoric linkages between *extracted* elements and pronouns. My original research subsumed these facts under the rubric 'crossover phenomena', a term taken to cover considerably more data, much of which subsequent work indicates is distinct from (1). Specifically, Postal (1971) failed to distinguish what Wasow (1972) I think properly differentiated as *strong* versus *weak* crossover binding violations, the former represented by (1), the latter by, for example, (2):

(2) a. ⊄Who_1 did all of his_1 associates detest t_1?
   b. ⊄the proposal $which_1$ your rejection of it_1 led me to abandon t_1
   c. ⊄[Whatever $starlet]_1$ they convinced her_1 employer that you had interviewed t_1, . . .

A major distinction is their different ranges of applicability. Some extractions induce no weak effects but do induce strong ones, for example, English topicalizations of *definite referential NPs*; see (3):

(3) a. Strong Crossover Case: ⊄Jenny₁ I am sure she₁ thinks you really dislike t₁.
     b. Weak Crossover Case: ⊂Jenny₁ I am sure her₁ husband thinks you really dislike t₁.

This English-internal difference correlates with the cross-linguistic fact that there do not even seem to be purported counterexamples to the strong effect; in contrast, *weak* effect variation exists even between French and English; see Postal (1993b).[2]

This study, which is restricted to strong violations, has two aspects. First, it is an extended rejection of the validity of the assertion in (4) that strong effects reduce to one of the elements of Chomsky's binding theory:

(4) Chomsky (1981: 193)
     "Principle (C) gives the basic facts of strong crossover in the sense of Wasow 1972, 1979) . . ."

Referencing a notion of *binding* based on coindexing and c-command, Chomsky's Principle C requires so-called *R(eferring)-expressions* to be unbound.[3] Second, intertwined with the argument for the inadequacy of a reduction of strong effects to Principle C is an argument that the standards utilized in the work that supposedly supports claim (4) are so low as to qualify as junk syntax.

Although Chomsky (1982b) transitorily abandoned the Principle C view of strong violations, it appears today to be standard and rarely challenged received wisdom about strong effects. Occasional alternatives like the proposal by Higginbotham (1980b) or that of Koopman and Sportiche (1982/1983) or the NP Structure proposals of Riemsdijk and Williams (1981, 1986) have few current echoes. Some sense of the scope of recent support for (4) is seen in (5):

(5) a. McCloskey (1990: 212)
         "Sentence (34b) is ungrammatical because the lexical NP *John* is c-commanded by, and coindexed with, the epithet *the bastard*. Sentence (34c) is ungrammatical because the embedded subject trace is A-bound by the epithet *the bastard*, giving rise to a Condition C (strong crossover) violation."
     b. Georgopoulos (1991: 37)
         "Strong crossover (SCO) is an effect of principle C of the binding theory or an equivalent c-command condition, which prevents a variable or an r-expression from having an antecedent in a c-commanding A-position."
     c. Ristad (1993: 85)
         "Recall that strong crossover is the configuration where an anaphoric element c-commands the trace of a displaced wh-phrase and intervenes between the wh-phrase and its trace as well."
     d. Other Works That Invoke a Principle C Account of the Strong Crossover Effect
         Cinque (1990: 150), Cowper (1992: 170), Culicover (1997: 316, 325, 326), Fiengo and May (1994: 279–280), Fox (2000: 132, note 21), Haegeman (1991: 380), Harbert

(1995: 182), Hornstein (1995: 21), Huang (1995: 139), Kennedy (1997: 702), Lasnik and Uriagereka (1988: 41; notably, though, this work, pages 137–138, expresses strong doubts about the Principle C account based on observations of Higginbotham), Müller (1995: 163), Napoli (1993: 487), Ouhalla (1994: 214–215), Roberts (1991: 17; 1997: 147), and Sells and Wasow (1999: 21).

Despite this broad acceptance, I argue that no Principle C account of the strong effect has ever been viable. The discussion is limited to English, which imposes no serious implications since at issue is the correctness of a claimed *universal* account. Therefore, a showing that it fails for English is entirely sufficient.

The attempt to reduce the strong effect to Principle C violations is inevitably linked to independent proposals. These include notably those of (6):

(6) Key Assumptions Linked to a Principle C View of the Strong Effect
   a. The assumed 'gaps' in the relevant sentences, that is, cases of putative movement to so-called nonargument positions, are taken to be filled by objects called *traces*. Like all traces, these are bound by the assumed extractees in the relevant constructions.
   b. The postulated traces must be characterized as R-expressions, because that is the (only) category that Principle C restricts.

Assumptions (6a and b) each involve potential weaknesses, some of which, I claim, are genuine flaws. Even granting (6a and b) however, the specific factual requirement in (7) must be met:

(7) Each gap that induces a strong violation, a gap taken to be a trace under assumption (6a), must be c-commanded by the pronoun whose link to the gap position yields the violation.

Assumption (7) holds since the concept 'binding' Principle C appeals to is only instantiated by pairs of constituents in a c-command relation. The link to c-command also creates a potential weakness argued to be irreparable.

The trace-based Principle C view of the strong effect grew out of Chomsky's own earlier trace-theoretic description of the effect, in turn a development of the account in Wasow (1972), whose key idea was attributed to Peter Culicover. See (8) and (9):

(8) Wasow's (1972, 1979: 160) number (10)
   a. $<_{S1}$ He said $<_{S2}$ Mary kissed someone $_{S2}> _{S1}>$
   b. $<_{S1}$ Who did he say $<_{S2}$ Mary kissed Δ $_{S2}> _{S1}>$
   c. Wasow (1972, 1979: 160)
      "The transformation of WH-fronting converts a structure like (10a) into one like (10b). Now, if who and he in (10b) are to be allowed to enter into an anaphoric relation, the Transitivity Condition requires that Δ and he also be anaphorically related. Consequently, the resultant sentence will be ungrammatical for the same reason that (11) is."
   d. Wasow's (11) was my *(10b).

(9) a. Chomsky (1976, 1977a: 195)
         "Thus we can account for the full range of interpretations in (74) by appeal to inde-
         pendently motivated principles of anaphora, again on the assumption (72) that sur-
         face structure determines LF with the natural additional assumption that bound
         variables function (to first approximation) as names."
     b. Chomsky (1976, 1977a: 195)
         "[N]or need we invoke any principle beyond established principles of anaphora that
         apply in (77)–(79)."

Space precludes discussion of these earlier approaches, but a crucial idea in all
of them, as in the Principle C view, is that strong effects reduce to the anaphoric linkage restriction in *nonextraction* examples like (10):

(10) a. ⊄She$_1$ convinced me that I should help Isabelle$_1$.
      b. ⊄He$_1$ said Mary kissed someone$_1$.

Such a reduction played no role in the account of Postal (1971) and, much more
importantly, is argued here to be incorrect.

The traces invoked in the original Principle C proposal were so-called *empty
categories*. More recently, its formulator has adopted the different account in (11),
the so-called *copy theory of traces*:

(11) Chomsky (1995b: 202)
      "[T]he trace left behind is a copy of the moved element, deleted by a principle of the
      PF component in the case of overt movement. But at LF the copy remains, providing
      the materials for 'reconstruction'."

The two alternative views of traces yield two variants of the claim that strong effects
follow from Principle C; these have different factual consequences and hence potentially distinct truth values. I argue that *neither* is tenable, beginning with the initial,
empty category proposal.

2. Older objections to Principle C accounts

2.1. Remarks

Despite its frequent invocation, at least four defects of the empty category version of
the Principle C approach *already* appear in the literature.

2.2. Defect 1: stipulation of "R-expression" status

Principle C can at best yield the strong effect only via the claim that the traces left by
movements to nonargument positions *are* R-expressions. Unless this categorization
follows from something, the degree of explanatory success achieved even if the strong
effect could reduce in this way to Principle C would be less than claimed. Even sym-
pathizers with Chomsky's approach recognize this defect. Thus Higginbotham (1983:

407) calls taking variables as R-expressions "rather unnatural" before giving cases where it does not work correctly (under a Principle C approach). Koster (1987: 68–69) calls the assignment an "unnecessary stipulation." And Lasnik and Uriagereka (1988: 42) defend the stipulation only by the faint praise that if all NPs have to be assigned to some category, "R-expression seems a not unreasonable candidate."

But the requirement does not follow since even if it is claimed that all movements leave traces, not all can be claimed to leave *R-expression* traces. This is impossible for so-called head movements and, of course, for movements to *argument* positions, whose traces must be anaphors. Very different consequences would obtain if movements to argument positions left R-expression traces and those to nonargument positions anaphors, both left anaphors, or both left R-expressions. So the actual choice from the four logical possibilities remains unprincipled. Moreover, Meyers (1994: 285) observes that subsuming only those traces linked to movement to nonargument positions and ordinary lexical NPs under a blanket category 'R-expression' is independently suspicious, for the former require antecedents, like the traces of movement to argument positions, but the latter do not. So the needed grouping links elements that contrast in required antecedence and fails to include others that do require antecedence. The original Principle C treatment then requires a dubious *stipulation* like (12):

(12)   Traces of movement to nonargument positions are R-expressions.

2.3. Defect 2: non-NP extractions

A second problem for the original Principle C account also relates to dependence on (12). For this is too general, since 'R-expression' is only a category of NPs, while non-NPs are also taken to move to nonargument positions. Chomsky's binding theory that includes Principle C is exclusively an account of certain NP properties. Incidentally, the recent invocation of DPs instead of NPs has no relevant consequences here and will here be ignored. Hence (12) has to be replaced, by something like (13):

(13)   (Only) traces of movement *of NPs* to nonargument positions are R-expressions.

Therefore, a claim that the strong effect reduces to Principle C entails that such effects are never induced by *non*-NP extraction, specifically not by Prepositional Phrase (PP) extraction. This follows since Chomskyan traces of moved PPs must be PPs, hence not 'R-expressions'. If the trace of a moved PP were an NP, a violation of Chomsky's (1981) projection principle would ensue. As Lasnik and Uriagereka (1988: 41) put it: "In accord with Trace Theory, let us assume that <u>who</u> leaves a trace when it moves. This trace is obviously an NP, a fact ensured by Trace Theory, which essentially says that, upon movement, an item leaves behind a syntactic silent copy of itself."

But the entailment is wrong. For as Koster (1987: 82) indicates:

If a PP containing a Wh-word is preposed, we have a really crucial example:

(130)   *[With whom$_i$] did he$_i$ say that Mary talked [$_{PP}$ t]

This is a normal case of strong crossover. It is not possible to construct a reading in which there is a binding relation between *he* and (the variable corresponding to) *whom*. In this case, the example is not ruled out by the binding theory, because the binding theory says nothing about PP-traces.[4]

While I will not in general quarrel with Principle C itself, it has known inadequacies and a possibly not so well known one. Namely, since Chomsky's binding theory is restricted not only to argument positions but also to NPs, an evident difficulty is that the bad CP anaphora case in (14a) is unblocked although the no more impossible gerundive NP version is properly blocked:

(14)   ⊄It$_1$suggests that Mike thought a. [that 2 and 2 is 4]$_1$/b. about [2 and 2 being 4]$_1$.

Example (14a) satisfies Principle C since the <u>that</u> clause, a CP, is thereby not an R-expression. The lack of induced binding failure in (14a) leads to a further non-NP related crossover problem linked to examples like (15a):

(15)   a. ⊄[That Ted is a spy]$_1$, I now realize that it$_1$ indicates that Bob knew t$_1$.
        b. *Ted adores/condoned/criticized/studied/ that Marsha is a vampire.
        c. *[That Marsha is a vampire]$_1$, Ted adores/condoned/criticized/studied t$_1$.

Such CP topicalizations are in general only licit when the t$_1$ position otherwise accepts <u>that</u> clauses, as (15b and c) illustrate, which suggests (15a) represents <u>that</u> clause topicalization. But via the same logic by which Principle C fails to block of (14a), it would also wrongly not yield a Principle C violation in the strong effect case (15a), either.

2.4. Defect 3: the secondary strong crossover effect

A third difficulty with the original Principle C claim relates to data like (16), also found in Postal (1971: 90):

(16)   a. [Whose$_1$ cousin]$_2$ did you convince ⊄him$_1$/⊄him$_2$ I had run over t$_2$?
        b. the nurse [[whose$_1$ father's]$_2$ sisters]$_3$ I convinced ⊄her$_1$/⊄him$_2$/⊄them$_3$ that you would contact t$_3$

Here the trace Chomsky's analysis posits, even if categorized as an R-expression and c-commanded by a pronoun, is only wrongly bound under Principle C when linked to the *entire* questioned or relativized phrase. But anaphoric linkage is equally banned for the contained NPs, which do not link to any traces. Further terminology is helpful. I take restrictions that ban anaphoric linkages like that between pronouns and the entire extracted phrases in (1) and (16) to represent the *Primary* strong effect and those that ban such linkages between the pronouns and (certain) *sub*constituents of the entire extracted phrase to constitute the *Secondary* strong effect. The latter has been extensively discussed; see, for example, Barss (1986), Chomsky (1981: 89), Culicover (1997), Engdahl (1986: 302), Higginbotham (1980a, 1980b, 1983), Jacobson (1976, 1977), Koopman and Sportiche (1982/1983), Koster (1987: 81), Kuno (1987: 55f, 60), Lasnik and Uriagereka (1988), Riemsdijk (1982), Riemsdijk and Williams (1981,

1986), and Safir (1996, 1998). But there seems to be no firmly established trace-theoretic solution.

And as Kuno (1987: 61) asserts: "Chomsky [(1981)] admits that there are many problems that arise in this connection but says that it is beyond the scope of his book. He dismisses trace theory with structured trace and continues to adopt trace theory with empty category. He thus leaves unexplained the fact that <u>he</u> cannot be coreferential with <u>whose</u> in (8.14)." Kuno's (8.14) is an example like (16a).

Minimally then, Principle C applied to the Surface Structure, which is what was originally claimed,[5] fails to induce all the attested strong effects. So the secondary strong effect undermines the original idea that recognition of traces could reduce the strong effect to a c-command condition that references *Surface* Structures.[6] Much discussion of the secondary effect involves appeal to so-called *reconstruction*, which time precludes discussing. But I return to the issue in effect when discussing the copy trace view.

2.5. Defect 4: the asymmetry property

The gravest previously noted defect of Principle C accounts of the strong effect relates to an asymmetry. In standard strong effect cases like (1), the extractee is *the antecedent of the pronoun* whose 'crossing' yields the violation. It is such cases, which involve question phrases or relative pronouns, that Culicover, Wasow, and Chomsky concentrated on almost exclusively; for them, a Principle C approach might have some initial plausibility.

But consider (17):

(17)   a. Postal (1971: 143): $\subset$Myself$_1$, I$_1$ can't begin to understand t$_1$.
       b. Postal (1971: 143): $\subset$[To myself$_1$]$_2$, I$_1$ never send things t$_2$.

Evidently, early strong effect work considered anaphoric linkages where a topicalized reflexive pronoun or PP that contained such was well formed in typical strong effect contexts. Chapter 16B of Postal (1971) was devoted to the fact that pronouns could licitly topicalize over their antecedents. Special devices were proposed to deal with the contrast between these cases and (18):

(18)   a. $\not\subset$Fred$_1$, he$_1$ can't begin to understand t$_1$.
       b. $\not\subset$[To Fran$_1$]$_2$, she$_1$ never sends things t$_2$.

Yet under Chomsky's empty category Principle C account the *well-formed* binding in (17a) yields no less a violation of Principle C than the *ill-formed* binding of (18a), as Kuno (1987: 81) already observed: "But trace theory does not distinguish . . . the trace of a full NP and that of a pronominal or reflexive, and therefore is incapable of distinguishing the two situations. This casts a serious doubt on the very foundation of trace theory."

The same factual pattern emerges in cleft structures and the restriction to extraction to the front of the clause *immediately* containing the antecedent characteristic of (17) is arbitrary:

(19) a. ⊂Herself$_1$, I am sure that Gladys$_1$ doesn't want to vote for t$_1$.
      b. ⊂It is herself$_1$ that I am sure that Gladys$_1$ doesn't want to vote for
      c. ⊂Himself$_1$, they found out that Eddy$_1$ had talked to Edna about t$_1$.
      d. ⊂It was himself$_1$ that they found out that Eddy$_1$ had talked to Edna about t$_1$.

Postal (1971) gave one well-formed example, namely, (20), which contained an extracted *non*reflexive pronominal:

(20) Postal (1971: 158): ⊂[To him$_1$]$_2$, [the man]$_1$ claimed you were engaged t$_2$.

But that work took (20) to be exceptional and assumed topicalization of a *nonreflexive* pronoun in standard strong effect configurations yielded violations; see (21):

(21) Postal (1971: 143) (see also Postal [1971: 145, 149])
      a. ⊄Her$_1$,Barbara$_1$ claimed that Tony hated t$_1$.
      b. ⊄Him$_1$, Harold$_1$ wanted Betty to visit t$_1$.
      c. Postal (1971: 158): ⊄Him$_1$, the man$_1$ claimed you were engaged to t$_1$.

In retrospect, my earlier claims about (21) seem fundamentally mistaken. While certain speakers reject such examples,[7] they do not present the sharply impossible anaphoric linkages of true strong effect violations. Topicalized pronoun examples of this sort should thus *not* be assimilated to sentences obtained by interchanging the relevant antecedents and pronouns, which yields unchallenged strong effect violations like (22):[8]

(22) a. ⊄Tony$_1$, he$_1$ said Harry insulted t$_1$.
      b. ⊄[That man]$_1$, he$_1$ claimed you were engaged to t$_1$.
      c. ⊄It was Tony who$_1$ he$_1$ said Harry insulted t$_1$.
      d. ⊄It was that man whom$_1$ he$_1$ claimed you were engaged to t$_1$.

Summarizing then, the strong effect is limited as in (23):

(23) Strong effects occur only in structures in which:
      a. There exist phrases A, B such that A antecedes B;
      b. A is extracted.

While (23a) restates a banality, (23b) distinguishes cases like (22) from those where a pronominal is extracted, as in (21) and (i) of note 8. I refer to this difference as *the Asymmetry Property*.
      A viable account of the strong effect must deal with minimal Asymmetry Property contrasts like (24):

(24) a. ⊄Who$_1$ did the directors convince him$_1$ that Jane should vote for t$_1$?
      b. ⊂It was himself that$_1$ the directors convinced Jane that he$_1$ should vote for t$_1$.
      c. ⊄the dancer who$_1$ I promised her$_1$ that you would visit t$_1$
      d. ⊂Her(self)$_1$, Joan$_1$ never promised me that you could visit t$_1$.

But Chomsky's original Principle C account draws no such distinction and so is again robustly counterexemplified by data easily available in Postal (1971). The work cited in (4) simply ignored these facts.[9]

More generally, the asymmetry problem was apparently not recognized internal to *published* trace-theory literature until fairly late in the 1980s, although it is noted in earlier unpublished theses; see Barss (1986), Browning (1987), and Sportiche (1983). For published trace-theoretic work, the earliest citations seem to be Williams (1986: 288) and Koster (1987: 78–79). The latter remarks:

> If there is a construal chain that makes it possible to identify the trace with reflexive features, the sentence is grammatical, even if the trace is A'-bound from COMP:
>
> (122)   Himself$_i$ [O$_i$ [he$_i$ does not really like t$_i$]]

Lasnik and Uriagereka (1988: 81–82, 157) consider material parallel to that in Kuno (1987: 81–82), showing the Principle C account makes erroneous predictions about topicalization of reflexive and nonreflexive pronouns. But this work treats the issue as newly noted, ignoring the extensive support for this conclusion in Postal (1971).[10]

2.6. Summary

So far then I have cataloged those objections to Chomsky's original Principle C approach to the strong effect already found in the literature and listed in (25):

(25)   a.   the stipulative character of the critical assignment of relevant traces to the category R-expression;
   b.   the existence of strong crossover effects in *non-NP* extraction cases;
   c.   the secondary strong crossover effect; and
   d.   most seriously of all, the Asymmetry Property.

3. New objections to Principle C accounts

3.1. Remarks

Flaws in the original Principle C approach *not* to my knowledge already found in the literature include diverse cases where the c-command condition required for Principle C relevance fails to hold between offending pronoun and extraction site.

3.2. Defect 5: the offending pronoun is in a prepositional phrase

The first such case is relatively minor. Example (26) shows that at best, c-command is not the right notion for any Principle C formulation intended to capture strong effects:

(26)   a.   ⊄[Which lawyer]$_1$ did Mike fail to mention [$_{PP}$ to her$_1$] that we had praised t$_1$?
   b.   ⊄[Which lawyer]$_1$ did Mike fail to tell her$_1$ that we had praised t$_1$?

Since the pronoun in (26a) fails to c-command the trace position, no Principle C violation can be induced. Nonetheless, anaphoric linkage is as impossible as in (26b). This problem parallels others PPs raise for anaphoric description and might just support replacing c-command with the notion suggested for related reasons in (27):

(27)   Pesetsky (1995: 173)
        "For example, we might define a relation called *EBPP-command* ('everything-but-PP-command') as a component of the notion 'binding' (cf. Lasnik's [1976] notion of Kommand).

> (453)   a. α EBPP-commands β if and only if the first non-PP that dominates α also dominates β.
>   b. α binds β if and only if α EBPP-commands β, α precedes β, and α and β are coindexed.

        "Such a theory would account for the interaction of prepositions with binding phenomena. Nonetheless, (453) would not explain this interaction. (453) cannot tell us why PPs fail to count for command, precisely because this fact is stipulated."

A restatement of Principle C in terms of (27) would correctly block (26) and is independently motivated for Principle C by *noncrossover* data like (28):

(28)   a. $\not\subset$Mike failed to mention [$_{PP}$ to [some lawyer]$_1$] that he respected [that lawyer]$_1$.
        b. $\subset$Mike talked [$_{PP}$ to Sharon$_1$] about herself$_1$.

So (26) indicates further sloppiness in earlier proposals that the strong effect reduces to Principle C but not a grave technical problem.

3.3.   Defect 6: the offending pronoun is in a coordinate phrase

The issue for a Principle C account raised by PP data has a partial analog in *coordination* data like (29), which represents the second new c-command problem.

(29)   a. $\not\subset$[Which nurse]$_1$ did Mike convince Jim and her$_1$ that you voted for t$_1$.
        b. $\not\subset$It was that nurse whom$_1$ Jim and she$_1$ said that you would hire t$_1$.
        c. $\not\subset$It doesn't matter [what nurse]$_1$ they arranged for Jim and her$_1$ to tell you that I would hire t$_1$.
        d. $\not\subset$[What woman]$_1$ did they place an alligator between Jim and her$_1$ while interviewing t$_1$?

These examples illustrate what I believe is the general truth in (30):

(30)   If a context C that induces strong violations is mapped into a different one *solely* by replacing the offending pronoun P in C by a conjunction of NPs *that include* P, binding of P by the extractee *remains impossible*.

Evidently, though, given that the pronoun in such coordinate structures is a subconstituent of a larger NP, it cannot c-command the trace position, and PP invisibility would not help. Designing some analog to (27) that ignores *coordinate* nodes would be misguided, given (31):

(31)   a. ⊂Mike convinced Jim and her$_1$ that you voted for [that nurse]$_1$.

        b. ⊂Jim and she$_1$ apparently (both) said that you would hire [that nurse]$_1$.

        c. ⊂They arranged for Jim and her$_1$ to tell you that I would hire [that nurse]$_1$.

        d. ⊂They placed an alligator between Jim and her$_1$ while interviewing [that woman]$_1$.

These data show informally that undoing extractions like those in (29) yields examples that do *not* contain anaphoric linkage violations. So, contrary to instances considered so far, where violations in putative strong effect cases parallel those found between pronoun positions and premovement extractee positions, not so in (29)/(31).

    With respect to this and other cases introduced later, a Principle C defender might deny that the problematic cases, here (29), represent strong effects. Such an approach is suspect because it means recognizing some *independent* binding constraint to block (29). Worse, examples like (29) manifest key defining features of the strong effect; they are insensitive to the PP/NP distinction, manifest the Asymmetry Property, and reveal primary and secondary variants; see (32):

(32)   a. ⊄Jane$_1$, [from whom$_1$]$_2$ Ted and she$_1$ said the police had hidden the truth t$_2$,

        b. ⊄Jane, who(m)$_1$ Ted mentioned to Mike and her$_1$ that you would call t$_1$.

        c. ⊂It was her who(m)$_1$ Mike and Jane$_1$ said you would call t$_1$.

        d. ⊄[Whose$_1$ niece]$_2$ did Mike and ⊄she$_1$/⊄she$_2$ claim that you had insulted t$_2$?

The Principle C account's failure to handle coordination facts is thus hardly to be rectified by invoking a phenomenon distinct from the strong effect.

    While the coordinate data just cited raise real issues for a Principle C account, these are relatively tame when compared to facts like (33):

(33)   a. ⊄It was [Jane$_1$ and Barbara$_2$]$_{1,2}$ who$_{1,2}$ Mike respectively convinced her$_1$ that you would call t$_1$ and tried to convince her$_2$ that I would call t$_2$.

        b. ⊄[Which two women]$_{1,2}$ did Mike respectively convince her$_1$ that you would call t$_1$ and try to convince her$_2$ that I would call t$_2$?

Here a Principle C treatment based on traces not only fails to induce the manifested strong effects. Rather, movement/trace approaches to extraction have not even shown how to provide basic analyses of such structures and, of course, standard treatments of extraction in general do not even mention them.

3.4. Defect 7: the offending pronoun is in an exceptive structure

The third new objection connected to a failure of c-command between pronoun and extraction site relates to *exceptive* structures such as (34):

(34) a. ⊄[Nobody but/except (for)/other than Vanessa$_1$]$_2$ could they convince her$_1$ you would invite t$_2$.
      b. ⊂[Nobody related to/fond of/interested in Vanessa$_1$]$_2$ could they convince her$_1$ you would invite t$_2$.
      c. ⊂[Nobody but her$_1$]$_2$ could they convince Vanessa$_1$ you would invite t$_2$.
      d. ⊄Vanessa$_1$, they convinced [everybody but her$_1$]$_2$ that you would invite t$_1$.
      e. ⊂Her$_1$, they convinced [everybody but Vanessa$_1$]$_2$ that you would invite t$_1$.

While it might be claimed that (34a) is not really a *new* problem, since it represents essentially only a further type of *secondary* strong effect, this is really wrong, for normally there is no secondary strong effect with *definite referential* NPs, as the contrasting (34b) shows. With respect to this property, there may, however, be individual variation; for instance, the anaphoric linkage in (35) is marked bad, while for me it is perfect:

(35) Pesetsky (1995: 270)
      ⊂/⊄[Which picture of Tom$_1$]$_2$ did he$_1$ say Sue had purchased t$_2$?

Example (34c) is not incompatible with a Principle C account, as that condition is satisfied. But a further genuine problem is seen in (34d). This does manifest illicit anaphoric linkage, although the pronoun cannot c-command the extraction site; so Principle C is not invoked. That (34a and d) are nonetheless strong effects is argued by the well-formed anaphoric linkages in (34c and e), which show that anaphoric linkages here manifest the Asymmetry Property.

A Principle C account defender might invoke here some analog of the concept proposed by Pesetsky or, alternatively, might claim that the index associated with the *inner* NP in an exceptive structure somehow percolates up to the outer NP. This could yield Principle C violations by converting (34a) to (36a) and (34d) to (36b):

(36) a. ⊄[Nobody except Vanessa$_1$]$_2$/$_1$ could they convince her$_1$ you would invite t$_2$.
      b. ⊄Vanessa$_1$, they convinced [nobody but her$_1$]$_2$/$_1$ that you would invite t$_1$.

In (36), the traces are arguably illicitly bound under Principle C by coindexed nodes. Precedents for such moves appear in trace-theoretic work on anaphora, for example, Safir (1984, 1996), who proposes such a mechanism for structures like those involved in secondary strong effects; see (37):

(37) Safir (1996: 325)
      "(31) a. Q-chain
            A Q-chain is a sequence of adjacent Ā-binding constituents [O$_1$, O$_2$, . . . ,O$_n$] such that O$_{m-1}$ binds a variable in O$_m$. The initial O$_1$ of the Q-chain is the Q-chain head. The variable bound by 0$_n$ is the Q-chain variable.
            The Q-Chain Convention
            Add the index of the Q-chain head to that of the Q-chain variable.
            The extractions that create and extend Q-chains are predicated on the LF movement of the class of elements that move scopally at LF, namely, the so-called true quantifiers."

But the *particular* mechanism Safir advanced could not function for exceptives, as it only creates secondary index assignment that originates from *quantificational* expressions, not with definite referential ones like <u>Vanessa</u> in (34a).

Moreover, claiming that the inner index of an exceptive is in general obligatorily assigned to the outer NP is untenable, given (38b, c, and d):

(38) a. $\not\subset$[Nobody except Vanessa$_1$]$_2$/$_1$ praised her$_1$.
   b. $\subset$[Nobody except ??her$_1$/herself$_1$]$_2$/$_1$ praised Vanessa$_1$.
   c. $\subset$[Nobody except Vanessa$_1$]$_2$/$_1$ praised Vanessa$_1$.
   d. $\not\subset$[Nobody except Vanessa$_1$]$_2$/$_1$ praised herself$_1$.

Obligatory secondary assignment would be not only consistent with (38a) but also supported by it, given that it would block the bad anaphoric linkage under anything like Chomsky's binding Principle B. But it is nonetheless counterexemplified by (38b and c), where it would *wrongly* create Principle C violations, and by (38d), which it would wrongly claim *satisfies* Principle A. It is not directly relevant here that the reflexive variant of (38b) creates a problem for any analog of Chomsky's *Principle A*, as there is no obvious way the apparent anaphor <u>herself</u> could be bound.

Thus even if appeal to index reassignment mechanisms is allowed, it offers no way to keep Principle C consistent with data like (34a and d), under the empty category view of traces.

Facts rather parallel to those with exceptives are found with phrases constructed with <u>only</u> and <u>even</u>; see for example (39):

(39) a. $\not\subset$Vanessa$_1$, they convinced [even/only her$_1$]$_2$ that you would invite t$_1$.
   b. $\not\subset$Vanessa, who$_1$, they convinced [even/only her$_1$]$_2$ that you would invite t$_1$, . . .
   c. $\subset$Vanessa$_1$, they convinced [her$_1$ mother]$_2$ that you would invite t$_1$.
   d. $\subset$Vanessa, who$_1$, they convinced [her$_1$ mother]$_2$ that you would invite t$_1$, . . .

Contrasts like that between (39a, c) and (39b and d) argue against treating (39a and b) as *weak* crossover violations.

Space forces me to pass over the rather parallel ordinary quantifier structures in (40) and (41):

(40) a. $\not\subset$[Each one/All/None of [those starlets]$_1$]$_2$ praised them$_1$.
   b. $\not\subset$[None of [those stars]$_1$]$_2$ could they convince them$_1$ that you would invite t$_2$.
   c. ?$\not\subset$[None of [them$_1$]]$_2$ could they convince [those stars]$_1$ that you would invite t$_2$.
   d. ?$\not\subset$[Those stars]$_1$, they could convince [none of [them]$_1$]$_2$ that you would invite t$_1$.
   e. $\subset$Them$_1$, they convinced [none of [those stars]$_1$]$_2$ that you would invite t$_1$.

(41) $\not\subset$[All of them$_1$/*themselves$_1$]$_2$/$_1$ praised [those stars]$_1$.

3.5. Defect 8: the noncrossover effect

A fourth largely new objection to a Principle C treatment linked to its reliance on c-command involves data that *lacks* a property invariably present in all the strong effects cited so far. In previous data, the extraction site uniformly *follows* the pronoun that the extractee cannot antecede. This property is not relevant to the Principle C account, but it was, of course, to the proposal of Postal (1971), where it determined choice of the term 'crossover'. Nonetheless, (42) exemplifies cases that manifest the key features of standard strong effects other than the word order property whose extraction sites nonetheless *precede* the pronouns with which anaphoric linkage is impossible:

(42)   a. Jacobson (1976: 12) attributed to William Leben
          (i) *⊄Who$_1$ did the wolf mention his planning to eat t$_1$ to her$_1$?
          (ii) *⊄Who$_1$ did Hamlet talk about his overhearing t$_1$ to him$_1$?
        b. Koopman and Sportiche (1982/1983: 149) and Safir (1984 :605)
           ⊄Who$_1$ did you give a picture of t$_1$ to him$_1$?
        c. ⊄Who$_1$ did you paste photos of t$_1$ on him$_1$?
        d. ⊄the nurse who$_1$ they bought sketches of t$_1$ from her$_1$
        e. ⊄Jerome$_1$, Ira expressed contempt for t$_1$ near him$_1$.
        f. ⊄It was Jerome$_1$ that Ira expressed contempt for t$_1$ near him$_1$.

While (42a–f) resemble standard primary strong effect violations in having extracted NPs that cannot anaphorically link to certain pronouns, they contrast in another respect. As in the coordinate cases, the corresponding *pre*-extraction structures violate *no* constraint on anaphoric linkages and so not Principle C; see (43):

(43)   a. ⊂You gave a picture of Claude$_1$/[some officer]$_1$/someone$_1$ to him$_1$.
        b. ⊂They bought sketches of [some/that nurse]$_1$ from her$_1$.
        c. Koopman and Sportiche (1982/1983: 148) explicitly note the lack of c-command between the antecedent and pronoun positions in cases like (43a and b).

Actually, some speakers reject the *indefinite* versions of (43). I find them at worst stylistically heavy. Moreover, anaphoric linkage is less problematic when the pronouns are replaced by anaphoric lexical NPs; see (44):

(44)   ⊂Earl gave a picture of [some officer]$_1$ to [that officer]$_1$.

This is relevant because such anaphora is also subject to strong effects.
    I refer to the anaphoric linkage violations revealed in (42) as *noncrossover* effects. Some might hope to reduce noncrossover effects to the c-command requirement of Principle C via special constituent structure assumptions. Given that the linguistics from which the Principle C account arose is given to a vast expansion of recognized constituents, for example, functional projections that include agreement constituents, multiple constituents with empty heads, recursions on nodes like VP, and so forth, the possibilities are not small. Nonetheless, good evidence that such moves, whatever their independent validity, cannot succeed in reducing noncrossover effects to c-command conditions is provided by the fact that the extraction position can even be inside a subject.
    The relevance of this requires a brief codicil. Even granting that, as generally claimed, subjects are *islands*, which in general bar extraction, and ignoring marginal

acceptability cases like (45), one can still use such *ungrammatical* extractions to test binding hypotheses because of principle (46):

(45)   Reinhart (1983: 120)
       ?[Which businessman]$_1$ did the gossip about t$_1$ cause a national scandal?

(46)   Mere extraction from an island, even when yielding severe ill-formedness, does *not* inherently block anaphoric linkages if such are licit in the pre-extraction structure itself.

The truth of (46) appears in the fact that while (47b, d, and f) are sharply ungrammatical, there is no more interference with the indicated anaphoric linkages than there is in the nonextraction cases (47a, c, and e):

(47)   a. ⊂I found that Jane and Mark$_1$ both said you would hire him$_1$.
       b. ⊂*It was Mark who$_1$ I found that Jane and t$_1$ both said you would hire him$_1$.
       c. ⊂I compared nobody but Michelle$_1$ to the woman who hated her$_1$.
       d. ⊂*It was Michelle who$_1$ I compared nobody but t$_1$ to the woman who hated her$_1$.
       e. ⊂Because Carla$_1$ was surly, Mike wouldn't call her$_1$.
       f. ⊂*It was Carla who$_1$ because t$_1$ was surly, Mike wouldn't call her$_1$.

Returning to noncrossover effects, regardless of the status of extraction from the subject, anaphoric linkage is impossible in (48a, b), (49b), and (50b), instantiating the noncrossover effect with a subject-internal extraction site.

(48)   a. ⊄*[Which businessman]$_1$ did gossip about t$_1$ annoy him$_1$?
       b. ⊄*a businessman$_1$ who$_1$ gossip about t$_1$ was infuriating to him$_1$

(49)   a. ⊂[Several friends of Jerome's$_1$] are talking about him$_1$.
       b. ⊄*Jerome$_1$, who$_1$ several friends of t$_1$ are talking about him$_1$,

(50)   a. ⊂[No future teacher]$_1$ did several friends of Vanessa's$_2$ describe t$_1$ to her$_2$.
       b. ⊄*It was Vanessa who$_2$ [no future teacher]$_1$ did several friends of t$_1$ describe t$_1$ to her$_2$.

No tenable constituency assumptions could reduce these antecedence blockages to Principle C, because a subconstituent of a subject cannot c-command elements of the VP even under the wildest proliferation of nontraditional categories.
      Space also forces ignoring (51):

(51)   a. ⊂[Most articles about Mary$_1$]$_2$, I am sure she$_1$ hates t$_2$.
       b. ⊄*It is Mary who$_1$ [most articles about t$_1$]$_2$, I am sure she$_1$ hates t$_2$.

Reinforcing the point that strong effects are found in environments that lack c-command between a pronoun and its potential antecedent, (52) illustrates that the exceptive and noncrossover cases can be combined, with the expected strong effects:

(52)   a. ⊄[No professor except Marsha$_1$]$_2$ did they hand [pictures of t$_2$] to her$_1$.
     b. ⊄It was Marsha who$_1$ they handed [pictures of t$_1$] to no one but her$_1$.

For noncrossover effects then, the idea that anaphoric linkage constraints associated with extractions reduce to constraints holding in pre-extraction structures, which has been the base of all trace-theoretic approaches to the strong effect, seems entirely untenable, which suggests that the violations are in some way induced by extractions themselves.

That traditional strong effects and what are here called noncrossover effects are special cases of one unified phenomenon is supported by the existence of the four clear parallels between them listed in (53); see (54)–(66).

(53)   Similarities between Standard Strong Effects and Noncrossover Effects
     a. Both effects have primary and secondary variants.
     b. Both types of secondary effect fail to appear when the extractees are, for example, definite referential NPs.
     c. Both effects also exist in cases of anaphorically linked lexical NPs instead of pronouns, a property noted for the standard strong effect in McCloskey (1990).
     d. Both effects manifest the Asymmetry Property.

First, there are restrictions that parallel those in secondary strong effect examples like (16), which leads directly to a distinction between primary and secondary noncrossover effects. As far as I can determine, the latter have the same general properties as secondary strong effects. So, alongside the primary noncrossover effect example (54a) are secondary noncrossover violations like (54b and c). See also (55):

(54)   a. ⊄[Which man]$_1$ did you paste photos of t$_1$ on him$_1$?
     b. ⊄[[Which man]$_1$'s dog]$_2$ did you paste photos of t$_2$ on him$_1$?
     c. ⊄the man [[whose$_1$ dog's]$_2$ trainer]$_3$ you pasted photos of t$_3$ on ⊄him$_1$/⊄him$_2$/⊄him$_3$

(55)   a. Secondary Strong Effect: Higginbotham (1983: 407)
       ⊄[Which biography of [which artist]$_2$]$_1$ do you think he$_2$ wants to read$_1$?
     b. Secondary Noncrossover Effect
       ⊄[Which biography of [which artist]$_2$]$_1$ do you think I should show a review of t$_1$ to him$_2$?

Secondary noncrossover effect cases also parallel extraction from subject primary noncrossover effects such as (48b) and (49b); see (56):

(56)   a. ⊄a businessman [whose$_1$ son]$_2$ gossip about t$_2$ was infuriating to him$_1$
     b. ⊄Jerome$_1$, [whose$_1$ sister]$_2$ several friends of t$_2$ are talking to him$_1$,

A second parallel between the two secondary effects strengthens their suggested unity. As touched on earlier, unlike question and restrictive relativization, certain extractions, topicalization, clefting, and some nonrestrictive relatives may fail to yield *secondary* strong crossover effects, as in (57). These same extractions also fail to induce *secondary* noncrossover effects under analogous circumstances; see (58):

(57) a. ⊂[Carl's$_1$ neighbor]$_2$, they did not introduce him$_1$ to t$_2$.
      b. ⊂It was [Carl's$_1$ neighbor]$_2$ that they introduced him$_1$ to t$_2$.
      c. ⊂Carl, [whose$_1$ nurse]$_2$, they did not introduce him$_1$ to t$_2$,

(58) a. ⊂[Carl's$_1$ neighbor]$_2$, they did not paste any pictures of t$_2$ on him$_1$.
      b. ⊂It was [Carl's$_1$ neighbor]$_2$ that they pasted some pictures of t$_2$ on him$_1$.
      c. ⊂Carl, [whose$_1$ neighbor]$_2$, they did not paste any pictures of t$_2$ on him$_1$,

Consider (59a, b, c), where lexical NPs can be anaphorically linked:

(59) a. ⊂He gave a picture of a troll$_1$ to that troll$_1$.
    / b. ⊂He pasted a picture of a troll$_1$ on that troll$_1$.
      c. ⊂Never show unflattering pictures of any trolls$_1$ to [those trolls]$_1$.

These are consistent with Chomsky's binding theory since the NP pairs satisfy Principle C, the only constraint relevant to anaphoric linkage between lexical NPs. That is, since in (59) in none of the lexical NP pairs does one c-command the other, neither binds the other. This contrasts with the situation in, for example, (60):

(60) ⊄A troll$_1$ (said he$_1$ had) pasted a picture of Rhonda on [that troll]$_1$.

But in extraction correspondents of the well-formed (59b), such as (61), there is, as for noncrossover effects with pronouns, an effect not reducible to properties of pre-extraction structures:

(61) a. ⊄[Which troll]$_1$ did he paste a picture of t$_1$ on [that troll]$_1$?
      b. ⊄List all the trolls$_1$ that$_1$ he pasted pictures of t$_1$ on [those trolls]$_1$.

For any traces inside the picture NPs in (61) neither bind nor are bound by the demonstrative NPs. So an analog of the primary noncrossover effect exists for anaphoric lexical NPs. Principle C would again at best have to be supplemented by some further principle. Riemsdijk and Williams's treatment also fails for (61) since application of the non-c-command constraint on the NP-structures of the examples would not block them.

That the primary noncrossover effect exists with nonpronouns provides a third parallelism with the primary strong effect. For as McCloskey (1990) observed, the latter also has a nonpronominal analog; see (62). Moreover, variants of both secondary effects also exist with lexical NPs; see (63):

(62) a. ⊄[Which nurse]$_1$ did you convince that nurse$_1$ that you would hire t,?
      b. ⊄a troll, [which troll]$_1$ I saw [that troll]$_1$ pretend t$_1$ was an elf,

(63) a. ¢[Which biography of [which space alien]$_2$]$_1$ did that space alien$_2$ prove t$_1$ was slanderous?

b. ¢[Which biography of [which space alien]$_2$]$_1$ did Ernest write a letter about t$_1$ to that space alien$_2$?

The conclusion that the noncrossover and strong effects reflect the same principles is supported in a fourth way by the Asymmetry Property, for a similar feature arguably holds for the noncrossover effect. Compare (64a, b):

(64) a. ¢It was Laura$_1$ whom$_1$ I described several photos of t$_1$ to her$_1$?

b. ⊂It was her(self)$_1$ whom$_1$ I described several photos of t$_1$ to Laura$_1$.

(65) ⊂I described several photos of her(self)$_1$, to Laura$_1$.

(66) a. ¢It was Laura$_1$ whom$_1$ I persuaded her$_1$ that you might hire t$_1$.

b. ⊂It was her(self)$_1$ whom$_1$ I persuaded Laura$_1$ that you might hire t$_1$.

The anaphoric linkage in (64b) lacks the impossible status of that of (64a), typical of strong effect violations, and seems as good as the nonextraction case (65). Significantly, the properties of (64) seem to be essentially identical to those of analogs in classical strong effect environments like (66). So the noncrossover effect also only exists when antecedents are extracted, as in (23).

The extensive paradigmatic similarities between strong effects and noncrossover effects support taking both to reflect the same underlying principles. Since these cannot be reduced to Principle C for the strong noncrossover effect, it follows that this is incorrect for strong crossover effects as well.

Chomsky considered a single noncrossover effect in passing as in (67), stating that (67ai and ii) were *weak* crossover violations:

(67) a. Chomsky (1982b: 38) echoing Koopman and Sportiche (1982/1983: 149)

(i) ¢Who$_1$ did you give a picture of t$_1$ to him$_1$?

(ii) ¢Who$_1$ did you give a picture of him$_1$ to t$_1$?

(iii) "Both examples violate weak crossover as determined by the Bijection Principle."

b. ¢Anthony$_1$, I gave a picture of t$_1$ to him$_1$.

c. ¢It was Anthony who$_1$ I gave a picture of t$_1$ to him$_1$.

d. ¢Anthony, who$_1$ I gave a picture of t$_1$ to him$_1$, . . .

e. ¢Anthony$_1$ was hard to give pictures of t$_1$ to him$_1$.

But this claim is undermined by the fact that (67b, c, d, and e), which also involve illicit anaphoric linkages, have definite referential extractees. For as noted at the outset and discussed in the works in (68a), such extractees do not in general induce *weak* crossover effects, as illustrated by the lack of effect in (68b, c, d):

(68) a. Lasnik and Stowell (1991), Postal (1993b), and Safir (1996)

b. ⊂It was Anthony whom$_1$ his$_1$ boss displeased t$_1$.

c. ⊂Anthony, whom$_1$ his$_1$ boss displeased t$_1$, . . .

d. ⊂Anthony$_1$ was hard to describe his$_1$ new office to t$_1$.

While seemingly favoring Chomsky's claim, the badness of the anaphoric link-age in the definite extractee correspondent of (67aii) seen in (69a) is, I suggest, irrele-vant. For I would argue that this anaphoric linkage violation is *not* a weak crossover effect but only a reflection of the requirement, whatever its basis, for a *reflexive* form in this environment; the presence of the latter yields the fine (69b):

(69)   a. ⊄Anthony, who$_1$ I gave a picture of him$_1$ to t$_1$, . . .
       b. ⊂Anthony, who$_1$ I gave a picture of himself$_1$ to t$_1$, . . .

Example (69b) violates the Bijection Principle no less than (69a), indicating contra Koopman, Sportiche, and Chomsky the irrelevance of that condition to the facts under discussion.

3.6. Defect 9: extraction from adjuncts

A fifth objection to Principle C accounts based on empty category traces connected to a failure of c-command involves extraction from *adjuncts*. Since this is often barred, principle (46) is again potentially crucial. As is well known, backward linking of a pronoun object to an antecedent in an adjunct is frequently *permitted*, as in (70c, e):

(70)   a. ⊄The doctor told her$_1$ that you loved Gladys$_1$.
       b. ⊄It was Gladys who$_1$ the doctor told her$_1$ that you loved t$_1$.
       c. ⊂The doctor told her$_1$ that story while treating Gladys$_1$.
       d. ⊄It was Gladys who$_1$ the doctor told her$_1$ that story while treating t$_1$.
       e. ⊂It was her who$_1$ the doctor told Gladys$_1$ that story while treating t$_1$.
       f. [Which patient's$_1$ child]$_2$ did the doctor tell ⊄her$_1$/⊄her$_2$ that story while treating t$_2$?

Here (70a) is an ordinary Principle C violation given that the object c-commands everything in the complement clause; (70b) is then a standard strong effect case at-tributed to Principle C, seemingly reducing to the same principle as (70a). Example (70c) is of course generally taken to show that an object does *not* c-command an element in an adjunct like that in (70c). If not, it is completely unexpected under a Principle C account that extraction from the position of <u>Gladys</u> in (70c) would yield a strong effect. But (70d) shows that it does. The contrast between (70d and e) re-veals the Asymmetry Property, arguing that (70d) is a genuine strong effect, as does the secondary strong effect in (70f).

Parallel facts are seen in the different adjunct cases in (71) and (72):

(71)   a   ⊂The doctor jumped up enraged at her$_1$ after arguing with Gladys$_1$.
       b. ⊄It was Gladys who$_1$ the doctor jumped up enraged at her$_1$ after arguing with t$_1$.
       c. ⊂?It was her who$_1$ the doctor jumped up enraged at Gladys$_1$ after arguing with t$_1$.
       d. [Which patient's$_1$ child]$_2$ did the doctor jump up enraged at ⊄her$_1$/⊄her$_2$ after argu-ing with t$_2$?

(72)   a. ⊂The suggestion was never made to him$_1$ that you might consult [Dr. Felix]$_1$.
       b. *⊄[Dr. Felix]$_1$, the suggestion was never made to him$_1$ that you might consult t$_1$.

c. *⊂Him$_1$, the suggestion was never made to [Dr. Felix]$_1$ that you might consult t$_1$.

d. *[Which patient's$_1$ child]$_2$ was the suggestion made to ⊄her$_1$/⊄her$_2$ that you could play with t$_2$?

The problem these cases raise is that to allow the anaphoric linkages in (70a), (71a), and (72a), the object pronoun position must *not* c-command into the adjunct. But to reduce the anaphoric blockages in, for example, (70b), (71b), and (72b) to Principle C, the object pronoun position must c-command into the adjunct. Such results are not jointly possible, since the positions in the corresponding good and bad cases are seemingly identical.

These adjunct cases would, though, *not* be problematic if the suggestion of Williams given in full in (73) were valid. This claims that extraction from such adjuncts is permitted only because *reanalysis* turns the adjunct into a complement of the main verb. If so, c-command between pronoun and extraction position would be established, reducing the strong effect to Principle C:

(73)   Williams (1994: 71–72)

"Suppose there is a reanalysis rule that moves the adjunct from adjunct position to complement position. In that position it will be able to participate in feature passing under the definition of relativized head:

(100)   [[leave]$_{VP}$ [with t]]$_{VP}$ ⇒   [leave [with t]]$_{VP}$

"The reanalysis will not affect the fact that the adjunct is not an argument and so will not endow it with the ability to originate a scope index; but it will permit it to pass up scope indexes that originate in arguments within it. So the trace, which is an argument of the preposition *with*, will be able to pass up its scope index in the reanalyzed structure. The reanalysis rule must be regarded as a 'marked' possibility, to account for the semi-ungrammaticality of extraction from adjuncts."

Williams's description of this putative reanalysis is so terse and informal that I cannot see what the output structure would be in complex cases. As argued in Baltin and Postal (1996) and chapter 8, other common invocations of reanalysis fail remarkably, which suggests that great caution is in order about this one as well.

Moreover, Williams's specific reanalysis suggestion is untenable. First, if grammatical extractions from adjuncts depended on reanalysis of adjuncts as complements, such extractions would show the properties of extraction from complements. These include maximum freedom of category for extractees, whereas genuine extraction from adjuncts is extraction from selective islands (see Postal, 1998) and normally incompatible with most non-NPs, predicate nominals, and so forth. But extractions from the adjuncts at issue do not behave like extractions from complements but are only possible for a restricted range of nonsubject *NPs*. Compare previous object NP extraction examples with the bad cases of (74) that involve extractions of other elements:

(74)   a. *the woman [for whom]$_1$ the doctor told me that while buying the ring t$_1$.

b. *[How long]$_1$ did the doctor tell you that while washing his hands t$_1$?

c. *[What kind of a specialist]$_1$ did the doctor tell you that story long after becoming t$_1$?
d. *[Underneath no elm tree]$_1$ did the doctor tell you that story after sitting t$_1$.

These data show that taking the extractions from adjuncts to involve reanalysis as complements just gives the wrong answer.

Second, if reanalysis existed in these cases, logic requires that it be either optional or obligatory. If *obligatory*, the good nonextraction case anaphoric linkages like those in (70a), (71a), and (72a) could not exist. Therefore, the putative reanalysis must be *optional*. But if it is in general *optional*, then the bad extraction anaphoric linkages would have nonreanalysis structures and so could not follow from Principle C on the structure where reanalysis is *absent*.

The only way to avoid this conclusion would be to claim that the 'backward pronominalization' can only exist when there is *no* reanalysis but that extraction from the apparent adjuncts is only possible *given* reanalysis. This is in effect claimed by Williams, who generalizes to the assertion that backward pronominalization into an adjunct is uniformly banned in the presence of extraction from that adjunct. This entails that such binding is banned even when there is no potential strong effect. The only actual support cited for this claim is (75):

(75) Williams (1994: 72)
      ⊄What$_1$ should I warn her$_2$ before giving Mary$_2$ t$_1$?

But even if the anaphoric linkage in (75) *is* bad, which I doubt, I do not find that the relevant type of backward anaphora is in general incompatible with extraction. For me, the anaphoric linkages in all of (76) are fine:

(76) a. ⊂What$_1$ they warned her$_2$ sternly before providing Mary$_2$ with t$_1$ was a rocket-propelled bicycle.
      b. ⊂What$_1$ did the doctor try to talk to her$_2$ while poking Gladys$_2$ with t$_1$?
      c. ⊂[Which principle]$_1$ did the professor make fun of them$_2$ while lecturing [the first-year students]$_2$ about t$_1$?
      d. ⊂[Which principle]$_1$ did the professor make fun of them$_2$ while lecturing about t$_1$ to [the first-year students]$_2$?
      e. ⊂It was orange sherbet that$_1$ Sonia giggled at him$_2$ while feeding t$_1$ to [little Bobbie]$_2$.

If correct, the data in (76) provide another reason that nothing like Williams's proposal offers an alternative to the view that (70b), (71b), and (72b) are strong effects whose offending pronouns fail to c-command the extraction site.

4. The copy trace version

4.1. Remarks

I turn to the copy trace version of the Principle C account of the strong effect. This conception of traces actually goes back at least to Chomsky (1981: 89–90), where it was considered to deal with the secondary strong effect problem but *not* adopted:

"The natural way to work this out in the present framework would be to establish the convention for Move-α that when α is moved it is not deleted but left unchanged, apart from a feature D indicating that it is to be deleted in the PF-component."[11]

At first glance, this modification seems to eliminate an array of defects that haunted the empty category trace version. Specifically, it seems to give a reason that the relevant traces *are* R-expressions. Second, it seems to solve the problem of strong effects induced by PP extraction, seen in, for example, (26b), and with no special assumptions about PPs. Third, it seems to resolve the secondary strong effect cases, treating these essentially like Riemsdijk and Williams's NP Structure account without the latter's special assumptions. Fourth, the copy theory of A-bar traces seems to resolve the asymmetry issue. For, remarkably, it seems to incorporate without special cost a version of Barss's (1986) modification of Chomsky's original proposal, under which the trace of each moved category is of the same type with respect to the *binding* theory as the extractee.

The copy trace variant of the Principle C proposal thus seemingly yields correct answers for the cases in (77), all of which except for *a* are *mis*analyzed by the empty category version:[12]

(77)   a. $\not\subset$Who$_1$ did you persuade him$_1$ that Joan would marry t$_1$ = [who$_1$]?
        b. $\subset$Him$_1$, I persuaded Joe$_1$ that Joan would marry t$_1$ = [him$_1$].
        c. $\subset$Herself$_1$, I persuaded Mike that Joan$_1$ would discuss t$_1$ =[herself$_1$].
        d. $\not\subset$[To Marsha$_1$]$_2$, I persuaded her$_1$ to get Bill to talk t$_2$ = [to Marsha$_1$]$_2$.

A violation ensues in (77a) but not in (77b, c), just as desired, since only in the former is the copy trace an R-expression. Moreover, a violation is properly specified for (77d), because the pronoun improperly binds the occurrence of <u>Marsha</u> *inside* the copy trace.

Despite these improvements though, the proposal remains nonviable. Least seriously, it does not solve the defect of 'crossed' pronouns inside PPs, as in (26); the copy trace structure still fails to induce a strong effect violation under a c-command statement of Principle C for cases like (78):

(78) $\subset$ Marsha$_1$, I mentioned to her$_1$ that Bill was infatuated with t$_2$ = [Marsha$_1$]$_2$.

And it also fails to induce a Principle C violation in CP topicalization cases like (15a).

I consider other unresolved flaws presently. But a deeper issue is the independent tenability of the assumption that each extraction can be associated with a trace copy of the extractee.

4.2. The general untenability of the copy view of traces

Real doubts about this claim should have arisen given that thirty-one years ago Perlmutter, in a rarely if ever credited work, arguably among the first associating tracelike elements with movements, suggested a view in which each extraction left a resumptive pronoun, under a different name; see (79):

(79)   Perlmutter (1972: 73)

"(1) Rules that 'chop' constituents over variables in the sense of Ross (1967) do not exist. (2) Rules that appear to be 'chopping rules' are actually 'copying rules' that leave behind a *shadow pronoun* in the position of the constituent that has apparently been 'chopped.'"

Moreover, Perlmutter gave factual arguments for the pronominal character of the invisible elements. While works like Cinque (1975) and Hirschbühler (1975) soon probably refuted the *general* claim, nothing to my knowledge has ever refuted the *particular* assertion that French nonrestrictive relative extraction sites manifest pronominal properties. Despite this, that extraction type induces strong effects just as English nonrestrictive relative extraction does. So, in terms of the copy trace based Principle C theory, these French cases would have to be assigned R-expression traces, thereby failing to account for the pronominal characteristics Perlmutter documented. Somehow assigning them pronominal traces would account for Perlmutter's observations but would fail to yield the strong effects.

One need not depend on French; an argument with the same logic arises from observations about the class of English extractions referred to as *B-extractions* in Postal (1994a, 1998). These include NP topicalization, NP clefting, and nonrestrictive NP extraction. Using Perlmutter's methodology, I have argued that these extractions manifest *pronominal* gaps. The factual basis for this claim is that the extractions in question, though not the other NP extractions called *A-extractions*, are incompatible with positions, called *Antipronominal Contexts*, that ban *weak* definite pronouns.[13] At issue then are facts like (80)–(84), which reveal correlations between *ill-formed* B-extraction sites and antipronominal contexts. These sites are, however, critically, *not* incompatible with A-extractions:

(80)   a. Marshall painted his trailer green/*it.
        b. *Green$_1$/[*That color]$_1$, Marshall never painted his trailer t$_1$.
        c. *It was that color that$_1$ Marshal painted his trailer t$_1$.
        d. *Green$_1$, which$_1$ Marshall painted his trailer t$_1$,
        e. [Which color]$_1$ did Marshall paint his trailer t$_1$?
        f. the color that$_1$ Marshall painted his trailer t$_1$

(81)   a. Jerome was speaking in Latin/*it.
        b. *[That language]$_1$, no one was speaking in t$_1$.
        c. *It was Latin that$_1$ Herman was speaking in t$_1$.
        d. *Latin$_1$, which$_1$ Herman was speaking in t$_1$, . . .
        e. [Which language]$_1$ was Herman speaking in t$_1$?

(82)   a. Joe met some other woman/*her yesterday who was telepathic.
        b. [Some other woman]$_1$, Joe met t$_1$ yesterday (*who was telepathic).
        c. It was some other woman whom$_1$ Joe met t$_1$ yesterday (*who was telepathic).
        d. Some other woman, whom$_1$ Joe met t$_1$ yesterday (*who$_1$ was telepathic), screamed.
        e. [Which other woman]$_1$ did Joe meet t$_1$ yesterday (who was telepathic)?

(83)   a. It was that death ray/*it that Mike used.
        b. *[Some other death ray]$_1$ it was t$_1$ that Mike used.
        c. *It was that death ray that$_1$/which$_1$ it was t$_1$ that Mike used.
        d. *that death ray, which$_1$ it was t$_1$ that Mike used, . . .
        e. [Which death ray]$_1$ was it t$_1$ that Mike used?
        f. [Whichever death ray]$_1$ it was t$_1$ that Mike used, it didn't work.

(84)   a. The concert lasted the whole week/*it.
        b. *[The whole week]$_1$, the concert lasted t$_1$.
        c. *It was the whole week that$_1$ the concert lasted t$_1$.
        d. *The whole week, which$_1$ the concert lasted t$_1$, . . .
        e. [What length of time]$_1$ did the concert last t$_1$?
        f. [No matter how long]$_1$ the concert lasted t$_1$, . . .

These and numerous other cases of the same type argue that English B-extraction sites are linked to nonovert resumptive pronouns. But as is well known and has been touched on variously earlier, these B-extractions nonetheless induce strong effects when the extractee is of the type characterized as an R-expression in Principle C terms; see (85):

(85)   a. ⊄[That woman]$_1$, Joe persuaded her$_1$ that you would hire t$_1$.
        b. ⊄It was that woman whom$_1$ Joe persuaded her$_1$ that you would hire t$_1$.
        c. ⊄That woman, whom$_1$ Joe persuaded her$_1$ that you would hire t$_1$, is waiting.

So, as in the French cases Perlmutter studied, the copy view of traces is incompatible with evidence that shows the pronominal character of a certain proper subset of all extraction sites, including those of English B-extractions, a pronominal character *not* dependent on *pronoun* extraction.

A parallel argument against the copy trace view is derivable from the observations in Cinque (1990) and Postal (1993a, 1994b, 2001a, 2001b) that involve parasitic gaps (P-gaps). These works argue that nominal P-gaps are pronominal in the sense just characterized.[14] For instance, P-gaps are impossible in the antipronominal contexts of (80)–(84), as only partly illustrated in (86):

(86)   a. *[Whatever color]$_1$ Marshall hated t$_1$ after painting his trailer pg$_1$, . . .
        b. *[What length of time]$_1$ did Alice waste t$_1$ while trying to prove the concert lasted pg$_1$?
        c. [What woman]$_1$ did Joe watch t$_1$ play tennis who was telepathic?
        d. [What woman]$_1$ did Joe discuss t$_1$ while watching pg$_1$ play tennis (*who was telepathic)?

Here the bad version of (86d) reinforces the point by showing the contrast between ordinary extraction, which is insensitive to antipronominal contexts, and P-gap extraction, whose gaps are pronominal.

Despite that, P-gaps induce strong effects, as probably first noted in Barss (1986), and thus contrast with topicalized or clefted visible pronouns. In Principle C terms then, they should involve copy traces of the R-expression type. But this is incompatible with the pronominal nature of the gaps. These points are illustrated in (87):

(87) a. Barss (1986: 378)

⊄It's John who$_1$ Mary voted for t$_1$ after he$_1$ asked someone to nominate pg$_1$.

b. Cinque (1990: 150)

⊄Who$_1$ did they find t$_1$ hostile before he$_1$ realized they wanted to help pg$_1$?

c. ⊄[What woman]$_1$ did Joe discuss t$_1$ while she$_1$ tried to persuade Mike to hire pg$_1$?

That (87) involves genuine strong effects is supported by the fact that the Asymmetry Property manifests, although there is one difficulty; see (88):

(88) Barss (1986: 377)

⊂It was himself that$_1$ John$_1$ nominated t$_1$ before he$_1$ voted for pg$_1$.

The difficulty is that while Barss (1986: 378) claimed that the anaphoric linkage in (89a) that involved an extracted pronoun rather than reflexive was acceptable, for me it is impossible, as is that in (89b). But perhaps these judgments are linked to the fact that despite accepting things like (89a) and the short forms of (89b and c), I find the full versions of (89b and c) ungrammatical:

(89) a. Barss (1986: 378)

C$_{Barss}$/⊄$_{Postal}$It was him that$_1$ John$_1$ claimed Mary liked t$_1$ even though he$_1$ knew she hated pg$_1$.

b. ⊄It was himself that$_1$ John$_1$ claimed Mary liked t$_1$ (*even though he$_1$ knew she hated pg$_1$).

c. It was himself that$_1$ John$_1$ claimed Mary liked t$_1$ (*even though I knew she hated pg$_1$).

When we put all these facts together and assume (89) is somehow resolved consistently with the Asymmetry Property, P-gaps are seen to be systematically pronominal and yet to induce strong effects, inconsistent with a Principle C account based on the copy trace view, which could only predict the strong effects by taking the relevant P-gaps to be R-expressions.

An additional general problem for the copy trace view relates to the fact known since the 1960s illustrated in (90):

(90) a. ⊄She$_1$ criticized some of the men who visited Betty$_1$.

b. Postal (1971: 85)

⊂[Which of the men who visited Betty$_1$]$_2$ do you think she$_1$ criticized t$_2$?

Left extractions of the sort that induce strong effect violations have the effect of *eliminating* certain pre-extraction anaphoric blockages that would be due to Principle C under Chomsky's binding theory. Under a direct modification of (90b) in terms of the copy trace theory, the result, as in effect previously noted by Kuno, is (91), which *wrongly* induces a Principle C violation:

(91) See Kuno (1987: 63)

⊂[Which of the men who visited Betty$_1$]$_2$ do you think she$_1$ criticized t$_2$ = [Which of the men who visited Betty$_1$]$_2$

With no reference to Kuno's criticism, it has been proposed by Chomsky (1995b) following Lebeaux (1991) that adjuncts, which include restrictive relative clauses, are introduced by generalized transformations in a way that avoids the violation, presumably by yielding a copy trace in (91) that does *not* contain <u>Betty</u>. Such proposals are supported by citing supposed contrasts from Riemsdijk and Williams (1981) and Freidin (1986) to the effect in (92):

(92)   Chomsky (1995b: 204)
      a. ⊄[Which claim that John$_1$ was asleep]$_2$ was he$_1$ willing to discuss t$_2$?
      b. ⊂[Which claim that John$_1$ made]$_2$ was he$_1$ willing to discuss t$_2$?

I do not perceive this distinction and find the anaphoric linkages in *both* (92a and b) acceptable. And I find it even clearer that the anaphoric linkages are well formed in (93a and b), just as much as in the adjunct case (93c), a judgment supported by its consistency with (93d and e):[15]

(93)   a. ⊂[The claim that [the director]$_1$ was corrupt]$_2$, he$_1$ was unwilling to discuss t$_2$.
      b. ⊂[That [the director]$_1$ was corrupt]$_2$, everyone knew that he$_1$ would always be able to deny t$_2$ with a straight face.
      c. ⊂[The claim that [the director]$_1$ made t$_2$]$_2$, he$_1$ was unwilling to discuss t$_2$.
      d. Ross (1973: 198)
         ⊂[That Ed$_1$ was under surveillance]$_2$ he$_1$ never realized t$_2$.
      e. Culicover (1997: 333)
         ⊂[That John$_1$ had seen the movie]$_2$, he$_1$ never admitted t$_2$.

Consequently, the complement versus adjunct distinction does not seem relevant, Lebeaux's strategem does not work, the problem for the copy trace theory raised by the incorrect implications of (91) remains undealt with, and so yields a further objection to the copy trace theory.

Still further direct problems for the copy trace view are found in (94), which involve reflexives that evidently some, including me but not all speakers, accept:

(94)   a. Barss (1986: 276)
         ⊂It was himself whom$_1$ John$_1$ said Mary loves t$_1$.
      b. *⊄Mike$_1$ said that Gladys would never marry himself$_1$.
      c. ⊂Mike$_1$ said that himself$_1$ Gladys would never marry t$_1$.
      d. ⊂It was himself whom$_1$ Mike said that Gladys would never marry t$_1$.
      e. Lasnik and Saito (1992: 110)
         ⊂John$_1$ thinks that himself$_1$ Mary likes t$_1$.
      f. Pollard and Sag (1992: 295)
         ⊂It was herself that$_1$ Mary$_1$ thought Bill admired t$_1$ most.
      g. ⊂Herself$_1$, I heard Barbara$_1$ claim that Tony hated t$_1$.
      h. ⊂Himself$_1$, I couldn't convince Harold$_1$ to let Betty visit t$_1$.
      i. ⊂It was himself that$_1$ they told Jim$_1$ to have Betty tutor t$_1$.

For in these cases a copy trace view induces reflexive traces in positions where actual reflexives are impossible.

Finally, recall the various different non-PP cases where the empty category view of traces permitted no reduction of strong effects to Principle C because the offending pronoun failed to c-command the extraction site. These were the coordinate, exceptive, noncrossover effect, and extraction from adjunct cases. Obviously, enrichment of the structure of traces has no effect whatever on this flaw; so the second version of the Principle C reduction idea inherits the defect of not inducing strong effects in a range of structures where they actually occur.

I have tried to show then that despite a certain initial *relative* success compared to the empty category version, the copy trace version of a Principle C account ultimately cannot rescue the Principle C view of strong effects. More generally, I have attempted to indicate that the copy trace idea is itself untenable as a general conception of the nature of extractions, for various reasons, some touched on by Perlmutter more than thirty years ago.

5. Substantive conclusions

To conclude, Chomsky's claim (4) was clearly untenable when made, remained untenable through the period that preceded adoption of the copy view of traces, and is also untenable under that view, which is itself in general untenable. Moreover, given the problems the overall conception faces, which include a rich range of cases where strong effects exist in the absence of any c-command between pronoun and extraction site, the prospects for future successful revision seem extremely poor. Further, the Principle C account incorporates the idea that strong effects can, via appeal to traces, be reduced to the principle that bars anaphoric linkage between a form F and an anaphoric form A where A is found in a higher constituent than F. Considerable evidence was presented that this more general idea, which dates to the original trace proposals of Culicover and Wasow, is also wrong.

If correct, given the limited current alternative descriptions of the strong effect, the conclusions show that the nature of the principles that *truly* underlie this phenomenon should be regarded as essentially open.

Further, the Principle C account of the strong effect is often, as in (95), cited as evidence that supports the postulation of the *nonpronominal* traces on which it depends:

(95)   Lasnik and Uriagereka (1988: 41)
        "Note that this account of so-called strong crossover demands that Condition C be applicable to derived structure, a conclusion we reached on other grounds in section 1.3.2. Furthermore, to the extent that this analysis is successful, it provides a second argument for the basic tenet of Trace Theory—that movement rules leave traces. If there were no traces, then there would be no R-expression for Condition C to constrain."

Significantly then, our conclusions here support the claim that there is no real factual support for any tracelike objects connected with extraction *except* invisible resumptive pronouns of the sort originally posited by Perlmutter.

For the latter I believe substantial evidence is available, in Obenauer (1984, 1985, 1986, 1992) as well as in Cinque (1990) and Postal (1994a, 1998), although this claim is sharply challenged in Levine (2001). This support is of essentially the sort that, as argued in Sag and Fodor (1995), has *never* successfully been provided for *non*-pronominal traces.

6. Methodological conclusions

A theoretical linguistic proposal like Chomsky's Principle C hypothesis about the strong effect could have been, as was, I believe, the proposal in Postal (1971), wrong without being disgraceful But as the text and notes 4, 6, 9, 10, and 11 support, the moves to introduce claim (4), that Chomsky's (1981) Principle C explained the strong effect, not only embody a factually and theoretically untenable grammatical proposal but also flout minimal standards of reasonable linguistic scholarship. In particular, it was shown that in addition to saturating the claim with theoretical and factual inadequacies that were not treated openly, no attempt was made even to keep claim (4) consistent with the original strong effect data in Postal (1971). The assertion ten years later that Principle C entailed the strong effect has been shown to have ignored (i) induction of strong effects by non-NP extractions, (ii) the secondary strong effect, and (iii) the Asymmetry Property, all of which were documented in Postal (1971).[16]

There is another aspect of the inadequacy of the development of (4) as a linguistic claim worth stressing. While it has been taken to be an actual linguistic discovery that the strong effect is an entailment of Principle C (given its supporting assumptions about traces, traces as R-expressions, etc.), it is notable that this claim exists only as scattered passing remarks in various works. Not only is there no complete section of any work, no article, no monograph devoted to its justification, there is hardly a full paragraph. Surely this fact, combined with the extraordinary shoddiness of the support for the proposal and the disdain for standards involved in its promulgation, should suggest a moral: When someone claims in passing to have a major theoretical syntactic result but can neither produce nor cite any work devoted to justifying the supposed accomplishment, one must rightly suspect that, as in this case, one is dealing with junk syntax.

8

Junk Syntax 2

*"There Remain a Few As Yet
Unexplained Exceptions"*

1. Background

During the now nearly five decades during which the ideas of generative transformational grammar have been applied to English syntax, *passive* constructions such
as (1) have been a continuing focus:

(1) a. Claudia was interviewed by that company.
     b. Few linguists were considered by Marie capable of solving that problem.

If these ideas were sound, one could today reasonably expect a basic analysis that
embodied a core of insight into English passive structures to have emerged. Such
has often been implied, as in the implicit suggestion in (2), which yielded the title of
this chapter, that the only problems that persisted (as of 1977; presumably even a
few of *those* would have *since* been resolved) are at the margins:

(2) Chomsky (1977a: 14, note 14)
     "On the analysis of passive constructions, see *Reflections on Language*, Chapter 3. There
     remain a few as yet unexplained exceptions."

I am aware of no repudiation since by the author of this remarkably optimistic view
of the level of success achieved by his transformational movement view of English
passivization.

Moreover, as is well known, in the overall Principles and Parameters tradition that represents the later evolution of the ideas of the author of (2), the description of passives continues to share a great deal with that of the period of the remark. It is as much standard doctrine now as in 1977 that English (verbal) passives are properly described transformationally, via (DP) movement of a specific type (now called A-movement); see, for example, Culicover (1997: 89–101) and, more recently still, Hornstein and Nunes (2002: 28–29). If so, the unrepudiated optimism of (2) should not be less tenable today than in 1977.

But the burden of this chapter is twofold: first, to suggest that beyond (partially) capturing the gross semantic/selectional similarities between active object and passive subject and active subject and passive by phrase already noted in 1957 (see [3]) there is little about the relevant construction that transformational accounts get right; second, and more important, to argue that the exposition and justification of transformational views of passivization have been prototypical instances of junk syntax. It is argued that claim (2) was then and would be today not only wrong but also deeply irresponsible.

2. The beginning: *syntactic structures*

The earliest generally available statement of a transformational view of English passives is represented by the informal account in (3):

(3)   Chomsky (1957: 42–43)

"Passive sentences are formed by selecting the element *be+en* in rule (28iii). But there are heavy restrictions on this element that make it unique among the elements of the auxiliary phrase. . . .

"Finally, note that in elaborating (13) into a full-fledged grammar we will have to place many restrictions on the choice of *V* in terms of subject and object in order to permit such sentences as: 'John admires sincerity,' 'sincerity frightens John,' 'John plays golf. . . . John drinks wine,' while excluding the 'inverse' non-sentences' 'sincerity admires John,' 'John frightens sincerity,' 'golf plays John,' 'wine drinks John.' But this whole network of restrictions fails completely when we choose *be+en* as part of the auxiliary verb. In fact, in this case the same selectional dependencies hold, but in the opposite order. That is, for every sentence NP_1–V–NP_2, we can have a corresponding sentence NP_2–*is* + V*en*–*by* + NP_1. If we try to include passives directly in the grammar (13), we shall have to restate all of these restrictions in the opposite order for the case in which *be* + *en* is chosen as part of the auxiliary verb. This inelegant duplication, as well as the special re- strictions involving the element *be* + *en*, can be avoided only if we deliberately exclude passives from the grammar of phrase structure, and reintroduce them by a rule such as:

(34)   If S_1 is a grammatical sentence of the form

$NP_1 - Aux - Y - NP_2$,

then the corresponding string of the form

$NP_2 - Aux + be + en - V - by + NP_1$

is also a grammatical sentence.

"For example, if *John–C–admire–sincerity* is a sentence then *sincerity – C + be + en – admire – by + John* (which by [29] and [19] becomes '*sincerity is admired by John*') is also a sentence."

This passage introduced one clearly correct insight of the transformational description—namely, the existence of corresponding selections. Beyond that, from the beginning there was vast exaggeration, a remarkable detachment from the facts of English, as well as outright distortion—that is, aspects of junk syntax. Most significant in particular is the claim that for *every* sentence of the form [NP$_1$ V NP$_2$] there is a corresponding passive of the form [NP$_2$ is + Ven by NP$_{1]}$]. One might assume today in defense that this long-ago falsehood (see later discussion) was due to mere naïveté, carelessness, or the inevitable limits of a beginning field. But consider passage (4) from the author's thesis of 1955, a study finished *two years before* the publication of the volume from which (3) is drawn:[1]

(4) Chomsky (1975a: 565)
    "There are many exceptions to the transformations that we have set up . . .
    "We might mention several incidental exceptions (whether real or apparent, only future investigation can determine) to the transformations we have constructed. As instances of actives with no corresponding passive we have:

471 (a) this costs a lot of money   (g) he had an accident
     (b) this weighs three pounds   (h) no one foresaw any improvement
     (c) John traveled three days   (i) he didn't like either of them
     (d) Mary married John   (j) he only likes certain people
     (e) misery loves company   (k) the artist redecorated it completely"
     (f) he got his punishment

That is, the author was aware several years before the publication of claim (3) in 1957 that it was false, had even said that there were many exceptions to his transformations in general, and knew in particular that his passive mapping failed for, for example:

(5) a. [NP John] [traveled] [NP three days]   ⇒   * three days were traveled by John
     b. [NP this] [costs] [NP a lot of money]   ⇒   * a lot of money is cost by this
     c. [NP he] [had] [NP an accident]   ⇒   *an accident was had by him

Further, Chomsky noticed (1975a: 534) that (6b and d) were ungrammatical, which means that the claim in (3) was also false for (6a and c), the latter example explicitly mentioned:

(6) a. John saw himself in the mirror.
     b. *Himself was seen by John in the mirror
     c. John ate dinner by himself.
     d. *Dinner was eaten by himself.

More generally, as amply (but still only in part) illustrated later, the degree to which the 'every' claim fails is extraordinary. One can only speculate as to why such a deliberate falsification was advanced in (3). But one can hardly avoid consideration of the fact that it appears in the author's first *published* attempt to tout the virtues of transformational grammar. Nor can one ignore the truism that a view always looks better if it can claim exceptionless principles, rather than rough approximations. Putting these together seems not to leave much mystery as to the ground for the falsification. In any event, the junk linguistic feature of outright fact distortion to render a proposal more attractive than it is had evidently surfaced in the first work that advocated a transformational view of English passives.

Moreover, claim (3) also contains the unsupportable assertion that the duplication of selectional and other restrictions that Chomsky had argued were associated with a phrase structural account of passive cases could *only* be avoided via a rule like the author's (34). This linked to similar exaggeration on page 78, where it was claimed that "any grammar that can distinguish singular from plural is sufficiently powerful to enable us to prove that the passive requires inversions of nouns phrases," and on page 79, where it was stated that "[s]uch verbs prove quite conclusively that the passive must be based on an inversion of subject and object." Critical is the occurrence of the strong 'prove' and still stronger 'prove quite conclusively' in these claims. The unfounded, exaggerated character of such remarks is shown entirely internal to the development of the author's own views.

For he has, of course, long since abandoned the idea that there is inversion of DPs in passives and only recognizes movement of objects; see section 5. So what was "proved (quite conclusively)" by X in 1957 was not even considered true by X a couple of decades later. Evidently there was no proof but only empty claims of such, raising minimally another issue of conduct. For the later abandonment of the conclusion was not to my knowledge associated with any public retractions of the false claims. A distinct strand of junk linguistic practice is illustrated. Claim something quite strong, using words like prove, later abandon the claim if it proves a burden, but never discuss or admit the lack of basis for the earlier admittedly false and exaggerated assertion.

And there was more:

(7)   Chomsky (1957: 82–83)

 "As another example of a similar type, consider the sentence

 (108)   John came home.

  "Although 'John' and 'home' are NP's, and 'came' is a Verb, investigation of the effect of transformations on (108) shows that it cannot be analyzed as a case of NP – Verb – NP. We cannot have 'home was come by John' under the passive transformation, or 'what did John come' under the question transformation T. We must therefore analyze (108) in some other way (if we are not to complicate unduly the description of these transformations), perhaps as NP – Verb – Adverb. Apart from such considerations as these, there do not appear to be very strong reasons for denying to (108) the completely counterintuitive analysis NP – Verb – NP, with 'home' the object of 'came.'"

In the discussion, the author encounters a failure of passivization, represented by (8b):

(8) a. John came home.
     b. *Home was come by John.

Passage (7) does not indicate that the problem is general across the class of intransitive verbs that accept a postverbal home:

(9) a. John crawled/dashed/flew/hopped/ran/swam home.
     b. *Home was crawled/dashed/flown/hopped/ran/swam by John.

The author's reaction to (8b) was remarkable. Although the passage already says that John is an NP, came is a verb, and home is an NP, it then claims bizarrely that (8a) *cannot* be analyzed as a case of [NP – Verb – NP], because if it is, it is wrongly predicted that, for example, (8b) is good. It is suggested that it should be given some other analysis, perhaps [NP – Verb – Adverb], to block the bad case. This proposal is incoherent. Stating that home was an NP had already granted that (8a) has the analysis [NP Verb NP].[2] Thus one need not depend on passages from Chomsky (1975a). Under its own constituency assumptions, the 1957 volume itself contains a counterexample to its claim in (3) that *every* [NP$_1$ V NP$_2$] structure yields a passive.

It is, moreover, irrelevant to any current point whether it is claimed that *in addition* the structure of cases like (8a) includes a subtree of the form (10), fig. 8.1:

(10)   Adverb

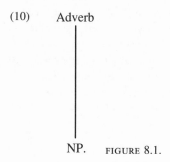

        NP.   FIGURE 8.1.

For the author's conceptions of transformational grammar have always been such that such a subtree would not block application of a rule defined in terms of NP – Verb NP.[3]

The only conclusion then is that the author had, as in the case of the counterexamples in (4), already noticed another anomaly for his transformational view of passive in cases like (8b) and had no coherent solution for it but failed to make that situation explicit.

As an account of the relation between English active and passive structures, (3) was clearly radically false; see sections 4–6 for an extensive listing of counterexamples to it. Moreover, other classes of data, while not counterexamples, also show its extreme inadequacy. These involve uncontroversial passives that do not correspond to actives of the form cited in (3). The most visible group of such seemingly exceptional cases are the prepositional passives or *pseudopassives*. Section 6 treats these exceptions to principles like those embodied in (3).

Evidently then, fundamental junk linguistic features were already highly visible in the work that introduced a transformational description of English passives to the general linguistic public. Despite this, the view that there is a viable, moreover insightful, transformational account of English passives had great fairly immediate *popular* success, which has persisted to the present day. The implication is that just because a junk linguistic proposal is awful linguistics or offends decent standards of inquiry, that doesn't begin to determine that it will not be widely accepted. Parallels are clear with the remarks in chapter 7 about the social success of the Principle C account of strong crossover phenomena despite its incompatibility with data published a decade before that account surfaced.

3. "Applies blindly"

The falsehood in (3) that *every* English [NP + V + NP] structure yields a corresponding passive received, in effect, a more elaborate and abstract formulation by its author during the 1970s. Associated with that development was an unheralded, repeated appeal to protective devices, elements that in effect can defend the formulation against any data. This is illustrated in (11):

(11)   Chomsky (1973); reprinted in Chomsky (1977a: 82–83) (emphasis mine: PMP)
        "[T]he Passive transformation (reducing it to essentials) applies to any phrase marker that can be 'factored' into five successive substrings in such a way that the second and fourth are noun phrases, the third a verb of a particular category (perhaps determined by some semantic property), and the first and fifth anything at all (including nothing). Thus the structural condition defining the transformation can be given in the form (Z, NP, V_x, NP, Y). The transformation rearranges the noun phrases in a fixed way. It will, therefore, apply to the phrase markers underlying the sentences of (1), converting them to the corresponding passive forms:

    (1)   a. Perhaps-John-read-the book-intelligently
         b. John-received-the book
         c. John-regards-Bill-as a friend
         d. John-painted-the wall-gray
         e. John-expects-the food-to be good to eat

        "Evidently, the semantic and grammatical relation of the main verb to the following noun phrase varies in these examples (there is no relation at all in [e]), but these relations are of no concern to the transformation, which *applies blindly* in all cases."

Although position (11) offers a refined formulation of the ideas of the *Syntactic Structures* account, it is similar in most key ways. Passivization continues to be characterized via NP/DP movement of both underlying postverbal DP and subject DP. But there are new emphases; specifically, transformations are stipulated to be *blind* to semantic and grammatical relations. So passivization in particular is thereby taken to be independent of these features.[4] The highlighted claim of blind application only appears strong since the associated hedge that a verb-instantiating term three of the structural description has to be "of a particular category," not characterized (moreover, one possibly determined by some unspecified semantic relation), renders claims of blind application vacuous. Any potential counterexamples, for example, those of (5) or (8b), could be handled merely by stipulating that their verbs are not of the right category. Such assignments could never be wrong since no independent criteria for membership in that category were presented. So, as a conception of the conditions that permit an English active structure to have a corresponding passive, proposal (11) embodies only the tautology that for a fixed active A, A has a corresponding passive or not, depending on whether A's verb belongs to category V_x or not.[5]

As (12) documents, the author of (11) made similar or related pseudostrong claims on other occasions during the 1970s, which indicates that the position cannot be dismissed as a temporary aberration:

(12) (all emphases mine: PMP)

a. Chomsky (1971: 30–31)

"In all cases, the passive is formed by the rule informally described a moment ago. The rule pays no attention to the grammatical and semantic relations of the main verb to the noun phrase that follows it. Thus in 'I believed your testimony,' the noun phrase is the grammatical object of 'believe.' In 'I believed your testimony to be false,' it bears no relation to 'believe,' and is the subject of 'be false.' In 'I believed your testimony to have been given under duress,' it bears no relation to 'believe' and is the grammatical object of the embedded verb 'give.' Yet in all cases, the rule *applies blindly*, caring nothing for these differences.' Thus in an important sense, the rules are structure-dependent and only structure-dependent. Technically, they are rules that apply to abstract labeled bracketing of sentences (abstract, in that it is not physically indicated), not to systems of grammatical or semantic relations."

b. Chomsky (1972b: 118)

"The basic property of transformations is that they map phrase-markers into phrase-markers. Each transformation applies to a phrase-marker on the basis of the formal configurations expressed in it, and quite independently of the meanings or grammatical relations expressed by these formal configurations. Thus such sentences as *John received the book*, *John read the book*, *John expected the book to be good*, *John gave Bill the book*, and so on, undergo the passive transformation in exactly the same way. The transformation *applies blindly* to any phrase-marker of the proper form, caring nothing about meanings or grammatical relations. This situation is typical; I know of no exceptions, and no counterarguments that amount to more than terminological revision."

While no insight into passives is visible in (11) or (12), they do reveal something about general principles of junk linguistics. These involve the tactic of making proposals *seem* significant by stating them in a vividly strong form ('applies blindly'/ 'independent of grammatical relations') while at the same time covering oneself against potentially embarrassing counterexamples via background tempering with protective hedges that render them safe from any data. The particular hedges in (11) are among a variety of mechanisms invoked by its author to eliminate testability of an otherwise strong claim about a transformational description of English passives. Other such devices with similar functions will be touched on presently.

Hedging the sort of transformational views promoted in the 1970s so that they could not be falsified was well motivated. Despite boasts like (2), *considerable* data incompatible with an unhedged formulation had accumulated by the time claims like (11) and (12) were made. For example, Fillmore (1965), a well-known and prominently reviewed work of the time (see Kuroda, 1968; and Wilson, 1966), had discovered several generalizations about one type of English, his own (and, incidentally, mine). The generalizations concerned *double object* or *ditransitive* cases like (13):

(13)   a. Armand sold her the six Uzis.
        b. Armand bought her the six Uzis.

Fillmore observed that in the type of English at issue, structure (13a), call it a *type A ditransitive*, corresponds to two distinct passives, while structure (13b), call it a *type B ditransitive*, corresponds to none.

(14)   a. She was sold the six Uzis by Armand.
        b. The six Uzis were sold her by Armand.

(15)   a. *She was bought the six Uzis by Armand.
        b. *The six Uzis were bought her by Armand.

Fillmore noted, moreover, that it was in significant part predictable whether a double object structure was of type A or B. The type A variety was such that the first object alternated with a structure with a PP in *to*, while the type B was such that the first object alternated with a structure with a PP in <u>for</u>.

(16)   a. Armand sold the six Uzis to her (for Rhonda).
        b. *Armand bought the six Uzis to her (for Rhonda).

Evidently, nothing in proposals (11)/(12) offers any insight into these facts. Moreover, (15a, b), and so on, are further prima facie counterexamples to the claim in (3) about "every" transitive active and to any factual content to a claim that there is some rule that "applies blindly." And (14b), an instance of the *tertiary passives* of Postal (1986a), challenges the assumption that only directly postverbal DPs passivize in English. If those assertions had been serious, they would have had to take into account Fillmore's observations and advance some proposal to keep the double object data consistent with the formulation. But typically for junk linguistics, formulations like (11)/(12) were advanced, multiply published, and defended as if Fillmore's observations, uncited, had never been made.

And it is entirely impossible that the author of (3), (11), and (12) was unaware of the dual passive possibilities of cases like (14). Least of all, it was traditionally documented; see, for example, Jespersen (1927: chapter 15). Moreover, amazingly, he *had himself noted this fact before Fillmore*. The point is made explicitly in his thesis, noted earlier to have preceded Fillmore's work by a decade, despite its publication delay by the same amount. Chomsky (1975a: 493) cites the type A ditransitive cases:

(17)   a. he was given several books by the teacher.
       b. several books were given him by the teacher.

Worse:

(18)   Chomsky (1975b: 242, note 43)
       "In ordinary passives such as (55), the rule of NP-preposing disregards the grammati-
       cal relation between the verb and the NP following it, at least if we use the term 'gram-
       matical relation' in something like its traditional sense. Thus in (55), the rule moves
       the direct object, but in such cases as 'John was told to leave' or 'John was promised
       that he would get the job,' it is the indirect object that is preposed (cf. 'John was told
       a story,' 'a story was told to John'; 'our promise to John . . .'. . .)."

That is, a decade *after* the appearance of Fillmore (1965), the author of (11) and (12) cited double object passives *selectively* as *supporting* his view that passive movement ignores grammatical relations, with no mention of his own or Fillmore's earlier observations, work that minimally is problematic for that view. This was fea-sible only by carefully picking examples of type A ditransitives and none of type B manifesting, as Fillmore documented, unpassivizable direct and indirect objects, and arguing that passivization does not disregard the type A/type B distinction, which nothing in the structures the author was offering distinguished. Moreover, it was necessary as well to avoid mention of type A tertiary passive examples like (14b) and (17b), since their citation would have inevitably raised issues for which no solu-tions were available. So where genuine linguistics would have manifested a real at-tempt to handle the facts Fillmore had discussed, some of which the author of (18) had noted even earlier, one finds instead spurious boasts like (2). The fact that claims like (11), (12), and (18) ignore the relevant ditransitive observations is in itself an excellent indication of the junk linguistic character of the passive proposals at issue.

More generally, the history of generative discussion of passives like (14b) is arguably an exceptional illustration of the grip of junk linguistics. Although such examples are commonly cited in traditional descriptions of British English (see Curme, 1931: 117; Jespersen, 1927: 301–312; and Sweet, 1891:113) and were analyzed for American English in Fillmore (1965), Oehrle (1976), and Postal (1986a), many linguistic works of the last twenty years, especially more recent ones, deny the exis-tence of American English passives like (14b); see, for example, Boeckx (1998, 451–452), Bresnan (1982c: 25–29; 2001: 316), Lasnik (1999a: 198), Ouhalla (1994: 175), Pesetsky (1995: 124), Riemsdijk and Williams (1986: 117), Runner (1999: 155), and Ura (2000: 244–248). Evidently, many Americans, especially younger ones, do not accept them.

But for many American speakers, including me, many examples are perfect. Example (17b) shows that the inventor of transformational ideas about passives being criticized here was in 1955 among them. And Christopher Potts kindly provides the following published written examples:

(19) a. He was a man of many holdings—many of them handed him, as each ancestor fin-
         ished his life's run and passed the stick forward, handed him in a lineal descent of
         bonds and a bank, of glass birds and dishes, land, houses, and attitudes.
         M. Malone. *Dingley Falls* (p. 88)
      b. The young men crunched ice cubes and wolfed cheese sandwiches brought them
         by Chris Henry.
         M. Malone. *Dingley Falls* (p. 127)
      c. Lagniappe: a small gift given a customer by a merchant at the time of purchase.
         Webster's 3rd New International Dictionary
      d. Included meanwhile in the epic consolations given the conservationists . . . were
         more than two million acres along the Yukon between Eagle and Circle.
         John McPhee. *Coming into the Country* (p. 246, hardcover)
      e. The friendship extended him by his classmates.
         Richard Russo. *Mohawk* (chap 16, p. 1)
      f. Cooper (1983) is the most explicit and fully developed attempt to pursue the first
         strategy, but the semantic techniques involved are significantly more complex than
         those afforded us by PC.
         Gennaro Chierchia and Sally McConnell-Ginet. *Meaning & Grammar* (p. 119)

So, given that many speakers reject them, a serious treatment of tertiary passives
should have, even ignoring British English, throughout dealt with what are clearly
partially contrasting grammatical systems. A proper account of American English
passives evidently needs to specify how these differ, a point explicitly made in Bach
(1980: 325) and Iwakura (1987: 94). Instead, it has, probably under the pressure of
various theoretical assumptions, come to be widely accepted in generative circles,
despite clear evidence to the contrary, that tertiary passives do not exist in American
English.

To see the truly bizarre character of this, one finds that, for example, Stroik (1997:
43), a work that explicitly develops the recent ('minimalist') transformational ideas
of Chomsky (1993, 1995a, 1995b), does not flinch from deriving *support* for specific assumptions from their ability to predict the *impossibility* of such passives. That
is, in 1997 one finds someone putatively developing the theoretical ideas of author
A and claiming support for a version of those ideas from the purported fact that they
predict the impossibility of sentences richly exemplified in the literature and that A
himself had documented for his own NL in 1955. Perhaps even more tellingly, in a
work submitted to a Web site of papers to honor the author of (18), Romero (1998),
someone associated with that author's own institution, asserts as part of a theoretical
discussion of passives crosslinguistically that only 'goal' passives are possible in
English ditransitives and cites:

(20) a. Almodovar was given the awards
      b. *The awards were given Almodovar

So here someone is "honored" by theoretical discussions that assume the essential
contrary of what the honoree had documented (in [17b]) forty-three years earlier.
This might be said to go beyond junk linguistics to a form of unintended parody.

One further point about the interaction of ditransitive structures and passivization is worth highlighting. A fact rarely discussed in transformational terms is the existence of passive constituents embedded under get. Notably, while, for example, (18) correctly cites various ditransitive first (indirect) objects as being passivizable and (17b) correctly indicates certain ditransitive second objects are, even those that have that property in standard settings with be lack it in get cases:

(21) a. The wrong books were/got ordered.
     b. The house was/got destroyed.
     c. The books were/got sold to Mike.
     d. Mike was/*got sold the books.
     e. Mike was/*got told several stories.
     f. Several books were/*got given him by the teacher.
     g. Nobody wants to be/*get sent threatening letters.

A parallel point holds for passive constituents embedded under causative verbs like have:

(22) a. Stella had the wrong books ordered.
     b. Stella had the house destroyed.
     c. Stella had the books sold to Mike.
     d. *Stella had Mike sold the books.
     e. *Stella had Mike told several stories.
     f. *Stella had several books given him.

Needless to say, nothing in the proposals about transformational descriptions of English passives accounts for these gaps. No aspect of (3), (11), or (12) seems to have any application. Indicated, I believe, is that the standard idea that all English passivization is to be reduced to a single undifferentiated operation is misguided. But in any event, the contrast between unsupported dreams like (2) and the factual reality of English is again quite palpable.

Statements (11) and (12) assert that transformations, specifically that involved in passivization, apply blindly and are indifferent to grammatical relations. But consider:

(23) Chomsky (1971: 29–30)
     "Consider next the sentence 'I believe the dog's owner to be hungry.' Applying the postulated operation, we locate the main verb 'believe' and the noun phrase 'the dog' following it, as before, and form 'The dog is believed's owner to be hungry.' Obviously, this is incorrect. What we must do is choose not the noun phrase 'the dog,' but rather the noun phrase of which it is a part, 'the dog's owner,' giving then: 'The dog's owner is believed to be hungry.' The instruction for forming passives was ambiguous: the ambiguity is resolved by the overriding principle that we must apply the operation to the largest noun phrase that immediately follows the verb. This, again, is a rather general property of the formal operations of syntax."

Here a really blindly applying rule would wrongly allow the impossible passivization of the genitive phrase. But instead of admitting that talk of blind application was vacuous, the author invokes an auxiliary hypothesis, in effect, the A-over-A principle. But if one is allowed to invoke some new curative hypothesis every time blind application fails, the claim obviously has no testable consequences. Moreover, it was untenable even in 1971 to invoke a *general* A-over-A principle. Ross (1967/ 1986) devoted a whole chapter to the general untenability of such, work that Chomsky is silent about. But the really key point is that the failed passive of the genitive discussed in (23) is *exactly* the sort of case that is properly *excluded* if passivization is, contra the claims, sensitive to grammatical relations—in particular, if one views passivization in anything like traditional relational terms such as those in (52) ahead. For in no one's sense is the genitive phrase any kind of object of the verb in whose clause it is unpassivizable. So, like the "applies blindly" claim, the supposed independence of passivization from grammatical relations was also interpreted in such a way as to admit of no falsification, at the same time it was proclaimed with great emphasis.

At a certain point, it was assumed that the transformational DP preposing putatively crucial for characterizing verbal passives was the same operation as one that putatively yielded certain prenominal genitive DPs; see Fiengo (1977, 1980) and Hoekstra (1984: 133–136). So, for example, (24a and b) were both taken to involve preposing of a DP, a theory-internal way of saying both are passive structures:[6]

(24)   a. The city was destroyed by the giant gorilla.
        b. the city's destruction by the giant gorilla

But Chomsky (1975b: 242, note 41), citing Joseph Emonds, noted a contrast between seeming nominal and verbal passives, as follows:

(25)   a. the lecture yesterday ⟹ yesterday's lecture
        b. he lectured yesterday ⟹ *Yesterday was lectured by him.

He then added:

(26)   Chomsky (1975b: 242, note 41)
        "I think that in many cases, perhaps all, the discrepancies can be attributed to other factors."

Crucially, the author does not say that his formulations of the NP preposing rule are *wrong*. Again, for a rule said to "apply blindly" the fact that it fails to apply in a case where its formulation says it should apply is not taken to show that the "apply blindly" claim is wrong. Rather than abandon the claim, in the particular case of (25), the author appeals instead to something he calls the *subject-predicate relation*, hypothesizing it to be defined on the surface structures of sentences but not on nominals:

(27)   Chomsky (1975b: 242, note 41)
        "[I]t might be plausibly argued that 'was lectured (by NP)' is not a possible predicate of 'yesterday' accounting for the ungrammaticalness."

In effect, (27) claims that some semantic principle that involves predication blocks (25b) but is inapplicable to the good (25a) because the subject-predicate relation is undefined for NPs/DPs. Nothing about this proposal is serious. First, the author has not defined the putative subject-predicate relation or given any evidence that there is such a thing and not shown independently a single fact it accounts for. So there is no visible justification for assuming any such subject-predicate relation defined on surface structures. Rather, the contrary is true, given, for example, (28a, b), where grammatical passive subjects are expletives, meaningless phrases of which it would make no sense to predicate anything:

(28)   a. It was proved that Disneyland is toxic.
      b. There are assumed to be space aliens in Congress.

Still worse for the author's proposal, there are perfectly fine English sentences that have exactly the sort of subject NPs that are bad in passives like (25b):

(29)   a. Yesterday found Mike in Detroit.
      b. Yesterday saw the Yankees lose to the Red Sox.
      c. Yesterday was found to be a poor day to launch the Space Shuttle.

What reason could there be that it is correct to predicate <u>found Mike in Detroit,</u> <u>saw</u> <u>the Yankees lose to the Red Sox,</u> or <u>was found to be a poor day to launch the Space</u> <u>Shuttle</u> of <u>yesterday</u> but not <u>was lectured by him</u>? None is of course given.

In short, the casual, unsupported attempt to defend the NP preposing rule in Chomsky (1975b: 142) was entirely spurious and no genuine basis whatever was offered for the ungrammaticality of (25b). Nonetheless, the same account is in effect repeated in Chomsky (1977a: 177–178). The very appeal to it shows clearly the emptiness of claims about movement rules "applying blindly." If the term 'junk linguistics' did not exist, it would arguably need to be invented for this invocation of an unmotivated and indefensible semantic principle of predication just to block the application of a rule that, if the "'applies blindly" terminology had any content, would have to apply even if the predication principle were real.[7]

Moreover, the procedure of proposing a desperate, ad hoc patch for an otherwise factually leaking proposal about passivization seen in (27) is not unique. That junk linguistic characteristic recurs; when the author notes factual problems for his transformational approach to passivization, he appears *never* to contemplate even the possibility that these show it is false. A second highly revealing instance is found in Chomsky (1981: 147, note 108), which considers (30):

(30)   They forced John to wait.

This is taken to be a *control* structure, in the author's terms, one with an invisible PRO complement subject coindexed with one in the including phrase, here <u>John</u>. One assumes this would be taken to be the right analysis for the whole range of <u>force</u> + infinitive cases like, for example, (31):

(31)   a. Mike forced Selma to do the dishes.
       b. Germany forced Holland to surrender.

Suspiciously though, the author gives no argument for a control analysis and considers no alternatives. Moreover, the various novel tests appealed to in chapter 2 to differentiate control from raising structures unambiguously indicate that infinitival complements with <u>force</u> are raising, not control, cases:

(32)   a. Middles
          The occupying power forced Uruguayan police to bribe cheaply.
       b. Metonymous Stock Structures
          Not even Zeus could force Lucent Technologies to go up.
       c. Partial Control
          *The director forced his subordinate to meet at noon.

That is, it was seen that control complements could not be middles or the metonymous structures and that raising complements could not manifest partial control. In all three respects then, the <u>force</u> complements behave like raising cases.

The arguably wrong control assumption putatively leads to an expectation, not explained, that cases like (33) are *bad*:

(33)   a. they forced it to rain (by seeding the clouds).
       b. the forced better care to be taken of the orphans (by passing new laws).

But according to the author (I agree) these seem "moderately acceptable." A straightforward reaction would have been to simply reject the control analysis, the source of the false expectation about (33). But this idea was not even considered.

Instead, it was proposed that these examples "are only derivatively generated (in the sense of Chomsky (1965, p. 227; 1972 pp27f.)." The former reference yields a discussion that claims that an adequate grammar directly generates all the perfect sentences but "derivatively generates" imperfect ones with, in some unspecified way, an account of how they are imperfect. The latter offers parallel claims with indication that what is being talked about is to be interpreted in part in terms of *analogy*, in terms of speakers "failing to take note of a certain distinction of grammaticalness." And the author goes so far as to insist:

(34)   Chomsky (1972c: 28)
       "There is no doubt that such processes of derivative generation exist as a part of grammar in the most general sense."

One observes that (33) represents further cases where the sort of "blind application" views of passivization advocated by the author, if interpreted substantively, fail, since the following are bad:

(35)   a. *it was forced to rain.
       b. *better care was forced to be taken of the orphans.

But, as in his discussion of the contrast between DP preposing in clauses and nominals, instead of seeing some problem with his formulation, the author again seeks an ad hoc solution, this time, in effect choosing to criticize the examples and to exclude them from the NL or to claim that they involve violations that speakers are failing to notice. Despite the undefended and indefensible (34), there is evidently no reason to see this as anything but junk linguistics. Support for that conclusion is that the author gives no substance to the claim that (33) is 'derivatively generated'. How is this done? What principle or aspect of the grammar do they putatively violate? No answers are offered.

But the author does go on to offer what is called "evidence supporting this conclusion," namely, the fact that they resist "further grammatical operations," this a reference to the ungrammaticality of *passives* like (35). This putative evidence would have to have a logic of the following form:

(36)   a. There are structures, for example, (33), putatively 'derivatively derived', that satisfy the input conditions for the author's passivization (DP-preposing) rule.
        b. The output of that rule on the cited structures is ungrammatical.
        c. Fact b. supports the 'derivatively derived' claim for the structures of (33).

But no logical connection between premisses and conclusion is visible here; one could hardly better instantiate the notion 'non sequitur'. Further, what is stated in (36) is that an operation, once said to apply blindly, gives as output from a grammatical input structure that satisies its requirements something ungrammatical. Instead of concluding from that that the rule is wrong, the author leaps to a view of the input in entirely obscure and unanalyzed terms as 'derivatively derived'. But evidently state of affairs (36b) is exactly that which could show that a factual claim involved in the transformational passivization rule is false. Again then the author makes ominously clear that in his methodology nothing will be allowed to lead to that conclusion for a proposal he favors. Instead, he decided to attempt to marginalize the facts under the obscure rubric 'derivatively derived', making it at least rhetorically unnecessary to deal with them seriously.

The thoroughly junk linguistic character of that move is shown differently by the fact that its logic, (36), would require taking *every* passive failure to indicate 'derivative generation' of the input. For some idea of the scope of the absurdity of this, see in particular section 7. Two additional cases would be:

(37)   a. The chimp has a peach. ⇒
        b. *A peach is had by the chimp.
        c. Therefore, a. is 'derivatively derived'.
        d. Wanda got a puppy. ⇒
        e. *A puppy was got(ten) by Wanda.
        f. Therefore, d. is 'derivatively derived'.

Moreover, as remarked in Postal and Pullum (1988: 657), Chomsky has himself not in general followed that logic and has on multiple occasions there referenced concluded merely that a passive failure indicates the existence of some linguistic constraint that blocks the output. Obviously, that is what he did with respect to the nominal/clausal contrast of (25). The junk linguistic character of methodology (36) then includes the fact that its advocate refuses to even follow it consistently.

The author then moves on from (33) and (35) to examples like (38):

(38)   they prevented it from raining.

Here he says bizarrely (1981: 147, note 108) that it "should also be ungrammatical if prevent assigns a θ-role to its object." This is bizarre because even if one adopts a framework that sanctions concepts like 'assign a θ-role', no independent reason is cited to make the assumption for the particular case and there is none:

(39)   a. He prevented *tabs* from being kept on her movements.
       b. God prevented *it* from being nice in the Congo.
       c. Only the president can prevent *there* from being a strike.
       d. The director prevented *it* from being revealed that the treasury was empty.

That is, the post-prevent position allows all sorts of DPs (highlighted) that the author has otherwise assumed cannot receive θ-roles.

Moreover, the novel tests that distinguish raising from control complements again indicate that the prevent cases are raising structures:

(40)   a. Middles
          The occupying power prevented Uruguayan police from bribing cheaply.
       b. Metonymous Stock Structures
          Not even Zeus could prevent Lucent Technologies from going down.
       c. Partial Control
          *The director prevented his subordinate from meeting at noon.

So the author's unsupported factual assumptions were clearly wrong.

It was then claimed there is a parallel between his (35) and the force cases because supposedly the corresponding passive is again impossible:

(41)   *it was prevented from raining

Here, though, as discussed in Postal and Pullum (1988: 657), the facts are wrong, since in general speakers find passives like (41) and (42) essentially perfect:

(42)   a. Only through the use of nuclear weapons can it be prevented from raining.
       b. It could not for long be prevented from being noticed that he was dead.

The author says about (38) that "it has been proposed as an argument for raising-to-object," referring without citation to one of the arguments in Postal (1974). But Chomsky asserts that no argument can be based on it "since the rules for generating it would appear to be idiosyncratic." This illustrates a further junk linguistic lack of logic for several reasons. First, since no actual rules are given or cited, there is no way to evaluate any claim about them. If there is no such set or if its putative members were not correct, nothing could follow. But second, even if the author had in mind a relevant set of correct and idiosyncratic rules, nothing would follow. For no known logic determines that arguments can't be based on idiosyncratic rules. They can be based on any facts and, even, in the case of reductio arguments, on false assertions. The "no argument" claim is entirely junk linguistic bluff.

Thus the passages just discussed show again the emptiness of claims of blind application But they also illustrate the more harmful characteristic that when faced with data incompatible with some putatively significant claim, the author systematically refuses to contemplate its falsehood and instead has sought to invoke the most ill-defined and far-fetched protective moves, instantiating a solid strand of junk linguistics. A variety of other proposals that either inoculate his passive proposals from falsification or show that claims of "blind application" are empty have been made by the author of (11) and (12). Besides those already touched on, others are found in the list in Postal and Pullum (1988: 656–657).[8]

Overall then, the transformational passive proposals of the 1970s I have been discussing had the following junk linguistic characteristic: strong, prestigious-sounding claims systematically bound to one or another hedging device that guaranteed their factual emptiness. Not surprisingly, such spurious proposals coexisted with a flagrant disregard of well-documented and publicly known facts, such as those from Fillmore (1965), some even earlier noted in Chomsky (1975a).

4. Evolution of ideas

The accounts of transformational description discussed so far, (3), (11), (12), and so on, all fall within an earlier set of transformational assumptions. From the mid-1970s through the mid-1980s, the theoretical framework that underlay these descriptions underwent significant evolution. At least *six* innovations are potentially relevant to subsequent discussion of passives in transformational terms:

(43) a. Each transformational movement was ultimately taken to leave an invisible *trace* in the position of origin.
   b. It was ultimately claimed that individual transformational rules, which included movements, were properly subsumed under general, construction-independent schema like *Move θ*.
   c. It was ultimately claimed that transformations could move elements to positions higher in trees but never to lower positions.
   d. It was ultimately claimed that there was a system of abstract *case* assignment so that NPs/DPs in particular were associated with invisible cases, subject to various principles called Case Theory.
   e. It was ultimately claimed that there was a system of assignment (in some not clear way) of elements called *θ roles* to DPs, subject to various principles called Theta Theory.
   f. It was ultimately claimed that moved phrases and their traces formed objects called *chains*, subject to various conditions.

It is not my intention to describe any of these changes in detail. They are all well known and much discussed. Accounts better than any I could provide are found in such works as Culicover (1997), Lasnik and Uriagereka (1988), Ouhalla (1994), Riemsdijk and Williams (1986), Roberts (1997), and Webelhut (1995). Roberts (1986) probably gives the description most closely tied to passive issues.

These innovations and in certain cases the various theoretical losses they entail have diverse consequences for the description of passives. The recognition of traces in the two varieties null and copy, already discussed in a different context in chapter 7, need play little role in this discussion. However, not so for the shift from a view of individually formulated transformations that characterize specific constructions to one like (43b). That does have significant relations to this discussion, as seen in the early specification of it in (44):

(44)   Chomsky (1986b: 72–73)

"Correspondingly, the study of NP movement led to the conclusion that the various cases reduce to Move-NP. In the earliest work, there was, for example, a 'passive trans-formation' converting (29i) to (29ii) by a rule with the structural description and struc-tural change indicated informally in (30), moving the third term to the position of the first, adding *be-en* to the second term *see* (which becomes *be see-en* = *be seen* by a later rule; we overlook here the placement of tense), to the third position where it is assigned *by*:

(i) John saw Bill   (29)
(ii) Bill was seen by John

(NP, V, NP) → (3, be-en 2, by 1)   (30)

"Similarly, the rule of raising that converts (31i) to (31ii) was expressed as a transfor-mation (32), moving the third term of the structural description to the position of the first, which is empty in the underlying D-structure generated by phrase structure rules:

(i) e seems [John to be happy]   (31)
(ii) John seems [e to be happy]

(NP, V, [NP, X]) → (3, 2, 4)   (32)

"With appropriate formulation of general principles on rules and representations, both (30) and (32) reduce simply to Move-NP, so that there is no passive or raising rule but simply an interaction of principles of UG yielding various constructions, differing from language to language as a consequence of options that the languages allow. Further-more, the differences between Move-*wh*, Move-NP, Move-PP, and so forth can be in large part (perhaps completely) explained in other terms, so that we are left with the rule Move-α, α being an arbitrary category. It would be too strong to claim that this conclusion has been demonstrated, but it is a reasonable hypothesis, and many par-ticular cases appear well substantiated."

Recourse to such schemas yields a major modification of earlier descriptions of passives like that of (3), (11), and (12). The specific formulation of passive as in, for example, (11), which simply vanishes in the 'Move-α' framework, in itself imposed putatively correct, although, as has been seen and will be further, massively wrong, limitations on which DPs in actives were in principle subject to passivization; it was, modulo the dodge about verb category already touched on, simply those directly postverbal DPs. But on its own, the Move-α approach *imposes no conditions whatever on those DPs subject to passivization*, and, as the jargon goes, vastly 'overgenerates'. In effect then, the original transformational theory of constraints on passives, versions of which are seen in (3), (11), and (12) and (66), is abandoned. Something additional is obviously needed. An early recognition of this is seen in (45):

(45)   Chomsky (1976); reprinted in Chomsky (1977a: 174)
"Evidently, a grammar limited to such rules as (7) or (8) will overgenerate massively, since intricate constraints cannot be built into specific transformations. Consider the case of NP-preposing; i.e., the leftward movement case of (7). By general conditions on recoverability of deletion (the correct formulation of which is a nontrivial matter; cf. Peters and Ritchie [1973]), the second NP can move only to an NP position that is empty of any lexical material. Assuming that the left NP position, which is to receive the moved NP, is empty, either by virtue of prior NP-postposing or for some other reason, we will have such instances of NP-preposing as the following:

(10)   a. John is believed [t is incompetent]
       b. John is believed [t to be incompetent]
       c. John('s) was read [t book]
       d. John seems [t to like Bill]
       e. John seems [Bill to like t]
       f. yesterday was lectured t
       g. yesterday's lecture t

"In each case, *t* is the trace left by movement of the NP (*John, yesterday*). Of these examples, only (b), (d), and (g) are grammatical, although NP-preposing has applied in a comparable way in all cases. Thus the rule overgenerates, specifically, in cases (a), (c), (e), and (f).

"There are two general approaches to the problem of overgeneration in such cases as these: we may try to impose (i) conditions on the application of rules or (ii) conditions on the output of rules, i.e., on surface structures. The latter may be related to rules of semantic interpretation that determine LF, under the assumptions of EST."

Two points about (45) are obvious.[9] First, the passage does not go beyond generalities to real conditions which would properly reduce the vast excess of an unconstrained Move-α description of passivization. Second, although such descriptions no longer specify that a passivizable phrase must be immediately postverbal, the cases cited arbitrarily met this condition, which raises the question of whether the author had faced the magnitude of unwanted possibilities allowed by rule schemata. Notably, a decade later, one finds, as in (44), the reduction of passivization to a variant of the Move α-(schema being described in effect as an *accomplishment*, with no specification of problems or unsolved issues. What is unquestionable is that the overall issue of precisely describing the facts of passivization has largely vanished into some much vaster and unfocused problem of controlling the outputs of Move-α. Given the evolutions in question, it is much less obvious that transformational claims about passives are false because it is more difficult to determine what, if anything, the relevant claims are.

One additional point is that the adoption of the Move-α view abandons the proposal in (66) that compatibility with manner adverbials is a defining property of English passives, one that excludes the objects of what were called middle verbs from passivizing. One would have expected that fact to have been discussed and justified. But as far as I know, it never was.

Finally, the claim of "blind application," seen to combine prestigious apparent force with vacuity-determining hedges, of course *necessarily* vanishes in a Move-α(framework, implicitly granting that its only significance was the junk linguistic function of associating some unearned glamour with a factually and conceptually inadequate view.

5. The cavalier treatment of the by phrase

The earliest *transformational* accounts of English such as (3) and (11) involved the posit of two distinct (though linked) nominal movements for passive clauses like (46a):

(46)   a. Gloria was bitten by the snake.
        b. The snake bit Gloria.

One involved the 'promotion' of a VP-internal DP (here Gloria) to subject position of the auxiliary; the other, a 'demotion' of the underlying subject (here the snake) of an activelike structure to a position that, in some way, ended up being inside a PP. The latter mapping was problematic, as it was unclear how to guarantee the derived PP structure if, as in the earliest accounts, the structure on which passivization operated was essentially like that of the corresponding activelike (46b). One subsequent approach to this problem, that of Chomsky (1965: 104), posited an underlying P with a following empty (dummy element) NP position into which the active subject could move. A later version of this is (47):

(47)   Chomsky (1976); reprinted in Chomsky (1977a: 169)
        "For example, we might formulate the passive transformation in English with the following SD:

        (3)   (*vbl*, NP, Aux, V, NP, *by*, #, *vbl*)

        In this formulation, the two terms *vbl* are (end-) variables, so that the first and last factors of a string X to which the transformation applies are arbitrary. The second and fifth factors must be NP's (each is an NP), the third an Aux(iliary), the fourth a V, the sixth *by* and the seventh # (*by* and # are terminal symbols; we may think of # as an 'abstract' representative of NP)."

In this view, the 'demotion' of subject part of passivization is taken to involve substitution of the subject DP for an empty post-P DP. This view was still evidently quite inadquate as, like the *Syntactic Structures* version, it fails to indicate that the passive by + DP form a PP.

Moreover, a few years later, in Chomsky (1981), the 'demotion' aspect of the original transformational description of passivization had been completely abandoned. Rather, the underlying form of (46a) was claimed to be more like (48) than like (46b):

(48)   [e] was bitten Gloria by the snake.

This approach establishes no obvious connection between the object of a passive by phrase and the subject of an active. One motivation for the rejection of subject postposing as a feature of passive description may have been a realization that such was incompatible with a principle like (49), already referenced in (43c):

(49)   Chomsky (1975b: 107):
   "[T]he permissible rules are rules of 'upgrading' which move a noun phrase closer to the 'root of the sentence,' that is, to a less embedded position; the impermissible rules are rules of 'downgrading,' which increase the embeddedness of the noun phrase. We might stipulate, then, that upgrading rules are permitted, but not downgrading rules."

For subject postposing in passives would, of course, be an instance of putatively banned downgrading.

But other, more theory fundamental, reasons for abandoning the earlier postulation of subject 'demotion' are inherent in the ideas of Chomsky (1981) and subsequent work. The earlier analysis would end up violating the Theta Criterion of Chomsky (1981), as the DP moved to subject position would be assigned θ roles in both that and its original position. And problems also arise from the fact that the preposed DP would apparently have to appear in a position of the trace of the postposed DP. Details are not relevant here.

What is relevant, though, is that while the proposals of Chomsky (1981) abandon the demotion analysis of passive by phrases, nowhere in that work is there any explicit justification for the move or any proposed treatment of the immediate consequences of it.[10] The same lack of discussion is seen in a still later work, where one is only given an indication that that the full by phrase is present at all stages of the passive:

(50)   Chomsky (1986b: 73)
   "The same will be true of the passive rule if we assume that the structure immediately underlying the S-structure form is not (29i) but rather (33):
      e was *see-en* Bill (by John) (33)"

Inter alia, the consequences that involve partially undermining the original motivations for transformational descriptions of the passive, which included, as specified in (3), the need to capture the identical selectional/semantic relations that link active subject and passive by phrase object. There was, one recalls, even reference in (3) to the existence of NP interchange having been *proved*.

But in 1981 the author of (3) abandoned that idea without comment and with no exploration of alternative means of dealing with what had been 'proved' to require subject demotion. Moreover, in discussing passive it was claimed:

(51)   Chomsky (1981: 124)

"The traditional characterization of passive as involving a change of object to subject is correct in one important sense: this is the core case of passive."

Not only does this fail to reference the author's own earlier ideas, for example, (3), with their explicit recognition of a syntactic relation between active subject/ by phrase, but it also distorts the "traditional characterization," which of course included such a relation:

(52)   Jespersen (1924: 164)

"In most cases this shifting is effected by means of the passive turn (B is preceded by A). Here what was the object (or one of the objects) in the active sentence is made into the subject, and what was the subject in the active sentence is expressed either by means of a propositional group, in English with *by* (formerly *of*), in French with *par* or *de*, in Latin with *ab*, etc., or in some languages simply by means of some case form (instrumental, ablative)."

The disdain for the development of ideas evident in the failure of (51) to mention the subject/by phrase relation, traditionally explicit as in (52), or the author's own earlier recognition of this seen in (3), should be regarded as another junk linguistic feature.

If there is no transformational relation between active subject/passive by phrase object, then the unchallenged selectional/semantic relations that link them (see, e.g., Baker, Johnson and Roberts, 1989; Jaeggli, 1986: 599; and Roberts, 1986: 27) must be described by some mechanisms M *distinct from* transformational derivation. Chomsky (1981, 1986b) provided no account of M or even any indication that it was necessary. This issue does not seem to have been faced in transformational terms until Jaeggli (1986) and Baker (1988a: chapter 6). These works proposed idiosyncratic accounts of mechanism M. Both accounts appealed to manipulations of so-called θ roles, arguably the most obscure and undeveloped aspect of the framework at issue.[11] For Jaeggli (1986: 600) the basic idea was "that the passive suffix *en* is crucially involved in transferring the external θ-role onto the NP in the by-phrase in a passive sentence." This was elaborated in a complex way. Baker (1988a: 335–336) refined and expanded Jaeggli's proposal by claiming that the external θ role of the verb is assigned to the passive morpheme and that the by phrase 'doubles' the θ role of the passive morpheme. The latter is taken to parallel the features of pronominal clitics. To partly formalize these ideas, Baker proposed a special type of coindexing, which linked the passive morpheme and the by phrase. It seems fair to see in these complexities a forced, far-fetched attempt to recapture part of what the simple identity of active subject and passive *by* phrase recognized in other approaches, which include that of (3), elegantly yielded.

Moreover, the question arises why mechanisms of the type M, however elaborated, could not supply an alternative to that part of the DP movement description of English passives, DP preposing, which post-1981 transformational accounts *main-*

tained. Surely, one reply to this question would reference idiom pieces, for one of the standard arguments for a transformational description of English passives has for decades appealed to idiomatic pieces of VPs, as in (53); see, for example, Culicover (1976: 167–168) and Radford (1988: 422–424).

(53)   a.   The doctors took/*brought/*found/*grabbed/*grasped little heed of her problems.
      b.   Little heed was taken/*brought/*found/*grabbed/*grasped of her problems by the doctors.

The claim has been that the transformational aspect of the passive is revealed not merely by the selectional/semantic relations but precisely by the passivizability of pieces of structure that either are not directly semantic or do not bear a direct semantic relation to the verb in whose clause they passivize. Exactly this view was expressed by Chomsky (1975b: 114), where it was claimed that if there were no passives such as inter alia those that involved idioms, there would be no motivation for a transformational derivation of passives. The idea is that the relations can be stated only once with respect to the active structure, with the transformational movement as it were projecting them to passives without cost. This argument about idioms is of course maintained even under the altered, 'demotion'-rejecting transformational conception of passives; see, for example, Chomsky (1981: 85).

From this point of view then, rejection of the earlier transformational derivation of the passive by phrase object claims that there should not be corresponding subject demotion cases. That is, the post-1981 transformational view of the passive implicitly denies that there are instances in which an *idiomatic subject piece* of a structure T appears as the by phrase object of a passive that corresponds to T. Such an absence would apparently justify a difference between capturing the object/subject selectional similarities via one mechanism (e.g., movement) but the subject/by phrase ones by another, some instantiation of M.

Testing this claim, evidently, requires first finding active clauses that have both idiomatic subjects and otherwise passivizable objects. However, if the claims of Marantz (1984: 26–27) were fully correct, there could be none. Marantz discussed a putative asymmetry in which there are many verb + object idioms that combine with nonidiomatic subjects but apparently no subject + verb idioms that combine with nonidiomatic, nonfixed objects. While Marantz noted the existence of idioms like (54a), he stressed that in these the object is as fixed as the subject; in any event, no passive is possible, as in (54b, c):

(54)   a.   The shit hit the fan. ('things went bad')
      b.   *The fan was hit. (ok a physical fan was struck; *'things went bad')
      c.   The fan was hit by the shit (*'things went bad')

However, while English cases of the sort Marantz denied are not common, they are, contrary to his claims, *not* nonexistent, as illustrated first in (55):

(55)   a.   The lovebug bit Ted/your uncle/the guy next door/several policemen last year = "Ted/etc. fell in love last year"
      b.   The lovebug has bitten Ted/your uncle/the guy next door/several policemen again.

There should be no doubt about idiomaticity here; the term <u>lovebug</u> occurs only with the verb <u>bite</u>, and this verb in such contexts does not denote dental activities.

(56)   The lovebug *chewed/*clawed/*grabbed/*licked/*mangled/*overwhelmed/*seized Ted.

Expressions like (55) have two properties that Marantz claimed could not exist: (i) an idiomatic subject coexisting with a freely choosable (human) object and (ii) an idiomatic subject occurring in expressions whose overall form is not that of a fixed phrase. So the post-1981 'no demotion' transformational view of English passivization determines that cases like (55) have no corresponding grammatical passives where the idiomatic subject phrase of the active occurs as object of a passive *by* phrase But this is false; they do:[12]

(57)   a. Ted was bitten *by the lovebug*.
       b. Most romantics are bitten *by the lovebug* at least once during their lives.

Moreover, the same morphological elements <u>bite</u> and <u>bug</u> also form a distinct but more productive idiomatic sequence. This is illustrated by (58) from Bresnan (2001: 15), credited to Avery Andrews:

(58)   The photography bug has bitten/*chewed up/*disturbed/*killed Fred.

That is, there seems to be an idiom of the form $[_{DP} D + Noun_x + bug]$ Aux <u>bite</u> DP_2; the whole is interpreted to mean something like "DP_2 has become strongly interested in Noun." While the verb seems to be fixed as <u>bite</u> and <u>bug</u> must be present, $Noun_x$ is seemingly not fixed as long as it can be taken to designate an activity of people; that is, roughly $Noun_x$ must be able to appear also in the context [DP is into $[_{DP}$ (D) $Noun_x$ + (plural)]]:

(59)   a. The chess/golf/heroin/Internet/poker/polo/skiing/television/tennis/video game/
         categorial grammar bug has bitten Fred.
       b. Fred is into chess/heroin/the Internet/poker/polo/skiing/swimming/television/video
         games/categorial grammar.

As in the idiomatic usage in (55), passivization is possible:

(60)   Fred has been bitten by the chess/golf/heroin/Internet/poker/polo/skiing/television/
       tennis/video game/categorial grammar bug.

A third case of the same sort as (55) is, I think, seen in (61):

(61)   a. A little bird told/*promised/*sang/*wrote/*informed me (of) that.
       b. I was told/*promised/*sung/*informed (of) that *by a little bird*.

The stars in (61b) mark only the case where <u>a little bird</u> is interpreted idiomatically as designating not a small object of possible ornithological interest but a person/source that the speaker is explicitly indicating (s)he is refraining from identifying.

Further, as mentioned in note 6 of chapter 2, Nunberg, Sag, and Wasow (1994) observed that certain figurative idiom pieces like <u>birds of a feather</u> can occur in restricted cases as subjects of certain control complements. Now, a few control structures like that of (62) permit a passive whose subject is extraposition <u>it</u>:

(62) a. Those kids decided to hang out together.
       b. It was decided by those kids to hang out together.

Notably then, (63b) seems to me no worse than (62b), while (63d) has the impossible character of (63c):

(63) a. Birds of a feather may decide to flock together.
       b. It may be decided by birds of a feather to flock together.
       c. *Birds of a feather may decide to surf the Net.
       d. *It may be decided by birds of a feather to surf the Net.

This amounts then to a fourth case where an idiomatic active subject piece can appear in a passive <u>by</u> phrase.

And a fifth is provided by (64), where only the noncanine reading of <u>old dogs</u> is relevant:

(64) a. Old dogs may even decide to learn new tricks.
       b. It may even be decided by old dogs to learn new tricks.
       c. *Old dogs may even decide to stop drinking.
       d. *It may even be decided by old dogs to stop drinking.

Contrary to expectations under a view where the passive <u>by</u> phrase is not syntactically related to active subjects, clear cases have been found of subject idiom chunks in passive <u>by</u> phrases. Since for transformational views the passivizability of idiomatic VP phrase pieces is taken to support a DP 'promotion' of passive subject/ active object relations, parity of reasoning indicates that the facts in (57), (60), (61b), (63b), and (64) support a 'demotional' view of passive *by* phrase/active subject relations.[13] This does not yield support for a transformational treatment of passivization; it just means that within that framework an *asymmetric* 'promotion only' view is factually untenable. It also falls out that the claims of Baker (1988a) and Jaeggli (1986) that the relations between active clause subject DPs and passive <u>by</u> phrase DPs can be taken as completely mediated by the manipulation of θ-roles is untenable. Even if there are such things, they cannot suffice for this function.

To conclude, the history of the treatment of passive <u>by</u> phrases in transformational terms is an instructive illustration of junk linguistics. Beginning with the exaggerated claims in (3) of a *proof* that the object DPs of passive <u>by</u> had to be moved subjects, one finds an evolution where the 'proved' view is later not even taken as true. And when it was abandoned, no reference to the earlier claims was made and a distorted view of pregenerative views of passive was offered. Moreover, the abandonment was linked to no explicit discussion of how to deal with the facts that motivated what had been claimed to have been proved. Subsequent work like that of

Baker (1988a) and Jaeggli (1986) grappled openly with the problems created but offered only rather convoluted appeals to obscure θ-role notions. And the evolved view yields proposals that inherently make the false claim that passive by phrase objects cannot be the sort of restricted DPs whose behavior as passive subjects has standardly been taken to justify transformational movement. Moreover, no facts appear to conflict with the view that by phrase objects are realizations of syntactic subjects. The historical rejection of this idea seems to have been entirely concept-driven. So, nearly a half-century after the claimed provably needed DP interchange in (3), there evolved a set of ideas arguably descriptively worse with respect to passive by phrases than the original 1957 view.[14]

6. Reanalysis

Previous to the conceptual evolutions listed in (43), the transformational view in (3), (11), and (12) faced, as alluded to in section 2, a vast problem of *under*generation with respect to *pseudopassives* like (65b):

(65) a. Myron referred to the problem.
      b. The problem was referred to by Myron.

Such cases seem to fall outside the schema of description in (3), (11), and (12) since the passivized phrase is *apparently* not immediately postverbal in what would be the passive rule input. There seem to have been two different transformational approaches to this issue, a transient one in Chomsky (1965) and a standard one.

The former was described as follows:

(66) Chomsky (1965: 103–104)
      "These observations suggest that the Manner Adverbial should have as one of its real-izations a 'dummy element' signifing that the passive transformation must obligato-rily apply. That is, we may have the rule (55) as a rewriting rule of the base and may formulate the passive transformation so as to apply to strings of the form (56), with an elementary transformation that substitutes the first NP for the dummy element *passive* and places the second NP in the position of the first NP:

      (55)   Manner → *by* ∩ *passive*

      (56)   NP— Aux—— V—. . .—NP —. . .-*by- passive* -

      (where the leftmost . . . in (56) requires further specification—e.g., it cannot contain an NP).

      "This formulation has several advantages over that presented in earlier work on transformational grammar (such as Chomsky, 1957). First of all, it accounts automati-cally for the restriction of passivization to Verbs that take Manner Adverbials freely. That is, a Verb will appear in the frame (56) and thus undergo the passive transforma-tion only if it is positively specified, in the lexicon, for the strict subcategorization feature [—NP ∩ Manner], in which case it will also take Manner Adverbials freely.

Second, with this formulation it is possible to account for the derived Phrase-marker of the passive by the rules for substitution transformations. This makes it possible to dispense entirely with an *ad hoc* rule of derived constituent structure that, in fact, was motivated solely by the passive construction (cf. Chomsky, 1957, pp. 73–74). Third, it is now possible to account for 'pseudopassives,' such as 'the proposal was vehemently argued against,' 'the new course of action was agreed on,' 'John is looked up to by everyone,' by a slight generalization of the ordinary passive transformation. In fact, the schema (56) already permits these passives. Thus 'everyone looks up to John by *passive*' meets the condition (56), with *John* as the second NP, and it will be converted into 'John is looked up to by everyone' by the same elementary transformation that forms 'John was seen by everyone' from 'everyone saw John.'"

The key currently relevant idea in this proposal is the variable represented by the first set of three dots, constrained not to contain an NP. This broadens the class of NPs/DPs allowed to prepose in passives from the immediately postverbal ones picked out by (3). It basically allows anything to occur between the verb and a passivizable DP except a DP. Even though (66) would properly allow passivization of postverbal PP objects, it hardly represented a correct analysis of these. First, it was still too restricted; even the vast freedom of choice would not have permitted description of, for example, (14b). Moreover, the only principle (66) offered distinguishing V + PP structures that yielded pseudopassives from those that did not was compatibility with manner adverbs. It is seen in the following discussion of reanalysis that this is nowhere near correct. Moreover, it would arguably have wrongly allowed passivization of DPs out of infinitives, as in (67):

(67) a. Jerome decided <to become famous in Europe> in an obsessed way.

     b. *Europe was decided to become famous in in an obsessed way by Jerome.

In any event, (66) seemingly vanished from the transformational framework without a trace (no pun intended), and without any arguments being offered for abandoning it. Instead, the standard resolution for pseudopassives came to appeal to something called *reanalysis*, a device more often invoked than defined. So Pesetsky (1995: 275) rightly says: "The preposition in these constructions must be affixed to V by a morphological process whose exact nature is unclear." The core assumption is that an operation like (68a) can remove a preposition from a PP and incorporate it into a preceding verb, converting a Verb + PP structure into one of the form Verb + DP, hence subject to the transformational passive defined on postverbal DPs.[15] This idea originates, as (68b) shows, in pregenerative work, although Curme never seems to be credited:

(68) a. Reanalysis (schematic)

     $<_{\varphi}<_V X> + <_{PP} P_a + DP_b> \rightarrow <_{\varphi}<_V X + P_a > + DP_b>$

    b. Curme (1931: 99)

     "In modern times the list of transitive verbs has been greatly increased by the addition of a large number of verbs originally intransitive which took a prepositional object, as 'to depend upon a man,' 'to laugh at a person,' 'to talk over a matter.' In course of time the preposition here has become attached to the verb as an integral part of it, so that the object is no longer a prepositional object but a direct object of the compound verb. This becomes apparent in the passive, where the object becomes subject and the preposition remains with the verb: 'They were laughed at by everybody.'"

One might easily assume that invocation of a Move-α view of passivization would have rendered appeal to reanalysis unnecessary. For under the schematic view, every DP in a clause except its subject, PP object or not, is potentially passivizable without special indication. But, in fact, Move-α does not yield this benefit when combined with later ideas, which include Case Theory, θ-role assignment, and chains, for reasons that need not concern us. Thus reanalysis continues to be appealed to even *after* passivization is claimed to be described properly by a combination of Move-α and other later assumptions:

(69)   Chomsky (1981: 123)
"There seems to be no difference in θ-role assignment in the examples of (20), though (i) (like [19iv]) can be passivized as (iii), while (ii) cannot be passivized as (iv):

(20)   (i)   they spoke to John
        (ii) they spoke angrily to John
        (iii) John was spoken to
        (iv) *John was spoken angrily to

"It may be, as has frequently been proposed, that in such cases as (19iv), (20iii), the verb-preposition construction has been reanalyzed as a verb, and as is well-known, this device is more readily available when the combination is somehow 'verb-like' in its semantic properties."

The appeal to reanalysis to describe pseudopassives, which persists in later views, is, though, arguably a major flaw. For as previously argued in Postal (1986a) and Baltin and Postal (1996), the hypothesis that pseudopassive formation depends on the reanalysis of Ps out of PPs into verbs in cases like (65b) is untenable and, unless supplemented by ad hoc restrictions, induces numerous false entailments. Eight are briefly described and illustrated in (70):

(70)   Although reanalysis putatively creates new transitive verbs and direct object structures (to feed passive formation via Move-α, etc.),
        a.   (i)   while *middles* are formed (only) on verbs with direct objects, the putative re-analysis never feeds middle formation (see Keyser and Roeper, 1984: 408; Roberts, 1986: 222; and Fagan 1988, 1992):
              (ii) Such principles are easily cited/discovered/referred to.
              (iii) Such principles cite/discover /*refer to easily.
        b.   (i)   while *nominalizations in of* are formed (only) on direct objects, reanalysis never feeds such nominalizations:[16]
              (ii) your citation/discovery/*reference to of that principle
              (iii) the citation/discovery/*reference to of that principle by Myra

c. (i) while direct object DPs can feed *Complex DP Shift* and PP objects cannot (Ross, 1967/1986), the putatively reanalyzed objects needed to feed pseudopassivization behave like PP objects, not like verbal objects:

   (ii) Steve cited often/discovered easily/*referred to frequently the principle you just explicated.

d. (i) the putatively reanalyzed Ps of (some) pseudopassives appear in contexts that make it essentially *impossible to regard them as verb-internal*:

   (ii) The bridge was climbed off of/onto by the chimp.

   (iii) The bridge was climbed onto by the gorilla and then, a few minutes later, off of by the chimp.

   (iv) The bridge was flown over (but) never, (I am quite sure), under by the daredevil pilot.

   (v) The bridge was flown over on Sunday by Sheila and under on Saturday by Louise.

e. (i) *gapping*, while clearly zeroing verbs, cannot (at least in the NL of many) yield the zeroing of a P without the zeroing of its complement DP; although supposedly incorporated in verbs, the putatively reanalyzed Ps of pseudopassive also obey this gapping constraint:

   (ii) Sandra cited/discovered/praised Plato and Steve Aristotle.

   (iii) Sandra argued about/referred to Plato and Steve about/to Aristotle.

   (iv) *Sandra argued about/referred to Plato and Steve Aristotle.

f. (i) *pseudogapping* has the same property as gapping:

   (ii) Although Steve didn't cite/discover Plato, he did Aristotle.

   (iii) Although Steve didn't argue about/refer to Plato, he did about/to Aristotle.

   (iv) *Although Steve didn't argue about/refer to Plato, he did Aristotle.

g.   there are no *nominal* pseudopassives:

   (i)   That issue was discussed/argued about by Greg.

   (ii) the discussion of/argument about that issue by Greg

   (iii) that issue's discussion/*argument about by Greg

   (iv) That scholar was cited/referred to by Greg

   (v)   the citation of/reference to that scholar by Greg

   (vi) that scholar's citation/*reference to by Greg

h. (i) while subject to semantic constraints, transitive verbs take the derivational prefix *re-*, no structure putatively reanalyzed as a transitive verb permits re-, even when the semantics seems acceptable:

   (ii) Such principles are easily cited/considered/discovered/discussed/referred to/talked about/reflected on.

   (iii) Such principles should be recited/reconsidered/rediscovered/*rereferred to/*rereflected on/*retalked about.

Thus quite systematically, the verbal phrase structures of the sort persistently taken to undergo reanalysis to yield pseudopassives in transformational terms systematically fail to manifest the behavioral features of common structures of the form $[_{VP} [_V X]] [_{DP} Y]$. Rather, they manifest the behavior of ordinary verb + PP structures. It is striking that all of the evidence just cited against reanalysis as a basis for pseudopassivization in no way impunes a passive-particular statement like (66).

A slightly different piece of evidence against reanalysis is derivable from the discussion of NEX ('locative inversion') clauses in chapter 1. There was cited an observation of Bresnan (1994) that pseudopassive clauses and NEX clauses do not intersect. It was claimed that this followed under the analysis of chapter 1 from the fact that visible expletive *there* cannot be the subject of a pseudopassive.

(71) a. In that article several strange principles were advanced/cited/developed.
      b. In that article there were advanced/cited/developed several strange principles.
      c. In that article were advanced/cited/developed several strange principles.

(72) a. In that article several strange principles were argued against/depended on/referred to.
      b. *In that article there were argued against/depended on/referred to several strange principles.
      c. *In that article were argued against/depended on/referred to several strange principles.

The contrasts between (71b, c) and (72b, c) are entirely unexpected under a reanalysis approach, which claims that, for example, argue against/depend on/refer to have the structure of complex transitive verbs like those of (71). Again, the implications of reanalaysis proposals are not verified. Note, too, that an analysis like (66) offers no insight into the locative inversion and expletive there facts.

A last point about the failure of reanalysis to provide a serious treatment of English pseudopassives is linked to the fact that, of course, many V + P + DP combinations do *not* sanction related pseudopassives, and these include many that cannot in any way be subsumed under independent constraints that bar, for whatever reason, the passivization of unaccusative structures.[17] So one observes for instance:

(73) a. The audience cheered for the home team.
      b. *The home team was cheered for by the audience.
      c. Irving fled from/to Peoria.
      d. *Peoria was fled from/to by Irving.
      e. Herb graduated on that date.
      f. *That date was graduated on by Herb.
      g. Emily lives with some chimp.
      h. *Some chimp was lived with by Emily.
      i. Nancy never mentioned to them to bring wine.
      j. *They were never mentioned to to bring wine.
      k. Helen rowed toward the island.
      l. *The island was rowed toward by Helen.
      m. Wendell was waiting for Nora.
      n. *Nora was being waited for by Wendell.
      o. Mildred told on Tony.
      p. *Tony was told on by Mildred.

It is worth remarking that the compatibility with manner adverbial criterion of (66) would not help here since all the actives are compatible with such adverbs. In reanalysis terms, whatever principle putatively incorporates Ps into verbs, and so forth, must be blocked in cases like (73). It might seem that this is not another argument against re-analysis on the ground that *any* view of passives needs to build in analogous restrictions.

However, a further quite strong argument against a reanalysis view nonetheless derives from facts like (73). This is based on an observation discussed and elaborated in Postal (1990b), whose original element was due to David Perlmutter. The following holds:

(74)   In wide range of cases, the ban against forming pseudopassives (like those of [73]) is matched by parallel bans against a range of other constructions, which I will for convenience call *Q constructions*; they include those referred to here as *object raising*, *object deletion*, *parasitic gaps*, and *nominal object raising*.

So alongside a pseudopassive contrast like (75a, b) there are corresponding nonpassive contrasts like (76):

(75)   a. The fort was fired at by the soldiers.
       b. The fort was crawled under(*neath) by the soldiers.

(76)   a. The fort was difficult to fire at.
       b. The fort was difficult to crawl under(*neath).
       c. The fort was too distant to fire at.
       d. The fort was too distant to crawl under(*neath).
       e. Which fort did they discuss before firing at?
       f. Which fort did they discuss before crawling under(*neath)?
       g. a strange fort to fire at
       h. a strange fort to crawl under(*neath)

And alongside a pseudopassive contrast like (77c, d), there are corresponding contrasts like those of (78):

(77)   a. The thief pleaded with the judge to free the woman.
       b. The thief pleaded with the judge to be allowed to free the woman.
       c. The judge was pleaded with (by the thief) to free the woman.
       d. *The judge was pleaded with (by the thief) to be allowed to free the woman.

(78)   a. The judge was hard to plead with to free the woman.
       b. *The judge was hard to plead with to be allowed to free the woman.
       c. The judge was too cruel to plead with to free the woman.
       d. *The judge was too cruel to plead with to be allowed to free the woman.
       e. Which judge did he call after pleading with to free the woman?
       f. *Which judge did he call after pleading with to be allowed to free the woman?
       g. a strange judge to plead with to free the woman
       h. *a strange judge to plead with to be allowed to free the woman.

The reason these correlations between bad pseudopassives and bad instances of the Q constructions are lethal for a reanalysis view of the former is this: The Q constructions are in general much freer than pseudopassives and accept as 'target' gaps such a broad range of positions as to make any invocation of reanalysis *for them* out of the question. So there is no hope of analyzing the Q constructions as limited to direct objects, which reanalysis is supposed to render feasible in simple clauses for passivization. Specifically, the gaps involved in Q constructions can be complements of a wide range of PPs not contiguous to verbs:

(79) a. Jerome is difficult to talk about that problem to.
      b. Jerome is too young to tell Betty to contact Ruth for.
      c. Who did they discuss after telling Betty not to talk to Ruth about that in front of?
      d. a strange judge to get people to tell their children not to talk about personal issues with

Therefore, the correlations sampled in (75)–(78) cannot be treated by any analog of reanalysis for the nonpassive constructions. So whatever blocks the pseudopassives in, for example, (73) cannot be attributed to reanalysis, but must rather hold of a wide class of PP objects of which those that pseudopassivize are one subset. Previous arguments show that the putative direct objects produced by posits of renanalysis do not behave like direct objects. This one shows in a different way that the PPs in the active correspondents of pseudopassives behave like genuine PPs in that one subset of them is subject to a set of constraints common to the PPs of object-raising, and so on, structures.

Overall then, under an interpretation of reanalysis as a factual hypothesis about English pseudopassives, it is incorrect. But (66) aside, transformational grammar, regardless of variety, has never really offered any other approach to pseudopassives.[18] So it seems fair to say that pseudopassives were clear exceptions to early versions of the transformational approach to passives like those in (3), (11), and (12) and remain exceptions to a Move-α/Case Theory approach. The latter view is not compatible with (66), so its only mechanism for treating them is some variant of Curme's (1931) mistaken invocation of reanalysis. Reanalysis might be viewed in part as a device to keep the 'applies blindly' transformational view of passivization (ignoring the hedges that render this vacuous) consistent with pseudopassives. But it does not. Overall, the failure of reananlysis proposals to describe pseudopassivization reveals in its own way the junk linguistic nature of a claim like (2).[19]

7. Arrays

Preceding sections have presented a bit of data incompatible with the claim of (3) that 'every' English active transitive structure corresponds to a grammatical passive and to the unfounded idea of (2) that exceptional cases with respect to some extant view of English passive structures are few and marginal. But while scattered examples that support the falsehood of such claims are found throughout the literature, some, as seen, even in the writings of their own author, no single work systematically lists enough such examples to give a true measure not only of their falsehood but also of their genuine absurdity.[20] But only such a measure permits an accurate evaluation of the extent to which such assertions are, beyond false, instances of junk linguistics. More significantly, it turns out, I claim, that counterexamples are to a significant extent not random but correlate with other grammatical features that transformational accounts have completely missed. And this cannot be seen in a few random examples.

So consider, for example, (80a)–(106a), where each a. example seemingly satisfies the input conditions for putative transformational passivization but for none of which is there a grammatical passive.

(80)   a. The express train could not approach the station.
       b. *The station could not be approached by the express train.

(81)   a. A fish course began the dinner.
       b. *The dinner was begun by a fish course.

(82)   a. Karen's remarks betrayed contempt for linguists.
       b. *Contempt for linguists was betrayed by Karen's remarks.

(83)   a. The audience didn't buy my argument.
       b. *My argument wasn't bought by the audience.

(84)   a. Armand caught the flu.
       b. *The flu was caught by Armand.

(85)   a. Bertrand croaked something unintelligible.
       b. *Something unintelligible was croaked by Bertrand.

(86)   a. The express departed Grand Central at 11 A.M.
       b. *Grand Central was departed by the express at 11 A.M.

(87)   a. Deborah lacked a pleasing personality.
       b. *A pleasing personality was lacked by Deborah.

(88)   a. The key couldn't enter the lock.
       b. *The lock couldn't be entered by the key.

(89)   a. This theory fits the facts.
       b. *The facts are fit by this theory.

(90)   a. Snakes don't give milk.
       b. *Milk is not given by snakes.

(91)   a. Horace heard that from Mildred.
       b. *That was heard from Mildred by Horace.

(92)   a. The cabinet includes the secretary of defense.
       b. *The secretary of defense is included by the cabinet.

(93) a. Saddam inspired loathing.
      b. *Loathing was inspired by Saddam.

(94) a. The affair involved foreign banks.
      b. *Foreign banks were involved by the affair.

(95) a. US 95 will lead you to New Haven.
      b. *You will be led to New Haven by US 95.

(96) a. Ellen left Chicago in June.
      b. *Chicago was left by Ellen in June.

(97) a. Evelyn doesn't mind profanity.
      b. *Profanity isn't minded by Evelyn.

(98) a. The *Titanic* neared the iceberg.
      b. *The iceberg was neared by the *Titanic*.

(99) a. The dean's decision permitted Nancy to remain in class.
      b. *Nancy was permitted to remain in class by the dean's decision.

(100) a. Hugh quit the police.
      b. *The police were quit by Hugh.

(101) a. The package never reached Gwen.
      b. *Gwen was never reached by the package.

(102) a. The Eiffel Tower resembles the Washington Monument.
      b. *The Washington Monument is resembled by the Eiffel Tower.

(103) a. Carmen can't stand sushi.
      b. *Sushi can't be stood by Carmen.

(104) a. The chimps couldn't tell (that is, 'determine') the distance to the chasm.
      b. *The distance to the chasm couldn't be told by the chimps.

(105) a. Tom wanted pizza.
      b. *Pizza was wanted by Tom.

(106) a. That experiment yielded a strange result.
      b. *A strange result was yielded by that experiment.

These twenty-seven cases represent an arbitrarily chosen subset of a group I refer to as *Array 1*. To avoid taking such data as clearly falsifying claims like (11), one would have to specify that none of the verbs of Array 1 is a member of the V_x category of (11). One might, for instance, propose that only members of that category have passive participles, that English passive participles are requisite for English passive clauses, and thus that the data of Array 1 follows.

Aside from such an ad hoc division of verbs motivated only by the failure of some to permit grammatical passives, the only other proposal in decades of transformational remarks about passives that offers anything is apparently the remarks in (107), related to (66) earlier:

(107)   Chomsky (1965: 103)
"Thus Verbs generally take Manner Adverbials freely, but there are some that do not—for example: *resemble, have, marry* (in the sense of 'John married Mary,' not 'the preacher married John and Mary,' which does take Manner Adverbials freely); *fit* (in the sense of 'the suit fits me,' not 'the tailor fitted me,' which does take Manner Adverbials freely); *cost, weigh* (in the sense of 'the car weighed two tons,' not 'John weighed the letter,' which does take Manner Adverbials freely); and so on. The Verbs that do not take Manner Adverbials freely Lees has called 'middle Verbs' (Lees, 1960a, p. 8), and he has also observed that these are, characteristically, the Verbs with following NP's that do not undergo the passive transformation. Thus we do not have 'John is resembled by Bill,' 'a good book is had by John,' 'John was married by Mary,' 'I am fitted by the suit . . . ten dollars is cost by this book,' 'two tons is weighed by this car,' and so on (although of course 'John was married by Mary' is acceptable in the sense of "John was married by the preacher," and we can have 'I was fitted by the tailor,' 'the letter was weighed by John,' etc.)."

If we combine these observations with proposal (66), it might, ignoring the fact that the latter is long abandoned, be claimed that Array 1 cases are simply middle verbs in the sense of Lees (1960). Putatively, these would preclude passivization, which requires compatibility with a manner adverb, while middle verbs do not combine with such adverbs. While I would agree that Lees' middle verbs are essentially instances of what I am calling Array 1, it is not true that this class is picked out by incompatibility with manner phrases. Of the twenty-seven cases cited, I find at least eleven compatible with these *on the uses illustrated*, namely, approach, betray, catch, croak, depart, enter, leave, permit, quit, reach, and tell.

Further, no appeal to an ad hoc V_x category like that of (11) or to compatibility with manner adverbials could defend the transformational account against Array 1 data. The reason is that the object DPs in the active examples share properties not really fully characterizable by appeal to such notions. The passive failures are simply one of a whole set of properties of Array 1 structures with respect to which they contrast with standardly passivizable clauses. Other properties shared by Array 1 members include those of (108):

(108)   Array 1 structures also:
a. have no corresponding *middles*
b. have no corresponding *nominalizations* in of (lack is the only exception I know of)
c. have no corresponding nominalized *incorporation* forms
d. have no corresponding –able forms
e. have no corresponding *object raising* (with difficult, easy, etc.) forms

    f. have no corresponding *object deletion* (with <u>too</u>/<u>enough</u>) forms
    g. have no corresponding parasitic gap forms
    h. have no corresponding *nominal object-raising* form
    i. have no corresponding <u>there</u>/<u>have</u> forms

It can be seen that included in (108) are the failure of Array 1 cases to occur grammatically in what were called Q constructions in section 6.

Space precludes documenting these claims fully, but (83')–(105') illustrate the sort of facts at issue for six corresponding Array 1 cases:

(83')   a. *Such arguments don't buy easily.
      b. *the/Clara's buying of such arguments
      c. *argument buying
      d. *That argument is unbuyable.
      e. *That argument is difficult to buy.
      f. *That argument is too weak for anyone to buy.
      g. *Which argument did he analyze carefully before buying?
      h. *That is a strange argument to buy.
      i. *There are/He has several arguments for you to buy.

(85')   a. *Such things don't croak frequently.
      b. *the croaking of threats
      c. *threat croaking
      d. *Such threats are uncroakable.
      e. *Such threats are difficult to croak.
      f. *That threat was too horrible to croak.
      g. *a threat that he considered without ever croaking
      h. *That is a strange threat to croak.
      i. *There is/She has something to croak.

(90')   a. *Milk gives frequently.
      b. *that cow's giving of poisoned milk
      c. *milk giving
      d. *Chocolate milk is ungivable.
      e. *Half-and-half is impossible for most cows to give.
      f. *That kind of milk is impossible for cats to give.
      g. *That is the kind of milk the cow promised to give without ever giving.
      h. *That is a strange kind of milk to give.
      i. *There is no milk for that cow to give.

(91')   a. *Such islands don't near easily.
      b. *the destroyer's nearing of the island
      c. *iceberg nearing
      d. *That island is unnearable.
      e. *That sort of island is hard to near.
      f. *That sort of island is too radioactive for us to near.
      g. *Which island did he survey after nearing?
      h. *That is a bizarre island to near.
      i. *There are few islands in this sector for us to near.

(100') a. *Such units don't quit easily.
     b. *Bob's quitting of the police
     c. *police quitting
     d. *The police are unquittable.
     e. *That sort of organization is impossible to quit.
     f. *That sort of organization is too unforgiving for me to quit.
     g. *Which unit did he criticize without quitting?
     h. *That is a bad unit to quit.
     i. *There are other organizations for Mike to quit.
(105') a. *Pizza wants too often.
     b. *Marsha's wanting of pizza
     c. *pizza wanting
     d. *Such food is unwantable.
     e. *Marshmallow pizza is hard to want.
     f. *Marshmallow pizza is too yucky for anyone to want.
     g. *What sort of pizza did he discuss before wanting?
     h. *That is an easy type of pizza to want.
     i. *There is nothing else for me to want.

A few comments about particular cases are in order. First, one should compare paradigm (83'), based on a use of buy that means "accept as correct," with the corresponding forms for the standard meaning of this verb. These have fine passives, as in (109), see (83"):

(109) a. The customer didn't buy my radio.
     b. My radio wasn't bought by the customer.

(83") a. ?Such radios don't buy easily.
     b. ?the/Clara's buying of the radio
     c. radio buying
     d. ?That radio is unbuyable.
     e. That radio is difficult to buy.
     f. That radio is too beat up for anyone to buy.
     g. Which radio did Irving praise after buying?
     h. That is a strange radio to buy.
     i. There are/He has several radios for you to buy.

The broad contrast between the two paradigms is a good indication of the systematic linking of the negative properties that define Array 1 but are totally missing in a standard object paradigm like (83").

Second, paradigm (85') is parallel to those for other so-called *manner of speaking* verbs, many of which are listed in (110):

(110) Other Manner of Speaking Verbs (Zwicky, 1971)
     bellow, chirp, cry, drawl, groan, growl, grunt, hiss, howl, moan, mumble, mutter, roar, scream, shout, shriek, snap, snarl, squeak, stammer, wail, whimper, whine, yell

Third, paradigm (90') contrasts with standard uses of <u>give</u>, which allow passives freely as (111) shows and which do not really bar any of the constructions in (108), with <u>able</u> forms a possible exception; see (90"):

(111)   Milk products should not be given to children for Christmas.
      (90")   a. ?Milk products don't give frequently for Christmas.
             b. that monster's giving of poisoned milk to the children
             c. gift giving for Christmas
             d. ?Chocolate milk is ungivable to lactose-intolerant individuals.
             e. That much milk is impossible for Australia to give to that country.
             f. That kind of milk is impossible for us to give to those children.
             g. What kind of milk did he purify before giving to those children?
             h. That is a bizarre kind of milk to give to those children.
             i. There is no milk for us to give to those children.

Even this overly brief survey of Array 1 shows the following: First, the idea that [DP Verb DP] structures systematically have corresponding passives is not just falsified by a few random counterexamples but by whole classes of structures. Second, for some of these classes, appeal to, for example, lexical absence of past participles or to compatibility with manner adverbials are not possible accounts, as the passive failures are not isolated properties. Each is just one among many failures of the same DPs to enter into constructions normally possible for direct objects and in some cases for a range of PP objects. These constructions are in general independent of issues of past participles or manner adverbials.

Next, I turn to what I will call *Array 2*, illustrated in (113)–(124):

(112)   a. Mary never answered Greg.
       b. *Greg was never answered by Mary.

(113)   a. The general never cabled Louisa.
       b. *Louisa was never cabled by the general. (ignore irrelevant reading that involves pieces of cable)

(114)   a. Her name eludes me.
       b. *I am eluded by her name.

(115)   a. The navy had failed her in several ways.
       b. *She had been failed by the navy in several ways.

(116)   a. 1998 found Becky in Paris.
       b. *Becky was found in Paris by 1998.

(117)   a. The truth just hit me.
       b. *I was just hit by the truth.

(118)   a. A six-pack doesn't last Marshall very long.
        b. *Marshall isn't lasted very long by a six-pack.

(119)   a. The brute could not let Sally go (= 'let go of', 'release')
        b. *Sally could not be let go by the brute.

(120)   a. Quentin was putting people down. (= 'demeaning')
        b. *People were being put down by Quentin.

(121)   a. That movie starred Madonna.
        b. *Madonna was starred by that movie.

(122)   a. Laura struck everyone as intelligent.
        b. *Everyone was struck as intelligent by Laura/by Laura as intelligent.

(123)   a. That did not suit the dean.
        b. *The dean was not suited by that.

(124)   a. Claude never wrote Irene.
        b. *Irene was never written by Claude.

These thirteen additional cases might just seem to be further instances of Array 1. This conclusion would be especially easy to reach given that for all of them not only are passives impossible but so are the other properties of (108). Paradigm (121') illustrates only for case (121):

(121')   a. *Old people don't star too often.
         b. *that film's starring of Madonna
         c. *foreigner starring
         d. *Such actors are unstarable.
         e. *Marshall is hard for a good movie to star.
         f. *Marshall is too sick for any movie to star.
         g. *That is the ex-wrestler that every movie that starred tended to displease.
         h. *Marshall is a strange person for any movie to star.
         i. *There is no other person for my film to star.

However, while sharing all the restrictions of Array 1, Array 2 forms are grammatically distinct because they also systematically manifest various constraints *not* associated with Array 1. These properly include those of (125):

(125)   Properties of Array 2 *Not* Shared with Array 1
        a. The object DP cannot be a target of left extraction.
        b. The object DP cannot be a target of Complex Phrase Shift.
        c. The object DP cannot be a target of Right Node Raising.
        d. The object DP does not permit subconstituent left extraction.

    e. The object DP does not strand under gapping.

    f. The object DP is not subject to partitive phrase (of + pronoun) suppression.

I illustrate in (126) and (127) for only two Array 2 verb cases, those of (121) and (124), contrasting them with *ordinary* verbal object structures, meaning by that term those subsumed by *neither* Array 1 nor Array 2:

(126)   a. [What actress]$_1$ did that movie enrich/*star t_1?

       b. That movie enriched t_1 enormously/*starred t_1 in the lead role—[a strange foreign actress]$_1$.

       c. The former film might have enriched t_1/*starred t_1 and the latter film did enrich/star [the foreign actress in question]$_1$.

       d. [Which actress]$_1$ did that film enrich/*star several friends of t_1?

       e. *The first film may have enriched/*starred Jim and the second film Tim.

       f. As for those foreigners, his films enriched/*starred many.

(127)   a. [Which actress]$_1$ did Melvin contact t_1/*write t_1?

       b. Melvin called t_1/*wrote t_1 several times [the actress in question]$_1$.

       c. Melvin may have contacted t_1/*written t_1 and Tom certainly did contact t_1/*write t_1 [that strange foreign actress]$_1$.

       d. [Which actress]$_1$ did Mike call/*write several friends of t_1?

       e. Mike may have contacted/*written Lois and Ed Selma.

       f. As for those foreigners, Mike may have contacted/*written several.

I must leave it to readers to verify that, on the contrary, none of the properties of (125) hold of Array 1 structures.

    While all the Array 2 objects cited so far are *animate*, there exist inanimate object instances of the pattern, as in (128):

(128)   a. The soldier/oil filled the bottle.

       b. The bottle was filled by the soldier/*oil.

       c. [Which bottle]$_1$ did the soldier/*oil fill t_1?

       d. The soldier/*Oil filled t_1 at that time [most of the large bottles]$_1$.

       e. The soldier/*Oil may have filled t_1 and the sailor/gasoline certainly did fill t_1 [the large bottles on the shelf]$_1$.

       f. [Which bottle]$_1$ did the soldier/*oil fill half of t_1?

       g. The soldier/*Oil filled the large bottle and the sailor/gasoline the small bottle.

       h. As for those bottles, the soldier/*oil filled several.

    Other inanimate object cases whose membership in Array 2 must be left to the reader to verify include those of (129):

(129)   a. Water covered the town.

       b. The pipe was oozing a dark liquid.

       c. The tank was dripping green muck.

       d. The bottle leaked sodium tribenzoate.

       e. Hedges surrounded the mansion.[21]

One might note that as with Array 1, there is no systematic correlation between Array 2 verbs and those that preclude manner adverbials. While some do, <u>answer</u>, <u>cable</u>, <u>fail</u>, <u>let go</u>, <u>put down</u>, and <u>write</u> accept them without problem.

There are several other arrays of forms whose incompatibility with passivization correlates with that for other constructions, including the Q constructions. Space precludes documenting this in detail. But (130) lists some relevant cases and (131) gives one illustration of a correlation for each of types (130a–h):

(130)   a. W-verb + DP + infinitive (e.g. *Helen wishes Greg to call Sonia.*)
        b. Causative verb + DP + *to*-less infinitive (e.g., *Helen let Greg call Sonia.*)
        c. Verb + predicate nominal DP (e.g., *They made a center fielder out of that guy.*)
        d. Expletive + verb + DP (e.g., *It disgusts her, the things they write.*)
        e. Verb + lexically determined <u>it</u> (see Bach, 1980: 305; and Postal and Pullum, 1988) (e.g., *Serena made it to Memphis.*)
        f. Verb + ambient *it* (see Napoli, 1988, 1993: 348–351) (e.g., *George loves it in Seattle.*)
        g. Cognate object cases (e.g., *She lived an exemplary life.*)
        h. Intellectual product subject cases (e.g., *That book proved something important.*)

(131)   a. *Greg was wished by Helen to call Sonia.
        b. *Greg was impossible for Helen to wish to call Sonia.
        c. *Greg was let call Sonia by Helen.
        d. *Greg was too boorish for Helen to let call Sonia.
        e. *A center fielder was made out of that guy by the local team.
        f. *What kind of center fielder did they need before making out of that guy?
        g. *She is disgusted by it, the things they write.
        h. *She is easy for it to disgust, the things they write.
        i. *It was made to Memphis by Serena.
        j. *It was too late for Serena to make to Memphis.
        k. *It is loved in Seattle by George.
        l. *It is a strange thing to love in Seattle.
        m. *An exemplary life was lived by Martha.
        n. *An exemplary life is hard to live.
        o. Something important was proved by that book.
        p. That was hard for that book to prove.

Let us consider type (130h) in a bit greater detail, though.

(132)   a. That author/Joe/Your uncle argues/asserts/claims/demonstrates/insists/proves/shows/states/that every set is a member of itself.
        b. That article/book/chapter/monograph/report/story argues/asserts/claims/demonstrates/insists/proves/shows/states/that every set is a member of itself.

While the verbs of the class illustrated in (132) normally take human or mind-possessing type subjects, one sees that they also permit subjects that denote, for example, documents. Notably, while the former cases have corresponding passives, not so for the document subject cases. This gap yields counterexamples to a strong interpretation of the claim of Roberts (1986: 26) that "[e]xactly those complement-taking Verbs which have thematic subjects can passivize." Moreover, again there are correlations, since the human cases allow all of the Q constructions while the document ones allow none:

(133)   a. That every set is a member of itself was claimed/demonstrated by Joe.
        b. That every set is a member of itself was difficult for Joe to claim/demonstrate.
        c. That every set is a member of itself is too absurd for Joe to claim/demonstrate.
        d. That every set is a member of itself, no one should claim without demonstrating.
        e. That every set is a member of itself is a strange thing for Joe to claim.

(134)   a. *That every set is a member of itself was claimed/demonstrated by that book.
        b. *That every set is a member of itself was difficult for that book to claim/demonstrate.
        c. *That every set is a member of itself is too absurd for that book to claim/demonstrate.
        d. *That every set is a member of itself, no book should claim without demonstrating.
        e. *That every set is a member of itself was a strange thing for that book to claim.

Moreover, there are further regularities:

(135)   a. That there are three ranks was proved by Jespersen/*Analytic Syntax.
        b. That there are three ranks was unprovable by ?Jespersen/*Analytic Syntax.
        c. the proof by Jespersen/*Analytic Syntax that there are three ranks
        d. Jespersen's/*Analytic Syntax's proof that there are three ranks

Clearly then, some systematic characteristic of document subject clauses with the verbs of (132) must block not only passives but all the Q constructions, able forms, nominalizations, and so on. What have five decades of transformational grammar offered in this connection? The answer, as far as I can see, is that none of the ideas of this framework that have been applied to English passives have anything to say at all. This paradigm alone suggests how deeply claim (2) was junk linguistics.

    The intellectual product subject cases differ from Array 1, Array 2, and so on, in the following way: They seem to be systematically related to sentences with the same verbs with animate subjects. That is, (132b) does not represent a distinct class of verbs from (132a). Each verb seems to have the same semantics in each corresponding a/b pair. There is nothing visible in transformational grammar that permits saying this, however.[22]

    Moreover, systematic relations between paradigms with the same verbs only one of which blocks passivization do not seem isolated. Consider the pair:

(136)   Frank punched Mike (back).

It was noted in Fraser (1965/1974: 52) that the particular particle back of (136), call it *retaliatory* back, blocks passivization:

(137)   Mike was punched (*back) by Frank.

Fraser did not, though, observe that the passivization failure is not isolated. In a range of ways parallel to those of earlier arrays, retaliatory <u>back</u> yields gaps in various constructions, which include the Q constructions:

(138)　a.　Great boxers don't punch (*back) easily.
　　　　b.　Great boxers are difficult to punch (*back).
　　　　c.　That boxer is too skilled to punch (*back).
　　　　d.　Which boxer did he tangle with without punching (*back)?
　　　　e.　He is a bad person to punch (*back).

　　Again, though, it would make no sense to say that a verb without <u>back</u> is of a different category than the same verb occurring with it. Moreover, it is thoroughly obscure what sort of constraint a transformational approach could propose to block all the relevant constructions in the <u>back</u> case. Notably, the considerations relevant to the 1Advancement Exclusiveness Law mentioned in note 17 are irrelevant to this case, as the semantics of the subject is identical in both the paradigm with and without <u>back</u>.
　　Overall then, the various arrays show in a distinctive way that there is nothing like a current account of conditions that allow or fail to allow passive correspondents to active clauses. Moreover, whatever principles deal with the passive facts for the arrays must evidently be special cases of more general ones that also control a range of distinct constructions, which include the Q constructions. Viewed against these facts, it is clear again that self-congratulatory claims like (2) have the character of junk linguistics.

8. Complement passivization and nonpassivization

Despite the fact that passives are, in the transformational terms being criticized in this chapter, systematically described as manifesting movement of a postverbal DP that ends up as passive subject, it has been known for decades (see Rosenbaum, 1967: 10) that, for example, <u>that</u> clauses can be the subjects of passives in ways seemingly parallel to DPs:[23]

(139)　a.　Gina proved that/that the turtle was clever.
　　　　b.　That/That the turtle was clever was proved by Gina.

In fact, in Chomsky (1975a: 496) not only were examples like the long form of (139b) noted, but they were also taken to be a prima facie argument that <u>that</u> clauses were NPs. Moreover, as already touched on in note 19, there are also <u>that</u> clause pseudopassives:

(140)　a.　That the perpetrators might be space aliens was agreed on by the authorities.
　　　　b.　That he will come on time cannot be counted on by anyone.
　　　　c.　That not every cube has right angles was referred to by the professor.

　　Since such clauses were originally categorized as NPs/DPs, *that* clause passivizability did not originally raise a theoretical problem in transformational grammar. But following the work of Emonds (1969, 1976) almost all transformationalists subsequently *abandoned* this idea and now generally claim that that clauses are not DPs (but CPs). That makes it obscure how to subsume clausal passives under transformational accounts of passivization like (11) and their descendants in terms of Move-α, traces, Case Theory, and so forth.

Schemas like Move-α would of course allow non-DPs/CPs to move without special stipulation. But CP movement nevertheless does *not*, under standard assumptions, directly solve the problem raised by the long form of (139b). For in general trace-theoretic terms, movement of a phrase of category K must link two positions *of category K*. Recall the discussion of traces and specifically quote (141) cited in chapter 7:

(141)   Lasnik and Uriagereka (1988: 41)
   "In accord with Trace Theory, let us assume that *who* leaves a trace when it moves. This trace is obviously an NP, a fact ensured by Trace Theory, which essentially says that, upon movement, an item leaves behind a syntactic silent copy of itself."

Moreover, the requirement that moved elements and their traces be of the same category is now a fundamental element of the much-touted copy theory of traces, also discussed in chapter 7. Consistent with this view would then be an analysis of the type in (142) given by Webelhut (1992: 96):

(142)   [$_{CP}$ That John would be unqualified] had been expected [$_{CP}$ e]

However, given that assumption, if the moved phrases in, for example, the long form of (139b) and (140) are CPs, both the subject position and position of origin must be CPs. And given the failure of reanalysis proposals already argued, clausal pseudo-passives like (140) would, in transformational terms, then have to involve CP movement out of positions *where CPs are barred*, yielding what Bresnan (2001: 17) refers to as a *movement paradox*.

Webelhut's (1992) nonstandard (I believe) solution to this situation is in effect to reject the principle in (141) (hence implicitly the copy theory of traces) and allow CP movement to link to DP traces. Minimally, this yields a conceptually undesirable less general statement of category relations in movement chains. Martin (1999: 21, note 13) also confronts the problem under discussion. He offers, though, barely three lines in a footnote that contemplates two entirely different proposals; in one, CPs (= that clauses) optionally have Case features. In another, rather similar to Webelhut's suggestion, these CPs optionally link to null DPs in argument positions.

One finds then a much-discussed and frequently praised general theoretical framework of movement, which seemingly involves a general condition of categorial identity between moved element and trace. But decades after Chomsky's 1955 documentation of that clause passives, no adequate description of them is integrated with that view. A serious attempt like that of Webelhut (1992) to achieve descriptive adequacy proposes something inconsistent with the generally praised theory. But that description is not presented as a criticism of the theoretical framework. More general works seem to ignore the problem. One has been told (see the introduction) that researchers should *hope* their proposals are false. And, according to Webelhut, the proposal of moved element/trace identity has to be false because of, for example, that clause pseudopassives. And yet I have encounted nothing that touts this result as progress. One suspects a junk linguistics disconnect between strong theoretical claims maintained in a partial factual vacuum and descriptive proposals incompatible with the theory. The former is not allowed to control the descriptive work and the latter is not taken to falsify the theory. This yields both strong-sounding general theoretical claims and descriptive proposals sensitive to the facts but no confrontation between them: ideal circumstances for junk linguistics.

Moreover, it would be a mistake to become overly sanguine about the factual adequacy of a proposal like that of Webelhut (1992). It does not address a variety of problems related to complement clause/passive interactions, including those of note 19. Further, while the proposal requires recognition of CP movement, inter alia to subject and topic positions, a variety of CPs lack a distribution compatible with this property:

(143) a. You should learn that he is a thief/if he is a thief.
       b. That he is a thief/*If he is a thief should be learned by everyone.
       c. That he is a thief/*If he is a thief, Ted will end up learning.[24]

(144) a. I loved that he did that/when he did that.
       b. That he did that/*When he did that was loved by most students.
       c. That he did that/*When he did that, most students loved.

(145) a. The children saw that the Romans invaded Samoa/how (*else) the Romans invaded Samoa.
       b. That the Romans invaded Samoa/*How (else) the Romans invaded Samoa was seen by the children.
       c. That the Romans invaded Samoa/*How (else) the Romans invaded Samoa, the children never saw.

(146) a. Amanda arranged (for you) to be picked up at the airport.
       b. *(For you) to be picked up at the airport was arranged (for) by Amanda.
       c. *(For you) to be picked up at the airport, Amanda did not arrange (for).

Nothing in Webelhut's proposal accounts for the contrast between such facts and those for *that* clauses. Nor is there any standard solution in the transformational framework.

Evidently, for an active structure that involves a complement clause and a fixed verb, there can be, as in (147b, c), two distinct types of corresponding passive, call them *it passives* and *clausal passives*:

(147) a. Greg proved that <two and two were seven>. <. . .> = X.
       b. It was proved by Greg that X.
       c. That X was proved by Greg.

As illustrated in (148)–(151), there is a four-way division of English that clause complement-taking *verbs* with respect to passivization. Every logical possibility is instantiated: Some take both it passives, and clausal passives, some neither, some only it passives, and some only clausal ones:

(148)   Type I. Both it Passives and Clausal Passives
   a. Myron asserted that X.
   b. It was asserted by Myron that X.
   c. That X was asserted by Myron.

(149)   Type II. Neither it Passives nor Clausal Passives
   a. Myron meant that X.
   b. *It was meant by Myron that X.
   c. *That X was meant by Myron.

(150)   Type III. it Passives but No Clausal Passives
   a. Myron thought that X.
   b. It was thought (?by Myron) that X.
   c. *That X was thought (by Myron).

(151)   Type IV. No it Passives but Clausal Passives
   a. *That theory expresses that X.
   b. *It is expressed by that theory that X.
   c. That X is expressed by that theory.

Types I and II do not require much comment. Type III has been the subject of some discussion, including Chomsky (1981: 122), Marantz (1984: 133), Postal (1986a: 96–99), and Williams (1981). Marantz concluded that Type III cases like (150c) argue against a 'promotion' analysis of English passives. But the discussion in Postal (1986a) indicates why this is not the case. Type IV has been discussed in Dowty and Jacobson (1988: 103), Grimshaw (1982), Hukari and Levine (1991: 116–117), Jacobson (1992b) and Postal (1998: 108–114).

I am aware of no overall account of the four-way division. But several writers, including Davies and Dubinsky (2001: 254–255), Marantz (1984 : 132–134), and Webelhut (1992: 96–97) and have noted *part* of it, namely, the simple partition into those that permit clausal passives and those that do not, illustrated further by (152):

(152)   a. Myron accepted that <the senator was guilty> = X.
   b. That X was accepted by Myron.
   c. Myron added that X.
   d. *That X was added by Myron.
   e. Myron answered that X.
   f. *That X was answered by Myron.
   g. Myron believed that X.
   h. That X was believed by Myron.

i.   Myron charged that X.
j.   *That X was charged by Myron.
k.   Myron couldn't conceive that X.
l.   *That X couldn't be conceived by Myron.
m.   Myron determined that X.
n.   That X was determined by Myron.
o.   Myron feared that X.
p.   *That X was feared by Myron.
q.   Myron heard that X.
r.   *That X was heard by Myron.
s.   Myron meant that X.
t.   *That X was meant by Myron.
u.   Myron mentioned that X.
v.   That X was mentioned by Myron.
w.   Myron mumbled that X.
x.   *That X was mumbled by Myron.
y.   Myron thought that X.
z.   *That X was thought by Myron.

The contrast divides even such everyday verbs as believe (good clausal passive) and think (bad clausal assive). What in the historical realm of transformational ideas about passives explains such a division? The only proposals I am aware of involve the recurring idea of Davies and Dubinsky (2001), Marantz (1984: 133), and Webelhut (1992). They have all suggested in effect that the difference lies in generalization (153):

(153)   Only those verbs that select DPs permit clausal passives.

So in such terms, for example, (152f) would be bad because answer does not select a DP object understood in the way that the CP it selects is understood and Marantz's (1984: 133) (154c) would be bad because of (154b):

(154)   a. Myron answered *that/*something.
        b. *I said the announcement in a loud voice.
        c. *That Elmer had the the best porcupines in the business was said around the financial district.

The attempt to integrate division (152) into standard terms via (153) is reasonable. But even though I believe the lattter claim true, it does not fully determine partition (152). For many verbs that allow both DP objects and that clause complements nonetheless *still do not allow clausal passives*. So while (153) can predict that verbs that do *not* allow DP objects do not allow clausal passives, it cannot predict what is arguably the case, that even many verbs that permit DP objects to alternate with clausal complements still do not.

To see this, observe first that many of the verbs that bar clausal passives nonetheless allow their complement to be the focus of a pseudocleft:

(155) a. What Jerome answered was X.
      b. *X was thought by Tom.
      c. What Tom thought was X.

To claim that (155b) follows from a lack of a DP object would force a surely undesirable denial that the pseudocleft <u>what</u> is a DP.

    Second, and worse, a number of <u>that</u>-clause complement-taking verbs that bar clausal passives take unchallengeable object DPs understood to be in the same semantic relation to the verb as the <u>that</u> clause they alternate with:

(156) a. Stan felt/found/heard that the chimp was intelligent.
      b. *That the chimp was intelligent was felt/found/heard by Stan.
      c. Stan felt/found/heard that.
      d. The (only) thing that Stan felt/found/heard was that the chimp was intelligent.
      e. Stan found/heard something, namely, that the chimp was intelligent.
      f. Stan had never heard such a(n) (absurd) thing.
      g. What did Stan hear, that the chimp had escaped?

(157) a. Stella couldn't conceive that/such a thing/anything of the sort/that the chimp was intelligent.
      b. *That the chimp was intelligent couldn't be conceived by Stella.

(158) a. Theodore held that the chimp was immortal.
      b. *That the chimp was immortal was held by Theodore.
      c. Theodore never held that/such a view.

(159) a. Irma intended that you see the results.
      b. *That you see the results was intended by Irma.
      c. Irma didn't intended that/any such thing.

(160) a. This means that we will be indicted.
      b. *That we will be indicted is meant by this.
      c. This has got to mean that/something.
      d. Whatever this means is irrelevant to me.

(161) a. Aristotle pledged that he would resign.
      b. *That he would resign was pledged by Aristotle
      c. Aristotle did not pledge that/anything.
      d. The only thing that Aristotle pledged was . . .

    Given these facts, there seems to be no way to reduce the clausal passivizability contrast to a simple distinction between <u>that</u> clause-taking verbs that also allow parallel DP objects and those that do not. So even accepting the truth of (153), the behavior of <u>that</u> clauses with respect to passivization still shows the serious current limitations on the insight that transformational grammar has yielded with respect to English passivization.

Moreover, whatever the answer to the contrasts seen in (152), it cannot involve some ad hoc division of complement-taking verbs into those that permit passives and those that do not. First, it passives are possible with many (though not all) of the verbs of (152), including many of those that *bar* clausal passives, as the following partially illustrates:

(162)   It was accepted/added/*answered/believed/charged/determined/feared/*heard/*meant/ mentioned/?mumbled/ thought by Myron that X.

Second, and far more significantly, the division of complement-taking verbs in (152) as to passivization is very closely matched by parallel divisions that involve the possibility of the that clause occurring as topic, as the subject of object-raising structures (e.g. with hard/easy), as the subject of object deletion structures (e.g., with too/enough), and so forth, that is with what I have been calling Q constructions. I illustrate only fragmentarily with believe and think:

(163)   a. That X, Myron does not believe/*think.
        b. That X was hard for Myron to believe/*think.
        c. That X was too complicated for Myron to believe/*think.
        d. That X, Myron asserted without believing/*thinking.[25]
        e. That X was a strange thing for Myron to believe/*think

Assuming the generalizations just suggested are valid, for example, that the facts in (163) are not accidental, there is evidently a systematic distinction required in the analysis of that clause complements, one that decades of transformational discussion of English have not provided. Moreover, that distinction must group together the possibility of that clause passives, that clause topics, and that clauses in the Q constructions,. There is no hint in the transformational literature of the basis of these divisions.

It is not my goal here to account for the partition of that clause behavior just documented. But the verb set in (152) that divides into those that permit clausal passives and the other cited constructions and those that do not manifests a remarkable independent correlation:

(164) Those that clause-taking verbs that permit clausal passives, and so on, permit their object to be a weak definite pronoun of the sort that can be anteceded by a that clause; the others do not.

So compare the corresponding cases of (152) and the following:

(165)   a. Myron accepted that <the senator was guilty> = <X>, but I did not accept it.
        c. *Myron added that X, but I did not add it.
        e. *Myron answered that X, but I did not answer it.
        g. Myron believed that X, but I did not believe it.
        i. *Myron charged that X, but I did not charge it.
        k. *Myron couldn't conceive that X, but I could conceive it.

m. Myron couldn't determine that X, but I could determine it.
o. *Myron feared that X, but I didn't fear it.
q. *Myron heard that X, but I didn't hear it.[26]
s. *Myron meant that X, but I didn't mean it.
u. Myron mentioned that X, but I didn't mention it.
w. *Myron mumbled that X, but I didn't mumble it.
y. *Myron thought that X, but I didn't think it.

Earlier work by Postal (1990b, 1993a, 1994a, 1994b, 1998, 2001a, 2001b), provided a partial basis for correlations between topicalization and the distribution of weak definite pronouns and for parallel correlations with most Q constructions. The basis is a claim that these constructions all involve invisible pronouns in the gap positions. No other way to capture the correlations with that clause passivization is evident; that is, it seems motivated to claim that English clausal passives involve invisible object pronouns. Of course, this would be an ad hoc condition if limited only to those passives.

But there is evidence that it is not and that it is a general feature of the construction. For there are such correlations as the following, where that clauses are not involved:

(166) a. They couldn't determine/tell the weight of the beast with that instrument.
       b. The weight of the beast couldn't be determined/*told with that instrument.
       c. As for the weight of the beast, they couldn't determine/*tell it.

(167) a. They made that guy/him into a center fielder.
       b. That guy was made into a center fielder.
       c. They made an excellent center fielder/*it/*him out of that guy.
       d. *An excellent center fielder was made out of that guy.

Such correlations are entirely outside the scope of transformational claims about the conditions that govern passivization, and, of course, cases like (166b) and (167b) are further instances that falsify the "every" claim of (3) and show that (2) was not serious.

At the same time, there are problems with the claimed passivization/weak pronoun correlation, such as why many of the verbs of (152) permit it passives. If passive clauses *in general* require object pronouns and these verbs bar visible object pronouns, why do they allow even it passives? Clearly, vastly more research is needed on the topics just gone over, which will hardly be stimulated by junk linguistic claims that "there remain a few exceptions" or that descriptive success, if achieved "is not a real result."

9. A remark about coordination

A remarkable feature of transformational accounts of (inter alia) passives is that to an extraordinary extent they have been developed and promoted in isolation from

one of the most fundamental aspects of NL, coordination. Even simple passive/
coordinate paradigms like (168) are rarely discussed in such terms in detail:

(168)   Janet was praised + by Rodney, criticized + by Sidney, and ignored + by Gregory.

In terms of an A-movement/trace view of movement, each of the passive VPs should
have had its own object move to subject position leaving its own trace. And yet the
subject position contains only a single DP, which must somehow apparently link to
three distinct traces. Clearly some mechanisms specific to coordination must be invoked. But which? And where are they described? I cannot answer.

But before deciding to invest time in searching, one should recognize that the
transformational ideas that have been applied to passives independently of coordination run into enormously greater problems than (168), as seen in (169):

(169)   a. Jill praised Otto.
         b. Otto was praised by Jill.
         c. Otto and Erhard were praised by Jill.
         d. Otto and Erhard were respectively praised by Jill and criticized by Linda.
         e. The two students were respectively praised by Jill and criticized by Linda.

Suppose it made sense, as evolved forms of transformational analysis claim, to
provide an analysis of (169b, c) as involving movement of an object DP into a higher
subject position leaving a trace of the subject, conjoined or not, after praised. If a
parallel analysis is adopted for structures like (169d), referred to as containing *inter-
woven dependencies* in Postal (1998), with, for example, a single trace linked to the
conjoined subject after some conjoined verbal constituent or with coindexed traces
similarly linked after the two verbs, the grammar would fail to indicate that one of
the subject conjuncts links semantically and selectionally to only one verb, the other
with only the other verb. That is, at best, something like (170) would be required:

(170)   [Otto$_1$ and Erhard$_2$]$_3$ were respectively praised t$_1$ by Jill and criticized t$_2$ by Linda.

But the usual mechanisms of movement provide no way to obtain such a structure.

For (169e), the situation is, if anything, worse, as there are no surface DPs to
link to distinct traces with the two passive verbs. It is difficult to see how such cases
can be integrated into an overall grammar without in some way providing a coordinate analysis with distinct conjuncts for at least *some* plural phrases, including the
two students in (169e). That idea has never been part of the conceptual schemes of
the chief developer of transformational views of passive, and he rejected its general
form during the generative semantics dispute and has not, as far as I know, otherwise discussed it; see (171):

(171)   Chomsky (1972b: 123, note 26)
         "The argument is based on the assumption that such *respectively* constructions are
         derived by transformation from conjunctions . . . This assumption, however, is un-
         tenable. Consider, for example, the problem of deriving in this way: *The successive*

STUDIES OF JUNK LINGUISTICS

descendants of my fruit fly will be heavier, respectively, than the successive descendants of yours, or any case involving an infinite set or finite set of unknown size."

I will say nothing further about problematic facts like (169d and e), which can be replicated for a wide range of constructions distinct from passives and for which no solution in any known framework may exist. But the fact that after most of half a century transformational grammar has provided no way even to keep its view of passives consistent with relatively simple coordination-containing clauses like those in (169d and e) clashes mightily with the common doctrinal promotion of this framework as offering some deep insights into the structure of sentences, not to say with boasts like (2). And, as with other aspects of grammar, a most disturbing aspect, indicative of the role of junk linguistics, is the failure to face the problem.

10. Conclusion

The goal of this chapter has been essentially negative. First, I have wished to debunk an idea that surfaced in 1957, namely, that the concepts of transformational grammar provide a viable and insightful account of English verbal passive clauses. I have considered a range of phenomena, certainly not intended to be complete, which neither the original transformational accounts nor their evolutions in terms of Move-α, traces, and so on, handle properly or, in some cases, at all. These included:

(172)   a. 'overgeneration' problems, failures to block in fact ill-formed passive correspondents of a range of active verbal phrases that contain DPs or complement clauses; see, for example, (15a, b), (21d, e), (25b), (35a, b), (37a, b), all of the cases of Array 1 and Array 2 plus those that correspond to the other Arrays of (130), (137), and (138), failures to block many in fact barred clausal passives as the bad cases of (156)–(158), and failure to bar bad clausal and <u>it</u> passives in, for example, (149) and bad <u>it</u> passives like (151b).
   b. 'undergeneration' problems, failures to allow tertiary passives like (14b) and, overwhelmingly, failure to give a viable account of pseudopassives, and, perhaps most striking of all, failure to provide, and mostly to even try to provide, a serious account of the interaction of passivization with coordination.
   c. failure to provide an adequate account of the nature of the <u>by</u> phrase

Any *one* of (172a, b, or c) suffices to belie the claim in the title of this chapter. Taken together, they cannot fail to indicate that the historical claims for the adequacy of transformational views of English passives have to be regarded as deeply unfounded.

Moreover, second, it has been documented that repeatedly the discussion of passives has been indelibly stained with aspects of junk linguistics. These included distortion of known facts to make proposals seem more adequate than they in fact were, suppression by an author X of relevant known data found even in X's earlier work, repeated strong-sounding claims ("applies blindly"/"care nothing for grammatical relations") hedged in multiple ways well beyond the point of emptiness, lack of coherent methodology, invocation of vague undefined principles, unfounded cavalier treatment of serious facts, replacement of theoretical view A with a distinct view B without justification or argument, failure to take seriously even one's own conceptual requirements when faced with descriptive problems, and a serious neglect of whole classes of facts, most notably coordination, to name only some.

With respect to the inadequacies that have been gone over, a remark parallel to that made in chapter 7 with respect to accounts of the strong crossover phenomenon and its putative explanation via Principle C is surely apropos. As in that case, there appears here also in transformational terms to be nothing like a full-length publication, monograph, or even substantial refereed article that seeks to analyze English passives in all of their variety and richness and to justify a transformational treatment.[27] Instead, what one finds since 1957 are scattered remarks and paragraphs, which treat in isolation one or another problematic aspect but without an integrated treatment. A reader is thereby denied the perspective needed to see the overall extraordinary weakness of what is being said vis-à-vis the whole construction and to see the full range of distinct, ad hoc, undesirable conceptual proposals (e.g., spurious interpretive rules, ill-defined appeals to analogy) that are needed, or the actual domain of facts that are not handled. As before, this approach is a recipe for junk linguistics and no one should be surprised at the shoddiness of the resulting product.

9

Junk Ethics 1

Advances in Linguistic Rhetoric

$\mathbf{L}$inguistics can be hard work. The attempt to develop insightful descriptions or theories of NLs can be extraordinarily taxing to the mind/brain. Almost every day another promising linguist keels over from the strain of marshaling facts, drawing distinctions, and postulating entities. Reliable techniques for stress reduction and lifestyle management are thus an urgent necessity for the linguistics community. It is toward the goal of meeting this need that attention is turned in the following remarks.

How can linguists successfully struggle against those who, like hungry vultures, hover ready to criticize, counterexemplify, refute? The answer is rhetoric, the art of convincing one's audience without benefit of logic. (More accurately, regardless of logic. No one has shown that it is actually disadvantageous to have a sound argument on one's side; it is merely unnecessary in linguistics, I will argue.)

Great strides are being made in linguistic rhetoric, whose progress puts the stasis in mere description and theorizing to shame. In the great rhetoric laboratories of the northeastern United States, defensive shields are being perfected that can render any theory virtually impervious to factual corrosion.

Moreover, essentially no risk attaches to the rhetorical techniques reviewed here. Each one simply generalizes techniques already effectively used by leading (often tenured) linguistics practitioners and published in top linguistics journals or in books by reputable international publishers. The only contribution of the guide offered here is to codify and publicize already developed methods so that they can be utilized by the broad mass of the overburdened linguistic workforce and not just by an elite few.

Let us begin with a familiar problem. You have a desired consequence that explains your data just right but face the demanding, perhaps impossible task of showing that it is a consequence of your general linguistic theory. Ideally, you would like a proof; but such are very hard to construct and call for a degree of explicitness that makes one go queasy just thinking about it. The solution? Simply assert. Nothing could be easier than simply saying that the desired consequence follows from your theory without giving any proof.

Risky? Disreputable? Hard to get away with? Not at all. This procedure, *the Phantom Theorem Move*, has worked for others, and *it can for you, too*. For example, Chomsky and Lasnik (1977: 453) assert that a generalization about the distribution of subject extraction follows from something called trace theory (don't ask; it's not called trace theory now). It doesn't, of course (Postal, 1982). But no one questions Chomsky and Lasnik's result on this score or demands a proof. They have asserted it aggressively; that is enough.

In any case, if anyone had exhibited the bad taste to question the claimed consequence, nothing would have been simpler for the authors than to accuse the complainer of *naive falsificationism* (Koster, 1978, 566) or, even more effectively, simply to ignore them.

Advanced players should be aware of an even bolder move. This takes the unproven assertion that one's factual generalization follows from one's theory and appends a disarming admission that one has no proof of this logical connection or (most daring of all) an admission that no proof of such a connection is even possible. Although this may sound outrageous and unfeasible, it has already worked perfectly well, as in the following much-admired piece of daredevil rhetoric:

(1) Freidin (1978: 539)
     "By taking (54a–e) as axioms of the theory of grammar, we derive the empirical effects
     of the strict cycle as a theorem."
     [Footnote 26] "This is not to say that we have a formal proof; clearly we do not. In fact,
     it seems unlikely at this point that a formal proof can be constructed."

One strength of this sophisticated bluff is that it provides quite an effective defense against any claims of trying to fool anyone. If accused of having no proof or argument that the theory entails the claim made, one replies, "Of course not. I said that quite explicitly on page 539; can my critic have failed to note that I said very clearly in footnote 26 that I don't even believe one is possible?" (Instant collapse of logic-chopping opponent. How can anyone so forthright be questioned further?)

Another sophisticated ploy for similar situations is *the Phantom Reference Move*. Under this procedure, one sketches a *portion* of an argument that apparently would show that one's theory does entail one's linguistic claim. One then stipulates that only with *further* assumptions does the argument really go through (the latter of course not being specified). One then adds the equivalent of "see below," but without giving any page, section, or even chapter references. A fine example is provided in (2):

(2) Chomsky (1981: 125)
     "Plainly, (24) is closely related to 2.6.(40), and a more general formulation is possible
     including as well ergative verbs that assign no Case to their object and no θ-role to their
     subjects . . . I will return directly to some tacit assumptions that are required for this

argument to go through in full generality. Let us assume now that these gaps can be filled."

This procedure is maximally effective when performed on an early page of a reasonably long work. Research indicates that those actually willing to scan through dozens, still less hundreds, of pages to determine whether you actually give these "further assumptions," and if so where, and even *try* to show anything follows from them are fewer than those who send the IRS unsolicited letters claiming they owe *more* income tax than they have been assessed for.

If showing facts follow from some principle is tedious, no less fatiguing is creating a principle in the first place. Fortunately, although often overlooked, the health-stressing activity of principle formulation is superfluous in theoretical linguistics. One need only propose some name N that sounds as if it could well be the designation of a linguistic principle.

To appear serious, of course, one should avoid principle names like "Rumple-stiltskin" or "Debby Does Dallas." Select something like "The Contraction Determination Condition" or "Recoverability." The procedure is then simply to assert that whatever facts you want follow from the principle of which N is the name. The charm of this strategy, normally called *the Phantom Principle Move*, is that nobody can ever show that the facts do not follow from N. And if the claim that they follow is not false, it must, according to propositional logic, be true.

As before, an advanced version is available: Append to your principle (say P) an explicit claim that you have not formulated P. Then announce forcefully that this does not matter since, of course, we *know* that P must exist, perhaps because, for example, children could not possibly learn the facts that follow (see preceding) from the principle. To quote again from a rhetorical masterpiece:

(3)   Chomsky and Lasnik (1977, 446–447)
      "We assume that this possibility is excluded by the recoverability principle for dele-
      tion. Exactly how to formulate this principle is a nontrivial question, but there is little
      doubt that such a principle is required."

Tests have shown that invocation of moves like these will prevent all but the really self-destructive from trying to hassle you about the content of P.

Moreover, the efficacy of such moves is long-lasting and stable over time. Thus Riemsdijk and Williams (1986: 103) appeal to the same phantom recoverability principle as Chomsky and Lasnik (1977): "The principle for recoverability that would allow this deletion remains to be given, but it is plausible to assume . . ." (plausible assumption omitted). Nine years had elapsed, and the phantom principle remains unformulated. I see no reason that the situation will be different nine years from now, or ever.[1] Hence there are grounds for believing that the procedures surveyed in this article can remain applicable over unlimited time periods.

A recurrent problem faced by the working linguist is to find something to say justifying his or her own treatment of some data and dismissing an opposing view. Substantive or logical arguments in favor of one's own or against the competition are useful but not easily found. No matter. If, as is here recommended, one has the good judgment to adopt views entirely within the current mainstream, one can always appeal for these purposes to the ever-effective *Social Conformity Move*. This is based on implying, possibly even truthfully, that one's opponent's views are incompatible with generally accepted wisdom while one's own are highly conformist.

A good and typical example is found in (4), where it functions effectively in lieu of a substantive criticism of a proposal about Georgian by Alice Harris:

(4)   Anderson (1984: 182)
      "As a result, the formulation of Inversion becomes global in character (since it must refer simultaneously to the fact that a given argument is a subject, and to the fact that it was initially a subject), a consequence which most views of syntax would reject."

This kind of stuff can only leave your opponent whining impotently about not all popular ideas being true, an outsider's complaint that will rarely cut any ice in or out of linguistics.

Once effective use is made of the devices discussed in the foregoing paragraphs, linguistic life quickly becomes much less taxing. But things are better yet; current linguistic rhetorical ingenuity offers many further aids. Suppose, for example, you have impulsively made public some description that could (because the described NL actually exists) conceivably be wrong. This might cause work if some negatively oriented, untheoretical linguist were to develop some evidence or argument against your description. To protect yourself against this kind of irrational hostility, you should have already published an item, easily composable on a plane flight, that contains your "philosophy of linguistics." This can say, inter alia, and very humbly: "Of course, a description may be wrong. In fact, we *hope* that our descriptions will be wrong." Thus:

(5)   Koster (1978: 566)
      "Interesting theories do not avoid conflicts with the data, but rather create clashes on purpose."

Note also the following exhibition of a positive lust for error:

(6)   Chomsky (1982b: 76):
      "Suppose that counterevidence is discovered—as we should expect and as we should in fact hope, since precisely this eventuality will offer the possibility of a deeper understanding of the real principles involved."

And in the same vein, one finds:

(7)   Riemsdijk and Williams (1986: 320)
      "[B]ut this is exactly what one wants of a strong proposal: that it lead immediately to a great deal of empirical difficulty."

The rhetorical strategy these expressions of yearning for counterevidence implement is, of course, the cunning *Epistemology of Desired Error Move*, which enables you to cover all the bases. If the description you have offered turns out to be right, you claim the credit and, naturally, squelch the critic for inadequate criticism. But if your description is wrong, as the critic claims, and you are somehow forced to admit it, you just say, "Of course. It is exactly as we should hope. After all, linguistics is a living field." (Upwardly mobile students should practice this several times daily, staring into a mirror with a look of utter conviction and sincerity.)

Again, suppose you are an advocate of some popular linguistic theory and are working on an exotic NL (one not used by European settlers of the thirteen American colonies) and you uncover a neat analysis of some sentences that is unfortunately inconsistent with some principle of the linguistic theory of which you are a vocal defender. This could, unpleasantly, force you to think about which to give up: (i) the theoretical principle; (ii) the analysis; or, boldly, (iii) logic. Obviously, (i) could annoy the many, often illiberal, defenders of the theory, (ii) would waste a lot of your time, and (iii), although not to be excluded a priori, is going to raise some eyebrows even in linguistics.

Happily, there are alternatives. Instead of getting rid of any of (i)–(iii), you can simply say that A only violates the letter of the principle but not its spirit. Too desperate even for linguistics? Not at all. The technique involved, called *the Sophisticated Interpretation Move*, has already been successfully introduced and tested:

(8)   Burzio (1986: 48)

"Two points can be made regarding the analysis in (70). The first is that such an analysis violates more the letter than the spirit of the projection principle."

Since you are as well equipped as anyone to know what the spirit of the crucial principle is (I assume, as recommended previously, that the principle has not actually been stated), nobody is going to give you any trouble on this point. Extensive testing indicates that no one will ever say that the analysis must be rejected because it really does violate P's spirit. It is simply not that easy working with principle spirits. Hence you can keep your pleasing analysis, not annoy the peer group that espouses and protects your chosen theory—and not even have to get rid of logic.

Even better, you can now say that your analysis supports the spirit of the theoretical principle, thereby actually pleasing the peer group. It is best to leave it a little vague as to how your analysis supports the spirit of the relevant principle; in particular, you should neither assert nor deny that it does this just by being inconsistent with its letter.

Another exhausting problem an advocate of a theory can face is writing a concluding chapter to, for example, a book about some NL that uses some theory (or conversely). A good quick way to end and one sure to be popular with the theory's support group is to say your work on the designated NL has confirmed some of its principles. At the end, it is better to say "confirmed P" than "confirmed the spirit of P," since it sounds more scientific. Luckily, research reveals that many health-conscious linguists, seeking to reduce reading stress, look only at concluding chapters, so that this will conveniently provide such readers with a solid and nonspiritual dose of the assurance they seek.

People tend to think you can only say that work on some NL has confirmed a given theory by showing that some facts actually follow from it. Fortunately, given the Phantom Theorem Move discussed above, you can always confidently say this and, given the Phantom Principle Move, you always have some trouble-free principle to say it about.

But things are even better: you can also say your work confirms some principle of a desired theory if that work supports an analysis of the facts that is in fact inconsistent with that principle. As already seen, the analysis could confirm the principle's spirit, given the Sophisticated Interpretation Move. Further, after all, if it weren't for the principle, you never would have been able to notice that the analysis was incompatible with it and nobody would have realized how important the analysis was. What could confirm a principle more than that? Naturally, then, one finds Burzio (1986: 437) concluding, despite the earlier admission that his analysis was incompatible with the Projection Principle: "Some of the above will in turn confirm the correctness of the projection principle." Some of it certainly will, given accepted standards in the field. Confirmation comes in many forms, after all, and warm words of support for the spirit must surely count for something.

One of the truly annoying and tiring things in linguistics is that other linguists often act as if they had a right to disagree with you, even about matters that should be quite obvious to them. For example, you may have been saying for a long time that some concept, say "subject of," has to be defined terms of the theory, and still somebody might have the temerity to suppose that the relevant ideas or ones pretty like them are primitive terms. You could try to give some arguments that they are not, but formulating arguments is exactly the sort of thing that migraine specialists warn against; besides, the average linguist probably would not be able to follow the sophisticated and robust argumentation that would be necessary. Anyway, how much time can you be expected to spend on such basic points? The only reasonable procedure in such cases is to formulate a methodological principle that simply makes it illicit for the concept concerned to be primitive, as in (9):

(9)   Chomsky (1981: 10)
       "But it would be unreasonable to incorporate, for example, such notions as "subject of a sentence" or other grammatical relations within the class of primitive notions, since it is unreasonable to suppose that these notions can be directly applied to linguistically unanalyzed data."

Of course, you don't have to, and should not, allow the methodological principle to constrain your own choice of future primitives if it is inconvenient. This is illustrated, in a passage within thirty pages of (9):

(10) Chomsky (1981: 37)
       "We can bring subcategorization and θ-marking together more closely by inventing a new θ-role, call it #, for non-arguments that are subcategorized by heads, e.g., *advantage* in 'take advantage of'."

Is one to suppose that the notion 'bears the θ-role #' "can be directly applied to linguistically unanalyzed data" in a way that subject cannot? Hardly, but no upwardly mobile linguist will raise the question provided that several pages of text have intervened since the methodological principle was introduced and used to exorcise evil assumptions. Trust me; its power will never rebound against the user.

Nor need you worry that most primitives you yourself have appealed to before springing the new methodology violate it just as much as, for example, # does, because the aim of introducing a new methodological principle is to prevent a lot of well-intentioned people from mistakenly wasting their time worrying about whether the given concepts are primitive or not. Why should you follow such an irritatingly restrictive methodology when you are yourself in no danger of this kind of pointless activity? It would be like a grown-up being forbidden to speak to strangers on the way to the corner store.

A delicate point in the search for a less stressful linguistic existence is reached when it becomes necessary to incorporate in your work ideas already advanced by individuals who have mostly wrong assumptions and mislead a lot of gullible people. It would be a serious error to actually cite them or give them any credit, which could only increase their credibility and hence their ability to lead others astray in the many domains (most, no doubt) in which their ideas remain misguided and objectionable. For example, suppose some proponent, like McCawley, of the unquestionably wrong and stupid Basic Semantics (BS) movement has, accidentally, hit on one or two ideas you need to use, say, hypothetically, the notion that surface quantifiers are connected to logiclike representations by transformational movement operations sensitive to syntactic constraints or something like that.

When adopting this idea, assuming that you wish to do so, it would be an obvious rhetorical error to cite any proponents of BS. Not only would this waste a lot of serious linguists' time if they were persuaded to actually read such misguided stuff, but it might also mislead less sophisticated thinkers than you into thinking something about BS was right. So the correct procedure is to proclaim and get others to proclaim, over a long period, many times, that BS is totally wrong, misguided, unscientific, and so on. Then, quietly, simply use whatever BS ideas you want without warning and without any tiring citational or attributional material. A well-known principle of scholarly law known as *Right of Salvage* guarantees that you cannot be held accountable for this. This principle determines that one need not make attributions to theoretical traditions already "generally established as stupid and not part of rational inquiry."

There are many other topics that should be discussed in a treatment of the subject matter here. A fuller account would cover rhetorical moves that are best suited to live verbal interaction, in conference question sessions or similar environments— moves like the *Argument from Bravery* ("Look, so-and-so may be wrong, but at least he has a theory") and the *Argument from Notoriety* ("Oh, those facts about nonrestrictive relatives are notorious"—i.e., my theory does not have to be compatible with them). But space constraints prevent our treating here such topics as the beautiful *Psychic Alternation Move* ("This criticism of A's claim is not valid, because although A admittedly made the claim, he could easily have made a different, correct claim instead"), which must await another occasion.

I would also have wished to cover the black art of refereemanship, where even the minimal constraints imposed on scholars by the fact that their names will be publicly seen above their words are absent. Here truth counts for little and rhetoric holds sway; see chapter 10.

Junk Refereeing

Our Tax Dollars at Work

$\mathbf{R}$ecall from chapter 9, page 292, the remark: "I would also have wished to cover the black art of refereemanship, where even the minimal constraints imposed on scholars by the fact that their names will be publicly seen above their words are absent. Here truth counts for little and rhetoric holds sway." This passage, which owed a great deal to Geoffrey K. Pullum, was, I will here argue, a bit prescient, supported by the subsequent appearance of the following successful[1] anonymous referee subpassage, which was part of the most negative report (Overall Rating: Poor) received for my NSF Proposal SBR-9808169 (*Diversity among English Objects*).[2] To facilitate its analysis and to justify my claim that this is junk refereeing, I have numbered the parts therein by associating a prefixed angle bracketed numeral with each or with major clauses within them:

<1> In my opinion, the broader impact of this work will be negligible, <2> simply because the whole approach is founded upon assumptions that have not been current in the field for some time now. <3> The whole domain of the data presented here is now considered by 99% of researchers in the field <4> to involve complex relations between (at least) (i) phrase structure configurations (possibly of a quite ornate type), (ii) argument structure configurations and properties (highest/lowest argument, particular thematic relations), and (iii) more detailed semantic properties. <5> This observation about theoretical assumptions should not be taken as mere trendiness; <6> far from it, for the general consensus concerning (i–iii) has not been arrived at by accident, but rather through 30 years of looking at semantics-syntax interactions, <7> and it is in some clear sense "correct." <8> Additionally, I think this whole body of work has shown a greater depth of insight and explanation than

could ever follow from the highly one-dimensional notation-crunching approach presented here. <9> Consequently, the various generalizations that are presented in this proposal . . . strike me as completely uninformative and totally lacking in any insight—<10> they are merely mechanical descriptions.

Beginning with section <1>, one notes that it consists exclusively of unchallengeable speculation about the future. Such could be offered about any proposal whatever. Does such speculation belong in a putative scientific referee report?

Section <2> asserts, more or less correctly, that the approach of the proposal is founded upon currently nonpopular assumptions (roughly, those of relational grammar). This might be relevant to a work on the sociology of the field. But what is its relevance to an evaluation of the scientific worth of the ideas and a proposal based on them?

Section <3> tells us that 99% of those studying the domain covered by the proposal have certain beliefs. No evidence of polling, sampling, and so forth, is offered, so one is safe in concluding that this remark involves hyperbole that uses made up numbers unsupported by any actual data. But how would even the truth of the concocted sociological claim bear on the scientific evaluation of the proposal? Is one really to accept the implication of an invariant correlation between correctness and popularity? Is there no chance the putative 1% are right about any point of disagreement?

Section <4> spells out the putative belief of the putative 99% of workers. One could only wonder if all of them accept all these with the same degree of confidence.

Section <5> reassures us that the observation in section <4>, which seems like an assertion of mere trendiness, is not. This reveals a laudable twinge of guilt rather rare in junk linguistics. It has occurred to the author perhaps that what (s)he has said so far has no actual substantive content, since it contains no specific critique of the logic or factual content of the proposal.

Section <6> reveals why the seeming appeal to mere trendiness is not. It is because the purportedly generally accepted trendy view was not arrived at by accident (whatever that would mean) but rather by thirty years of looking at semantics-syntax interactions. Again the remark fills a gap that should be filled by something of substance. That is, the twinge of guilt has failed to lead to anything of value.

Section <7> makes it final. The trend that took thirty years to develop is "in some clear sense" *correct*. It would be petty to ask "what clear sense." For it is always pretty convincing to be told flatly by an opponent O that O's position is correct.

In section <8>, the referee actually criticizes the proposal being refereed, and in three ways. First, it is said to be inferior in depth of insight and explanation to the views supposedly held by 99% of the researchers in the field. But no insight or explanation of anything superior to that in the proposal is cited. So criticism one here is empty. Second, the proposal view is disparaged as being "highly one-dimensional" and, third, it is equally disparaged as involving "notation-crunching." Let us suppose that one could assign some content to the notion of being "highly one-dimensional" and even agree further that the proposal has this property. It would still need to be shown that having said property is undesirable, a task the referee does not attempt. As for "notation-crunching," this also is unexplained and a bit obscure. I infer (but who knows) that the referee is, via a pun on the known form 'number-crunching', referring to the fact that the proposal utilizes the standard relational grammar notation for some grammatical relations of numerical signs like "1," "2," and so on. Why this choice of notation might be worse than another (what other?) is not specified, nor is it addressed why or how a nonsubstantive choice of notation could be relevant to evaluating a scientific proposal.

Section <9> lets on that the proposal contains generalizations but rejects them as "completely uninformative" and "lacking in any insight."[3] These claims are, though, entirely unsupported. The referee does not discuss the actual generalizations and does not cite any counterexamples to them or any way in which they are insufficiently general. No specific reason is given that they could be stated better in some other terms. The putative criticism is then empty and the identical words could equally be levied against any proposal whatever in any field, even one that contains thoroughly established scientific laws. Not even the law of contradiction in logic would be safe from such pseudocriticism.

Finishing with a flourish, section <10> demeans the generalizations of the proposal still further. Here they are said to be "merely mechanical." The chief characteristic of this phrase is that it is undefined. But, curiously, <u>mechanical</u> is a word used in formal studies as a positive requirement, for example, as when one speaks of a 'mechanical procedure', an algorithm; see Partee, ter Meulen, and Wall (1993: 515–516). Why would the referee think that being mechanical is a *flaw*? The point would seem to be that unwilling or unable to actually discuss and analyze the content of the proposal but nonetheless determined to reject it, the referee is forced to invent pseudoproperties that then permit rejection of the proposal on the ground that it fails to have them, if it is stipulated that they are good, or has them, if it is stipulated that they are bad. That is, starting from a different cast of mind, a referee might have written: "What a wonderful proposal! Its generalizations are mechanical and even reveal *extensive* notation-crunching."

The reader's report I have quoted pretends to be an instance of proposal refereeing but is, I have argued, junk refereeing. The referee does not actually analyze the material in the proposal but contents him- or herself with such empty and meaningless criticisms as that the approach is founded on ideas that are not currently popular, is one-dimensional (dimensions undefined), and involves notation-crunching, and the referee makes unsupported assertions that some opposing view is "in some clear sense 'correct,'" makes unanalyzed claims that its "generalizations . . . are . . . completely uninformative and totally lacking in any insight," and finally asserts that the descriptions are merely mechanical. It is obviously much easier to write such things than to find genuine counterexamples to the claims or to provide actual alternatives that cover the same facts and do not appeal to the notions utilized in the work supposedly being reviewed, substantive tasks this referee scrupulously avoided.

To conclude, the reader's method is not only an instance of junk refereeing, it also can be taken as a model of that enterprise. Believe me, esteemed reader, if the need arises, you can adopt this approach and apply it to reject any proposal you wish. It doesn't have to be one that, for example, 99% of the researchers in the field can confidently (though without evidence) be said to already know has got to be wrong.

Junk Ethics 2

The Most Irresponsible Passage

Consider a contest to determine the most *irresponsible* passage written by a professional linguist in the entire history of linguistics. Contestants will no doubt differ in their choice of entries; here I specify and try to justify mine.

The most irresponsible passage ever written by a linguist about the overall subject matter of linguistics is, I suggest, the five paragraphs (here broken up) quoted in (1). To facilitate its analysis and discussion, I have numbered the twenty successive sentences therein by associating a prefixed angle bracketed numeral with each. I have also suppressed from the quoted text the author's footnote numerals.

(1)   Chomsky (1999: 33–34)
       "<1> A broader category of questions has to do with the 'internalist' conception of language adopted in this discussion, and in the line of inquiry from which it derives for the past 40 years, a branch of what has been called 'biolinguistics.' <2> FL (= faculty of language : PMP) is considered to be a subcomponent of Jones's mind/brain; Jones's (I -) language L is the state of his FL, which he puts to use in various ways.
       <3> We study these objects more or less as we study the system of motor organization or visual perception, or the immune or digestive systems.
       <4> It is hard to imagine an approach to language that does not adopt such conceptions, at least tacitly.
       <5> So we discover, I think, even when it is strenuously denied, but I will not pursue the matter here.
       <6> Internalist biolinguistic inquiry does not, of course, question the legitimacy of other approaches to language, any more than internalist inquiry into bee communication in-

validates the study of how the relevant internal organization of bees enters into their social structure.

<7>The investigations do not conflict; they are mutually supportive. <8> In the case of humans, though not other organisms, the issues are subject to controversy, often impassioned, and needless.

<9>We also speak freely of derivations, of expressions EXP generated by L, and of the set of such EXPs—the set that is called 'the structure of L' in Chomsky (1986), where the I-/E- terminology is introduced.

<10> Evidently, these entities are not 'internal.' <11> That has led to the belief that some externalist concepts of 'E-linguistics' are being introduced. <12> But that is a misconception. <13> These are not entities with some ontological status; they are introduced to simplify talk about properties of FL and L, and can be eliminated in favor of internalist notions. <14> One of the properties of Peano's axioms PA is that PA generates the proof 'P of 2+2 = 4' but not the proof 'P' of 2+2 = 7' (in suitable notation).

<15> We can speak freely of the property 'generable by PA,' holding of P but not P' and derivatively of lines of generable proofs (theorems) and the set of theorems, without postulating any entities beyond PA and its properties. <16> Similarly, we may speak of the property 'generable by L,' which holds of certain derivations D and not others, and holding derivatively of an expression EXP formed by D and of the set {EXP} of those expressions. <17> No new entities are postulated in these usages beyond FL, its states L, and their properties. <18> Similarly, a study of the solar system could introduce the notion HT = {possible trajectories of Halley's comet within the solar system}, and studies of motor organization or visual perception could introduce the notions {plans for moving the arm} or {visual images for cats (vs. bees)}. <19> But these studies do not postulate weird entities apart from planets, comets, neurons, cats, . . . <20> There is no 'Platonism' introduced, and no 'E-linguistic' notions: only biological entities and their properties."

Sentence <1> reveals that at issue in this passage are questions of the *ontology of NL* rather than particular linguistic facts and their description and explanation. As the sentence only cites the existence of questions and recognizes its author's own 'internalist' conception, it is itself unobjectionable.

Sentence <2> fills in the author's standard and well-known view; NL is taken to be a biological aspect of human nature. In the author's sense, the NL of an individual I is taken to be a state of I's brain. Irresponsibility has begun to appear since this view, although multiply repeated by the author over the years and widely adopted by others, has also been criticized sharply and even argued to be incoherent.[1] Responsibility would thus require, if not reply to such criticisms, at a minimum reference to them with full citations. Instead, the relevant works and their authors are left as phantoms that need not be named and whose arguments need not be cited. This irresponsibly minimizes the reader's chances of objectively comparing the contrasting positions.

The irresponsibility of <3> is perhaps clouded by the sheer absurdity of its claim. Note that it is a claim and not, for example, a suggestion. The "we" must clearly be understood to mean "linguists" or at the least "linguists (including trivially the author of <3>) who accept the claims and linguistics-characterizing assumptions in <1> and

<2>." But barring a perverse interpretation of "more or less" as meaning "in largely distinct ways," it must be clear to anyone who has read a sample of the author's linguistic research writings that they bear no serious connection to the study of immune or digestive systems.

Consider the latter. Since digestive systems are physical objects, which exist in space and time, the biological and medical scientists who study them of course seek physical records, for instance, those yielded by probes, dissection, photographs, and slides and, in more recent years, those produced by X rays, MRIs, and so forth. Those who have had the personal experience of a medical study of their own digestive system are not likely to be bluffed into imagining it shared some feature with the author's inquiries into, for example, subjacency, binding, or expletive associates. The author's work involves no analog of the collection of physical records. Nor does it have the slightest plausibility that he could remain unaware of the enormity of the nonparallels between, in particular, his own linguistic research and the physical study of digestive systems. No one could be unaware that his own work had after more than four and half decades failed to produce a single *physical* record of any of the postulated objects (syntactic component, lexicon, LF, move-α, syntactic trees, and so on.) parallel to the physical records that are the everyday feature of the study of digestive systems. To paraphrase a formulation due to Everett (2001), if linguistics were what the author claims, syntactic trees would be visible in CAT scans.

Sentence <3> is then a crude and arguably deliberate distortion of the truth.

Sentence <4> develops the irresponsible character of <3> further. The "it is hard to imagine" locution is to be taken either literally or as a harmless, relatively standard way of indicating a claim of extreme implausibility. But in this context, neither interpretation can defend the remark against its truly deceptive character. Even if the author were, implausibly, sufficiently limited imaginatively as to be personally unable to even conceive an alternative to his own ontological position, others then not so limited have long ago done the work for him and not only proposed but also justified such an alternative, with specific discussion of the relative inferiority of his own position; see note 1. Moreover, the author could not in general be unaware of such work.[2] So the only viable interpretation of <4> is that it is a pretense that adoption of the author's ontological position is imposed by a sort of necessity due to the lack of an alternative; see chapter 13. The remark illegitimately substitutes for the missing substantive answer to the all too real but never answered challenges already issued to the author's ontology and reveals an extraordinary lack of willingness to grapple openly and fairly with the threat of the alternative.

Sentence <5> is irresponsible in several ways. It seeks to rhetorically support the distortion of <4> by a claim unsupported by argument or fact, thereby empty, that other approaches in fact ("we discover") adopt the author's position *even when they deny it.* An objective or even inquisitive reader might be interested in knowing who are those shadowy and misguided workers who think they have an alternative (recall that for the author in <4> such was "hard to imagine") and what it is. Irresponsibly, nothing is said and <4> and <5> together can support nothing about the author's position.

Sentence <6> tells us that "internalist biolinguist inquiry," that is, in effect, the author, does not question the legitimacy of other approaches to NL. Could the author have forgotten that just a couple of lines before <6> he had told us that it was hard to imagine approaches that did not adopt his 'internalist' viewpoint? So <6> declares, then with entirely hypocritical magnanimity, that the author does not question the legitimacy only of something whose existence is putatively essentially beyond his imagination.

Sentence <7> is parasitic on <6> and seems to tell us that two inquiry types, one the author's own and one whose existence he cannot imagine, do not conflict.

Sentence <8> is irresponsible principally in being largely empty. The irresponsible implication, though, is clear: Some misguided individuals (but not the author) are engaged in impassioned and needless controversy over something, but he is evidently unwilling or unable to tell us who they are, what they are arguing about, and why it is needless. How easy it is with no intellectual content to portray oneself as objective, above the fray, and not drawn into needless emotionalism like certain (unnamed) inferiors, whose inferiority the reader is, though, thereby denied any means of verifying.

Awful as sentences <2>–<8> are separately and offensive as they are as a whole to any serious standards of scholarship, it still might not be a sure thing to enter them in the contest on their own. Fortunately for the viability of this contest entry, the *really* bad stuff in passage (1) has not yet even begun to be dealt with.

Although the author does not indicate this, sentence <9> introduces an issue that is a major source of incoherence in his overall ontological position. By the standards of the overall passage, <9> is itself only mildly irresponsible. Basically, it introduces the fact known to all that linguistics deals with sentences, avoiding that term in favor of 'expressions'. It begs the question of whether NL sentences *have derivations* and whether there is a set (here called EXP) of them that can be generated, the former of which is denied in many types of linguistics (e.g., HPSG[3]) and the latter of which was argued to be impossible in some long ago published works, such work being systematically ignored by the author.[4] The issue introduced is how can these expressions, which linguistics in some sense seems to be about, be made sense of in terms of the author's ontology represented by <1>–<3>? Although the author does not explicate, the issue is what status sentences can have if an individual's NL is a state of his or her mind/brain.

With sentence <10>, more irresponsibility enters immediately. The facile "evidently" covers up the fact that readers are not told the reason. Moreover, in a work by the same author published shortly after this one and whose proofs would no doubt have been read roughly simultaneously with the writing of this one, one finds (2):

(2)   Chomsky (2000c: 160)
    "The internalist study of language also speaks of 'representations' of various kinds, including phonetic and semantic representations at the 'interface' with other systems. But here too we need not ponder what is represented, seeking some objective construction from sounds or things. The representations are postulated mental entities, to be understood in the manner of a mental image of a rotating cube, whether it is the consequence of tachistoscopic presentations or a real rotating cube, or stimulation of the retina in some other way; or imagined, for that matter."

Remark (2) states that 'representations' are mental entities, where 'representations' are clearly sentences or parts of sentences, that is, just the 'expressions' in (1).

They are, we are told, to be understood on analogy with mental images, that is, therefore as mental, internal.[5] There is then in short a crude contradiction between <10> and an almost contemporaneous claim by the author, with no explication, no cross-references, no indication of how these claims could fail to be contradictory. Revealed is an extraordinary failure on the author's part to take even his *own* assertions seriously.

In sentence <10> the core question at stake in (1) is joined. Precisely at issue in the whole discussion is a surreptitious attempt to back away from any claim of sentence internality like (2). But if sentences are not internal, then since, for the author, NL *is* internal, sentences can't be part of it. A new contradiction then threatens, one distinct from that *between* the separately published positions of Chomsky (1999) and Chomsky (2000c) and entirely internal to claim (1). Because if NL is internal and sentences are as claimed in this work not internal, then maintenance of position (2), which takes sentences to be mental things, is incoherent and must be replaced. But by what?

Sentences <11> and <12> jointly reject the idea, developed and justified at length in work such as that cited in note 1, that sentences are real things, just nonmental ones. The now repeated irresponsibility on the author's part of rejecting positions without citation and without therefore indicating how to overcome their unpleasant opposing arguments is manifest.

By the end of his sentence <12> the author of (1) has driven himself to the conclusions that (i) NL is a biological thing, hence 'internal'; (ii) sentences (usually called by the author expressions, representations, or symbolic objects) are, contrary to Chomsky (1999: 160), not 'internal'; and (iii) sentences are not 'external', either.

Via logic alone, (i)–(iii) can only mean that sentences are not real. And it is this claim that forms a major kernel of the deepest irresponsibility in (1) and which sentence <13> makes explicit. That is, there is no other way to interpret in context the assertion that X "are not entities with some ontological status" than as saying X "has no ontological status," which is to say X "do not exist." Moreover, only this is consistent with the second clause of <13>, which invokes a rather standard type of philosophy of science reductionism, claiming that sentences "can be eliminated" and actually involve a mere *façon de parler* to simplify discussion of the putatively real things, FL and L, a biological object and one of its states respectively, that is, purely internal things.[6]

Before continuing to delve into the post–sentence <13> remarks that the author offers in the attempt to justify claim <13>, it should be commented immediately that for the author to adopt <13> is trivially incoherent/contradictory and, with a further dose of irresponsibility, contradictory in ways already explicated in the literature as an objection to just the sort of putatively biological ontology the author is trying to rescue here. This is true since for almost five decades the author has claimed consistently that NL has the property of (denumerable) *infinitude*. And this is maintained in Chomsky (2000c: 3) and also, albeit more obliquely, in Chomsky (1999).[7] Evidently, NL is only denumerably infinite if there is some aspect of it that can be put in one-to-one correspondence with the full set of natural numbers, and the only aspect of NL with this property is some collection, for example, the collection of sentences. But the author has now claimed that an NL is simply a *state* of a mind brain, an obviously *finite* object (since any brain state has physical and temporal boundaries), and that there are no sentences, entailing thereby that their collection is the null set, maximally far from a collection in one-to-one correspondence with the full set of natural numbers. In short, as observed in Katz and Postal (1991: 547–548) and Langendoen and Postal (1984: 131–132), one of the incoherences of the author's ontology is to both claim that NL is infinite and yet deliberately recognize no aspect of linguistic reality that could have this property.[8]

Evidently, in the face of uniform previous recognition of the existence of sentences in NLs and his own previous forty-five-plus-year history consistent with this, as in Chomsky (2000c: 160), a sudden denial of the reality of sentences is a bit much to simply *declare*, even for this author. Unacknowledged recognition of this then leads him to seek a bit of justification. But instead of attacking directly the challenge of making sense of a linguistic claim that sentences are not real, as would minimally be required in a responsible account, the author proceeds via a purported analogy. This carries the discussion into levels of shoddiness orders of magnitude beyond even the ominous levels already documented.

The author's sentence <14> introduces the notion of Peano's axioms, well-known basic principles of number theory. A version of these is given in (3):

(3)   Partee, ter Meulen, and Wall (1993: 214)

"(8-40) *Peano's axioms*. There are two primitive predicates, N and S. The intended interpretation of N is 'is a natural number' and that of S is 'is the (immediate) successor of.' There is one primitive constant, 0, whose intended interpretation is the natural number zero.

P1) $N0$

P2) $\forall x(Nx \rightarrow \exists y(Ny \ \& \ Syx \ \& \ \forall z(Szx \rightarrow z = y)))$

P3) $\sim\exists x(Nx \ \& \ S0x)$

P4) $\forall x \forall y \forall z \forall w((Nx \ \& \ Ny \ \& \ Szx \ \& \ Swy \ \& \ z=w) \rightarrow x=y)$

P5) If Q is a property such that

(a) $Q0$

(b) $\forall x \forall y((Nx \ \& \ Qx \ \& \ Ny \ \& \ Syx) \rightarrow Qy)$,

then $\forall x(Nx \rightarrow Qx)$

"Peano, like Euclid, conceived of the primitive terms of the system read having known meaning, and of the axioms as the smallest set of true statements about the natural number series from which its other properties could be derived."

While <14> might seem innocuous, it is actually irresponsible, since it falsely takes PA to be generative/proof-theoretic principles analogous to the rules of a generative grammar when they are in fact evidently *statements*, formulas that can be assigned truth values. As such, like other axioms, PA cannot generate proofs. Proofs can be built from them only with the help of an actual proof system that provides appropriate instructions for forming the legitimate formal objects (e.g., sequences of lines of symbols) that are proofs. Since the author knows what a proof is, his confusion of PA with proof-theoretic principles is irresponsible distortion.[9] That is, the analogy the author later (sentence <16>) draws between PA-based proof derivations and generative grammar derivations fails.

Sentence <15> is the core of the analogy intended to justify the author's claim of the nonexistence or unreality of NL sentences. The point is, irresponsibly made since not explicit, that where mathematicians think of PA as formalizing the properties of real objects, the natural numbers, as in Partee, ter Meulen, and Wall's description, <15> in effect denies the reality of natural numbers, since these are precisely the entities one can supposedly avoid postulating. Rather, a reader is to believe that talk of these can tenably just be taken as some sort of simplification of "real" talk about proofs from PA. Evidently the reader is not supposed to ask, as Chomsky seemingly has not, what sense one could make of questions of the *choice* of sets of axioms like PA if there is no real domain independent of the axioms for them to formulate truths about. Why should one be talking about PA and not, for example, a set of axioms like (4a, b)?

(4)   a. O is not a number.
       b. Neither is anything else.

This pair of absurdities in fact seems to say about numbers what the author claims. Is one supposed to query mathematicians about why they do not adopt the simpler system (4a, b)?

The ground is then laid in <15> for defending by analogy the claim that NL sentences are not real, though the mental grammar = brain state that generates them supposedly is.[10] The reader is supposed to conclude that this is viable from the just asserted viability of the claim that PA (presumably real in some sense[11]) generates proofs of theorems about numbers even though the latter don't exist.[12]

Sentence <16> makes the analogy explicit. And sentence <17> then draws the inference that is the whole point of the exercise. The entities that are not postulated, that is, supposedly need not be postulated, are exactly NL sentences.

There are then two major sorts of inept irresponsibility here. The justification of the relevant conclusion that sentences do not exist depends solely on an analogy with arithmetic. Even if the characterization of the latter and PA that the author has sketched were tenable, this would be no actual argument for a relevant property of *NL*. A skeptic could simply deny that NL is like arithmetic and justifiably deny it *without argument* since the author has given no argument that it is relevantly like *his* conception of the number system in the pertinent respects. So the analogy could provide no ground for the conclusion about NL sentence nonexistence *even if the characterization of PA and the number system made sense.*

Moreover, the highlighted hypothetical is false, in fact, grotesquely so, as already indicated. A vivid additional way to see this is to recognize that it is broadly agreed that the greatest result of modern logic is provided by K. Gödel's incompleteness theorems. So, for example, Suppes (1957: 70) indicates: "Gödel's theorem on the incompleteness of elementary number theory is probably the most important theorem in the literature of modern logic." Hintikka (2000: 3) goes even further: "Gödel had indeed proved such a result. This result is known as his first incompleteness theorem. It is arguably one of the most important and challenging discoveries in twentieth-century science, comparable with Einstein's theory of relativity or Heisenberg's uncertainty relation."

We need not say much about the highly technical substance of Gödel's theorems, except that one result shows that no axiomatization of elementary number theory, that is, inter alia, no set of axioms like PA, can be both complete and logically consistent. To understand this conclusion, one needs to understand the relevant property of *completeness*. Informally, an axiomatization A of a domain D is complete if every truth about D is a theorem of A. In the case of arithmetic then, to consider the question whether, for example, a system like PA is complete, one must consider the relation between two sets: the set of theorems of A and the set of truths about D.

To understand the truly outrageous character of the author's account of PA in <15>, it suffices then to observe this: Were it correct, not only would it be impossible to *prove* Gödel's incompleteness theorems, but it also would be impossible even to *formulate* them. Because the author's account of PA in <15> entails precisely that there is no set of truths about the relevant D. For D is then the domain of all natural numbers, just the entities the author says do not need postulating. But there are no truths about things that are not. We cannot answer questions like "How tall was the first female president of the United States elected before 1940?" And yet, as Boolos and Jeffrey (1974: 180) indicate: "And perhaps the most significant consequence of Theorem 6 (Gödel's first incompleteness theorem: PMP) is what it says about the notions of *truth* (in the standard interpretation for the language of arithmetic) and *theoremhood*, or *provability* (in any particular formal theory): that they are in no sense the same." That is, the author's claim <16> totally ignores and directly conflicts with one of the luminous results of modern logic.

So, to accept <15> one would have to accept that arguably the greatest modern logician and the community of subsequent logicians who have expounded his incompleteness results and touted their greatness have simply been misguided fools who failed to recognize the nonexistence of any truths about numbers and thus the chimera of all talk of (in)completeness. One need not linger over the absurdity of such a conclusion.

Moreover, the author's assertion here is even more irresponsible than it might seem. One cannot, for example, imagine sympathetically that he merely *fails to understand* the general outlines of the notion of completeness and Gödel's incompleteness results or that he does not know that there is a set of truths of elementary number theory distinct from any questions of proofs from axioms. For he already knew this forty years ago:

(5) Chomsky (1963: 356)
     "There are, furthermore, perfectly reasonable sets that are not recursively enumerable; for example, the set of true statements in elementary number theory or the set of all satisfiable schemata of quantification theory."

It is impossible to render quote (5) consistent with sentence <15>. Since the set of all generated proofs is a recursively enumerable set, if the set of true statements were only a *façon de parler* for talking about proofs, no interpretation of "true statements in elementary number theory" could define a nonenumerable set.

In short, sentence <15>, the core of the author's 1999 attempted defense of his *biological* ontology for NL, is inconsistent with his own 1963 understanding of basic facts of logic. Even minimal responsibility would then have required that he explicate this contradiction and justify the 1999 branch of it as against Gödel's results, accepted by all logicians for seventy years. Instead, as with the contradiction between Chomsky (2000c: 160) and <13>, the author fails to allude to the issue, to his own earlier position, or to standard ideas in logic and thus irresponsibly obscures with silence the awful character of his claims. There is no textual basis for doubting that <15> represents something the author knows to be nonsense but states anyway in a scandalously unscrupulous attempt to prop up a bankrupt ontology.

The issues about logic just gone over provide a further insight into the irresponsibility of (1). Surely if the author had any genuine work product whatever dealing with elementary number theory that even *hinted at* calling into question the validity (still less the sense) of Gödel's results or called into doubt the existence of a collection of truths of elementary number theory, the only thing to do with such a result would be to submit it to a *professional journal in logic*, where it could be reviewed by experts. Of course, the author has not presented anything that represents even an iota of such a result. Instead, with enormous cynicism, he has to the contrary buried his ludicrous claim, contradicting even his own earlier statement and entirely unsupported by argument, in an article for linguists, assuming no doubt that most will not be able to recognize the incompetence of his account about a domain that is not their area of expertise.[13]

Sentences <18>–<20> require little comment. They introduce a further pointless analogy between linguistics and various physical studies. The key feature is the use of the undefined but clearly pejorative term 'weird' to describe the sort of entities these studies do not postulate. Sentence <20> with its passing remark about Platonism, as usual with no reference to proponents, no citation, and no discussion of opposing arguments, irreponsibly makes it clear that what is at issue throughout, as stated here, is defense of the author's biological perspective against the Platonist alternative. And what is the defense in these sentences? It consists essentially of the empty name-calling 'weird'. There is also the illegitimate invited inference that if astronomy, vision studies, felinology, and such, need not posit abstract objects of the sort advocated by Platonists, then linguistics (thereby) need not, either. The inference is question-begging non sequitur, because the author has chosen arbitrarily to mention only fields that study physical objects. Why exclude, for example, logic, which can hardly be assumed to deal with "biological entities and their properties"? But whether linguistics need not appeal to abstract objects, as the author claims or whether it studies exactly those (sentences and collections of sentences) like logic and mathematics, as Platonists claim, is exactly the point at issue in the ontological discussion the author has entered into in (1).

To sum up then, what (1) represents is no more and no less than a deception. Faced with, although never explicitly admitting, the contradiction between his claim that NL is mind/brain internal and the fact that sentences cannot be, a contradiction pointed out years ago by opponents of the author precisely to show the impossibility of his ontology, the author has retreated to a distinct but equally incoherent position, one that denies that sentences even exist. The only basis for this claim is a purported analogy with a characterization of elementary number theory. And this characterization is a travesty at odds with modern logic and even with the author's own correct 1963 understanding of that.[14] To make things worse, although the author knows there are opposed ontological positions in linguistics and that these have in fact been crafted in large part as explicit critiques of the failures of his own ontology, he deliberately fails to reference any such work and engages in empty name-calling, empty talk of "needless controversy," pretense that there is no alternative to his position, and in general nonsubstantive and purely rhetorical attempts to denigrate an opposing position he is evidently unequipped to face openly. It appears fair to conclude that one encounters here sheer desperation. Revealed is an ontological position so deeply lacking seriousness that its "defense" is an ever steeper descent into the absurd, but one that the author tries to pretend fancifully is imposed by some sort of necessity.

The chief intended and, unfortunately, probably to some extent real victims of the intended deception in (1) are, I suspect, two classes of naive readers. One consists of those willing, given the author's influential status, to take almost any claim of his at face value. The other consists of those linguists little versed in logical and mathematical questions, including especially many relatively new in the field, such as the author's own students, that is, the very people whose education he has been paid to further.

This concludes my analysis of (1) and justification for my belief that it is the most irresponsible passage in the history of linguistics. Find worse if you can. My own suspicion, though, is that not only will it not be possible to come close to (1) in this regard, but also most linguists would, blessedly, be incapable of inventing anything worse, even if they set out with that goal in mind.[15]

Junk Reasoning 1

If It Doesn't Follow Automatically, *Then It's Pretty Much Got to at Least* Virtually *Follow, and If Not, Don't Worry; It Is Still* Unquestionably Natural

1. Automatic logical connections

A locution found in the writings of linguists is highlighted in (1):

(1)   a. It *follows automatically* from assumptions $A_1 \ldots A_n$ that B.
       b. B *follows automatically* from assumptions $A_1 \ldots A_n$.
       c. B falls out *automatically* from assumptions $A_1 \ldots A_n$.
       d. B is an *automatic* consequence/result of assumptions $A_1 \ldots A_n$.
       e. $A_1 \ldots A_n$ predict B automatically.
       f. B *automatically* satisfies $A_1 \ldots A_n$

There follow a few entirely random quoted examples of the usages in (1):

(2)   a. Chomsky ([1955], 1975a: 566)
        "And it will also automatically give 'no improvement was foreseen by anyone' as the passive of case (h), thus eliminating one discrepancy in what appears to be a simple and intuitively correct manner."
      b. Chomsky (1965: 104)
        "First of all, it accounts automatically for the restriction of passivization to Verbs that take Manner Adverbials freely."
      c. Postal (1972b: 221)
        "This could be an automatic consequence of a higher trigger cyclic formulation . . ."

d. Bresnan and Grimshaw (1978: 372)

"But in examples (167a–c), the P is deleted as an automatic consequence of Controlled Pro Deletion, which deletes the terminal string of PP [Pro] and coindexes the trace PP with the controller PP in head position."

e. Gazdar (1982: 174)

"The major advantage of the present analysis over that proposed by Bresnan and Grimshaw, apart from its basis in a more constrained linguistic metatheory, is that it automatically predicts the badness of examples like (9.17)."

f. Aissen and Perlmutter (1983: 366)

"A grammar that accounts for the phenomenon by means of a rule of Clause Reduction, however, cannot generate *(16–17) and thereby automatically predicts that these senences will be ungrammatical."

g. Baker (1988a: 119)

"The result of this discussion is that Incorporation automatically satisfies the case theory requirements of the NP whose head is incorporated."

h. Hukari and Levine (1987: 203, note 8)

"From such a definition, the 'double hole constraint' discussed by Maling and Zaenen (1982) falls out automatically."

i. Culicover and Jackendoff (1995: 258)

"Rather, we will argue, the proper analysis of X *else* falls in naturally with that of reflexives and pronouns; the apparent differences between them are an automatic consequence of our analysis."

j. Ladusaw (1996a: 212)

"Under the assumptions made here, this fact follows automatically from the treatment of the NPI as an indefinite, because on this construal, the If condition for the NPI is not met: though the NPI indefinite is in the scope of a licensing operator, it is not roofed by it."

k. Newmeyer (2000: 234)

"Given her theory that only direct objects can be 'promoted' to subject position in passivization, the ungrammaticality of (19b) follows automatically."

l. Chomsky (2001: 24)

"Proper positioning might be automatic under various assumptions: e.g., if the simultaneous satisfaction of properties of _v_ involves an internal cyclic order, with raising of OBJ first, then 'tucking in' of externally Merged SU."[1]

m. Den Dikken (2001: 15, note 19)

"On Kayne's (1994) analysis of *that*-relative clauses, where the moved constituent is an *NP*, not a DP, this will be an automatic result."

Since the citations in (2) are drawn from works that span almost five decades, from the 1950s to the present, they can by no means be regarded as mere slips of the pen or aberrational. Moreover, they do not seem limited to any particular school of syntactic thought.[2]

At issue specifically is the modifying form automatic(ally), used in the broader culture most often in connection with machinery, devices, and technology, for example, when one speaks of an automatic transmission in a vehicle, that is, one that shifts gears without specific mechanical inputs from a driver; an automatic shutoff valve, that is, one that one does not have to be opened or closed by hand; or a program or automaton that carries out some task automatically, such as one that debits a bank account. Various questions arise about the appearance of this locution in linguistic works like those in (2).

The uses of automatic(ally) in (1) appear substantively unrelated to the ordinary technological usage.[3] Rather, the term shows up in contexts where one is talking about *logical consequences*. Anyone who writes one of the variants of (1) surely intends to indicate *some* logical connection between a set of premises $A_1 \ldots A_n$ and some proposition B. One would *like* to assume that the implication is that if $A_1 \ldots A_n$ are all true, then necessarily B is also. This is consistent with the role of, for example, follows in standard discourse about logical connection. The adjectival/adverbial usage of linguists in (1) is then puzzling.

For consultation of works in logic reveals automatic(ally) to be unused there, as indicated inter alia by its absence from logic book indexes. Would a logician not rewrite, for example, (1a) simply by striking the word automatically, which yields (3):

(3)   It follows from assumptions $A_1 \ldots A_n$ that B.

Why then do linguists not systematically do likewise? Does the word automatic(ally) in linguistic uses like those in (2) make some (perhaps subtle) substantive contribution, one that affects truth functionality? If it *does*, one should be able to specify precisely the logical difference between (1a) and (3). If it does *not* make such a contribution but is *still* not totally redundant, then linguists should be in a position to give some *other*, non–truth functional justification for its discourse-complicating inclusion. There is then a minor mystery here, which I briefly address.

Genuine logical entailment admits no degrees, approximations, or manners; either something is a logical consequence of a fixed set of assumptions or not. Given that, the uses of automatic(ally) in (1) could, *if* the forms being modified manifested their wider culture *strictly logical* sense, contribute no truth functional substance. While one can perhaps not fully exclude the possibility of total redundancy, persistent use of terms over a long period by a wide range of linguists in a seemingly systematic way renders such a view implausible. So one suspects that at least most occurrences have a different basis. This could initially be taken to mean that standard linguistic uses of logic-invoking terms like follow combined with automatic(ally) have meanings at least partially distinct from their logical usages.

Assuming that requires seeking some way in which linguists' use of automatic(ally) could be rationalized under an assumption that it is *not* modifying a strict logical use of forms like follow and is thereby not redundant. This demands some view of how logic-invoking terms like follow are used in linguistics when they occur *without* the modifiers of relevance. Several colleagues have proposed the following possibility: Roughly, a usage like (1a) might differ from one like (3) in that the modifier expresses an *exclusion* of the need for *auxiliary assumptions* beyond $A_1 \ldots A_n$ to render B an actual logical consequence, whereas the usage in (3), at least among linguists, leaves open this requirement. This initially plausible hypothesis has several implications.

First, unexpectedly and a bit paradoxically, (1a) would then just translate as the logical equivalent of (3) on its strict logical sense, which seemingly leads again to a view of the modifier as <u>logically</u> redundant. Second, invocation of the idea that claims like (3) must or at least can be interpreted against a background posit of inexplicit auxiliary assumptions means that when linguists write something like (3), they are *not* committed in general to the existence of any actual logical connection per se between $A_1 \ldots A_n$ and B. What then exactly would be implied by claims like (3) under this interpretation? A first approximation might be something like (4):

(4)   (In linguistics), "B follows from $A_1 \ldots A_n$" (can be used to) mean(s) only that there is *some* set of premises $C_1 \ldots C_m$ such that B is a logical consequence of the *union* of $A_1 \ldots A_n$ and $C_1 \ldots C_m$. Here $C_1 \ldots C_m$ would be the auxiliary assumptions required to yield a genuine logical consequence.

But, evidently, a usage characterized *merely* as in (4) would be inappropriate to any intellectual pursuit. Ignoring the trivial case where some $C_i = B$, given that every proposition is a logical consequence *of a contradiction*, (4) alone would sanction assertion of "X follows from Y" for any arbitrary X and Y. Any of the infinitely many extant contradictions would union with Y to entail X. Thus minimally, to rationalize usages like (3) via a schema like (4), relevance constraints would have to be imposed on $C_1 \ldots C_m$. A further suggestion I have received is that a reconstruction like (4) of, for example, (3) is to be interpreted such that $C_1 \ldots C_m$ represent (part of) *some commonly understood theory*, presumably a contradiction-free part.

This helps a little but only subject to important reservations. Schema (4) so clarified might in principle describe a reasonable usage in a field at a state of development where the $C_1 \ldots C_m$ are uniquely identified, well-known, well-established principles. For example, internal to the elementary number theory part of mathematics, $C_1 \ldots C_m$ could be Peano's axioms (see chapter 11). Then it would be quite clear that something like (3) was in effect shorthand for (5):

(5)   The union of $A_1 \ldots A_n$ and Peano's axioms entails B.

For fixed $A_1 \ldots A_n$, this makes a checkable claim just because elementary number theory has a fixed set of precise, accepted axioms. However, one need not stress that contemporary linguistics is nothing like that; there is not even a hint in current work on syntax, for example, of an analog of Peano's axioms. What would fill the role of well-known, well-established precise principles whose truth is accepted even by *most* syntacticians? The closest one could come is probably the Coordinate Structure Constraint. But even today, thirty-six years after Ross (1967) proposed it, it remains most often entirely informal and what its actual formulation should be is obscure, and there are those who have denied the validity of the informal generalization.[4]

Minimally then, in linguistics, interpreting arbitrary uses of the form (3) against a schema like (4) means that as often as not it will be unclear what the background $C_1 \ldots C_m$ are supposed to be.

So, consider the quotations in (2) of actual uses of the logic-invoking forms (irrelevantly for this point, occurring with the modifier at issue here). One finds first, that in certain cases it is unclear whether it is relevant to invoke *any* set of auxiliary assumptions at all. So (2d) states that the deletion of a particular form is an automatic consequence of a *specific deletion rule*. Second, and more generally, there is no single common set of auxiliary assumptions that could be taken to underly this range of uses. That of Chomsky ([1955]/1975c) would involve the earliest notions of transformational generative grammar, that of Chomsky (1965) would have to involve the transformational assumptions of that work, but those were very sketchy and incomplete. That of Postal (1972b: 221) would have to involve some set of assumptions relevant to an early but somewhat latter stage of transformational grammar, but which set? That of Bresnan and Grimshaw (1978: 372) would invoke a later (but still, e.g., pre-GB stage) stage and again it is unclear what the precise set of axioms would be. The claim of Gazdar (1982: 174) would have to involve assumptions of the beginning stage of GPSG, that of Aissen and Perlmutter (1983: 366) the never-formalized assumptions of early RG, those of Baker (1988a: 119) an idiosyncratic variant of GB, those of Hukari and Levine (1991: 203) some variant of HPSG, those of Culicover and Jackendoff (1995) some unique mixture of Principles and Parameters work (e.g., probably as described in Culicover, 1997), and those of Jackendoff's (1983, 1990) quite different and specific views. The assumptions of Ladusaw (1996a: 212) would have to involve his own interpretation of a Montague semantics approach, those of Chomsky (2001: 24) some variant of the Minimalist Program, and finally those of Den Dikken (2001) some unspecified variant of the Principles and Parameters framework. No three of these could involve common assumptions and it is unclear even that any two of them do.

Given such states of affairs and the rapidity of conceptual turnover in linguistics, a reader can have no reliable method for determining for any fixed linguistic usage of <u>follows</u>, and so forth, how to interpret it against a background view like (4). That is, it is quite doubtful that there is an effective way to *actually find some unique, appropriate set of principles $C_1 \ldots C_m$*. Without that, assertions of the form (3) are always in danger of being unverifiable and hence significantly contentless on that ground alone.

Worse, many linguistic views that might be invoked as sources for $C_1 \ldots C_m$ are hardly clearly or precisely developed; they cannot be seriously compared to sets of precise formulas like Peano's axioms; some linguistic theoreticians have even downplayed the importance of precise formulations.[5] So, even if one knows, for example, that a logical consequence claim is to be interpreted against *some* set of background $C_1 \ldots C_m$ drawn from some view V it is unclear that one would be able to determine the specific *parts* of V that could justify actual talk of logical consequence *even under unioning as in* (4). Skepticism here seems requisite.

Moreover, assume one can determine the view V that underlies a claim P of the form (3) and can isolate a subset of V that can be taken as $C_1 \ldots C_m$ in (4). It will still in general be unclear whether P's advocate has ever constructed a demonstration of B from the union of $A_1 \ldots A_n$ and $C_1 \ldots C_m$, whose mere display could satisfy a skeptic. So ask yourself how many instances one finds in the linguistic literature of such demonstrations. One can be assured that in many cases at least, none has actually been constructed.[6] Rather, linguists have most often *at best* only intuited that one is possible. But even sincere intuitions of this form should not be relied on. Anyone who has ever faced the task of proving some proposition from a fixed set of axioms of a nontrivial character will recognize that it is anything but straightforward. Therefore, it should arguably be mandatory to demand a demonstration of any merely claimed consequence whose status can reasonably be doubted.

The conclusion then is that interpreting linguists' use of the expressions in (1) without the modifier <u>automatic(ally)</u> against a schema like (4) leaves great potential unclarity as to the nature of any truth claim. As in the case of any inference, a reader must minimally determine what precise propositions B and each of $A_1 \ldots A_n$ represent. But far beyond that, one would then in addition be obliged to somehow figure out what set of auxiliary assumptions $C_1 \ldots C_m$ is required and what precise proposition each of those represents. Only then is there any real hope of verifying the existence of an actual logical consequence. Possibly all this would be doable in certain cases, but the chances do not in general seem very high.

So a usage characterizable essentially as in a refined version of (4), while not inherently incapable of having a place in genuine inquiry, contains great latitude for *potential* abuse. Under the lure of achieving the sort of prestigious results associated with the rigor of formal fields like logic and mathematics, (some) linguists could end up using the range of logic-invoking terms like 'B follows from A' and synonyms illustrated in (1) in ways that not only fail to represent their strict logical usage but also fail to represent any *genuine* instantiation of even the enormously weaker schema (4). The latter requires that there exists some actual set of extant auxiliary assumptions $C_1 \ldots C_m$ whose union with $A_1 \ldots A_n$ yields a real logical entailment. But since the actual "location" of the auxiliary assumptions, their identity, and the rigor with which they are formulated are all left maximally vague, the way is open to literary sanctioning of declarations that "B follows from $A_1 \ldots A_n$" under circumstances broad enough to shade off into sheer wishful thinking.

There is good reason to think that the cited danger is real. It is one where <u>follow</u> and so forth, have a use, call it the *dream interpretation*, which involves no more content than that their author *hopes* to show some logical relation and *promises* that it can be done. Although such a use is obviously never made explicit, it is, for instance, reasonable to see the instances of <u>follow</u> in (6) as instantiating a dream interpretation:

(6) a. Chomsky (1980a: 9)
        "Assuming that the notion 'reciprocal' falls into its natural place within universal grammar, it will follow from (16) that *each other* must have an antecedent, in fact, a plural antecedent." (Here the author's [16] is: *Each other* is a reciprocal phrase: PMP.)
     b. Chomsky (1980a: 9)
        "If we assume the NP-trace relation to be simply a case of bound anaphora, then the general properties of movement rules also follow."
     c. Chomsky (1980a: 12)
        "Since Opacity governs trace, the familiar properties of movement rules also follow."
     d. Chomsky (1999: 9)
        "The computational burden is further reduced if the phonological component can 'forget' earlier stages of derivation. That follows from the Phase Impenetrability Condition (PIC)."

e. Chomsky (2000b: 120)

"The raised element typically c-commands its trace in the original position, but where true, that follows from independent properties of C_{HL}."

Although the overall contexts (6a–e) are suggestive of logical connection, it would be impossible to provide genuine demonstrations from the putative premisses themselves to the alleged conclusions.[7] One could then appeal to a schema like (4). The difference between, for example, taking some cited principle to be backed up by a precise axiom system like Peano's axioms and something very different then emerges clearly. One has no real idea of, for example, what in (6a) "the natural place" of a reciprocal in universal grammar is. And for (6b, c) it is not even specified what the "familiar properties" are, so the whole question of a logical demonstration that their presence follows from something cannot arise. For (6d) what is supposed to follow is a property denoted by a word in quotes, indicating that it is not a technical term and has not been defined. Moreover, it is obscure what that denotes. Is it "that the computational burden is reduced" or "that the phonological component can forget"? So again questions of genuine demonstration could hardly arise, even if one could tell what the appropriate auxiliary assumptions were. It would be simply utopian to assume that the author of such remarks has actually constructed (but nonetheless failed to make public!) a demonstration of the purported consequence from some fixed set of assumptions that includes the cited one. For (6e), something is claimed to follow from "independent properties," the latter unspecified. Once more, questions of demonstration can hardly be posed.

The correctness of recognizing a dream usage for <u>follow</u> and a range of its synonyms is supported by the occurrence of these forms where the lack of denotation of actual logical consequence along with "yearned for" connections is made contextually palpable, when, for instance, propositions that embody putative logical connections are under the scope of modals like <u>would</u>/<u>should</u>. And such usages are not difficult to find (all emphases mine: PMP):

(7)   a. Chomsky (2000b: 108)

"The Phase-Impenatrability Conditions yields a strong form of Subjacency. For A-movement, it *should* follow from the theories of Case/agreement and locality."

   b. Chomsky (2000b: 109)

"The remaining properties of (5) *should* follow from the theories of Case/agreement and locality, to which we will turn shortly."

   c. Chomsky (2000b: 115)

"Basic properties of chains *should* then follow from elementary derivational principles."

   d. Chomsky (2000b: 121)

"To the extent that such ideas can be given substance, it *would* follow that the dislocation property is required."

   e. Chomsky (2001: 5)

"However PIC is formulated exactly, it *should* have as a consequence that at the phase ZP containing phase HP:

(6) The domain of H is not accessible to operations, but only the edge of HP."

Usages like (7a, b, c, d, and e) are clearly consistent with a dream use of the logical terms. So, for example, (7d) makes it pretty clear that "such ideas" have yet to be given substance. Nonetheless, in the discourse type under discussion one putatively knows what *would* follow from such un–worked out ideas *before* this is done, knows that in the dreamed of (let's grant possible) world where they are worked out, certain things will follow from them.[8, 9] Similarly, in (7e) it is explicit that PIC has not been formulated, so that only in fantasy can questions of its consequences arise. Further evidence of the reality of a dream usage would appear superfluous.[10]

I have been exploring a rationalization of the use of the modifier automatic(ally) in linguistics as in (1) via appeal to a schema like (4). This is taken as a reconstruction of at least allowable usages of those forms without the modifier. It has been suggested that such a reconstruction is fraught with problems; so the usage "B follows from A" under an interpretation like even a refined version of (4) is open to such vagueness and obscurity that the actual truth conditions of the claim are difficult, if not impossible, to determine. A collapse into the self-indulgent form of discourse seen in (6) and (7) is in no way excluded. This utilizes words with the prestigious connotations of real logical connection to represent at best mere yearning for connections that have never been established. The result is a systematic shift to a dream-oriented discourse in which the mere wish for an established consequence suffices for public presentation and even submission for publication.[11, 12]

To sum up so far, I hope to have shown the following:

(8) a. Linguists use logic-invoking terms like follows in ways that do not represent their strict logical usage.

   b. It may be correct that many of these usages are (intended) to be interpreted against an elaborated schema like (4).

   c. Such a schema is quite weak and, without considerable specification in particular cases, it is impossible to make an actual assessment of what the wider set of assumptions $(C_1 \ldots C_m)$ are, still less whether they guarantee the truth of the claimed consequent, that is, yield an actual logical entailment.

   d. Given the enormous slack between the assertion "B follows from $A_1 \ldots A_n$," under the view (4), such a usage is open to a variety of abuses, one of which amounts to nothing more than the dream interpetation.

   e. The dream interpetation can be attested.

Conclusions (8a–e) do not argue that (4) is not a reconstruction of the actual way linguists use the logic-oriented expressions of (1) but only that this usage is one open to obscurities, problems, and abuse. But in our context, whose core goal is to try to understand the appearance of the modifier automatic(ally), the very intellectual inadequacy of the uses that (4) sanctions may offer a requisite *insight*. For it suggests a function for the modifier of interest.

Namely, perhaps due to cognizance at some level of the weakness (or even emptiness) of claims in linguistics like "B follows from $A_1 \ldots A_n$" *tout court*, the modifier usage unknown in logic has developed to permit signaling a claim of a stronger connection than the minimum sanctioned by something like (4), open even to the dream interpretation. It may be that having been exposed to many discourses where the logic-invoking terms of (1) are used in ways that leave obscure what, if any, logical connections exist and between what and even having been exposed to discourses like (6) and (7), linguists are at least subconsciously aware that simply writing something like "B follows from A" allows and possibly even favors a vastly weaker interpretation than they feel they want to communicate. Thus one can consider a partly vague, informal assumption, call it *the Seriousness Hypothesis*, that the modifier usage has arisen to permit specification of a degree of seriousness about claimed logical connections higher than the low level otherwise fairly current. That is, possibly the modifier automatic(ally) is used because of an implicit recognition that occurrences in linguistic writings of the logic-invoking terms not so modified often represent a level of seriousness appropriate only for junk linguistics.

The thesis that in general the forms modified by automatic(ally) in (1) are used with questionable seriousness has a number of potentially testable implications. A first expectation would involve the most obvious instantiations of *nonserious* use of the logic-invoking forms, represented by the dream usage, for example, in (7d). The Seriousness Hypothesis suggests that the more a context indicates that occurrence of follow and so on, have a dream usage, the more preposterous should addition of the modifier automatic(ally) seem. Adding it to, for example, (7c) yields

(9)   Basic properties of chains *should* then follow automatically from elementary deriva-
        tional principles.

This does perhaps sound even sillier than the original.

Second, if it is true that the usages in (1) flourish only against a background intuition of nonserious use of the unmodified terms, it should seem wrong to use the modifiers in contexts where claimed language abuse in linguistics is irrelevant. So, for instance, presence of the modifier in (10) should seem ridiculous, which to me it does:

(10)   a. If today is Sunday, then it follows (automatically) that tomorrow is Monday.
        b. Since he is in Paris and Paris is in France, it is a(n) (automatic) consequence that he
           is in France.

Third, if in specific other fields of inquiry F words that have genuine logical uses like follow are *not* used as weakly as (4) allows, one would expect that the discourse of F would not instantiate the use of automatic(ally) illustrated in (1). I have not made the (evidently inherently enormous commitment) required to even begin to evaluate this claim.[13]

Fourth, suppose that even in linguistics *certain* logic-invoking terms lack a nonserious use of the sort that follow has. The Seriousness Hypothesis leads to the expectation that such forms would *not* occur in linguistics with the modifiers of (1). I suspect that the entail, entailment paradigm exemplifies this situation. That is, whatever impulse one might have to interpret (11a) via a schema like (4) seems to me absent for (11b and c):

(11) a. B follows from A.
      b. A entails B.
      c. B is an entailment of A.

The latter two really do seem to assert the existence of a genuine relation of logical connection between B and A. If correct that a schema parallel to (4) is always irrelevant for <u>entail</u>, <u>entailment</u>, then it is no accident that dream proposal (6a) is expressed with <u>follow</u> and not with a sentence that contains a corresponding usage of <u>entail</u>, as in (12):

(12) "Assuming that the notion 'reciprocal' falls into its natural place within universal grammar, (16) will entail that *each other* must have an antecedent, in fact, a plural antecedent."

If <u>entail</u> and <u>entailment</u> lack the nonserious uses richly illustrated for <u>follows</u> and so forth, addition of the modifier of (1) with such forms would, according to the Seriousness Hypothesis, never be motivated. This would ground the apparent fact that one does not seem to encounter the usages in (13), which, moreover, strike me as simply ungrammatical:

(13) a. Assumptions $A_1 \ldots A_n$ automatically entail B.
      b. Assumptions $A_1 \ldots A_n$ are an automatic entailment of B.

A fifth type of support for the Seriousness Hypothesis is that it provides a reason that the <u>follows automatically</u> usage is impossible in a context that really *forces* a strict logical interpretation of <u>follow</u>. There are at least three distinct subcases. The first involves a context with the form of *an actual proof*:

(14) a. Axiom 1
      b. . . . .
      c. Axiom n
      d. Therefore, it follows (automatically) that Q.

Even for linguists, use of <u>automatic(ally)</u> in a context like (14d) should, it seems to me, appear preposterous; I thus guess that it cannot be attested. The Seriousness Hypothesis grounds this, since the very structure of (14) enforces a strict usage of the logic-invoking term, which renders any signal of greater than usual seriousness entirely redundant.

A second, related, instance where <u>automatic(ally)</u> seems equally out of the question in a context that forces a strict logical interpretation is one that actually *cites a rule of inference* that justifies a conclusion:

(15) It follows (automatically) *via Modus Ponens* that B.

Here also, the Seriousness Hypothesis finds no ground justifying the modifier.

For a third case, recall Freidin's usage remarked in note 12:

(16)   It follows (automatically) as a theorem (automatically) from $A_1 \ldots A_n$ that B.

Here the presence of <u>as a theorem</u> also seems to force a strict logical sense of <u>follow</u>, and again the modifier seems bizarre. The Seriousness Hypothesis justifies that situation, too, since the context makes interpretation of <u>follow</u> via schema (4) unavailable.

The last issue I can raise about the usage in (1) and its connection to the Seriousness Hypothesis involves negation:

(17)   a. B follows automatically from $A_1 \ldots A_n$.
        b. B follows from $A_1 \ldots A_n$.
        c. B does not follow automatically from $A_1 \ldots A_n$.
        d. B does not follow from $A_1 \ldots A_n$.

While nothing in general English rules of syntax or interpretation justifies that (17c) is (any more than [17d]) bizarre, I find the usage odd and I cannot cite any instantiations of (17c) in the literature. Regularly, one would expect that in (17c) the scope of negation is restricted to the adverbial. Why then is this negation peculiar? I think that the Seriousness Hypothesis offers some basis for this.

For implicit in the latter is the idea that the modifiers in (17) do not really modify a minimal meaning to give a more complex meaning. Rather, they simply signal that a word is being used in a strict sense when custom in the field allows very unstrict uses. Under that view, <u>follow</u> in (17a) is *truth functionally* simply the reciprocal of <u>entail</u>. So a commitment to (17a) simply asserts the strict sense of (17b). Therefore, to deny (17a) is just to deny (17b). And a short way to do that is to assert (17d). Moreover, the motivations that, according to the Seriousness Hypothesis, lead to expression of the strict sense of (17b) as (17a) do not likewise motivate expressing the strict sense of (17d) as (17c). For *lack* of a logical consequence relation between a proposition B and an arbitrary set of assumptions $A_1 \ldots A_n$ *is the default*. One is thus in general motivated to *deny* such a connection only in the face of an *assertion* of its existence. Therefore, one is motivated to assert the negation of (17a) at best only when someone has asserted (17a). But to reject a claim of the form (17a), it suffices to use (17d). Invocation of the 'seriousness marker' <u>automatic(ally)</u> is unmotivated because merely by using it any defender of (17a) has already *renounced* appeal to an interpretation of <u>follow</u> via a weak schema like (4). Thus nothing motivates one who denies (17a) to *also* renounce it.

The Seriousness Hypothesis is the best account I have been able to develop of the a priori puzzling linguistic usage schematized in (1). I certainly have not meant to suggest that this vague, primitive, and unformalized proposal is a serious lexical analysis, and I invite others to pursue the development of the latter.

Recognition that "B follows from $A_1 \ldots A_n$" even in contexts that seem to involve logical connection does not in linguistics commit an author to a genuine logical connection raises the question of whether appending <u>automatic(ally)</u> does so. To deny this is to allow that e.g. even 'B follows *automatically* from $A_1 \ldots A_n$' involves no commitment to established logical consequence. That would seem to open the door to the nihilistic conclusion that nothing linguists say can so commit them. Such a conclusion strikes me as going beyond skepticism to genuine cynicism. However, the following section indicates that linguists utilize other terms in ways which explicitly undermine commitment to real logical consequence. So even mere skeptics might well keep in mind the saying that "no matter how cynical one is, one can't keep up."

2. If it's just about true, it can't be false, can it?

Another usage that has a special connection to forms with logical import in ordinary discourse and seems to have achieved some currency in linguistics is schematized in (18):

(18)   X *virtually* holds.

Examples include:

(19)   a. Chomsky (1981: 136)
           "Base rules are virtually eliminated."
       b. Chomsky (1982b: 89)
           "[A]nd the components of transformations in the sense of earlier work can be vir-
           tually abandoned."
       c. Chomsky (1982b: 34)
           "An important property of these three types of EC is that they (virtually) partition
           the distribution of NP."
       d. Chomsky (2000c: 120)
           "There is reason to believe that the computational system is invariant, virtually."
       e. Chomsky (2000c: 122)
           "Each language, then, is (virtually) determined by a choice of values for lexical
           parameters;"

A survey of logic works again provides no grounding for the adverb. In this case, though, I believe the use of the adverbial form is less mysterious than that of <u>auto-matically</u>. It always functions substantively; its suppression to yield (20) clearly changes things truth functionally.[14]

(20)   X holds.

For anyone who writes an instance of (18) must admit (21):

(21)   X does not hold.

This is clear since <u>virtually</u> in contexts like (18) is, like the <u>in part</u> discussed in note 9, a kind of weakening hedge but one probably even vaguer than <u>in part</u>. No one would claim (18) *if* they were in the position to demonstrate or argue for (20) itself.[15]

This is evident for (19a, b), where, if the author had thought it was really support-able that base rules in the first case or transformational components in the second could in his terms just flatly be abandoned, he would not have felt the need for hedg-ing. Even more clearly, for the case of (19c), the author himself appended a footnote (his 29) that makes explicit that the claim without the hedge is false.

Given then that (18) expresses (21), why would linguists write (18)? The only answer I see is that it is a relatively safe way of at least implying more good things about one's proposals than is justified. This is why it is hard to imagine anyone *ever* writing (18) as part of a criticism of someone *else's* analysis whose *rejection* one is defending. If one is criticizing analysis A, which supposedly explains B, and one can really show that A simply doesn't entail B, one would surely simply assert something like (21). One only uses things of the form (18), I believe, to talk about conclusions one *likes* and *supports*. For in saying (18) one gives the, of course illusory, impression of some sort of result. The implication is that the logical connection holds except in some insignificant way; one at least implicitly grants in the background (to cover oneself) that it is not literally true but vouschafes that in some inchoate sense (one need never specify) this does not matter to serious folk like contemporary linguists. In short, such usages terminologically facilitate the claim of a significant result in the absence of one.

Among the infinite set of natural numbers, some are even and some odd. Just so, some are primes and some are not. Notably, the intersection of the even natural numbers and the prime natural numbers contains only one member, 2. Linguists who are prepared to look with indulgence on the use in linguistics of <u>virtually</u> as in (18) might then consider (22):

(22) a. All primes are odd.
      b. The distribution of the properties even and odd among the primes virtually follows from (22a).

What was said before determines that (22b) requires:

(23) The distribution of the properties even and odd among the primes does *not* follow from (22a).

And (23) is, as already indicated, true. But if one considers some sort of measure of degree of falsehood in terms of cases, then (22a) (and consequently [22b]) is not bad. After all, there are $\aleph_0$ cases that support (22a) and only one that falsifies it. It is doubt-ful that any linguistic usage of <u>virtually</u> could even aspire to such grounding. And yet clearly (22a) is an absurdity.[16] The imposed conclusion then is that talk like (18) in linguistics is a thinly veiled attempt to imply a result or stronger results than could be justified by any available argument or evidence.

The two usages discussed so far, <u>follows automatically</u> and <u>virtually</u>, are inde-pendent and in principle could be combined, and at least once they have been:[17]

(24) Hukari and Levine (1991: 119–120)
      "Apart from a remarkable structural parallel between these and subject-extraction con-texts, there is considerable evidence that AP and A[1] must ccontain the agreement fea-

ture AGR, thus making it locally accessible to the UDC feature associated with the gap, from which connectivity follows virtually automatically."

Happily, previous research aids us in translating any claim of the form (25a) into truth functionally more transparent assertions:

(25)   a. It follows virtually automatically that X.
        b. It follows automatically that X.

For it has been established that (25a), which hedges (25b), can only be true if (26) holds:

(26)   It does not follow automatically that X.

And the prior discussion of such uses of <u>automatically</u> in linguistics indicates that the odd (26) is simply a way of asserting and in any event entails

(27)   It does not follow that X.

Normally, in inquiry if one has not established any connection between states of affairs, one can save time, energy, ink, and so forth, by simply not claiming one has. As touched on in the previous section, that is the default. Why then is it at least modestly acceptable in current linguistics to formulate the nonresult (27) as the better-sounding but obscuring (25a)? Why do referees and editors allow such verbiage to be distributed with the imprimatur of a scientific journal? It may not be fun to inquire into such matters, especially for those who doubt that our field contains a good dose of what should rightfully be called junk linguistics.

3. My accounts are natural; don't you wish yours were!

It would be only *natural* in a skeptical essay concerned like this one with usages in linguistics to focus on the concept <u>natural</u>, for example, in contexts like the following (all highlighting mine: PMP):

(28)   a. Chomsky (1975b: 94–95)
           "I have elaborated a version of this position elsewhere, and shown how some fairly complex examples can be handled from this point of view in what seems a rather *natural* way."
        b. Chomsky (1975b: 241, note 27)
           "There is, in fact, a rather *natural* analysis of rules into several categories in terms of their position in the system of linguistic rules and the conditions that apply to them."
        c. Chomsky (1988: 83)
           "Given the quite *natural* representation in (22), we can . . ."

    d. Chomsky (1988: 89–90)

       "[A]nd it is a fact of some interest that a *natural* logical structure is directly repre-
sented in the mental representations that underlie the actual expressions of language."

    e. Chomsky (1999: 12)

       "A *natural* principle, which has been suggested in various forms, is (14)." (The
author's [14] is: "Maximize matching effects.")

    f. Chomsky (1999: 31)

       "These conclusions too follow *naturally* if overt V-to-T raising, T-to-C raising, and
N-to-D raising are phonological properties . . ."

    g. Chomsky (2000b: 113)

       "Relations that enter into C_{HL} either (i) are imposed by legibility conditions or (ii)
fall out in some *natural* way from the computational process."

While a detailed investigation of this usage is currently beyond my powers,
(29a–d) seem correct.

(29)   The term
     a. is undefined and unanalyzed,
     b. adds nothing of substance,
     c. is subjective, and
     d. is used by writer W as a totally safe (since contentless) way of being positive about
       a proposal, almost always one of W's.

It is of course of some note, given earlier remarks, that the empty <u>naturally</u> appears in (28f) as a modifier of <u>follow</u>. Again the combination is unknown in logic
for reasons parallel to those mentioned about <u>automatic(ally)</u>. One must suspect that
the modified usage involves the dream interpretation of <u>follow</u>.

Observe that in (28g) things are said to fall out in *some* (unspecified) natural
way, indicating that, in the author's view, there are more than one. Are there better
and worse *natural* ways in which things fall out? Again one is clearly very remote
from the realm of discussion of actual logical consequences, which either hold or
fail to and which need no contentless compliments like <u>natural</u>.

With respect to (29d), the intended claim is that one can be confident that a pur-
veyor of this use of <u>natural</u> would never say anything like (30a, b):

(30)   a. So and so's proposal must be rejected because it is natural and gets the facts wrong.
     b. This analysis of the sentences at issue is misguided and quite natural.

It is probably accurate then to say that the use of <u>natural</u> in the contexts in question
approximates in objective content and in subjective positive attitude the youthful <u>cool</u>;
see presumably interchangeable fine-sounding pairs like (31a) and interchangeable
but bad-sounding ones like (31b):

(31)   a. The analysis I have here provided of these facts is natural/cool.
     b. So and so's analysis is completely wrongheaded, lacking in scientific value, and
       quite natural/cool.

Statement (31a) evidently totally lacks truth functional content, and in (31b) neither version of the third conjunct adds any substance.

Consider, too, how (equally) absurd it would be to argue *against* claims like (32a) in the form (32b):

(32)   a. Linguist W: It follows in a natural/cool way from $A_1 \ldots A_n$ that B.
       b. Linguist X: While B may follow from $A_1 \ldots A_n$, it is simply not true that it follows in a natural/cool way.

That is, no one but a drunk in a bar is going to quarrel with a claim of naturalness and argue *tout court* that some proposal is *not* natural.

The characteristic <u>natural</u> of linguistics is then a purely rhetorical device to give a positive-sounding though content-free (but, happily, thereby universally available) boost to any proposal a writer wishes. Those who doubt the existence of junk linguistics might ask why those who waste time, energy, ink, and space with this empty verbiage (think they) need to.

4. Virtually self-evident natural conclusions that follow automatically (surely) from something

I have in the previous sections focused on three usages rather prevalent in linguistic writings of the sort falling under the topic of these essays. Evidently, I have only touched the surface of a serious analysis of these forms. I invite others with greater analytic powers, more patience, and more insight to do more.

That said, I hope to have said enough to indicate that each of these usages has unfortunate features incompatible with serious writings concerned with a search for the truth about NL. The trouble with the <u>automatic(ally)</u> usage is that it can, as far as I see, be rationalized as other than a total waste of words only against a background of more or less debased usages of <u>follows</u> and other terms from logic. If one could by magic exclude the excessively obscure uses of logic-invoking <u>follows</u>, and so forth, allowed by a schema like (4), uses open even to the dream interpretation, what purpose could <u>automatic(ally)</u> serve? Put differently, the evidently widely felt need for this usage should be taken as a warning sign, like that provided by expired canaries in the coal mines of an earlier era, that something toxic is present. In this case, the toxic material is called junk linguistics.

The <u>virtually</u> usage might seem less ominous. It is a wider culture hedge and might seem to be used in linguistics in partially standard ways. The problem, though, is that it is arguably leaking into contexts where *it simply is not appropriate to hedge*. At certain points, one just has to face the fact that if one has not established that conclusion C holds, there is not only no postive value but also on the contrary considerable negative value in penning the weaker "C virtually holds." First, there is a real possibility of fooling readers into thinking more has been established than has been. Second, and possibly even worse, there is a possibility of fooling oneself into not pursuing the search for actual results, those that need no hedging.

322   STUDIES OF JUNK LINGUISTICS

As for <u>natural(ally)</u>, it, too, has a bit of the aspect of the warning canaries. The impulse to use this term is an admission that an author wishes to say more positive things about a proposal than there is any substantive basis for saying. Such a wish alone is unworthy but being largely subjective must be dealt with by individuals for themselves. But one who actually indulges the wish by penning <u>natural(ally)</u> carries discourse toward the realm of junk linguistics, whose essential nature is, after all, to advance pretensions to the discovery of some truth(s) about NL in the absence of any such discovery. To the extent that a real linguistics provides actual discoveries, they will impose themselves by their truth and will induce no felt need to gild them with empty compliments.

Overall then, caution about the discourse of linguists is advisable; one must subject instances of logic-invoking terms like <u>follow</u> to strict analysis, one must question why one should care about claims about positively regarded conclusions that are only *virtually* true (that is, are false), and one should strongly suspect that the degree to which work is infected with the virus of junk linguistics is in part measured by the number of times one is told some proposal is cool or natural.

13

Junk Reasoning 2

'(Virtually) Conceptually Necessary'

1. A bit of sarcasm

A good move internal to junk linguistics if you want to advance a proposal P about some NL or NL in general but have no genuine evidence or factual argument for P is to say that it is (*virtually*) *conceptually necessary* for P to hold. First of all, this is pretty deep-sounding, the more so since nobody can be sure what 'conceptually necessary' means and it makes it seem like you really have a good reason to assume P. Second, once you have said P is necessary, even modifying it with the modifier 'conceptually', the likelihood is high of bluffing many readers since a lot of people are going to be reluctant to argue with P. After all, who wants to put themselves in the position of arguing against something *that is necessary*?[1] Hedging with 'virtually' is also a fine idea because it covers you in case someone suggests that the relevant NL or all of NL is such that P doesn't hold. Most likely, no one is going to care that, given the meaning of <u>virtually</u> (see chapter 12), a claim that P is 'virtually conceptually necessary' admits that it is *not* conceptually necessary. But if some negative and malevolent person, not lacking in our profession, does attack you, an excellent defense is thereby always available: You can simply observe that since you yourself said it was only *virtually* necessary, of course a small-minded, petty individual could waste people's time by focusing on the trivial aspect in which it isn't.

To address any feeling that the preceding paragraph is *unfair* sarcasm, in what follows, I analyze three actual claims of 'conceptual necessity'. The discussion will show, I hope, that, while admittedly sarcastic, the initial remarks are anything but unfair. Talk of 'conceptual necessity' can be seen as a terminology whose junk lin-

323

guistic function is to facilitate question begging and the acceptance of arguably base-
less claims, those for which no argument has ever been provided, and, in specific
cases, claims for which no viable argument could be provided (since they are false).

2. An operation called 'Copy'

Chomsky (1995b: 168–169) asserts:

(1) "Another standard assumption is that a language consists of two components: a lexicon
     and a computational system. The lexicon specifies the items that enter into the compu-
     tational system, with their idiosyncratic properties. The computational system uses these
     elements to generate derivations and SDs. The derivation of a particular linguistic ex-
     pression, then, involves a choice of items from the lexicon and a computation that con-
     structs the pair of interface representations. So far we are within the domain of virtual
     conceptual necessity, at least if the general outlook is adopted."

These ideas are evidently quite basic to much of the work in what is called the
minimalist program. No argument is offered for them, and the conceptual necessity
terminology suggests that none is necessary.

But this is erroneous, since inter alia as it stands (1) is question-begging about
the nature of proper grammars for NLs. Built into the remarks are never-justified
assumptions that such grammars must be generative/constructive/proof-theoretic
devices. As was discussed in chapter 6, this assumption is quite gratuitous and an
extant, never answered challenge to it has existed for at least twenty years. In Johnson
and Postal (1980) and Langendoen and Postal (1984) an informal sketch of a nongenerative, model-theoretic approach to grammars was provided. Moreover, chapter 6 argued in a new way that no NL can have a proof-theoretic grammar. The issue
here is not which view is right. It is only that discourse like (1) builds into its very
foundations a refusal to *face the alternative*, exactly the sort of refusal expected of
junk linguistics.[2]

A key aspect of (1) is the idea that grammars bifurcate into two components,
one a lexicon. Implicit is a view of the lexicon as in effect analogous to a computer
file, which is somehow accessed to provide the (lexical) basis for a construction of
sentences. Aoun, Choueiri, and Hornstein (2001) attempt to flesh out this picture
involving the lexicon in a particular way so as to putatively bring out more clearly
the sense in which sentence construction relates to the lexicon, as follows:

(2) Aoun, Choueiri, and Hornstein (2001: 400)
     "We believe that Copy is similarly conceptually necessary, in the sense of following
     from a very uncontroversial design feature of Universal Grammar. It rests on the fact
     that there is a (virtually unanimously held) distinction between the lexicon and the com-
     putational system and that words are accessed from the lexicon. How does Copy follow
     from this fact? It is universally assumed that the atoms manipulated by the computa-
     tional system come from the lexicon. How does the computational system access the
     lexicon? It does so by *copying* elements from the lexicon to the computational system.

That accessing the lexicon involves copying is clear from the fact that the lexicon gets no smaller when it is accessed and words are obtained for manipulation by the syntax. If this is correct, then grammars that distinguish the lexicon from the computational system conceptually presuppose an operation like Copy. As virtually every approach to grammar assumes something like a distinction between lexicon and grammar, Copy is a 'virtually conceptually necessary' operation for much the same reason that Merge is."

Evident is that this account depends totally on the basic question begged in (1) of whether grammars are constructive devices that build sentences in the way a computer program creates some output. Only the idea that they are, argued to be not only not necessary but not even tenable in chapter 6, underlies the claim that there needs to be an *operation* that accesses the lexicon and copies its entries as part of a sentence-building procedure. The authors just cited are concerned with the question "how does the computational system access the lexicon?" But this query obviously depends on an assumption that there is such a system and that it accesses things, claims that are denied by any view that takes an NL grammar to consist of model-theoretically interpreted statements, not operations. So an inevitable aspect of any remarks about 'conceptual necessity' is that they presuppose the existence of the feature claimed to be necessary. Therefore, even if one assumed it made sense to talk about 'conceptual necessity' for aspects of NL, which I do not, one should minimally never take seriously claims that such and such feature is a conceptually necessary feature of NL in the absence of strong evidence that it is, first of all, a feature. Use of the substantively empty 'conceptually necessary' to talk about a supposed copy operation then merely fills space that should be taken up with argument that there is such an operation. In what follows, it is shown that any claim that the existence of lexical items and phrasal combinations of them requires the existence of an operation is entirely false.

3. An operation called 'Merge'

Another key claim of the minimalist program is that there is an operation called Merge:

(3) Chomsky (1995b: 226)
     "The simplest such operation takes a pair of syntactic objects (SO_i, SO_j) and replaces them by a new combined syntactic object SO_{ij}. Call this operation *Merge*. We will return to its properties, merely noting here that the operations Select and Merge, or some close counterparts, are necessary components of any theory of natural language."

(4) Chomsky (1995b: 378)
     "Something like Merge is inescapable in any languagelike system . . ."

(5) Chomsky (2000b: 101)
     "First, what operations enter into this component of C_{HL}? One is indispensable in some form for any language-like system: the operation *Merge*, which takes two syntactic objects (α, β) and forms $K(\alpha, \beta)$ from them."

Again, though, nothing motivates talk of any operation-combining syntactic objects other than the question begging that grammars should be generative/proof-theoretic. The claim at the end of (3) and in (4) and (5), hedged only by talk of 'close counterparts', that the existence of such is a *necessary* feature of any theory of NL is not grounded in any way. So talk of necessity again fills space that should have been taken up by arguments for proof-theoretic grammars and/or arguments against model-theoretic ones, the latter nowhere to be found. The junk linguistic character of the preceding is brought out most sharply by the lack of reference anywhere in such writings even to the existence of alternatives to generative grammars. And this failure is of course well motivated. To make the model-theoretic alternative explicit would be to highlight the need for an argument that favored generative grammars and the need for responses to extant arguments against proof-theoretic limitations. Since there is no sign that such arguments could be constructed, talk about 'necessity' usefully (from a junk linguistic point of view) obfuscates that actually highly controversial and in fact unsupportable assumptions are simply being advanced as items of dogma, with no intellectual foundation or justification.

Just as Aoun, Choueiri, and Hornstein (2001) attempt to elaborate the putative conceptual necessity of Copy, they proceed in the same way with Merge, stating as in (6):[3]

(6)   Aoun, Choueiri, and Hornstein (2001: 399)
       "Chomsky (1993) has argued that Merge is a virtually conceptually necessary opera-
       tion. In what sense is this so? Its conceptual necessity rests on its link to a very obvious
       feature of natural languages: sentences are composed of words that are arranged in larger
       phrasal structures. Given this fact, there must be some operation for composing words
       into phrases, and this operation is Merge. What makes Merge 'virtually conceptually
       necessary' is that every theory needs an operation like it in order to accommodate this
       obvious fact about natural language."

For convenience of reference, I break up their passage into individual sentences and clauses placed in numbered angled brackets:

(7)   <1> Chomsky (1993) has argued that Merge is a virtually conceptually necessary
            operation.
       <2> In what sense is this so?
       <3> Its conceptual necessity rests on its link to a very obvious feature of natural languages:
       <4> sentences are composed of words that are arranged in larger phrasal structures.
       <5> Given this fact, there must be some operation for composing words into phrases,
            and this operation is Merge.
       <6> What makes Merge 'virtually conceptually necessary' is that every theory needs an
            operation like it in order to accommodate this obvious fact about natural language.

The authors' footnote 31 refers to (7) as involving *reasoning*. If one accepts this, one can examine that reasoning by attempting to construe (7) as an actual formal argument. Certain conclusions are immediate. Subparts <1>, <2>, and <3> could be of no relevance to the reasoning. The premiss is <4>. Sentence <5> claims that there follows from <4> at least the existence of some operation that composes words into phrases = Merge, and possibly some necessity (via the 'must'). Statement <6> repeats that such an operation exists and concludes that it is conceptually necessary (hedged with 'virtually') and that every theory needs it. So the structure of the putative argument is (8):

(8) a. Premiss   = Sentences are composed of words arranged in larger phrasal structures.
     b. Intermediate Conclusion   = There is some operation, Merge, that composes words into phrases.
     c. Ultimate Conclusion   = That operation, Merge, is virtually conceptually necessary.

As it stands, though, this putative reasoning consists only of non sequiturs. No known logic permits any deduction of b. from the premiss, of c. from b., or of c. from the premiss. As it stands, no valid logical connection at all is established between the premiss and the final conclusion c. or the intermediate conclusion b.

What would have to be done to convert (8) into an actual argument? Needed are further premises that relate (8a) to the existence of operations. One of these would need to be an analog of an axiom of infinity of set theory (see, e.g., Partee, ter Meulen, and Wall, 1993, 216; and Stoll, 1979: 298). Because if there are only finitely many compositions of words in the collection, they could be listed just like the atoms of the lexicon, and no operations to form them could conceivably be required. So necessary for conversion of (8) into an argument is an additional premiss something like (9):

(9) The collection of phrasal combinations of words contains infinitely many members.

But that still doesn't permit an entailment of (8b) by known logic. One would evidently need a more articulated premiss like (10):

(10) The existence of an infinite collection of (phrasal) combinations of a finite number of objects (words) entails the existence of an *operation* of object (word/phrase) combination.

With an axiom like (10) one could develop a version of the original argument in which (8b) actually followed logically. But just to advance (10) as an axiom *without supporting argument* is no more and no less than to make explicit a specification of the question begging of whether NL grammars are proof-theoretic or model-theoretic. Moreover, no serious argument for (10) could ever be advanced, since it is just false. For it is of course standard in formal studies to specify the membership of infinite collections of complex objects (set-theoretically "built" of simpler ones) without operations via the specification of an axiom system together with a model-theoretic interpretation of the statements the axioms represent.[4]

It is important enough to illustrate the possibility of non-proof-theoretic characterizations of (infinite) collections that I will instantiate it for the case at hand, by taking a trivial though infinite linguistic model and showing how one can characterize precisely all and only the allowed combinations with no analog whatever of a Merge operation. The model, already specified in chapter 6, consists of the full infinite collection whose *initial* elements are listed in (11):

(11)   a. My father died.
       b. My father's father died.
       c. My father's father's father died.
       d. My father's father's father's father died.
       e. My father's father's father's father's father died.

As chapter 6 noted, this infinite collection can be schematized via the Kleene star notation as (12):

(12)   {My + (father+'s)* + father + die+ ed}

But for simplicity, I will regard <u>father's</u> and <u>died</u> as unanalyzed lexical atoms. So the total lexicon for the collection at issue in something like the terms of the authors being criticized is the four-word set in (13):

(13)   {my, father, father's, died}

   I will also assume that the notion 'arranged in larger phrasal structures' of the quoted material simply means that the linguistic objects are *linguistic trees* in the standard sense defined by various well-known explicit axiom systems such as that in Partee, ter Meulen, and Wall (1993: 441–442). The task then is to define an infinite collection that includes at least one such tree for each element of the collection schematized by (12) and no structure for anything else.[5] For concreteness, I assume that the relevant constituent structures are defined by the following constituency assumptions: Full sentences involve trees whose root nodes are labeled S and consist exclusively of NP + Verb. Subjects of clauses are defined by nodes labeled NP. Intuitive possessor phrases of the form <u>my</u> are defined by nodes labeled Pos^A, intuitive possessor phrases of the form <u>father's</u> are defined by nodes labeled Pos^B, and there is a larger possessive constituent defined by nodes labeled Pos^C.

   The following ten axioms then suffice to characterize the relevant collection:

(14)   The sentence collection schematized in (12) consists of all and only the members of
       the collection {X}, such that
       a. $x \varepsilon$ {X} if and only if X is a linguistic tree in the sense of Partee, ter Meulen, and
          Wall (1993: 441–442), whose nodes are a subset of $\{n_a, \ldots n_q\}$, whose nonterminal
          labels are a subset of $\{S, NP, V, Pos^A, Pos^B, Pos^C\}$ and whose terminal labels are
          those of (13); and
       b. a node n_j is labeled S if and only if it is a root node; and
       c. a node n_j is a root if and only if there are two nonterminal nodes n_k and n_l such that
          n_j immediately dominates n_k and n_l, and n_k is labeled NP and n_l is labeled V; and:
       d. a node n_j is labeled V if and only if there is a terminal node n_k that (i) is immediately dominated by n_j and (ii) is labeled <u>died</u> and;
       e. a node n_j is labeled NP if and only if there are nodes n_k and n_l such that n_j immediately dominates n_k and n_l, and n_k is labeled Pos^C and n_l is labeled N; and
       f. a node n_j is labeled N if and only if there is a terminal node n_k that (i) is immediately dominated by n_j and (ii) is labeled <u>father</u> and

g. a node n_j is labeled Pos^C if and only if there are nodes n_k and n_l such that n_j immediately dominates only nodes n_k and n_l and n_k is labeled Pos^A and either $n_k = n_l$ or n_l is labeled Pos^B; and

h. a node n_j is labeled Pos^A if and only if there is a terminal node n_k that (i) is immediately dominated by n_j and (ii) is labeled <u>my</u>, and;

i. a node n_j is labeled Pos^B if and only if either (i) there are nodes n_k and n_l such that n_j immediately dominates only nodes n_k and n_l and either $n_k = n_l$ and there is a terminal node n_m immediately dominated by n_k and labeled <u>father's</u> or (ii) $n_k \neq n_l$ and both n_k and n_l are labeled Pos^B; and

j. If n_k and n_l are sister nonterminal nodes, then n_k linearly precedes n_l if n_k is labeled NP or n_k is labeled Pos^A or n_k is labeled Pos^C.

The nonobvious aspect of these axioms is that the form <u>my</u> is the only representative of the Pos^A constituent and has no other analysis, that <u>father's</u> is the only *lexical* instantiation of Pos^B and that the recursion that renders the collection (denumerably) infinite is due to the fact that a node labeled Pos^B can immediately dominate two other nodes labeled Pos^B (permitting unbounded left branching, right branching, or center embeddings for Pos^B nodes; for the notions 'left branching,' and such, see Chomsky, 1965: 12–13). I claim that the set of strings schematized in (12) is exactly the union of the yields of the set of trees that satisfy the logical conjunction of the tree-defining axioms and the axioms of (14).

This overall axiom set is satisfied by, for example, clauses containing NPs like those in (15) but not satisfied by those that contain NPs like those in (16):

(15) Good Structures, that is, Models of (14, figs. 13.1a–c)

a.

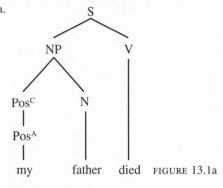

my   father   died   FIGURE 13.1a

b.

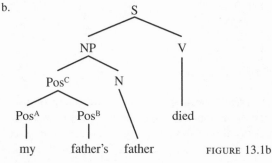

my   father's father   FIGURE 13.1b

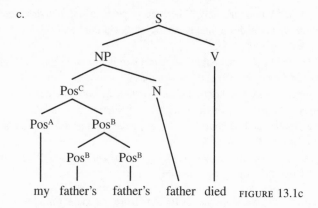

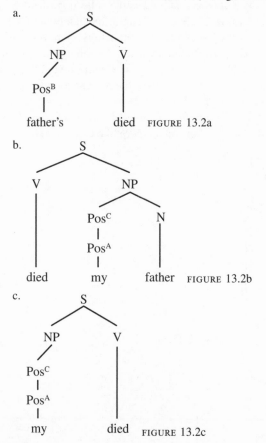

c.

FIGURE 13.1c

(16)   Bad Structures, that is, non-Models of (14, figs. 13.2a–c)

a.

FIGURE 13.2a

b.

FIGURE 13.2b

c.

FIGURE 13.2c

Clearly then, one can perfectly well specify the membership of a collection, more specifically, a collection of standard linguistic trees, with no appeal to *any* operation, hence no appeal to Merge, and equally with no appeal to a lexical access operation like Copy. Claims that such operations are (virtually) conceptually necessary/inevitable/inescapable, and so forth, are mere propaganda that cannot cover up the fact that such operations have never been argued to serve any proper function in a linguistic theory. To show that they did, one would at the least need an argument that proof-theoretic grammars that embody operations (like Copy, Merge, Move, etc.) are superior to model-theoretically interpreted grammars that consist of *statements* (like, e.g., those of [14]). As far as I know, though, the literature is entirely free of any such argument. Moreover, chapter 6 argued at length, as did Langendoen and Postal (1984) before it, for the claim that a variety of well-attested properties make it impossible to actually formulate adequate proof-theoretic grammars of NLs.

If one had solid, fact-based arguments for a position P, one would, I suggest, never be motivated to talk about P's conceptual necessity. One must then suspect (the reader should check it out) that whenever such an idiom is used, one is in the realm of junk linguistics, an activity in which one seeks to promulgate or defend P *despite* the fact that one has no argument or evidence for it.

4. A property called 'displacement'

There is much talk in recent minimalist writings about a putative property called *displacement*, which seems to be no more than a renaming (for unknown reasons) of what was formerly called movement. This is more often cited than explained, but one does find the following:

(17)   Hornstein (2001: 4)
       "[s]entences show displacement properties in the sense that expressions pronounced in one position are interpreted in another."

This highly informal account is only modestly informative. The notion of being 'interpreted in a position' is hardly clear. For instance, what is a position? Is it a feature of the superficial form of sentences, of some abstract 'logical structure', or what? So, in what positions exactly are the *phonetically empty* elements, recognized en masse in the views that talk about displacement, interpreted? Moreover, consider for example the DP subject in (18b), which seems to yield the same overall clausal interpretation as that in (18a):

(18)   a. Each of the gorilla leaders was taller than any woman.
       b. The gorilla leaders were each taller than any woman.

The phrase the gorilla leaders in (18b) is, I guess, pronounced in subject position. Is it interpreted there, hence in a different position than the same words with the same meaning in (18a)? Further, in what position is a phrase with the meaning of the subject of (18a) interpreted in (18b), if it is?

Setting aside such issues, the notion, whatever it means, seems too narrow. So the highlighted WH-phrases in (19a, b) seem to have equal claim to being interpreted in, for example, an object position of the verb buy:

(19)   a. It is a car *which* you won't regret agreeing to buy.
      b. It is a car *which* years from now you won't have to ask yourself why you agreed to buy it.

And yet, given the resumptive pronoun in (19b), historically only the WH phrase in (19a) has been taken to involve movement/displacement.

Consider, too, paired topicalization and left dislocation cases like (20) and (21):

(20)   a. Marsha wants that/*that you pet her gerbil.
      b. That/*[That you pet her gerbil]$_1$, Marsha wants t$_1$ very badly.
      c. That/*[That you pet her gerbil]$_1$, Marsha wants it$_1$ very badly.

(21)   a. Marsha sought it/to outrun the grizzly/*outrunning the grizzly.
      b. Marsha considered it/outrunning the grizzly.
      c. *[Outrunning the grizzly]$_1$, Marsha should never have sought t$_1$/it$_1$.
      d. [Outrunning the grizzly]$_1$, Marsha should never have considered t$_1$/it.

The key fact is that in these cases left dislocatees, which link to resumptive pronouns, obey the same strict categorization constraints as do topics and the same as would the same phrases in the position of the gap/resumptive pronoun. This means that if topics are taken to instantiate displacement but left dislocatees are not, "generalizations are lost." This argument would be very strong if it were true, as seems to be widely accepted, that strict subcategorizations of the type in question are required to be local in a very limited sense.

The problem is perhaps worse in

(22)   That two and two is seven, that, I am quite sure of.

Here, the clausal topic would seem to have a call to be interpreted as the object of the preposition, a position where it could never be pronounced. But if anything has been displaced from that position in the terms at issue it would have to be *that*. Examples at least grossly parallel to (22) are common in Germanic languages, such as Swedish; see, for example, Andersson (1982: 35).

All this is just to indicate that the current terminological incarnation of the earlier notion of a transformationally moved phrase is not at all clear in its extension. Despite this, one reads:

(23)   Chomsky (2001: 8)
      "[A]nd Merge yields the property of 'displacement,' which is ubiquitous in language and must be captured in some manner in any theory."

(24)   Chomsky (2001: 8–9, note 29)
      "Recourse to any device to account for the displacement phenomena also is mistaken, unless it is independently motivated (as is internal Merge). If this is correct, then the radically simplified form of transformational grammar that has become familiar ('Move

α' and its variants) is a kind of conceptual necessity, given the undeniable existence of the displacement phenomena."

(25)   Hornstein (2001: 6)
"It is self-evident that natural languages manifest 'displacement' in the sense that expressions in a sentence are heard in one position yet interpreted from another."

In such declarations, one is told, problematically, that there is some NL property, displacement; but implicit and more than problematic is the additional assumption that this property represents transformational movement, an idea made explicit in (24). Once more, talk of conceptual necessity is supposed to make it seem beyond question that such *movement* is an undeniable feature of NL. But the transition from recognition of the sort of facts putatively taken in some frameworks to motivate talk of transformations to a claim that thereby one *must* recognize transformational mechanisms is a non sequitur.

The very unclarity of the notion displacement already touched on in itself renders suspect a claim that any hypothesis about how it can be described (that is, movement) has any kind of necessity. And suspicion should expand by orders of magnitude when it is recognized that there are, of course, a variety of nontranformational ways of describing each of the phenomena characterized in minimalist terms as displacement. To justify any claim of necessity, it would be requisite to show minimally that movement accounts are superior to available alternatives, for example, those of HPSG, LFG, categorial grammar, and so forth. But attempts to do this seem to be nonexistent.

In their place, one finds only substantively empty, self-serving comments like the following:

(26)   Chomsky and Lasnik (1995: 25)
"The transformational rules still exist . . . Such devices appear to be unavoidable in one or another form, whether taken to be operations forming derivations or relations established on representations."

Similarly:

(27)   Chomsky (2000a: 24) (as clarified by his personally checked editors' remarks [2000a: 37])
"Every theory of language has some way of capturing the displacement property; so they all have transformations or some counterpart."

And also:

(28)   Epstein and Seely (2002: 10)
"This represents a significant shift from defining binding-theoretic domains on trees to seeking an explanation of them in terms of independently motivated, and seemingly ineliminable, apparatus (movement theory)."

That is, without argument, transformations are claimed to be unavoidable although the phenomena they are claimed to describe have for more than twenty years been described in a variety of distinct frameworks *that avoid them*, which include GPSG, HPSG, LFG, APG (see Johnson and Postal, 1980), categorial grammar (see, e.g., Jacobson, 1992a; and Steedman, 1996) and others. Again then claims of (conceptual) necessity, inevitability, and ineliminability are found as the only justification for the arbitrary and factually unsupported decision to adopt some view, here that to invoke a framework that utilizes grammatical transformations, rather than extant alternatives. A serious basis for such a choice in the late twentieth and early twenty-first centuries would have required substantive arguments for the superiority of transformational descriptions over those available in, inter alia, the other frameworks mentioned.[6] But in junk linguistics it suffices to invoke an invented conceptual necessity or inevitability. One must surely suspect that the reason for this invocation is that those who advance such with respect to transformational mechanisms are at some level aware of their inability to argue for their adoption on genuine substantive grounds.[7]

5. Conceptual necessity based on 'nonexistent' objects

There is a further aspect about the claims that have been considered to the effect that Copy, Merge, and Move are conceptually necessary, hedged or not. The attempted justifications for this hinge, as we have seen, on appeal to lexical items and their composition into larger phrases, up to sentence-level phrases. Recall, though, that chapter11 considered in detail the claim of Chomsky (1999: 34) that "[t]hese are not entities with some ontological status; they are introduced to simplify talk about properties of FL and L, and can be eliminated in favor of internalist notions." Here the 'these' clearly denoted sentences.

But the *combination* of these views is incoherent independently of the incoherence of the ontological view on its own. For although Chomsky (1995b) and the works by Hornstein and others attempt to justify Copy and Merge, that is, parts in their terms of the FL (faculty of language) and L (the internal grammar), via appeal to the properties of words and phrases built out of them, Chomsky (1999) has declared that such words and phrases, parts of sentences or expressions in his terms, *are not real things* and can be eliminated in terms of the internalist notions. I derided this view in chapter 11. But in our context here, the view is even more laughable since, combined with the conceptual necessity claims, it yields a totally vicious circle. The union of the "not entities with some ontological status" view with the conceptual necessity claim means that the putatively conceptually necessary features of FL/L can only be justified as such by appeal to things *claimed not to exist*. So, in such terms, for example, Merge is putatively conceptually necessary to form phrasal combinations of words, ultimately whole sentences, which Chomsky (1999) has declared not to be real things. The appropriate analogy is to a claim on page 3 of a housing development proposal that incorporation of a special supersensitive security system is (virtually) conceptually necessary in all new houses to ward off *ghosts* following a statement on page 2 that ghosts are not real.

At the beginning of this chapter, I suggested that what followed would show that while the first paragraph was sarcastic, it was not *unfairly* so. I think I have met that burden. And in the process I hope to have shown the versions of junk linguistics at issue in the proper light. For what could be a better (partial) characterization of the sort of playacting at linguistics that junk linguistics represents than a documentation that it seeks to show some aspect of something is (virtually) conceptually necessary by appealing to properties of things it has claimed have no independent existence!

The perhaps jarring term 'playacting' just used deserves a bit of exegesis. First, it entered the linguistic literature no later than when Chomsky (1958: 39) wrote apropos of some contentless claims by B. F. Skinner: "To speak of 'conditioning' or 'bringing previously available behavior under control of a new stimulus' in such a case is just a kind of play-acting at science." Second, if, as I believe, that terminology was appropriate in the case of Skinner's empty claims, how could it not be appropriate apropos of an equally empty and deceptive claim that talk of a feature of a putative mechanism is conceptually necessary to characterize properties of objects claimed to be a mere *façon de parler* of that mechanism? Third, and most significant, how is it that the same individual who at the beginning stages of the generative grammar movement he initiated recognized the presence of playacting in others now, more than four decades later, produces discourse of comparable quality? Reflection on such a question is critical, I would say, if one is to gain some appreciation of the scope and role of junk-linguistic activity in contemporary linguistics.

6. Conclusion

I have argued in this chapter that invocations of (virtual) conceptual necessity take their place as part of a longstanding and fundamental program of question begging about the nature of grammars. One should confront this claim with declarations such as (29):

(29)   Chomsky (2001: 3)
       "The minimalist program is the attempt to explore these questions. Its task is to examine every device (principle, idea, . . .) that is employed in characterizing languages to determine to what extent it can be eliminated in favor of a principled account in terms of general conditions of computational efficiency and the interface condition that the organ must satisfy for it to function at all."

Setting aside issues about whether characterizing NLs has anything to do with organs (see chapter11 and references therein), one must recognize that the apparently laudable program of examining "every device, (principle, idea, . . .) that is employed in characterizing languages," a program that, so limited, *anyone* could support, has so far never led to any examination whatever of whether or not the whole idea of generative/constructive/proof-theoretic (as opposed to model-theoretic) machinery is appropriate (still less, required) for NL grammars. Until this is done, and I would not advise losing any sleep waiting, all the apparent open-minded examination of notions employed in characterizing NLs is actually conceptually internal to questions that have now been begged in the tradition represented by (29) for going on fifty years.

Use of termnology like '(virtually) conceptually necessary' and 'inevitable' by authors to characterize the properties of their own ideas can be viewed as an attempt to provide certain views with a sort of priveleged status, with the goal of placing them at least rhetorically beyond the demands of serious argument or evidence. One would not be surprised then to find that the utilizers of such expressions invoke other sorts of priveleged status claims as well. Observe then:

(30)   Chomsky (2001: 1)

> "A stronger thesis is that the biolinguistic approach has a kind of privileged status, in that every constructive approach to human language and its use presupposes it, or something similar, at least tacitly. That too seems to me tenable, but I will not pursue the issue here."

Here work W informs its readers that the foundational position that underlies W has a *privileged* status. One is not told what that means, but clearly an author only says such a thing with a persuasive goal. The implication is that *opposing* positions, of course not cited, if any, need some sort of extra or special justification. The only putative reason given for this status is a mere claim, exactly as unsupported as the claim of privilege, that every 'constructive' approach to NL presupposes the author's position, or something similar, at least tacitly.

Cutting through the forest of associated hedges ('constructive', 'something similar', 'tacitly'), one sees only the same unsupported and false assertions analyzed in chapter 11 that everyone accepts (must accept?) the foundational assumptions of the author. In short, it is more of the same sort of junk linguistic attempt to establish fake security for the indefensible. The underlying theme is that "I do not have to argue for my position, but you have to argue for yours, because mine is privileged." Significant about such a transparently illegitimate rhetorical move is that it again manifests the attempt to avoid justifying an in fact enormously controversial and ill-founded position by pretending that it has a status that does not require any justification.

Anyone can of course claim that their position is privileged in some way.[8] But one can be sure that unless such a claim is buttressed with detailed and viable argument, one is deep into the realm of junk linguistics that involves question begging, pretense, and propaganda. Real linguistics would have no need for such really desperate attempts to keep attention away from alternatives because its results would impose themselves by their truth and the evidence for them and it would not need to fear comparison with alternatives. But the practitioner of junk linguistics is ever insecure, aware at some level of facing not only the risk of being wrong, the everyday possibility for every genuine researcher, but also the more serious danger of having the unsupported pretense on which junk linguistic work is based revealed for what it is. Real research *should* involve some fear of error and falsehood. But for junk linguistic activity, the principal threat will inevitably be from the truth.

Junk Linguistics

The Bottom Line

I assume the previous seven chapters have given good grounds for the belief that junk linguistics is not only existent but also widespread and well entrenched. This raises the inevitable question of how to deal with it.

My suggestions are these: It seems proper and reasonable to consider junk linguistics as a kind of pollution of the scholarly environment. Viewed from that vantage point, if one wants less of it, then one should proceed as in (1)–(5):

(1) No matter what one's place in the linguistic world, with respect to junk linguistics:
   a. Don't produce it.
   b. Don't pretend it doesn't exist.
   c. Don't justify it.
   d. Don't excuse it.
   e. Don't praise it by only faintly damning it.
   f. Do tell others not to produce it, pretend it doesn't exist, justify it, or excuse it.
   g. Do try to deepen one's understanding of the difference between junk linguistics and real linguistics.
   h. To the extent one can, try to expose it for what it is.

(2) If one is a referee or reader, then:
   a. Don't accept it.
   b. Don't cover it up.

(3) If one is an editor or publisher's representative, then:
   a. Don't publish it.

(4) If one is an authority in a linguistics department, then:
   a. Try to strengthen whatever in the curriculum and organization of the department hinders it.
   b. Try to consider what, if anything, in the curriculum and organization of the department could favor it.

(5) If one is a student,
   a. Beware.
   b. Be skeptical.[1]

NOTES

Introduction

1. One can make the claim in the text without in any way accepting the view that linguistic theory is a theory of NL learning. The latter view inter alia confuses NL and knowledge of NL; see Katz (1981, 1984, 1996, 1998), Katz and Postal (1991), Langendoen and Postal (1984), and chapter 11 for relevant discussion.

Moreover, even a linguistics oriented toward the study of NL learning need hardly accept claims like those in (1). See Culicover (1999) for a contrasting position based on a highly detailed analysis of a wide array of facts.

One might add that it is, moreover, hard to understand why, if GB was such a great success, its inventor has jettisoned so much of its content in his transition to the 'minimalist' framework. See, e.g., Hornstein (2001: chapter 1) for some specification and Lappin, Levine, and Johnson (2000a, 2000b, 20001) and Seuren (2000) for relevant comment.

2. The current negative evaluation of claims for the achievements of the GB/Principles and Parameters framework is hardly unique. Quite a detailed basis for such a judgment is found, for instance, in Ackerman and Webelhut (1998: 123–127), who remark inter alia:

(i) (1998: 126)
   "To conclude this section: a systematic comparison of the hypothetical insights of the principles and parameters framework with its actual achievements shows a wide gulf between the two."

And:

(ii) (1998: 127)
   "In sum, we believe that much of the literature systematically overestimates the value of the principles and parameters framework in several ways:

"(22)   (i) by pointing to individual successes it has achieved but failing to mention that this success does not generalize to one single inherently consistent theory of grammar of the kind that has been successfully implemented in HPSG or LFG;

"(ii) by failing to recognize that many proposals within the principles and parameters framework, despite being articulated in some respects, are ultimately schematic and unlikely to carry over into extended analyses that meet the higher descriptive standards of competing theories like HPSG or LFG;

"(iii) by failing to mention that the principles and parameters theory lacks a generally accepted and empirically adequate theory of lexical representations that can deal with lexical idiosyncrasies, idiomaticity, etc."

3. The dismissal of the importance of accurate descriptions seen here is not new and has advanced so far in the past as to yield a claim that one should *hope* one's descriptions are wrong; see Chomsky (1982b: 76), Koster (1978: 566), Riemsdijk and Williams (1986: 320), and chapter 9. Noteworthy is, e.g., Chomsky (1981: 281), which claims: "As theoretical work advances and proposals become more significant, we expect—in fact, hope—that serious empirical and conceptual problems will arise. That is what makes progress possible." Such material seems designed to make life hard for a caricaturist. The latter is perhaps reduced to imagining a journal devoted to junk linguistics (titled, of course, the *Journal of Non-Junk Linguistics*) whose call for papers, in order to maximize progress, specifically limits descriptive analysis submissions to those that their authors *hope* are incorrect.

4. A clear instance of the junk linguistic procedure of attributing a view to someone without any textual basis or justification is seen, I believe, in Smith (1999). In the course of an attempted defense of the ontological position about linguistics of Noam Chomsky (see chapter 11), Smith (1999: 148) claims: "Katz is aware of the I-language/E-language distinction, but he still argues that since the grammar of any individual (uncontroversially) characterizes an infinite set of sentential constructs, *it must itself be infinite* [my emphasis: PMP]." The highlighted assertion is accompanied by neither any reference to a page nor that to a specific work. The same claim is then in effect repeated a few lines later when Smith asserts: "Katz's critique appears to rest on the mistaken assumption that because a finitely represented device, the I-language, has an infinite range, it must itself be infinite."

Having worked with the target of criticism (the renowned philosopher of language Jerrold J. Katz) and being familiar with his work, I was certain both that no such explicit claim ever appeared in his writings and that nothing that did appear in them entailed such an absurd consequence. This suggested that the position that Smith attributed to Katz was an invention, taken as a target in lieu of the latter's real position. So, before constructing this note, I sought in E-mail of November 9, 2002, to elicit from Professor Smith references or materials that support his claim. His reply of November 11, 2002, offered nothing more than the statement that what he wrote was his understanding of Katz's putatively difficult-to-understand position.

5. Although the term was not used in any of these works, I believe it accurate to characterize much of the material in the two series of articles in (i) and (ii) as in effect previous revelations of, and attacks on, junk linguistics:

(i)   Postal (1981, 1982, 1983, 1984)
(ii)   Postal and Pullum (1978, 1979, 1982, 1986)

And an analogous remark could be justified for Postal and Pullum (1988).

The term 'junk linguistics' is used here essentially to refer to the linguistic subvariety of the term 'spurious science' of the following:

(iii)   Seuren (2000: 1):
"This book is a sustained argument purporting to show that Chomsky's linguistic theory, especially in the form recently presented as the minimalist programme (MP) (Chomsky 1995a, 1998) is a prime example of spurious science. It fails to satisfy the basic criteria for sound scientific work, such as respect of data, unambiguous formulations, falsifiability, and also, on a different level, simple good manners."

6. The issue arises as to what extent *self*-deception plays a role for at least some of those involved in junk linguistics. I will have nothing to say about this question here. But I do not doubt its relevance in many cases.

7. In other fields, part of the professional curriculum involves courses in professional ethics. Presumably, a course in professional ethics for linguists would consider the dangers of junk linguistics and provide help in avoiding its production and uncovering it where it does exist. But in more than forty years in linguistics, not only have I never heard of the existence of a professional ethics course in linguistics but I also have never heard anyone even mention the possibility.

8. I tried this not too long ago with respect to the assertion of Smith (2000: vii) in his foreword to Chomsky (2000) that the volume's author defends a certain claim "with a series of imaginative analyses." Since I could find *no analyses at all* in the volume, I naturally did not see how there could be imaginative ones. I asked Smith in two E-mails (of July 2000) on what pages of the cited work anything characterizable as an analysis (in the sense of something acceptable in a refereed journal in linguistics) could be found. The most precise "information" I could extract, though, (E-mail of July 12, 2000) was "passim," a transparent falsehood. This incident illustrates, I believe, that, unaccustomed to demands to justify junk claims, purveyors of them do poorly when faced with such. All the more reason to relentlessly challenge them.

9. The 'one language' claim is also found in Chomsky (1999: 7), who says: "The Martian scientist might reasonably conclude that there is a single human language, with differences only at the margins." A similar claim occurs in Pinker (1994: 232), who says: "According to Chomsky, a visiting Martian scientist would surely conclude that aside from their mutually unintelligible vocabularies, Earthlings speak a single language." Note the "surely." One sees that the 'one language' claim is not an *isolated*, onetime aberration.

The reference to "mutually unintelligible vocabularies" in the last quote comes closest to representing a testable claim. It might be interpreted to suggest that for any pair of distinct-seeming NLs Q_1 and Q_2, any well-formed sentence $S_a(Q_1)$ in Q_1 maps with only trivial adjustments to a well-formed sentence $S_b(Q_2)$ in Q_2, where $S_b(Q_2)$ differs from $S_a(Q_1)$ by the replacement of the relevant vocabulary items in $S_a(Q_1)$ by the corresponding Q_2 vocabulary items. But one need not look beyond NLs as closely related culturally and historically as French and English to see that any such claim is entirely untenable, even when one picks sentences of the two NLs where perfect equivalences exist for the nongrammatical vocabulary items.

For instance, all of the following a. examples are fine French sentences based on only a tiny vocabulary, each of whose ten or so items has an equivalent in the corresponding English b. examples. But none of the latter are grammatical:

(i)   a. Ca mange beaucoup de viande, un requin.   b. *That eats much/lots (of) meat, a shark.

(ii) a. Un requin, ça mange beaucoup de viande.   b. *A shark, that eats much/lots (of) meat.

(iii) a. Un oiseau, ça (ne) mange pas de viande.   b. *A bird, that (?) eats not (of) meat.
(iv)   a. Les requins, ça (ne) se mange pas.   b. *(The sharks), that does not eat (i.e.
                                                         'one does not eat them')

10. So Milsark (2001) reviews Smith (1999) quite favorably and nowhere mentions the 'one language' claim.

11. The idea that the generative linguistics under discussion is lacking in real results may seem strange, shocking, even irresponsible, given the vast literature and public promotion that has over time been devoted to praising it and stressing its supposed accomplishments. But one need not take my word for it. Comments of the inventor of this approach himself are consistent with the claim. For a telling exemplification, in the course of a relatively recent interview by Adriana Belletti and Luigi Rizzi, two researchers who are, notably, entirely *sympathetic* to his approach, the inventor was twice asked to list the results (Chomsky, 2002: 151):

> AB & LR: Taking for granted the obvious fact that nothing is definitively acquired in empirical science, what are those aspects that you would consider "established results" in our field?
> NC: My own view is that almost everything is subject to question, especially if you look at it from a minimalist perspective.

After that, the interviewee rambled on for more than eight hundred words, without ever committing himself to a single established result.

Apparently unsatisfied, the interviewers then in effect tried again somewhat indirectly (Chomsky, 2002: 153–155):

> AB & LR: Sometimes speaking with specialists of other disciplines, people ask: what are the results of modern linguistics? Is there a way of phrasing some of the results independently from the technical language that makes them opaque for the public at large?

Again the interviewee responds at length, here for more than three hundred words, but once more without invoking a single actual result.

12. See Lappin, Levine, and Johnson (2000a, 2000b, 20001) for extensive discussion of this point, as well as responses to a number of critics who strongly disagreed. Levine (2002) also provides a good deal of insight into the quality of minimalist claims.

13. It would be hard to see as insignificant the fact that the author of these strange claims is, as of 2002, a member of the associate editorial board of the same journal.

1. A Paradox in English Syntax

1. Irrelevantly to our concerns here, one might strengthen this claim to 'always'. This depends on the status of inter alia apparent PP subjects like that highlighted in (i), discussed later, and WH infinitives, such as that highlighted in (ii):

(i)   *Inside the closet* is a fine place to hide the snake.
(ii) Was *when to use a microscope* ever discussed?

2. Various principles in different frameworks have been proposed that would arguably require an S3 in a wide range of clauses, subject perhaps to specific structural factors and/or parametric variation. These include the relational grammar *Final 1 Law* (see Perlmutter and Postal, 1983b: 100–101), the lexical-functional grammar Subject Condition (see Dalrymple, 2001: 18–19), and the government-binding *Extended Projection Principle* (see Chomsky, 1981: 25–27).

3. Hoekstra and Mulder (1990: 31) seem to view the construction at issue as defined by locative PP preposing in particular. For instance, they specifically cite such PPs in saying: "[O]ur hypothesis predicts that unergative verbs of the type sleep, eat, etc. can also be ergativized in this way. English preposing constructions provide direct evidence for the correctness of our hypothesis, as we find constructions with these verbs with postverbal subjects, but only if there is a locative PP in sentence initial position." They then cite:

(i)   In this bed has slept an important member of the royal family.
(ii) In this restaurant used to eat the famous encyclopedists.

But these very verbs permit NEX clauses with *nonlocative* PPs:

(iii) Only with the help of drugs could finally succeed in sleeping soundly a number of the most gravely ill patients.
(iv) For that reason were sleeping late most of the members of the mime troupe.
(v)   In that artificial style/manner appear to have ostentatiously eaten many of the visiting foreigners.

4. Bresnan (1976: 486) cited, e.g., (i), claiming that the highlighted phrase was a subject, one that then falsified the claim of Postal (1974: 91) that subjects cannot be the targets of Complex DP Shift:

(i)   Over my windowsill climbed *an entire army of ants*.

She cited two arguments for the subject status: (i) the DP in question determines verb agreement, and (ii) the DP satisfies a definition of 'subject' in Postal (1974). The latter, having been long abandoned, can be ignored. The former point was also cited in Bresnan (1977: 186), who said: "I assume that the PP in (65) is not a subject, on the ground that subjects can induce number agreement of the verb."

The factual reason was then the verb agreement. But as observed in Postal (1977), a reply to Bresnan (1976), the same agreement determination typical of subjects is seen with the postverbal DPs of there insertion sentences like (ii), clear non-S3s:

(ii) Over my windowsill there were/*was climbing thousands of huge ants.

Bresnan's claim did not control for this fact and thus gave no real grounds for choosing a view that the DP in (i) is a subject, in effect view (4b) of this work, as against the view, in effect (4c) of this work, that it has the status of the postverbal DP in (ii). I return to this point.

5. Notably, though, Bresnan (1977: 179, 180, 186) cited cleft extraction cases like (i):

(i)   = Bresnan's (41a)
      It's in these villages that are found the best examples of this cuisine

6. Contrary to Pesetsky's remark and the implications of the quote from Bresnan (1994), Postal (1977) *nowhere* claimed that the X-PPs underwent subject raising.

7. One might add that a non-top-level subject can also coordinate with a top-level subject, yielding alongside (10d) the following:

(i)   She's someone that—likes cooking and I expect—will hate jogging.

8. And the following matches (12a):

(i)   That's the old graveyard in which __ will be buried the president and they say __ is buried a treasure.

9. Although the Adverb Effect was introduced into grammatical discussion with great emphasis in the 1990s in the work of Culicover, arguably this phenomenon was discovered

by Bresnan (1977: 194, note 6). I am indebted to Ivan Sag for this information. Bresnan noted then that her constraint (17), proposed to account for the Anticomplementizer Constraint, allows all of the following, which she then characterized as only awkward:

(i)   Who did she say that tomorrow—would regret his words?
(ii) an amendment which they say that next year—will be law
(iii) Which doctor did you tell me that during an operation—had had a heart attack?

But until Culicover's work of the last few years, much discussion of the Anticomplementizer Constraint seems to have ignored the Adverb Effect.

   10. Davies and Dubinsky (2001: 252–253) criticize Bresnan's proposal and suggest an alternative of the form (i):

(i)   [_{DP} [_D Ø] [_{PP} under the bed]]] is a good place to hide

They argue that Bresnan's proposal, with a zeroed noun, is dubious because of (ii):

(ii) ??the location (of) under the bed is a good place to hide.

But replacement of the definite by an indefinite article yields a perfect result, so this argument cannot show much. In any event, the difference between Bresnan's proposal and that of Davies and Dubinsky has no relevance to our concerns here. Both are agreed that the superficial subject PPs in fact are parts of subject DPs, a view adopted here.

   11. A distinct and not directly relevant question is whether P-subjects can link to SFQs. I would claim no for my dialect; so the following are simply terrible:

(i)   *Into the cafeteria have both just rushed the students I was telling you about.
(ii) *From this pulpit have both preached Cotton Mather's closest and most trusted associates.

But Culicover and Levine (2001: 301) cite essentially these examples as well formed.

   12. Cases previously discussed such as (i) also preclude NFQs:

(i)   Under the table and/or under the chair are good places (*each) to hide the heroin.

There is no great mystery here, as NFQs are in general bad with predicate nominals, regardless of the subject they link to:

(ii) The table and the chair were good places (*each) to hide the heroin (*each).

   13. Actually, it is of great significance that, while valid for cases like those cited in the text, this claim is not true across-the-board. So some restriction is needed to allow the (for me) perfectly grammatical extraction case correspondents in (ib and d) of the impossible reflexive forms in (ia and c):

(i)   a. *Herself was described to Sylvia by Martin.
      b. Herself, they proved had never been described to Sylvia by Martin.
      c. *Themselves had been praised by the prizewinners.
      d. It was themselves who had been praised by the prizewinners.

The point of the argument in the text is maintained by restricting attention to cases where, independently, extraction does *not*, as in (ib and d), repair reflexivization violations.

   14. Green (1985: 125–126) considered the relation between expletive there sentences and NEX sentences and concluded that the correlation was not perfect and that there were many gaps. Examples included (i):

(i)   a. Into the game now is the fullback Jenkins.
      b. *Into the game now there is the fullback Jenkins.

But such real paradigmatic gaps in no way determine the inadequacy of a linkage between NEX cases and expletive <u>there</u>. The issue is what hypothesis gives the best overall account of all the data.

15. As indicated in Postal (1998: 111), I believe the right constraint on these verbs is that they are incompatible with clausal extraposition structures. This is something of the opposite of the constraint on verbs like <u>feel</u> and <u>hold</u>, which require their underlying complement clause to occur in that structure.

16. It might seem that (59) explains, and thereby gains further support from, the fact cited in Tellier (1988: 135) (taken from Stowell, 1981), that A-Parentheticals cannot be formed that correspond to subject <u>that</u> clauses, which are unextraposable because of the presence of object complements:

(i)   a. That John owns the gun shows that he is guilty.
      b. *It shows that he is guilty that John owns the gun.
      c. That Jenny is famous convinced Jim to visit her.
      d. *It convinced Jim to visit her that Jenny is famous.
      e. *John owns the gun, as shows that he is guilty.
      f. *Jenny is famous, as convinced Jim to visit her.

However, this argument does not stand up for two reasons. First, while (id) is for me impossible, (ib) is merely awkward. Second, these verbs permit extraposed structures like (ii), which still lack corresponding A-Parentheticals:

(ii) a. It must show something that he owns a gun.
      b. *He owns a gun, as it must show something.

Appeal to (59) is thus not strong enough to block all the bad A-Parentheticals with these verbs. It might be, as suggested in Tellier (1988), that something like appeal to the principle that an A-Parenthetical cannot be based on a logical subject <u>that</u> clause is relevant. If so, the cases in (i) do not support (59, as they would be independently precluded. My own view is that what is involved is the notion Quace of section 9. That is, clauses that are logical subjects, whether extraposed or not, are assigned 1-Quace, which precludes <u>as</u> formation. Very likely this is linked to the fact that 1-Quace on a complement makes it an island, since in general islands are incompatible with <u>as</u> formation.

17. This conclusion falsifies the claim of Bresnan (1994: 103) to the effect that in English, unlike other Germanic NLs such as Dutch, Faroese, German, and Icelandic, null expletive subjects are lacking in inter alia extraposition cases. The evidence cited shows that, while this is generally true, null expletive subjects are found in restricted classes of embedded extraposition cases.

18. The third claim is not incompatible with the assertion of Coopmans (1989: 733), who cites (i) as well formed:

(i)   Out of which barn ran which horse?

Nonetheless, I find (i) impossible.

19. For reasons I do not understand, facts like these seem much clearer when the P-subject is plural.

20. Note, though, that both types of clausal structures are grammatical when combined with passives of transitives that take predicate nominals:

(i)   a. They turned Maurice into a doctor.
      b. In that way (there) were turned into doctors several previously unsuccessful immigrants.

(ii)   a. The community elected Sarah and Jane councilwomen.
       b. At that time (there) were elected councilwomen several previously unsuccessful candidates.

21. This observation should probably be theoretically linked to the long-known fact that the French extraposition of indefinite construction is also incompatible with adjectival clauses; see Kayne (1975: 332) and Ruwet (1972: 21).

22. Full generality of the claim in the text is hostage to the analysis of cases like (i):

(i)   Levin and Hovav (1995: 248)
      and on it are engraved three pyramids.

Such cases form part of a grammatical pattern also illustrated in the following:

(ii)   On the blackboard (there) were written several threats.
(iii) In his notebook (there) were pasted several nude photos.
(iv)   On his passport (there) were stamped several secret identifications.
(v)   Into the rock (there) was carved the image of a deity.

If the short versions of (i)–(v) are NEX versions of adjectival passives, as suggested in Landau (forthcoming: 105), then the generalization in the text is not right. But this would not really bear on current concerns, since, to my ear, the longer versions of these examples with explicit there are also grammatical. It is notable, though, that in contexts that force an adjectival analysis, such as those where the negative prefix un is present and/or where the putative adjective is embedded below the main verbs go or remain, analogs of (i)–(v) seem totally bad:

(vi)   a. *On her passport (there) remained unstamped any identification marks.
       b. *In our notebooks (there) went unpasted any nude photos.

23. WH infinitives and WH finite clauses can be P-subjects, as in (i) and (ii):

(i)   a. At that time should certainly be asked how to find the remaining witnesses.
      b. In that way can no doubt be determined when to add the other ingredients.
(ii) a. Through the use of these new research tools will probably be discovered what happened to the missing villages.
      b. In our lab can now easily be calculated how long it will take for the planet Jupiter to shrink to the size of a walnut.

24. Other exceptional forms include idiom chunks, as in (i) and (ii):

(i)   a. They prevented tabs from being kept on her movements.
      b. *Tabs were prevented from being kept on her movements.
(ii) a. Only that prevented all hell from breaking loose.
      b. *All hell was prevented from breaking loose.

25. For discussion of middles, see Ackema and Schoolemmer (1995), Fagan (1988), Fellbaum and Zribi-Hertz (1989), Hale and Keyser (1986), Keyser and Roeper (1984), Roberts (1987), Stroik (1992, 1995, 1997, 1999), and Zribi-Hertz (1993).

26. Bresnan's claim that the shifted phrases (my P-subjects) in NEX clauses must be *thematic* objects is, on several grounds, clearly untenable under any substantive interpretation of 'thematic'. First, it fails for exactly the reasons that Levin and Rappaport (1986: 634–635) argue that a parallel claim about the phrases that can be subjects of adjectival passives is untenable. Specifically, both of the postverbal phrase types of cases like (i) can form the subjects of adjectival passives and be P-subjects:

(i)   a. They provided such corn chips to the students.
      b. They provided the students with such corn chips.
(ii) a. Such corn chips remain unprovided to the students.
      b. Those students remain unprovided with such corn chips.
(iii) a. At that time were provided to the students several varieties of corn chips.
      b. At that time were provided with corn chips several groups of students.

But clearly if <u>such corn chips</u> in (ia) is thematic, <u>the students</u> in (ib) cannot be.

Second, a major claim of Bresnan's more recent work on NEX structures is that they are impossible with transitive clauses, those that contain a direct object; see Bresnan (1994: 77–78). This claim is in accord with a broad range of previous work (see Langendoen, 1979; and Postal, 1977) and there is ample apparent evidence in favor of this position, as attempts to form NEX structures with standard direct objects present invariably fail:

(iv) a. *In that office have written valuable papers several philosophers.
      b. *At that time will file important charges a large number of state attorneys.

But in spite of the agreement and the rich body of evidence that apparently supports the claim that NEX clauses are incompatible with direct objects, no such constraint really holds. Although there is a constraint that blocks most transitive cases, this is not a direct ban on direct objects.
    In support of this consider (v):

(v)   a. In the second bathroom was grooming *Bob/himself a short foreign-looking old man.
      b. At that nightclub were amusing themselves/*Glen and Louise a trio of bankers on vacation.

For me, a good number of reflexive direct objects do not preclude NEX structures. For at least some speakers, this may also be true of *reciprocal* direct objects:

(vi) a. Near the Xerox machine were consoling each other two of the victims of the hurricane.
      b. Inside the blimp seem to have been hassling each other two very macho parachutists.

Clearly, in any cases like the good versions of (v) and (vi) the P-subject is not a theme in Bresnan's terms.
    Third, clearly, in cases like (vii) the P-subject is in Bresnan's terms an agent:

(vii) a. At that time were proven to have committed perjury several congresswomen.
      b. During that hearing were found to be lying all of the witnesses with guilty expressions.

    27. There are other constructions, e.g., middles, that seem to show a similar antimetaphoric sensitivity:

(i)   Such armies/groups/well-trained troops don't massacre/obliterate/crush easily.
(ii) a. The Yankees really massacre/obliterate/crush such teams.
      b. Such teams don't massacre/obliterate/crush easily.

I find that (iib) lacks the sports reading of "defeat in a contest" possible in (iia) and has only the same literal, physical violence reading of (i).
    28. In work that appeared long after the bulk of this chapter was completed, Culicover and Levine (2001) observe a similarity between NEX clauses and those with extracted S3s, which they take to support a subject view of X-PPs. This involves weak crossover effects (WCO). They note (p. 289) contrasts like (i):

(i)   a. *Into every dog's₁ cage its₁ owner peered.
      b. Into every dog's₁ cage peered its₁ owner.

That is, in the non-NEX case (ia) there is WCO, but in the NEX clause (ib) there is not. Culicover and Levine (2001) take this to support a subject analysis of the X-PP in (ia), as in Bresnan's (1994) analysis, because of the parallelism with the lack of WCO in clear cases of extracted S3s like (iia), compared to WCO effects in extracted non-S3s:

(ii) a. Who₁ appears to his₁ mother to be a genius?
      b. ?*Who₁ is his₁ mother grilling obsessively?

However, this argument does not work against the proposal of this essay, since the lack of WCO in (ib) is also found in cases with audible expletive *there*; so (iii) is just like (ib), not like (ia):

(iii) Into every dog's₁ cage there peered its₁ outraged owner.

See also:

(iv) a. *To some nurse₁ her₁ own father's care was/seems to have been entrusted.
      b. To some nurse₁ there was/seems to have been entrusted her₁ own father's care.
      c. To some nurse₁ was/seems to have been entrusted her₁ own father's care.

29. Of course, (161b) is irrelevantly well formed on a reading that involves object extraction and subject verb inversion of <u>Marie</u>.

30. As in previous works on Metagraph Grammar, beginning with Johnson and Postal (1980), this account appeals to a class of primitive nodes as well as a class of primitive arcs; such a development is also standard in graph theory, the branch of mathematics that in effect underlies the structures at issue; see, e.g., Gould (1988). However, I believe it is possible to construct a form of this framework with only primitive arcs, one in which nodes would be defined in terms of the set of primitive relations between arcs.

31. The reason for this choice is that I vaguely suspect that quirky 1-Quace, 2-Quace, and 3-Quace all have distinct instantiations in diverse English constructions and choice of a contrasting Quace is thereby suggested to keep distinct constraints distinct. Elaboration of this point is not relevant here.

32. In the framework of Johnson and Postal (1980), expletive constituents were defined as those that corresponded to heads of a certain type of arc (type defined in terms of its sponsor relations) called a *ghost arc*. Expletive arcs in general were simply all the remote successors of ghost arcs.

33. To embed examples like (179) in Bresnan's (1994) view that the Anticomplementizer Constraint is defined over extracted S3s demands, evidently, taking predicational phrases like <u>lying on the table</u> to be S3s. Besides the intuitively odd character of such a claim, it would require some special stipulations to allow, for instance, for the choice of tag:

(i)   Lying on the table were two sick gerbils weren't there/*it/*them.

But this would be expected if, as for NEX cases, it is claimed that such examples involve invisible expletive <u>there</u> S3s.

34. This statement could be made more compact by appeal to the notion *Erasable* (*A*, *B*) 'A is erasable by B' of Postal (1990a), but I will not bother here.

35. An issue being glossed over here involves the existence of extractions that link to resumptive pronouns in the extraction site. In Metagraph terms, such a case, say one that involves extraction of a subject, would, I suggest, have the substructure in (i, figure 1.11), assuming all Quace arcs are suppressed:

(i)

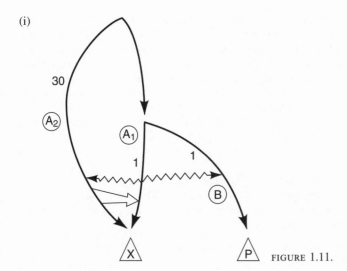

FIGURE 1.11.

Now, in terms of definition (167), A_1, whose head represents the extracted constituent, and B, whose head constituent represents the resumptive pronoun, would both qualify, quite undesirably, as final 1-arcs. In the terms of Johnson and Postal (1980), arc B represents a type called a *replacer* (of A_1). In such a case, the presumed final subject would be the resumptive pronoun. This suggests the following: First, one must take definition (167) to define a slightly distinct concept, call it *prefinal arc*, and define a *final arc* as a prefinal arc, *which is not replaced*. Second, the development of Quace assignment and Quace agreement in the text was assumed to "begin" with final Nominal-arcs. Evidently, if the previous suggestions are taken, this should be refined to prefinal Nominal-arcs. Third, the issue arises as to the relation between the Quace of a replacer arc like B and that of its sponsor, A_1. My assumption would be that this should be an instance of identity mediated by another type of Quace agreement. Roughly:

(ii)   If A is a prefinal arc whose Quace Marker has the Relational Marker M and B replaces A, then B's Quace Marker has the Relational Marker M.

36. There is a potential problem inherent in what has been said. Namely, suppose two distinct constituents extract from below a fixed complementizer C_n to positions higher than C_n. Then, according to the development so far, it might seem that the CT-arc headed by C_n would have to agree in Quace with two distinct 30-arcs, which, if the latter have distinct Quace Markers, could be impossible and would be in every case where the Relational Marker of one Quace Marker was not a proper initial sequence of that of the other.

Multiple extractions in English are rare but not unknown. Many people, including myself, accept (i) for example, and (ii) does not seem too bad, either:

(i)   Janet, I am sure that the police will interrogate everyone who knew.
(ii)   Janet, never did I believe (that) they interrogated.
(iii) *Janet, never did I believe (**that) interrogated the suspects.

And while even the short version of (iii) is bad, it is clear that the Anticomplementizer Constraint still manifests, since presence of a pronounced complementizer is much worse than its absence.

While it is difficult to investigate this matter in English, the proposal I would make relates to the ideas of Postal (1998). There it was claimed that extraction from (selective) islands must involve invisible resumptive pronouns, at most optional for other extractions. Moreover, I would assume that each extraction "creates" an island. If so, then at least one of the extractions in multiple intersecting extraction cases must involve (selective) island extraction. One obvious way to keep such phenomena consistent with the development of this section is to assume that while "ordinary" extractions involve 30-arc successors, extractions from selective islands involve at least one other type, say 40-arcs; these would be subject to an analog of the Uniformity Condition for 30-arcs.. The constraint of Postal (1998) could then be informally that extractions that involve 40-arc successors must determine resumptive pronouns. Given these assumptions, the CT-arc headed by the complementizer that in cases like (ii) and (iii) will be a neighbor of both a 30-arc and a 40-arc. But it is only required by Condition (190) to agree in Quace with the former.

However, this could not be the end of the matter, since nothing yet guarantees that in, e.g., (iii) it is the subject extraction (of Janet) that involves a 30-arc, while the extraction of never involves 40-arc successors. Perhaps then one needs to either specify (iv) or determine that it follows from something more general:

(iv)   If A is a 1-arc Start arc remote foreign predecessor of some Overlay-arc, then A's foreign successor is a 30-arc.

Clearly, one would want to link (iv) to the well-known fact that in many cases extraction of final subjects from selective islands is banned, as in (va); but one must also allow for the improvement when the subject is not the subject of the highest clause in the island, as in (vb), or is in an Adverb Effect environment, as in (vc):

(v)   a. *What candidate did Janet learn whether could speak Spanish?
      b. ??What candidate did Janet learn whether Tom thought could speak Spanish?
      c. ?? What candidate did Janet learn whether under a deep form of hypnosis could speak Spanish?

Plausibly, the improvement here is linked to Condition (195), which would determine that the highest arc in the adjunct headed by What candidate in both (vb) and (vc) would have finished 2-Quace, not the finished 1-Quace which the highest such arc in (va) would have. This relation could be captured by refining (iv) to something like (vi):

(vi)   If A is a 1-arc Start arc remote foreign predecessor of some arc B that is a 30-arc predecessor of an Overlay-arc C, then B has finished 2-Quace.

However, real exploration of these issues is again well beyond possible discussion here.

37. The notion represented by the highlighted subexpression is here left totally informal.

38. It remains unexplained, of course, why (197c) is bad. One can suspect that this state of affairs is due to whatever principle (see Grimshaw, 1997, for discussion in terms very removed from those of these remarks) precludes a null complementizer in the case of complement-internal extractions:

(i)   a. Mason believes that/*Ø Sonia, Kim will never hire.
      b. Mason believes that/* Ø never will Kim hire Sonia.
      c. Mason believes that/* Ø no matter who Kim hires, she will complain.
      d. Mason believes that/* Ø such large lights, Kim will never agree to install them.

I will not attempt to say more about this feature; I suspect, though, that it is related to the fact that complement-internal extractions like those of (i) map clauses that are otherwise not islands into islands. For it is generally true that a nonrelative clause structure of the form [X [$_\alpha$ that Y] Z], where the constituent is an island with respect to anything external to it, cannot alternate with one in which that is replaced by Ø.

39. Kayne (1984: 5) claims that a contrast exists between (i) and (ii):

(i)   a. the man who I believe has left
      b. the man who I think is quite intelligent
(ii) a. the man whom it is obvious likes you
      b. the man whom it is likely admires her

He regards those in (ii) as ungrammatical. But neither I nor my colleague Mark Baltin perceives a contrast between such cases. Equally clear to me is that the adjectival and verbal variants of (iii) do not differ:

(iii) a. the woman who he is sure/recognizes loves you
      b. the only doctor who I am confident/know can help you

All the examples of (i)–(iii) really deserve question marks, but none obviously more than the others. For Kayne the perceived contrast between (i) and (ii) is due to the fact that the former pair involves a higher *verb*, the latter pair a higher *adjective*, and in the GB terms Kayne was adopting verbs, but not adjectives, assign case. It would be possible, though a priori undesirable, to build a verb/adjective distinction into a variant of principle (195).

40. A problem for condition (205) is visible in pairs like (i):

(i)   a. the guy who once hired Joan and they now claim I should hire
      b. *the guy who they claim I should hire and once hired Joan

Here, in both cases, a main clause subject is combined under coordination with an embedded object. Since neither subcontext of principle (195) determines any 2-Quace for the higher subject, combination with the lower object would be predicted by the discussion in the text to be bad. This is clearly correct for (ib) but seems wrong for (ia). So the question is what analysis of the latter is possible consistent with (205). I do not have a good answer, but perhaps (ia) involves a phenomenon linked to relative pronouns. That is, perhaps (ia) is related by some form of relative pronoun that zeroes to (ii), which is not constrained by (205):

(ii) the guy who once hired Joan and who they now claim I should hire

Note that analogs of (ia) do not seem so good if not based on structures that arguably contain relative pronouns:

(iii) a. What manager once hired Joan and do they now claim I should hire.
      b. ?What manager once hired Joan and do they now claim I should hire.
(iv) a. No engineer (both) praised Jack and claims I should praise Jerome.
      b. *No engineer (both) praised Jack and do they now claim I should praise.

2. A Putatively Banned Type of Raising

I am greatly indebted to Idan Landau for very helpful comments on an earlier version of this chapter. These have significantly improved the text and helped avoid some unfortunate errors. Needless to say, remaining problems are entirely my responsibility.

1. The ungrammaticality of Bresnan's (72a) and other related examples like those in (ib, c) should be related to other cases of unextractable PPs, some discussed in Postal (1998: 127–129), such as those in (ii):

(i)   a. *It is on John that Mary relies to dress himself.
      b. *the person on whom Mary relies to dress himself
      c. *On which person does Mary rely to dress himself?

(ii)　a. Laura made light of the death of the chimp.

　　　b. Which chimp did Laura make light of the death of?

　　　c. *Of which chimp did Laura make light of the death?

That is, the notion of 'unextractable PP' seems to be a feature of English. Remarkable about cases like (i), though, is that the parallel PP with the same verb(s) is extractable when no infinitive is present:

(iii)　a. Mary relies on John.

　　　b. It is on John that Mary relies.

　　　c. the person on whom John relies

　　　d. On which person does Mary rely the most?

　　2. I find no discussion of relevant cases or the overall topic in Bresnan (2001). But Kaplan and Bresnan (1995: 75) invoke the principle that led to Bresnan's original claims, that is, the principle that functional controllers must be SUBJ, OBJ, or OBJ$_\theta$ and hence not Obliques. And Dalrymple (2001: 345) appears to reiterate the same point.

　　3. Since, as was indicated, the LFG framework utilizes the notion of functional control for both raising and control structures, it is unclear to me how, internal to these ideas, it would be possible to reconstruct the view of Pollard and Sag (1987, 1994) that there is a contrast between the two phenomena with respect to whether the main clause pivot phrase can be the complement of a P. That is, the framework described by Bresnan (1982b) should be just as incompatible with the control structure taken by Pollard and Sag to manifest in the appeal variant of (i) as with a raising structure for the rely on cases:

(i)　Herman asked/appealed to Gertrude to aid the runaway gerbils.

Here, too, the only possibility would seem to be to appeal to reanalysis and to attempt to reduce appeal to to the single verb status of, e.g., ask. But data like (ii) shows the untenability of such a proposal:

(ii)　a. Herman appealed repeatedly to Gertrude to aid the runaway gerbils.

　　　b. Herman appealed to Gertrude or to Lydia to aid the runaway gerbils.

　　　c. Herman appealed not to Gertrude but to Lydia to aid the runaway gerbils.

　　　d. Herman appealed not only to Gertrude to aid the gerbils but to Lydia to aid the mice.

　　　e. *Herman appealed to to aid the runaway gerbils the woman he had met at the animal protection league.

　　4. Stowell argues that what McCloskey (1984) took to be RCP is actually raising to subject position and that what McCloskey took to be prepositions are actually irregular (quirky) case markers. Obviously, regardless of validity of Stowell's claims for Irish, the type of approach to protecting GB ideas he was taking has no application to English on verb cases, where it is out of the question to talk about raising to subject position, the latter being filled independently by obvious subjects. McCloskey's cases involved intransitive/possibly impersonal verbs. This makes English cases even more important as arguments for raising. For if they stand up, they accomplish what McCloskey's argument was intended to do without offering the target that Stowell tried to take advantage of.

　　5. Although, as in Postal (1974: 363–364), I list bank and bet as members of the class, I will mostly ignore them in giving examples. The reason is that I find many infinitival examples with these strained or artificial at best, for unknown reasons.

　　6. Some of the at least metaphorical idiom chunks do occur in control cases, as noted by Nunberg, Sag, and Wasow (1994). See for instance:

(i)   a. Birds of a feather flock/*hang out/*go/*travel/*fly together.
      b. Birds of a feather intend/like/love to flock/*hang out/*go/*travel/*fly together.
      c. Old dogs can't be taught/*instructed about new tricks.
      d. Old dogs don't want to be taught/*instructed about new tricks.

Such cases are simply irrelevant to differentiating control from raising contexts, as they occur in both. So:

(ii) a. It is easy to prove birds of a feather to flock together.
      b. It is easy to convince birds of a feather to flock together.
      c. It is impossible to depend on birds of a feather to flock together.

7. In the earliest variants of generative grammar, it was assumed that control structures involved matching NPs in the main and complement clauses and deletion of the complement NP by a rule called Equi (NP deletion); see, e.g., McCawley (1971: 7, 28, 85, 161; 1981: 129, 467). So (ib) would involve a reduction of (ia):

(i)   a. Winston wants Winston to succeed.
      b. Winston wants to succeed.

This works out badly on semantic grounds for cases with nonreferential NPs, like those of (ii); see McCawley (1971: 108–109; 1981: 129):

(ii) a. Every representative wants every representative to succeed.
      b. Every representative wants to succeed.

For clearly the meaning of (iib) is not captured by a structure like (iia).

In Postal (1970) I proposed that a controlled subject was a pronoun with a special feature, Doom. This analysis was adopted in effect in Chomsky (1981) via postulation of the element PRO, though without attribution, as noted in Larson, Iatridou, Lahari, and Higginbotham (1992: ix).

8. The situation would be a bit complicated if, as argued in chapter 3, certain instances of raising leave invisible resumptive pronouns as complement subjects, an idea with a certain historical track record; see Grinder (1972) and Pullum (1976).

9. For discussion and exploitation of the notion of antipronominal context, see Postal (1993a, 1993c, 1994a, 1994b, 1998, 2001a, 2001b).

10. As observed in Kayne (1984: 112), French in general allows apparent analogs of cases like (53f) with verbs of the believe/croire semantic class. Since these verbs are subject to an analog of the constraint referred to as DOC in the text but allow extraction cases where the extracted DP would correspond to a raised subject, one can suspect that the French cases have an analysis parallel to that suggested here for English claim:

(i)   Kayne (1984: 111–112)
      a. *Je reconnais Jean être le plus intelligent de tous.
         "I recognize Jean to be the most intelligent of all."
      b. Quel garçon reconnais-tu être le plus intelligent de tous?
         "What boy do you recognize to be the most intelligent of all?"
      c. Je reconnais avoir fait une erreur.
         "I recognize to have made an error."

11. Chomsky (1977a: 190–191; 1980a: 6) proposed that control structures *in general* involve reflexive phrase deletion. That hypothesis would, of course, lose the distinction stressed here between raising structures, a tiny few of which are here taken to involve reflexive deletion, and control structures. The difference is evidently key to the factual contrasts between them, e.g.:

(i)   a. Control   *Uruguayan police wish to bribe cheaply.
      b. Raising + Reflexive Deletion   Uruguayan police claim to bribe cheaply.
(ii) a. Control   *They dissuaded Uruguayan police from bribing
                                                              cheaply.
      b. Raising   They prevented Uruguayan police from bribing
                                                              cheaply.
(iii) a. Control   The director wanted to have gotten together by 10 A.M.
      b. Raising + Reflexive Deletion   *The director claimed to have gotten together by 10 A.M.
(iv) a. Control   They dissuaded the director from meeting before 10 A.M.
      b. Raising   *They prevented the director from meeting before 10 A.M.

12. For discussions of de se interpretations, see Chierchia (1989), Fiengo and May (1994), Fodor (1975: 133–138), Higginbotham (1992), Landau (2000, 2002), Schlenker (1999), and Tancredi (1997).

13. Despite permitting clear raising structures like (ia), expect in structures like (ib) involves control, not raising plus reflexive deletion, as argued by middle, stock, and partial control facts like (ii):

(i)   a. Jeremy expects Rhonda to call him.
      b. Jeremy expects to call Rhonda.
(ii) a. *Uruguayan police expect to bribe cheaply.
      b. *Microsoft expects to go up
      c. The boss expected to have gotten together by 10 A.M.

14. Actually, things are more complicated than the text discussion implies. At issue are several implications:

(i)   If a complement does allow partial control, it is not a raising complement (hence is a control complement).
(ii) If a complement does not allow partial control, it is not a control complement (hence is a raising complement).

Now, the relevant partial control data that involve on verb complements in this chapter instantiate the conditional part of (ii), rather than that of (i). However, while Landau (1999, 2000) has argued that (i) is true, he did not assume (ii) and in fact claimed that there are three types of *control* complements that, like raising complements, preclude partial control.

To the extent that that is true, even a correct showing in particular that the infinitival complements of on verbs bar partial control does not as such justify the claim that these infinitives are raising complements. Strictly, all that is supported, even given the (I think uncontroversial) view adopted here that the raising/control distinction exhausts the domain of subjectless complements, is a disjunction of something like the form:

(iii) The infinitival complements of on verbs are *either* raising complements *or* some type of control complements that bar partial control.

While this initially weakens the case for a raising analysis of on verbs derivable from the incompatibility of their infinitival complements with partial control, it does not eliminate it, for two reasons. First, given that the other classical and new tests support a raising view of these complements, the best overall analysis will clearly choose the first disjunct of (iii). Second, Landau has argued that those control complements that nonetheless bar partial control fall into three independently existing semantically characterizable classes, which he designated as (iv):

(iv) a. implicative verbs, e.g., <u>manage</u>
      b. aspectual verbs, e.g., <u>begin</u>
      c. modal verbs, e.g., <u>have to</u>

The issue is a bit clouded by the fact that there are good grounds to assume that some instances of the verbs of (ivb and c) are raising, not control, verbs. Note, for instance, that they allow expletive subjects and middle complements and permit the metonymous stock structures:

(v)   a. There began to be opposition.
      b. Uruguayan police began to bribe more cheaply/easily.
      c. Microsoft began to drop.
(vi) a. There have to be some changes.
      b. Uruguayan police have to bribe pretty cheaply.
      c. Microsoft has to go up.

Significantly, these contrast with the implicative case:

(vii) a. *There managed to be opposition.
      b. *Uruguayan police managed to bribe cheaply/easily.
      c. *Microsoft managed to go up. (good only irrelevantly as personification)

Nonetheless, Landau (2000) has argued that some instances of these verbs cannot be treated as raising cases and yet their complements still resist partial control. But this turns out not to really undermine the claim that their incompatibility with partial control supports the raising character of the infinitival complements of <u>on</u> verbs. For given his assumption that there is a contrast between infinitivals as to whether they incorporate tense or not, Landau proposes:

(viii) Landau (2000)
        Control verb complements allow partial control if and only if they contain tense.

Accepting (viii), disjunction (iii) immediately strengthens to (ix):

(ix)   The infinitival complements of <u>on</u> verbs are *either* raising complements *or* partial control barring *control* complements that do not have tense.

Condition (ix) greatly strengthens the case from partial control that <u>on</u> verb complements are raising structures, since the tests that Landau exhibits argue that the infinitival complements of <u>on</u> verbs are tensed. Given that, the disjunction in (ix) reduces to its first disjunct.

I conclude then that despite the complications discussed in this note, the partial control phenomenon does contribute substantively to supporting a raising analysis of <u>on</u> verb infinitival complement structures.

3. A New Raising Mystery

1. See Lasnik (1999a, 1999b) and Lasnik and Saito (1991) for some revisionist thinking in the tradition that formerly *rejected* raising to object analyses.

2. To make this claim concrete, one can give an account in the Metagraph framework of Johnson and Postal (1980), Postal (1990a, 1992, 1996), and chapter 1, section 9, along the following lines: Assume that the R(elational)-signs of arcs that define Complex DP Shift and Right Node Raising belong to a class denoted R-extract. Then one could say that the principle at work in cases like, e.g., (28c) is essentially:

(i)   If A is a 2-arc type I foreign successor of a 1-arc, B, and a foreign predecessor of an R-extract-arc, then B is copied (that is, replaced by a copy arc).

Since all replacers have the same R-sign as the arcs they replace, (i) guarantees the presence of a 1-arc replacer of the 1-arc, B, that defines the origin of the raising. For (i) to cover both the raising to object cases and the raising to subject cases discussed later, one needs to assume that raising to subject involves raising to 2 with subsequent advancement to 1, an idea often considered independently in the relational literature; see Perlmutter and Postal (1983a: 68–69).

3. While positing (invisible) resumptive pronouns in a subset of English raising cases might seem somewhat radical, the idea is not new. As discussed in Pullum (1976), Grinder (1972) proposed that raising to subject always involved such a pronoun, although his motivations for this claim, which involved issues of transformations applying cyclically or not, were entirely distinct from our concerns here.

4. A straightforward interpretation of (48) as a universal claim makes predictions about NLs like Niuean; see Massam (2001) and Seiter (1980, 1983). Niuean appears to have raising of both subjects and direct objects to both subject and direct object. Interpretation of condition (48bi) as a universal would then entail that in the direct object-raising cases resumptive pronouns are present. No evidence for this is currently available, and the predicted resumptive pronouns would have to be forced to be invisible.

5. The reason for the inability of the work at issue to analyze cases like (52) and (54) in terms of raising involves claims that movement out of tensed clauses (setting aside the role of previous movement to the Comp constituent or its Specifier) is impossible. This view dates to Chomsky's (1973) Tensed S Condition but has always been maintained in successive systems despite radical revisions, replacements, and additions; see Chomsky (1986b: 176–179) and Culicover (1997: 104–106).

6. Recent statements of the purported central role of cyclic application include:

(i) Chomsky (1999: 9)
     "Derivation is assumed to be strictly cyclic, but with the phase level of the cycle playing a special role."
(ii) Chomsky (2001: 4)
     "Assume that all three components are cyclic, a very natural optimality requirement and fairly conventional."

The claim that rules apply cyclically links to the key question of whether NLs are properly described via generative/proof-theoretic rules. If, as I suggest, they are not, the question of rules applying cyclically simply cannot arise, since the question of their applying cannot. For then the rules of NL grammars, being statements, not analogs of computer program subparts, are not operations. Thus the issue of how/when/at what stage rules apply can no more arise for NL grammars than it can, for example, for the axioms of set theory or for Peano's axioms. Whether grammars are generative/proof-theoretic or nongenerative/model-theoretic and whether this question has been begged in the generative literature are treated in chapters 6 and 13.

4. Chromaticity

1. While small, the class of nonchromatics is not really rigidly closed in the sense that, e.g., the class of tense endings is. For instance, vulgar slang forms like jack, jack-shit, and squat are nonchromatics but seem to be relatively recent additions to standard English.

2. Moreover, if, as is indicated for reasons touched on later, interrogative when, where, how, and why are nonchromatic, the claim is even less tenable.

3. Kishimoto actually gives a somewhat more complex structure for theoretical reasons that has no grounding in any of the facts considered here.

4. It cannot be maintained that "Only someone spoke Spanish" is bad because <u>only</u> requires stress on the N, while nonchromatics like <u>someone</u> do not permit this. For note the contrast:

(i)   Only SOME chimp spoke Spanish.
(ii) *Only SOMEone spoke Spanish.

That is, <u>only</u> is content with strong stress on the D of a chromatic DP but not on a nonchromatic form. This makes a pure stress account difficult to defend.

5. One finds, of course, also the grammatical, though literary, expression <u>all else</u>:

(i)   All else is illusion.
(ii) When all else fails, . . .

This may be analyzable as a variant of the more transparent <u>everything else</u>, although <u>all else</u> seems limited to subject position:

(iii) Shelly threw out everything/*all else.
(iv)   Shelly gave everything/*all else a lot of thought.
(v)   Shelly argued about everything/*all else.
(vi)   What I don't understand is everything/*all else.

Beyond the presence of *else*, the nonchromatic character of <u>all else</u> is shown by facts like (vii):

(vii) a. *Everything else/*All else/Every week/part/moment of the month was spent _{<temporal>} in study.
       b. Everything else/All else/*All the problems that was/were the matter with her liver was minor.

6. All the single-word "adverbial" interrogatives <u>when</u>, <u>where</u>, <u>why</u>, and <u>how</u>, like the nonadverbial interrogatives <u>what</u> and <u>who</u>, permit <u>else</u>:

(i)   a. When else can we meet?
      b. Where else can we meet?
      c. Why else would she have said that?
      d. How else can we discover the truth?
      e. What else did she say?
      f. Who else did she insult?

This plus their single-word character, which requires postposed adjectives (if any), suggests the nonchromatic character of all of these, as touched on in note 2.

Arguably, too, it is only the nonchromatic relative pronoun forms that delete:

(ii) a. the only time (when) I can go
      b. the only place (where) I can live
      c. the only reason (why) he did that
      d. the only way (*how) he can do that

Note, for instance, that the only locative forms that can occur in the relative-internal gap position in (iib) are nonchromatic:

(iii) I can live *some town/*some ranch/somewhere/someplace.

A parallel point holds for, e.g., the manner case if one makes the assumption that the nonchromatic manner relative pronoun is obligatorily not optionally null and that there are no noninterrogative nonchromatic manner forms that correspond to the locative <u>somewhere/anywhere</u>.

(iv)   a. He can do that in some way.
    b. *He can do that someway.
    c. *He can't do that anyhow.

7. I take the last example of (19d) to indicate that the noun <u>stuff</u> has a chromatic analysis. Other data, e.g., that in (19c) and (31a) and (32a), argue that it also has a nonchromatic analysis. This is also supported by pseudocleft data:

(i)   *What Milo likes is stuff.
(ii)   What Milo likes is cheap stuff.

While the two instances of <u>stuff</u> in (19c and d) contrast in the presence or not of an adjective, the relation between this noun and adjectival occurrence is not straightforward. That is, while the nonchromatic <u>stuff</u> of (19c) has no adjective, the cases in (31a) and (32a) suggest that nonchromatic <u>stuff</u> can also occur with an adjective. Given that, one issue then is why the last example of (19c) is ill formed. One possibility would be to say that *chromatic* <u>stuff</u> is only possible in the presence of some sort of "modifier." Given the ban on inanimate genitive nonchromatics, this would properly predict contrasts like (iii) and (iv):

(iii)   a. cheap stuff's cost
    b. *stuff's cost
(iv)   a. evil stuff's implications
    b. *stuff's implications

8. The chromatic analysis of the weak definite pronouns is what permits grammatical expressions like (i), given the earlier conclusion that inanimate genitive nonchromatics are impossible:

(i)   their motors
(ii)   its engine

9. Actually, there is a grammatical usage for clauses like that starred here, one extremely common at least in New York area English and represented by (i):

(i)   What did he drive in last year, sixty runs?

This usage seems to form pseudopolite weak assertions "disguised" as questions. Thus (i) is roughly equivalent to (ii):

(ii)   He drove in roughly sixty runs last year, didn't he?

Notably, on this use, the form <u>what</u> is semantically quite distinct from the normal interrrogative <u>what</u> and means "how many." So (i) is also roughly equivalent to

(iii)   How many runs did he drive in last year, sixty?

Arguably, this usage of <u>what</u> is not restricted to the category nonchromatic. For it is possible for it to link to a gap in a position that must be chromatic and <u>else</u> is impossible:

(iv)   a. What (*else) language (*else)/*What (else) does he speak?
    b. What (*else) does he speak, ten languages?

This might support an analysis of cases like (iv) that relates them to those with chromatic DPs like that in (v):

(v)   How many languages does he speak?

A parallel argument indicates that the somewhat different noninterrogative <u>what</u> of examples like (vi), also characteristic of New York English, is also not restricted to chromatic contexts:

(vi)   a. What (*else) is he, an idiot!
       b. What (*else) are you, a clown!

These are insulting assertive reactions to perceived inept remarks or acts, equivalent respectively to a bit weakened forms of "He is an idiot," and "You are a clown." Notably, though, they are possible linked to chromatic gap positions:

(vii) a. *What are you speaking? (request for information)
       b. What (*else) are you speaking, an/some ape language! (an insult)
       c. *What are you attending $_{<\text{matriculation}>}$? (request for information)
       d. What (*else) are you attending $_{<\text{matriculation}>}$, a school for idiots! (an insult)

This also might suggest an analysis of cases like (viib and d), which involve underlying chromatic DPs, e.g., something like X + some ape language and X + a school for idiot. How to execute such an analysis is, though, not obvious.

10. This point is strengthened by the fact that like agreement in person, number, and gender, chromaticity value agreement is also found between what are usually considered distinct sentences in a discourse, e.g., question/answer pairs:

(i)   a. Who did the boy$_1$ call? He$_1$/*She$_1$/*They$_1$ called the director.
       b. Was Jane studying *something$_1$/some language$_1$? Yes, but she didn't speak it$_1$.

11. However, one difference that involves conjunction is discussed in section 6.

12. Examples like (72g) indicate that nonchromatic DPs, though usually grammatically singular, need not be. See also:

(i)   a. The things that are the matter with his liver are not life-threatening.
       b. Lots of things are eating Gilbert.
       c. The things they thought about naming him were silly.
       d. Those things, I am sure, are no longer wrong with him.
       e. Most of the things that are still wrong with him are minor.

13. Speakers differ, sometimes radically, in which subset of, in particular, the forms in (75c) they use and/or know.

14. This is the case in, e.g., the NL Mohawk of the Iroquoian family; see Baker (1996) and Postal (1979).

15. I must confess, though, that although I reject (84), it is nonetheless possible in my speech, as apparently in that represented in that example, to form a partly plural-looking reflexive themself, whose existence is also noted in Huddleston and Pullum (2002: 426, 494). But I seem to restrict it essentially to just the set of antecedents found in (81):

(i)   a. If everyone$_1$/someone$_1$/no one$_1$ praises themself$_1$/*themselves$_1$, . . .
       b. Who$_1$ praised themself$_1$?
       c. Whoever praised themself$_1$/*themselves$_1$ was not modest.
(ii)   a. *If every guy$_1$/some guy$_1$/no guy$_1$ praises themself$_1$, . . .
       b. *What guy$_1$ praised themself$_1$?
       c. *Whatever guy$_1$ praised themself$_1$ was not modest.

The first vowel of this very nonstandard themself is a schwa and must be unstressed. The grammatical cases of (i) are prescriptively even less acceptable than those of (81), a prescriptivism built into my version of Microsoft Word, which doggedly insists on changing themself to themselves. I suspect that many people who use "fake plurals" would still not use themself. Moreover, I do not believe this reflexive can be used as an *emphatic* reflexive, which yields contrasts like (iii):

(iii)   a. Somebody was criticizing himself/themself.
      b. Everyone wanted to buy himself/themself a new dress.
      c. If someone is himself/*themself incapable of distinguishing right from wrong, . . .

16. No doubt there is speaker variation with respect to singular they. So Huddleston and Pullum (2002: 493) cite several examples, which include (ia, b, and c) as grammatical:

(i)   a. The patient$_1$ should be told . . . how much they$_1$ will be required to pay.
     b. But a journalist$_1$ should not be forced to reveal their$_1$ sources.
     c. A friend of mine$_1$ has asked me to go over and help them$_1$ with an assignment.

But I find these quite impossible.
    That said, comments from Christopher Potts and further reflection suggest that the claim in the text is too strong. Potts observes that for him, examples like (i) with the general noun person are grammatical, and they are for me, too:

(i)   a. If a person$_1$ thinks they$_1$ are a genius, beware.
     b. Any person$_1$ who thinks they$_1$ are immortal should not buy life insurance.

This seems to indicate that the nonchromaticity requirement for antecedent of fake plural pronouns is at least slightly too strong, weakening support for the category from this phenomenon. It seems that gender neutrality is relevant, given contrasts like (ii):

(ii)   If an individual$_1$/being$_1$/*guy$_1$/*stud$_1$/*dude$_1$/*babe$_1$/*chick$_1$ thinks they$_1$ are a genius, beware.

However, more is involved, since even the gender neutral nouns of (iii) also make terrible antecedents:

(iii)   If a(n) *doctor$_1$/*earthling/*jerk/*idiot/*programmer$_1$/*linguist$_1$/*politician$_1$/*server$_1$ thinks they$_1$ are a genius, beware.

I think it relevant that the good antecedent nouns of (i) and (ii) are maximally general, restricting the individuals they denote only to being sentient and possibly human, while the bad cases impose further constraints on possible denotata. Possibly then, the nonchromatic category I have argued for is actually a subtype of a slightly larger 'colorless' noun category, which includes being, individual, and person but not earthling, politician, etc.
    There is actually a bit of additional ground for this. Consider the question of what nouns can compound. It seems that none of the few potential compounders here characterized as nonchromatic can:

(iv)   a. room/car/cabin/boat/equipment/gear cleaning
     b. *stuff/*thing cleaning

However, the bad cases of (ivb) cannot be blocked by mere appeal to nonchromaticity, since we saw that the two nouns involved are ambiguously members of both the chromatic and nonchromatic classes. A restriction that bars compounding of nonchromatics only accounts for the badness of (ivb) on one analysis.
    Moreover, limiting noncompounders to nonchromatics is independently too limited; see (v):

(v)   a. earthling/guy/stud/dude/babe/chick/humanoid chasing
     b. *person/*individual/*being chasing

That is, those general human nouns known to me that seem, along with nonchromatics, to be able to antecede fake plural pronouns also fail to compound, which suggests that there is a grammatical characterization here. Further study is obviously in order.

Finally, I should note that I became aware of Lagunoff's (1997) full-length study of singular they only after essential completion of this chapter and thus too late to take account of its rich database.

5. The Structure of One Type of American English Vulgar Minimizer

I dedicate this chapter to the memory of James D. McCawley, whose loss at a much too early age leaves an enormous gap and whose many and perceptive observations about negation have been a great aid in achieving what little understanding I have of this domain.

I would like to thank William Ladusaw and Laurence Horn for a good deal of early advice and instruction about minimizers and vulgar minimizers in particular. Their input was particularly useful and required considerable indulgence, as it came at a time when I could hardly have distinguished a minimizer from an atomizer. Needless to say, they bear no blame whatever for any inadequacies of this text.

Finally, much of anything that is of value in this chapter owes a great deal in ways that mere citations fail to indicate to observations of and discussions with Haj Ross over a number of years.

1. In the fall of 2000, I found that a class of twenty-three undergraduates all met this condition. Most could use squat in particular, also the form I am most comfortable with and which I hence use in most examples. My speculative sociology is that these forms were until fairly recently restricted to substandard and regional dialects and were quite vulgar. But some of them have become part of standard American English, and their vulgarity aspect is notably diminishing or vanishing, as indicated by their use even by elegant middle-class women in television dramas and by such data as a cartoon that appeared in the *New Yorker* of July 19, 1999.

The cartoon shows a rhinoceros with an impressive horn talking to a creature like a tiger or a leopard. The caption read:

(i)   It's supposed to be some kind of aphrodisiac, but it hasn't done jack for me.

First, I am confident that the editors of the *New Yorker*, producers of a publication with a rather genteel style, saw no special vulgarity in the caption. Second, the rhinoceros is clearly speaking standard American English; no special inferences about his social status, class, educational background, etc., are possible. Contrast that with a situation where, instead, the caption had been (ii):

(ii)   It hasn't done nothin(g) for me.

This could have expressed the same meaning but would have revealed that the rhinoceros was, or was trying to pass for, a substandard speaker and hence was not the sort of rhinoceros who could, for instance, reasonably be assumed to have been a Yale graduate.

2. The alternative types property has been recognized by previous commentators; see (16)–(19). But some speakers seem to allow only one or another usage of at least some vulgar minimizers. So David Perlmutter has informed me that for him, squat only has usages of the "anything" type. And for me, fuck-all only seems to have uses of the "nothing" type.

3. Examples (ia and b) illustrate one other case of apparent irrelevance of negation:

(i)   a. She could not (*at all/*ever) care (*at all) less about their/*anyone else's agenda (*at all) (could/*couldn't she?). =
      b. She could care less about their /*anyone else's agenda (*at all) (?could/*couldn't she?).

It is a challenge to explicate why the real negative in (ia), its reality indicated inter alia by its ability to determine a positive confirmation tag and total inability to permit a negative tag and its power to permit the negation sensitive (n)either (see section 2), is strangely impotent to license negative polarity items like anyone/at all. Compare the more regular use of care in (ii):

(ii)   She did not (at all) care about their/anyone else's agenda.

4. I do not at all intend (15a) to preclude the possibility of a still deeper analysis of any. In fact, I think that such can be justified and that the matter bears heavily on the proper analysis of type A vulgar minimizers. But these issues are way beyond the scope of my remarks here. See Postal (in preparation b).

5. Neither type A nor type Z vulgar minimizers accept modifiers, including parenthetical modifiers like not even + X. This fact weakens any support derivable from (26d) for the non-negative structure of type Z vulgar minimizers.

6. During a lecture on these forms at Ohio State University in March 1999, a number of audience members seemed to accept examples like (30a), which I and others (e.g., Haj Ross) robustly reject.

7. I take no position here on the correctness of Déprez's suggestion for the French facts that motivated it.

8. The justification for this claim is nonobvious and depends on issues of the analysis of type A vulgar minimizers, matters beyond the scope of this discussion.

9. I ignore here and throughout another possible reading of nothing that, when present, renders the starred version of (49a) irrelevantly grammatical. This is a reading in which the DP nothing is equivalent to one of roughly the form something which was nothing, that is, with the meaning "something insignificant/trivial." This reading yields semantically an increasing (upward-entailing) DP, rather than the decreasing DP yielded by ordinary no forms or zero forms. Now, in general, it is impossible to topicalize decreasing DPs. Notably then, the reading under discussion permits topicalization, normally banned for no forms, yielding contrasts like (i):

(i)   a. Nothing, he will often be shocked by.
       b. *No problem/outrage/joke/quip/remark, he will often be shocked by.

The same point holds for the construction in (ii), which also is in general impossible with decreasing DPs:

(ii)   a. Nothing, that is what he was shocked by.
       b. *No problem/outrage/joke/quip/remark, that is what he was shocked by.

6. The Openness of Natural Languages

Any discernible virtues in this chapter exist only thanks to the remarkable work on the foundations of linguistics over the last two decades by Jerrold J. Katz; see Katz (1981, 1984, 1996, 1998). It is with great appreciation that I dedicate this work to his memory.

I am greatly indebted to Marcel den Dikken, Ray Jackendoff, David Johnson, Christopher Potts, Geoffrey K. Pullum, Haj Ross, and Pieter Seuren for comments on earlier versions of this chapter, which have substantively improved the result. None of them, however, can be assumed to accept any specific claim made here And I alone am responsible for any deficiencies.

1. A (recursively) enumerable set is one that falls under the following characterization (Boolos and Jeffrey, 1974: 4): "To say that a set A is enumerable is to say that there is a function all of whose arguments are positive integers and all of whose values are members of A, and that each member of A is a value of this function: for each member a of A there is at least one positive integer n to which the functions assigns a as its value."

2. The reviews in question were Abbott (1986), Lapointe (1986), McCawley (1987), Rauff (1989), Sgall (1987), and Thompson (1986). Wilks (1984) is also a review of sorts; although it does not mention the actual argument of Langendoen and Postal (1984) and badly misconstrues a number of points, it also fails to contain even any claimed refutation of the argument.

3. Cantor's Theorem states that for any set V the power set of V, that is, the set of all subsets of V, is of a higher cardinality than V; see Stoll (1979: 86).

4. This despite Lapointe's (1986: 238) remarkably inaccurate quasi prediction that "if Chomsky takes L&P's comments at all seriously, we can anticipate a lengthy response from him in the near future."

5. See Chomsky (1975b, 229, note 8, 244–245, note 1, 246, note 9, 251, note 38; 1978, 311–312; 1980b, 267, note 28; 1982a, 33; 1984, 47; 2000c, 49–50).

6. Clearly then, the argument of Langendoen and Postal (1984, 1985), though publicly unchallenged, has had no effect on Chomsky's assertions. It would be instructive to have a specification and defense of some principles of proper scholarly conduct or "rational inquiry" that could justify continuing assertion of the contrary of a published claim A in the absence of any refutation or criticism of the argument for A, indeed without even any mention of A. Here I believe one touches on the topic of part II of this work, junk linguistics.

7. The existence of nonfinite sentences was not a premiss of the basic argument but a consequence of its underlying assumption. So if one could show that every NL sentence is a finite object, one would have falsified the argument by proving the negation of one of its entailments. Such a reductio demonstration remains unknown, however.

8. This prejudice is strong in philosophy as well as in linguistics; see Langendoen and Postal (1984: 95–96). And more recently Sorensen (1998) claimed without argument:

This context sensitive approach is designed to work within a single, learnable language—such as English. However, such a language has only denumerably many sentences. Supplementing the language with indices might ensure that there will be a sentence for any thought in the super-denumerable queue. But the language will not have a sentence for each and every thought in the queue. For there are uncountably many thoughts and only countably many sentences.

Sorensen's unsupported claim is directly inconsistent with the arguments of Langendoen and Postal (1984, 1985).

9. Not surprisingly, the doctrine in question has migrated to popularizations of generative grammar, where it is treated as an established fact. So Pinker (1994: 76) asserts: "The way language works, then, is that each person's brain contains a lexicon of words and the concepts they stand for (a mental dictionary) and a set of rules that combine the words to convey relationships among concepts (a mental grammar)."

10. The argument that only closed collections of sentences can be enumerated and hence that Chomsky's claim (3d) can only hold if NLs are closed can evidently be stated in terms of gödel numbering, described by Boolos and Jeffrey (1974: 170) as follows:

A *gödel numbering* is an assignment of natural numbers (called "gödel numbers") to expressions (in some set) that meets these conditions: (1) different gödel numbers are assigned to different expressions: (2) it is effectively calculable what the gödel number of any expression is; (3) it is effectively decidable whether a number is the gödel number of some expression in the set, and, if so, effectively calculable which expression it is the gödel number of.

Such a numbering provides a way of mapping any denumerable set of elements into a distinct set of gödel numbers. Put differently, a gödel numbering provides a way of coding any denumerable set into an isomorphic set of natural numbers. If, contrary to (3d), at least some NL sentences contain minimal elements *m* not drawn from a finite list, there is no way to calculate any assignment of gödel numbers to *m* and hence a set of sentences some of whose members contain elements of *m* cannot have a complete gödel numbering and is thereby not denumerable.

11. Earlier, Partee (1973: 411–412) contemplated the idea that the correct representation of a direct speech component was simply a phonological representation. But her remarks were terse and she did not address the problems of extending this idea to foreign segments, nonlinguistic noises, etc.

12. As the number of segments increases, the size of the set of alternative bracketings becomes staggeringly large; see Pullum (1982: 211) for a relevant formula for calculating the cardinality of such sets.

13. The careless implication built into Chomsky's singular/definite phrase 'the sign language of the deaf' that there is *only one* such NL is a falsehood that clashes with modern research on nonphonetically expressed NLs; see, e.g., Perlmutter (1986). Neidle, Kegl, Maclaughlin, Bahan, and Lee (2000: 6–7) indicate rather: "Contrary to popular misconception, there is no single, universal signed language. As with spoken languages, distinct signed languages are found in different parts of the world. Moreover, individual signed languages exhibit dialectal variation. For example, there are regional variations in the use of ASL."

14. That there are such in particular in ASL, the NL of the deaf in the United States, is argued in Lee, Neidle, and Maclaughlin (1997); many thanks to Carol Neidle for making me aware of this work and providing a copy.

15. The claim that the class of planar figures is of the order of the real numbers can be justified as follows. A planar figure is a set of *lines*, each line being a set of *points*. But the number of points on a line is itself of the order of the real numbers. As Davis and Hersh (1981: 224) put it:

> The first, the infinity of the natural numbers (and of any equivalent infinite sets) is called aleph nought ($\aleph_0$). Sets with cardinality $\aleph_0$ are called countable. The second kind of infinity is the one represented by a line segment. Its cardinality is designated by a lower-case German *c* (c) for 'continuum.' *Any* line segment of arbitrary length, has cardinality c. So does any rectangle in the plane, any cube in space, or for that matter all of unbounded *n*-dimensional space, whether *n* is 1, 2, 3 or 1,000.

So the number of lines in the plane is of the order of real numbers. Since each planar form consists of at least one line, the result is immediate.

16. As with direct speech segments, the issue arises of which contexts permit metalinguistic constituents like <u>by nos</u> and <u>by al que</u> in (37b). One might suggest that this is possible simply after the passive agent marker <u>by</u>. However, a more plausible alternative is that such examples involve invisible forms of a noun that denotes 'expression' or the like. For such forms are part of paradigms with visible nouns with similar denotations:

(i)   One of the traces must be bound by the element/expression/form/morpheme/word <u>nos</u> . . .

Recognition of an invisible element of this paradigm in examples like (37b) would permit a much more limited and context-restricted specification of the environments that allow foreign metalinguistic expressions.

17. The reasons for the hedge in this claim are explicated in section 10.

18. Actually, Kathol and Levine (1993: 210) seem to be casting doubt even on the constituency of direct speech segments, as follows:

> Thus, consider examples such as (based on Peters 1984:108):
> (11)   a.   "I intend", said Melicent rather grandly, because . . . , "to take the veil, and would like to be among the Benedictine sisters of Polesworth."

    b. "I intend to take the veil," said Melicent rather grandly, "and would like to be . . ."

    c. "I intend to take the veil, and would like," said Melicent rather grandly, "to be . . ."

It is difficult to see how in anything remotely like an X-bar based syntax the quoted material which appears to be fronted to the left of the inverted verb could be taken to be a projection of some lexical category—especially given the fact that this material need not be grammatical, or even correspond to human speech. Given that the quotation cannot be characterized as even a grammatical category, we find it extremely implausible that it could arise in its fronted position via a syntactic relation which is only well-defined between syntactic categories, such as that which relates a filler to the empty category it is linked to.

Questions of X-bar theoretic assumptions being irrelevant to issues of constituency per se, it is not made explicit in this quote, nor is it very clear, what the argument against the constituency of the quoted material is supposed to be. I take it, though, that the key element in the argument is the discontinuous character of the quotes. That is, presumably there would be no argument if the only example were (i):

(i)   "I intend to take the veil, and would like to be . . . ," said Melicent rather grandly.

But a general principle to the effect that segments of a surface sentence whose discontinuity is due to separation by a parenthetical element cannot correspond to an abstract constituent would seem to have unacceptable consequences. Consider for instance:

(ii)   Herb, (I guess/suppose) Bob, and (I assume/am nearly certain) Ted will vote for Sheila.

Clearly, without the parentheticals it is uncontroversial that there is a complex conjoined constituent [Herb, Bob, and Ted], a DP that is the subject of the clause. It seems then that the only argument derivable from the data Kathol and Levine (1993) cite in apparent opposition to the constituency of direct speech segments would equally yield an argument that denies that there is a subject DP constituent in the long versions of (i) that is a conjunction of three other DPs. An alternative in both cases is to allow certain appearances of parentheticals inside certain constituents. If I have understood them, this is the view of discontinuous direct speech cases taken by Collins and Branigan (1997: 10–11) for cases like their (iii):

(iii)   "When on earth," asked Harry, "will the fishing begin again?"

To suggest such a 'parenthetical insertion' view is not of course to give a precise account or even a rough conceptualization of it. This is no trivial matter and it is obscure to me what even the basic conditions that allow the kind of positional alternations illustrated by Kathol and Levine are. For me, though, it seems that such insertions are very narrowly limited and, bizarrely, I find that they depend on the fact that the quoted material is English. Thus I see sharp contrasts between, e.g., (iv) and (v):

(iv) a. "I don't give a damn about Bananastan," shouted Felicia in English.
     b. "I don't give a damn," shouted Felicia in English, "about Bananastan."
     c. "I don't give," shouted Felicia in English, "a damn about Bananastan."

(v) a. "Je m'en fous de Bananastan," shouted Felicia in French.
     b. *"Je m'en fous," shouted Felicia in French, "de Bananastan."
     c. *"Je m'en," shouted Felicia in French, "fous de Bananastan."

That is, the possibility of a discontinuous direct speech constituent may depend in part on the possibility of analyzing the latter according to the rules of the NL in which it is quoted.

19. That is, the elided parts of ellipsis constructions and their antecedents that involve direct speech constituents seem to obey the same type of identity conditions as those discussed for standard elided constituents in, e.g., Fiengo and May (1994).

20. Evidently, this view requires recognition of a vast number of distinct NLs, even internal to mutually intelligible speech communities. This consequence is not only harmless but also entirely in line with parallel conclusions based on distinct observations about NLs. So Kayne (2000: 7–8) observes: "My own experience in observing the syntax of English speakers . . . makes me think that it is entirely likely that no two speakers of English have exactly the same syntactic judgements." Based on such an assumption, Kayne then is led to an estimate, with whose bases I agree, that "[e]xtrapolating to the world at large, one would reach the conclusion that the number of syntactically distinct languages/dialects is at least as great as the number of individuals presently alive (i.e., more than 5 billion)." From this point of view, the cardinality of specifiable NLs due to partially distinct lexicons seems unremarkable.

21. See Katz (1981, 1984, 1996, 1998), Katz and Postal (1991), and Langendoen and Postal (1984: chapter 6) for extended arguments for the abstract object character of NLs. The specification that NL sentences are sets is elaborated in Langendoen and Postal (1984: 165–166).

22. The set of marbles is not to be confused with the marbles. For instance, the latter are physical objects, located on the table, but the former is an abstract object and has no space/time location at all.

23. An analogy with the set of presidents of the United States is apt. While one can specify the cardinality of the subset of presidents up to a fixed date, the cardinality of the set itself is at present indeterminate to mere mortals.

24. Specification (50) does not require that the token *denoted* by a use U of an unregimented constituent is distinct from the actual token that is U. Such a specification would make a false claim in a case like the performance of (i):

(i)   I just said 'smekto'.

That is, on one interpretation (i) could be truly uttered by a person whose total lifetime pronunciations of smekto were unitary. It could also be truly uttered by a person at 10:15 who had uttered smekto at 10:10. On the former reading, a distinctness specification would yield a false claim, since the utterance is in an obvious sense self-referential.

The normal communication that a direct speech constituent use U, as in (ii), denotes some token distinct from U itself must be an implicature from various pieces of contextual information:

(ii)   Bob said 'smekto' yesterday.

More specifically, in enunciating (ii) a speaker is referencing a past action; therefore, the token that instantiates a present time use of the unregimented constituent in (ii) must be distinct from the token denoted, given that tokens have time coordinates and that the same token cannot have distinct time coordinates.

25. Quite positively, though, Jackendoff (1984: 36) did avoid being bluffed by a reader's attempt to dismiss his observations:

One reader has remarked that these constructions "lie at the edge of linguistic structure—in my judgment, just at the point where linguistic structure slides off into chaos," and that "one would presumably not want to use them to throw light on the core of linguistic theory." My conclusion, however, is quite the opposite. The only "chaos" in these constructions lies in the appearance of the free expression E, and the judgments seem to me no more delicate or unreliable than those in contemporary discussions of "core" matters such as control.

Jackendoff's rejection of the reader's attempt to justify ignoring the constructions at issue here was evidently correct. The reader provided no argument at all that the facts Jackendoff was discussing were not internal to NL. The illegitimacy of his or her approach to the matter is then clear from the fact that the reader's exact words could otherwise be used to dismiss any set of facts that any theorist found embarrassing. Consider, for example, "the difficulty of determining the facts of, e.g., weak crossover, where linguistic structure slides off into chaos so that one would presumably not want to use them to throw light on the core of linguistic theory, etc."

7. Junk Syntax 1

1. The gap/coindexing notation in (1a, b) and throughout is a descriptive device. It represents no commitment to the linguistic reality of traces or coindexing.

In (1) and hereafter, the notations in (ic, d) indicate the success or failure of indicated anaphoric linkages. In some cases, failure is associated with ungrammaticality; in others, not. Some examples are thus doubly marked.

(i)   Notations:
   a. $*$ = as standard, the indicated expression is *ill formed*.
   b. absence of $*$ = as standard, the indicated expression is *well formed*
   c. $\subset$ = the anaphoric linkage indicated by the cosubscripting is *well formed*
   d. $\not\subset$ = the anaphoric linkage indicated by the cosubscripting is *ill formed*

2. I would like to take this opportunity to (admittedly, very belatedly) make up for unfortunate failures of attribution in Postal (1993b). Three observations of that essay should have referenced May (1985). In particular, the content of example (3b) there, that the weak crossover effect is not found in English restrictive relative clauses, is made in May (1985: 24, ex. [54] and [55]). The content of example (42b) there, that the weak crossover effect is not found in English in the presence of resumptive pronouns, is noted in May (1985: 155, ex. [80]). Finally, the content of example (41) there, the absence of the weak crossover effect in the presence of resumptive pronouns in Hebrew, is noted in May (1985: 156, ex. [83]). I am grateful to Robert May (personal communication, 1993) for pointing out these regrettable oversights.

3. The following indicates that the essence of Principle C is due to George Lakoff:

Lakoff (1976: 301)
(i)   "(166) is . . . an output condition that applies only to anaphoric noun phrases that are not pronouns."
(ii)   Lakoff's (166) was:
Structural Description
$X \cdot NP_i - X - NP_i - X$
1   2   3   4   5

The sentence is unacceptable if: (i) 2 is the antecedent of 4; (ii) 2 commands 4, and (iii) 4 is not a pronoun.

Lakoff's formulation differs from Chomsky's later one chiefly in using command rather than c-command, in appealing to a notion of antecedent, and in being offered as a rule of English rather than a universal.

4. This permits the first of several asides about the *seriousness* of the proposal under discussion. Formulation of a theory that denies that the strong effect is induced by PP extraction a decade after the initial work on the topic was, to put it indulgently, remarkably careless; data that show the contrary are found in the original source and other early work; see (i):

(i)   a. ⊄Who₁ did he₁ claim you were engaged to t₁?
      b. Postal (1971: 157, ex. [30.67b])
          ⊄[To whom₁]₂ did he₁ claim you were engaged t₂?
      c. Lakoff (1976: 278)
          ⊄[Near John₁]₂, he₁ saw a snake t₂.

Just as Koster (1987: 82) remarked about his example, nothing suggests that the anaphoric violation in the non-NP extraction case (ib) differs from the strong effect in the NP case (ia). Moreover, the page on which (ib) appeared contained generalization (ii):

(ii) Postal (1971: 157)
      "[I]n every case crossing restrictions are unaffected by whether or not a preposition travels with its following NP under the operation of either WH-Q movement or WH-Rel movement."

So Chomsky's original Principle C account failed to take seriously the previously known database.
      5. See Chomsky (1981: 197): "[T]hese examples provide *prima facie* evidence that the binding theory applies at S-structure, . . ."
      6. As a second aside, one sees that the original Principle C proposal had in effect been refuted (via the secondary strong effect) before it was made.
      7. Examples like (21) are explicitly rejected in Jacobson (1976: 5).
      8. A revised judgment about (21) is supported by explicit remarks of a number of linguists who cite cases like (21) as well formed:

(i)   Some Writers Who Accept Sentences Similar to (21)
      a. Lasnik and Uriargereka (1988: 157) and Williams (1986: 288)
      b. Kuno (1987: 81) claims that many speakers consider (c) acceptable:
      c. Bill₁ thinks that Mary is in love with Tom, and Jane is . . . ⊂Him₁, he₁ thinks Martha is in love with t₁.
      d. Pollard and Sag (1994: 247) cite e. = their {6.23a}
      e. [Senator Dole]₁ doubted that the party delegates would endorse his wife.
          ⊂But HIM₁ he₁ was sure they would support t₁.
      f. Barss (1986: 275)
(ii) It's him who₁ John₁ said Mary loves t₁ with all her heart.
(iii) Him₁, John₁ said Mary loves t₁ with all her heart.

      9. Works by Chomsky that discuss and make proposals about the strong crossover effect but ignore the Asymmetry Property include Chomsky (1975b: 98–101; 1977a: 194–195; 1977b: 83; 1981:183f, 193f, 278–279; 1982b: 20, 23; 1986b: 78, 109, 182, 207n; 1995b: 71–72).
      10. So, as a third aside about seriousness, over a considerable period Chomsky and followers assumed an account of the strong effect already refuted by unchallenged data prominent in the original work on the phenomenon, data taken in Postal (1971) to require distinguishing extracted antecedents from extracted pronominal forms.
      11. Chomsky's discussion is criticized in Kuno (1987: 61–64). Chomsky's feature D here and its use parallel almost entirely the Doom feature of Postal (1970: 486–493). But the latter is not referenced.
      12. There is another type of case of the strong crossover effect that no Principle C/trace account (nor any other to my knowledge) has ever been shown to properly analyze, illustrated by (ib):

(i)   a. It was [[his₁] mother]₂ that₂ I told him₁ that I had praised.
      b. ⊄It was [His₁] Holiness/Honor/Majesty] that I told him₁ that I had praised.

Despite the superficial similarity between the possessive structures of (ib) and the more standard structure in (ia), only the former manifests a strong effect. Despite its superficial possessive form, a phrase like <u>His Majesty</u> behaves, in terms of a Principle C account of the strong effect, like a referring expression, moreover one with the same index as its initial possessive form DP. My suggestion is that cases like (ib) fall under the discussion of *camouflage* phenomena in Johnson and Postal (1980: 620–621). The analysis there permits an underlying nonpossessor DP to take on the status of a possessor DP of a denotationally empty larger DP. To make such an analysis yield the strong effect, the latter would have to be characterized in such a way as to reference in cases like (ib) the status of the possessor DP independently of the camouflage phenomenon.

13. The resumptive pronoun-linked account of a subset of extractions appealed to in the text here is strongly criticized in the context of a review of Postal (1998) by Levine (2001). While some of Levine's observations are surely valid, I disagree with his overall negative conclusion about the matter. But this is not the place where that disagreement can be discussed.

14. I expand and refine this view in Postal (2001a). As in the remarks of the previous note, Levine (2001) also strongly criticizes the claims about the pronominal properties of nominal P-gaps, as do Levine, Hukari, and Calcagno (2001).

15. I also find the anaphoric linkages in the following examples unexceptionable:

(i)   ⊂Your insulting Bob₁, I never discussed her reaction to with him₁.
(ii) ⊂Which claim that some senator₁ groped some intern₂ did that senator₁/that intern₂ confirm?

16. It is of some historical note that claim (4) does not reference Postal (1971) but rather Wasow (1972), published as Wasow (1979), which adds little or nothing to the database in Postal (1971) apropos of the strong effect. There is in fact, to my knowledge, nothing that would support a conclusion that Chomsky ever consulted Postal (1971).

8. Junk Syntax 2

Thanks to Haj Ross for many useful comments on this chapter.

1. This work's publication was delayed until 1975; see Chomsky (1975a: 2–4) for its history and relation to Chomsky (1957).

2. It is irrelevant here that the categorial analysis was inadequate; data like (i) argue that the naked <u>home</u> of (8b) should be seen as a PP with an invisible P:

(i)   a. Joe came right/straight home/to his office.
      b. Joe visited (*right/*straight) his office.
      c. Joe ran right/straight (to his) home.
      d. Joe discussed (*right/*straight) his home.
      e. (Straight) home/*office came Joe.

3. This is, for instance, visible in remarks like those of (i):

(i)   Chomsky (1973); reprinted in Chomsky (1977a: 88–89)
      "(18) [s [NP I] [VP [V believe] [s [NP the dog] [VP to be hungry]]]]
      Under any formulation of the theory of transformations so far proposed, it would require an extra condition on the transformation to exclude (18) from the domain of the Passive with the structural condition (X, NP, V, NP, Y)."

That is, (i) makes clear that the extra structure represented by the S-labeled bracket in the author's (18) does not block application to the NP.

4. My view is that rather than being *blind* to grammatical relations, passivization is essentially relational, an idea assumed in traditional grammar (see [52]), developed in the relational grammar of the 1970s and 1980s (see Perlmutter, 1984; and Perlmutter and Postal, 1983c, 1984a, 1984b), borrowed into the LFG framework (see Bresnan, 1982c), developed in a modified fashion in Postal (1992, 1996), and expounded in detail in Postal (in preparation a).

5. To make the empty hedge fully effective, it will, of course, be necessary in some cases to recognize homonymous verbs, e.g.:

(i)   a. Mischa wrote a letter.
      b. A letter was written by Mischa.
(ii) a. Mischa wrote a senator.
      b. *A senator was written by Mischa.

To save the "apply blindly" view in this case, one must minimally say that the <u>write</u> of (i) belongs to V_x while the <u>write</u> of (ii) does not.

6. This was seemingly denied in Bresnan (1982a: 358). However, evidence that nominals with <u>by</u> phrases involve passives is not lacking. Note the parallelisms for the 'document' and Array 1 paradigms discussed in section 7:

(i)   a. Karen/That article demonstrated something important.
      b. Something important was demonstrated by Karen/*that article.
      c. Karen's/that article's demonstration of something important
      d. the demonstration of something important by Karen/*that article
(ii) a. Jerome lacks wisdom.
      b. *Wisdom is lacked by Jerome.
      c. Jerome's lack of wisdom
      d. *the lack of wisdom by Jerome

7. None of the discussion of parallels between passivelike structures in nominals and those in clauses notes, still less accounts for, as far as I know, such contrasts as (i) and (ii):

(i)   the editorializing of/by that columnist yesterday
(ii) yesterday's editorializing *of/by that columnist

To the extent that these structures are related to passives, they represent further facts unaccounted for by transformational treatments of that domain.

8. The casual appeals to analogy by an author who for decades has stressed the importance of *restrictiveness*, that is, of a narrowly constrained universal system of NL grammar, represent a striking failure to take seriously the deepest ideas of his own conceptual system. That characteristic can be regarded as itself a strand of junk linguistics. One should, that is, contrast the invocation of undefined notions of analogy and derivative generation with pronouncements like (i):

(i)   Chomsky (1981: 10)
      "Since virtually the origins of contemporary work on generative grammar, a major concern has been to restrict the class of grammars made accessible in principle by UG."

9. Moreover, the appeal to something called recoverability of deletion is significant. As observed in chapter 9 and chapter 12, note 10, this *principle name* is something of a running joke in the sense that year after year it is putatively invoked to explain this or that, although a serious formulation of the principle supposedly named is never undertaken.

10. Notably, of the roughly seventy English passive clauses cited in chapter 2 of that work, almost all are short passives, with only two or three containing <u>by</u> phrases, facilitating ignoring the problems raised by the latter. About them all that is said is (Chomsky 1981: 103):

"[I]f an agent phrase (e.g., *by everyone*) is added, then a θ-role is assigned to its NP by the preposition *by*, and this θ-role is similar to (perhaps identical with) the θ-role assigned to the agent by the VP in the corresponding sentence." See the following note for comments on this talk of assignment, etc.

11. There are several senses in which so-called θ-roles are obscure linguistic concepts. First, although they are usually described as having something to do with semantics, most appeal to them has no more semantic relevance than expressing that the meaning of some DP is an argument of some functor. Second, even this weak connection is abandoned, as noted in Postal and Pullum (1988: 663–664), when Chomsky (1981: 37) invents a θ-role # for the form <u>advantage</u> of the idiom <u>take advantage</u>, which even its inventor noted was an artifice. This move indicates that in the understanding of their introducer into transformational theory they are no more than arbitrary syntactic elements that hide behind traditional quasisemantic names like 'agent'.

Even more serious than any of this is the fact that the formal structures represented by θ-roles were essentially unspecified in Chomsky (1981) and mostly remain so. So one observes that the standard terminology of "A assigns a θ-role to B" is *relational*; but how this relation is to be formally marked, what an input structure to such assignment looks like, and how the output differs are questions with no received answers. The whole question of how θ-roles formally integrate with phrase structure, etc., has been mostly left open.

It would be reasonable, in my opinion, to view the posit of θ-roles in Chomsky (1981) as the recognition of the need for *primitive grammatical relations*, which relational grammar work had then been arguing for a half-dozen years. The failure to make this character explicit could thereby be explicated by the notable fact, then a clear instance of junk linguistic deception, that Chomsky (1981: 10) specifically *rejects* the notion of primitive grammatical relations; see some further discussion of the connection between this and the θ-role # in chapter 9.

It is notable that a work like Baker (1988b), which attempts to exploit notions of θ-role, provides six nonstandard diagrams. Each is an otherwise standard tree structure annotated with arrows between labeled nodes, these arrows sometimes labeled with θ and pointing at nodes labeled with common names for putative θ-roles like ben, instr, etc. Such diagrams seem to make explicit a view that needs to appeal to a formal notion of arc, as in relational frameworks like that of chapter 1, section 9, but formally has no place for them.

It would also, I believe, be justified to take talk of 'case assignment' in the same framework also to be a hidden introduction of a distinct set of primitive grammatical relations. And again the questions of formal integration are mostly unanswered or even unasked.

12. Cases like (57) seem to me to counterexemplify Roberts's (1986: 28) claim that "the *by*-phrase *must* receive a θ-role." Even if, unlike me, one believes there are things like θ-roles, it would be a heavy burden indeed to justify claiming that *the lovebug* has one. This assumes, of course, that talk of phrases having θ-roles involves testable semantic claims and is hence more than a mere arbitrary syntactic marking, as with the # of note 11. If, as for the latter, there is no independent test for the existence of putative θ-roles, claims about phrases "having to" receive them are rendered essentially contentless.

13. The <u>lovebug</u>, etc., cases are entirely consistent with arc-based approaches to passive as described in chapter 1 and references cited there. For in these, passive <u>by</u> phrase DPs can be treated as demoted subjects. Moreover, what I believe is the core of truth in the "no downgrading" argument for abandoning subject postposing in transformational terms can be captured in arc terms without abandoning the view of passive <u>by</u> phrase objects as demoted subjects.

14. To avoid this conclusion, a defender of the position of Chomsky (1981) might stress the *restricted number* of cases like (57), (60), (61b), (63b), and (64), to talk of exceptions,

marginality, special cases, etc.. There are two rebuttals. First, given Marantz's observation that idiomatic subjects that occur with unfixed objects are very rare, there is only a tiny space of possibilities within which the claim of nonpassivizability in such cases can be tested. From that point of view, the five cases cited here where they *do* passivize is not really so few. Second, and far more important, as a matter of logic, principles that entail P are falsified by even a *single* bona fide instance of not-P. In this case, a view that fails to link the syntax of active subjects and passive by phrases claims that there should be *no* semantically unspecifiable links between such pairs, not merely few. But (57), (60), (61b), (63b), and (64) show that there are, arguing for a syntactic connection between active subject/passive by phrase object.

15. Extensive discussions of reanalysis are found in Riemsdijk (1976) and Stowell (1981); see also: Baker (1988a: 259–263), Hoekstra (1984: 134–135), Hornstein and Weinberg (1981), Radford (1981: 347–348), and Riemsdijk and Williams (1986: 148–149).

16. A lovely instance of this was discussed in Jackendoff (1977: 86). He noted that there are two uses of the verb approve, one that takes a direct object, the other a PP in of:

(i)   Mildred approved the plan.
(ii) Mildred approved of the plan.

The uses differ in meaning: That in (i) refers to an action by someone with authority; that in (ii) refers to a subjective evaluation. Jackendoff's key observation was that while both uses have nominalizations of the form (iii), only the direct object use has one of the form (iv):

(iii) the approval of the plan by Mildred
(iv)   the plan's approval by Mildred

Jackendoff's generalization was that only a DP that was a direct object in the clausal correspondent could have a form like (iv). Again then reanalysis gets it wrong, since in that view, (v) requires a reanalysis treatment, rendering the DP a direct object in both cases; thus the basis of the distinction Jackendoff noted is lost:

(v)   The plan was approved of by Mildred.

Hoekstra (1984: 134–135) argues that the failure of reanalysis in nominals is not an argument against a generalized rule of passivization operative in both clauses and nominals because, in some way associated with the markedness of reanalysis, it is limited to clausal categories. To give this argument any chance of viability, though, it must be denied that there is a systematic relation between nominalizations and the verbal structures they relate to; that is, the latter must not "feed" the former.

While I will not argue against this view here, it seems to face serious difficulties given that, e.g., derivational elements like *re-* seem to manifest in nominalizations only if they manifest in the corresponding verbal forms:

(v)   a. Alice (re)occupied/visited the family ranch.
      b. Alice's (re)occupation/visiting of the family ranch
(vi) a. Alice (*re)abandoned/(*re)left the family ranch.
      b. Alice's (*re)abandonment/(*re)leaving of the family ranch

Note that even if the nominalization case is erased from (70), the case against reanalysis is formidable.

17. By independent constraints I am alluding in particular to principles like the 1 Advancement Exclusiveness Law of Perlmutter and Postal (1984a); see also Baker (1988a: chapter 6), Baker, Johnson, and Roberts (1989), Farrell (1993, 1994), and Marantz (1984).

18. Postal (1986a and 1996) present arc-based accounts of English pseudopassives entirely independent of reanalysis. Notable about the latter work is its claim that English

pseudopassives are structurally parallel in significant ways to French examples like (ib), claimed to stand in roughly a passive relation to actives like (ia) (with the main verb *se faire* having a function analogous to the auxiliary *be* of English verbal passives):

(i)   a. Lucille s'est moquée d'André.
      Lucille self is mocked of Andre = "Lucille made fun of Andre"
      b. André s'est fait moquer de *lui* par Lucille.
      "Andre got made fun of by Lucille"

The crucial point is that the highlighted form in (ib) *is a resumptive pronoun*. This supports the view of Postal (1986a, 1996) that English pseudopassives are also resumptive pronoun structures, with their stranded Ps arising from a requirement absent in the French cases that those pronouns be null.

   19. Significant additional problems with reanalysis treatments of passivization touched on in Baltin and Postal (1996: 139–141, note 12) involve complement clauses. There are contrasts like the following:

(i)   That every student will turn in a superb paper cannot be counted on (with much confidence).
(ii) *One cannot count on (with much confidence) that every student will turn in a superb paper.
(iii) It cannot be counted on (with much confidence) that every student will turn in a superb paper.

Reanalysis approaches claim that the pseudopassive (i) can exist only because some mapping has turned <u>counted on</u> into a single verb, so that passivization does not involve a PP. But (ii) seems like a standard case of a barred <u>that</u> clause object of a preposition. So an unexplained fact is why reanalysis fails to save it via a putative structure that includes (iv):

(iv) [$_V$ count on] (with much confidence) [$_{CP}$ that every student will turn in a superb paper]

Moreover, it is generally claimed in transformational terms that the difference between (i) and (iii), like that between (v) and (vi), involves the fact that CPs, not requiring case, need not move to subject position in passives, so that in (iii) and (vi) putatively nothing would have preposed:

(v)   That every student will turn in a superb paper cannot be proved.
(vi) It cannot be proved that every student will turn in a superb paper.

See, e.g., Chomsky (1981: 125) and Lasnik and Uriagereka (1988: 19). But this view leaves it equally mysterious why (ii) and (iii) contrast, since it must be allowed that <u>count</u> (<u>on</u>) subcategorizes for a CP, which then cannot occur in the reanalysis environment.

   20. Bach (1980) provides a large number of problems for accounts of English passivization, arguing *against* a transformational approach. Seuren (1996: 132) lists fourteen nonpassivizable cases. Responding to the question he poses as to why the relevant cases have no passives, he says: "There is no known answer to these questions, and no attempt is made here to find one. This area of syntax and semantics is still relatively obscure."

   21. Baker, Johnson, and Roberts (1989: 221) and Marantz (1984: 129) cite (i) as a grammatical passive, which would counterexemplify the claim about (129e):

(i) The house is surrounded by trees.

However, while (i) is grammatical, there are strong reasons to doubt it is a passive. The predicate expression can be taken as an adjectival one, supported by the fact that it occurs with the adjectival prefix <u>un</u>:

(ii)   The house still remains unsurrounded by trees.

That is, (i) should, I suggest, be distinguished from the genuine passive:

(iii)   The house was deliberately (*un)surrounded by the police.

A clear difference is the possibility of the verbal prefix re:

(iv)   a. The house was (*re)surrounded by trees. (The long version is grammatical only on
        a personification reading.)
        b. The house was (re)surrounded by the police.

(iva) is like an uncontroversial adjectival case:

(v)   The relocated house was (*re)adjacent to/(*re)far from the nearest highway.

My suspicion is that the relation in (vi) is an irregular variant of the one in (vii):

(vi)   a. Trees surrounded the house.
        b. The house was surrounded by trees.
(vii)   a. Water covered the floor.
        b. The floor was covered/remains uncovered with/*by water

22. Farrell (1993, 1994) discusses a number of similar cases, providing a relational treatment of the related paradigms. However, nothing in his approach explicates, I believe, the
correlations between passive and Q construction constraints.

23. Although occasionally one finds cited a grammatical instance of a passivized non-WH
infinitive, as in (i), in general, passivization of such infinitives is impossible, as in (ii) and (iii):

(i)   Rosenbaum (1967: 14)
        To remain silent was preferred by everyone.
(ii)   a. Rosenbaum (1967: 14)
           *To play with his little brother often was tended by John.
        b. The doctor hoped/prepared/tried to reduce the patient's discomfort.
        c. *To reduce the patient's discomfort was hoped/prepared/tried by the doctor.
(iii)   a. The doctor arranged for the nurse to stay with the patient.
        b. *For the nurse to stay with the patient was arranged (for) by the nurse.

But WH infinitives passivize productively:

(iv)   a. How to read minds was discovered by Dr. Zaslofsky.
        b. When to eat with a fork was not totally grasped by Willie.
        c. Where to buy peanut butter sushi was being looked into by Hilda.

In usual terms, this would seem to motivate treating WH infinitives but not simple ones as
DPs. How this might be done while recognizing a CP structure with a locus for the WH form
is a topic that seems to be little discussed.

24. Although noting their general ungrammaticality, Adger and Quer (2001: 114) cite
some cases of if clause subjects as grammatical, e.g.:

(i)   If he is guilty can be shown by our evidence.
(ii)   If a vaccine is synthesizable is usually discovered a few years after the outbreak of the
        disease.

But I find these to be badly ill formed.

25. Example (163d) has, of course, an irrelevant reading on which the without constituent contains no parasitic gap.

26. Example (165q) doesn't sound so bad, but that may be due to the fact that in a case where the antecedent of it is, e.g., a regular DP, the example is fine:

(i)   Myron heard that but I didn't hear it.

27. Even given the limits of our understanding of passive structures, there is no reason to believe this lack is inherent in the situation. For instance, Fiengo and May (1994) manage a careful, detailed, and rigorous approach to verb phrase ellipsis with rich factual coverage and citation of previous work and results. There is no reason that serious linguistics could not have produced the same for passives.

9. Junk Ethics 1

I would like to thank Geoffrey K. Pullum and James D. McCawley for many suggestions that have greatly improved this chapter.

1. The prediction here, made in 1988, turned out to be quite accurate. As shown in chapter 12, note 10, the same move was instantiated in 1995.

10. Junk Refereeing

1. By "successful" I mean that it succeeded in its goal of preventing funding of the proposal.
2. Since I tout in these essays the virtue of skepticism, to avoid any suspicion that I am leaving out or distorting parts of the referee report that would undermine these criticisms, I present the report in full. As NFS proposals are public documents, it should be possible for those who move beyond skepticism to real suspicion to obtain a copy of the original from the NSF.

SBR = 9808169

Paul M. Postal "Diversity among English Objects"

Overall Rating: Poor

The intellectual merits of this proposal lie in the fact that it may bring to light new facts about English objects, and may uncover new generalizations about distributions in the data.

In my opinion, the broader impact of this work will be negligible, simply because the whole approach is founded upon assumptions that have not been current in the field for some time now. The whole domain of the data presented here is now considered by 99% of researchers in the field to involve complex relations between (at least) (i) phrase structure configurations (possibly of a quite ornate type), (ii) argument structure configurations and properties (highest/lowest argument, particular thematic relations), and (iii) more detailed semantic properties. This observation about theoretical assumptions should not be taken as mere trendiness; far from it, for the general consensus concerning (i–iii) has not been arrived at by accident, but rather through 30 years of looking at semantics-syntax interactions, and it is in some clear sense "correct." Additionally, I think this whole body of work has shown a greater depth of insight and explanation than could ever follow from the highly one-dimensional notation-crunching approach presented here. Consequently, the various generalizations that are presented in this proposal, such as (70), (73), (76), (88), (92), strike me as completely uninformative and totally lacking in any insight—

they are merely mechanical descriptions. The one putative "argument" in the present proposal for the irrelevance of thematic relations is extremely unconvincing.

In terms of the assumptions that the author makes that strike me as out of touch with current practice, it is stated that GRs are given in terms of phrase structure representations by such statements as "subject is specifier of " and "object is comple-ment of V." With regard to objects, the focus of this proposal, the latter statement hardly seems to touch on the wide range of object properties that have been de-scribed in the late GB and Minimalist literature, where various structural relations to abstract components of an overt verb-form during the course of a complex deri-vation have been considered.

Similarly, lexical alternations are considered in the 1982 LFG mode of rules, rather than the underspecification/Lexical Mapping Theory approach which has been current for around 10 years now, in which rules are replaced by underspecification regarding the surface expression of arguments, and where direct connections to thematic properties are part of the explanatory vocabulary.

3. It is of course not in the slightest relevant here to specify the content of the generali-zations contained in the proposal. The goal here is not to defend the proposal. Nonetheless, just so the reader is not left floating totally in the dark, two of the informal generalizations were the following:

(i)   Get passives are only possible for 2s.
(ii)   Only the heads of 2s incorporate.

Principle (i) was intended to distinguish, e.g., (iva, b, c), given the undifferentiated (iiia, b, c), while principle (ii) was intended to differentiate, e.g., (via, b) given the undifferentiated (va, b):

(iii)   a. The servant was sent to her accidentally.
        b. She was sent it accidentally.
        c. It was sent her accidentally.
(iv)   a. The servant got sent to her accidentally.
        b. *She got sent it accidentally.
        c. *It got sent her accidentally.
(v)   a. That machine answered my question.
        b. Those remarks answered my question.
(vi)   a. question-answering machines
        b. *question-answering remarks

11. Junk Ethics 2

I am indebted to Barbara Partee and Christopher Potts for criticisms of an earlier version of this chapter. The usual exonerations hold.

1. See Katz (1981, 1984, 1996, 1998), Katz and Postal (1991), and Langendoen and Postal (1984).

2. So, a few lines in Chomsky (1986b: 33–36, 49–50) *purport* to reply to the argument of Katz (1981). However, as argued in great detail in Katz and Postal (1991), a work never answered by Chomsky, this "reply" is mostly bluff and the core of the position has never really been addressed by the author.

3. See, e.g., Pollard and Sag (1994: 4), who specify: ". . . and therefore HPSG shares the property of 'non-derivationality' with CG, GPSG, APG, and LFG, in contradistinction to GB and its derivational kin."

4. See Langendoen and Postal (1984, 1985).

5. Independently of questions of responsibility, it would not be entirely trivial to find a *worse* account of the ontology of sentences than one that analogizes sentences to mental images. Specifically:

(i)   Sentences are objective; images are subjective. You may have an image at time t, I may not at time t or ever. But a sentence like, e.g., "Sentences are not like images" adheres to no one.

(ii) Images enter into causal relations (e.g., are caused); but sentences are neither caused nor cause.

(iii) Images have temporal boundaries; they begin at time t and end at time t + n. Sentences have neither temporal beginnings nor conclusions.

(iv) Insofar as images are physical, they are bounded in space. Thus if X has an image IM and a large bomb goes off next to X, IM ceases to exist. But nothing can destroy a sentence.

(v)   There are infinitely many sentences, but the number of images in any mind/brain over a life span is finite.

6. The possibility that the author would deny the reality of sentences was in effect foreseen in Langendoen and Postal (1984: 128).

7. Chomsky's (1999: 2) account recognizes infinitude obliquely via its talk of a 'recursive system'. The quality of the discussion of infinity in Chomsky (2000c: 4) is revealed by the fact that it discursively treats the topic in just the sort of baby talk terms ("and that they go on forever") that Partee, ter Meulen, and Wall (1993: 55) warn students against: "A definition employing the terms 'never ending' . . . would be defective, since these expressions are themselves no clearer than the term 'infinite' that is to be explicated."

8. Work by the author published after the bulk of this chapter was written brings out still more clearly a lack of a minimally coherent view of the nature of sentences. So Chomsky (2000a: 18) asserts: "Take any sentence you like, . . . 'John had a book stolen.' Take that sentence in English. It has lots of empirical properties, including certain very curious multiple ambiguities, which are not matched in similar languages." So here, with no reference to the 1999 pasage under discussion in this chapter, which claims sentences *have no reality*, the author takes sentences to have empirical properties. But clearly, things with empirical properties must exist.

Further, in Chomsky (2002: 48) one is told, again with no cross-referencing to work like Chomsky 1999:

Each internal language has the means to construct the mental objects that we use to express our thoughts and to interpret the limitless array of overt expressions that we encounter. Each of these mental objects relates sound and meaning in a particular structured form. A clear understanding of how a finite mechanism can construct an infinity of objects of this kind was reached only in the twentieth century.

Here evidently sentences are taken to be real mental objects, again inconsistent with the 1999 assertion that they are not real. And the position is, moreover, glaringly internally inconsistent, since there is somehow supposed to be an infinite number of mental objects, whereas minds, viewed in the author's terms, as biological objects, are finite. The fact that such contradictions were pointed out in, e.g., Katz and Postal (1991) and Langendoen and Postal (1984), works not mentioned by Chomsky, reveals in another way the sort of irresponsibility at issue in this chapter. What could better illustrate junk linguistics then the repetition of contradictions years after these had been pointed out in works the repetitions do not mention?

9. So, one finds Chomsky (1995b: 226–227): ". . . any more than proof theory is concerned with a sequence of lines that does not satisfy the formal conditions that define 'proof'."

10. The identification of a grammar with a brain state is a crude category mistake, equivalent to identifying, e.g., Microsoft Word with the state of some computer in which it is installed. Again, the brain state or computer state is destructible, but a grammar and Microsoft Word are sets, abstract objects, beyond space, time, and causation. See Langendoen and Postal (1984: 147–148).

11. Actually, it is incoherent to object on ontological grounds to the reality of sentences and NLs as collections of sentences and yet accept the reality of PA. All of the properties of note 5 (i)–(v) characteristic of sentences are equally characteristic of logical axioms. This should not be obscured by a confusion between axioms and some physical representation of them.

12. Claims that numbers are not real should be juxtaposed with the most appropriate remark of Boolos (1998: 129): "To maintain that there aren't any numbers at all because numbers are abstract and not physical objects seems like a demented way to show respect for physics, which everyone of course admires. But it is nuts to think Wiles could have spared himself all those years of toil if only he had realized that since there are no numbers at all, there are no natural numbers x, y, z, n > 2." "Wiles" here refers to the British mathematician Andrew Wiles, who in 1994, after years of work on the problem, completed a proof of Fermat's Last Theorem, which mathematicians had been seeking for some three hundred and fifty years.

13. Talk of journals reminds us that *refereeing* plays a large role in real science: In their study of fraud and deceit in science, Broad and Wade (1982: 17) note:

> He [a scientist: PMP] must publish the results of his research in a scientific journal, but before publication his article is sent out by the journal editor to scientific reviewers, known as referees. The referees advise the editor as to whether the work is new, whether it properly acknowledges the other researchers on whose results it depends, and most importantly, whether the right methods have been used in conducting the experiment and the right arguments in discussing the results.

Combining this central role of refereeing in (physical) science with Chomsky's (1999) repeated claim that his linguistics is biological physical science, one would expect to find that scientific refereeing of his work had played a major role. But while I have not studied this question in detail, it seems that appearance of the author's work in refereed journals has been marginal in his overall career and that in more recent decades it has been almost nonexistent. For instance, although the author began speaking of his 'minimalist program' early in the last decade, I am aware of no work published by him on this topic in a refereed journal. Essentially none is cited in Chomsky (1999, 2000a, 2000c, 2002).

14. It is ironic to compare the toxic irrationality of the material criticized here with Smith's (1999: 181) highlighting of Chomsky's *supposed* relation to rationality:

> [S]o what is surprising is that many scholars systematically reject or ignore standard canons of rationality. There are at least three different categories. First, there is the uninteresting class of those who simply substitute emotional rhetoric for argument: many of Chomsky's detractors fall into this category. Second, there are those who assert contradictions, and are hence technically irrational, but who do so for reasons of propaganda, and rely on the reader's gullibility or prejudice to escape detection. This is the category of those "drowning in their own hypocrisy" that Chomsky has concentrated on most, and who will be discussed below.

Since instantiations of these two categories of "ignoring standard canons of rationality" have both been richly illustrated in the text and are in other chapters as well, Smith is arguably looking for hypocrisy in partly the wrong places.

15. This entry is submitted for judgment independently of questions of the degree of influence of the writer whose passage is criticized. But of course, the degree of educational and scholarly irresponsibility in publishing proposals must in part be assessed by the degree of influence of the writer, which is a partial measure of the potential harm of the documented irresponsibility. And the exceptional influence of the author is well known. So Smith in his laudatory introduction to Chomsky (2000a: vi) states: "[A]nd he has dominated the field of linguistics ever since." Given that, the irresponsibility documented here is magnified to an extent that would be hard to exaggerate.

12. Junk Reasoning 1

1. It seems correct to take <u>automatic</u> in (211) as elliptical for <u>an automatic consequence</u>.

2. While I would like to be able to claim I have never utilized <u>follows automatically</u>, etc., (2c), alas, already shows I have, and I suspect this is not the only instance. However, I hope I have not used it in at least several decades.

3. One possible exception, relevant at most to (2d), is that the use of <u>automatic(ally)</u> in linguistics might be linked to the technological meaning via the assumption that grammars are a variety of automata. I disregard this possibility in this essay, although it bears looking into.

4. Lakoff (1986) rejects the existence of a syntactic constraint properly reconstructed as the Coordinate Structure Constraint. His arguments are analyzed and rejected in Postal (1998: chapter 3).

5. See Pullum (1989) for documentation and Chomsky (1990) for a not very responsive response.

6. Postal (1982) analyzes in detail a claim of Chomsky and Lasnik (1977) that some substantive generalization follows from something called *trace theory*, which would instantiate the variable V in the text. The results more than justify the skepticism expressed here.

7. These remarks about the claimed consequences in (6) are highly skeptical of course, but that is appropriate in what were announced to be skeptical essays. Moreover, anyone skeptical of *my* claims here could easily show they are false merely by (and only by) providing the demonstrations I have claimed cannot be provided.

8. With respect to the overall implication of this section of this volume that much in today's linguistics is junk linguistics, it is appropriate to ask how many other fields there are where one could document pages being taken up not with establishing actual logical connections but with expressions of mere hope about connections that hold under some imagined sets of circumstances

9. The debasement of language represented by the dream usage internal to a putative science is hardly the only one of the relevant terms that can be found. Consider:

(i)   Chomsky (2000b: 103)
       "Property (5a) follows in part from the θ-theoretic principle (6), which is implicit in the conception of θ-roles as a relation between two syntactic objects, a configuration and an expression selected by its head."

Here the critical notion is "B follows in part from A." Surely <u>in part</u> is here a hedge, but one so vague and unexplicated that it is impossible to determine whether (iia or b) or something else is intended:

(ii)   a. Property (5a) is a logical consequence of a set of principles that include principle (6) and a non-null set of others not mentioned here.
       b. Some but not all cases where (5a) holds are consequences of principle (6).

380 NOTES TO PAGES 313-314

Clear under either radically distinct interpretation is that, despite the logiclike usages of follows from and principle, no logical consequence relation (is even claimed to) exist between principle (6) and property (5a). That is, no one would be led to use follows in part as in (i) unless the actual situation were as follows:

(iii)   Property (5) has not been shown to be a logical consequence of principle (6).

10. Dream usages in linguistics are not limited to the expressions of (1). Consider:

(i)   Chomsky and Lasnik (1995: 65)
      "A strong form of *recoverability of deletion* would presumably prevent the deletion of an element with φ-features."

Claim (i) is properly characterized as dreaming because it references consequences of a principle not actually formulated. Notable is that the highlighted *principle name* invoked in (i) figured in my 1988 parody reprinted here as chapter 9, where it instantiated one of the explicit targets of ridicule. So it was there observed (chapter 9, page 288) that the same principle name invoked with no formulation of a principle by Chomsky and Lasnik (1977) to account for a fact was equally invoked by other linguists nine years later, again with no formulation. And I quoted in (ii) Chomsky and Lasnik (1977: 446–447).

(ii)   We assume that this possibility is excluded by the recoverability principle for deletion. Exactly how to formulate this principle is a nontrivial question, but there is little doubt that such a principle is required.

And I then noted: "Thus Riemsdijk and Williams (1986, p. 103) appeal to the same phantom recoverability principle as Chomsky and Lasnik (1977)" and quoted the former authors:

(iii)   The principle for recoverability that would allow this deletion remains to be given, but it is plausible to assume . . . [plausible assumption omitted].

I then concluded: "Nine years have elapsed, and the phantom principle remains unformulated. I see no reason why the situation will be different nine years from now, or ever." (i) justifies the latter conclusion as one sees that seven years later (hence eighteen years after the initial reverie), the dream usage of *recoverability* is yet again invoked by these authors.

11. Whatever success this form of discourse achieves depends of course on a highly indulgent audience. Merely submitting dreams to putative scientific outlets in linguistics can only lead to publication with the cooperation of the editorial authorities. The prevalence of such publication and the lack of discernible outcry about it thus suggest that indulgent audiences and cooperative editors are not lacking.

12. Recall the remark of Freidin (1978: 539) mentioned in the introduction and already discussed in chapter 9: "By taking (54a–e) as axioms of the theory of grammar, we derive the empirical effects of the strict cycle as a theorem." This "derive as a theorem" claim, which seems stronger than the dream usage and at least as strong as the intentions of follows automatically, was then followed by an explicit admission that no proof was extant, accompanied by doubts that any was possible. This usage does not fit the dream pattern since the author was seemingly perfectly cognizant of, and up-front about, the *lack* of logical consequence. Perhaps involved here was a simple lack of understanding of the equivalence between "theorem of axioms A_1 . . . A_n" and "conclusion of a valid proof from A_1 . . . A_n." The remaining mystery is what the author thought "deriving X as a theorem from axioms" *does* mean. About that I have no clue.

13. But Christopher Potts has made a small start. Surprisingly (to me), he informs me (personal communication, April 30, 2002) that via Internet searches he has found usages of "follows automatically" outside of linguistics, in other academic disciplines. He offers data like the following:

(i)   From a page titled "The Abstract Group Concept":
      "As for permutations the associative law follows automatically for operators."
      http://www-groups.dcs.st-and.ac.uk/~history/HistTopics/Abstract_groups.html
(ii) From a page titled "Re: Quaternionic C*-Algebras":
      "This equation follows automatically from the abstract nonsense given above—we don't
      need to put it in by hand."
(iii) From a page titled "Relation Expansion":
      "Sometimes the congruence property follows automatically because the relation and
      (constructor and selector) signatures involved are the default choices."
      http://www.cs.ucsd.edu/groups/tatami/handdemos/doc/rexp.htm
(iv) From a tutorial on basic logic:
      "A strong (or sound) argument is one in which (1) the premises of that argument are
      true and (2) the conclusion follows automatically from its premises."
      http://www.molloy.edu/academic/philosophy/sophia/reading/evaluation.htm

These occurrences seem to me to have unpleasant implications for the fields in which they
occur, but I will have to leave it to those who work in these fields to worry about it.

   14. In this respect, <u>virtually</u> is like <u>almost</u>/<u>practically</u>. So all of (i) seems to determine
the negative (ii):

(i)   Andre is almost/practically/virtually penniless.
(ii) Andre is not penniless.

In ordinary discourse, these forms have perfectly *reasonable* uses, specifically when the predicate they modify denotes something evaluable on a scale. So consider:

(iii) This (football game) is virtually over.

Such a remark is reasonable and contentfully interpretable if said, e.g., with twenty seconds
remaining and a score of 56–3. The reason is that <u>over</u> said of games (and, e.g., elections) has
an ambiguity. On one reading, where <u>virtual</u> in (iii) would *not* be appropriate when used as
described, a game is over when the rules that define it specify that it has come to completion.
In football, this is when and only when the fixed time period (sixty minutes in professional
games) has elapsed. In this sense, a game cannot sensibly be said to be "virtually over," since
it either is or isn't. But on a second sense, a game is over when the conditions (the score) are
such that no matter what the team/player in the inferior position is assumed to do, it/(s)he
cannot alter the relative status. That is, on the second reading, <u>over</u> means something like
"the outcome is determined." It is reasonable to hedge this because such determinations, unlike those that involve the technical definition of completion, concern scalar inference and
judgment. So, as one gradually decreases the gap (here 53) and increases the remaining time,
it becomes less and less reasonable to say the game is "virtually over."

   The reader will note that the reasonableness of utilizing <u>virtual</u> with predicates evaluated on a scale offers no rationalization whatever for uses of this term in linguistics like
those in (19).

   15. Beyond the remarks of note 14, one can imagine at least one sort of context in which
one might reasonably say, "It virtually follows from A that B," namely, one in which one
then immediately concludes that one must, to establish a logical connection, also assume C,
thereby going on to assert: "It follows from A and C that B." The uses of <u>virtually</u> being
quarreled with here do not occur in such contexts.

   16. Of course, it would *not* be an absurdity if one could adopt the exceptionally clueless
view of mathematical truth of Smith (1999: 148) that "mathematical systems have no properties of their own, except those we stipulate." For (22a) is as good a stipulation as any, Smith

not even having required, e.g., any notion of consistency for his stipulations. One must wonder then whether Smith believes something analogous about logic. Since he holds that, e.g., the property that every number is smaller than its successor is at best just a stipulation one could (therefore) suspend, is, e.g., logical consistency, too, for him just an arbitrary stipulation? Is the property of inference embodied in the rule of Modus Ponens also a mere stipulation? In fact, it is hard to see how Smith's view could permit any defense of the idea that truth in logic is more than stipulation. If Smith sees a fundamental break between truth in mathematics (mere stipulation) and truth in logic, how would he account for the extensively successful attempt of Whitehead and Russell to reduce talk of mathematics to talk about logic (so that Quine [1953: 80] could say: "In Whitehead and Russell's *Principia Mathematica* we have good evidence that all mathematics is translatable into logic")?

One cannot help but wonder, too, how Smith accounts to himself for the fact that mathematicians sometimes devote their whole careers to solving certain problems, acting as if there were some truth there. Why don't they, to save time, simply stipulate whatever answer they like or whatever answer someone will pay them for and then do something real? And what could be the difference in Smith's terms between a proven mathematical result and an open question, e.g., Goldbach's Conjecture (that every even natural number is the sum of two primes)? Since there is no truth beyond what is stipulated, everyone is free to make it come out however they want. Smith (1999) expresses other clueless ideas about mathematics, such as (p. 231) that a nondenumerably infinite set is one that can be put in one-to-one correspondence with the collection of real numbers. This claims, contrary to all of modern set theory, that there are only two sizes for infinite sets and, specifically contrary to Cantor's Theorem (see note 3 of chapter 6), that there are sets S whose power sets are not greater in size than S.

17. I have as yet encountered no usage of the form "B automatically virtually follows from $A_1 \ldots A_n$." I suppose that, given what has been said, this would have to mean that B is not an actual logical consequence of the premises. And this not being the sort of thing linguists want to say about their own favored ideas, there is no motivation for its occurrence.

Other logically possible but so far unattested combinations of various hedges and modifiers discussed in preceding text are listed in (i):

(i)   a. B automatically follows in part from $A_1 \ldots A_n$.
       b. B virtually follows in part from $A_1 \ldots A_n$.
       c. B automatically virtually follows in part from $A_1 \ldots A_n$.
       d. B follows virtually automatically in part from $A_1 \ldots A_n$.

Only someone with stronger masochistic tendencies than mine would want to inquire seriously into their truth conditions.

13. Junk Reasoning 2

Comments from Robert D. Borsley have led to significant improvements in earlier versions of this chapter.

1. In an earlier, more religious historical context, one might have said, with no less basis or content and probably similar hoped for opposition-numbing effect, that "It is God's will that P holds."

2. The issue of choice between proof-theoretic and model-theoretic approaches to grammar is clouded by inadequate accounts of the history of ideas. Consider:

(i)   Chomsky (1995b: 162)
       "I [Chomsky: PMP] have *always* understood a generative grammar to be *nothing more* [both emphases mine: PMP] than an explicit grammar."

This is easily seen, though, to be an extreme falsehood; it clearly contradicts both (1c) of chapter 6, repeated in (ii), and (iii):

(ii) Chomsky (1959: 138)
      "The weakest condition that can significantly be placed on grammars is that F be included in the class of general, unrestricted Turing machines."
(iii) Chomsky (1957: 13)
      "The grammar of L will thus be a device that generates all of the grammatical sequences of L and none of the ungrammatical ones."

Both these quoted assertions from the 1950s are evidently (grotesquely) incompatible with claim (i). A model-theoretic grammar is not a Turing machine at all and thus cannot be included in the class of such. Moreover, such a grammar does not generate anything in the technical sense, since there is no requirement that the collection it specifies be a recursively enumerable set or even a set; see Langendoen and Postal (1984, 1985).

Claim (i) appears in a footnote, where it functions as part of a distorted reply to the correct remarks of McCawley (1988), who concluded that Chomsky's (1986b) position represented, as Chomsky (1995b: 162) quoted: "a sharp change in my [Chomsky's: PMP] usage that gives the enterprise an entirely different cast from that of the 1960s, when the task was taken to be 'specifying the membership of a set of sentences that is identified with a language.'" As (iii) shows, despite the denials, McCawley's claim was grounded in historical reality. Chomsky (1995b: 162–163) then went on to claim: "But the characterization he gives does not imply that 'generative' means anything more than 'explicit'; there is, furthermore, no change in usage or conception, at least for me, in this regard." But quotes (ii) and (iii) show the falsity of the claim that 'generative' was intended to denote only "explicit," which would have been historically bizarre given that it was a technical notion from logic and one that has rich content far beyond any appeal to "explicitness." Thus Chomsky (1965: 9) specified: "The term 'generate' is familiar in the sense intended here in logic, particularly in Post's theory of combinatorial systems." And any technical specification of 'generative' reveals the same point. So Partee, ter Meulen, and Wall (1993: 435) specify: "A formal grammar (or simply grammar) is essentially a deductive system of axioms and rules of inference (see Chapter 8), which generates the sentences of a language as its theorems." Like any such account, this clearly brings out the specific proof-theoretic character of generative grammars, which are built out of the analogs of logical rules of inference, not out of statements, like model-theoretic grammars. But either type could be explicit.

3. The same concepts of conceptual necessity appealed to by Aoun, Choueiri, and Hornstein (2001) are found in Hornstein (2001: 211–212), with, however, no additional tenable support.

4. According to the view being criticized, an operation, Merge, is virtually conceptually necessary. And it is part of a putative overall computational system, that is, one that, by definition, characterizes a recursively enumerable set of objects. Given the latter, if, contrary to fact, the existence of phrasal combinations of words over an infinite range really rendered Merge conceptually necessary, this would have important consequences for *mathematics*.

For it is of course well known, as touched on in chapter 6, that any recursively enumerable set can be coded as a set of numbers via the device of gödel numbering. Therefore, the output of the computational procedure claimed to be the heart of the minimalist notion of grammar can be regarded as a recursively enumerable set of numbers. If it were true that specification of such a set entailed the existence of an operation (e.g., Merge), it would follow that *number theory* requires analogous operations to, e.g., specify the collection of natural numbers, normally specified via Peano's axioms. But of course number theory invokes no analog of Merge at all. Is this basic mathematical theory, developed over millennia by multitudes of history's finest mathematicians, thereby inadequate? The absurdity of such a consequence gives some measure of the lack of seriousness of the claim of Merge's conceptual necessity.

5. Arguably, the idea that a collection of trees can be specified without generative mechanisms goes back to McCawley's (1968) (reprinted in McCawley, 1971) discussion of 'node admissability conditions'. The root idea was attributed by him to a personal communication of Richard Stanley.

6. One should note that in the early stages of generative grammar, say from 1955 to 1978, to justify appeal to a transformational mechanism for the description of some phenomenon Q it sufficed to argue (i) that Q was a syntactic phenomenon and (ii) that a transformational description of Q was superior to a phrase structural one, these two classes of devices arguably being the only syntactic ones available. The current situation, though, bears no relation to that one.

7. The question begging involved in current talk about displacement is by no means limited to the few authors cited here in this connection. It is, for instance, built into the very structure of an October 2002 conference, Triggers, held at Tilburg University, The Netherlands. Its call, found at http://kubnw8.kub.nl/~breitbar/triggers/index.html (A. Breitbarth, A.Breitbarth@kub.nl)d), begins:

> Phrase structure and displacement are prominent universal properties of natural language. While some approaches have tried to eliminate transformational operations, displacement continues to play a crucial role in derivational theories such as Minimalism. Concentrating on displacement we can ask ourselves two different questions:
>
> (i)   Why does it exist in human language? and
> (ii) How is it implemented?

Thus although the authors of this document correctly observe that some approaches to syntax do not appeal to transformational devices, the entire outlined structure of the conference ignores this and takes displacement as a known fact. So a key question is putatively why it exists. But the richly outlined structure of the conference makes clear that *none of it* will be devoted to arguing that transformational movement exists or to countering arguments that it does not.

8. One might ask whether my invocation of the notion of *best theory* in Postal (1972a) was an earlier illegitimate appeal to privilege of the sort just criticized. I would suggest not. The reasons are that (i) the claim of privilege, that is, that one type of framework was inherently superior to another, was buttressed by argument, which it was the whole purpose of the article to elaborate; and (ii) the overall claim had the form of a standard Occam's Razor simplicity argument. And it is universally acknowledged that if one theoretical system S_1 is a proper subset of another S_2 but has the same factual implications, S_1 is superior to S_2, that is, is privileged. These remarks are entirely independent of any issues that concern the *validity* or *soundness* of the purported Occam's Razor argument.

14. Junk Linguistics

1. The recommended skepticism has nothing in common with an arrogant dismissal of others' positions or a dogmatic assurance that such and such view is right or wrong. Genuine skepticism wll always begin fundamentally with one's own views.

After essentially finishing this volume, I came across (at http://www.bpagency.com/pages/linguistics.htm) the following remarks (I have corrected some grammatical and spelling errors) in a promotional statement for a new book by Kewal Krishan Sharma, entitled *Linguistics: Facets and Issues*: "If you are just starting your studies in linguistics, the first piece of advice I have seems rather odd. It is this: beware of all books on linguistics. And that includes the one you are now reading. A healthy skepticism is not a bad thing. Most books on linguistics raise expectations of understanding which they cannot fulfill." These remarks, by an author with whose work I was unfortunately not previously familiar, seem to me to represent the same attitude that underlies much of this volume.

REFERENCES

Abbott, Barbara (1986) Review of Langendoen and Postal (1984) *Language* 62, 154–157.

Ackema, Peter, and Maaike Schoolemmer (1995) "The Middle Construction and the Syntax-Semantics Interface" *Lingua* 93, 59–90.

Ackerman, Farrell, and Gert Webelhut (1998) *A Theory of Predicates*, Stanford, California, CSLI.

Adger, David, and Josep Quer (2001) "The Syntax and Semantics of Unselected Embedded Questions" *Language* 77, 107–133.

Aikhenvald, Alexandra Y., Robert M. W. Dixon, and Masayuki Onishi (eds.) (2001) *Non-Canonical Marking of Subjects and Objects*, Amsterdam, Holland, John Benjamins.

Aissen, Judith (1975) "Presentational there-Insertion: A Cyclic Root Transformation" in Robin E. Grossman, L. James San, and Timothy J. Vance (eds.), *Papers from the Eleventh Regional Meeting of the Chicago Linguistic Society*, Chicago, Chicago Linguistic Society.

Aissen, Judith, and Jorge Hankamer (1972) "Shifty Subjects: A Conspiracy in Syntax?" *Linguistic Inquiry* 3, 501–504.

Aissen, Judith and David M. Perlmutter (1983) "Clause Reduction in Spanish" in David M. Perlmutter (ed.), *Studies in Relational Grammar 1*, Chicago, University of Chicago Press.

Allwood, Jens, Lars-Gunnar Andersson, and Östen Dahl (1997) *Logic in Linguistics*, Cambridge, England, Cambridge University Press.

Anderson, Stephen R. (1984) "On Representations in Morphology: Case Marking, Agreement and Inversion in Georgian" *Natural Language and Linguistic Theory* 2, 157-218.

Andersson, Lars-Gunnar (1982) "What Is Swedish an Exception To?" in Elisabet Engdahl and Eva Ejerhed (eds.), *Readings on Unbounded Dependencies in Scandinavian Languages*, Stockholm, Sweden, Almqvist and Wiksell.

Aoun, Joseph (1985) *A Grammar of Anaphora*, Cambridge, Massachusetts, MIT Press.

Aoun, Joseph, Lina Choueiri, and Norbert Hornstein (2001) "Resumption, Movement, and Derivational Economy" *Linguistic Inquiry* 32, 371–403.

Atlas, Jay David (1996) "'Only' Noun Phrases, Pseudo-Negative Generalized Quantifiers, Negative Polarity Items, and Monotonicity" *Journal of Semantics* 13, 265–328.

Atlas, Jay David (1997) "Negative Adverbials, Prototypical Negation and the De Morgan Taxonomy" *Journal of Semantics* 14, 349–367.

Atlas, Jay David (2001) "Negative Quantifier Noun Phrases: A Typology and an Acquisition Hypothesis" in Jack Hoeksema, Hotze Rullman, Victor Sánchez-Valencia, and Ton van der Wouden (eds.), *Perspectives on Negation and Polarity Items,* Amsterdam, Holland, John Benjamins.

Bach, Emmon (1977) Review of Postal (1974) *Language* 53, 621–654.

Bach, Emmon (1980) "In Defense of Passive" *Linguistics and Philosophy* 3, 297–342.

Bach, Emmon (1982) "Purpose Clauses and Control" in Pauline Jacobson and Geoffrey K. Pullum (eds.), *The Nature of Syntactic Representation*, Dordrecht, Holland, D. Reidel.

Baker, Mark C. (1988a) *Incorporation*, Chicago, University of Chicago Press.

Baker, Mark C. (1988b) "Theta Theory and the Syntax of Applicatives in Chichewa" *Natural Language and Linguistic Theory* 6, 353–389.

Baker, Mark C. (1996) *The Polysynthesis Parameter*, Oxford, England, Oxford University Press.

Baker, Mark C., Kyle Johnson, and Ian Roberts (1989) "Passive Arguments Raised" *Linguistic Inquiry* 20, 219–251.

Baltin, Mark (2003) "The Interaction of Ellipsis and Binding: Implications for the Sequencing of Principle A" *Natural Language and Linguistic Theory* 21, 215–246.

Baltin, Mark, and Paul M. Postal (1996) "More on Reanalysis Hypotheses" *Linguistic Inquiry* 27, 127–145.

Barss, A. (1986) *Chains and Anaphoric Dependence: On Reconstruction and Its Implications*, Cambridge, Massachusetts, MIT Doctoral Dissertation.

Beghelli, Fillipo (1994) "Asymmetries with Decreasing QPs" in *Proceedings of the Thirteenth West Coast Conference on Formal Linguistics*, Stanford, California, CSLI.

Boeckx, Cédric (1998) *A Minimalist View on the Passive*, Working Papers in Linguistics, Occasional Papers, Issue 2, Storrs, University of Connecticut.

Boolos, George S. (1998) *Logic, Logic, and Logic*, Cambridge, Massachusetts, Harvard University Press.

Boolos, George S., and Richard C. Jeffrey (1974) *Computability and Logic*, Cambridge, England, Cambridge University Press.

Bowers, John S. (1976) "On Surface Structure Grammatical Relations and the Structure-Preserving Hypothesis" *Linguistic Analysis* 2, 225–242.

Bresnan, Joan W. (1972) *Theory of Complementation in English Syntax*, Cambridge, Massachusetts, MIT Doctoral Dissertation.

Bresnan, Joan W. (1973) "Syntax of the Comparative Clause Construction in English" *Linguistic Inquiry* 4, 275–343.

Bresnan, Joan W. (1975) "Comparative Deletion and Constraints on Transformations" *Linguistic Analysis* 1, 25–74.

Bresnan, Joan W. (1976) "Nonarguments for Raising" *Linguistic Inquiry* 7, 485–501.

Bresnan, Joan W. (1977) "Variables in the Theory of Transformations" in Peter W. Culicover, Thomas Wasow, and Adrian Akmajian (eds.), *Formal Syntax*, New York, Academic Press.

Bresnan, Joan W. (1982a) "Control and Complementation" in Joan W. Bresnan (ed.), *The Mental Representation of Grammatical Relations*, Cambridge, Massachusetts, MIT Press.

Bresnan, Joan W. (1982b) *The Mental Representation of Grammatical Relations*, Cambridge, Massachusetts, MIT Press.

Bresnan, Joan W. (1982c) "The Passive in Lexical Theory" in Joan W. Bresnan (ed.), *The Mental Representation of Grammatical Relations*, Cambridge, Massachusetts, MIT Press.

Bresnan, Joan W. (1989) "The Syntactic Projection Problem and the Comparative Syntax of Locative Inversion" *Journal of Information Science and Engineering* 5, 287–303.

Bresnan, Joan W. (1991) "Locative Case vs. Locative Gender" in *Proceedings of the Seventeenth Annual Meeting of the Berkeley Linguistics Society*, Berkeley, California, Berkeley Linguistics Society.

Bresnan, Joan W. (1994) "Locative Inversion and the Architecture of Universal Grammar" *Language* 70, 72–131.

Bresnan, Joan W. (1995) "Category Mismatches" in Akinbiyi Akinlabi (ed.), *Theoretical Approaches to African Languages*, Trenton, New Jersey, African World Press.

Bresnan, Joan W. (2001) *Lexical-Functional Syntax*, Oxford, England, Blackwell.

Bresnan, Joan W., and Jane Grimshaw (1978) "The Syntax of Free Relatives in English" *Linguistic Inquiry* 9, 331–391.

Bresnan, Joan W., and Jonni M. Kanerva (1989) "Locative Inversion in Chichewa: A Case Study of Factorization" *Linguistic Inquiry* 20, 1–50.

Bresnan, Joan W., and Jonni M. Kanerva (1992) "The Thematic Hierarchy and Locative Inversion in U.G. A Reply to Paul Schachter's Comments" in Eric Wehrli and Thomas Stowell (eds.), *Syntax and Semantics 24: Syntax and the Lexicon*, New York, Academic Press.

Broad, William, and Nicholas Wade (1982) *Betrayers of the Truth*, New York, Simon and Schuster.

Browning, Marguerite (1987) *Null Operator Constructions*, Cambridge, Massachusetts, MIT Doctoral Dissertation.

Burzio, Luigi (1986) *Italian Syntax*, Dordrecht, Holland, D. Reidel.

Cantrall, William R. (1969) *On the Nature of the Reflexive in English*, Urbana, University of Illinois Doctoral Dissertation.

Carstens, Vicki (1985a) "Adjunct ECP Effects in Yoruba" in *Proceedings of NELS 15*, Amherst, University of Massachusetts, GLSA.

Carstens, Vicki (1985b) "Proper Government in Yoruba" in *Proceedings of the Fourth West Coast Conference on Formal Linguistics*, Stanford, California, Stanford Linguistics Association.

Chierchia, Gennaro (1984) *Topics in the Syntax and Semantics of Infinitives and Gerunds*, Amherst, University of Massachusetts Doctoral Dissertation.

Chierchia, Gennaro (1989) "Anaphora and Attitudes de se" in Rennata Bartsch, Jeremy van Benthem, and P. van Emde Boas (eds.), *Semantics and Contextual Expression*, Dordrecht, Holland, Foris.

Chierchia, Gennaro, and Pauline Jacobson (1985) "Local and Long Distance Control" in *Proceedings of NELS 16*, Amherst, GLSA, University of Massachusetts.

Chomsky, Noam (1957) *Syntactic Structures*, The Hague, Mouton.

Chomsky, Noam (1958) Review of B. F. Skinner, *Verbal Behavior in Language* 35, 26–58.

Chomsky, Noam (1959) "On Certain Formal Properties of Grammars" *Information and Control* 2, 137–167.

Chomsky, Noam (1963) "Formal Properties of Grammars" in R. Duncan Luce, R. Bush, and Eugene Galanter (eds.), *Handbook of Mathematical Psychology*, New York, John Wiley.

Chomsky, Noam (1965) *Aspects of the Theory of Syntax*, Cambridge, Massachusetts, MIT Press.

Chomsky, Noam (1971) *Problems of Knowledge and Freedom*, New York, Random House.

Chomsky, Noam (1972a) *Language and Mind*, New York, Harcourt Brace Jovanovich.

Chomsky, Noam (1972b) "Some Empirical Issues in the Theory of Transformational Grammar" in Stanley Peters (ed.), *Goals of Linguistic Theory*, Englewood Cliffs, New Jersey, Prentice-Hall.

Chomsky, Noam (1972c) *Studies on Semantics in Generative Grammar*, The Hague, Holland, Mouton.

Chomsky, Noam (1973) "Conditions on Transformations" in Stephen R. Anderson and Paul Kiparsky (eds.), *A Festschrift for Morris Halle*, New York, Holt, Rinehard and Winston; reprinted in Chomsky, *Essays on Form and Interpretation*, Amsterdam, Holland, North-Holland.

Chomsky, Noam (1975a) *The Logical Structure of Linguistic Theory*, Chicago, University of Chicago Press.

Chomsky, Noam (1975b) *Reflections on Language*, New York, Pantheon.

Chomsky Noam (1976) "Conditions on Rules of Grammar" *Linguistic Analysis* 2, 303-351; reprinted in Chomsky (1977a).

Chomsky, Noam (1977a) *Essays on Form and Interpretation*, Amsterdam, Holland, North-Holland.

Chomsky, Noam (1977b) "On WH-Movement" in Peter W. Culicover, Thomas Wasow, and Adrian Akmajian (eds.), *Formal Syntax*, New York, Academic Press.

Chomsky, Noam (1978) "An Interview with Noam Chomsky" *Linguistic Analysis* 4, 301–319.

Chomsky, Noam (1980a) "On Binding" *Linguistic Inquiry* 11, 1–46.

Chomsky, Noam (1980b) *Rules and Representations*, New York, Columbia University Press.

Chomsky, Noam (1981) *Lectures on Government and Binding*, Dordrecht, Holland, Foris.

Chomsky, Noam (1982a) *The Generative Enterprise*, Dordrecht, Holland, Foris.

Chomsky, Noam (1982b) *Some Concepts and Consequences of the Theory of Government and Binding*, Cambridge, Massachusetts, MIT Press.

Chomsky, Noam (1984) *Modular Approaches to the Study of the Mind*, San Diego, California, San Diego State University Press.

Chomsky, Noam (1986a) *Barriers*, Cambridge, Massachusetts, MIT Press.

Chomsky, Noam (1986b) *Knowledge of Language*, New York, Praeger Scientific.

Chomsky, Noam (1988) *Language and Problems of Knowledge*, Cambridge, Massachusetts, MIT Press.

Chomsky, Noam (1990) "On Formalization and Formal Linguistics" *Natural Language and Linguistic Theory* 8, 143–147.

Chomsky, Noam (1993) "The Minimalist Program for Linguistic Theory" in Kenneth Hale and Samuel J. Keyser (eds.), *The View from Building 20*, Cambridge, Massachusetts, MIT Press.

Chomsky, Noam (1995a) "Bare Phrase Structure" in Gert Webelhuth (ed.), *Government and Binding Theory and the Minimalist Program*, Oxford, England, Blackwell.

Chomsky, Noam (1995b) *The Minimalist Program*, Cambridge, Massachusetts, MIT Press.

Chomsky, Noam (1999) "Derivation by Phase" *MIT Occasional Papers in Linguistics 18*, Cambridge, Massachusetts, Department of Linguistics, MIT.

Chomsky, Noam (2000a) *The Architecture of Language*, New Delhi, Oxford University Press.

Chomsky, Noam (2000b) "Minimalist Inquiries: The Framework" in Roger Martin, David Michaels, and Juan Uriagereka (eds.), *Step by Step*, Cambridge, Massachusetts, MIT Press.

Chomsky, Noam (2000c) *New Horizons in the Study of Language and Mind*, Cambridge, England, Cambridge University Press.

Chomsky, Noam (2001) "Beyond Explanatory Adequacy," *MIT Occasional Papers in Linguistics 20*, Cambridge, Massachusetts, Department of Linguistics, MIT.

Chomsky, Noam (2002) *On Nature and Language*, Cambridge, England, Cambridge University Press.

Chomsky, Noam, and Morris Halle (1968) *The Sound Pattern of English*, New York, Harper and Row.

Chomsky, Noam, and Howard Lasnik (1977) "Filters and Control" *Linguistic Inquiry* 8, 425–504.

Chomsky, Noam, and Howard Lasnik (1995) "The Theory of Principles and Parameters" in Noam Chomsky, *The Minimalist Program*, Cambridge, Massachusetts, MIT Press.

Chung, Sandra (1998) *The Design of Agreement*, Chicago, University of Chicago Press.

Chung, Sandra, and James McCloskey (1987) "Government, Barriers, and Small Clauses in Modern Irish" *Linguistic Inquiry* 18, 173–237.

Cinque, Guglielmo (1975) "The Shadow Pronoun Hypothesis and 'Chopping' Rules in Romance" *Linguistic Inquiry* 6, 140–145.

Cinque, Guglielmo (1990) *Types of Ā-Dependencies*, Cambridge, Massachusetts, MIT Press.

Collins, Chris, and Phil Branigan (1997) "Quotative Inversion" *Natural Language and Linguistic Theory* 15, 1–41.

Coopmans, Peter (1989) "Where Stylistic and Syntactic Processes Meet: Locative Inversion in English" *Language* 65, 728–751.

Cowper, Elizabeth A. (1992) *A Concise Introduction to Syntactic Theory*, Chicago, University of Chicago Press.

Culicover, Peter W. (1976) *Syntax*, New York, Academic Press.

Culicover, Peter W. (1991) "Polarity, Inversion and Focus in English" in *ESCOL 91*, Columbus, Ohio State University.

Culicover, Peter W. (1993a) "The Adverb Effect: Evidence against ECP Accounts of the *that-t* Effect" in *Proceedings of NELS 23*, Amherst, GLSA, University of Massachusetts.

Culicover, Peter W. (1993b) "Evidence against ECP Accounts of the THAT-T Effect" *Linguistic Inquiry* 24, 557–561.

Culicover, Peter W. (1997) *Principles and Parameters*, Oxford, England, Oxford University Press.

Culicover, Peter W. (1999) *Syntactic Nuts*, New York, Oxford University Press.

Culicover, Peter W., and Ray Jackendoff (1995) "*Something Else* for the Binding Theory" *Linguistic Inquiry* 26, 249–275.

Culicover, Peter W., and Robert D. Levine (2001) "Stylistic Inversion in English: A Reconsideration" *Natural Language and Linguistic Theory* 19, 283–310.

Culicover, Peter, and Paul M. Postal (eds.) (2001) *Parasitic Gaps*, Cambridge, Massachusetts, MIT Press.

Curme, George O. (1931) *Syntax*, Boston, D. C. Heath.

Dalrymple, Mary (2001) *Lexical Functional Grammar*, New York, Academic Press.

Davies, William D., and Stanley Dubinsky (2001) "Functional Architecture and the Distribution of Subject Properties" in William D. Davies and Stanley Dubinsky (eds.), *Objects and Other Subjects*, Dordrecht, Holland, Kluwer Academic.

Davis, Philip J., and Reuben Hersh (1981) *The Mathematical Experience*, Boston, Houghton Mifflin.

Déprez, Viviane (1997) "A Non-Unified Analysis of Negtive Concord" in Danielle Forget, Paul Hirschbühler, France Martineau, and María-Luisa Rivero (eds.), *Negation and Polarity*, Current Issues in Linguistic Theory 155, Amsterdam, Holland, John Benjamins.

Dikken, Marcel Den (2001) "A Polar Whole: Dutch Heel 'Whole' as a Special Kind of Negative Polarity Item," Unpublished Paper, New York, CUNY Graduate Center.

Dowty, David (1985) "On Recent Analyses of the Semantics of Control" *Linguistics and Philosophy* 8, 291–331.

Dowty, David, and Pauline Jacobson (1988) "Agreement as a Semantic Phenomenon" in *Proceedings of the Fifth Eastern States Conference on Linguistics*, Columbus, Ohio State University.

Dresher, Bezalel Elan, and Norbert Hornstein (1979) "Trace Theory and NP Movement Rules" *Linguistic Inquiry* 9, 151–175.

Dryer, Matthew S. (1985) "The Role of Thematic Relations in Adjectival Passives" *Linguistic Inquiry* 16, 320–326.

Emonds, Joseph E. (1969) *Root and Structure-Preserving Transformations*, Cambridge, Massachusetts, MIT Doctoral Dissertation.

Emonds, Joseph E. (1976) *A Transformational Approach to English Syntax: Root, Structure-Preserving, and Local Transformations*, New York, Academic Press.

Engdahl, Elisabet (1985) "Parasitic Gaps, Resumptive Pronouns, and Subject Extractions" *Linguistics* 23, 3–44.

Engdahl, Elisabet (1986) *Constituent Questions*, Dordrecht, Holland, D. Reidel.

Engdahl, Elisabet, and Eva Ejerhed (1982) *Readings on Unbounded Dependencies in Scandanavian Languages*, Stockholm, Sweden, Almqvist and Wiksell.

Epstein, Samuel David, and Norbert Hornstein (1999) "Introduction" in Samuel David Epstein and Norbert Hornstein (eds.), *Working Minimalism*, Cambridge, Massachusetts, MIT Press.

Epstein, Samuel David, and T. Daniel Seely (2002) "Introduction: On the Quest for Explanation" in Samuel David Epstein and T. Daniel Seely (eds.), *Derivation and Explanation in the Minimalist Program*, Oxford, England, Blackwell.

Everett, Dan (2001) "Discussion: On Nonobjects of Syntactic Study" *LINGUIST List*: Volume 12, number 1816, July 13, 2001.

Fagan, Sarah M. B. (1988) "The English Middle" *Linguistic Inquiry* 19, 181–203.

Fagan, Sarah M. B. (1992) *The Syntax and Semantics of Middle Constructions*, Cambridge, England, Cambridge University Press.

Falk, Yehuda (1983) "Subjects and Long-Distance Dependencies" *Linguistic Analysis* 12, 245–270.

Farrell, Patrick (1993) "A Last Look at the 1AEX" in *Proceedings of the Eleventh West Coast Conference on Formal Linguistics*, Stanford, California, CSLI.

Farrell, Patrick (1994) *Thematic Relations and Relational Grammar,* New York, Garland.

Fauconnier, Gilles (1975a) "Polarity and the Scale Principle" *Papers from the Eleventh Regional Meeting of the Chicago Linguistic Society*, Chicago, Chicago Linguistic Society.

Fauconnier, Gilles (1975b) "Pragmatic Scales and Logical Structure" *Linguistic Inquiry* 6, 353–375.

Fauconnier, Gilles (1976) *Etude de certains aspects logiques et grammaticaux de la quantification et de l'anaphore en français et en anglais*, Paris, Thèse de quatrième cycle de l'université de Paris VII.

Fauconnier, Gilles (1979) "Implication Reversal in Natural Language" in Franz Guenther and S. J. Schmidt (eds.), *Formal Semantics and Pragmatics for Natural Languages*, Dordrecht, Holland, D. Reidel.

Fellbaum, Christine, and Anne Zribi-Hertz (1989) "La construction moyenne en français et en anglais: Étude de syntaxe et de sémantique comparées" *Recherches Linguistiques* 18, 19–57.

Fiengo, Robert (1977) "On Trace Theory" *Linguistic Inquiry* 8, 35–81.

Fiengo, Robert (1980) *Surface Structure*, Cambridge, Massachusetts, Harvard University Press.

Fiengo, Robert, and Howard Lasnik (1974) "Complement Object Deletion" *Linguistic Inquiry* 5, 535–571.

Fiengo, Robert, and Robert May (1994) *Indices and Identity*, Cambridge, Massachusetts, MIT Press.

Fillmore, Charles J. (1965) *Indirect Object Constructions in English and the Ordering of Transformations*, The Hague, Holland, Mouton.

Fodor, Jerry A. (1975) *The Language of Thought*, Cambridge, Massachusetts, Harvard University Press.

Fox, Danny (2000) *Economy and Semantic Interpretation*, Cambridge, Massachusetts, MIT Press.

Fraser, Bruce (1965/1974) *An Examination of the Verb-Particle Construction in English*, Cambridge, Massachusetts, MIT Doctoral Dissertation; published as *The Verb-Particle Combination in English*, Tokyo, Taishukan, 1974.

Freidin, Robert (1978) "Cyclicity and the Theory of Grammar" *Linguistic Inquiry* 9, 519–550.

Freidin, Robert (1986) "Fundamental Issues in the Theory of Binding" in Barbara Lust (ed.), *Studies in the Acquisition of Anaphora*, Dordrecht, Reidel.

Gazdar, Gerald (1981) "Unbounded Dependencies and Coordinate Structure" *Linguistic Inquiry* 12, 155–184.

Gazdar, Gerald (1982) "Phrase Structure Grammar" in Pauline Jacobson and Geoffrey K. Pullum (eds.), *The Nature of Syntactic Representation*, Dordrecht, Holland, D. Reidel.

Georgopoulos, Carol (1991) "Canonical Government and the Specifier Parameter: An ECP Account of Weak Crossover" *Natural Language and Linguistic Theory* 9, 1–46.

Giannakidou, Anastasia (1998) *Polarity Sensitivity as (Non) Veridical Dependency*, Amsterdam, Holland, John Benjamins.

Giannakidou, Anastasia (1999) "Affective Dependencies" *Linguistics and Philosophy* 22, 367–421.

Giannakidou, Anastasia (2001) "Varieties of Polarity Items and the (Non) Veridicality Hypothesis" in Jack Hoeksema, Hotze Rullman, Víctor Sánchez-Valenica, and Ton van der Wouden (eds.), *Perspectives on Negation and Polarity Items*, Amsterdam, Holland, John Benjamins.

Gould, Ronald (1988) *Graph Theory*, Menlo Park, California, Benjamin/Cummings.

Green, Georgia M. (1985) "The Description of Inversions in Generalized Phrase-Structure Grammar" *Proceedings of the Eleventh Annual Meeting of the Berkeley Linguistics Society*, Berkeley, California, Berkeley Linguistic Society.

Grimshaw, Jane (1979) "Complement Selection and the Lexicon" *Linguistic Inquiry* 10, 279–326.

Grimshaw, Jane (1981) "Form, Function, and the Language Acquisition Device" in C. L. Baker and John J. McCarthy (eds.), *The Logical Problem of Language Acquisition*, Cambridge, Massachusetts, MIT Press.

Grimshaw, Jane (1982) "Grammatical Relations and Subcategorization" in Annie Zaenen (ed.), *Subjects and Other Subjects: Proceedings of the Harvard Conference on Grammatical Relations*, Bloomington, Indiana University Linguistics Club.

Grimshaw, Jane (1997) "Projection, Heads, and Optimality" *Linguistic Inquiry* 28, 373–422.

Grinder, John (1972) "On the Cycle in Syntax" in John Kimball (ed.), *Syntax and Semantics 1*, New York, Academic Press.

Gross, Maurice (1975) *Méthodes en syntaxe*, Paris, Hermann.

Haegeman, Liliane (1991) *Introduction to Government and Binding Theory*, Oxford, England, Blackwell.

Hale, Kenneth, and Samuel J. Keyser (1986) "A View from the Middle" *Lexicon Working Paper 7*, Cambridge, Massachusetts, MIT Center for Cognitive Science.

Halmos, Paul R. (1960) *Naive Set Theory*, Princeton, New Jersey, D. Van Nostrand.

Harbert, Wayne (1995) "Binding Theory, Control and Pro" in Gert Webelhuth (ed.), *Government and Binding Theory and the Minimalist Program*, Oxford, England, Blackwell.

Harris, Zellig (1979) *Mathematical Structures of Language*, Huntington, New York, Robert Krieger.

Heim, Irene (1984) "A Note on Negative Polarity and Downward Entailingness" *Proceedings of NELS 14*, Amherst, GLSA, University of Massachusetts.

Higginbotham, James (1980a) "Anaphora and GB: Some Preliminary Remarks" in *Proceedings of NELS 10*, Ottawa, Canada, University of Ottawa.

Higginbotham, James (1980b) "Pronouns and Bound Variables" *Linguistic Inquiry* 11, 679–708.

Higginbotham, James (1983) "Logical Form, Binding, and Nominals" *Linguistic Inquiry* 14, 395–420.

Higginbotham, James (1992) "Reference and Control" in Richard K. Larson, Sabine Iatridou, Uptal Lahari, and James Higginbotham (eds.), *Control and Grammar,* Dordrecht, Holland, Kluwer Academic.

Hintikka, Jaakko (2000) *On Gödel*, Belmont, California, Wadsworth.

Hirschbühler, Paul (1975) "On the Source of Lefthand NPs in French" *Linguistic Inquiry* 6, 155–165.

Hockett, Charles F. (1966) "Language, Mathematics, and Linguistics" in Thomas A. Sebeok (ed.), *Current Trends in Linguistics 3: Theoretical Foundations*, The Hague, Holland, Mouton.

Hoeksema, Jack (1983) "Negative Polarity and the Comparative" *Natural Language and Linguistic Theory* 1, 403–434.

Hoeksema, Jack (1986) "Monotonicity Phenomena in Natural Language" *Linguistic Analysis* 16, 25–40.

Hoeksema, Jack (1996) Review of Progovac (1994) *Studies in Language* 20, 196–207.

Hoeksema, Jack (2000) "Negative Polarity Items: Triggering, Scope, and C-Command" in Laurence R. Horn and Yasuhiko Kato (eds.), *Negation and Polarity*, Oxford, England, Oxford University Press.

Hoeksema, Jack, Hotze Rullman, Victor Sánchez-Valencia, and Ton van der Wouden (2001) "Introduction" in Jack Hoeksema, Hotze Rullman, Victor Sánchez-Valencia, and Ton van der Wouden (eds.) *Perspectives on Negation and Polarity Items*, vii–xii, Amsterdam, Holland, John Benjamins.

Hoekstra, Teun (1984) *Transitivity: Grammatical Relations in Government-Binding Theory*, Dordrecht, Holland, Foris.

Hoekstra, Teun, and Renee Mulder (1990) "Unergtives as Copular Verbs: Locational and Existential Predication" *Linguistic Review* 7, 1–79.

Horn, Laurence R. (1985) "Metalinguistic Negation and Pragmatic Ambiguity" *Language* 61, 121–174.

Horn, Laurence R. (1995) "Negative Polarity and the Dynamics of Vertical Inference" in Danielle Forget, Paul Hirschbühler, France Martineau, and María-Luisa Rivero (eds.), *Current Issues in Linguistic Theory 155: Negation and Polarity*, Amsterdam, Holland, John Benjamins.

Horn, Laurence R. (1996a) "Exclusive Company: *Only* and the Dynamics of Vertical Inference" *Journal of Semantics* 13, 1–40.

Horn, Laurence R. (1996b) "Flaubert Triggers, Squatitive Negation, and Other Quirks of Grammar" *Taalkundig Bulletin* 26, 183–205; reprinted in Jack Hoeksema, Hotze Rullman, Víctor Sánchez-Valenica, and Ton van der Wouden (eds.) (2001), *Perspectives on Negation and Polarity Items*, Amsterdam, Holland, John Benjamins.

Horn, Laurence R. (2000) "Pick a Theory (Not Just Any Theory)" in Laurence R. Horn and Yasuhiko Kato (eds.), *Negation and Polarity*, Oxford, England, Oxford University Press.

Horn, Laurence R. (2001) *A Natural History of Negation*, Stanford, California, CSLI.

Horn, Laurence R., and Yasuhiko Kato (eds.) (2000) *Negation and Polarity*, Oxford, England, Oxford University Press.

Horn, Laurence R., and Young-Suk Lee (1995) Review article on Progovac (1994) "Progovac on Polarity" *Journal of Linguistics* 31, 401–424.

Hornstein, Norbert (1995) *Logical Form,* Oxford, England, Blackwell.

Hornstein, Norbert (2001) *Move! A Minimalist Theory of Construal,* Oxford, England, Blackwell.

Hornstein, Norbert, and Jairo Nunes (2002) "On Asymmetries between PG and ATB Constructions" *Syntax* 5, 26–54.

Hornstein, Norbert, and Amy Weinberg (1981) "Case Theory and Preposition Stranding" *Linguistic Inquiry* 12, 55–91.

Huang, C.-T. (1995) "Logical Form" in Gert Webelhuth (ed.), *Government and Binding Theory and the Minimalist Program,* Oxford, England, Blackwell.

Huddleston, Rodney, and Geoffrey K. Pullum (2002) *The Cambridge Grammar of the English Language,* New York, Cambridge University Press.

Hukari, Thomas E., and Robert D. Levine (1987) "Parasitic Gaps, Slash Termination and the C-Command Condition" *Natural Language and Linguistic Theory* 5, 197–222.

Hukari, Thomas E., and Robert D. Levine (1991) "On the Disunity of Unbounded Dependency Constructions" *Natural Language and Linguistic Theory* 9, 97–144.

Israel, Michael (1996). "Polarity Sensitivity as Lexical Semantics" *Linguistics and Philosophy* 19, 619–666.

Israel, Michael (1998) *The Rhetoric of Grammar: Scalar Reasoning and Polarity Sensitivity,* La Jolla, University of California at San Diego Doctoral Dissertation.

Iwakura, Kunihiro (1978) "On Root Transformations and the Structure-Preserving Hypothesis" *Linguistic Analysis* 4, 321–364.

Iwakura, Kunihiro (1987) "A Government Approach to Double Object Constructions" *Linguistic Analysis* 17, 78–98.

Jackendoff, Ray (1971) "Gapping and Related Rules" *Linguistic Inquiry* 2, 21–36.

Jackendoff, Ray (1972) *Semantic Interpretation in Generative Grammar,* Cambridge, Massachusetts, MIT Press.

Jackendoff, Ray (1977) $\bar{X}$ *Syntax: A Study of Phrase Structure,* Cambridge, Massachusetts, MIT Press.

Jackendoff, Ray (1983) *Semantics and Cognition,* Cambridge, Massachusetts, MIT Press.

Jackendoff, Ray (1984) "On the Phrase *the Phrase* 'the Phrase'" *Natural Language and Linguistic Theory* 2, 25-37.

Jackendoff, Ray (1990) *Semantic Structures,* Cambridge, Massachusetts, MIT Press.

Jacobson, Pauline (1976) *Crossover and Some Related Problems,* Berkeley, University of California at Berkeley Master's Dissertation.

Jacobson, Pauline (1977) *The Syntax of Crossing Coreference Sentences,* Berkeley, University of California at Berkeley Doctoral Dissertation.

Jacobson, Pauline (1992a) "Flexible Categorial Grammars: Questions and Prospects" in Robert D. Levine (ed.), *Formal Grammar: Theory and Implementation,* Oxford, England, Oxford University Press.

Jacobson, Pauline (1992b) "The Lexical Entailment Theory of Control and the *Tough*-Construction" in Ivan A. Sag and Anna Szabolcsi (eds.), *Lexical Matters,* Stanford, California, CSLI.

Jaeggli, Osvaldo A. (1986) "Passive" *Linguistic Inquiry* 17, 587–622.

Jespersen, Otto (1924) *The Philosophy of Grammar,* London, George Allen and Unwin.

Jespersen, Otto (1927) *Syntax 2: A Modern English Grammar on Historical Principles, Part III,* London, George Allen and Unwin.

Johnson, David E., and Paul M. Postal (1980) *Arc Pair Grammar,* Princeton, New Jersey, Princeton University Press.

Johnson, Kyle (2001) "What VP Ellipsis Can Do, and What It Can't, but Not Why" in Mark Baltin and Chris Collins (eds.), *The Handbook of Contemporary Syntactic Theory*, Oxford, England, Blackwell.

Joseph, Brian D. (1979) "Raising to Oblique in Modern Greek" *Proceedings of the Fifth Meeting of the Berkeley Linguistics Society*, Berkeley, California, Berkeley Linguistics Society.

Joseph, Brian D. (1990) "Is Raising to Prepositional Object a Natural Language Grammatical Construction?" in Brian D. Joseph and Paul M. Postal (eds.), *Studies in Relational Grammar 3*, Chicago, University of Chicago Press.

Kaplan, Ronald M., and Joan Bresnan (1982) "Grammatical Representation" in Joan W. Bresnan (ed.), *The Mental Representation of Grammatical Relations*, Cambridge, Massachusetts, MIT Press.

Kaplan, Ronald M., and Joan Bresnan (1995) "Lexical-Functional Grammar: A Formal System for Grammatical Representation" in Mary Dalrymple, Ronald M. Kaplan, John T. Maxwell III, and Annie Zaenen (eds.), *Formal Issues in Lexical Functional Grammar*, Stanford, California, CSLI.

Kathol, Andreas, and Robert D. Levine (1993) "Inversion as a Linearization Effect" *Proceedings of NELS 23*, Amherst, GLSA, University of Massachusetts.

Katz, Jerrold J. (1981) *Language and Other Abstract Objects*, Totowa, New Jersey, Rowman and Littlefield.

Katz, Jerrold J. (1984) "An Outline of Platonist Grammar" in Thomas G. Bever, John M. Carroll, and Lance A. Miller (eds.), *Talking Minds: The Study of Language in Cognitive Science*, Cambridge, Massachusetts, MIT Press.

Katz, Jerrold J. (1996) "The Unfinished Chomskyan Revolution" *Mind and Language* 11, 270–294.

Katz, Jerrold J. (1998) *Realistic Realism*, Cambridge, Massachusetts, MIT Press.

Katz, Jerrold J., and Paul M. Postal (1991) "Realism vs. Conceptualism in Linguistics" *Linguistics and Philosophy* 14, 515–554.

Kayne, Richard S. (1975) *French Syntax*, Cambridge, Massachusetts, MIT Press.

Kayne, Richard S. (1976) "French Relative 'que'" in F. Hensey and Marta Luján (eds.), *Current Studies in Romance Linguistics*, Washington, D.C., Georgetown University Press.

Kayne, Richard S. (1984) *Connectedness and Binary Branching*, Dordrecht, Holland, Foris.

Kayne, Richard S. (2000) *Parameters and Universals*, Oxford, England, Oxford University Press.

Kempson, Ruth (1985) "More on Any: Reply to Ladusaw," *Proceedings of NELS 15*, Amherst, GLSA, University of Massachusetts.

Kennedy, Christopher. (1997) "VP Deletion and 'Nonparasitic' Gaps" *Linguistic Inquiry* 28, 697–707.

Keyser, Samuel Jay, and Thomas Roeper (1984) "On the Middle and Ergative Constructions in English" *Linguistic Inquiry* 15, 381–416.

Kiparsky, Carol, and Paul Kiparsky (1970) "Fact" in Manfred Bierwisch and Karl E. Heidolph (eds.), *Progress in Linguisitics*, The Hague, Mouton.

Kishimoto, Hideki (2000) "Indefinite Pronouns and Overt N-Raising" *Linguistic Inquiry* 31, 557–566.

Klima, Edward (1964) "Negation in English" in Jerry A. Fodor and Jerrold J. Katz (eds.), *The Structure of Language*, Englewood Cliffs, New Jersey, Prentice-Hall.

Koopman, Hilda (1982) "Control from COMP and Comparative Syntax" *Linguistic Review* 2, 365–391.

Koopman, Hilda (1984) *The Syntax of Verbs*, Dordrecht, Holland, Foris.

Koopman, Hilda, and Dominique Sportiche (1982/1983) "Variables and the Bijection Principle" *Linguistic Review* 2, 139–160.

Koopman, Hilda, and Dominique Sportiche (1986) "A Note on Long Extraction in Vata and the ECP" *Natural Language and Linguistic Theory* 4, 357–374.

Koster, Jan (1978) "Conditions, Empty Nodes, and Markedness" *Linguistic Inquiry* 9, 551–594.

Koster, Jan (1987) *Domains and Dynasties*, Dordrecht, Holland, Foris.

Krifka, Manfred (1990) "Some Remarks on Polarity Items" in D. Zaefferer (ed.), *Semantic Universals and Universals of Semantics*, Dordrecht, Holland, Foris.

Krifka, Manfred (1994) "The Semantics and Pragmatics of Weak and Strong Polarity Items in Assertions" in Mandy Harvey and Lynn Santelmann (eds.), *SALT IV*, Ithaca, New York, Cornell University.

Krifka, Manfred (1995) "The Semantics and Pragmatics of Polarity Items" *Linguistic Analysis* 25, 209–257.

Kuno, Susumu (1987) *Functional Syntax*, Chicago, University of Chicago Press.

Kuroda, Sige-Yuki (1968) Review of Fillmore (1965) *Language* 44, 374–378.

Ladusaw, William (1980) *Polarity Sensitivity as Inherent Scope Relations*, New York, Garland.

Ladusaw, William (1996a) "Configurational Expression of Negation" in Jaap van der Does and Jan van Eijck (eds.), *Quantifiers, Logic, and Language*, CSLI Lecture Notes No. 54, Stanford, California, CSLI.

Ladusaw, William (1996b) "Negation and Polarity Items" in Shalom Lappin (ed.), *The Handbook of Contemporary Semantic Theory*, Oxford, England, Blackwell.

Lagunoff, Rachel (1997) *Singular they*, Los Angeles, University of California at Los Angeles Doctoral Dissertation.

Lakoff, George (1976) "Pronouns and Reference" in James D. McCawley (1976) (ed.), *Syntax and Semantics 7: Notes from the Linguistic Underground*, New York, Academic Press.

Lakoff, George (1986) "Frame Semantic Control of the Coordinate Structure Constraint" in *Papers from the Twenty-second Regional Meeting of the Chicago Linguistic Society, Part 2, Papers from the Parasession on Pragmatics and Grammatical Theory*, Chicago, Chicago Linguistic Society.

Landau, Idan (1999) *Elements of Control*, Cambridge, Massachusetts, MIT Doctoral Dissertation.

Landau, Idan (2000) *Elements of Control, Structure and Meaning in Infinitival Constructions*, Dordrecht, Holland, Kluwer Academic.

Landau, Idan (forthcoming) *The Locative Syntax of Experiencers*.

Landau, Idan (in press) "Movement Out of Control" *Linguistic Inquiry*

Langendoen, D. Terence (1976) "On the Weak Generative Capacity of Infinite Grammars" *CUNY Forum* 1, 13–24.

Langendoen, D. Terence (1979) "More on Locative-Inversion Sentences and the Structure-Preserving Hypothesis" *Linguistic Analysis* 5, 421–437.

Langendoen, D. Terence, and Paul M. Postal (1984) *The Vastness of Natural Languages*, Oxford, England, Blackwell.

Langendoen, D. Terence, and Paul M. Postal (1985) "Sets and Sentences" in Jerrold J. Katz (ed.), *The Philosophy of Linguistics*, Oxford, England, Oxford University Press.

Lapointe, Steven G. (1986) Review of Langendoen and Postal (1984) *Linguistics and Philosophy* 9, 225–243

Lappin, Shalom, Robert D. Levine, and David E. Johnson (2000a) "The Structure of Unscientific Revolutions" *Natural Language and Linguistic Theory* 18, 665–671.

Lappin, Shalom, Robert D. Levine, and David E. Johnson (2000b) "The Revolution Confused: A Response to Our Critics" *Natural Language and Linguistic Theory* 18, 873–890.

Lappin, Shalom, Robert D. Levine, and David E. Johnson (2001) "The Revolution Maximally Confused" *Natural Language and Linguistic Theory* 19, 901–919.

Larson, Richard K., Sabine Iatridou, Utpal Lahari, and James Higginbotham (1992) *Control and Grammar*, Dordrecht, Holland, Kluwer Academic.

Lasnik, Howard (1976) "Remarks on Coreference" *Lingusitic Analysis* 2, 1–22.

Lasnik, Howard (1999a) "Chains of Arguments" in Samuel David Epstein and Norbert Hornstein (eds.), *Working Minimalism*, Cambridge, Massachusetts, MIT Press.

Lasnik, Howard (1999b) *Minimalist Analysis*, Oxford, England, Blackwell.

Lasnik, Howard (1999c) "A Note on Pseudogapping" in Howard Lasnik, *Minimalist Analysis*, Oxford, England, Blackwell.

Lasnik, Howard, and Mamoru Saito (1991) "On the Subject of Infinitives" in L. Dobrin, L. Nichols, and R. Rodriguez (eds.), *Papers from the Twenty-seventh Regional Meeting of the Chicago Linguistic Society*, Chicago, Chicago Linguistic Society; reprinted in Lasnik (1999b).

Lasnik, Howard, and Mamoru Saito (1992) *Move a*, Cambridge, Massachusetts, MIT Press.

Lasnik, Howard, and Tim Stowell (1991) "Weakest Crossover" *Linguistic Inquiry* 22, 687–720.

Lasnik, Howard, and Juan Uriagereka (1988) *A Course in GB Syntax*, Cambridge, Massachusetts, MIT Press.

Lawler, John M. (1977) "A Agrees with B in Achenese" in Peter Cole and Jerrold M. Sadock (eds.), *Syntax and Semantics 8: Grammatical Relations*, New York, Academic Press.

Lebeaux, David (1991) "Relative Clauses, Licensing, and the Nature of the Derivation" in Susan D. Rothstein (ed.), *Syntax and Semantics 25: Perspectives on Phrase Structure: Heads and Licensing*, New York, Academic Press.

Lee, Robert G., Carol Neidle, and Dawn Maclaughlin (1997) "Role Shift in ASL: A Syntactic Look at Direct Speech" in Carol Neidle, Dawn Maclaughlin, and Robert G. Lee (eds.), *Syntactic Structure and Discourse Function*, Report Number 4, American Sign Language Project, Boston, Massachusetts, Boston University.

Lees, Robert B. (1960) *The Grammar of English Nominalizations*, The Hague, Mouton.

Levin, Beth (1993) *English Verb Classes and Alternations*, Chicago, University of Chicago Press.

Levin, Beth, and Malka Rappaport (Hovav) (1986) "The Formation of Adjectival Passives" *Linguistic Inquiry* 17, 623–661.

Levin, Beth, and Malka Rappaport (Hovav) (1995) *Unaccusativity*, Cambridge, Massachusetts, MIT Press.

Levin, Nancy (1978) "Some Identity-of-Sense Deletions Puzzle Me. Do They You?" in *Papers from the Fourteenth Annual Meeting of the Chicago Linguistic Society*, Chicago, Chicago Linguistic Society.

Levin, Nancy (1986) *Main Verb Ellipsis in Spoken English*, New York, Garland.

Levine, Robert D. (1989) "On Focus Inversion: Syntactic Valence and the Role of a SUBCAT List" *Linguistics* 17, 113–155.

Levine, Robert D. (2001) "Review Article: The Extraction Riddle: Just What Are We Missing?" *Journal of Linguistics* 37, 145–174.

Levine, Robert D. (2002) Review of Juan Uriagareka, *Rhyme and Reason: An Introduction to Minimalist Syntax* (Cambridge, Mass., MIT Press), *Language* 78, 325–330.

Levine, Robert D., Thomas E. Hukari, and Michael Calcagno (2001) "Parasitic Gaps in English: Some Overlooked Cases and Their Theoretical Implications" in Peter W. Culicover and Paul M. Postal (eds.), *Parasitic Gaps*, Cambridge, Massachusetts, MIT Press.

Lightfoot, David (1976) "The Theoretical Implications of Subject Raising" *Foundations of Language* 14, 257–285.

Linebarger, Marcia (1981) *The Grammar of Negative Polarity*, Bloomington, Indiana University Linguistics Club.

Linebarger, Marcia (1987) "Negative Polarity and Grammatical Representation" *Linguistics and Philosophy* 10, 325–387.

Linebarger, Marcia (1991) "Negative Polarity and Linguistic Evidence" *Papers from the Twenty-seventh Regional Meeting of the Chicago Linguistic Society, Part 2, Papers from the Parasession on Negation*, Chicago, Chicago Linguistic Society.

Lobeck, Anne (1995) *Ellipsis*, Oxford, England, Oxford University Press.

Marantz, Alec (1984) *On the Nature of Grammatical Relations*, Cambridge, Massachusetts, MIT Press.

Martin, Roger (1999) "Case, the Extended Projection Principle, and Minimalism" in Samuel David Epstein and Norbert Hornstein (eds.), *Working Minimalism*, Cambridge, Massachusetts, MIT Press.

Massam, Diane (2001) "On Predication and the Status of Subjects in Nieuean" in William D. Davies and Stanley Dubinsky (eds.), *Objects and Other Subjects*, Dordrecht, Holland, Kluwer Academic.

May, Robert (1985) *Logical Form*, Cambridge, Massachusetts, MIT Press.

McCawley, James D. (1968) "Concerning the Base Component of a Transformational Grammar" *Foundations of Language* 4, 243–269.

McCawley, James D. (1971) *Grammar and Meaning*, Tokyo, Taishukan.

McCawley, James D. (1981) *Everything That Linguists Have Always Wanted to Know about Logic* *but Were Ashamed to Ask*, Chicago, University of Chicago Press.

McCawley, James D. (1987) Review of Langendoen and Postal (1984) *International Journal of American Linguistics* 53, 236–239.

McCawley, James D. (1988) Review of Chomsky (1986b), *Language* 64, 355–366.

McCawley, James D. (1998) *The Syntactic Phenomena of English*, Chicago, University of Chicago Press.

McCloskey, James (1984) "Raising, Subcategorization and Selection in Modern Irish" *Natural Language and Linguistic Theory* 1, 441–485.

McCloskey, James (1990) "Resumptive Pronouns, A-Binding, and Levels of Representation in Irish" in Randall Hendrick (ed.), *Syntax and Semantics 23: The Syntax of the Modern Celtic Languages*, New York, Academic Press.

Meyers, Adam (1994) *A Unification Approach to Government and Binding Theory*, New York, New York University Doctoral Dissertation.

Milsark, Gary (2001) Review of Smith (1999) *Language* 77, 599–600.

Moreau, M.-L. (1971) "L'homme que je crois qui est venu: qui, que: relatifs et conjonctions" *Langue Française* 11, 77–90.

Müller, Gereon (1995) *A-bar Syntax*, Berlin, Mouton de Gruyter.

Napoli, Donna Jo (1988) "Subjects and External Arguments: Clauses and Non-Clauses" *Linguistics and Philosophy* 11, 323–354.

Napoli, Donna Jo (1993) *Syntax*, New York, Oxford University Press.

Neidle, Carol, Judy Kegl, Dawn Maclaughlin, Benjamin Bahan, and Robert G. Lee (2000), *The Syntax of American Sign Languages*, Cambridge, Massachusetts, MIT Press.

Nejit, A. (1980) *Gapping*, Dordrecht, Holland, Foris.

Newmeyer, Frederick J. (2000) "The Discrete Nature of Syntactic Categories: Against a Prototype-Based Account" in Robert D. Borsley (ed.), *Syntax and Semantics 32: The Nature and Function of Syntactic Categories*, New York, Academic Press.

Nunberg, Geoffrey, Ivan Sag, and Thomas Wasow (1994) "Idioms" *Language* 70, 491–538.

Obenauer, Hans-Georg (1984) "On the Identification of Empty Categories" *Linguistic Review* 4, 153–202.

Obenauer, Hans-Georg (1985) "Connectedness, Variables, and Stylistic Inversion in French" in Jacqueline Guéron, Hans-Georg Obenauer, and Jean-Yves Pollock (eds.), *Grammatical Representation*, Dordrecht, Holland, Foris.

Obenauer, Hans-Georg (1986) "Déplacer α et Ā-liage local: dérivations vs. représentations" in Mitsou Ronat and Daniel Couquaux (eds.), *La grammaire modulaire*, Paris, Les éditions de minuit.

Obenauer, Hans-Georg (1992) "L'interprétation des structures Wh et l'accord du participe passé" in Hans-Georg Obenauer and Anne Zribi-Hertz (eds.), *Structure de la phrase et théorie du liage*, Paris, Presses Universitaires de Vincennes.

Oehrle, Richard (1976) *The Grammatical Status of the English Dative Alternation*, Cambridge, Massachusetts, MIT Doctoral Dissertation.

Ouhalla, Jamal (1994) *Transformational Grammar*, New York, Edward Arnold.

Partee, Barbara H. (1973) "The Syntax and Semantics of Quotation" in Stephen R. Anderson and Paul Kiparsky (eds.), *A Festschrift for Morris Halle*, New York, Holt, Rinehart and Winston.

Partee, Barbara H., Alice ter Meulen, and Robert E. Wall (1993) *Mathematical Methods in Linguistics*, Dordrecht, Holland, Kluwer Academic.

Partridge, Eric (1970) *A Dictionary of Slang and Unconventional English*, New York, Macmillan.

Perlmutter, David M. (1972) "Evidence for Shadow Pronouns in French Relativization" in Paul M. Peranteau, Judith N. Levi, and Gloria C. Phares (eds.), *The Chicago Which Hunt: Papers from the Relative Clause Festival*, Chicago, Chicago Linguistic Society.

Perlmutter, David M. (1984) "The Inadequacy of Some Monostratal Theories of Passive" in David M. Perlmutter and Carol G. Rosen (eds.), *Studies in Relational Grammar 2*, Chicago, University of Chicago Press.

Perlmutter, David M. (1986) "No Nearer to the Soul" *Natural Language and Linguistic Theory* 4, 515–523.

Perlmutter, David M., and Paul M. Postal (1983a) "The Relational Succession Law" in David M. Perlmutter (ed.), *Studies in Relational Grammar 1*, Chicago, University of Chicago Press.

Perlmutter, David M., and Paul M. Postal (1983b) "Some Proposed Laws of Basic Clause Structure" in David M. Perlmutter (ed.), *Studies in Relational Grammar 1*, Chicago, University of Chicago Press.

Perlmutter, David M., and Paul M. Postal (1983c) "Toward a Universal Characterization of Passivization" in David M. Perlmutter (ed.), *Studies in Relational Grammar 1*, Chicago, University of Chicago Press.

Perlmutter, David M., and Paul M. Postal (1984a) "Impersonal Passives and Some Relational Laws" in David M. Perlmutter and Carol G. Rosen (eds.), *Studies in Relational Grammar 2*, Chicago, University of Chicago Press.

Perlmutter, David M., and Paul M. Postal (1984b) "The 1-Advancement Exclusiveness Law" in David M. Perlmutter and Carol G. Rosen (eds.), *Studies in Relational Grammar 2*, Chicago, University of Chicago Press.

Pesetsky, David (1981/1982) "Complementizer-Trace Phenomena and the Nominative Island Condition" *Linguistic Review* 1, 297–343.

Pesetsky, David (1995) *Zero Syntax*, Cambridge, Massachusetts, MIT Press.

Pinker, Steven (1994) *The Language Instinct: How the Mind Creates Language*, New York, William Morrow.

Pollard, Carl, and Ivan A. Sag (1987) *Information-based Syntax and Semantics 1: Fundamentals*, Stanford, California, CSLI.

Pollard, Carl, and Ivan A. Sag (1992) "Anaphors in English and the Scope of Binding Theory" *Linguistic Inquiry* 23, 261–303.

Pollard, Carl, and Ivan A. Sag (1994) *Head-Driven Phrase Structure Grammar*, Chicago, University of Chicago Press.

Postal, Paul M. (1970) "On Coreferential Complement Subject Deletion" *Linguistic Inquiry* 1, 439–523.

Postal, Paul M. (1971) *Cross-Over Phenomena*, New York, Holt, Rinehart and Winston.

Postal, Paul M. (1972a) "The Best Theory" in Stanley Peters (ed.), *Goals of Linguistic Theory*, Englewood Cliffs, New Jersey, Prentice-Hall.

Postal, Paul M. (1972b) "On Some Rules That Are Not Successive Cyclic" *Linguistic Inquiry* 3, 211–222.

Postal, Paul M. (1974) *On Raising: One Rule of English Grammar and Its Theoretical Implications*, Cambridge, Massachusetts, MIT Press

Postal, Paul M. (1977) "About a 'Nonargument' for Raising" *Linguistic Inquiry* 8, 141–154.

Postal, Paul M. (1979) *Some Syntactic Rules in Mohawk*, New York, Garland.

Postal, Paul M. (1981) "A Failed Analysis of the French Cohesive Infinitive Construction" *Linguistic Analysis* 8, 281–323.

Postal, Paul M. (1982) "The Generalization (71) Follows from Trace Theory" *Linguistic Analysis* 9, 277–284.

Postal, Paul M. (1983) "On Characterizing French Grammatical Structure" *Linguistic Analysis* 11, 361–417.

Postal, Paul M. (1984) "French Indirect Object Cliticization and SSC/BT" *Linguistic Analysis* 14, 111–172.

Postal, Paul M. (1986a) *Studies of Passive Clauses*, Albany, State University of New York Press.

Postal, Paul M. (1986b) "Why Irish Raising Is Not Anomalous" *Natural Language and Linguistic Theory* 4, 333–356.

Postal, Paul M. (1990a) "French Indirect Object Demotion" in Paul M. Postal and Brian D. Joseph (eds.), *Studies in Relational Grammar 3*, Chicago, University of Chicago Press.

Postal, Paul M. (1990b) "Some Unexpected English Restrictions" in Katarzyna Dziwirek, Patrick Farrell, and Errapel Mejías-Bikandi (eds.), *Grammatical Relations: A Cross-Theoretical Perspective*, Stanford, California, CSLI.

Postal, Paul M. (1992) "Phantom Successors and the French *faire par* Construction" in Diane Brentari, Gary Larson, and Lynn MacLeod (eds.), *The Joy of Grammar: A Festschrift for James D. McCawley*, Amsterdam, John Benjamins.

Postal, Paul. M. (1993a) "Parasitic Gaps and the Across-the-Board Phenomenon" *Linguistic Inquiry* 24, 735–754.

Postal, Paul. M. (1993b) "Remarks on Weak Crossover Effects" *Linguistic Inquiry* 24, 539–555.

Postal, Paul M. (1993c) "Some Defective Paradigms" *Linguistic Inquiry* 24, 347–364.

Postal, Paul M. (1994a) "Contrasting Extraction Types" *Journal of Linguistics* 30, 159–186.

Postal, Paul M. (1994b) "Parasitic and Pseudo-Parasitic Gaps" *Linguistic Inquiry* 25, 63–117.

Postal, Paul M. (1996) "A Glance at French Pseudopassives" in Clifford S. Burgess, Katarzyna Dziwirek, and Donna B. Gerdts (eds.), *Grammatical Relations; Theoretical Approaches to Empirical Questions*, New York, Cambridge University Press, CSLI.

Postal, Paul M. (1998) *Three Investigations of Extraction*, Cambridge, Massachusetts, MIT Press.

Postal, Paul M. (2001a), "Further Lacunae in the English Parasitic Gap Paradigm" in Peter W. Culicover and Paul M. Postal (eds.), *Parasitic Gaps*, Cambridge, Massachusetts, MIT Press.

Postal, Paul M. (2001b) "Missing Parasitic Gaps" in Peter W. Culicover and Paul M. Postal (eds.), *Parasitic Gaps*, Cambridge, Massachusetts, MIT Press.

Postal, Paul M. (in press) "A Remark on English Double Negatives" in Christian Leclère, et al. (eds.), *A Festschrift for Maurice Gross*, Amsterdam, Holland, John Benjamins.

Postal, Paul M. (in preparation) *Negative Polarity Nominals as Negative Quantifiers.*

Postal, Paul M., and Geoffrey K. Pullum (1978) "Traces and the Description of English Complementizer Contraction" *Linguistic Inquiry* 9, 1–29.

Postal, Paul M., and Geoffrey K. Pullum (1979) "On an Inadequate Defense of Trace Theory" *Linguistic Inquiry* 10, 689–706.

Postal, Paul M., and Geoffrey K. Pullum (1982) "The Contraction Debate" *Linguistic Inquiry* 13, 122–38.

Postal, Paul M., and Geoffrey K. Pullum (1986) "Misgovernment" *Linguistic Inquiry* 17, 104–110.

Postal, Paul M., and Geoffrey K. Pullum (1988) "Expletive Noun Phrases in Subcategorized Positions" *Linguistic Inquiry* 19, 635–670.

Postal, Paul M., and Geoffrey K. Pullum (1997) "Murphy's Review of Barsky," *LINGUIST List*: Volume 8, Number 755, May 5, 1997.

Potts, Christopher (2002) "The Lexical Semantics of Parenthetical-*As* and Appositive-*Which*" *Syntax* 5, 55–88.

Progovac, Ljiljana (1993) "Negative Polarity: Entailment and Binding" *Linguistics and Philosophy* 16, 149–180.

Pullum, Geoffrey K. (1976) *Rule Interaction and the Organization of a Grammar*, New York, Garland.

Pullum, Geoffrey K. (1982) "Syncategorematicity and English Infinitival *To*" *Glossa* 16, 181–215.

Pullum, Geoffrey K. (1983) "How Many Possible Natural Languages Are There?" *Linguistic Inquiry* 14, 447–467.

Pullum, Geoffrey K. (1989) "Formal Linguistics Meets the Boojum" *Natural Language and Linguistic Theory* 7, 137–143.

Pullum, Geoffrey K., and Barbara C. Scholz (2001) "On the Distinction between Model-Theoretic and Generative-Enumerative Syntactic Frameworks" in *LACL 2001, Proceedings of the Conference on Logical Aspects of Computational Linguistics*, Berlin, Springer-Verlag.

Quine, Willard van Orman (1953) *From a Logical Point of View*, Cambridge, Massachusetts, Harvard University Press.

Radford, Andrew (1981) *Transformational Syntax*, Cambridge, England, Cambridge University Press.

Radford, Andrew (1988) *Transformational Grammar*, Cambridge, England, Cambridge University Press.

Rando, Emily, and Donna Jo Napoli (1978) "Definites in *THERE* Sentences" *Language* 54, 300–313.

Rappaport, Malka, and Beth Levin (1986) "A Case Study in Lexical Analysis: The Locative Alternation" Unpublished Manuscript, Cambridge, Massachusetts, MIT.

Rauff, James V. (1989) Review of Langendoen and Postal (1984) *Computational Linguistics* 15, 55–57.

Reinhart, Tanya (1983) *Anaphora and Semantic Interpretation*, Chicago, University of Chicago Press.

Reuland, Eric J., and Alice G. B. ter Meulen (1987) *The Representation of (In)Definiteness*, Cambridge, Massachusetts, MIT Press.

Riemsdijk, Henk van (1976) *A Case Study in Syntactic Markedness: The Binding Nature of Prepositional Phrases*, Dordrecht, Foris.

Riemsdijk, Henk van (1982) "Derivational Grammar vs. Representational Grammar" in *Linguistics in the Morning Calm: Selected Papers from SICOL—1981*, Seoul, Hanshin.

Riemsdijk, Henk van, and Edwin Williams (1981) "NP-Structure" *Linguistic Review* 1, 171–217.

Riemsdijk, Henk van, and Edwin Williams (1986) *Introduction to the Theory of Grammar*, Cambridge, Massachusetts, MIT Press.

Ristad, Eric S. (1993) *The Language Complexity Game*, Cambridge, Massachusetts, MIT Press.

Rizzi, Luigi (1990) *Relativized Minimality*, Cambridge, Massachusetts, MIT Press.

Roberts, Ian G. (1986) *The Representation of Implicit and Dethematized Subjects*, Dordrecht, Foris.

Roberts, Ian (1991) "NP-Movement, Crossover and Chain-Formation" in Hubert Haider and Klaus Netter (eds.), *Representation and Derivation in the Theory of Grammar*, Dordrecht, Holland, Kluwer Academic.

Roberts, Ian (1997) *Comparative Syntax*, New York, Edward Arnold.

Rogers, Andrew Daylon (1973) *Physical Perception Verbs in English: A Study in Lexical Relatedness*, Los Angeles, University of California at Los Angeles Doctoral Dissertation.

Romero, Juan (1998) "Passives, Agreement, and Equidistance" in *Celebration: An Electronic Festschrift in Honor of Noam Chomsky's 70th Birthday*, http:addendum@mitpress.mit.edu/celebration.

Rosenbaum, Peter S. (1967) *The Grammar of English Predicate Complement Constructions*, Cambridge, Massachusetts, MIT Press.

Ross, John Robert (1967/1986) *Constraints on Variables in Syntax*, Cambridge, Massachusetts, MIT Doctoral Dissertation; published as *Infinite Syntax*, Norwood, New Jersey, Ablex, 1986.

Ross, John Robert (1973) "Nouniness" in Osamu Fujimura (ed.), *Three Dimensions of Linguistic Theory*, Tokyo, TEC.

Ross, John Robert (1984) "Inner Islands" in *Proceedings of the Tenth Annual Meeting of the Berkeley Linguistic Society*, Berkeley, California, Berkeley Linguistics Society.

Runner, Jeffrey T. (1999) *Noun Phrase Licensing*, New York, Garland.

Ruwet, Nicolas (1972) *Théorie syntaxique et syntaxe du français*, Paris, Editions du Seuil.

Safir, Kenneth J. (1984) "Multiple Variable Binding" *Linguistic Inquiry* 15, 603–638.

Safir, Kenneth J. (1985) *Syntactic Chains*, Cambridge, England, Cambridge University Press.

Safir, Kenneth J. (1996) "Derivation, Representation, and Resumption: The Domain of Weak Crossover" *Linguistic Inquiry* 27, 313–339.

Safir, Kenneth J. (1998) "Vehicle Change and Reconstruction in A'-chains" Unpublished Paper, New Brunswick, New Jersey, Rutgers University.

Sag, Ivan A. (1976) *Deletion and Logical Form*, Cambridge, Massachusetts, MIT Doctoral Dissertation.

Sag, Ivan A., and Janet D. Fodor (1995) "Extraction Without Traces" in *Proceedings of the Thirteenth West Coast Conference on Formal Linguistics*, Stanford, California, CSLI.

Sainsbury, R. M. (1988) *Paradoxes*, Cambridge, England, Cambridge University Press.

Schlenker, Philippe (1999) *Propositional Attitudes and Indexicality: A Cross-Categorical Approach*, Cambridge, Massachusetts, MIT Doctoral Dissertation.

Seiter, William (1980) *Studies in Nieuean Syntax*, New York, Garland.

Seiter, William (1983) "Subject–Direct Object Raising in Nieuean" in David M. Perlmutter (ed.), *Studies in Relational Grammar 1*, Chicago, University of Chicago Press.

Sells, Peter, and Thomas Wasow (1999) "Anaphora" in Keith Brown, Jim Miller, and R. E. Asher (eds.), *Concise Encyclopedia of Grammatical Categories*, Oxford, England, Elsevier.

Seuren, Pieter (1996) *Semantic Syntax*, Oxford, England, Blackwell.

Seuren, Pieter A. M. (2000) *Chomsky's Minimalism*, Unpublished Manuscript, Nijmegen, Holland, Max Planck Institute for Psycholinguistics.

Sgall, Peter (1987) Review of Langendoen and Postal (1984) *Prague Bulletin of Mathematical Linguistics* 47, 63–68.

Siegel, Dorothy (1973) "Non-sources for Un-passives" in John Kimball (ed.), *Syntax and Semantics 2*, New York, Academic Press.

Smith, Neil (1999) *Chomsky: Ideas and Ideals*, Cambridge, England, Cambridge University Press.

Smith, Neil (2000) "Foreword" in Noam Chomsky, *New Horizons in the Study of Language and Mind*, Cambridge, England, Cambridge University Press.

Sorensen, Roy A. (1998) "Yablo's Paradox and Kindred Infinite Liars" *Mind* 107/425, 137–155.

Spears, Richard A. (1996) *NTC's Dictionary of American Slang and Colloquial Expressions*, Lincolnwood, Illinois, NTC.

Sportiche, Dominique (1983) *Structural Invariance and Symmetry in Syntax*, Cambridge, Massachusetts, MIT Doctoral Dissertation.

Stahlke, Herbert (1974) "Pronouns and Islands in Yoruba" *Studies in African Linguistics* 5, 171–204.

Steedman, Mark (1996) *Surface Structure and Interpretation*, Cambridge, Massachusetts, MIT Press.

Stoll, Robert R. (1979) *Set Theory and Logic*, New York, Dover.

Stowell, Timothy (1981) *Origins of Phrase Structure*, Cambridge, Massachusetts, MIT Doctoral Dissertation.

Stowell, Timothy (1989) "Raising in Irish and the Projection Principle" *Natural Language and Linguistic Theory* 7, 317–359.

Stroik, Thomas (1992) "Middles and Movement" *Linguistic Inquiry* 23, 127–137.

Stroik, Thomas (1995) "On Middle Formation: A Reply to Zribi-Hertz" *Linguistic Inquiry* 26, 165–171.

Stroik, Thomas (1997) *Minimalism, Scope, and VP Structure*, Thousand Oaks, California, Sage.

Stroik, Thomas (1999) "Middles and Reflexivity" *Linguistic Inquiry* 30, 119–131.

Suppes, Patrick (1957) *Introduction to Logic*, New York, D. Van Nostrand.

Sweet, Henry (1891) *A New English Grammar*, Oxford, England, Oxford University Press.

Tancredi, Chris (1997) "Pronouns and Perspectives" in Hans Bennis, Pierre Pica, and Johan Rooryk (eds.), *Atomism and Binding*, Dordrecht, Holland, Foris.

Tellier, Christine (1988) *Universal Licensing: Implications for Parasitic Gaps*, Montreal, McGill University Doctoral Dissertation.

Thompson, Henry (1986) Review of Langendoen and Postal (1984) *Journal of Linguistics* 22, 241–242.

Trask, R. L. (1993) *A Dictionary of Grammatical Terms in Linguistics*, London, Routledge.

Ura, Hiroyuki (2000) *Checking Theory and Grammatical Functions in Universal Grammar*, Oxford, England, Oxford University Press.

van der Wouden, Ton (1994) "Polarity and 'Illogical Negation'" in Makoto Kanazawa and Christopher Piñón (eds.), *Dynamics, Polarity, and Quantification*, Stanford, California, CSLI.

van der Wouden, Ton (1997) *Negative Contexts*, London, Routledge.

Wasow, Thomas (1972) *Anaphoric Relations in English*, Cambridge, Massachusetts, MIT Doctoral Dissertation.

Wasow, Thomas (1977) "Transformations and the Lexicon" in Peter W. Culicover, Thomas Wasow, and Adrian Akmajian (eds.), *Formal Syntax*, New York, Academic Press.

Wasow, Thomas (1979) *Anaphora in Generative Grammar*, Ghent, Holland, E. Story-Scientia.

Watanabe, Akira (2000) "Feature Copying and Binding: Evidence from Complementizer Agreement and Switch Reference" *Syntax* 3, 159–181.

Webelhut, Gert (1992) *Principles and Parameters of Syntactic Saturation*, Oxford, England, Oxford University Press.

Webelhut, Gert (1995) (ed.) *Government and Binding Theory and the Minimalist Program*, Oxford, England, Blackwell.

Whitney, William D. (1875/1979) *The Life and Growth of Language*, New York, Dover.

Wilks, Yorick (1984) Review of Langendoen and Postal (1984) *Times Literary Supplement*, June 15, 660–661.

Williams, Edwin (1981) "Argument Structure and Morphology" *Linguistic Review* 1, 81–114.

Williams, Edwin (1986) "A Reassignment of the Functions of LF" *Linguistic Inquiry* 17, 265–299.

Williams, Edwin (1994) *Thematic Structure in Syntax*, Cambridge, Massachusetts, MIT Press.

Wilson, Robert D. (1966) Review of Fillmore (1965) *International Journal of American Linguistics*, 405–409.

Woolford, Ellen (1987) "An ECP Account of Constraints on Across-the-Board Extraction" *Linguistic Inquiry* 18, 166–171.

Zaenen, Annie, and Joan Maling (1982) "The Status of Resumptive Pronouns in Swedish" in Elisabet Engdahl and Eva Ejerhed (eds.), *Readings on Unbounded Dependencies in Scandinavian Languages*, Stockholm, Sweden, Almqvist and Wiksell.

Zribi-Hertz, Anne (1993) "On Stroik's Analysis of English Middle Constructions" *Linguistic Inquiry* 24, 583–589.

Zwarts, Frans (1995) "Nonveridical Contexts" *Linguistic Analysis* 25, 286–312.

Zwarts, Frans (1996) "Facets of Negation" in Jaap van der Does and Jan van Eijck (eds.), *Quantifiers, Logic, and Language*, CSLI Lecture Notes No. 54, Stanford, California, CSLI.

Zwarts, Frans (1999) "Polarity Items" in Keith Brown and Jim Miller (eds.), *Concise Encyclopedia of Grammatical Categories*, New York, Elsevier.

Zwicky, Arnold (1971) "In a Manner of Speaking" *Linguistic Inquiry* 2, 223–233.

INDEX